Adobe®
PHOTOSHOP® CS5
COMPREHENSIVE

Gary B. Shelly

Joy L. Starks

Indiana University Purdue University Indianapolis

Alec Fehl

Asheville-Buncombe Technical Community College

COURSE TECHNOLOGY
CENGAGE Learning™

SHELLY
CASHMAN
SERIES®

Australia • Brazil • Japan • Korea • Mexico • Singapore • Spain • United Kingdom • United States

Adobe® Photoshop® CS5: Comprehensive
Gary B. Shelly, Joy L. Starks, Alec Fehl

Vice President, Publisher: Nicole Pinard

Executive Editor: Kathleen McMahon

Product Manager: Aimee Poirier

Editorial Assistant: Angela Giannopoulos

Director of Marketing: Cheryl Costantini

Marketing Manager: Tristen Kendall

Marketing Coordinator: Adrienne Fung

Print Buyer: Julio Esperas

Director of Production: Patty Stephan

Senior Content Project Manager: Jill Braiewa

Developmental Editor: Amanda Brodkin

QA Manuscript Reviewer: Susan Whalen

Copyeditor: Camille Kiolbasa

Proofreader: Kim Kosmatka

Indexer: Alexandra Nickerson

Art Director: Marissa Falco

Cover and Text Design: Lisa Kuhn, Curio Press, LLC

Cover Photo: Tom Kates Photography

Compositor: PreMediaGlobal

For product information and technology assistance, contact us at
Cengage Learning Customer & Sales Support, 1-800-354-9706

For permission to use material from this text or product,
submit all requests online at **cengage.com/permissions**
Further permissions questions can be emailed to
permissionrequest@cengage.com

Library of Congress Control Number: 2010935957
ISBN-13: 978-0-538-47391-0
ISBN-10: 0-538-47391-6

Course Technology
20 Channel Center Street
Boston, Massachusetts 02210
USA

Adobe, the Adobe logos, and Photoshop are either registered trademarks or trademarks of Adobe Systems Incorporated in the United States and/or other countries. THIS PRODUCT IS NOT ENDORSED OR SPONSORED BY ADOBE SYSTEMS INCORPORATED, PUBLISHER OF PHOTOSHOP.

Cengage Learning is a leading provider of customized learning solutions with office locations around the globe, including Singapore, the United Kingdom, Australia, Mexico, Brazil, and Japan. Locate your local office at:
international.cengage.com/region

Cengage Learning products are represented in Canada by Nelson Education, Ltd.

For your course and learning solutions, visit **www.cengage.com**

To learn more about Course Technology,
visit **www.cengage.com/coursetechnology**

Purchase any of our products at your local college bookstore or at our preferred online store **www.cengagebrain.com**

Credits
Chapter 1: Fig 1-1: Fred Starks; Fig 1-85: Mali Jones; Fig 1-86: John J.Mosesso/NBII. Gov; Fig 1-87: NASA/JPL-Caltech/Harvard-Smithsonian CFA; Fig 1-88: National Park Services; Fig 1-90: Misty Vermaat; Case and Places 1: Katie Starks; Cases and Places 2: Fred Starks; Cases and Places 3: Jeffrey Olson Sgt. Floyd Monument Sioux City Iowa **Chapter 2:** Fig 2-1: Fred Starks; Fig 2-73, 2-74, 2-75: Kevin Marshall; Fig 2-76, 2-77, 2-78, Cases and Places 1: Fred Starks; Cases and Places 3: Katie Starks **Chapter 3:** Fig 3 -1: Fred Starks; Fig 3-77, 3-78, 3-80: Kevin Marshall; Figure 3-79 Fred Starks **Chapter 4:** Fig 4-1, 4-76: Katie Starks; Fig 4-77, 4-78, 4-81: Kevin Marshall; Fig 4-79: Fred Starks **Chapter 5:** Fig 5-2, 5-66: Katie Starks; Fig 5-20, 5-54, 5-72: Fred Starks; Fig 5-26: Ethel Lykins; Fig 5-43: Anita Louks; Fig 5-48: Lourdes Nunez; Fig 5-68, 5-71: Kevin Marshall; Fig 5-70: Donna Reneau **Chapter 6:** Fig 6-1, 6-61, 6-64: Fred Starks; Fig 6-62, 6-67: Kevin Marshall; Fig 6-65: Katie Starks

Printed in the United States of America
1 2 3 4 5 6 7 16 15 14 13 12 11 10

Adobe PHOTOSHOP® CS5
COMPREHENSIVE

Contents

Appendices

Preface

The Shelly Cashman Series® offers the finest textbooks in computer education. We are proud of the fact that our previous Photoshop books have been so well received. With each new edition of our Photoshop books, we have made significant improvements based on the comments made by instructors and students. The Adobe Photoshop CS5 books continue with the innovation, quality, and reliability you have come to expect from the Shelly Cashman Series.

For this Photoshop CS5 text, the Shelly Cashman Series development team carefully reviewed our pedagogy and analyzed its effectiveness in teaching today's student. Students today read less, but need to retain more. They not only need to be able to perform skills, but to retain those skills and know how to apply them to different settings. Today's students need to be continually engaged and challenged to retain what they're learning.

With this Photoshop CS5 text, we continue our commitment to focusing on the user and how they learn best.

Objectives of This Textbook

Adobe Photoshop CS5: Comprehensive is intended for a course that offers an introduction to Photoshop and image editing. No previous experience with Adobe Photoshop CS5 is assumed, and no mathematics beyond the high school freshman level is required.

The objectives of this book are:

- To teach the fundamentals and more advanced features of Adobe Photoshop CS5
- To expose students to image editing and graphic design fundamentals
- To develop an exercise-oriented approach that promotes learning by doing
- To encourage independent study and to help those who are working alone

The Shelly Cashman Approach

A Proven Pedagogy with an Emphasis on Project Planning

Each chapter presents a practical problem to be solved, within a project planning framework. The project orientation is strengthened by the use of Plan Ahead boxes, that encourage critical thinking about how to proceed at various points in the project. Step-by-step instructions with supporting screens guide students through the steps. Instructional steps are supported by the Q&A, Experimental Step, and BTW features.

A Visually Engaging Book that Maintains Student Interest

The step-by-step tasks, with supporting figures, provide a rich visual experience for the student. Call-outs on the screens that present both explanatory and navigational information provide students with information they need, when they need to know it.

Supporting Reference Materials (Quick Reference, Appendices)

The appendices provide additional information about the application at hand, such as the Help Feature and customizing the application. With the Quick Reference, students can quickly look up information about a single task, such as keyboard shortcuts, and find page references of where in the book the task is illustrated.

Integration of the World Wide Web

The World Wide Web is integrated into the Photoshop CS5 learning experience by (1) BTW annotations; (2) a Quick Reference Summary Web page; and (3) the Learn It Online section for each chapter.

End-of-Chapter Student Activities

Extensive end of chapter activities provide a variety of reinforcement opportunities for students where they can apply and expand their skills through individual and group work.

Book Resources

🔒 **Instructor's Manual**
🔒 **PowerPoint Presentations**
🔒 **Solutions to Exercises (Windows)**
🔒 **Syllabus**
🔒 **Test Bank and Test Engine**
Additional Student Files
Data Files for Students (Windows)

Instructor Resources

The Instructor Resources include both teaching and testing aids and can be accessed via CD-ROM or at login.cengage.com.

Instructor's Manual Includes lecture notes summarizing the chapter sections, figures and boxed elements found in every chapter, teacher tips, classroom activities, lab activities, and quick quizzes in Microsoft Word files.

Syllabus Easily customizable sample syllabi that cover policies, assignments, exams, and other course information.

Figure Files Illustrations for every figure in the textbook in electronic form.

PowerPoint Presentations A multimedia lecture presentation system that provides slides for each chapter. Presentations are based on chapter objectives.

Solutions to Exercises Includes solutions for all end-of-chapter and chapter reinforcement exercises.

Test Bank & Test Engine Test Bank includes 112 questions for every chapter, featuring objective-based and critical thinking question types, including page number references and figure references, when appropriate. Also included is the test engine, ExamView, the ultimate tool for your objective-based testing needs.

Additional Activities for Students Consists of Chapter Reinforcement Exercises, which are true/false, multiple-choice, and short answer questions that help students gain confidence in the material learned.

Content for Online Learning

Course Technology has partnered with Blackboard, the leading distance learning solution provider and class-management platform today. The resources available for download with this title are the test banks in Blackboard- and WebCT-compatible formats. To access this material, simply visit our password-protected instructor resources available at login.cengage.com. For additional information or for an instructor username and password, please contact your sales representative. Other formats also are available.

CourseNotes

Course Technology's CourseNotes are six-panel quick reference cards that reinforce the most important and widely used features of a software application in a visual and user-friendly format. CourseNotes serve as a great reference tool during and after the course. CourseNotes are available for software applications such as Adobe Dreamweaver CS5, Adobe Photoshop CS5, Microsoft Office 2010, and Windows 7. There are also topic-based CourseNotes available for Best Practices in Social Networking, Hot Topics in Technology, and Web 2.0. Visit www.cengagebrain.com to learn more!

Adobe Photoshop CS5 30-Day Trial Edition

A copy of the Photoshop CS5 30-Day trial edition can be downloaded from the Adobe Web site (www.adobe.com). Point to Downloads in the top navigation bar, click Trial downloads, and then follow the on-screen instructions. When you activate the software, you will receive a license that allows you to use the software for 30 days. Course Technology and Adobe provide no product support for this trial edition. When the trial period ends, you can purchase a copy of Adobe Photoshop CS5, or uninstall the trial edition and reinstall your previous version. The minimum system requirements for the 30-day trial edition is a Intel® Pentium® 4 or AMD Athlon® 64 processor; Microsoft® Windows® XP with Service Pack 3, Windows Vista® Home Premium, Business, Ultimate, or Enterprise with Service Pack 1 (Service Pack 2 recommended), or Windows 7; 1GB of RAM; 1GB of available hard-disk space for installation; additional free space required during installation (cannot install on removable flash-based storage devices); 1024×768 display (1280×800 recommended) with qualified hardware-accelerated OpenGL graphics card, 16-bit color, and 256MB of VRAM; Some GPU-accelerated features require graphics support for Shader Model 3.0 and OpenGL 2.0; DVD-ROM drive; QuickTime 7.6.2 software required for multimedia features; and broadband internet connection required for online services.

About Our Covers

The Shelly Cashman Series is continually updating our approach and content to reflect the way today's students learn and experience new technology. This focus on student success is reflected on our covers, which feature real students from Bryant University using the Shelly Cashman Series in their courses, and reflect the varied ages and backgrounds of the students learning with our books. When you use the Shelly Cashman Series, you can be assured that you are learning computer skills using the most effective courseware available.

Textbook Walk-Through

Plan Ahead boxes prepare students to create successful projects by encouraging them to think strategically about what they are trying to accomplish before they begin working.

Overview

As you read this chapter, you will learn how to edit the photo shown in Figure 1–1a on the previous page by performing these general tasks:

- Customize the workspace.
- Display and navigate a photo at various magnifications.
- Crop a photo effectively.
- Create and modify a border.
- Stroke a selection.
- Resize and print a photo.
- Save, close, and then reopen a photo.
- Save a photo for the Web.
- Use Mini Bridge.
- Use Photoshop Help.

Plan Ahead

General Project Guidelines

When editing a photo, the actions you perform and decisions you make will affect the appearance and characteristics of the finished product. As you edit a photo, such as the one shown in Figure 1–1a, you should follow these general guidelines:

1. **Find an appropriate image or photo.** Keep in mind the purpose and the graphic needs of the project when choosing an image or photo. Decide ahead of time on the file type and decide if the image will be used on the Web. An eye-catching graphic image should convey a universal theme. The photo should grab the attention of viewers and draw them into the picture, whether in print or on the Web.

2. **Determine how to edit the photo to highlight the theme.** As you edit, use standard design principles, and keep in mind your subject, your audience, the required size and shape of the graphic, color decisions, the rule of thirds, the golden rectangle, and other design principles. Decide which parts of the photo portray your message and which parts are visual clutter. Crop the photo as needed.

3. **Identify finishing touches that will further enhance the photo.** The overall appearance of a photo significantly affects its ability to communicate clearly. You might want to add text or a border.

4. **Prepare for publication.** Resize the photo as needed to fit the allotted space. Save the photo on a storage medium, such as a hard drive, USB flash drive, or CD. Print the photo or publish it to the Web.

When necessary, more specific details concerning the above guidelines are presented at appropriate points in the chapter. The chapter also will identify the actions performed and decisions made regarding these guidelines during the creation of the edited photo shown in Figure 1–1b on the previous page.

Step-by-step instructions now provide a context beyond the point-and-click. Each step provides information on why students are performing each task, or what will occur as a result.

BTW

Screen Resolution
If your computer has a high-resolution monitor with a screen resolution of 1280 × 800 or higher, lowering that resolution to 1024 × 768 may cause some images to be distorted because of a difference in the aspect ratio. If you want to keep your high-resolution setting, be aware that the location of on-screen tools might vary slightly from the book.

Starting Photoshop

If you are using a computer to step through the project in this chapter, and you want your screen to match the figures in this book, you should change your screen's resolution to 1024 × 768. For information about how to change a screen's resolution, read Appendix C.

To Open a Photo

The following steps open the Cyclist file from a CD located in [...] might differ.

1
- Insert the CD containing the Data Files for Students that accompanies this book into your CD drive. After a few seconds, if Windows displays a dialog box, click its Close button.
- Click File on the menu bar to display the File menu (Figure 1–10).

Q&A What if I do not have the CD?
You will need the Data Files for Students to complete the activities and exercises in this book. See your instructor for information on how to acquire the necessary files.

Q&A Can I use a shortcut key to open a file?
Yes, the shortcut keys are displayed on the menu. In this textbook, the shortcut keys also are displayed at the end of each series of steps in the Other Ways box.

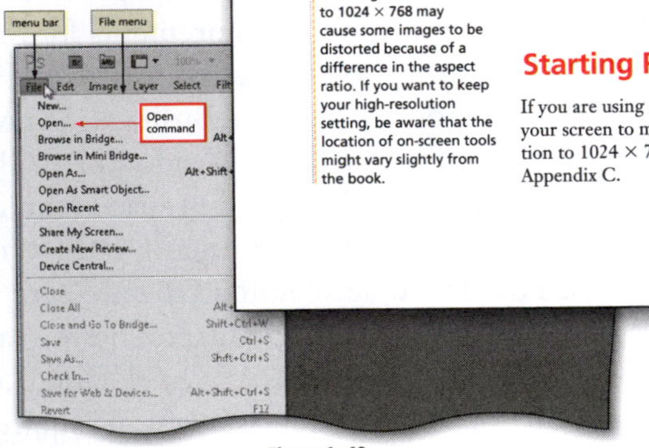

Figure 1–10

2
- Click Open on the File menu to display the Open dialog box.
- Click the Look in box arrow (Open dialog box) to display a list of the available storage locations on your system (Figure 1–11).

Q&A Are there other ways to navigate in the Open dialog box?
Yes, the Go To Last Folder Visited button and Up One Level button help you move through the folders on your computer. The navigation pane also displays links to common storage locations.

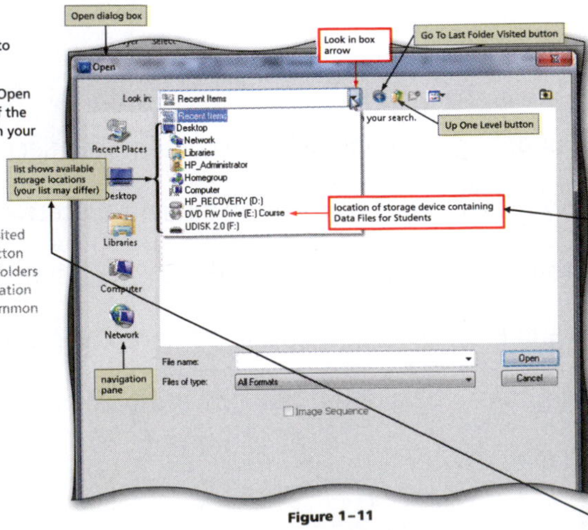

Figure 1–11

BTW

Screen Shots
Callouts in screenshots give students information they need, when they need to know it. The Series has always used plenty of callouts to ensure that students don't get lost. Now, color distinguishes the content in the callouts to make them more meaningful.

Navigational callouts in red show students where to click.

Explanatory callouts summarize what is happening on screen.

Optimization is the process of changing the photo to make it most effective for its purpose. The Save for Web & Devices command allows you to preview optimized images in different file formats, and with different file attributes, for precise optimization. You can view multiple versions of a photo simultaneously and modify settings as you preview the image.

Using the Save for Web & Devices Command

To optimize the cyclist photo for use on the Web, you need to make decisions about the file size and how long it might take to load on a Web page. These kinds of decisions must take into consideration the audience and the nature of the Web page. For example, Web pages geared for college campuses probably could assume a faster download time than those that target a wide range of home users. An e-commerce site that needs high-quality photography to sell its product will make certain choices in color and resolution.

The hardware and software of Web users also is taken into consideration. For instance, if a Web photo contains more colors than the user's monitor can display, most browsers will **dither**, or approximate, the colors that it cannot display, by blending colors that it can. Dithering might not be appropriate for some Web pages, because it increases the file size and therefore causes the page to load more slowly.

Many other appearance settings play a role in the quality of Web graphics, some of which are subjective in nature. As you become more experienced in Photoshop, you will learn how to make choices about dithering, colors, texture, image size, and other settings.

To Preview Using the Save for Web & Devices Dialog Box

The followings steps use the Save for Web & Devices command to display previews for four possible Web formats.

1
- With the Cyclist Resized photo open, click File on the menu bar to display the File menu and then click Save for Web & Devices to display the Save for Web & Devices dialog box.

- Click the 4-Up tab to display four versions of the photo.

- Click the upper-right preview, if necessary, to choose a high-quality, version of the photo (Figure 1–66).

Q&A
Why are there four frames?
Photoshop displays four previews — the original photo and three others that are converted to different resolutions to optimize download times on the Web.

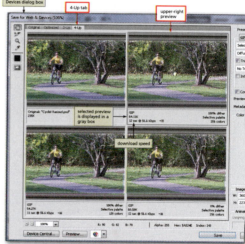

Figure 1–66

Other Ways
1. Press ALT+SHIFT+CTRL+S

To Adjust the Hue and Saturation

The following steps adjust the hue and saturation of the coffee table lay...

1
- Click the Layers panel tab to display the Layers panel, and then select the coffee table layer.

- Click the Adjustments panel tab to display the Adjustments panel, and then click the Hue/Saturation icon (shown in Figure 3–60 on page PS 183) on the Adjustments panel.

- Click the Clip to Layer button on the Adjustments panel status bar to adjust only the layer.

Figure 3–63

- Drag the Hue slider to +5. Drag the Saturation slider to −5. Drag the Lightness slider to −10 (Figure 3–63).

Experiment
- Drag the sliders to view the affect of hue and saturation settings to the layer. When you are done experimenting, drag the sliders to the settings listed in the step.

2
- Click the 'Return to adjustment list' button to display all of the adjustment icons and settings on the Adjustments panel.

Other Ways
1. Select layer, press CTRL+U, complete adjustments, right-click layer, click Create Clipping Mask

Brightness and Contrast

Brightness refers to color luminance or intensity of a light source, perceived as lightness or darkness in an image. Photoshop measures brightness on a sliding scale from −150 to +150. Negative numbers move the brightness toward black. Positive numbers compress the highlights and expand the shadows. For example, the layer might be an image photographed on a cloudy day; conversely, the image might appear overexposed by having been too close to a photographer's flash. Either way, editing the brightness might enhance the image.

Contrast is the difference between the lightest and darkest tones in an image, involving mainly the midtones. When you increase contrast, the middle-to-dark areas become darker, and the middle-to-light areas become lighter. High-contrast images contain few color variations between the lightest and darkest parts of the image; low-contrast images contain more tonal gradations.

To Adjust the Brightness and Contrast

Sometimes it is easier to create a layer adjustment from the Layers panel. The following steps edit the brightness and contrast of the Background layer using the 'Create new fill or adjustment layer' button on the Layers panel.

BTW
Layer Selection
Sometimes a menu or panel will cover the Layers panel, or a layer might be scrolled out of sight. You always can identify which layer you are working with by looking at the document window tab as shown in Figure 3–64 on the next page. The name of the current layer appears in parentheses.

Textbook Walk-Through

Other Ways boxes that follow many of the step sequences explain the other ways to complete the task presented.

2
- Click Adobe Photoshop CS5 in the search results on the Start menu to start Photoshop.

- After a few moments, when the Photoshop window is displayed, if the window is not maximized, click the Maximize button next to the Close button on the title bar to maximize the window (Figure 1–3).

Q&A What is a maximized window?

A maximized window fills the entire screen. When you maximize a window, the Maximize button changes to a Restore Down button.

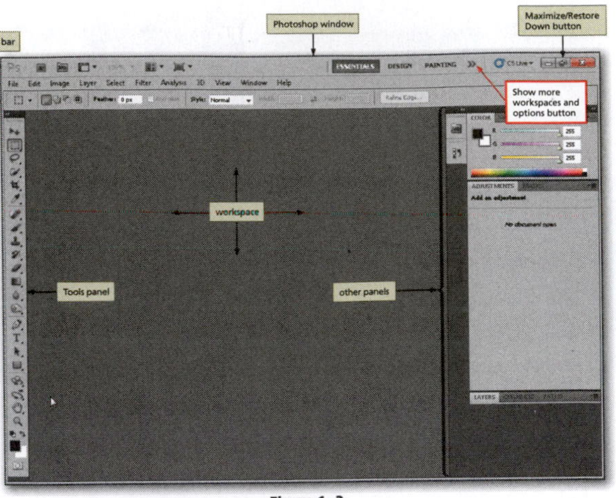

Figure 1–3

Other Ways
1. Double-click Photoshop icon on desktop, if one is present
2. Click Adobe Photoshop CS5 on Start menu

Customizing the Photoshop Workspace

The screen in Figure 1–3 shows how the Photoshop workspace looks the first time you start Photoshop after installation on most computers. Photoshop does not open a blank or default photo automatically; rather, the Application bar, a menu bar, and the options bar cross the top of the screen with a gray work area below the options bar. The Tools splayed on the left; other panels are displayed on the right. The gray work area are referred to collectively as the **workspace**.

ou work in Photoshop, the panels, the selected tool, and the options bar ght change. Therefore, if you want your screen to match the figures in this should restore the default workspace, select the default tool, and reset the r. For more information about how to change other advanced Photoshop e Appendix C.

use of a default preference setting, each time you start Photoshop, the p workspace is displayed the same way it was the last time you used p. If the panels are relocated, then they will appear in their new locations ime you start Photoshop. You can create and save your own workspaces, or shop's saved workspaces that show a group of panels used for certain tasks. ple, the Painting workspace displays the Brush presets panel and the Swatches ong others — all of which you would need when painting. You will learn more els later in this chapter. Similarly, if values on the options bar are changed or a ool is selected, they will remain changed the next time you start Photoshop. If to return the workspace to its default settings, follow these steps each time you oshop.

Photoshop Chapter 1

Chapter Summary

In this chapter, you gained a broad knowledge of Photoshop. First, you learned how to start Photoshop. You were introduced to the Photoshop workspace. You learned how to open a photo and zoom in and out. You learned about design issues related to the placement of visual points of interest. You then learned how to crop a photo to eliminate extraneous background. After you added a blended border, you resized the image.

Once you saved the photo, you learned how to print it. You used the Save for Web & Devices command to optimize and save a Web version. You learned how to use Adobe Mini Bridge to view files and Adobe Help to research specific help topics. Finally, you learned how to quit Photoshop.

The items listed below include all the new Photoshop skills you have learned in this chapter:

1. Start Photoshop (PS 5)
2. Select the Essentials Workspace (PS 7)
3. Reset the Tools Panel (PS 8)
4. Reset the Options Bar (PS 8)
5. Open a Photo (PS 10)
6. Save a Photo in the PSD Format (PS 19)
7. Use the Zoom Tool (PS 23)
8. Open the Navigator Panel (PS 25)
9. Use the Navigator Panel (PS 26)
10. Collapse the Navigator Panel (PS 26)
11. Use the Hand Tool (PS 27)
12. Change the Magnification (PS 27)
13. Change the Screen Mode (PS 28)
14. Display Rulers (PS 30)
15. Crop a Photo (PS 33)
16. Position the Rule of Thirds Overlay (PS 34)
17. Create a Selection (PS 35)
18. Stroke a Selection (PS 36)
19. Modify a Selection (PS 38)
20. Switch Foreground and Background Colors (PS 40)
21. Deselect (PS 41)
22. Save a Photo with the Same File Name (PS 42)
23. Close a Photo (PS 42)
24. Open a Recent File (PS 43)
25. Resize the Image (PS 44)
26. Save a Photo with a Different Name (PS 46)
27. Print a Photo (PS 47)
28. Preview Using the Save for Web & Devices Dialog Box (PS 48)
29. Choose a Download Speed (PS 49)
30. Preview the Photo on the Web (PS 51)
31. Save the Photo as a Web Page (PS 52)
32. Use Mini Bridge to View Files (PS 54)
33. Collapse the Panel (PS 57)
34. Access Photoshop Help (PS 58)
35. Use the Help Search Box (PS 59)
36. Quit Photoshop (PS 60)

Chapter Summary includes a concluding paragraph, followed by a listing of the tasks completed within a chapter together with the pages on which the step-by-step, screen-by-screen explanations appear.

Every chapter features a **Learn It Online** section that is comprised of six exercises. These exercises include True/False, Multiple Choice, Short Answer, Flash Cards, Practice Test, and Learning Games.

Apply Your Knowledge usually requires students to open and manipulate a file from the Data Files that parallels the activities learned in the chapter.

Learn It Online

Test your knowledge of chapter content and key terms.

Instructions: To complete the Learn It Online exercises, start your browser, click the Address bar, and then enter the Web address `scsite.com/psCS5/learn`. When the Photoshop CS5 Learn It Online page is displayed, click the link for the exercise you want to complete and then read the instructions.

Chapter Reinforcement TF, MC, and SA
A series of true/false, multiple choice, and short answer questions that test your knowledge of the chapter content.

Flash Cards
An interactive learning environment where you identify chapter key terms associated with displayed definitions.

Practice Test
A series of multiple choice questions that tests your knowledge of chapter content and key terms.

Who Wants To Be a Computer Genius?
An interactive game that challenges your knowledge of chapter content in the style of a television quiz show.

Wheel of Terms
An interactive game that challenges your knowledge of chapter key terms in the style of the television show *Wheel of Fortune*.

Crossword Puzzle Challenge
A crossword puzzle that challenges your knowledge of key terms presented in the chapter.

Apply Your Knowledge

Reinforce the skills and apply the concepts you learned in this chapter.

Editing a Photo in the Photoshop Workspace

Photoshop and perform the customization steps found on pages PS 6 through PS 9.
1 Water Park file in the Chapter 01 folder from the Data Files for Students. You can
les for Students on the CD that accompanies this book. See the inside back cover of this
ons on downloading the Data Files for Students, or contact your instructor for informa-
g the required files.
ill save the photo in its own folder. Then you will crop the photo, add a white border,
d photo, as shown in Figure 1–85. Next, you will resize the photo for printing and
nally you will reopen your edited photo, and then you will optimize it for the Web,
t.

ing tasks:
nenu, click Save As. When Photoshop displays the Save As dialog box, navigate to your
ve and then click the Create New Folder button. Type Apply 1-1 as the folder name
s the ENTER key. Double-click the folder to open it. In the File name box, type
ter Park Edited. Click the Format button and choose the PSD file format. Click the
o save the file.

Extend Your Knowledge

Extend the skills you learned in this chapter and experiment with new skills. You may need to use Help to complete the assignment.

Separating Objects from the Background

Instructions: Start Photoshop and perform the customization steps found on pages PS 6 through PS 9. Open the Extend 2-1 Flowers file in the Chapter 02 folder from the Data Files for Students and save it, in the PSD format, as Extend 2-1 Flowers Edited. You can access the Data Files for Students on the CD that accompanies this book; see the inside back cover of this book for instructions on downloading the Data Files for Students, or contact your instructor for information about accessing the required files.

The original flower image displays the flowers in their natural settings, with various colors in the background. After moving the frame and making a copy, you will select the flowers while preventing background colors from straying into the selection. Finally, you will position each flower in front of a frame as shown in Figure 2–74.

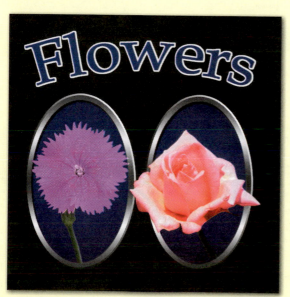

Figure 2–74

Extend Your Knowledge projects at the end of each chapter allow students to extend and expand on the skills learned within the chapter. Students use critical thinking to experiment with new skills to complete each project.

Textbook Walk-Through

Make It Right projects call on students to analyze a file, discover errors in it, and fix them using the skills they learned in the chapter.

In the Lab assignments require students to utilize the chapter concepts and techniques to solve problems on a computer.

Found within the Cases and Places exercises, the **Personal** activities call on students to create an open-ended project that relates to their personal lives.

Make It Right

Analyze a project and correct all errors and/or improve the design.

Changing a Photo's Focus and Optimizing It for the Web

Instructions: Start Photoshop and perform the customization steps found on pages PS 6 through PS 9. Open the Make It Right 1-1 Young Stars file in the Chapter 01 folder from the Data Files for Students and save it as Make It Right 1-1 Young Stars Edited in the PSD file format. You can access the Data Files for Students on the CD that accompanies this book. See the inside back cover of this book for instructions on downloading the Data Files for Students, or contact your instructor for information about accessing the required files.

Members of your Astronomy Club have selected the Young Stars photo (Figure 1–87) for the club's Web site. You are to edit the photo to more clearly focus on the cluster of stars and its trailing dust blanket, and then optimize the photo for the Web.

View the photo in different screen modes and at different magnifications.

Keeping the rule of thirds and the golden rectangle 5:8 ratio concepts in mind, crop the photo to change its focal point and resave it. Then save the photo for the Web as Make-It-Right-1-1 Young-Stars-for-Web using the optimal settings for a GIF file with maximum colors and width.

In the Lab

Design and/or create a project using the guidelines, concepts, and skills presented in this chapter. Labs are listed in order of increasing difficulty.

Lab 1: Cropping a Photo and Adding a Feathered Border

Problem: A nature magazine has accepted the submission of your photo of an American bald eagle, but they would like you to crop the photo more, add a feathered border, and resize it. Also, the editor would like the final version saved in the TIFF format. The edited photo is displayed in Figure 1–88. See the inside back cover of this book for instructions on downloading the Data Files for Students, or contact your instructor for information about accessing the required files.

Figure 1–88

Instructions: Start Photoshop. Perform the customization steps found on pages PS 6 through PS 9. Open the file, Lab 1-3 Tram, from the Chapter 01 folder of the Data Files for Students. Save the file in the PSD format with the name Lab 1-3 Tram Edited, in a new folder named Lab 1-3. (*Hint:* Use the Create New Folder button in the toolbar of the Save As dialog box.) Resize the photo to 500 pixels wide. Zoom to 50% magnification. Search Photoshop Help for help related to optimization. Read about optimizing for the Web. Print a copy of the help topic and then close the Photoshop Help window.

Use the Save for Web & Devices dialog box to view the 4-Up tab. Choose the best looking preview. Select the connection speed of your Internet connection. Save the HTML and Images in the Lab 1-3 folder using the name, Lab-1-3-Tram-for-Web. Use Mini Bridge to check your file structure and see your photos. Collapse the Mini Bridge panel. For extra credit, upload the HTML file and the accompanying Image folder to a Web server. See your instructor for ways to submit this assignment.

Cases and Places

Apply your creative thinking and problem-solving skills to design and implement a solution.

Note: To complete these assignments, you may be required to use the Data Files for Students. See the inside back cover of this book for instructions on downloading the Data Files for Students, or contact your instructor for information about accessing the required files.

1: Cropping a Photo for a Picture Directory

Academic

As a member of your high school reunion committee, it is your task to assemble the class photo directory. You are to edit a high school student photo and prepare it for print in the reunion directory. The photo needs to fit in a space 1.75 inches high and 1.33 inches wide. Each photo needs to have approximately the same amount of space above the headshot: .25 inches. After starting Photoshop and resetting the workspace, select the photo, Case 1-1 Student, from the Chapter 01 folder of the Data Files for Students. Save the photo on your USB flash drive storage device as Case 1-1 Student Edited, using the PSD format. Resize the photo to match the requirements. Use the rulers to help you crop the photo to leave .25 inches above the top of the student's head. Save the photo again with the file name Case 1-1 Student for Print and print a copy for your instructor.

2: Creating a Photo for a Social Networking Site

Personal

You would like to place a photo of your recent tubing adventure on your social networking site. The photo you have is of two people. You need to crop out the other person who is tubing. After starting Photoshop and resetting the workspace, select the photo, Case 1-2 Tubing, from the Chapter 01 folder of the Data Files for Students. Save the photo on your USB flash drive storage device as Case 1-2 Tubing Edited, using the PSD format. Crop the photo to remove one of the inner tubes, keeping in mind the rule of thirds, the golden rectangle, and the direction of the action. Save the photo again and print a copy for your instructor.

1 | Editing a Photo

Objectives

You will have mastered the material in this chapter when you can:

- Start Photoshop and customize the Photoshop workspace

- Open a photo

- Identify parts of the Photoshop workspace

- Explain file types

- Save a photo for both print and the Web

- View a photo using the Zoom Tool, Navigator panel, Hand Tool, and screen modes

- Display rulers

- Crop a photo using the Rule of Thirds overlay

- Create a blended border by stroking a selection

- Open a recent file

- Resize a photo

- Print a photo

- View files in Mini Bridge

- Access Photoshop Help

- Close a file

- Quit Photoshop

1 | Editing a Photo

What Is Photoshop CS5?

Photoshop CS5 is a popular image editing software program produced by Adobe Systems Incorporated. **Image editing software** refers to computer programs that allow you to create and modify **digital images**, or pictures in electronic form. One type of digital image is a digital **photograph** or **photo**, which is a picture taken with a camera and stored as a digitized file. The photo then is converted into a print, a slide, or used in another file. Other types of digital images include scanned images or electronic forms of original artwork created from scratch. Digital images are used in graphic applications, advertising, print publishing, and on the Web. Personal uses include private photos, online photo sharing, scrapbooking, blogging, and social networking, among others. Image editing software, such as Photoshop, can be used for basic adjustments such as rotating, cropping, or resizing, as well as for more advanced manipulations, such as airbrushing, retouching, photo repair, changing the contrast of an image, balancing, or combining elements of different images. Because Photoshop allows you to save multilayered, composite images and then return later to extract parts of those images, it works well for repurposing a wide variety of graphic-related files.

Photoshop CS5 is part of the **Adobe Creative Suite 5** and comes packaged with most of the suite versions. It also is sold and used independently as a stand-alone application. Photoshop CS5 is available for both the PC and Macintosh computer platforms. Photoshop CS5 Extended includes all of the features of Photoshop CS5 and some new features for working with 3D imagery, motion-based content, and advanced image analysis. The chapters in this book use Photoshop CS5 on the PC platform, running the Windows 7 operating system.

To illustrate the features of Photoshop CS5, this book presents a series of chapters that use Photoshop to edit photos similar to those you will encounter in academic and business environments, as well as photos for personal use.

Project Planning Guidelines

The process of editing a photo requires careful analysis and planning. As a starting point, choose a photo that correctly expresses your desired subject or theme. Once the theme is determined, analyze the intended audience. Define a plan for editing that enhances the photo, eliminates visual clutter, improves color and contrast, and corrects defects. Always work on a duplicate of an original image. Finally, determine the file format and print style that will be most successful at delivering the message. Details of these guidelines are provided in Appendix A. In addition, each chapter in this book provides practical applications of these planning considerations.

Project — Rack Card Graphic

A **rack card** is a popular form of advertising, typically measuring 4 × 9 inches and printed in color on both sides. Organizations print rack cards on sturdy paper so the publications can last longer and stand up in a rack. Interested parties, such as students, tourists, clients, or the public can see the rack card easily. Rack cards commonly use graphics to attract attention.

The project in this chapter uses Photoshop to enhance a photograph of a cyclist to be used on a rack card produced by a university to show prospective students some leisure-time activities on campus. Figure 1–1a displays the original photo. Figure 1–1b displays the edited photo. The enhancements will emphasize the cyclist by positioning the scene to make the layout appear more visually appealing and to crop some of the background. A complimentary border will make the photo stand out. Finally, you will resize the photo to fit on a rack card and then optimize it for the university's Web site.

(a) Original photo

(b) Edited photo

Figure 1–1

Overview

As you read this chapter, you will learn how to edit the photo shown in Figure 1–1a on the previous page by performing these general tasks:

- Customize the workspace.
- Display and navigate a photo at various magnifications.
- Crop a photo effectively.
- Create and modify a border.
- Stroke a selection.
- Resize and print a photo.
- Save, close, and then reopen a photo.
- Save a photo for the Web.
- Use Mini Bridge.
- Use Photoshop Help.

Plan Ahead

General Project Guidelines

When editing a photo, the actions you perform and decisions you make will affect the appearance and characteristics of the finished product. As you edit a photo, such as the one shown in Figure 1–1a, you should follow these general guidelines:

1. **Find an appropriate image or photo.** Keep in mind the purpose and the graphic needs of the project when choosing an image or photo. Decide ahead of time on the file type and decide if the image will be used on the Web. An eye-catching graphic image should convey a universal theme. The photo should grab the attention of viewers and draw them into the picture, whether in print or on the Web.

2. **Determine how to edit the photo to highlight the theme.** As you edit, use standard design principles, and keep in mind your subject, your audience, the required size and shape of the graphic, color decisions, the rule of thirds, the golden rectangle, and other design principles. Decide which parts of the photo portray your message and which parts are visual clutter. Crop the photo as needed.

3. **Identify finishing touches that will further enhance the photo.** The overall appearance of a photo significantly affects its ability to communicate clearly. You might want to add text or a border.

4. **Prepare for publication.** Resize the photo as needed to fit the allotted space. Save the photo on a storage medium, such as a hard drive, USB flash drive, or CD. Print the photo or publish it to the Web.

When necessary, more specific details concerning the above guidelines are presented at appropriate points in the chapter. The chapter also will identify the actions performed and decisions made regarding these guidelines during the creation of the edited photo shown in Figure 1–1b on the previous page.

BTW

Screen Resolution
If your computer has a high-resolution monitor with a screen resolution of 1280 × 800 or higher, lowering that resolution to 1024 × 768 may cause some images to be distorted because of a difference in the aspect ratio. If you want to keep your high-resolution setting, be aware that the location of on-screen tools might vary slightly from the book.

Starting Photoshop

If you are using a computer to step through the project in this chapter, and you want your screen to match the figures in this book, you should change your screen's resolution to 1024 × 768. For information about how to change a screen's resolution, read Appendix C.

To Start Photoshop

The following steps, which assume Windows 7 is running, start Photoshop, based on a typical installation. You may need to ask your instructor how to start Photoshop for your computer.

1

- Click the Start button on the Windows 7 taskbar to display the Start menu.

- Type **Photoshop CS5** as the search text in the 'Search programs and files' text box, and watch the search results appear on the Start menu (Figure 1–2).

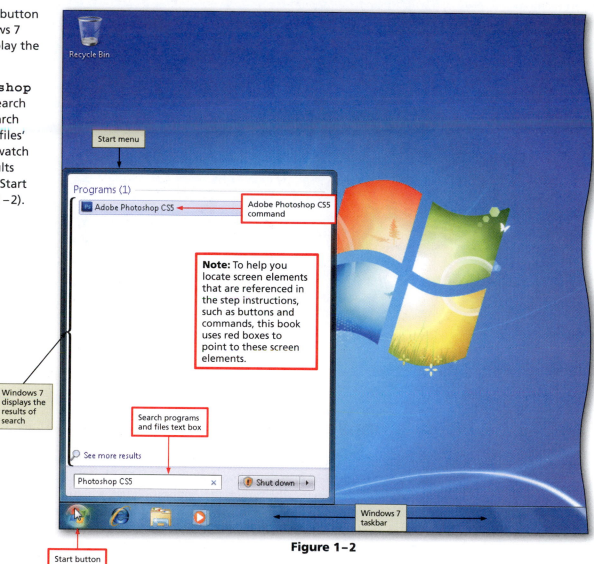

Start menu

Programs (1)

Adobe Photoshop CS5

Adobe Photoshop CS5 command

Note: To help you locate screen elements that are referenced in the step instructions, such as buttons and commands, this book uses red boxes to point to these screen elements.

Windows 7 displays the results of search

Search programs and files text box

See more results

Photoshop CS5

Shut down

Windows 7 taskbar

Start button

Figure 1–2

Q&A

Why do I have documents and files in my list of results?

Any documents containing the words, Photoshop CS5, and any files that have been opened with Photoshop CS5 may appear in your list.

2

- Click Adobe Photoshop CS5 in the search results on the Start menu to start Photoshop.

- After a few moments, when the Photoshop window is displayed, if the window is not maximized, click the Maximize button next to the Close button on the title bar to maximize the window (Figure 1–3).

Q&A

What is a maximized window?

A maximized window fills the entire screen. When you maximize a window, the Maximize button changes to a Restore Down button.

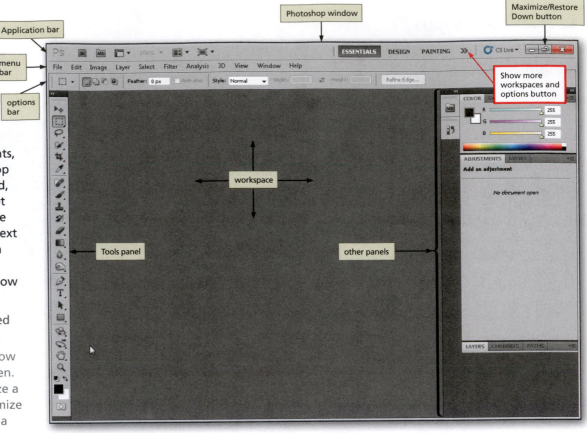

Figure 1–3

Other Ways

1. Double-click Photoshop icon on desktop, if one is present
2. Click Adobe Photoshop CS5 on Start menu

Customizing the Photoshop Workspace

The screen in Figure 1–3 shows how the Photoshop workspace looks the first time you start Photoshop after installation on most computers. Photoshop does not open a blank or default photo automatically; rather, the Application bar, a menu bar, and the options bar appear across the top of the screen with a gray work area below the options bar. The Tools panel is displayed on the left; other panels are displayed on the right. The gray work area and panels are referred to collectively as the **workspace**.

As you work in Photoshop, the panels, the selected tool, and the options bar settings might change. Therefore, if you want your screen to match the figures in this book, you should restore the default workspace, select the default tool, and reset the options bar. For more information about how to change other advanced Photoshop settings, see Appendix C.

Because of a default preference setting, each time you start Photoshop, the Photoshop workspace is displayed the same way it was the last time you used Photoshop. If the panels are relocated, then they will appear in their new locations the next time you start Photoshop. You can create and save your own workspaces, or use Photoshop's saved workspaces that show a group of panels used for certain tasks. For example, the Painting workspace displays the Brush presets panel and the Swatches panel, among others — all of which you would need when painting. You will learn more about panels later in this chapter. Similarly, if values on the options bar are changed or a different tool is selected, they will remain changed the next time you start Photoshop. If you wish to return the workspace to its default settings, follow these steps each time you start Photoshop.

To Select the Essentials Workspace

The default workspace, called Essentials, displays commonly used panels. The following steps select the Essentials workspace.

1
• Click the 'Show more workspaces and options' button on the Application bar to display the names of saved workspaces (Figure 1–4).

 Experiment

• Click each of the workspaces that are displayed in the list to view the different panel configurations. When you are finished, click the 'Show more workspaces and options' button again to display the list.

Figure 1–4

2
• If necessary, click Essentials to select the default workspace panels.

• Click the 'Show more workspaces and options' button again to display the list (Figure 1–5).

Q&A | What does the New Workspace command do?

The New Workspace command displays a dialog box where you can create a new workspace based on the currently displayed panels. You also can add the current keyboard shortcuts and menus to the new workspace.

Figure 1–5

3
• Click Reset Essentials to restore the workspace to its default settings and reposition any panels that may have been moved (Figure 1–6).

Q&A | My screen did not change. Did I do something wrong?

If Photoshop is a new installation on your system, you might notice few changes on your screen.

Other Ways

1. On Window menu, point to Workspace, click Essentials (Default)

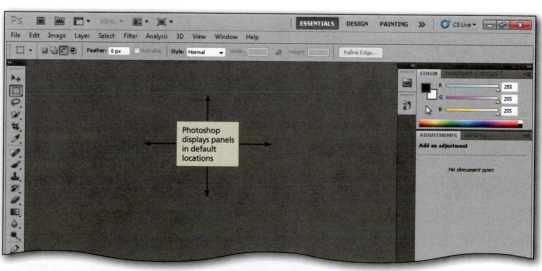

Figure 1–6

To Reset the Tools Panel

The following step resets the Tools panel to its default setting. When you select a tool on the Tools panel, the options bar reflects the settings of that tool.

1

- If necessary, click the second button from the top on the Tools panel to select it (Figure 1–7).

- If the tools in the Tools panel appear in two columns, click the double arrow at the top of the Tools panel.

Q&A

What appears when I point to the button?

When you point to many objects in the Photoshop workspace, such as a tool or button, Photoshop displays a tool tip. A **tool tip** is a short, on-screen note associated with the object to which you are pointing, which helps you identify the button. This button's name is the Rectangular Marquee Tool.

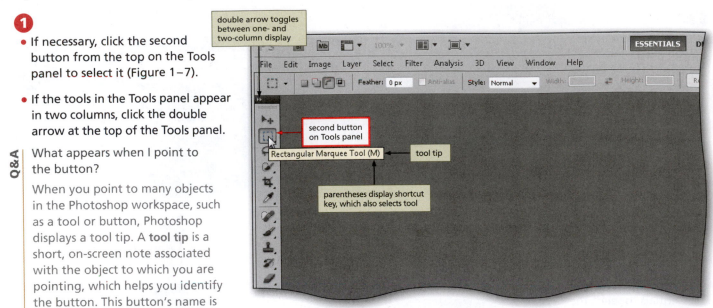

Figure 1–7

Other Ways

1. Press M

To Reset the Options Bar

As you work through the chapters, editing and creating photos, you will find that the options bar is **context sensitive**, which means it changes as you select different tools. In addition, the options and settings are retained for the next time you use Photoshop. To match the figures in this book, you should reset the options bar each time you start Photoshop using a context menu. A **context menu**, or **shortcut menu**, appears when you right-click some objects in the Photoshop workspace. The menu displays commands representing the active tool, selection, or panel.

The following steps reset all tool settings in the options bar using a context menu.

1

- Right-click the Rectangular Marquee Tool icon on the options bar to display its context menu (Figure 1–8).

Q&A

Why is my icon elliptical?

It is possible that a previous user has used the Elliptical Marquee Tool. Press SHIFT+M to return to the Rectangular Marquee Tool.

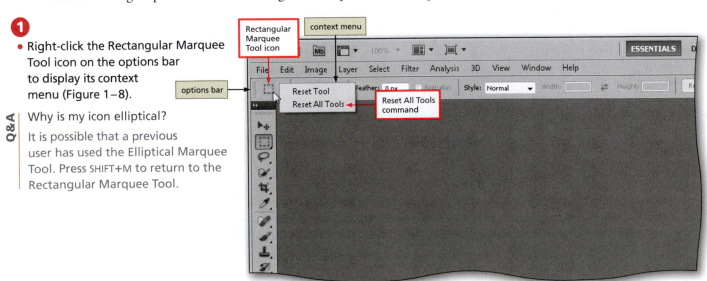

Figure 1–8

2

• Click Reset All Tools to display a confirmation dialog box (Figure 1–9).

3

• Click the OK button (confirmation dialog box) to restore the tools to their default settings.

Figure 1–9

Opening a Photo

To open a photo in Photoshop, it must be stored as a digital file on your computer system or on an external storage device. To **open** a photo, you bring a copy of the file from the storage location to the screen where you can **edit** or make changes to the photo. The changes do not become permanent, however, until you **save** or store the changed file on a storage device. The photos used in this book are stored on a CD located in the back of the book. Your instructor may designate a different location for the photos.

Find an appropriate image or photo.

Sometimes a person or business gives you a specific photo for use in a project. Other times, you are assigned a theme and asked to find or take the photo. An eye-catching graphic image should convey a universal theme or visually convey a message that is not expressed easily with words. Keep the audience in mind as you choose a photo. Photos generally fall into one of four categories:

• In advertising, a photo might show a product, service, result, model, or benefit.

• In a public service setting, a photo might represent a topic of interest, nature, signage, buildings, or a photo of historical importance.

• In industry, a photo might display a process, product, work organization, employee, facility, layout, equipment, safety, result, or culture.

• For personal or journalistic use, a photo might be a portrait, scenery, action shot, or event.

The images used in rack cards must fit into a small space. A picture on a rack card might contain text printed over the picture or a border to attract attention. A graphic designed for a rack card should be of high quality, use strong color, and must deliver a message in the clearest, most attractive, and most effective way possible.

Plan Ahead

BTW

Context Menus
Photoshop uses the term, context menu, for any short menu that appears when you right-click. Other applications may call it a shortcut menu. The two terms are synonymous.

To Open a Photo

The following steps open the Cyclist file from a CD located in drive E. The drive letter of your CD drive might differ.

1

- Insert the CD containing the Data Files for Students that accompanies this book into your CD drive. After a few seconds, if Windows displays a dialog box, click its Close button.

- Click File on the menu bar to display the File menu (Figure 1–10).

Q&A   What if I do not have the CD?

You will need the Data Files for Students to complete the activities and exercises in this book. See your instructor for information on how to acquire the necessary files.

Q&A   Can I use a shortcut key to open a file?

Yes, the shortcut keys are displayed on the menu. In this textbook, the shortcut keys also are displayed at the end of each series of steps in the Other Ways box.

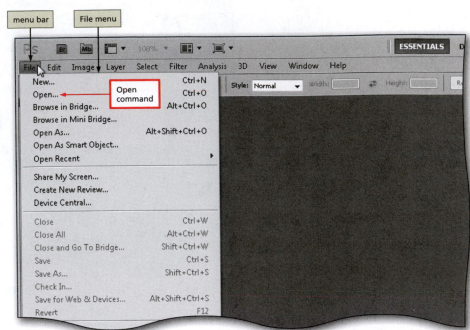

Figure 1–10

2

- Click Open on the File menu to display the Open dialog box.

- Click the Look in box arrow (Open dialog box) to display a list of the available storage locations on your system (Figure 1–11).

Q&A   Are there other ways to navigate in the Open dialog box?

Yes, the Go To Last Folder Visited button and Up One Level button help you move through the folders on your computer. The navigation pane also displays links to common storage locations.

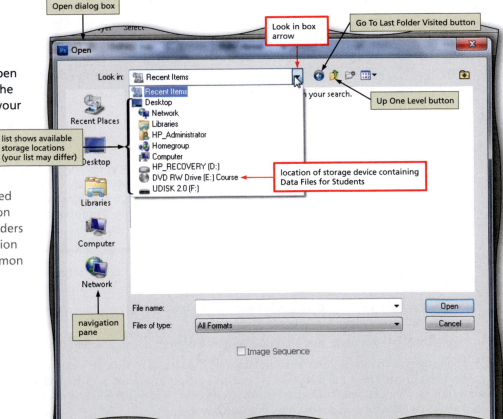

Figure 1–11

3

- Click DVD RW Drive (E:) Course, or the drive associated with your CD, to display its contents (Figure 1–12).

Q&A Why is the third button at the top of the Open dialog box disabled?

That button is the Create New Folder button. It is disabled because the CD is read-only.

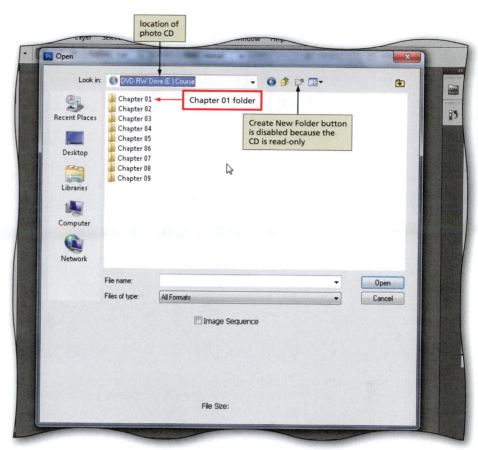

Figure 1–12

4

- Double-click the Chapter 01 folder and then click the file, Cyclist, to select the file to be opened (Figure 1–13).

Q&A Why does my file list look different?

Your list will vary. Also, the files in Figure 1–13 are displayed in List view. Click the View Menu button to verify your view.

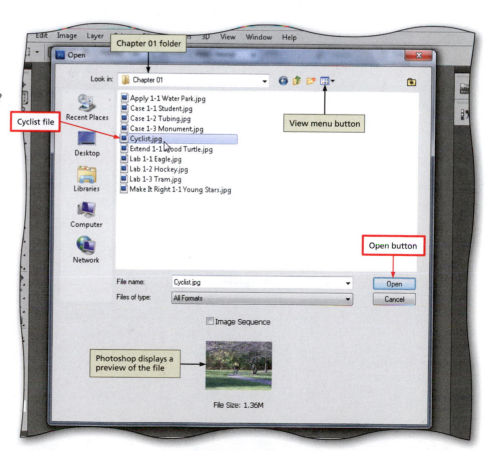

Figure 1–13

5
- Click the Open button to open the selected file and display the open photo in the Photoshop workspace (Figure 1–14).

Can I edit a printed photo?

Most of the images you will use in this book already are stored in digital format; however, when you have a print copy of a picture, rather than a digital file stored on your system, it sometimes is necessary to scan the picture using a scanner. A **scanner** is a device used to convert a hard copy into a digital form for storage, retrieval, or other electronic purposes. Photoshop allows you to bring a copy from the scanner directly into the workspace.

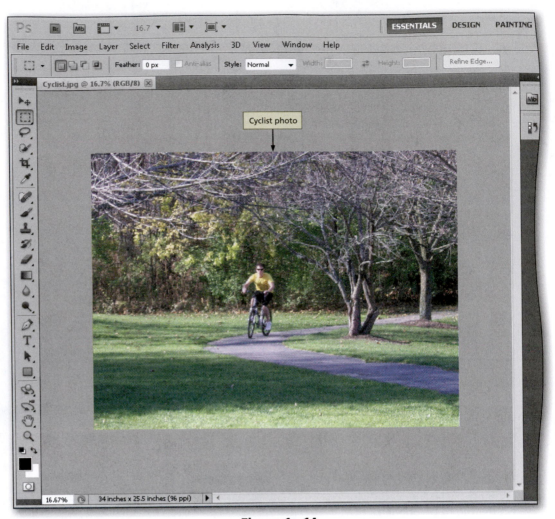

Figure 1–14

Other Ways

1. Press CTRL+O, select file, click Open
2. In Windows, right-click file, click Open with, click Adobe Photoshop CS5

The Photoshop Workspace

The Photoshop workspace consists of a variety of components to make your work more efficient and to make your photo documents look more professional. The following sections discuss these components.

The Application Bar

The Application bar appears at the top of the workspace (Figure 1–15). The Application bar contains the Launch Bridge button, the Launch Mini Bridge button, and commonly used controls related to document and workspace manipulation. On the right side of the Application bar are the CS Live button and common window clip controls. Your Application bar might contain different controls depending on the chosen saved workspace.

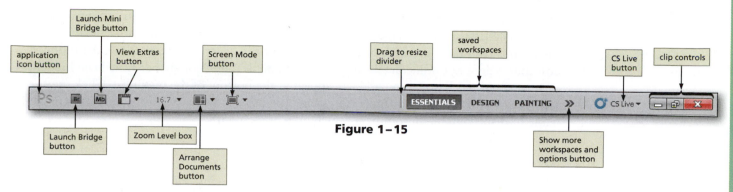

Figure 1–15

The Menu Bar

The menu bar appears at the top of the screen just below the Application bar (Figure 1–16). The **menu bar** is a toolbar that displays the Photoshop menu names. Each **menu** contains a list of commands you can use to perform tasks such as opening, saving, printing, and editing photos. To display a menu, such as the View menu, click the View menu name on the menu bar. If you point to a command on a menu that has an arrow on its right edge, as shown in Figure 1–16, a **submenu**, or secondary menu, displays another list of commands.

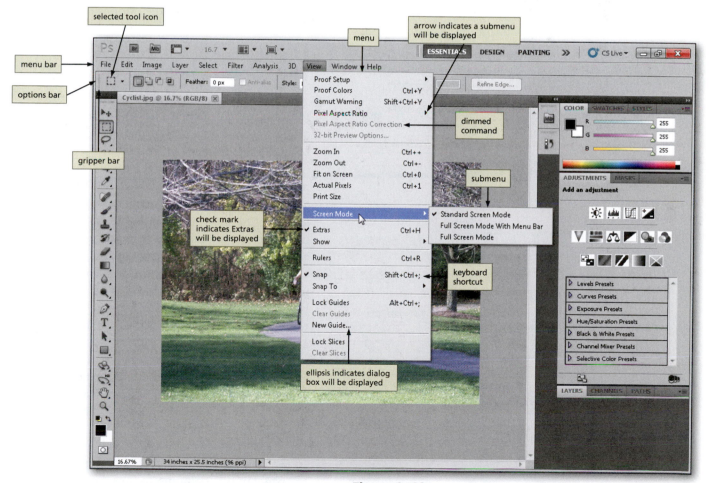

Figure 1–16

When Photoshop first is installed, all of the menu commands within a menu appear when you click the menu name. To hide seldom-used menu commands, you can click the Menus command on the Edit menu and follow the on-screen instructions. A **hidden command** does not immediately appear on a menu. If menu commands have been hidden, a Show All Menu Items command will appear at the bottom of the menu list. Click the Show All Menu Items command, or press and hold the CTRL key when you click the menu name to display all menu commands, including hidden ones.

The Options Bar

The options bar (Figure 1–16 on the previous page) appears below the menu bar. Sometimes called the Control panel, the options bar contains buttons and boxes that allow you to perform tasks more quickly than when using the menu bar and related menus. Most buttons on the options bar display words or images to help you remember their functions. When you point to a button or box on the options bar, a tool tip is displayed below the mouse pointer. The options bar changes to reflect the tool currently selected on the Tools panel. For example, a tool related to text might display a font box on the options bar, whereas a tool related to painting will display a brush button. The selected tool always appears as an icon on the left side of the options bar. As each tool is discussed throughout this book, the associated options bar will be explained in more detail.

You can **float**, or move, the options bar in the workspace by dragging the gray **gripper bar** on the left side of the options bar. You can **dock** or reattach the options bar below the menu bar by resetting the workspace. To hide or show the options bar, click Options on the Window menu.

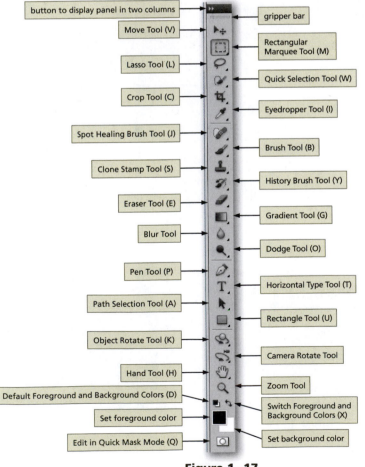

Figure 1–17

The Tools Panel

On the left side of the workspace is the Photoshop Tools panel. The Tools panel is a group of **tools**, or buttons, organized into a toolbar. Like the options bar, you can float, dock, hide, or show the Tools panel. Each tool on the Tools panel displays a **tool icon**. When you point to the tool icon, a tool tip displays the name of the tool including its shortcut key. You can expand some tools to show hidden tools beneath them. Expandable tools display a small triangle in the lower-right corner of the tool icon. Click and hold the tool button or right-click to see or select one of its hidden tools from the context menu. The default tool names and their corresponding shortcut keys are listed in Figure 1–17.

When you click a tool on the Tools panel to use it, Photoshop selects the button and changes the options bar as necessary. When using a tool from the Tools panel, the mouse pointer changes to reflect the selected tool.

The Tools panel is organized by purpose. At the very top of the panel is a button to display the panel in two columns, followed underneath by the gripper bar. Below that, the selection tools appear, then the crop and slice tools, followed by retouching, painting, drawing and type, annotation, measuring, and navigation tools. At the bottom of the Tools panel are buttons to set colors and create a quick mask. As each tool is introduced throughout this book, its function and options bar characteristics will be explained further.

The Document Window

The **document window** is the light gray area within the workspace that displays the active file or image. The document window contains a title bar, display area, scroll bars, and status bar (Figure 1–18).

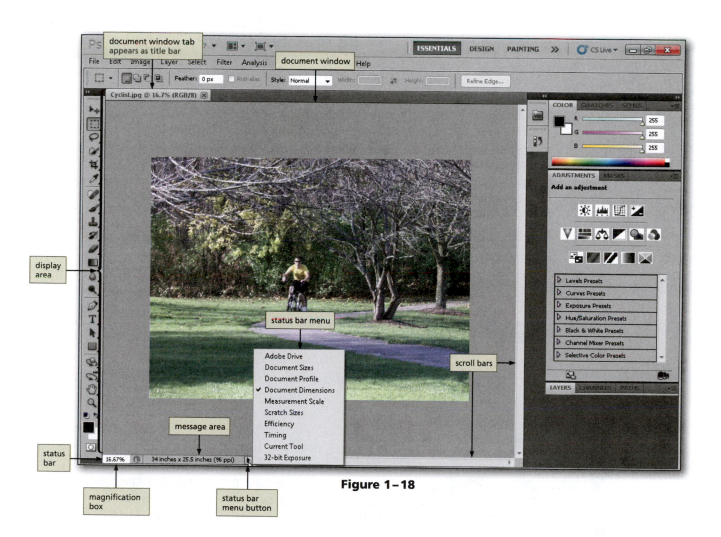

Figure 1–18

Title Bar Photoshop displays a **title bar**, or **document window tab**, at the top of the document window that shows the name of the file, the magnification, the color mode, and a Close button. If you have multiple files open, each has its own document window tab. You can move the document window by dragging the document window tab, or dock it again by dragging the title bar close to the options bar. When floating, the title bar expands across the top of the document window and displays Minimize, Restore Down, and Close buttons.

Display Area The **display area** (Figure 1–18 on the previous page) is the portion of the document window that displays the photo or image. You perform most tool tasks and edit the photo in the display area.

Scroll Bars **Scroll bars** appear on the right and bottom of the document window. When the photo is bigger than the document window, the scroll bars become active and display scroll arrows and scroll boxes to move the image up, down, left, and right.

Status Bar Across the bottom of the document window, Photoshop displays the **status bar**. The status bar contains a magnification box. **Magnification** refers to the percentage of enlargement or reduction on the screen. For example, a 50% indication in the magnification box means the entire photo is displayed at 50 percent of its actual size. Changing the magnification does not change the size of the photo physically; it merely displays it on the screen at a different size. You can type a new percentage in the magnification box to display a different view of the photo.

Next to the magnification box is the **message area**. Messages can display information about the file size, the current tool, or the document dimensions. When you first start Photoshop, the message area displays information about the document size in storage.

On the right side of the status bar is the status bar menu button that, when clicked, displays a status bar menu. You use the status bar menu to change the message area or to change to other versions of the document.

Your installation of Photoshop might display rulers at the top and left of the document window. You will learn about rulers later in this chapter.

BTW

Status Bar
The status bar may display different messages, depending upon your previous settings, the previous kind of file you had open, and your installation. If you want your status bar to match the figures in this chapter, click the status bar menu and then click Document Dimensions.

Panels

A **panel** is a collection of graphically displayed choices and commands, such as those involving colors, brushes, actions, or layers (Figure 1–19). Panels help you monitor and modify your work. Each panel displays a panel tab with the name of the panel and a panel menu button. When you click the panel menu button, also called the panel menu icon, Photoshop displays a context-sensitive menu that allows you to make changes to the panel. Some panels have a status bar across the bottom. A panel can display buttons, boxes, sliders, scroll bars, or drop-down lists.

Several panels appear in the Essentials workspace. Some panels are expanded to display their contents, and are grouped by general purpose. A **panel group** or **tab group** displays several panels horizontally. The panel group is docked vertically on the right side of the workspace. Two other panels are displayed as icons or buttons in a vertical docking between the document window and the expanded panels. Panels are **collapsed** when they appear as a button or **expanded** when they display their contents. Panels are **minimized** when they display only their tab. To collapse or expand a panel, click the double arrow in the panel title bar. To minimize a panel, double-click its tab. To close a panel, click Close on the panel

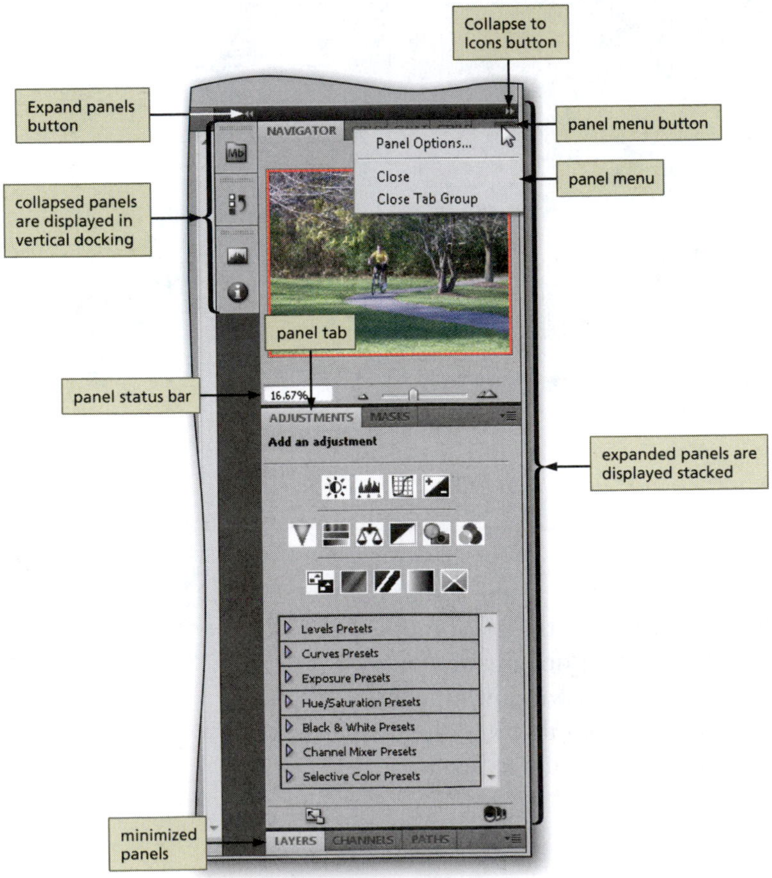

Figure 1–19

menu. To redisplay the panel, click the panel name on the Window menu or use a panel shortcut key.

You can arrange and reposition panels either individually or in groups. To move them individually, drag their tabs; to move a group, drag the area to the right of the tabs. To float a panel in the workspace, drag its tab outside of the vertical docking. You can create a **stack** of floating panels by dragging a panel tab to a location below another floating panel and docking it.

Sometimes you might want to hide all the panels to display more of the document window. To hide all panels, press the TAB key. Press the TAB key again to display the panels.

Photoshop comes with 26 panels, described in Table 1–1. As each panel is introduced throughout this book, its function and characteristics will be explained further.

Table 1–1 Photoshop Panels

Panel Name	Purpose
3D	to show the 3D layer components, settings, and options of the associated 3D file — available in Photoshop Extended only
Actions	to record, play, edit, and delete individual actions
Adjustments	to create nondestructive adjustment layers with color and tonal adjustments
Animation	to create a sequence of images or frames, displayed as motion over time
Brush	to select preset brushes and design custom brushes
Brush Presets	to create, load, save, and manage preset brush tips
Channels	to create and manage channels
Character	to provide options for formatting characters
Clone Source	to set up and manipulate sample sources for the Clone Stamp tools or Healing Brush tools
Color	to display the color values for the current foreground and background colors
Histogram	to view tonal and color information about an image
History	to jump to any recent state of the image created during the current working session
Info	to display color values and document status information
Layer Comps	to display multiple compositions of a page layout
Layers	to show and hide layers, create new layers, and work with groups of layers
Masks	to create precise, editable pixel- and vector-based masks
Mini Bridge	to assist in navigating folders and files, and to access other modules in the suite
Measurement Log	to record measurement data about a measured object — available in Photoshop Extended only
Navigator	to change the view or magnification of the photo using a thumbnail display
Notes	to insert, edit, and delete notes attached to files
Paragraph	to change the formatting of columns and paragraphs
Paths	to manipulate each saved path, the current work path, and the current vector mask
Styles	to view and select preset styles
Swatches	to select and store colors that you need to use often
Tools	to select tools
Tool Presets	to save and reuse tool settings

BTW

File Extensions
The default setting for file extensions in Photoshop is to use a lowercase three-letter extension. If you want to change the extension, do the following: Press SHIFT+CTRL+S to access the Save As dialog box. In the File name text box, type the file name, period, and extension within quotation marks. Click the Save button.

BTW

Saving Photos
When you save a photo on a storage device, it also remains in main memory and is displayed on the screen.

File Types

A **file type** refers to the internal characteristics of digital files; it designates the operational or structural characteristics of a file. Each digital file, graphic or otherwise, is stored with specific kinds of formatting related to how the file appears on the screen, how it prints, and the software it uses to do so. Computer systems use the file type to help users open the file with the appropriate software. A **file extension**, in most computer systems, is a three- or four-letter suffix after the file name that distinguishes the file type. For example, Cyclist.jpg refers to a file named Cyclist with the extension and file type JPG. A period separates the file name and its extension. When you are exploring files on your system, you might see the file extensions as part of the file name, or you might see a column of information about file types.

Graphic files are created using many different file types and extensions. The type of file sometimes is determined by the hardware or software used to create the file. Other times, the user has a choice in applying a file type and makes the decision based on file size, the intended purpose of the file — such as whether the file is to be used on the Web — or the desired color mode. A few common graphic file types are listed in Table 1–2.

BTW

File Name Characters
A file name can have a maximum of 260 characters, including spaces. The only invalid characters are the backslash (\), slash (/), colon (:), asterisk (*), question mark (?), quotation mark ("), less than symbol (<), greater than symbol (>), and vertical bar (|).

Table 1–2 Graphic File Types

File Extension	File Type	Description
BMP	Bitmap	BMP is a standard Windows image format used on DOS and Windows-compatible computers. BMP format supports many different color modes.
EPS	Encapsulated PostScript	EPS files can contain both bitmap and vector graphics. Most graphics, illustrations, and page-layout programs support the EPS format, which can be used to transfer PostScript artwork between applications.
GIF	Graphics Interchange Format	GIF commonly is used to display graphics and images on Web pages. It is a compressed format designed to minimize file size and electronic transfer time.
JPG or JPEG	Joint Photographic Experts Group	JPG files commonly are used to display photographs on Web pages. JPG format supports many different color modes. JPG retains all color information in an RGB image, unlike GIF format. Most digital cameras produce JPG files.
PDF	Portable Document Format	PDF is a flexible file format based on the PostScript imaging model that is cross-platform and cross-application. PDF files accurately display and preserve fonts, page layouts, and graphics. PDF files can contain electronic document search and navigation features such as hyperlinks.
PNG	Portable Network Graphics	PNG graphics display images without jagged edges, while keeping the file size small. The PNG format is used for clip art, Web graphics, and when graphics need to display transparent backgrounds rather than white.
PSD	Photoshop Document	PSD format is the default file format in Photoshop and the only format that supports all Photoshop features. Other Adobe applications can import PSD files directly and preserve many Photoshop features due to the tight integration among Adobe products.
RAW	Photoshop Raw	RAW format is a flexible file format used for transferring images between applications and computer platforms. There are no pixel or file size restrictions in this format. Documents saved in the Photoshop Raw format cannot contain layers.
TIF or TIFF	Tagged Image File Format	TIF is a flexible bitmap image format supported by almost all paint, image-editing, and page-layout applications. This format often is used for files that are to be exchanged between applications or computer platforms. Most desktop scanners can produce TIF images.

Saving a Photo

As you make changes to a file in Photoshop, the computer stores it in memory. If you turn off the computer or if you lose electrical power, the file in memory is lost. If you plan to use the photo later, you must save it on a storage device such as a USB flash drive or on your hard drive.

While you are editing, to preserve the most features such as layers, effects, masks, and styles, Photoshop recommends that you save photos in the **PSD format**. PSD, which stands for Photoshop Document Format, is the default file format for files created from scratch in Photoshop, and supports files up to two gigabytes (GB) in size. The PSD format also maximizes portability among other Adobe versions and applications.

To Save a Photo in the PSD Format

The following steps save the photo on a USB flash drive using the file name, Cyclist Edited. In addition to saving in the PSD format, you will save the photo with a new file name and in a new location, so that the original photo is preserved in case you need to start again. Even though you have yet to edit the photo, it is a good practice to save a copy of the file on your personal storage device early in the process.

1

- With a USB flash drive connected to one of the computer's USB ports, click File on the menu bar to display the File menu (Figure 1–20).

Q&A Do I have to save to a USB flash drive?

No. You can save to any device or folder. A **folder** is a specific location on a storage medium. You can save to the default folder or a different folder.

Q&A What if my USB flash drive has a different name or letter?

It is very likely that your USB flash drive will have a different name and drive letter and be connected to a different port. Verify that the device in your Computer list is correct.

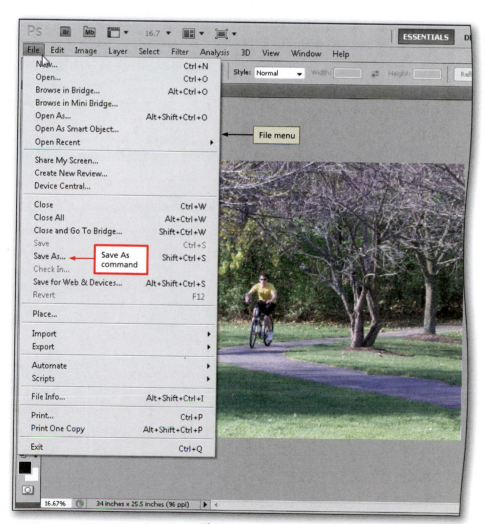

Figure 1–20

2

- Click Save As to display the Save As dialog box.

- Type **Cyclist Edited** in the File name text box (Save As dialog box) to change the file name. Do not press the ENTER key after typing the file name.

- Click the Save in box arrow to display the list of available drives (Figure 1–21).

Q&A

Do I have to use that file name?

It is good practice to identify the relationship of this photo to the original by using at least part of the original file name with some notation about its status.

Q&A

Why is my list of drives arranged and named differently?

The size of the Save As dialog box and your computer's configuration determine how the list is displayed and how the drives are named.

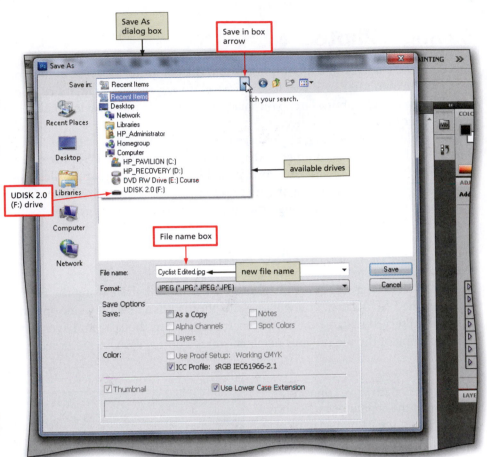

Figure 1–21

3

- Click UDISK 2.0 (F:), or the name of your USB flash drive, in the list of available storage devices to select that drive as the new save location.

- Click the Format button (Save As dialog box) to display the list of available file formats (Figure 1–22).

Q&A

Should I make a special folder for my photos?

You might want to create a folder for each chapter in this book. If so, click the Create New Folder button in the Save As dialog box. When the new folder is displayed, type a chapter name such as **Chapter 01** and then press the ENTER key. Double-click the new folder to open it.

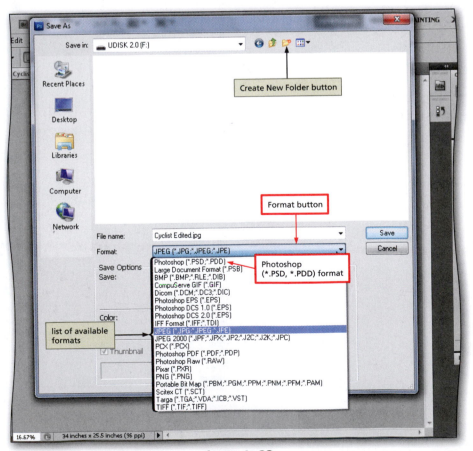

Figure 1–22

• Click Photoshop (*.PSD, *.PDD) to select it (Figure 1–23).

Q&A What is PDD?

The **PDD format** is used with images created by Photo Deluxe and other software packages. Some older digital cameras produce files with a PDD extension as well.

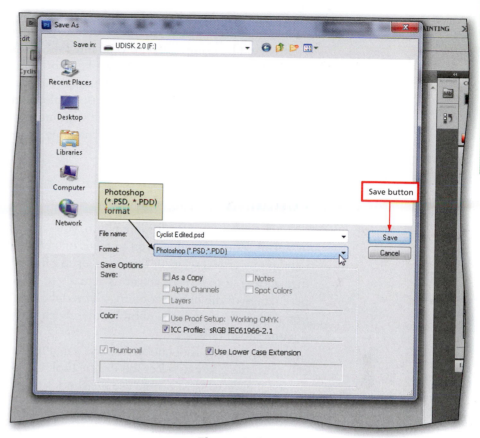

Figure 1–23

• Click the Save button (Save As dialog box) to save the document on the selected drive with the new file name (Figure 1–24).

Q&A How do I know that the project is saved?

While Photoshop is saving your file, it briefly displays a Working in Background mouse pointer. In addition, your USB drive might have a light that flashes during the save process. The new file name appears on the document window tab.

new file name is displayed in document window tab

Figure 1–24

Other Ways

1. Press SHIFT+CTRL+S, choose settings, click Save button

Viewing Photos

Photoshop allows you to view photos in many different ways, by adjusting the document window and by using different tools and panels. Using good navigation techniques to view images can help you edit the details of a photo or check for problems. For example, you might want to zoom in on a specific portion of the photo or move to a different location in a large photo. You might want to use a ruler to measure certain portions of the photo. Or you might want to view the image without the distraction of the panels and menu. Zooming, navigating, scrolling, and changing the screen mode are some ways to view the document window and its photo.

Zooming

To make careful edits in a photo, you sometimes need to change the magnification, or **zoom**. Zooming allows you to focus on certain parts of the photo, such as a specific person in a crowd scene or details in a complicated picture. A magnification of 100% means the photo is displayed at its actual size. Zooming in enlarges the magnification and percentage of the photo; zooming out reduces the magnification. Note that zooming does not change the size of the photo; it merely changes the appearance of the photo in the document window.

The Zoom Tool button displays a magnifying glass icon on the Tools panel. You also can press the z key to select the Zoom Tool. Choosing one over the other is a matter of personal choice. Most people use the shortcut key. Others sometimes choose the button because of its proximity to the mouse pointer at the time.

When you use the Zoom Tool, each click magnifies the image to the next preset percentage. When positioned in the photo, the Zoom Tool mouse pointer displays a magnifying glass, with either a plus sign, indicating an increase in magnification, or a minus sign, indicating a decrease in magnification. Right-clicking with the Zoom Tool in the photo displays a context menu with options to zoom in or zoom out, among others.

Figure 1–25 displays the Zoom Tool options bar, with buttons to zoom in and out. Other options include check boxes used when working with multiple photos, displaying the actual pixels, fitting the entire photo on the screen, filling the screen, and displaying the photo at its print size.

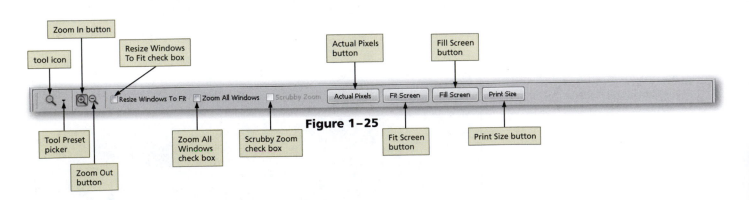

Figure 1–25

To Use the Zoom Tool

The following steps zoom in on the cyclist for careful editing later in the chapter.

1

- Click the Zoom Tool button on the Tools panel to select the Zoom tool.

- Move the mouse pointer into the document window to display the magnifying glass mouse pointer (Figure 1–26).

Q&A

Why does my mouse pointer display a minus sign?

Someone may have previously zoomed out and the setting has carried over. Click the Zoom In button on the options bar.

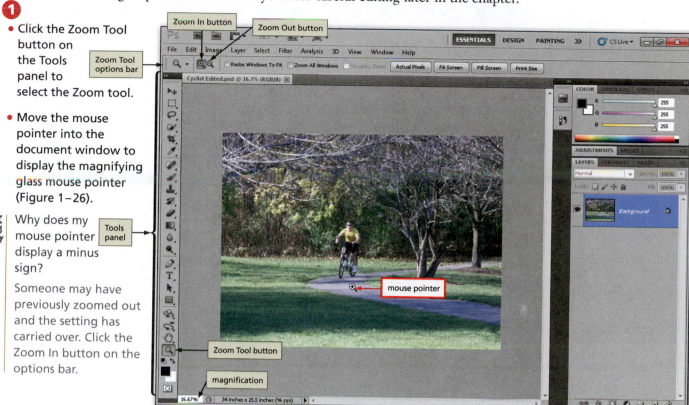

Figure 1–26

2

- Click the cyclist three times to zoom in (Figure 1–27).

Experiment

- On the options bar, click the Zoom Out button and then click the photo. ALT+click the photo to zoom in the opposite direction from the options bar setting. Zoom to 50% magnification.

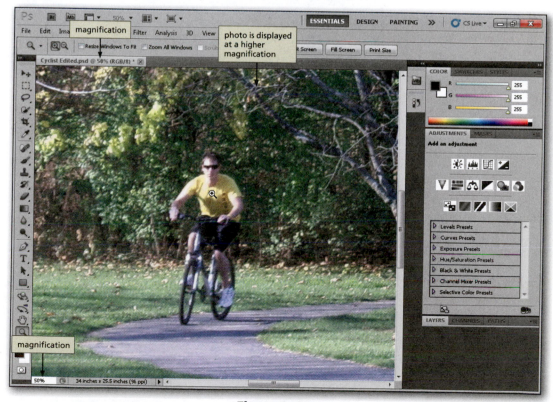

Figure 1–27

Other Ways

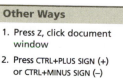

1. Press Z, click document window
2. Press CTRL+PLUS SIGN (+) or CTRL+MINUS SIGN (−)
3. On View menu, click Zoom In or Zoom Out

The Navigator Panel

Another convenient way to zoom and move around the photo is to use the Navigator panel. The Navigator panel (Figure 1–28) is used to change the view of your document window using a thumbnail display. To display the Navigator panel, choose Navigator from the Window menu.

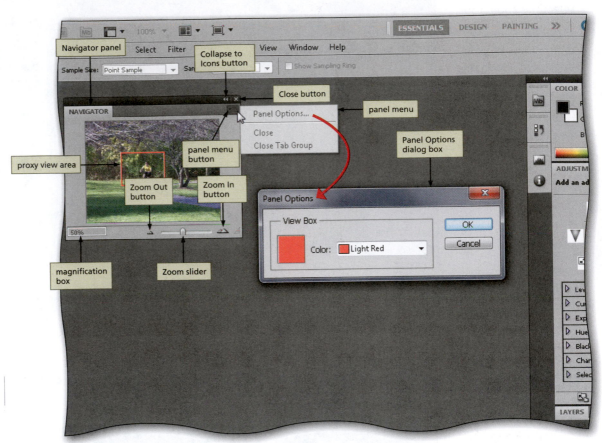

Figure 1–28

The rectangle with the red border in the Navigator panel is called the **proxy view area** or **view box**, which outlines the currently viewable area in the window. Dragging the proxy view area changes the portion of the photo that is displayed in the document window. In the lower portion of the Navigator panel, you can type in the desired magnification, or you can use the slider or buttons to increase or decrease the magnification.

In Figure 1–28, the Navigator panel menu appears when you click the panel menu button. The Panel Options command displays the Panel Options dialog box.

To move the panel, drag the panel tab. To collapse the panel, click the Collapse to Icons button. To close the panel, click the panel's Close button or click Close on the panel menu.

When you are using a different tool on the Tools panel, such as a text tool or brush tool, it is easier to use the Navigator panel to zoom in or out and move around in the photo. That way, you do not have to change to the Zoom tool, perform the zoom, and then change back to your editing tool.

To Open the Navigator Panel

The following steps open the Navigator panel.

1

● Click Window on the menu bar to display the Window menu (Figure 1–29).

Q&A

What do the check marks mean?

Each panel with a check mark already is displayed and expanded in the workspace.

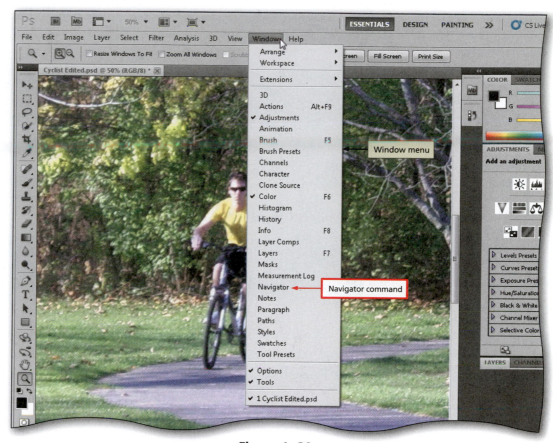

Figure 1–29

2

● Click Navigator on the Window menu to open the Navigator panel (Figure 1–30).

Q&A

Why does the Navigator panel extend into the document window?

Panels that are not part of the current workspace appear in the vertical panel docking. When displayed, they expand to the left.

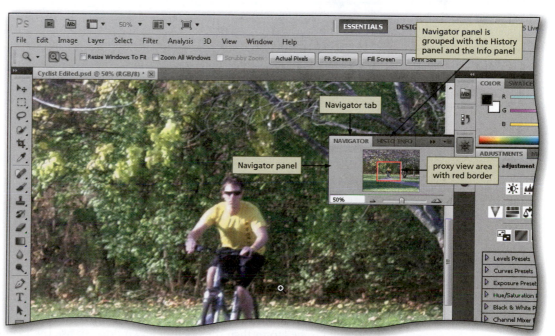

Figure 1–30

To Use the Navigator Panel

The following step repositions the view of the photo using the proxy view area.

1
- Drag the proxy view area on the Navigator Panel to display the lower-right portion of the photo (Figure 1–31).

🔍 **Experiment**
- Drag the proxy view area to display different portions of the photo, and then drag to display the lower-right portion of the photo.

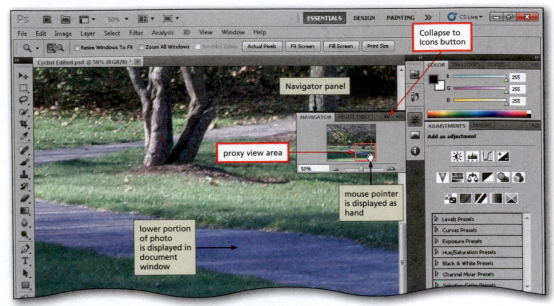

Figure 1–31

To Collapse the Navigator Panel

The following step collapses the Navigator panel.

1
- Click the Collapse to Icons button (shown in Figure 1–31) on the Navigator panel title bar to collapse the Navigator panel (Figure 1–32).

Q&A

How would I close the Navigator panel completely?

Click the panel menu button and then click Close on the panel menu.

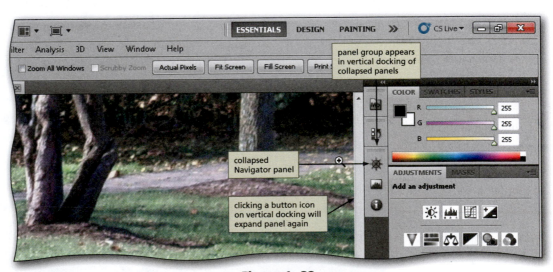

Figure 1–32

The Hand Tool

The Hand tool also can be used to move around in the photo if the photo has been magnified to be larger than the document window. To use the Hand tool, click the Hand Tool (H) button on the Tools panel, and then drag in the display area of the document window.

The Hand Tool options bar (Figure 1–33) displays boxes and buttons to assist you in scrolling and manipulating the document window.

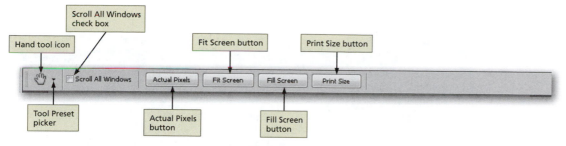

Figure 1–33

To Use the Hand Tool

The following step uses the Hand Tool to view a different part of the photo.

1

- Click the Hand Tool button on the Tools panel to select the Hand Tool.

- Drag in the document window to display the center portion of the photo (Figure 1–34).

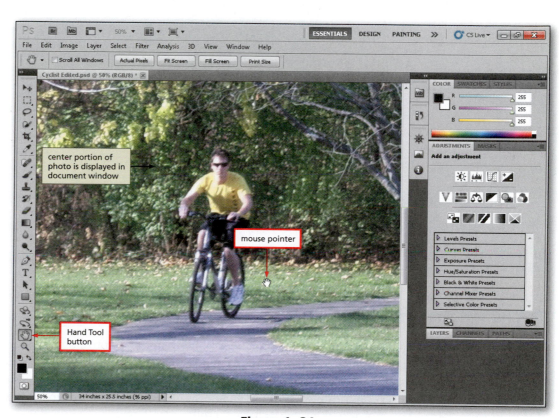

Figure 1–34

To Change the Magnification

The following steps use the magnification box on the status bar to change the magnification.

1

- Double-click the magnification box on the status bar to select the current magnification (Figure 1–35).

Figure 1–35

2

• Type 2 0 and then press the ENTER
key to change the magnification
(Figure 1–36).

photo is
displayed at 20%
magnification

magnification
is changed

20%   34 inches x 25.5 inches (96 ppi)

Figure 1–36

Other Ways

1. On Navigator panel, type
   percentage in magnification
   box

2. On Application bar, type
   percentage in magnification
   box

3. On Application bar, click
   Zoom Level box arrow,
   click desired percentage

To Change the Screen Mode

To change the way the panels, bars, and document window appear, Photoshop includes three **screen modes**, or
ways to view the document window. **Standard screen mode** displays the Application bar, menu bar, options bar, document window, scroll bars, and visible panels. **Full screen mode** displays only the image and rulers, if they are visible, on
a black background. **Full screen mode with menu** enlarges the document window to fill the workspace and combines
the Application bar and menu bar with no status bar or scroll bars. A fourth way to view the screen is to hide the panels.
The following steps view the document window in different modes.

1

• On the Application bar,
click the Screen Mode
button to display its
menu (Figure 1–37).

Q&A

Which mode is best?

It depends on what you are trying
to accomplish. While editing a single
photo, standard screen mode may
be the best, especially for beginners.
If you are working on multiple files,
screen space is at a premium and
you might want to use one of the
full screen modes.

Screen Mode button

Application
bar

20% ▾   ESSENTIALS

✓ Standard Screen Mode
Full Screen Mode With Menu Bar
Full Screen Mode   Full Screen Mode
command

File Edit Image Layer Select Filter An   elp

Scroll All Windows   Actual Pixels

Cyclist Edited.psd @ 20% (RGB/8) * [X]

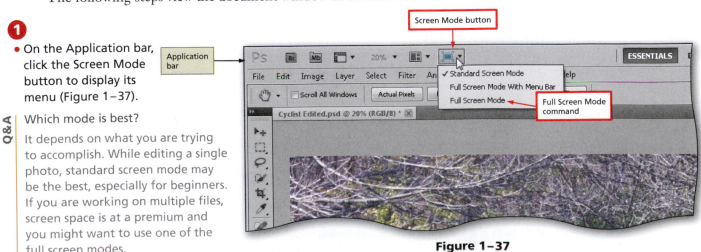

Figure 1–37

2

- Click Full Screen Mode to display the Message dialog box (Figure 1–38).

Q&A What does the 'Don't show again' check box do?

If you check this box, Photoshop will not display the Message dialog box the next time you select Full Screen Mode. Until you are familiar with how to manipulate the screen modes, you should not check this box. The message is a good reminder while you are learning.

Figure 1–38

3

- Click the Full Screen button (Message dialog box) to view the document in full screen mode (Figure 1–39).

- Press the F key to exit full screen mode.

Experiment

- Press the TAB key to hide the panels. Press the TAB key again to display the panels.

Figure 1–39

Other Ways
1. On View menu, point to Screen Mode, click desired mode

To Display Rulers

To make careful edits in a photo, sometimes it is necessary to use precise measurements in addition to zooming and navigating. In these cases, it is necessary to change the Photoshop document window to view the rulers. **Rulers** appear on the top and left sides of the document window. Rulers help you position images or elements precisely. As you move your mouse pointer over a photo, markers on the ruler display the mouse pointer's position.

The following steps display the rulers in the document window.

1
- On the Application bar, click the View Extras button to display its menu (Figure 1–40).

Q&A What are the other extras?

Guides are individual, nonprinting straight lines that you can drag from the rulers. Grids are a checkerboard of nonprinting straights lines that float above the photo. Both guides and grids help you position and align objects in the photo.

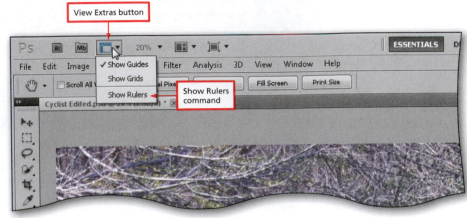

Figure 1–40

2
- Click Show Rulers to display the rulers in the document window. If the ruler does not display inches, right-click the ruler and then click Inches (Figure 1–41).

Q&A What unit of measurement do the rulers use?

Rulers display inches by default, but you can right-click a ruler to change the increment to pixels, centimeters, or other measurements.

Q&A Is the photo really 34 × 25 inches?

The resolution from photos taken with digital cameras is measured in **megapixels** or millions of pixels. The more megapixels you have, the better the photo resolution; however, it translates to very large print sizes. You will resize the photo later in the chapter.

Figure 1–41

Other Ways

1. Press CTRL+R
2. On View menu, click Rulers

Editing the Photo

Editing, or making corrections and changes to a photo, involves a wide variety of tasks such as changing the focus of interest, recoloring portions of the photo, correcting defects, adding new artwork, or changing the file type for specific purposes. Editing also is called **post-processing**, because it includes actions you take after the picture has been processed by the camera or scanner.

Table 1–3 suggests typical categories and types of edits you might perform on photos; there are many others. These edits commonly overlap; and, when performed in combination, they even can create new editing varieties. You will learn more about edits as you work through the chapters in this book.

Table 1–3 Photo Edits	
Category	**Types of Edits**
Transformations	cropping, slicing, changing the aspect, rotating, leveling, mirroring, warping, skewing, distorting, flipping, and changing the perspective
Enhancements and Layering	filtering, layering, cloning, adding borders and artwork, adding text, animating, painting, morphing, ordering, applying styles, masking, creating cutaways, selecting, adding depth perception, anti-aliasing, moving, adding shapes, rasterizing
Color	correcting, contrasting, blending, using modes and systems, using separations, screening, adjusting levels, ruling, trapping, matching, adjusting black and white
Correction	sharpening, fixing red-eye, fixing tears, correcting distortion, retouching, reducing noise, applying a blur, dodging, burning
File Type	camera raw, print, Web, animated images
Resolution	resampling, resizing, collinear editing, interpolating, editing pixel dimensions and document sizes

Editing the Cyclist Edited photo will involve three steps. First, you will crop the photo to remove excessive background. Next, you will add a border and fill it with color. Finally, you will resize the photo to fit the intended use and size requirements.

BTW

Cropping
To evaluate an image for cropping, print a copy. Using two L shapes cut from paper, form a size and shape rectangle to isolate a portion of the image. Draw lines on the printout to use as a guide when cropping in Photoshop.

Cropping

The first step in editing the cyclist photo is to **crop**, or cut away, some of the extra grass and visual clutter so the photo focuses on the cyclist. Photographers try to compose and capture images full-frame, which means the object of interest fills the dimensions of the photo. When that is not possible, photographers and graphic artists crop the photo either to create an illusion of full-frame, to fit unusual shapes in layouts, or to make the image more dramatic. From a design point of view, sometimes it is necessary to crop a photo to straighten an image, remove distracting elements, or simplify the subject. The goal of most cropping is to make the most important feature in the original photo stand out. Cropping sometimes is used to convert a digital photo's proportions to those typical for traditional photos.

Most photographers and graphic artists use the **rule of thirds**, also called the principle of thirds, when placing the focus of interest. Imagine that the scene is divided into thirds both vertically and horizontally. The intersections of these imaginary lines suggest four positions for placing the focus of interest. The position you select depends on the subject and its presentation in the photo. For instance, there might be a shadow, path, or visual line you wish to include. In the case of moving objects, you generally should leave space in front of them, into which they theoretically can move. When eyes are involved, it is better to leave space on the side toward which the person or animal is looking, so they do not appear to look directly out of the setting.

Because the cyclist photo will be used on a rack card, the photo's orientation should be **landscape**, or horizontal. In most cases, you should try to crop to a rectangular shape with an approximate short-side to long-side ratio of 5:8. Sometimes called the **golden rectangle**, a 5:8 ratio emulates natural geometric forms such as flowers, leaves, shells, and butterflies. Most digital cameras take pictures with a similar ratio.

The Crop Tool allows you to select the portion of the photo you wish to retain. Photoshop automatically displays handles and a rule of thirds overlay for further adjustments, if necessary. Then, when you press the ENTER key, the rest of the photo is cropped.

The Crop options bar displays boxes and buttons to assist cropping activities (Figure 1–42a). You can specify the exact height and width of the crop, as well as the resampling resolution which you will learn about later in the chapter. The Front Image button allows you to crop using the dimensions of another photo. Once you begin working with the Crop Tool, the options bar changes to include choices about the background display, crop guide overlay, color of the cropped area, and the ability to change the perspective while cropping (Figure 1–42b).

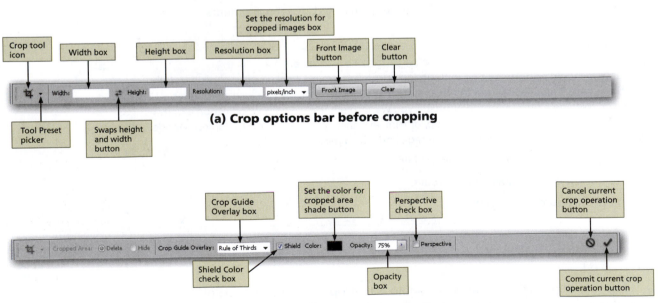

(a) Crop options bar before cropping

(b) Crop options bar during cropping

Figure 1–42

To Crop a Photo

To make the cyclist the focus of the photo, the extra background will be cropped to provide a line of sight to the right, keeping as much of the bike path as possible. The following steps crop the photo of the cyclist.

- Click the Crop Tool button on the Tools panel to select the Crop Tool (Figure 1–43).

Q&A Can I force the crop tool to use a 5:8 ratio?

Yes, on the options bar, you can enter 8 in the Width box and 5 in the Height box.

Figure 1–43

2

- Using the rulers as guides, drag a rectangle beginning 10 inches from the left side and 8 inches from the top. Drag down and to the right to include as much of the bike path as possible (Figure 1–44).

Q&A What if I change my mind or make a mistake when cropping?

If you make a mistake while dragging the cropping area and want to start over, you can click the 'Cancel current crop operation' button (Figure 1–42b) or press the ESC key, which cancels the selection. If you already have performed the crop and then change your mind, you have several choices. You can click the Undo command on the Edit menu, or you can press CTRL+Z to undo the last edit.

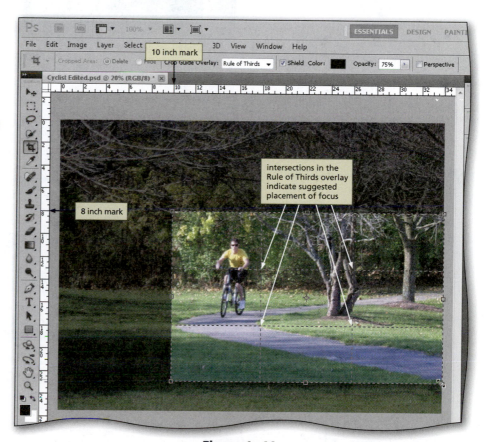

Figure 1–44

Other Ways
1. Press c, drag in photo   3. To crop, right-click cropping selection, click Crop on context menu 2. Select portion of image, on Image menu, click Crop

To Position the Rule of Thirds Overlay

The following steps move the crop selection to position the cyclist at the top-left intersection using the rule of thirds.

1

- Drag the upper-left intersection in the Rule of Thirds overlay to position it in the center of the cyclist (Figure 1–45).

Q&A

Can I turn off the rule of thirds overlay?

Yes, click the Crop Guide Overlay box arrow to display its list, and then click None.

Figure 1–45

2

- Press the ENTER key to complete the crop (Figure 1–46).

Experiment

- If you want to practice cropping, drag again. Press the SHIFT key while you crop to a perfect square. After each crop, press CTRL+Z to undo the crop.

Figure 1–46

Other Ways

1. Drag Rule of Thirds grid, click Commit current crop operation button

Break Point: If you wish to take a break, this is a good place to do so. You can quit Photoshop now. To resume at a later time, start Photoshop, open the file called Room Edited, and continue following the steps from this location forward.

Creating a Border

A **border** is a decorative edge on a photo or a portion of a photo. Photoshop provides many ways to create a border, ranging from simple color transformations around the edge of the photo, to predefined decorated layers, to stylized photo frames.

A border helps define the edge of the photo, especially when the photo might be placed on colored paper or on a Web page with a background texture. A border visually separates the photo from the rest of the page, while focusing the viewer's attention. Rounded borders soften the images in a photo. Square borders are more formal. Decorative borders on a static photo can add interest and amusement, but easily can detract from the focus on a busier photo. **Blended borders** are not a solid fill; rather, they blend a fill color from the outer edge toward the middle, sometimes providing a three-dimensional effect. A border that complements the photo in style, color, and juxtaposition is best. In the cyclist photo, you will create a border using selections of 100 black pixels with 50 pixels of overlapping white. A **pixel** is an individual dot of light that is the basic unit used to create digital images.

BTW

Reviewing Your Edits
Each edit or state of the photo is recorded sequentially in the History panel. If you want to step back through the edits or go back to a particular state, such as the previous crop, click the state in the History panel. You will learn more about the History panel in a future chapter.

> **Identify finishing touches that will further enhance the photo.**
> Adding a border or decorative frame around a photo sometimes can be an effective way to highlight or make the photo stand out on the page. A border should frame the subject, rather than become the subject. If a border is required by the customer or needed for lay-out placement, choose a color and width that neither overwhelms nor overlaps any detail in the photo. Using a border color that complements one of the colors already in the photo creates a strong, visually connected image. For more information about graphic design concepts, read Appendix B.

Plan Ahead

To Create a Selection

Specifying or isolating an area of your photo for editing is called making a **selection**. By selecting specific areas, you can edit and apply special effects to portions of your image while leaving the unselected areas untouched.

Selections can be simple shapes such as rectangles or ovals, or unusually shaped areas of a photo, outlining specific objects. Selections can be the entire photo or as small a portion as one pixel. A selection displays a marquee in Photoshop. A **marquee** is a flashing or pulsating border, sometimes called marching ants.

In the case of the Cyclist Edited photo, you will make a selection around the edge of the photo in order to create a border. The following steps select the photo.

1
- On the menu bar, click Select to display the Select menu (Figure 1–47).

Figure 1–47

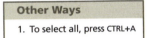

2

• On the Select menu, click All to display the selection marquee around all of the photo (Figure 1–48).

Q&A

Am I selecting all of the photo itself?

You are identifying the pixels along the edge of the image. Some commands apply to all of the pixels within the selection border, such as copying, deleting, or filling; other commands, such as stroking, apply only to the pixels along the edge of the selection.

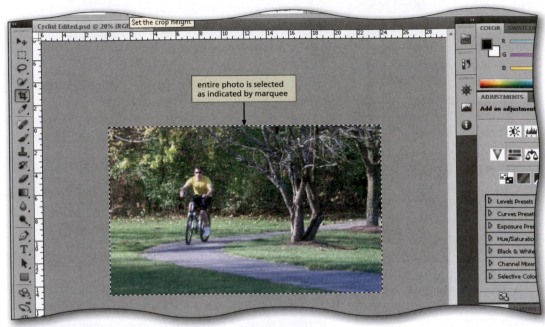

Figure 1–48

Other Ways

1. To select all, press CTRL+A

To Stroke a Selection

A **stroke** is a colored outline. When stroking a selection, you must specify the number of pixels to include in the stroke and the desired color. You also must decide to apply the stroke outside the selection border, inside the selection border, or centered on the selection border. Other stroke settings include blending modes and opacity which you will learn about in a later chapter.

The following steps stroke a selection.

1

• With the photograph still selected, click Edit on the menu bar to display the Edit menu (Figure 1–49).

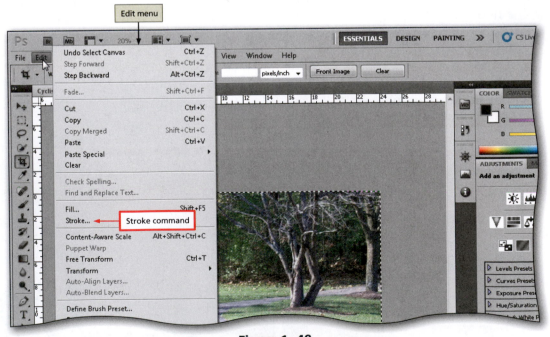

Figure 1–49

2

• Click Stroke to display the Stroke dialog box.

• Type **100** in the Width box.

• Click the Inside option button (Stroke dialog box) to select an inside stroke (Figure 1–50).

Q&A

Do I need to select a color?

No, the default value is the foreground color, black. If someone has changed your foreground color, click the Cancel button, press the D key to choose the default colors and start again with Step 1.

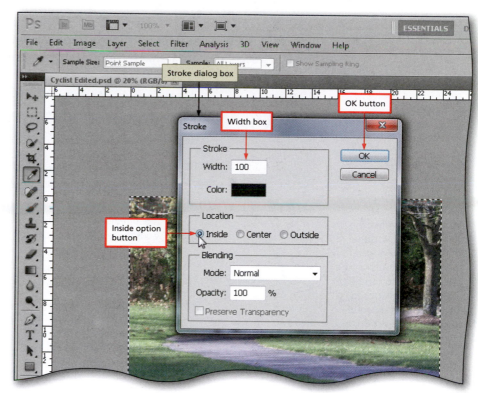

Figure 1–50

3

• Click the OK button to apply the stroke (Figure 1–51).

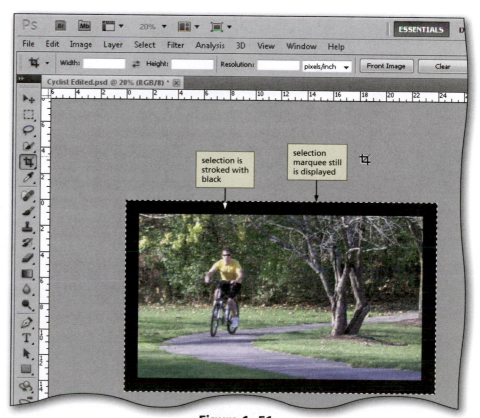

Figure 1–51

Modifying Selections

You can modify the selection border in several different ways. In the cyclist photo, you will modify the selection by increasing the number of pixels along the border so you can add a second color at that location. Table 1–4 displays the modify commands.

Table 1–4 Modify Commands	
Type of Modification	**Result**
Border	This command allows you to select a width of pixels, from 1 to 200, to be split evenly on either side of the existing selection marquee. If the selection is already on the edge, then half of the entered value will be included in the border.
Smooth	Photoshop examines the number of pixels in a radius around the selection. To smooth the selection, if more than half of the pixels already are selected, Photoshop adds the rest within the radius. If less than half are selected, the pixels are removed. The overall effect is to smooth sharp corners and jagged lines, reducing patchiness.
Expand	The border is increased by a number of pixels from 1 to 100. Any portion of the selection border running along the canvas's edge is unaffected.
Contract	The border is decreased by a number of pixels from 1 to 100. Any portion of the selection border running along the canvas's edge is unaffected.
Feather	This command creates a feather edge with a width from 0 to 250 pixels.

BTW

Selections
When you select all, Photoshop displays the photo with a marquee around all four edges. The selection tools on the Tools panel also can help you make selections in the photo. The marquee, lasso, Quick Selection, and Magic Wand tools will be discussed in Chapter 2.

To Modify a Selection

The following steps modify the selection.

1
• On the menu bar, click Select, and then point to Modify to display the Modify submenu (Figure 1–52).

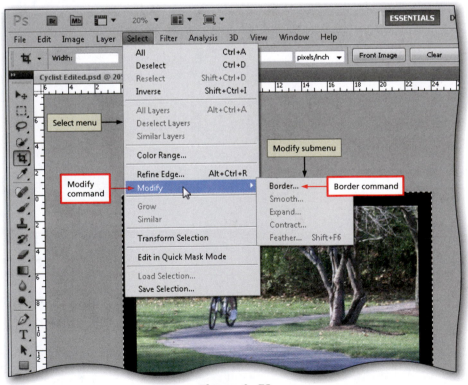

Figure 1–52

2

- Click Border on the Modify submenu to display the Border Selection dialog box.

- Type 2 0 0 in the Width box to create a border on each side of the photo (Figure 1–53).

Q&A Could I use the Contract command to contract the selection?

No, you must specify the border first. The Contract command is **grayed out** so you cannot select it, before choosing the Border command.

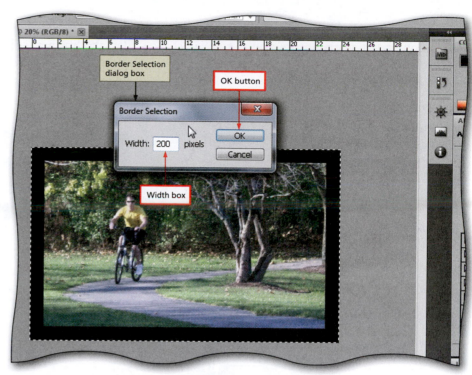

Figure 1–53

3

- Click the OK button in the Border Selection dialog box to define the selection (Figure 1–54).

Q&A Is the border 200 pixels wide?

No. Photoshop adds half of those pixels to either side of the selection marquee. Because the selection was already on the edge of the photo, the selection was moved only 100 pixels.

Experiment

- To practice smoothing the border, click the Select menu, point to Modify, and then click Smooth. Enter a value in the Sample Radius box and then click the OK button. Notice the rounded rectangle in the border marquee. Press CTRL+Z to undo the Smooth command.

Figure 1–54

To Switch Foreground and Background Colors

On the Tools panel, the default foreground color is black and the default background color is white. Photoshop uses the default foreground color in strokes, files, and brushes — in the previous steps when you stroked, the pixels became black. In order to create a white, overlapping stroke you must make white the foreground color. The following steps switch the foreground and background colors so white is over black.

1
- Click the Switch Foreground and Background Colors button to reverse the colors (Figure 1–55).

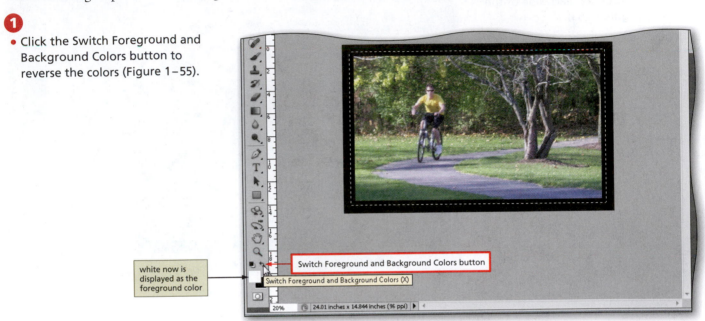

white now is displayed as the foreground color

Switch Foreground and Background Colors button

Switch Foreground and Background Colors (X)

20% | 24.01 inches x 14.844 inches (96 ppi)

Figure 1–55

Other Ways
1. Press X

To Stroke Again

1 Click Edit on the menu bar to display the Edit menu.

2 Click Stroke to display the Stroke dialog box.

3 Type **50** in the Width box.

4 Click the Center option button to select a center stroke.

5 Click the OK button to apply the stroke (Figure 1–56).

selection is stroked with white

selection marquee still is displayed

Levels Presets
Curves Preset
Exposure Pres
Hue/Saturation
Black & White P
Channel Mixer P
Selective Color

Figure 1–56

To Deselect

Because the border is complete, you should remove the selection indicator, or **deselect** it, so it no longer appears. The following step removes the selection.

- Click Select on the menu bar and then click Deselect to remove the selection (Figure 1–57).

Q&A Why does my mouse pointer still display the Crop Tool mouse pointer?

Deselecting does not change the current tool on the Tools panel. Whichever tool you used prior to the deselecting process will display its own mouse pointer.

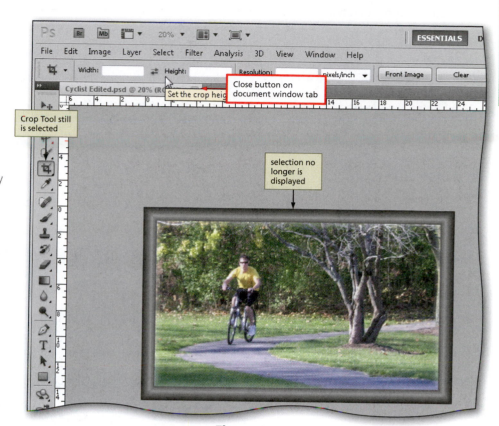

Figure 1–57

Other Ways
1. Press CTRL+D

To Switch Foreground and Background Colors

The following step uses the shortcut key to switch the foreground and background colors back to black over white.

1 Press the x key to switch the foreground and background colors.

Saving a Photo with the Same File Name

Because you have made many edits to the photo, it is a good idea to save the photo again. When you saved the document the first time, you assigned the file name, Cyclist Edited. When you use the following procedure, Photoshop automatically assigns the same file name to the photo, and it is stored in the same location.

To Save a Photo with the Same File Name

The following step saves the Cyclist Edited file with the changes you made.

1

- Click File on the menu bar and then click Save to save the photo with the same file name.

Other Ways

1. Press CTRL+S

Break Point: If you wish to take a break, this is a good place to do so. You can quit Photoshop now. To resume at a later time, start Photoshop, open the file called Room Edited, and continue following the steps from this location forward.

To Close a Photo

The following step closes the Cyclist Edited document window without quitting Photoshop.

1

- Click the Close button on the Document window tab (shown in Figure 1–57 on the previous page) to close the document window and the image file (Figure 1–58).

- If Photoshop displays a dialog box asking you to save again, click the No button.

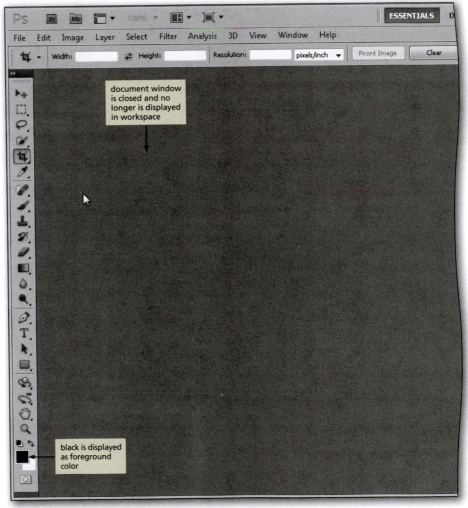

Figure 1–58

Other Ways

1. Press CTRL+W

Opening a Recent File in Photoshop

Once you have created and saved a document, you may need to retrieve it from your storage medium. For example, you might want to edit the photo or print it. Photoshop maintains a list of recently used files in order to give you quick access to them for further editing. Opening a recent file requires that Photoshop is running on your computer.

To Open a Recent File

Earlier in this chapter you saved your edited photo on a USB flash drive using the file name, Cyclist Edited. The following steps open the Cyclist Edited file using the Open Recent list.

1

- Click File on the menu bar and then point to Open Recent to display the Open Recent submenu (Figure 1–59).

Q&A

What does the Clear Recent command do?

If you click the Clear Recent command, your Recent list will be empty. To open a file, you have to click Open on the File menu and then navigate to the location of the file.

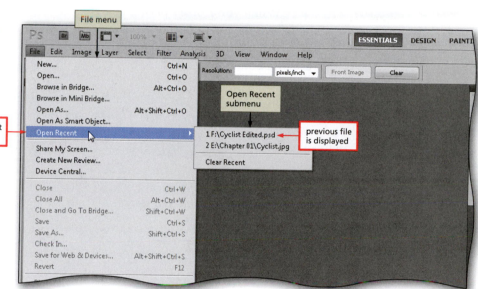

Figure 1–59

2

- Click Cyclist Edited.psd on the Open Recent submenu to open the file.

- If necessary, change the magnification to 25% (Figure 1–60).

Q&A

Why is the Crop Tool still selected?

Photoshop tools do not change until you select a new tool. You have been working in the menu system and have yet to choose a new tool in the Tools panel.

Figure 1–60

Changing Image Sizes

Sometimes it is necessary to resize an image to fit within certain space limitations. **Resize** means to scale or change the dimensions of the photo. Zooming in or dragging a corner of the document window to change the size is not the same as actually changing the dimensions of the photo. Resizing in a page layout program, such as Publisher, QuarkXPress, or InDesign, merely stretches the pixels. In Photoshop, resizing means adding to or subtracting from the number of pixels.

Photoshop uses a mathematical process called **interpolation**, or **resampling**, when it changes the number of pixels. The program interpolates or calculates how to add new pixels to the photo to match those already there. Photoshop samples the pixels and reproduces them to determine where and how to enlarge or reduce the photo.

When you resize a photo, you must consider many things, such as the type of file, the width, the height, and the resolution. **Resolution** refers to the number of pixels per inch, printed on a page or displayed on a monitor. Not all photos lend themselves to resizing. Some file types lose quality and sharpness when resized. Fine details cannot be interpolated from low-resolution photos. Resizing works best for small changes where exact dimensions are critical. If possible, it usually is better to take a photo at the highest feasible resolution or rescan the image at a higher resolution rather than resize it later.

In those cases where it is impossible to create the photo at the proper size, Photoshop helps you resize or **scale** your photos for print or online media.

BTW

Resolution
Graphics for print purposes are usually higher resolution than those for use on the Web. Images designed for the Web are limited by the resolution of the computer screen, which usually varies from 72 to 96 pixels per inch.

Plan Ahead

Prepare for publication.
Keep in mind the golden rectangle of well-designed photos and the limitations of your space. Resize the photo. Print a copy and evaluate its visual appeal. If you are going to publish the photo to the Web, determine the following:

- Typical download speed of your audience
- Browser considerations
- Number of colors
- File type

Finally, save the photo with a descriptive name indicating its completion.

To Resize the Image

Because the cyclist photo will be printed on a rack card at a specific size, you will change the width to 3.75 inches. The following steps resize the image to create a custom-sized photo for printing.

1
- Click Image on the menu bar to display the Image menu (Figure 1–61).

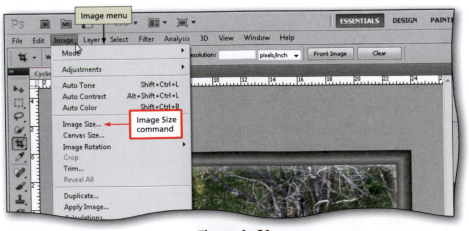

Figure 1–61

2

- Click Image Size to display the Image Size dialog box.

- In the Document Size area, double-click the value in the Width box and then type **3.75** to replace the previous value (Figure 1–62).

Q&A Why did the height change?

When you change the width, Photoshop automatically adjusts the height to maintain the proportions of the photo. Your exact height might differ slightly depending on how closely you cropped the original photo.

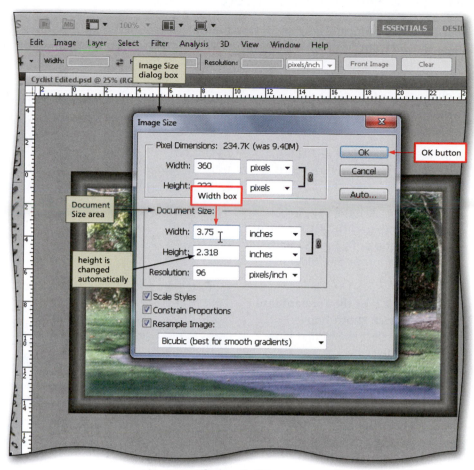

Figure 1–62

3

- Click the OK button (Image Size dialog box) to finish resizing the image.

- Change the magnification to 100% (Figure 1–63).

Other Ways

1. Press ALT+CTRL+I, change settings, click OK button (Image Size dialog box)

Figure 1–63

To Save a Photo with a Different Name

Many graphic designers will save multiple copies of the same photo with various edits. Because this photo has been resized to print properly, you need to save it with a different name. The following step renames the file.

1

- Click File on the menu bar and then click Save As to display the Save As dialog box.

- In the File name text box (Save As dialog box), type **Cyclist Resized**.

- If necessary, click the Save in box arrow and then click UDISK 2.0 (F:), or the location of your USB flash drive and appropriate folder in the list.

- If necessary, click the Format button and then click Photoshop (*.PSD, *.PDD) to select the format type (Figure 1–64).

- Click the Save button (Save As dialog box) to save the image with the new name.

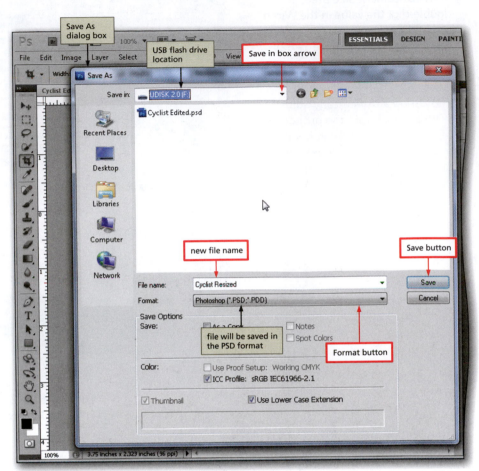

Figure 1–64

Other Ways

1. Press SHIFT+CTRL+S

Printing a Photo

BTW

Printing
When you use the Print One Copy command to print a document, Photoshop prints the photo automatically, using preset options. To print multiple copies, display the Print dialog box by clicking File on the menu bar, clicking Print, and then entering the number of copies you want to print.

The photo now can be printed, saved, taken to a professional print shop, or sent online to a printing service. A printed version of the photo is called a **hard copy** or **printout**. You can print one copy using the Print One Copy command on the File menu, or to display the Print dialog box, you can click Print on the File menu, which offers you more printing options.

The Print One Copy command sends the printout to the default printer. If you are not sure which printer is your default printer, choose the Print command. In the Print dialog box, click the Printer box arrow and choose your current printer. You will learn more about the Print dialog box in a later chapter.

After printing a copy of the photo, you will close the photo. Then, you will return to the version of the photo before resizing to prepare a Web version.

To Print a Photo

The following steps print the photo created in this chapter.

- Ready the printer according to the printer instructions.

- Click File on the menu bar and then click Print to display the Print dialog box.

- If necessary, click the Printer box arrow and then select your printer from the list. Do not change any other settings (Figure 1–65).

Q&A

Does Photoshop have a Print button?

Photoshop's Print commands are available on the menu or by using shortcut keys. There is no Print button on the options bar.

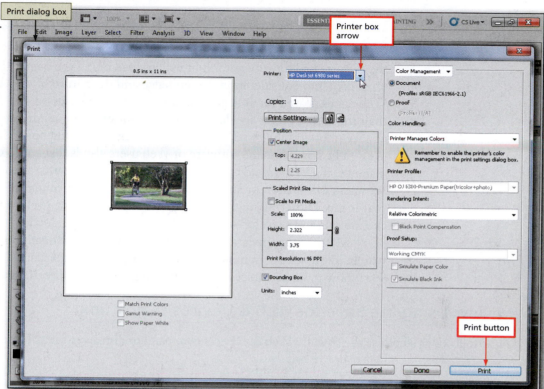

Figure 1–65

2

- In the Print dialog box, click the Print button to start the printing process. If your system displays a second Print dialog box or a Print Settings dialog box, unique to your printer, click its Print button.

- When the printer stops, retrieve the hard copy of the photo.

Other Ways

1. To print one copy, press ALT+SHIFT+CTRL+P

2. To display Print dialog box, press CTRL+P

Saving a Photo for Use on the Web

When preparing photos for the Web, you often need to compromise between the quality of the display and file size. Web users do not want to wait while large photos load from the Web to their individual computer systems. To solve this problem, Photoshop provides several commands to compress the file size of an image while optimizing its online display quality. Additionally, Photoshop allows you to save the photo in a variety of formats such as **GIF**, which is a compressed graphic format designed to minimize file size and electronic transfer time, or as an **HTML** (Hypertext Markup Language) file, which contains all the necessary information to display your photo in a Web browser.

Therefore, you have two choices in Photoshop CS5 for creating Web images: the Zoomify command and the Save for Web & Devices command. When you **zoomify**, you create a high-resolution image for the Web, complete with a background and tools for navigation, panning, and zooming. To zoomify, click Export on the File menu and then click Zoomify. In the Zoomify Export dialog box, you set various Web and export options. Photoshop creates the HTML code and accompanying files for you to upload to a Web server.

If you do not want the extra HTML files for the background, navigation, and zooming, you can create a single graphic file using the Save for Web & Devices command. The resulting graphic can be used on the Web or on a variety of mobile devices.

Optimization is the process of changing the photo to make it most effective for its purpose. The Save for Web & Devices command allows you to preview optimized images in different file formats, and with different file attributes, for precise optimization. You can view multiple versions of a photo simultaneously and modify settings as you preview the image.

Using the Save for Web & Devices Command

To optimize the cyclist photo for use on the Web, you need to make decisions about the file size and how long it might take to load on a Web page. These kinds of decisions must take into consideration the audience and the nature of the Web page. For example, Web pages geared for college campuses probably could assume a faster download time than those that target a wide range of home users. An e-commerce site that needs high-quality photography to sell its product will make certain choices in color and resolution.

The hardware and software of Web users also is taken into consideration. For instance, if a Web photo contains more colors than the user's monitor can display, most browsers will **dither**, or approximate, the colors that it cannot display, by blending colors that it can. Dithering might not be appropriate for some Web pages, because it increases the file size and therefore causes the page to load more slowly.

Many other appearance settings play a role in the quality of Web graphics, some of which are subjective in nature. As you become more experienced in Photoshop, you will learn how to make choices about dithering, colors, texture, image size, and other settings.

To Preview Using the Save for Web & Devices Dialog Box

The followings steps use the Save for Web & Devices command to display previews for four possible Web formats.

1
- With the Cyclist Resized photo open, click File on the menu bar to display the File menu and then click Save for Web & Devices to display the Save for Web & Devices dialog box.

- Click the 4-Up tab to display four versions of the photo.

- Click the upper-right preview, if necessary, to choose a high-quality, version of the photo (Figure 1–66).

Q&A Why are there four frames?

Photoshop displays four previews — the original photo and three others that are converted to different resolutions to optimize download times on the Web.

Figure 1–66

To Choose a Download Speed

For even faster downloads when the photo is displayed as a Web graphic, you can choose a download speed that will be similar to that of your target audience. The **annotation area** below each image in the Save for Web & Devices dialog box provides optimization information such as the size of the optimized file and the estimated download time using the selected modem speed.

The following steps change the download speed to 512 kilobytes per second (Kbps).

1
- In the annotation area below the upper-right preview, click the 'Select download speed' button to display the list of connection speeds (Figure 1–67).

Figure 1–67

2
- In the list, click Size/Download Time (512 Kbps Cable/DSL) or another appropriate speed (Figure 1–68).

Q&A

How fast will the picture download?

In Figure 1–66, the speed was 12 seconds at 56.6 Kbps. At 512 Kbps, the photo will download in 2 seconds, as shown in Figure 1–68. Your download times might differ slightly.

Figure 1–68

Experiment

- Click the Select download speed button to display the list of connection speeds and then click various connection speeds to see how the download times are affected. When finished, click Size/Download Time (512 Kbps Cable/DSL) in the list.

Other Ways
1. Right-click annotation area, select download speed

Options in the Save for Web & Devices Dialog Box

On the left side of the Save for Web & Devices dialog box, Photoshop provides several tools to move, zoom, select colors, and slice a portion of the selected preview (Figure 1–69). Along the bottom of the Save for Web & Devices dialog box are buttons to preview the image and perform file functions.

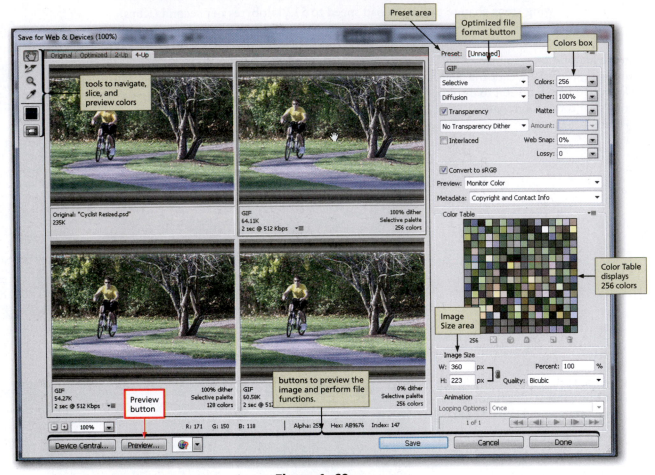

Figure 1–69

If you choose a preview other than the original located on the upper left, the Save for Web & Devices dialog box displays options in the Preset area on the right. The Preset area lets you make changes to the selected preview such as the file type, the number of colors, transparency, dithering, and photo finishes. Fine-tuning these kinds of optimization settings allows you to balance the image quality and file size.

Below the Preset area are the Color Table and Image Size areas. The Color Table area and its buttons and menu display different options based on the choices you made in the Preset area. The colors used in the selected preview can be locked, deleted, set to transparent, or adjusted for standard Web palettes. The Image Size area allows you to make changes to the size of the image similar to those changes you made using the Image Size command earlier in the chapter. Changing the image size affects all four previews. The settings are not permanent until you click the Save button. You will learn more about these settings in a later chapter.

To Preview the Photo on the Web

It is always a good idea to preview a photo before uploading it to the Web to check for errors. When Photoshop displays a Web preview of any photo, it also displays the characteristics of the file and the HTML code used to create the preview. The following steps preview the image in a browser.

1

- Click the Preview button (shown in Figure 1–69) to display the photo in a Web browser.

- If necessary, double-click the browser's title bar to maximize the browser window (Figure 1–70).

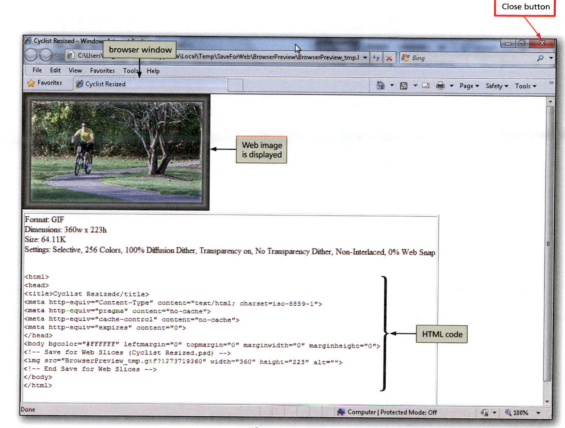

Figure 1–70

Q&A When I clicked the Preview button, the HTML code was displayed in Notepad. Should it open in a browser?

If Photoshop cannot detect a default browser on your system, you may have to click the box arrow next to the Preview button (Figure 1–69), and then click Edit List to add your browser.

Q&A How would I use the HTML code?

As a Web designer, you might copy and paste the code into a text editor or Web creation software, replacing BrowserPreview with the name of the file. After saving, the code, the HTML file, and the photo would need to be uploaded to a server.

2

- Click the Close button on the browser's title bar to close the browser window. If necessary, click the Adobe Photoshop CS5 button on the Windows 7 taskbar to return to the Save for Web & Devices dialog box.

To Save the Photo as a Web Page

When you click the Save button in the Save for Web & Devices dialog box, you will name the Web page and create a folder for the files, as performed in the following steps.

- In the Save for Web & Devices dialog box, click the Save button to display the Save Optimized As dialog box.

- Type **Cyclist-for-Web** in the File name text box (Save Optimized As dialog box).

- If necessary, click the Save in box arrow and then click UDISK 2.0 (F:), or the location of your USB flash drive and appropriate folder in the list.

- Click the Create New Folder button (Figure 1–71).

Q&A

Why are the words in the file name hyphenated?

For ease of use, it is standard for Web graphics to have no spaces in their file names.

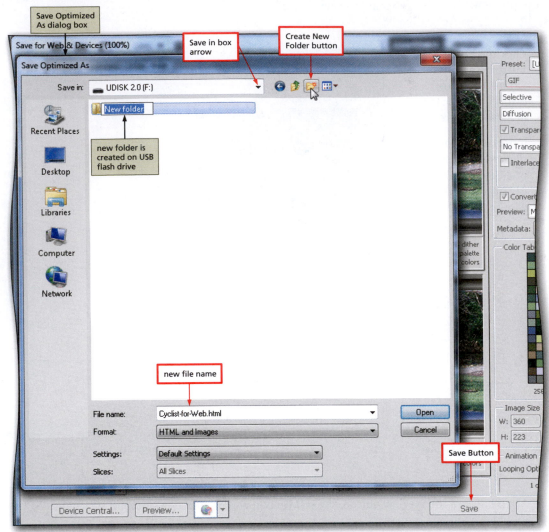

Figure 1–71

- Type **Cyclist Web Page Files** as the new name for the folder and then press the ENTER key (Figure 1–72).

Figure 1–72

- Double-click the new folder to open it.

- Click the Format button (Save Optimized As dialog box) to display the saving options (Figure 1–73).

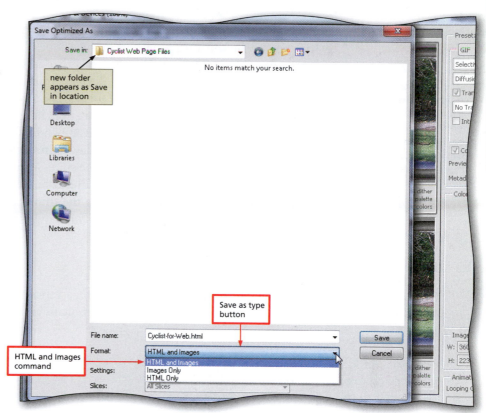

Figure 1–73

- Click HTML and Images in the list to direct Photoshop to save the HTML code and the Web version of the photo (Figure 1–74).

Q&A

What are the differences in the three ways to save for the Web?

The Images only option saves the photo itself in a Web-friendly format as a GIF file. The HTML only option saves the coding that creates the Web page, but not the photo. The HTML and Images option saves the Web page and creates an accompanying folder named images to go with the Web page file. Inside the images folder is a GIF version of the photo.

- Click the Save button to save the HTML and Image files.

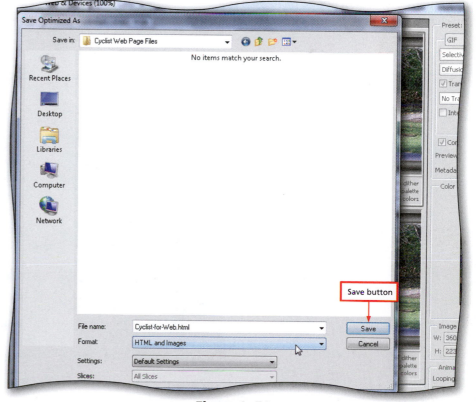

Figure 1–74

Adobe Bridge and Mini Bridge

Opening Files in Adobe Bridge
When working with multiple photos, or organizing your photos, it might be more convenient to use the Bridge tool to open files. In other cases, use the Open command on the Photoshop File menu if you only want to open a single photo for editing.

Adobe Bridge is a file exploration tool similar to Windows Explorer. Bridge can be used with any of the software programs in the Adobe Creative Suite. Using Bridge, you can locate, drag, organize, browse, and standardize color settings across your content for use in print, on the Web and on mobile devices. A useful Bridge tool allows you to attach or assign keywords, or **metadata**, used for searching and categorizing photos. Metadata is divided into three categories: file information, image usage, and image creation data. The Bridge interface is explained in detail in Appendix E.

A subset of Adobe Bridge is the new **Mini Bridge** that helps you navigate folders and files and access other modules in the suite. Mini Bridge provides a search mechanism, and interaction with Web sites such as Photoshop.com and Flickr.com. You can use Mini Bridge to open a file by double-clicking the **thumbnail**, or small picture. You also can view the files in a list, in a grid, or as a slideshow, among other ways.

To Use Mini Bridge to View Files

So far in this chapter, you have saved the edited cyclist photo, a version for printing, and a version for the Web. The following steps open Mini Bridge and view those files as thumbnails and then with details.

1
• Click the Mini Bridge button in the vertical docking to open the Mini Bridge panel (Figure 1–75).

 **Experiment**
• Point to each of the buttons and settings in the Mini Bridge panel to view the tool tips.

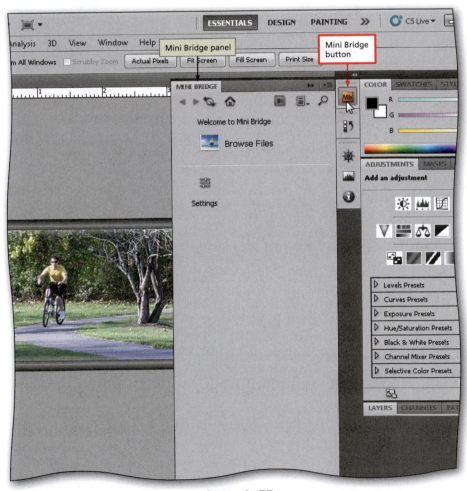

Figure 1–75

2
- Click the Panel View button to display the panel settings (Figure 1–76).

Q&A | What is a pod?

Pod is the term that Adobe uses for content viewing areas or sections within panels.

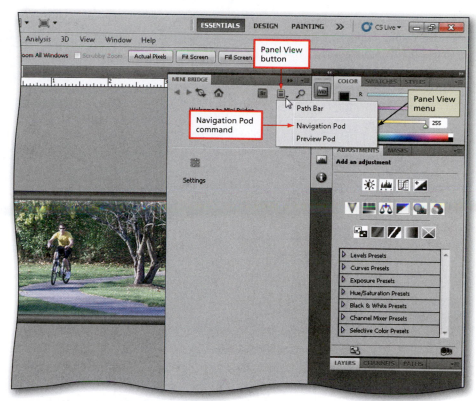

Figure 1–76

3
- Click Navigation Pod to display common and recent locations, as well as the Content area.

- If Photoshop displays a dialog box asking if you want to start Bridge each time you log in, click the No button.

- If necessary, click Recent Folders in the Navigation area, and then click your USB flash drive location to display its contents.

- If you created a Chapter 01 folder, double-click the Chapter 01 folder icon (Figure 1–77).

 Experiment

- Drag the slider at the bottom of the panel to display the thumbnails at different sizes.

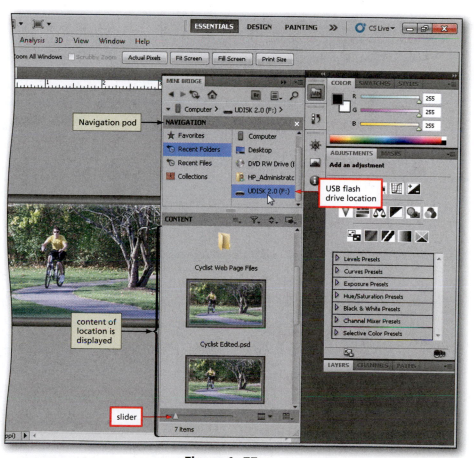

Figure 1–77

4

- In the lower-right corner of the Mini Bridge panel, click the View button to display a menu of other ways to view photos in Mini Bridge (Figure 1–78).

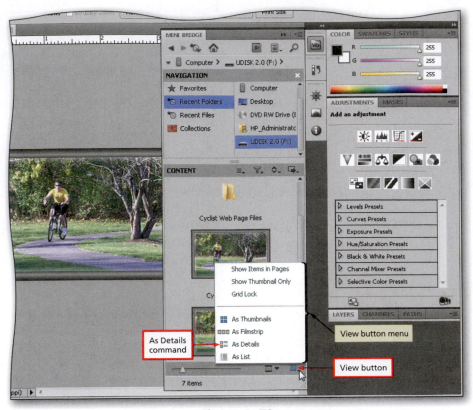

Figure 1–78

5

- Click As Details to show more information about each photo.

- If necessary, drag the slider to see more of the details (Figure 1–79).

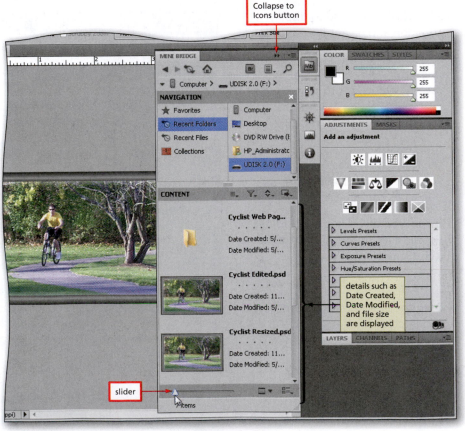

Figure 1–79

To Collapse the Panel

The following step collapses the Mini Bridge panel.

- Click the Collapse to Icons button on the Mini Bridge panel title bar to collapse the panel (Figure 1–80).

Figure 1–80

Photoshop Help

At anytime while you are using Photoshop, you can get answers to questions using **Photoshop Help**. You activate Photoshop Help either by clicking Help on the menu bar or by pressing the F1 key. The Photoshop Help command connects you, through the Web, to a wealth of assistance, including tutorials with detailed instructions accompanied by illustrations and videos. Used properly, this form of online assistance can increase your productivity and reduce your frustration by minimizing the time you spend learning how to use Photoshop. Additional information about using Photoshop Help is available in Appendix D.

BTW

Community Help
Community Help is an integrated Web environment that includes Photoshop Help and gives you access to community-generated content moderated by Adobe and industry experts. Comments from users help guide you to an answer.

To Access Photoshop Help

The following step accesses Photoshop Help. You must be connected to the Web if you plan to perform this step on a computer.

1

- With Photoshop open on your system, press the F1 key to access Photoshop Help online.

- If necessary, double-click the title bar to maximize the window (Figure 1–81).

Q&A

My help screen is asking me to download an update. Should I do that?

If you are in a lab situation, you should check with your instructor. Updates provide you with the latest help topics, videos, and tutorials, but downloading them takes time and disk space. You must be online to download the updates, and Photoshop might require you to restart your system.

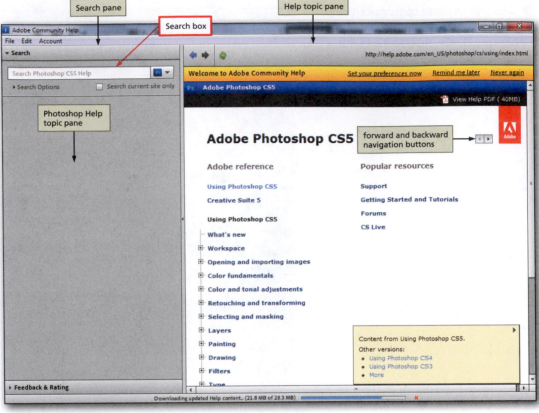

Figure 1–81

Other Ways

1. On Help menu, click Photoshop Help

Using the Search Box in Photoshop Help

The Search box allows you to type words or phrases about which you want additional information and help, such as cropping or printing images. When you press the ENTER key, Photoshop Help responds by displaying a list of topics related to the word or phrase you typed.

To Use the Help Search Box

The following steps use the Search box to obtain information about the Tools panel.

 1
- Click to display a check mark in the 'Search current site only' or 'Adobe reference only' check box.

- Click the Search box and then type **Tools** to enter the search topic (Figure 1–82).

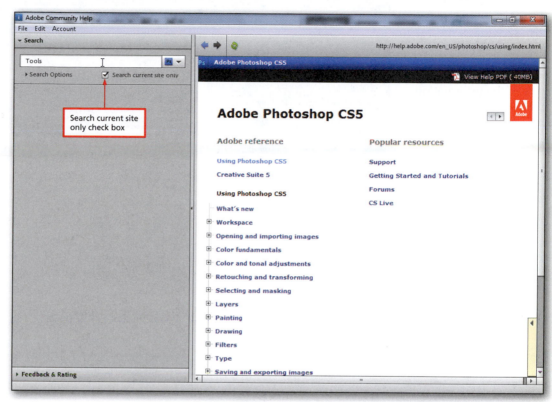

Figure 1–82

2
- Press the ENTER key to display the relevant links.

- Scroll down to display the link named Adobe Photoshop CS5 * Tools (Figure 1–83).

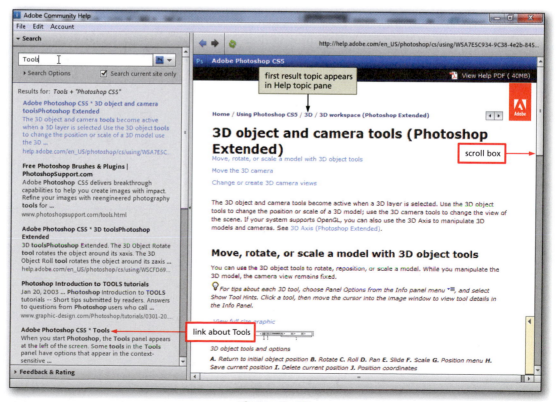

Figure 1–83

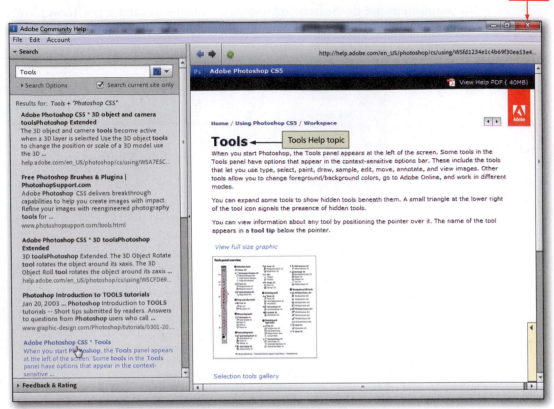

Figure 1–84

3
- Click the About Photoshop CS5 * Tools link to display the contents (Figure 1–84).

- Scroll as necessary to read the information about tools.

 Experiment
- Click other links to view more information, or search for other topics using the Search box.

4
- In the browser title bar, click the Close button to close the window, and then, if necessary, click the Adobe Photoshop CS5 button on the taskbar to return to Photoshop.

Other Ways
1. On Help menu, click Photoshop Help, enter search topic

To Quit Photoshop

The following steps quit Photoshop and return control to Windows.

1
- Click the Close button on the right side of the Application bar to close the window.

- If Photoshop displays a dialog box asking you to save changes, click the No button.

Other Ways
1. On File menu, click Exit
2. Press CTRL+Q

Chapter Summary

In this chapter, you gained a broad knowledge of Photoshop. First, you learned how to start Photoshop. You were introduced to the Photoshop workspace. You learned how to open a photo and zoom in and out. You learned about design issues related to the placement of visual points of interest. You then learned how to crop a photo to eliminate extraneous background. After you added a blended border, you resized the image.

Once you saved the photo, you learned how to print it. You used the Save for Web & Devices command to optimize and save a Web version. You learned how to use Adobe Mini Bridge to view files and Adobe Help to research specific help topics. Finally, you learned how to quit Photoshop.

The items listed below include all the new Photoshop skills you have learned in this chapter:

1. Start Photoshop (PS 5)
2. Select the Essentials Workspace (PS 7)
3. Reset the Tools Panel (PS 8)
4. Reset the Options Bar (PS 8)
5. Open a Photo (PS 10)
6. Save a Photo in the PSD Format (PS 19)
7. Use the Zoom Tool (PS 23)
8. Open the Navigator Panel (PS 25)
9. Use the Navigator Panel (PS 26)
10. Collapse the Navigator Panel (PS 26)
11. Use the Hand Tool (PS 27)
12. Change the Magnification (PS 27)
13. Change the Screen Mode (PS 28)
14. Display Rulers (PS 30)
15. Crop a Photo (PS 33)
16. Position the Rule of Thirds Overlay (PS 34)
17. Create a Selection (PS 35)
18. Stroke a Selection (PS 36)
19. Modify a Selection (PS 38)
20. Switch Foreground and Background Colors (PS 40)
21. Deselect (PS 41)
22. Save a Photo with the Same File Name (PS 42)
23. Close a Photo (PS 42)
24. Open a Recent File (PS 43)
25. Resize the Image (PS 44)
26. Save a Photo with a Different Name (PS 46)
27. Print a Photo (PS 47)
28. Preview Using the Save for Web & Devices Dialog Box (PS 48)
29. Choose a Download Speed (PS 49)
30. Preview the Photo on the Web (PS 51)
31. Save the Photo as a Web Page (PS 52)
32. Use Mini Bridge to View Files (PS 54)
33. Collapse the Panel (PS 57)
34. Access Photoshop Help (PS 58)
35. Use the Help Search Box (PS 59)
36. Quit Photoshop (PS 60)

Learn It Online

Test your knowledge of chapter content and key terms.

Instructions: To complete the Learn It Online exercises, start your browser, click the Address bar, and then enter the Web address **scsite.com/psCS5/learn**. When the Photoshop CS5 Learn It Online page is displayed, click the link for the exercise you want to complete and then read the instructions.

Chapter Reinforcement TF, MC, and SA

A series of true/false, multiple choice, and short answer questions that test your knowledge of the chapter content.

Flash Cards

An interactive learning environment where you identify chapter key terms associated with displayed definitions.

Practice Test

A series of multiple choice questions that tests your knowledge of chapter content and key terms.

Who Wants To Be a Computer Genius?

An interactive game that challenges your knowledge of chapter content in the style of a television quiz show.

Wheel of Terms

An interactive game that challenges your knowledge of chapter key terms in the style of the television show *Wheel of Fortune*.

Crossword Puzzle Challenge

A crossword puzzle that challenges your knowledge of key terms presented in the chapter.

Apply Your Knowledge

Reinforce the skills and apply the concepts you learned in this chapter.

Editing a Photo in the Photoshop Workspace

Instructions: Start Photoshop and perform the customization steps found on pages PS 6 through PS 9. Open the Apply 1-1 Water Park file in the Chapter 01 folder from the Data Files for Students. You can access the Data Files for Students on the CD that accompanies this book. See the inside back cover of this book for instructions on downloading the Data Files for Students, or contact your instructor for information about accessing the required files.

First, you will save the photo in its own folder. Then you will crop the photo, add a white border, and save the edited photo, as shown in Figure 1–85. Next, you will resize the photo for printing and print one copy. Finally, you will reopen your edited photo, and then you will optimize it for the Web, save it, and close it.

Perform the following tasks:

1. On the File menu, click Save As. When Photoshop displays the Save As dialog box, navigate to your USB flash drive and then click the Create New Folder button. Type Apply 1-1 as the folder name and then press the ENTER key. Double-click the folder to open it. In the File name box, type Apply 1-1 Water Park Edited. Click the Format button and choose the PSD file format. Click the Save button to save the file.

Figure 1– 85

2. Use the Zoom Tool to zoom the photo to 50% magnification, if necessary.

3. Use the Hand Tool to reposition the photo in the workspace to view different areas of the zoomed photo.

4. Use the Navigator panel to zoom out to 16.67%.

Continued >

Apply Your Knowledge *continued*

5. Use the Crop Tool to crop the photo, retaining the top patio of the water slide and the child on the right slide as shown in Figure 1–85 on the previous page. Include more water than sky. Use the Rule of Thirds guide to position the child in the lower-right intersection. (*Hint:* If your cropping selection does not look correct, you can press the ESC key to clear the selection before you press the ENTER key. Immediately after cropping the photo, you can click Undo on the Edit menu to undo the crop action.)

6. To create the border:

   a. Press the X key to reverse the foreground and background colors.

   b. Press CTRL+A to select all of the photo.

   c. Use the Select menu to modify the border to 100 pixels.

   d. Press SHIFT+F5 to display the Fill dialog box and then fill the border with white.

   e. Press CTRL+D to clear your selection when finished creating the border.

7. Press CTRL+S to save the Apply 1-1 Water Park Edited photo with the same file name in the same location.

8. Use the Image menu to resize the photo width to 5 inches wide to create a custom-sized photo for printing.

9. Save the resized file as Apply 1-1 Water Park for Print.

10. Print the photo and then close the file. If Photoshop displays a dialog box about saving again, click the No button.

11. Open the Apply 1-1 Water Park for Print file using the recent list.

12. Save the photo for the Web, displaying it in the 4-Up tab and zoomed to fit on the screen. Select the preview that looks the best for your download speed.

13. Preview the optimized photo in your browser, and print the browser page. Close the browser.

14. Save the photo with the name, Apply-1-1-Water-Park-for-Web, using the HTML and Images file type.

15. Close the Apply 1-1 Water Park for Print file without saving it and close Photoshop.

Extend Your Knowledge

Extend the skills you learned in this chapter and experiment with new skills. You may need to use Help to complete the assignment.

Exploring Border Width and Fill Options

Instructions: Start Photoshop and perform the customization steps found on pages PS 6 through PS 9. Open the Extend 1-1 Wood Turtle file in the Chapter 01 folder from the Data Files for Students and save it as Extend 1-1 Wood Turtle Edited in the PSD file format. You can access the Data Files for Students on the CD that accompanies this book. See the inside back cover of this book for instructions on downloading the Data Files for Students, or contact your instructor for information about accessing the required files.

The wood turtle photo (Figure 1–86) is to be added to a middle school science handout about amphibians and reptiles. Before the photo is inserted in the handout document, you must add a complementary border to the photo. The only requirement is that the border not be black or white.

complementary border color

Figure 1–86

Before you save the photo with a border, you need to explore different border widths and fill options to find the right combination. As you experiment with border options, you can press the CTRL+ALT+Z keys to quickly step back through the current editing history, returning the photo to a previous state.

Perform the following tasks:

1. Select the entire photo.

2. Specify a border width.

3. Review Table 1–4 on page PS 38. Use the commands on the Modify submenu to set the border fill contents, blending, and opacity options of your choice and apply them to the photo. Make a note of your width and fill settings for future reference.

4. After viewing the resulting border, press the CTRL+ALT+Z keys enough times to step back to the photo's original unedited state.

5. Repeat Steps 1–4 several times to experiment with different border widths and fills, then apply the border that best complements the photo and save the changes to the photo.

6. Close the photo and quit Photoshop.

Make It Right

Analyze a project and correct all errors and/or improve the design.

Changing a Photo's Focus and Optimizing It for the Web

Instructions: Start Photoshop and perform the customization steps found on pages PS 6 through PS 9. Open the Make It Right 1-1 Young Stars file in the Chapter 01 folder from the Data Files for Students and save it as Make It Right 1-1 Young Stars Edited in the PSD file format. You can access the Data Files for Students on the CD that accompanies this book. See the inside back cover of this book for instructions on downloading the Data Files for Students, or contact your instructor for information about accessing the required files.

Members of your Astronomy Club have selected the Young Stars photo (Figure 1–87) for the club's Web site. You are to edit the photo to more clearly focus on the cluster of stars and its trailing dust blanket, and then optimize the photo for the Web.

View the photo in different screen modes and at different magnifications.

Keeping the rule of thirds and the golden rectangle 5:8 ratio concepts in mind, crop the photo to change its focal point and resave it. Then save the photo for the Web as Make-It-Right-1-1-Young-Stars-for-Web using the optimal settings for a GIF file with maximum colors and 250 pixels in width.

Figure 1–87

In the Lab

Design and/or create a project using the guidelines, concepts, and skills presented in this chapter. Labs are listed in order of increasing difficulty.

Lab 1: Cropping a Photo and Adding a Feathered Border

Problem: A nature magazine has accepted the submission of your photo of an American bald eagle, but they would like you to crop the photo more, add a feathered border, and resize it. Also, the editor would like the final version saved in the TIFF format. The edited photo is displayed in Figure 1–88. See the inside back cover of this book for instructions on downloading the Data Files for Students, or contact your instructor for information about accessing the required files.

Figure 1–88

Continued >

In the Lab *continued*

Instructions:

1. Start Photoshop.

2. Click the 'Show more workspaces and options' button on the Application bar and then click Essentials to choose the workspace. Click the button again and then click Reset Essentials to restore the workspace to its default settings.

3. Select the second button on the Tools panel to reset the Tools panel.

4. Right-click the Rectangular Marquee Tool icon on the options bar and then click Reset all Tools to reset the options bar.

5. If black is not over white at the bottom of the Tools panel, click the Switch Foreground and Background Colors button.

6. Open the file, Lab 1-1 Eagle, from the Chapter 01 folder of the Data Files for Students or from a location specified by your instructor.

7. Click Save As on the File menu, and then type the new file name, Lab 1-1 Eagle Edited. Click the Format button and choose TIFF (*.TIF;*.TIFF) format. Click the Save button. If a TIFF Options dialog box is displayed, click the OK button.

8. Use the magnification box to zoom the photo to 50% magnification, if necessary.

9. If the rulers do not appear, press CTRL+R to view the rulers.

10. Select the Crop Tool. Position the mouse pointer at the top of the photo and 2 inches from the left side of the photo as measured on the ruler. Drag down and to the right to include all of the rock that the eagle is standing on.

11. Position the Rule of Thirds overlay so the eagle stands along the right inner line, with his shoulders along the top inner line.

12. Press the ENTER key. If your crop does not seem correct, click the Undo command on the Edit menu and repeat Steps 10 and 11.

13. Save the photo again.

14. Press CTRL+A to select all of the photo. Click Select on the menu bar, point to Modify to display the Modify submenu, and then click Border to display the Border dialog box. Type **100** in the Width box and then click the OK button.

15. Go the Modify submenu again, and click Feather. Type **50** in the Feather Radius box, and then click the OK button to create a second marquee with feathered edges.

16. If white is not the foreground color, press the x key to switch the foreground and background colors. Click Edit on the menu bar and then click Stroke. Type **50** in the Width box. Click the Inside option button in the Location area. Type **75** in the Opacity box. Click the OK button to stroke the selection.

17. Click the Image Size command on the Image menu. When the Image Size dialog box is displayed in the Document Size area, type **4.25** in the Width box. Click the OK button to resize the image.

18. Press CTRL+S to save the file again.

19. Use the Print One Copy command on the File menu to print a copy of the photo.

20. Close your file and quit Photoshop.

21. Send the photo as an e-mail attachment to your instructor, or follow your instructor's directions for submitting the lab assignment.

In the Lab

Lab 2: Creating a Smoothed Border

Problem: The local hockey team is preparing a flyer to advertise its next game. The marketing department would like you to take one of the pictures from the last game and crop it to show just the face-off players and the official. Because the flyer will be printed on white paper, you should create a white border so the photo blends into the background and adds to the ice rink effect. The edited photo is displayed in Figure 1–89. See the inside back cover of this book for instructions on downloading the Data Files for Students, or contact your instructor for information about accessing the required files.

Figure 1– 89

Instructions:

1. Start Photoshop. Perform the customization steps found on pages PS 6 through PS 9.

2. Open the file, Lab 1-2 Hockey, from the Chapter 01 folder of the Data Files for Students or from a location specified by your instructor.

3. Use the Save As command on the File menu to save the file on your storage device with the name, Lab 1-2 Hockey Edited, in the PSD format.

4. Click the Zoom Tool button on the Tools panel. Click the official to center the photo in the display. Zoom as necessary so you can make precise edits.

5. Crop the picture to display only the official and the two hockey players ready for the face-off. Use the golden rectangle ratio of approximately 5:8. The vertical line of the hockey stick and the visual line of the official should be positioned using the rule of thirds.

6. Save the photo again with the same name.

7. Close the file and open it again using the Recent submenu.

8. Press CTRL+A to select all of the photo.

9. To create the border, do the following:

   a. On the Select menu, point to Modify, and then click Border.

   b. When the Border Selection dialog box is displayed, type 100 in the Width Box. Click the OK button.

Continued >

In the Lab *continued*

    c. On the Select menu, open the Modify submenu, and click Smooth.

    d. When the Smooth Selection dialog box is displayed, type **50** in the Sample Radius box to smooth the corners. Click the OK button.

    e. Press SHIFT+F5 to access the Fill command.

    f. When the Fill dialog box is displayed, click the Use box arrow and then click White in the list.

    g. Click the Mode box arrow and then click Normal in the list, if necessary.

    h. If necessary, type **100** in the Opacity box. Click the OK button.

    i. Press CTRL+D to deselect the border.

10. Save the photo again.

11. Use the Print One Copy command on the File menu to print a copy of the photo.

12. Close the document window.

13. Quit Photoshop.

14. Send the photo as an e-mail attachment to your instructor, or follow your instructor's directions for submitting the lab assignment.

In the Lab

Lab 3: Preparing a Photo for the Web

Problem: As an independent consultant in Web site design, you have been hired by the Department of Tourism to prepare a photo of an aerial tram for use on the department's Web site. The edited photo is displayed in Figure 1–90. See the inside back cover of this book for instructions on downloading the Data Files for Students, or contact your instructor for information about accessing the required files.

Figure 1–90

Instructions: Start Photoshop. Perform the customization steps found on pages PS 6 through PS 9. Open the file, Lab 1-3 Tram, from the Chapter 01 folder of the Data Files for Students. Save the file in the PSD format with the name Lab 1-3 Tram Edited, in a new folder named Lab 1-3. (*Hint:* Use the Create New Folder button in the toolbar of the Save As dialog box.) Resize the photo to 500 pixels wide. Zoom to 50% magnification. Search Photoshop Help for help related to optimization. Read about optimizing for the Web. Print a copy of the help topic and then close the Photoshop Help window.

Use the Save for Web & Devices dialog box to view the 4-Up tab. Choose the best looking preview. Select the connection speed of your Internet connection. Save the HTML and Images in the Lab 1-3 folder using the name, Lab-1-3-Tram-for-Web. Use Mini Bridge to check your file structure and see your photos. Collapse the Mini Bridge panel. For extra credit, upload the HTML file and the accompanying Image folder to a Web server. See your instructor for ways to submit this assignment.

Cases and Places

Apply your creative thinking and problem-solving skills to design and implement a solution.

Note: To complete these assignments, you may be required to use the Data Files for Students. See the inside back cover of this book for instructions on downloading the Data Files for Students, or contact your instructor for information about accessing the required files.

1: Cropping a Photo for a Picture Directory

Academic

As a member of your high school reunion committee, it is your task to assemble the class photo directory. You are to edit a high school student photo and prepare it for print in the reunion directory. The photo needs to fit in a space 1.75 inches high and 1.33 inches wide. Each photo needs to have approximately the same amount of space above the headshot: .25 inches. After starting Photoshop and resetting the workspace, select the photo, Case 1-1 Student, from the Chapter 01 folder of the Data Files for Students. Save the photo on your USB flash drive storage device as Case 1-1 Student Edited, using the PSD format. Resize the photo to match the requirements. Use the rulers to help you crop the photo to leave .25 inches above the top of the student's head. Save the photo again with the file name Case 1-1 Student for Print and print a copy for your instructor.

2: Creating a Photo for a Social Networking Site

Personal

You would like to place a photo of your recent tubing adventure on your social networking site. The photo you have is of two people. You need to crop out the other person who is tubing. After starting Photoshop and resetting the workspace, select the photo, Case 1-2 Tubing, from the Chapter 01 folder of the Data Files for Students. Save the photo on your USB flash drive storage device as Case 1-2 Tubing Edited, using the PSD format. Crop the photo to remove one of the inner tubes, keeping in mind the rule of thirds, the golden rectangle, and the direction of the action. Save the photo again and print a copy for your instructor.

Continued >

Cases and Places *continued*

3: Creating a Rack Card Graphic with a Border

Professional

You are an intern with a tour company. They are planning a bus tour that follows the original Lewis and Clark trail and want to produce a rack card advertising the trip. On the back of the rack card, they would like a photo of one of the sites along the trail. The photo named Case 1-3 Monument is located in the Chapter 01 folder of the Data Files for Students. Save the photo on your USB flash drive storage device as Case 1-3 Monument Edited, using the PSD format. Rack cards typically measure 4×9 inches; the photo needs to fit in the upper half. Resize the photo to be 3.75 inches wide. Create a border of 200 pixels. Do not use smoothing. Fill the border with 50% black opacity.

2 | Using Selection Tools and Shortcut Keys

Objectives

You will have mastered the material in this chapter when you can:

- Explain the terms perspective, layout, and storyboard
- Describe selection tools
- Select objects using the marquee tools
- Move a selection
- Make transformation edits
- Use the History panel
- Use the Grow command and Refine Edges to adjust selections

- Employ the lasso tools
- Add and subtract areas from selections
- Use ruler grids and guides
- Select objects using the Quick Selection and Magic Wand tools
- Print to a PDF file
- Create and test new keyboard shortcuts

2 | Using Selection Tools and Shortcut Keys

Introduction

In Chapter 1, you learned about the Photoshop interface as well as navigation and zooming techniques. You cropped and resized a photo, added a border, and saved the photo for both Web and print media. You learned about online Help, along with opening, saving, and printing photos. This chapter continues to emphasize those topics and presents some new ones.

Recall that when you make a selection, you are specifying or isolating an area of your photo for editing. By selecting specific areas, you can edit and apply special effects to portions of your image, while leaving the unselected areas untouched. The new topics covered in this chapter include the marquee tools used to select rectangular or elliptical areas, the lasso tools used to select free-form segments or shapes, and the Quick Selection and Magic Wand tools used to select consistently colored areas. You also will learn how to use the Move Tool and transformation tools to duplicate, move, scale, skew, and warp those selections. Finally, you will print to a PDF file and create a new keyboard shortcut.

Project — Advertisement Graphic

An advertisement, or ad, is a form of communication that promotes a product or service to a potential customer. An advertisement tries to persuade consumers to purchase a product or service. An advertisement typically has a single message directed toward a specific audience.

A graphic designed for advertising, sometimes called an **advertising piece**, needs to catch the customer's eye and entice him or her to purchase the product. A clear graphic with strong contrast, item repetition, and visual lines will tell the story while enhancing any text that might be added later. Chapter 2 illustrates the creation of a department store advertising piece. You will begin with the image in Figure 2–1a that shows pieces from a set of dishes. You then will manipulate the image by selecting, editing, and moving the objects to produce a more attractive layout, creating Figure 2–1b to use in the advertisement.

Overview

As you read this chapter, you will learn how to create the advertisement graphic shown in Figure 2–1b by performing these general tasks:

- Select portions of the photo.
- Copy, move, rotate, and flip selections.
- Use the transformation commands to edit, scale, warp, and skew selections.
- Eliminate white space in and among objects in selected areas.
- Retrace editing steps using the History panel.
- Refine edges of selections.
- Print to a PDF file.
- Create a new shortcut key.

(a) Original Image

(b) Edited Image

Figure 2–1

General Project Guidelines

When editing a photo, the actions you perform and decisions you make will affect the appearance and characteristics of the finished product. As you edit a photo, such as the one shown in Figure 2–1a, you should follow these general guidelines:

1. **Choose the correct tool.** When you need to copy and paste portions of your photo, consider carefully which Photoshop selection tool to use. You want the procedure to be efficient and produce a clear image. Keep in mind the shape, background, purpose, and your expertise with various tools.

2. **Plan your duplications.** Use a storyboard or make a list of the items you plan to duplicate. Then decide whether it will be an exact duplication or a manipulated one, called a transformed copy. The decision depends on the visual effect you want to achieve.

3. **Use grids and guides.** When you are working with exact measurements, closely cropping and moving objects, or if you just want to align things easily, use grids and guides to display nonprinting lines across the document window. Use the Photoshop snapping function to align selections. Visual estimations of size and location are easier to perceive.

4. **Create files in portable formats.** You might have to distribute your artwork in a variety of formats depending on its use. Portability is an important consideration. It usually is safe to begin work in the Photoshop PSD format and then use the Save As command or Print command to convert to the PDF format. PDF files are platform and software independent.

When necessary, more specific details concerning the above guidelines are presented at appropriate points in the chapter. The chapter also will identify the actions performed and decisions made regarding these guidelines during the creation of the edited photo shown in Figure 2–1b.

Plan Ahead

Creating an Advertising Piece

Figure 2–2 illustrates the design decisions made to create the advertising piece. An attractive layout using multiple objects is a good marketing strategy, visually and subconsciously encouraging the viewer to purchase more than one item. **Layout** refers to placing visual elements into a pleasing and understandable arrangement. In the place setting advertisement, the layout is suggestive of how the product or products might look in a buyer's home. Advertising artists and product designers try to determine how the target consumer will use the product and group objects accordingly in the layout.

Figure 2–2

From a design point of view, creating visual diagonal lines creates perspective. **Perspective** is the technique photographers, designers, and artists use to create the illusion of three dimensions on a flat or two-dimensional surface. Perspective is a means of fooling the eye by making it appear as if there is depth or receding space in an image. Adjusting the sizes and juxtaposing the objects creates asymmetrical balance and visual tension between the featured products. The diagonal alignment of the glasses leads the viewer's eye to the background, as does the placement of smaller pieces in front of larger ones.

The **horizon line** in perspective drawing is a virtual horizontal line across the picture. The placement of the horizon line determines from where the viewer seems to be looking, such as down from a high place or up from close to the ground. In the dishes advertisement, the horizon line runs across the middle of the drawing, just below the center.

Using white space, or non-image area, is effective in directing the viewer to notice what is important. The products grouped this way are, in a sense, framed by the white space.

This product layout also helps other members of the design team when it is time to make decisions about type placement. The group of products can be shifted up or down, as one image, to accommodate the layout and text, including the font sizes, placement, title, description, and price information. Recall that the rule of thirds offers a useful means to make effective layouts for images and text.

Designing a preliminary layout sketch, similar to Figure 2–2, to help you make choices about placement, size, perspective, and spacing, is referred to as creating a **storyboard** or **rough**.

BTW

Photoshop Help
The best way to become familiar with Photoshop Help is to use it. Appendix D includes detailed information about Photoshop Help and exercises that will help you gain confidence in using it.

To Start Photoshop

If you are stepping through this project on a computer and you want your screen to match the figures in this book, then you should change your computer's resolution to 1024×768 and reset the tools and panels. For more information about how to change the resolution on your computer, and other advanced Photoshop settings, read Appendix C.

The following steps, which assume Windows 7 is running, start Photoshop based on a typical installation. You may need to ask your instructor how to start Photoshop for your system.

1 Click the Start button on the Windows 7 taskbar to display the Start menu and then type `Photoshop CS5` in the 'Search programs and files' box.

2 Click Adobe Photoshop CS5 in the list to start Photoshop.

3 If the Photoshop window is not maximized, click the Maximize button next to the Close button on the Application bar to maximize the window.

To Reset the Workspace

As discussed in Chapter 1, it is helpful to reset the workspace so that the tools and panels appear in their default positions. The following steps select the Essentials workspace.

1 Click the 'Show more workspaces and options' button on the Application bar to display the names of saved workspaces and then click Essentials to select the default workspace panels.

2 Click the 'Show more workspaces and options' button again to display the list and then click Reset Essentials to restore the workspace to its default settings and reposition any panels that may have been moved.

To Reset the Tools and the Options Bar

Recall that the Tools panel and the options bar retain their settings from previous Photoshop sessions. The following steps select the Rectangular Marquee Tool and reset all tool settings in the options bar.

1 If the tools in the Tools panel appear in two columns, click the double arrow at the top of the Tools panel.

2 If necessary, click the Rectangular Marquee Tool button on the Tools panel to select it.

3 Right-click the Rectangular Marquee Tool icon on the options bar to display the context menu and then click Reset All Tools. When Photoshop displays a confirmation dialog box, click the OK button to restore the tools to their default settings.

To Reset the Default Colors

Photoshop retains the foreground and background colors from session to session. Your colors might not display black over white on the Tools panel. The following step resets the default colors.

1 Press the D key to reset the default foreground and background colors.

BTW

Resetting Default Colors
At the bottom of the Tools panel, the Default Foreground and Background Colors button always sets black as the foreground color and white as the background color. You also can press the D key to reset the colors.

To Open a Photo

To open a photo in Photoshop, it must be stored as a digital file on your computer system or on an external storage device. The photos used in this book are stored in the Data Files for Students. You can access the Data Files for Students on the CD that accompanies this book. See the inside back cover of this book for instructions on downloading the Data Files for Students, or contact your instructor for information about accessing the required files.

The following steps open the file, Dishes, from a CD located in drive E.

1 Insert the CD that accompanies this book into your CD drive. After a few seconds, if Windows displays a dialog box, click its Close button.

2 With the Photoshop window open, click File on the menu bar, and then click Open to display the Open dialog box.

3 In the Open dialog box, click the Look in box arrow to display the list of available locations, and then click drive E or the drive associated with your CD.

4 Double-click the Chapter 02 folder to open it, and then double-click the file, Dishes, to open it.

5 When Photoshop displays the image in the document window, if the magnification shown on the status bar is not 25%, double-click the magnification box on the status bar, type 25, and then press the ENTER key to change the magnification (Figure 2–3).

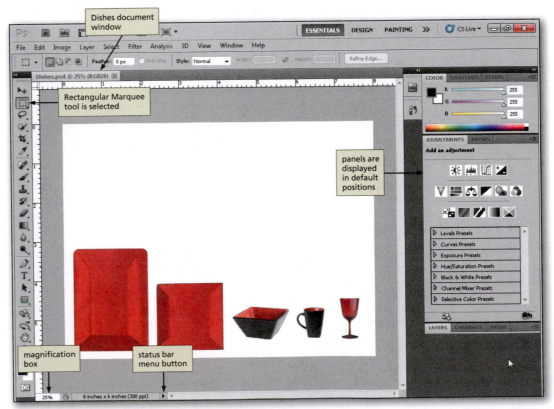

Figure 2–3

To View Rulers

The following steps display the rulers in the document window to facilitate making precise measurements.

1 If the rulers are not shown on the top and left sides of the document window, press CTRL+R to display the rulers in the workspace.

2 If necessary, right-click the horizontal ruler and then click Inches on the context menu to display the rulers in inches.

To Save a Photo

Even though you have yet to edit the photo, it is a good practice to save the file on your personal storage device early in the process. The following steps save the photo with the name Dishes Edited.

1 With your USB flash drive connected to one of the computer's USB ports, click File on the menu bar to display the File menu and then click Save As to display the Save As dialog box.

2 In the File name text box, type `Dishes Edited` to rename the file. Do not press the ENTER key after typing the file name.

3 Click the Save in box arrow and then click UDISK 2.0 (F:), or the location associated with your USB flash drive, in the list, if necessary.

4 Click the Save button in the Save As dialog box to save the file.

Break Point: If you wish to take a break, this is a good place to do so. You can quit Photoshop now. To resume at a later time, start Photoshop, open the file called Dishes Edited, and continue following the steps from this location forward.

The Marquee Tools

The **marquee tools** allow you to draw a marquee that selects a portion of the document window. Marquee tools are useful when the part of an image or photo that you wish to select fits into a rectangular or an elliptical shape. Photoshop has four marquee tools that appear in a context menu when you click the tool and hold down the mouse button, or when you right-click the tool. You can select any of the marquee tools from this context menu. Recall that Photoshop offers the added flexibility of selecting a tool with a single letter shortcut key. Pressing the M key activates the current marquee tool.

The Rectangular Marquee Tool is the default marquee tool that selects a rectangular or square portion of the image or photo. The Elliptical Marquee Tool allows you to select an ellipsis, oval, or circular area.

Dragging with the Rectangular or Elliptical Marquee tools creates a marquee drawn from a corner. If you press the SHIFT key while dragging a marquee, Photoshop constrains the proportions of the shape, creating a perfect square or circle. If you press the ALT key while drawing a selection, Photoshop creates the marquee from the center. Pressing SHIFT+ALT starts from the center and constrains the proportions.

The Single Row Marquee Tool allows you to select a single row of pixels. The Single Column Marquee Tool allows you to select a single column of pixels. A single click in the document window then creates the selection. Because a single row or column of pixels is so small, it is easier to use these two marquee tools at higher magnifications.

BTW

The Tool Preset Picker
Most tools display a Tool Preset picker on the options bar. When you click the button, Photoshop displays a list of settings used during the current Photoshop session or previously saved options bar settings. The list makes it easier to save and reuse tool settings. You can load, edit, and create libraries of tool presets in conjunction with the Tool Presets panel. To choose a tool preset, click the Tool Preset picker in the options bar, and then select a preset from the list.

Table 2–1 describes the four marquee tools.

Table 2–1 The Marquee Tools			
Tool	**Purpose**	**Shortcut**	**Button**
Rectangular Marquee	selects a rectangular or square portion of the document window	M SHIFT+M toggles to Elliptical Marquee	
Elliptical Marquee	selects an elliptical, oval, or circular portion of the document window	M SHIFT+M toggles to Rectangular Marquee	
Single Row Marquee	selects a single row of pixels in the document window	(none)	
Single Column Marquee	selects a single column of pixels in the document window	(none)	

Plan Ahead

Choose the correct tool.
When you need to copy, paste, and move portions of your photo, consider carefully which selection tool to use. You want the procedure to be efficient and produce a clear image. Keep in mind the following as you choose a selection tool:

- the shape of the selection
- the background around the selection
- the contrast between the selection and its surroundings
- the proximity of the selection to other objects
- your expertise in using the tool
- the availability of other pointing devices, such as a graphics tablet
- the destination of the paste

The options bar associated with each of the marquee tools contains many buttons and settings to draw effective marquees (Figure 2–4). The options bar displays an icon for the chosen marquee on the left, followed by the Tool Preset picker. The Tool Preset picker allows you to save and reuse toolbar settings.

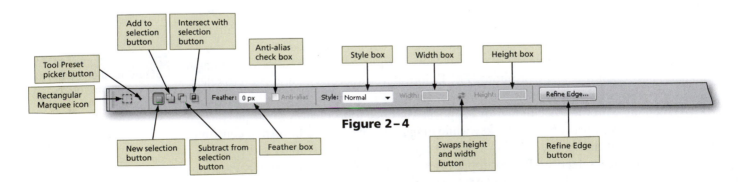

Figure 2–4

The next four buttons to the right adjust the selection. When selected, the New selection button allows you to start a new marquee.

The 'Add to selection' button draws a rectangle or ellipsis and adds it to any current selection. The 'Add to selection' button is useful for selecting the extra corners of an

L-shaped object or for shapes that do not fit within a single rectangle or ellipsis. To activate the 'Add to selection' button, you can click it on the options bar or hold down the SHIFT key while dragging a second selection. When adding to a selection, the mouse pointer changes to a crosshair with a plus sign.

The 'Subtract from selection' button allows you to deselect or remove a portion of an existing selection. The new rectangle or ellipsis is removed from the original selection. It is useful for removing block portions of the background around oddly shaped images, or for deselecting ornamentation in an object. To activate the 'Subtract from selection' button, you can click it on the options bar or hold down the ALT key while dragging a second selection. When subtracting from a selection, the mouse pointer changes to a crosshair with a minus sign.

The 'Intersect with selection' button allows you to draw a second rectangle or ellipsis across a portion of the previously selected area, resulting in a selection border only around the area in which the two selections overlap. To activate the 'Intersect with selection' button, you click it on the options bar, or hold down the SHIFT and ALT keys while dragging a second selection. When creating an intersection, the mouse pointer changes to a crosshair with an X.

To the right of the selection buttons, the options bar displays a Feather box. **Feathering** softens the edges of the selection. In traditional photography, feathering is called **vignetting**, which creates a soft-edged border around an image that blends into the background. Feathering sometimes is used in wedding photos or when a haloed effect is desired. The width of the feather is measured in pixels. When using the Elliptical Marquee Tool, you can further specify blending by selecting the Anti-alias check box. **Anti-aliasing** softens the block-like, staircase look of rounded corners. Figure 2–5 shows a rectangle with no feathering, one with five pixels of feathering, an ellipsis with no anti-aliasing, and one created with a check mark in the Anti-alias check box.

BTW

Anti-Aliasing
Anti-aliasing is available for the Elliptical Marquee Tool, the Lasso Tool, the Polygonal Lasso Tool, the Magnetic Lasso Tool, and the Magic Wand Tool. You must specify this option before using these tools. Once a tool selection is made, you cannot add anti-aliasing.

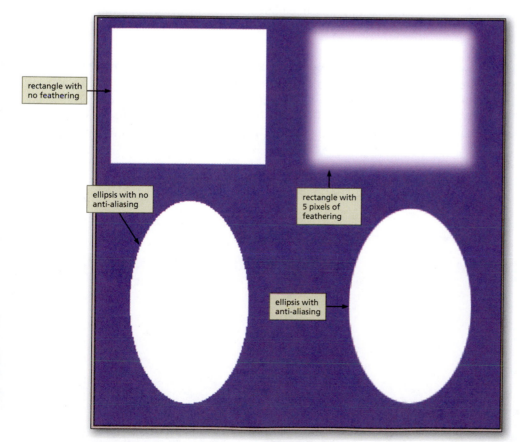

rectangle with no feathering

rectangle with 5 pixels of feathering

ellipsis with no anti-aliasing

ellipsis with anti-aliasing

Figure 2–5

BTW

Marquee Tool Selection
If you are using a different tool, and want to activate the marquee tools, you can click the Rectangular Marquee Tool button on the Tools panel or press the M key to select the tool. Once the tool is selected, pressing SHIFT+M toggles between the Rectangular and Elliptical Marquee tools. You must choose the Single Row and Single Column Marquee tools from the context menu — there are no keyboard shortcuts.

BTW

Single Row and Single Column Marquee Tools
To create interesting backgrounds, wallpapers, and color ribbons using the Single Row or Single Column Marquee tools, choose a colorful photo and create a single row or single column marquee. Press CTRL+T to display the bounding box. Then drag the sizing handles until the selection fills the document window.

BTW

Nudging Selections
Instead of dragging to move a selection, you can use the arrow keys on the keyboard to move the selection in small increments in a process called **nudging**.

When using the Rectangular Marquee Tool or the Elliptical Marquee Tool, you can click the Style box arrow (Figure 2–4 on page PS 80) to choose how the size of the marquee selection is determined. A Normal style sets the selection marquee proportions by dragging. A Fixed Ratio style sets a height-to-width ratio using decimal values. For example, to draw a marquee twice as wide as it is high, enter **2** for the width and **1** for the height, and then drag in the photo. A Fixed Size style allows you to specify exact pixel values for the marquee's height and width. Photoshop enables the Width box and Height box when you choose a style other than Normal. A button between the two boxes swaps the values, if desired.

Sometimes you need to make subtle changes to a selection marquee. For example, if the border or edge of a selection seems to be jagged or hazy, or if the colors at the edge of a selection bleed slightly across the marquee, you can use the Refine Edge button. When clicked, it opens a dialog box in which you can increase or decrease the radius of the marquee, change the contrast, and smooth the selection border.

Once you have drawn a marquee, you can choose from other options for further manipulation of the selected area. Right-clicking a selection displays a context menu that provides access to many other useful commands such as deselecting, reselecting, or selecting the **inverse**, which means selecting everything in the image outside of the current selection. Right-clicking a selection also enables you to create layers, apply color fills and strokes, and make other changes that you will learn about in future chapters. The Select menu also displays commands to manipulate selections.

If you make a mistake or change your mind when drawing a marquee, you can do one of three things:

1. If you want to start over, and the New selection button is selected on the options bar, you can click somewhere else in the document window to deselect the marquee, and then simply draw a new marquee. Deselecting also is available as a command on the Select menu and on the context menu.

2. If you have already drawn the marquee but wish to move or reposition it, and the New selection button is selected on the options bar, you can drag the selection to the new location.

3. If you want to reposition while you are creating the marquee, do not release the mouse button. Press and hold the SPACEBAR, drag the marquee to the new location, and then release the SPACEBAR. At that point, you can continue dragging to finish drawing the marquee. Repositioning in this manner can be done while using any of the four selection adjustment buttons on the options bar.

To Use the Rectangular Marquee Tool

The following step selects the rectangular tray in the Dishes Edited image using the Rectangular Marquee Tool.

1

- With the Rectangular Marquee Tool selected on the Tools panel, drag to draw a rectangle around the tray to create a marquee selection. Do not include the square plate (Figure 2–6).

🔍 **Experiment**

- Practice drawing rectangular and elliptical marquees. Press SHIFT+M to switch between the two. SHIFT+drag to look at the effects. When you are finished, redraw a marquee around the tray.

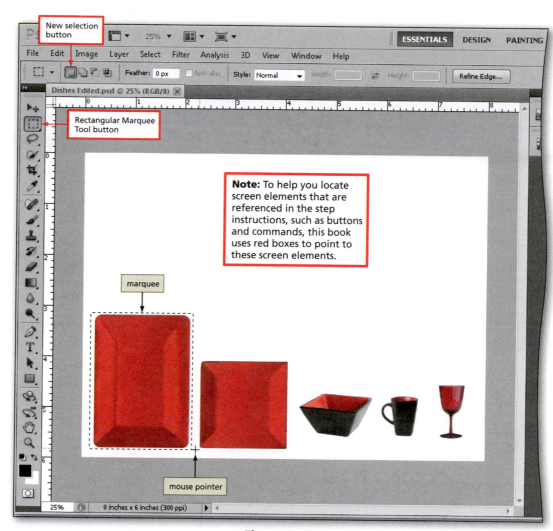

Figure 2–6

Other Ways

1. Press M key or SHIFT+M until Rectangular Marquee Tool is active, drag selection

The Move Tool

The Move Tool on the Photoshop Tools panel is used to move or make other changes to selections. Activating the Move Tool by clicking the Move Tool button, or by pressing the V key on the keyboard, enables you to move the selection border and its contents by dragging in the document window. When you first use the Move Tool, the mouse pointer displays a black arrowhead with scissors. To move the selection in a straight line, press and hold the SHIFT key while dragging. If you press and hold the ALT key while dragging, you duplicate or move only a copy of the selected area, effectively copying and pasting the selection. While duplicating, the mouse pointer changes to a black arrowhead with a white arrowhead behind it.

When you move selections, you need to be careful about overlapping images. As you will learn in Chapter 3, Photoshop might layer or overlap portions of images when you move them. While that sometimes is preferred when creating collages or composite images, it is undesirable if an important object is obscured. Close tracing while creating selections and careful placement of moved selections will prevent unwanted layering.

BTW

Quick Reference
For a table that lists how to complete the tasks covered in this book using the mouse, context menu, and keyboard, see the Quick Reference Summary at the back of this book or visit the Photoshop CS5 Quick Reference Web page (scsite.com/pscs5/qr).

The Move Tool options bar displays tools to help define the scope of the move (Figure 2–7). Later, as you learn about layers, you will use the Auto-Select check box to select layer groupings or single layers. The align and distribute buttons and the Auto-Align Layers button also are used with layers. The Show Transform Controls check box causes Photoshop to display transformation controls on the selection.

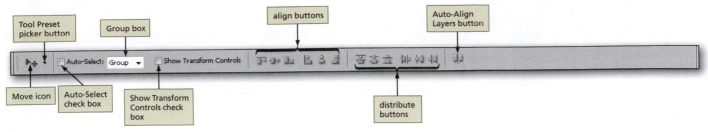

Figure 2–7

As you use the Move Tool throughout this chapter, be careful to position your mouse pointer inside the selection before moving. Do not try to move a selection by dragging its border. If you drag one by mistake, press the ESC key.

To Use the Move Tool

The following steps use the Move Tool to move the tray up and to the right.

1
- With the tray still selected, click the Move Tool button on the Tools panel to activate the Move Tool.

- If necessary, on the options bar, click the Auto-Select check box so it does not display a check mark. If necessary, click the Show Transform Controls check box so it does not display a check mark (Figure 2–8).

Q&A Are there any other tools nested with the Move Tool?

No, the Move Tool does not have a context menu. Tools with a context menu display a small black triangle in the lower-right corner.

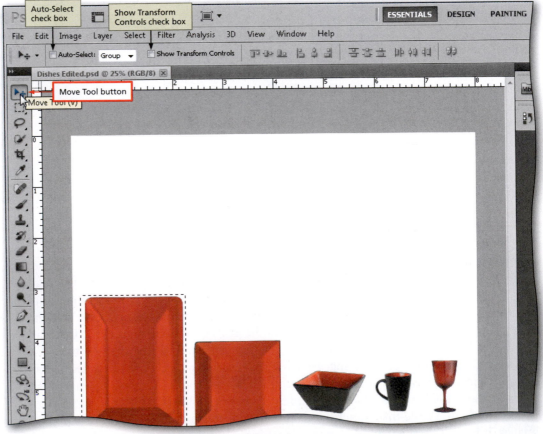

Figure 2–8

2

● Position your mouse pointer over the tray, within the marquee. Drag the selection to a position above the other dishes, near the top margin and approximately centered (Figure 2–9). Do not press any keys.

My document window shows a black square. What did I do wrong?

It is possible that the default colors on your system were changed by another user. Press CTRL+Z to undo the move. Press the D key to select the default foreground and background colors. Looking at the bottom of the Tools panel, if black is not showing as being on top, press the X key to exchange the black and white colors.

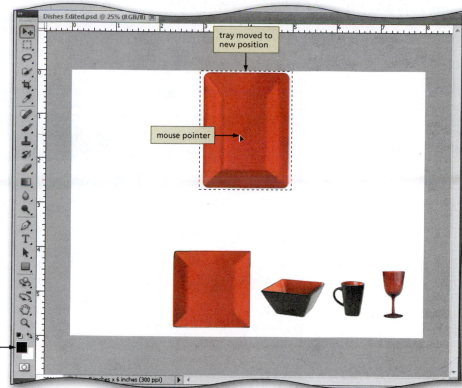

Figure 2–9

The Transformation Commands

In Photoshop, the word **transform** refers to making physical changes to a selection. To choose a transformation command, click the Edit menu, point to Transform, and then click the desired transformation. Alternatively, you can click Transform Selection on the context menu that is displayed when you right-click a selection.

When you choose to transform, Photoshop displays a **bounding box**, or border with six sizing handles around the selection (Figure 2–10). A small reference point appears in the center of the selection as a small circle with a crosshair symbol. A **reference point** is a fixed pivot point around which transformations are performed. You can move a reference point by dragging.

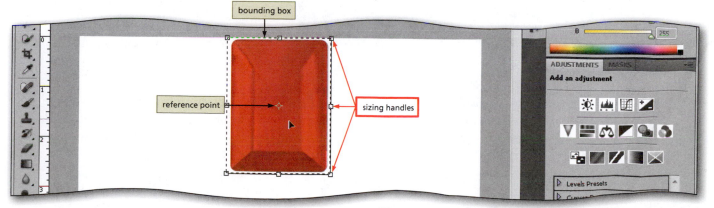

Figure 2–10

Table 2–2 lists the types of transformations you can perform on a selection, the techniques used to perform a particular transformation, and the result of the transformation. Many of the commands also are on the context menu when you right-click the bounding box. If you choose free transform rather than using the context menu, you must use the mouse techniques to perform the transformation.

Table 2–2 Transformation Commands

Using the Menu	Using the Mouse (Free Transform)	Using the Transform Options Bar	Result
Scale	Drag a sizing handle on the bounding box. SHIFT+drag to scale proportionately. ALT+drag to scale opposite sides at the same time.	To scale numerically, enter percentages in the Width and Height boxes, shown as W and H, on the options bar. Click the Link icon to maintain the aspect ratio.	Selection is displayed at a different size.
Rotate 180° Rotate 90° CW (clockwise) Rotate 90° CCW (counterclockwise)	Move the mouse pointer outside the bounding box border. It becomes a curved, two-headed arrow. Drag in the direction you wish to rotate. SHIFT+drag to constrain the rotation to 15° increments.	In the Set Rotation box, shown as a compass on the options bar, type a positive number for clockwise rotation or a negative number for counterclockwise rotation.	Selection is rotated or revolved around the reference point.
Skew	Right-click selection and then click Skew. Drag a side of the bounding box. ALT+drag to skew both vertically and horizontally.	To skew numerically, enter decimal values in the horizontal skew and vertical skew boxes, shown as H and V on the options bar.	Selection is tilted or slanted either horizontally or vertically.
Distort	Right-click selection and then click Distort. Drag a corner sizing handle to stretch the bounding box.	Enter new numbers in the location, size, rotation, and skew boxes.	Selection is larger on one edge than on the others.
Perspective	Right-click selection and then click Perspective. Drag a corner sizing handle to apply perspective to the bounding box.	Enter new numbers in the size, rotation, and skew boxes.	The selection appears larger on one edge than on the others, giving the larger edge the appearance of being closer to the viewer.
Warp	When the warp mesh is displayed, drag any line or point.	Click the Custom box arrow. Click a custom warp.	Selection is reshaped with bulge, arch, warped corner, or twist.
Flip Horizontal Flip Vertical	Flipping is available only on the menu.	Flipping is available only on the menu.	Selection is turned upside down or mirrored.

To display the Transform options bar, create a selection, and then choose Free Transform on the Edit menu, click a sizing handle, or press CTRL+T. Photoshop displays a Transform options bar that contains boxes and buttons to help you with your transformation (Figure 2–11).

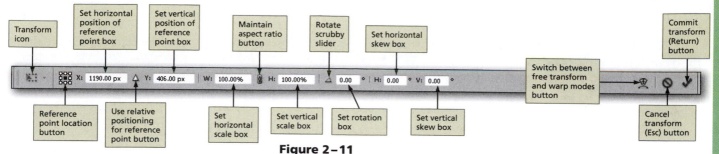

Figure 2–11

On the left side of the Transform options bar, Photoshop displays the 'Reference point location' button. Each of the nine squares on the button corresponds to a point on the bounding box. The default middle square represents the center reference point. To select a different reference point, click a different square on the 'Reference point location' button.

The X and Y boxes allow you to place the reference point at an exact pixel location in the document window by entering horizontal and vertical values. When you enter a value in one of those boxes, Photoshop moves the entire selection. If you click the Use relative positioning for reference point button, located between the X and Y boxes, the movement of the selection is relative to the current location.

The W and H boxes allow you to scale the width and height of the selection. When you click the 'Maintain aspect ratio' button between the W and H boxes, the aspect ratio of the selection is maintained.

To the right of the scale boxes is a Set rotation box. Entering a positive number rotates, or turns, the selection clockwise; a negative number rotates the selection counter-clockwise.

The H and V boxes, to the right of the Set rotation box, set the horizontal and vertical skews of the selection, measured in degrees. A positive number skews the selection to the right; a negative number skews to the left.

A unique feature is the ability to drag labels to change the box values. For example, if you drag the H, Y, W, or other labels, the values in the text boxes change. The inter-active labels, called **scrubby sliders**, appear when you position the mouse pointer over the label. When you point to any of the scrubby sliders on the Transform options bar, the mouse pointer changes to a hand with a two-headed arrow, indicating the ability to drag. Dragging to the right increases the value; dragging to the left decreases the value. Holding down the SHIFT key while dragging the scrubby slider accelerates the change by a factor of 10. Many options bars use scrubby sliders.

On the far right of the Transform options bar are three buttons. The first one switches between the Transform options bar and the Warp options bar. After you are finished making transformations, you commit changes, or apply the transformations by pressing the ENTER key or by clicking the 'Commit transform (Return)' button (the second button). Committing the transformation is the same as saving it. If you do not wish to make the transformation, press the ESC key or click the third button, the Cancel transform (Esc) button.

After transforming a selection, you must either commit or cancel the transformation before you can perform any other action in Photoshop.

To Display Transformation Controls

The following step displays the transformation controls, including the bounding box, the reference point and the Transform options bar.

1

• Press CTRL+T to display the bounding box and the Transform options bar (Figure 2–12).

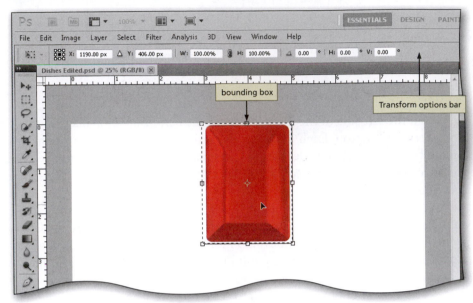

Figure 2–12

To Rotate a Selection

The following steps rotate the tray.

1

• Move the mouse pointer to the upper-right corner of the tray, just outside of the bounding box.

• When the mouse pointer displays a double-headed curved arrow, drag to the right and down until the tray appears on its side, as shown in Figure 2–13.

Q&A

How do you use the reference point?

The reference point serves as the pivot point during rotation. The default placement is in the center of the selection. If you drag the reference point to another location, any rotation performed on the selection will pivot around that new location.

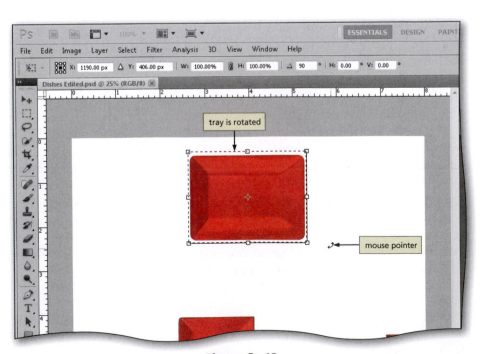

Figure 2–13

 Experiment

- On the options bar, drag the Rotate scrubby slider in either direction to watch the selection rotate. When you are done, rotate the tray to match Figure 2–13.

2

- Press the ENTER key to confirm the transformation.

Other Ways		
1. On Edit menu, click Free Transform, drag selection	2. On Edit menu, point to Transform, click desired rotate command	3. On options bar, enter degree rotation in Set Rotation box

To Deselect

The following step removes the selection marquee using the menu.

1 Click Select on the menu bar and then click Deselect to remove the selection marquee.

The Quick Selection Tool

The Quick Selection Tool draws a selection quickly using the mouse. As you drag, Photoshop creates a selection automatically, expanding outward to find and follow the defined edges in the image. The Quick Selection Tool is nested with the Magic Wand Tool on the Tools panel. You can access either tool from the context menu or by pressing the W key; if the Magic Wand Tool has been used previously, press SHIFT+W.

Dragging a quick selection is almost like painting a stroke with a brush. The Quick Selection Tool does not create a rectangular or oval selection; rather, it looks for a contrast in color and aligns the selection border to that contrast. It is most useful for isolated objects or parts of an image that contain a contrasting background. When using the Quick Selection Tool, the mouse pointer changes to a brush tip that displays a circle with a centered cross inside. You can decrease or increase the size of the brush tip by using the LEFT BRACKET ([ ) or RIGHT BRACKET ( ]) keys respectively, or by using the options bar.

The Quick Selection Tool options bar (Figure 2–14) displays the size of the brush and contains some of the same buttons as other selection tools. It also contains an Auto-Enhance check box that reduces roughness in the selection boundary when the box is checked.

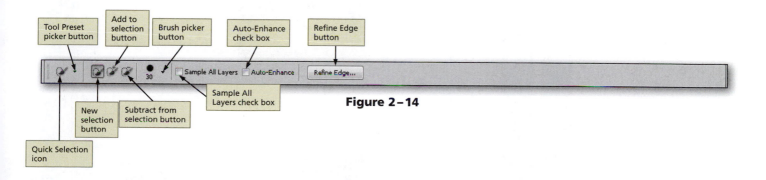

Figure 2–14

To Use the Quick Selection Tool

The following steps use the Quick Selection Tool to select the square plate.

1

- Right-click the Quick Selection Tool button on the Tools panel to display the context menu (Figure 2–15).

Q&A

What should I do if I make a mistake with the Quick Selection Tool?

If you make a mistake and want to start over, you can deselect by pressing CTRL+D, and then begin again.

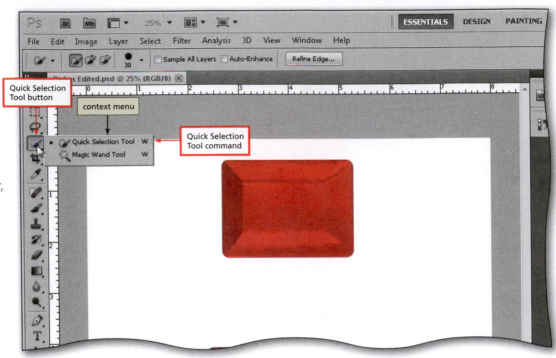

Figure 2–15

2

- If necessary, click Quick Selection Tool to select it.

- On the options bar, click the New selection button, if necessary. Click the Auto-Enhance check box so it displays a check mark, if necessary (Figure 2–16).

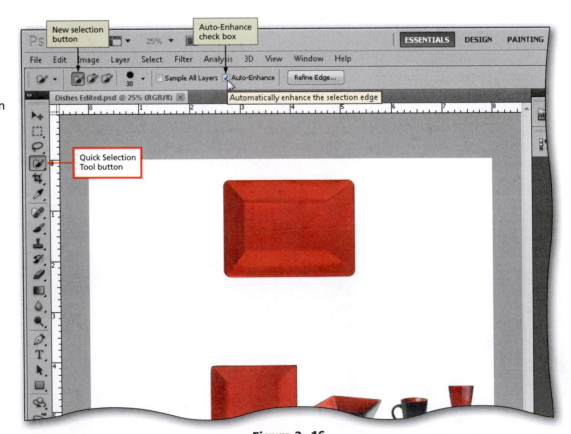

Figure 2–16

3
- Move the mouse pointer to the top-left corner of the square plate, and then slowly drag down and right to select only the plate (Figure 2–17).

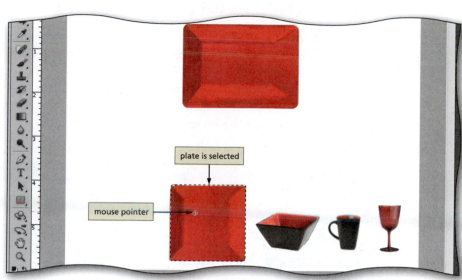

Figure 2–17

To Move a Selection

The following steps move the plate using the Move Tool. If you make a mistake while moving, press CTRL+Z and then move again. If you accidentally move a sizing handle or the center reference point, press the ESC key to cancel the transformation.

1 On the Tools panel, click the Move Tool button to select it.

2 Drag the selection up to a location in front of the tray (Figure 2–18). Do not press any keys.

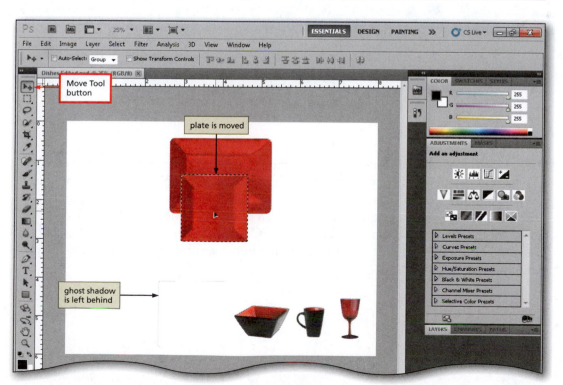

Figure 2–18

The History Panel

The History panel is displayed when you click the History button in the vertical docking of collapsed panels. The History panel records each step, called a **state**, as you edit a photo (Figure 2–19). Photoshop displays the initial state of the document at the top of the panel. Each time you apply a change to an image, the new state of that image is added to the bottom of the panel. Each state lists the name of the tool or command used to change the image.

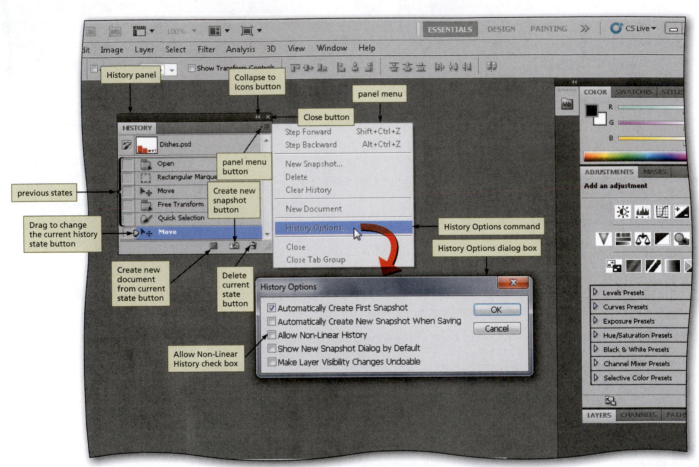

Figure 2–19

Like the Navigator panel that you learned about in Chapter 1, the History panel also has a panel menu where you can clear all states, change the history settings, or dock the panel. Buttons on the History panel status bar allow you to create a new document, save the selected state, or delete it. The panel can be collapsed by clicking the History button in the vertical docking or by clicking the Collapse to icons button. To redisplay a collapsed History panel, click the History button in the vertical docking or choose it again from the Window menu.

The History Panel
The History panel will list a Duplicate state when you use the ALT key to copy a selection. The word, Paste, will appear next to the state when you use the Copy and Paste commands from the keyboard or from the menu. The Copy command alone does not affect how the image looks; it merely sends a copy to the system Clipboard. Therefore, it does not appear as a state.

To Display the History Panel

The following step displays the History panel.

1
- Click the History button on the vertical docking of collapsed panels to expand the History panel (Figure 2–20).

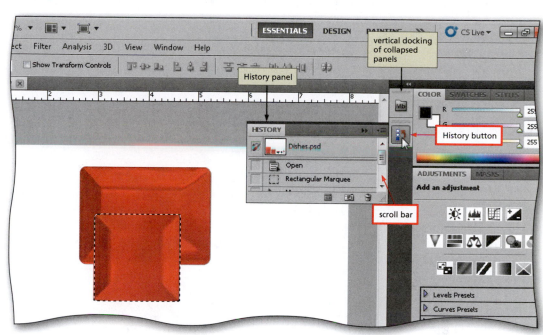

Figure 2–20

Using the History Panel

You can use the History panel in several different ways. When you select one of the states, the image reverts to how it looked when that change first was applied. Some users use the History panel to undo mistakes. Others use it to try out or experiment with different edits. By clicking a state, you can view the state temporarily or start working again from that point. You can step forward and backward through the states in the History panel by pressing CTRL+SHIFT+Z or CTRL+ALT+Z respectively.

Selecting a state and then changing the image in any way eliminates all the states in the History panel that came after it; however, if you select a state and change the image by accident, you can use the Undo command or CTRL+Z to restore the eliminated states. If you select the Allow Non-Linear History check box in the History Options dialog box (Figure 2–20) deleting a state deletes only that state.

You can use the History panel to jump to any recent state of the image created during the current working session by clicking the state. Alternatively, you can give a state a new name called a **snapshot**. Naming a snapshot makes it easy to identify. Snapshots are stored at the top of the History panel and make it easy to compare effects. For example, you can take a snapshot before and after a series of transformations. Then, by clicking between the two snapshots in the History panel, you can see the total effect, or choose the before snapshot and start over. To create a snapshot, right-click the step and then click New Snapshot on the context menu or click the Create new snapshot button on the History panel status bar. Snapshots are not saved with the image; closing an image deletes its snapshots.

Not all steps appear in the History panel. For instance, changes to panels, color settings, actions, and preferences are not displayed in the History panel, because they are not changes to a particular image.

BTW

Moving Among History Panel States
Photoshop uses many function keys to move easily among the states in the History panel. To step forward, press CTRL+SHIFT+Z. To step backward, press CTRL+ALT+Z. You also can use the History panel menu to step forward and backward.

By default, the History panel lists the previous 20 states. You can change the number of remembered states by changing a preference setting (see Appendix C). Photoshop deletes older states automatically to free more memory. Once you close and reopen the document, all states and snapshots from the last working session are cleared from the panel.

To Undo Changes Using the History Panel

Notice that in Figure 2–18 on page PS 91, a ghost shadow appears in the previous location of the plate. That sometimes happens with any of the selection tools, especially when fringe pixels are faded. The following steps undo the Move command.

1

• Scroll down in the History panel to display the last few states.

• Click the Quick Selection state in the History panel to go back one step and undo the move (Figure 2–21). Do not press any keys.

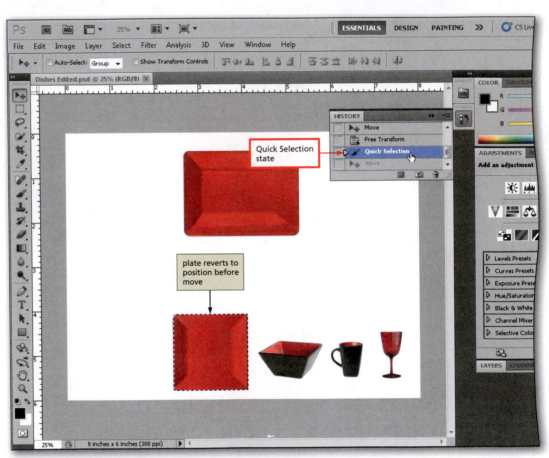

Figure 2–21

Could I have pressed CTRL+Z to undo the move?

Yes, if you only need to undo one step, pressing CTRL+Z will work. If you need to go back more than one step, you can press CTRL+ALT+Z or use the History panel.

What is the box to the left of each state?

The box sets the source for painting a clone-like image using the Art History Brush Tool.

Other Ways
1. Press CTRL+ALT+Z

To Collapse the History Panel

You can redisplay the History panel whenever you need it; however, the following step collapses the History panel to a button in the vertical docking so you can see more of the document window.

1

• Click the History button to collapse the panel (Figure 2–22).

Figure 2–22

Refining Edges

The Refine Edge button located on the options bar of each selection tool displays a dialog box where you can make choices about improving selections with jagged edges, soft transitions, hazy borders, or fine details and improve the quality of a selection's edges. Additionally, it allows you to view the selection on different backgrounds to facilitate editing (Figure 2–23).

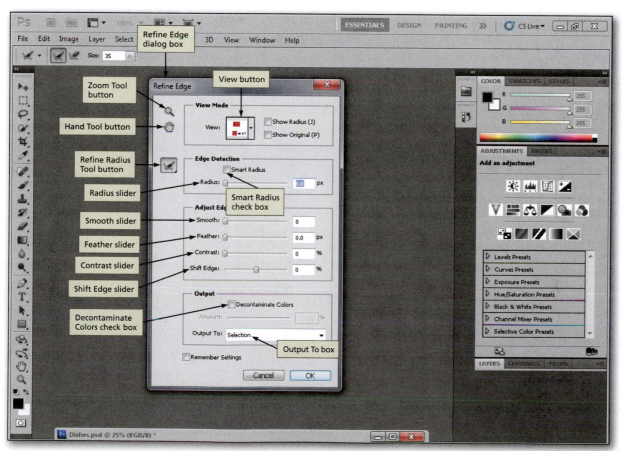

Figure 2–23

Table 2–3 describes some of the controls in the Refine Edge dialog box.

Table 2–3 Controls in the Refine Edge Dialog Box	
Control	**Function**
View Mode area	allows you to choose the background of the selection
Smart Radius check box	adjusts the radius edges automatically
Radius slider	adjusts the size of the selection boundary by pixels
Smooth slider	reduces irregular areas in the selection boundary to create a smoother outline with values from 0 to 100 pixels
Feather slider	softens the edges of the selection for blending into backgrounds using values from 0 to 250 pixels
Contrast slider	sharpens the selection edges to remove any hazy or extraneous pixels, sometimes called fuzzy artifacts or noise; increasing the contrast percentage can remove excessive noise near selection edges caused by a high radius setting
Shift Edge slider	enlarges or shrinks selection border
Decontaminate Colors check box	replaces fringe color fringes
Output To box	sets the output to a mask, layer or new document

The various settings in the Refine Edge dialog box take practice to use intuitively. The more experience you have adjusting the settings, the more comfortable you will feel with the controls. To improve selections for images on a contrasting background, you should first increase the radius and then increase the contrast to sharpen the edges. For grayscale images or selections where the colors of the object and the background are similar, try smoothing first, then feathering. For all selections, you might need to adjust the Shift Edge slider.

To Refine Edges

The following steps refine the edge of the selection to eliminate the ghost shadow.

 1

- On the Tools panel, click the Quick Selection Tool button to return to the Quick Selection Tool.

- On the Quick Selection Tool options bar, click the Refine Edge button to display the Refine Edge dialog box.

- Drag the Contrast slider (Refine Edge dialog box) until the Contrast box displays 35% to increase the contrast.

- Drag the Shift Edge slider until the percentage is +60% to expand the selection (Figure 2–24).

Experiment

- Drag the Shift Edge slider to various percentages and watch how the selection changes. Return the slider to +60%.

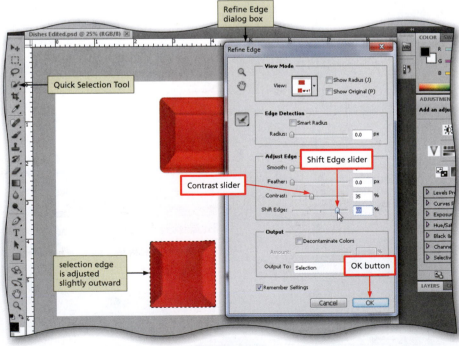

Figure 2–24

2

- Click the OK button (Refine Edge dialog box) to apply the changes and close the dialog box.

Q&A

Should I have any white area inside the selection marquee?

No. If your selection includes any white areas, select the 'Subtract from selection' button. Drag the white area carefully and slowly to remove it from the selection.

Other Ways

1. Right-click selection, click Refine Edge, choose settings, click OK

To Move Again

The following steps move the plate again, this time without leaving behind a ghost shadow.

1 Click the Move Tool button on the Tools panel to activate the Move Tool.

2 Drag the selection up and slightly right so the plate is in front of the tray, as shown in Figure 2–25.

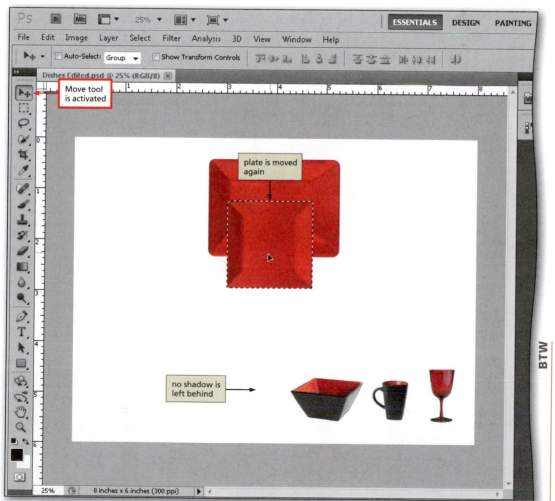

Ghost Shadows
After refining the edges, if you still have a ghost shadow, you can go back a step in the History panel, and then expand the selection even more, using the Refine Edge dialog box. Or, after you finish with the selection, you can use the Eraser tool to erase the shadow.

Figure 2–25

**Plan
Ahead**

Plan your duplications.

Creating a storyboard, either by hand or by using software, allows you to plan your image and make decisions about copies and placement. Some graphic artists annotate each copy in the storyboard with information about size, shape, location, and the tool they plan to use. For example, when you paste or drag a new copy of an image into a photo, you have two choices. You can keep the copy as an exact duplicate, or you can transform the copy. The choice depends on the visual effect you want to achieve and the customer requirements. Noting those requirements on your storyboard ahead of time will facilitate creating your image.

Use an exact copy to duplicate a logo or a border, or to create a tiled background. Commercial applications may create duplications to represent growth; or several duplications beside each other can emphasize a brand. Sometimes artists will duplicate an item several times when creating a quick sketch or a rough draft. Across photos, exact duplicates maintain consistency and product identification.

Transforming a copy or selection provides additional flexibility and diversity. You might want to create the illusion of multiple, different items to promote sales. Scaling, skewing, warping, and distorting provide interest and differentiation, and sometimes can correct lens errors. Flipping, rotating, or changing the perspective of the copy adds excitement to reproductions and creates the illusion of three dimensions.

BTW

Cutting and Pasting
Just as you do in other applications, you can use the Cut, Copy, and Paste commands from the Edit menu or shortcut keys to make changes to selections. Unless you predefine a selection area by dragging a marquee, the Paste command pastes to the center of the document window. Both the commands and the shortcut keys create a new layer when they copy or paste.

To Duplicate the Selection

Recall that pressing and holding the ALT key while dragging with the Move Tool creates a copy, or duplicates, the selection. The following step selects the Move Tool and creates a copy of the selected plate.

1

- With the plate still selected, if necessary, click the Move Tool button to select the Move Tool.

- Press and hold the ALT key while dragging to duplicate and move the selection to a location slightly down and right of the original, as shown in Figure 2–26. The copy will overlap the original.

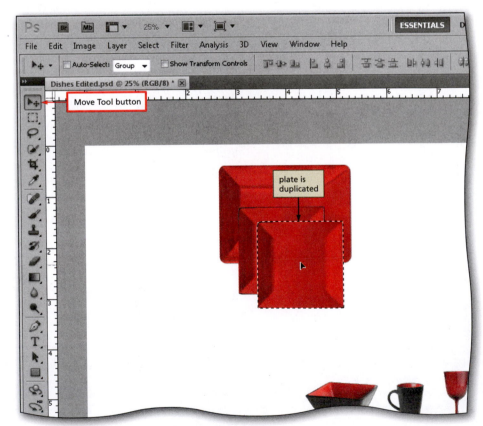

Figure 2–26

Other Ways

1. Press CTRL+C, press CTRL+V, press V, drag selection

2. Press V, ALT+drag selection

3. Select Magic Wand Tool, CTRL+drag selection

To Scale a Selection

As described in Table 2–2 (on page PS 86), when you scale a selection, you resize it by changing its width, height, or both. The following steps scale the duplicated plate.

1

• With the Move Tool button still selected, click the Show Transform Controls check box on the options bar to display the bounding box (Figure 2–27).

Q&A Could I use CTRL+T to display the bounding box?

Yes, you can use either the check box or those shortcut keys.

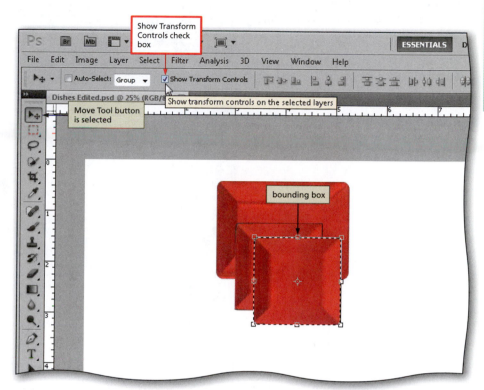

Figure 2–27

2

• SHIFT+drag the upper-right sizing handle toward the center of the plate until it is resized approximately 70 percent of the original (Figure 2–28).

Q&A How can I estimate 70 percent?

As soon as you begin to scale, the Move options bar changes to the Transform options bar. The values in the W: and H: boxes change as you scale the image. You can drag until they display approximately 70%.

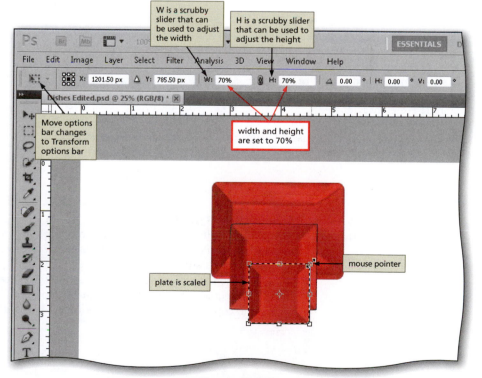

Figure 2–28

3
- Press the ENTER key to commit the change.
- Click the Show Transform Controls check box to remove the bounding box from the selection.
- Press CTRL+D to deselect (Figure 2–29).

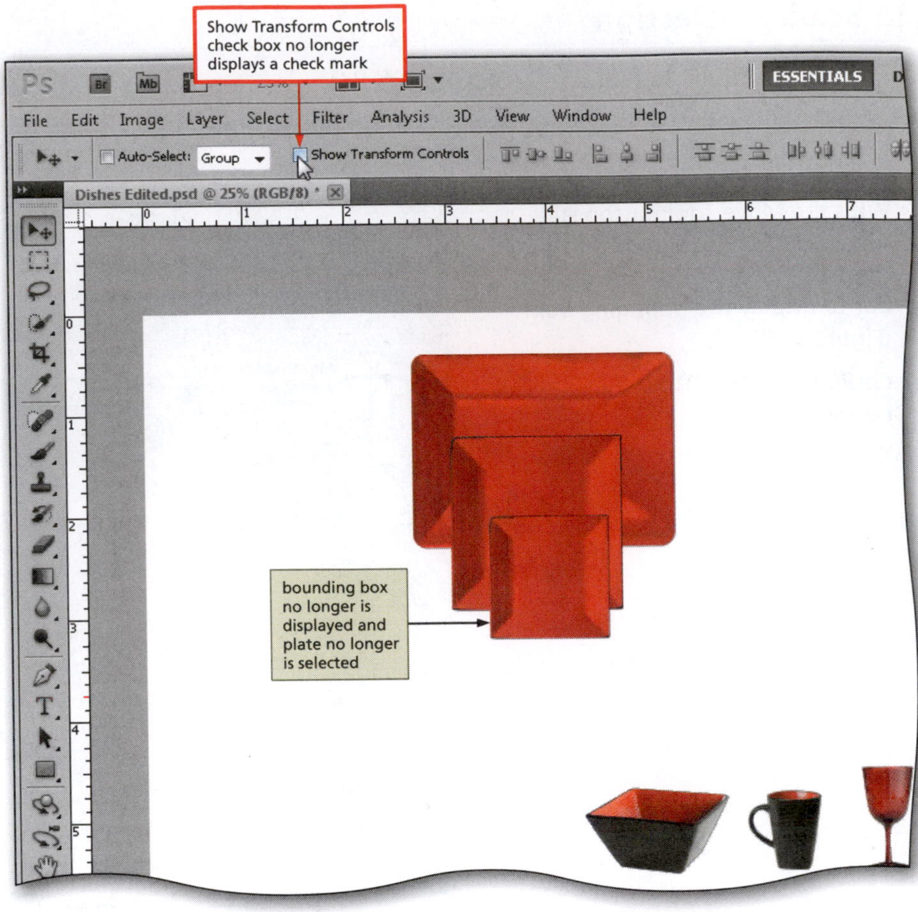

Show Transform Controls check box no longer displays a check mark

bounding box no longer is displayed and plate no longer is selected

Figure 2–29

Other Ways
1. On Transform options bar, enter new width and height, press ENTER
2. Press CTRL+T, right-click selection, click Scale, drag selection handle
3. On Edit menu point to Transform, click Scale, drag selection handle

Guides and Grids
You can change the color or style of guides and grids. On the Edit menu, point to Preferences, and then click Guides, Grid, & Slices.

Grids and Guides

Photoshop can show a grid of lines superimposed on an image. The **grid** is useful for laying out elements symmetrically or positioning them precisely. The grid can appear as nonprinting lines or dots. A **guide** is a nonprinting ruler line or dashed line that graphic designers use to align objects or mark key measurements. Both grids and guides help position selections precisely. You can change the color, style, and grid dimensions.

Plan Ahead

Use grids and guides.
Showing grids in your document window gives you multiple horizontal and vertical lines with which you can align selections, copies, and new images. Grids also can help you match and adjust sizes and perspective.

Create guides when you have an exact margin, location, or size in mind. Because selections will snap to guides, you easily can create an upper-left corner to use as a boundary when you move and copy. Grids and guides do not print and are turned on and off without difficulty.

Table 2–4 displays various ways to manipulate guides.

Table 2–4 Manipulating Guides

Action	Steps
Change color and style	Double-click guide.
Clear all guides	On the View menu, click Clear Guides.
Convert between horizontal and vertical guide	Select the Move Tool, ALT+CLICK guide.
Create	Drag from ruler into document window; or, on the View menu, click New Guide, and then enter the orientation and position.
Lock in place	On the View menu, click Lock Guides.
Move	Select the Move Tool, and then drag the guide to a new location.
Remove	Select the Move Tool, and then drag the guide to the ruler.
Snap guide to ruler tick	SHIFT+drag the ruler.
Turn on/off display	On the Application bar, click View Extras, and then click Show Guides; or, on the View menu, point to Show, and then click Guides; or press CTRL+SEMICOLON (;).

The term **snapping** refers to the ability of objects to attach, or automatically align with a grid or guide. For example, if you select an object in your image and begin to move it, as you get close to a guide, the object's selection border will attach itself to the guide. It is not a permanent attachment. If you do not wish to leave the object there, simply keep dragging. To turn on or off snapping, click Snap on the View menu.

In a later chapter, you will learn about smart guides that automatically appear when you draw a shape or move a layer. Smart guides further help align shapes, slices, selections, and layers. Appendix C describes how to set guide and grid preferences using the Edit menu.

BTW

Displaying Extras
On the View menu is an Extras command that you can use to show or hide selection edges, guides, target paths, slices, annotations, layer borders, and smart guides. You also can use CTRL+H to show or hide those items.

To Display a Grid

The following steps display the grid.

1
- On the Application bar, click the View Extras button to display its menu (Figure 2–30).

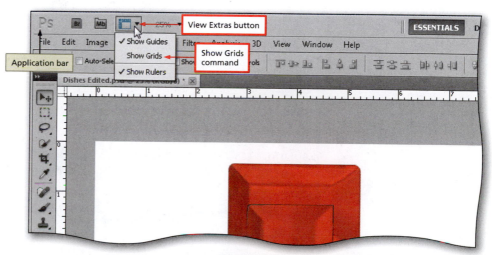

Figure 2–30

2

• Click the Show Grids command to display the grid (Figure 2–31).

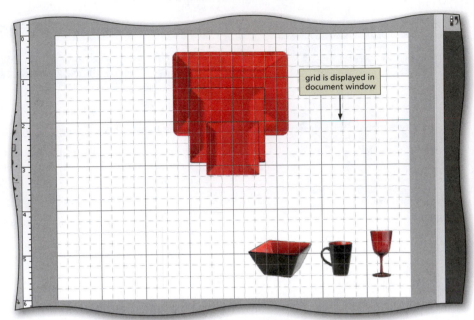

grid is displayed in document window

Other Ways

1. Press CTRL+APOSTROPHE (')

2. On View menu, point to Show, click Grid

Figure 2–31

To Turn Off the Grid Display

The display of a grid is a **toggle**, which means that you turn it off in the same manner that you turned it on; in this case, with the same command. The following step turns off the grid display.

1

• On the Application bar, click the View Extras button to display its menu.

• Click Show Grids to remove the check mark and remove the grid from the display (Figure 2–32).

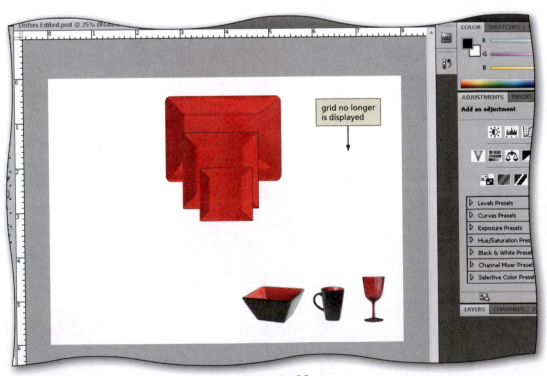

grid no longer is displayed

Figure 2–32

To Create a Guide

The following step creates a guide to help place the bowl and cup on the same horizontal plane.

- Position the mouse pointer in the horizontal ruler at the top of the document window and then drag down into the image to create a guide at approximately 3.5 inches.

- Release the mouse button (Figure 2–33).

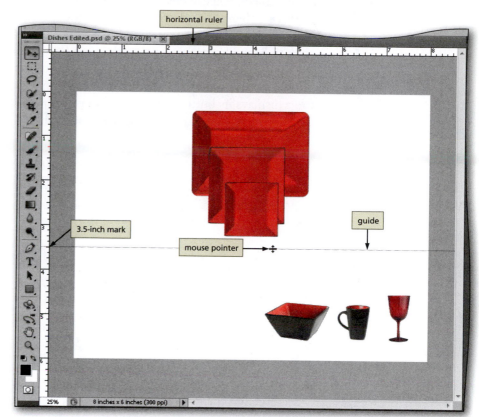

Figure 2–33

Other Ways

1. To show or hide guides, press CTRL+SEMICOLON (;)
2. To create guide, on View menu click New Guide, enter value, click OK

The Lasso Tools

The **lasso tools** draw freehand selection borders around objects. The lasso tools provide more flexibility than the marquee tools with their standardized shapes, and might be more suitable than the Quick Selection Tool when the object has a non-contrasting background. There are three kinds of lasso tools. The first is the default Lasso Tool, which allows you to create a selection by using the mouse to drag around any object in the document window. You select the Lasso Tool button on the Tools panel. You then begin to drag around the desired area. When you release the mouse, Photoshop connects the selection border to the point where you began dragging and completes the loop. The Lasso Tool is useful for a quick, rough selection.

The Polygonal Lasso Tool is similar to the Lasso Tool in that it draws irregular shapes in the image; however, the Polygonal Lasso Tool uses straight line segments. To use the Polygonal Lasso Tool, choose the tool, click in the document window, release the mouse button, and then move the mouse in straight lines, clicking each time you turn a corner. When you get back to the beginning of the polygon, double-click to complete the selection.

The Magnetic Lasso Tool allows you to click close to the edge of the object you wish to select. The Magnetic Lasso Tool tries to find the edge of the object by looking for

BTW

Lasso Tool Selection
If you are using a different tool, and want to activate a lasso tool, you can click the Lasso Tool button on the Tools panel or press the L key to select the Lasso Tool. After selecting the Lasso Tool, pressing SHIFT+L cycles through the three lasso tools.

the closest color change. It then attaches the marquee to the pixel on the edge of the color change. As you move the mouse, the Magnetic Lasso Tool follows that change with a magnetic attraction. The Magnetic Lasso Tool's marquee displays fastening points on the edge of the object. You can create more fastening points by clicking as you move the mouse, to force a change in direction or to adjust the magnetic attraction. When you get all the way around the object, you click at the connection point to complete the loop, or double-click to have Photoshop connect the loop for you. Because the Magnetic Lasso Tool looks for changes in color to define the edges of an object, it might not be as effective to create selections in images with a busy background or images with low contrast. Each of the lasso tools displays its button icon as the mouse pointer.

Table 2–5 describes the three lasso tools.

Table 2–5 The Lasso Tools

Tool	Purpose	Shortcut	Button
Lasso	used to draw freeform loops, creating a selection border	L SHIFT+L toggles through all three lasso tools	
Polygonal Lasso	used to draw straight lines, creating segments of a selection border	L SHIFT+L toggles through all three lasso tools	
Magnetic Lasso	used to draw a selection border that snaps to the edge of contrasting color areas in the image	L SHIFT+L toggles through all three lasso tools	

Each of the lasso tools displays an options bar similar to the marquee options bar, with buttons to add to, subtract from, and intersect with the selection, as well as the ability to feather the border. The Magnetic Lasso Tool options bar (Figure 2–34) also includes an Anti-alias check box to smooth the borders of a selection and a Contrast box to enter the contrast, or sensitivity of color, that Photoshop evaluates in making the path selection. A higher value detects only edges that contrast sharply with their surroundings; a lower value detects lower-contrast edges. The Width box causes the Magnetic Lasso Tool to detect edges only within the specified distance from the mouse pointer. A Frequency box allows you to specify the rate at which the lasso sets fastening points. A higher value anchors the selection border in place more quickly. A tablet pressure button on the right changes the pen width when using a graphic drawing tablet instead of a mouse.

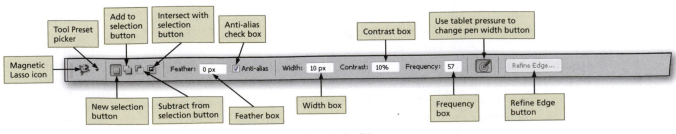

Figure 2–34

To Select Using the Polygonal Lasso Tool

The following steps select the bowl by drawing lines around it with the Polygonal Lasso Tool.

1

• Right-click the Lasso Tool button on the Tools panel to display the context menu (Figure 2–35).

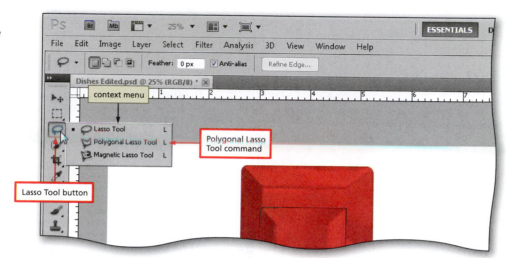

Figure 2–35

2

• Click the Polygonal Lasso Tool to activate the lasso.

• If necessary, on the options bar, click the New selection button to select it (Figure 2–36).

Experiment

• Practice using the Polygonal Lasso Tool to draw a triangle by doing the following: in a blank area of the photo, click to begin; move the mouse pointer to the right and then click to create one side. Move the mouse pointer up and then click to create a second side. Move the mouse pointer to the beginning point and then click to complete the lasso. When you are finished experimenting, press CTRL+D to deselect.

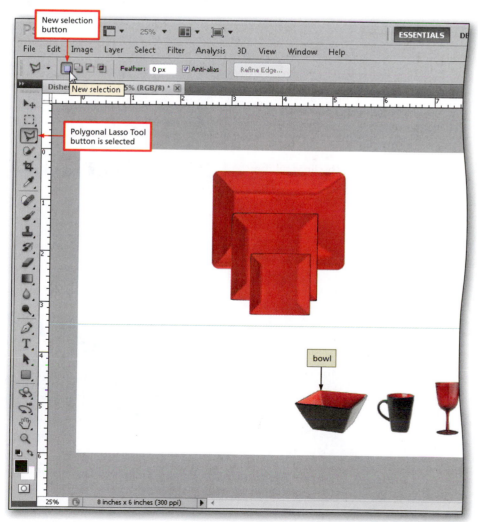

Figure 2–36

3

- Click the upper-left corner of the bowl and then move the mouse pointer to the right to create the first line.

- Click the upper-right corner of the bowl (Figure 2–37).

Q&A

Can I reposition the starting point if I make a mistake?

Yes. Press the ESC key and then start again.

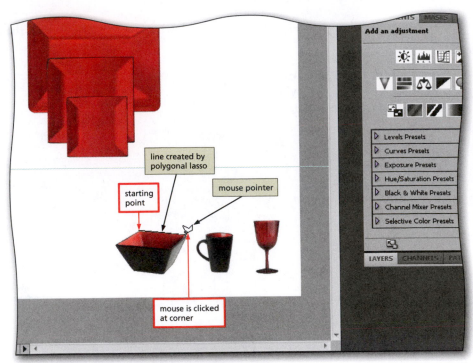

Figure 2–37

4

- Continue creating line segments by moving the mouse pointer and clicking each time you need to change direction.

- When you complete the lines all the way around the bowl, double-click to connect them and complete the selection (Figure 2–38).

Q&A

What was the small circle that appeared when I moved close to the beginning of the polygonal lasso?

When the mouse pointer moves close to where you started the polygonal lasso, Photoshop displays a small circle, which means you can click to complete the lasso. Otherwise, you have to double-click.

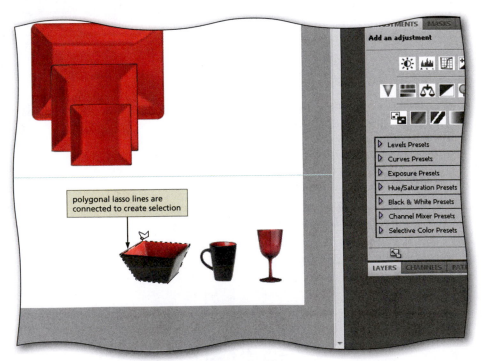

Figure 2–38

Other Ways

1. Press L or SHIFT+L until Polygonal Lasso Tool is active, click image, move mouse

To Grow the Selection

A quick way to increase the size of a selection without using the Refine Edge dialog box is to use the Grow command on the Select menu. The Grow command will increase, or grow, the selection border to include all adjacent pixels falling within the tolerance range as specified in the options bar of most selection tools. Choosing the Grow command more than once will increase the selection in increments. Similar to refining the edge, the Grow command helps to avoid leaving behind a ghost shadow when you move the selection.

The following steps grow the selection around the bowl, to prevent a ghost shadow.

1
• Click Select on the menu bar to display the Select menu (Figure 2–39).

Q&A

Will I notice a big difference after I use the Grow command?

You might not see the subtle change in the selection marquee; however, growing the border helps ensure that you will not leave behind a ghost shadow when you move the selection.

2
• Click Grow to increase the selection border.

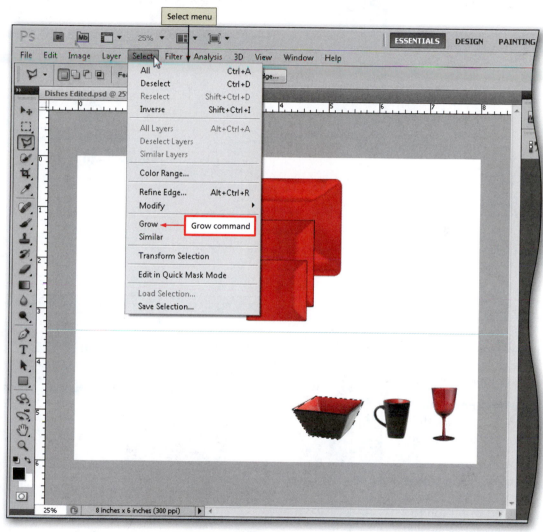

Figure 2–39

To Move and Snap the Bowl

1 Press the V key to activate the Move Tool.

2 Drag the bowl to a location in front of the plate, so the lower-right corner snaps to the guide, as shown in Figure 2–40 on the next page.

3 Press CTRL+D to deselect. If a shadow remains in the original location, you can press ALT+CTRL+Z several times and try again; or, you can ignore the shadow, as it will be cropped out of the image later in the chapter.

BTW

Snapping
To turn on or off the snapping capability, you can press SHIFT+CTRL+SEMICOLON (;).

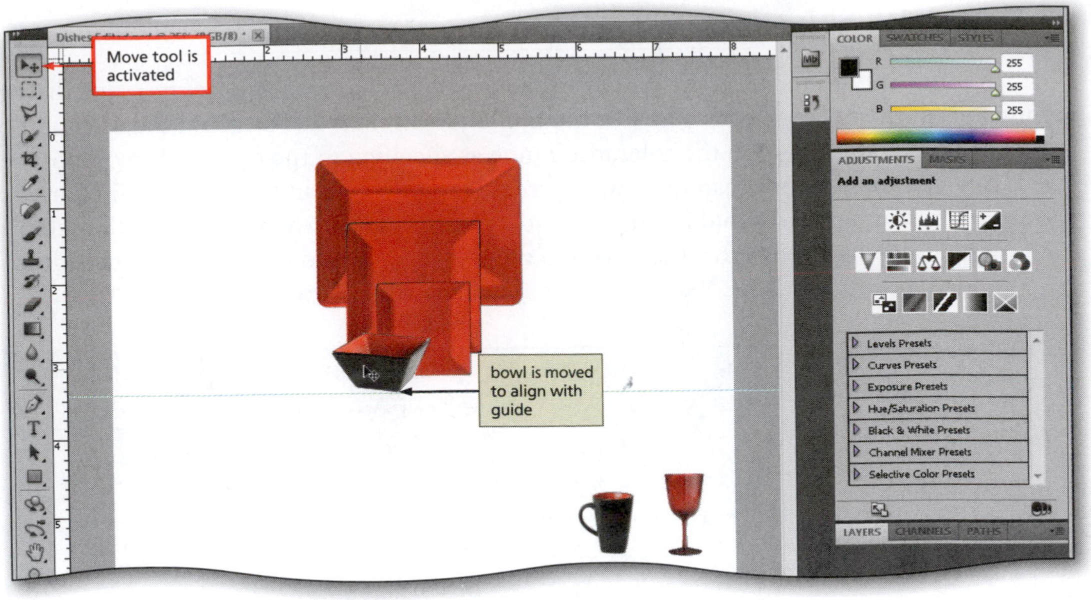

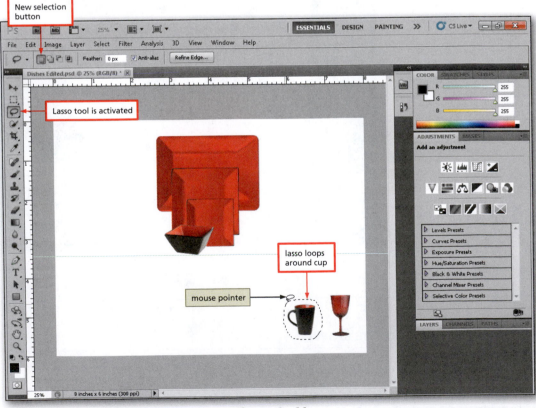

Figure 2–40

To Select Using the Lasso Tool

The following step uses the Lasso Tool to select the cup by dragging around it. As you will notice, the Lasso Tool leaves white space around the cup and inside the handle.

1
- Right-click the current lasso tool button on the Tools panel to display the context menu, and then click Lasso Tool to select it.

- If necessary, on the options bar, click the New selection button.

- Drag around the cup to create a completed lasso and then release the mouse button to connect the beginning and end points (Figure 2–41).

Q&A

How will I know if the lasso is complete?

When the lasso ends are connected, the marquee will pulsate. You also can double-click to connect the ends.

Figure 2–41

Other Ways

1. Press L or SHIFT+L until Lasso Tool is active, drag selection

The Magic Wand Tool

The Magic Wand Tool lets you select a consistently colored area with a single click. For example, if you wanted to select the blue sky in an image, clicking with the Magic Wand Tool would automatically select it, no matter what the shape of the blue area. When you use the Magic Wand Tool and click in the image, Photoshop selects every pixel that contains the same or similar colors as the location you clicked. The default setting is to select contiguous pixels only, but Photoshop allows you to change that setting to select all pixels of the same color. The Magic Wand Tool mouse pointer appears as a small line with a starburst, or magic wand, on the end.

The Magic Wand Tool options bar (Figure 2–42) contains the same selection adjustment buttons as the marquee tools, including the ability to create a new selection, add to or subtract from a selection, and intersect selections. The Magic Wand Tool options bar also has a Tolerance box that allows you to enter a value that determines the similarity or difference in the color of the selected pixels. A low value selects the few colors that are very similar to the pixel you click. A higher value selects a broader range of colors. As with the marquee tools, the Anti-alias check box smoothes the jagged edges of a selection by softening the color transition between edge pixels and background pixels. While anti-aliasing is useful when cutting, copying, and pasting selections to create composite images, it might leave behind a trace shadow after cutting or moving a selection.

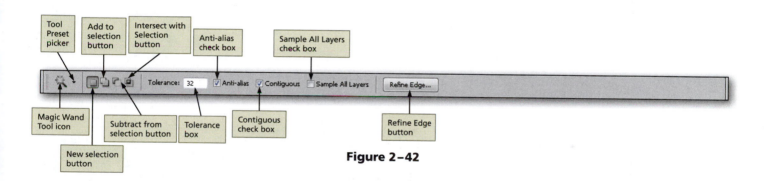

Figure 2–42

When checked, the Contiguous check box selects only adjacent areas using the same colors. Otherwise, Photoshop selects all pixels in the entire image that use the same colors. Finally, the Sample All Layers check box selects colors using data from all visible layers. Otherwise, the Magic Wand Tool selects colors from the active layer only.

Besides using the options bar, the Magic Wand Tool can be used with many shortcut keys. Holding down the SHIFT key while clicking adds to a Magic Wand Tool selection. Holding down the ALT key while clicking subtracts from the selection. Holding down the CTRL key while dragging with the Magic Wand Tool moves the selection.

To Subtract from a Selection Using the Magic Wand Tool

The following steps use the Magic Wand Tool to eliminate the white background in the selection, leaving only the cup inside the marquee.

- With the cup still selected, right-click the Quick Selection Tool button on the Tools panel to display the context menu.

- Click Magic Wand Tool to activate the tool.

- On the options bar, click the 'Subtract from selection' button and then click the Anti-alias check box so it does not display a check mark.

- If necessary, enter 32 in the Tolerance box, and click to display a check mark in the Contiguous check box (Figure 2–43).

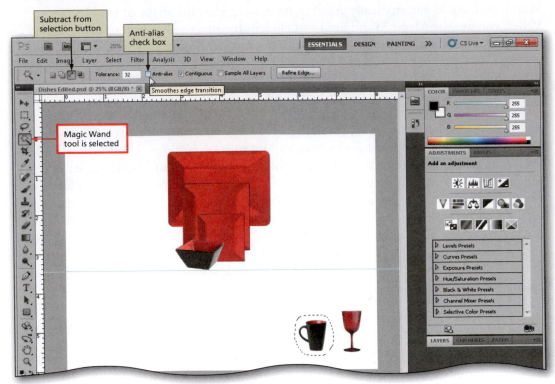

Figure 2–43

- Using the tip of the Magic Wand Tool mouse pointer, click the white space outside the cup, but inside the selection marquee, to remove the white color from the selection (Figure 2–44).

Q&A

What is the minus sign beside the mouse pointer?

The minus sign appears when you choose to subtract from a selection. A plus sign indicates an addition to the selection, and an X indicates an intersection.

Photoshop displays these signs so you do not have to glance up at the options bar to see which button you are using while you drag the selection.

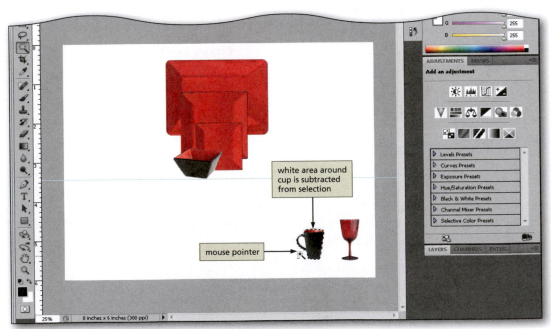

Figure 2–44

3

- Click the white space inside the cup's handle to remove it from the selection (Figure 2–45).

Q&A

What if I make a mistake and click the wrong color?

You can undo the latest edit by pressing CTRL+Z.

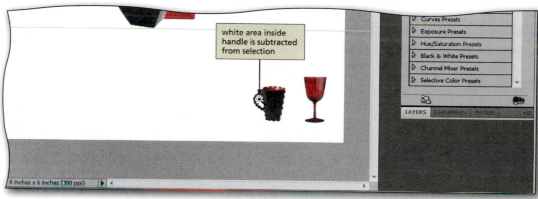

white area inside handle is subtracted from selection

Figure 2–45

Other Ways
1. To select Magic Wand Tool, press w or SHIFT+W until Magic Wand Tool is active   2. Select Magic Wand Tool, ALT+click selection   3. Select Magic Wand Tool, right-click photo, click Subtract from selection

To Flip a Selection

As described in Table 2–2 on page PS 86, when you flip a selection, Photoshop creates a mirror image with a horizontal flip, or an upside-down version of the selection with a vertical flip. Flipping is available on the Edit menu and its Transform submenu or on the context menu when you right-click. Flip transformations do not have to be committed.

The following steps flip the selection horizontally.

1

- With the cup still selected, click Edit on the menu bar and then point to Transform to display the Transform submenu (Figure 2–46).

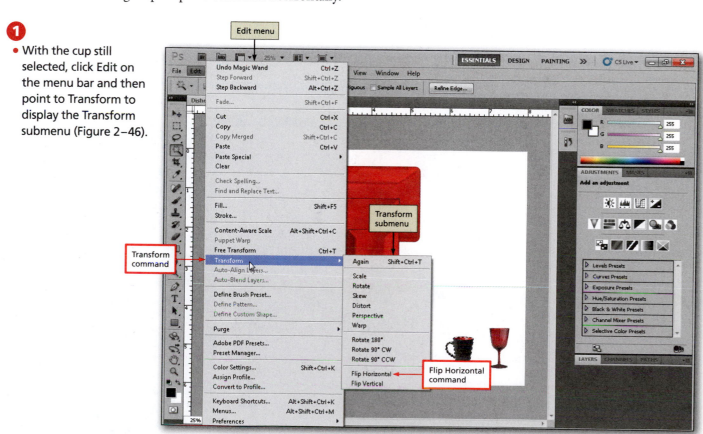

Figure 2–46

2
- Click Flip Horizontal to flip the selection horizontally (Figure 2–47).

Q&A

What if I make a mistake and flip or rotate the wrong way?

You can undo the latest edit by pressing CTRL+Z.

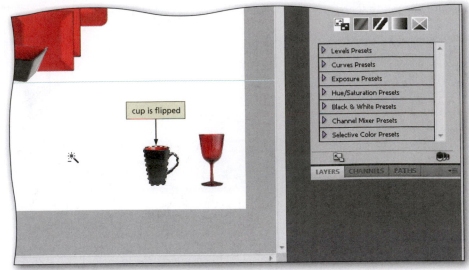

Figure 2–47

Other Ways

1. Press CTRL+T, right-click selection, click desired flip command

To Move the Cup

The following steps move the cup.

1 Press the V key to activate the Move Tool.

2 Drag the cup to a location, right of the bowl. The bottom of the cup should snap to the guide (Figure 2–48).

3 Press CTRL+D to deselect.

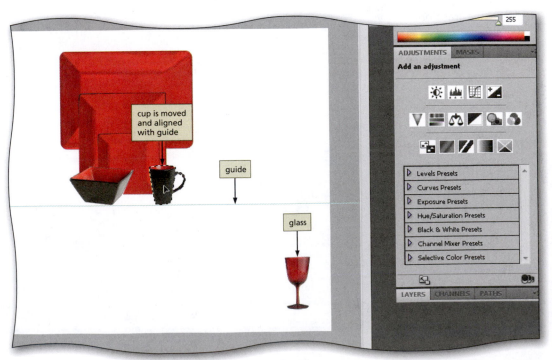

Figure 2–48

To Zoom In

The following steps zoom in on the glass to facilitate editing.

1 Press the z key to activate the Zoom Tool.

2 Click the glass four times to zoom in.

3 If necessary, use the scroll boxes to position the glass in the center of the document window (Figure 2–49).

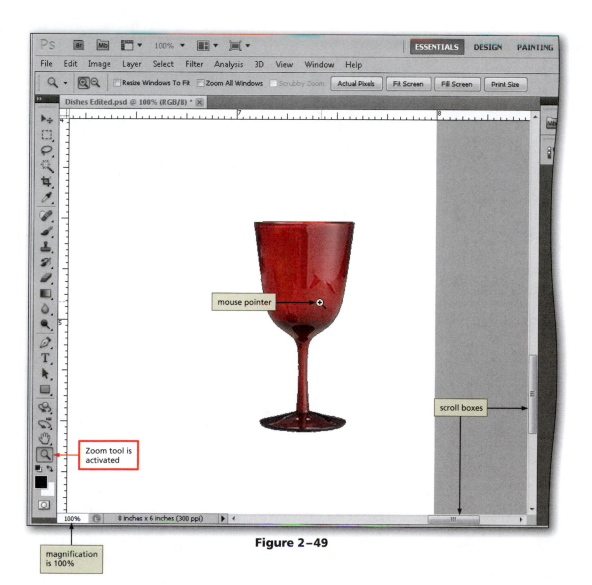

Figure 2–49

To Select Using the Magnetic Lasso Tool

The following steps use the Magnetic Lasso Tool to select the glass. Recall that the magnetic lasso selects by finding the edge of a contrasting color.

1
- Right-click the current lasso tool button and then click Magnetic Lasso Tool to select it from the context menu.

- If necessary, on the options bar, click the New selection button.

- Double-click the Contrast box and type 5 0 to replace the value (Figure 2–50).

Q&A
What is the effect of changing the value in the Contrast box?

Increasing the contrast helps detect the edges where red meets white, thereby increasing the magnetism of the edge of the glass.

Figure 2–50

2
- Click the upper-left edge of the glass to start the selection.

- Move, rather than drag, the mouse pointer slowly along the left edge of the glass to create the selection marquee (Figure 2–51).

Q&A
How do I correct a mistake?

As you use the Magnetic Lasso Tool, if you make a mistake, press the ESC key and begin again.

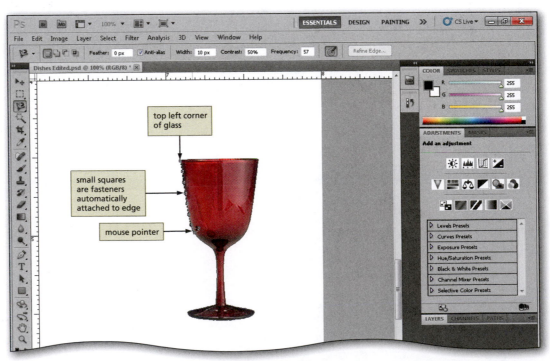

Figure 2–51

3

- Continue moving the mouse pointer around the edge of the glass. Click the mouse when turning a corner to create an extra fastening point.

- When you get all the way around the glass, double-click to finish the lasso (Figure 2–52).

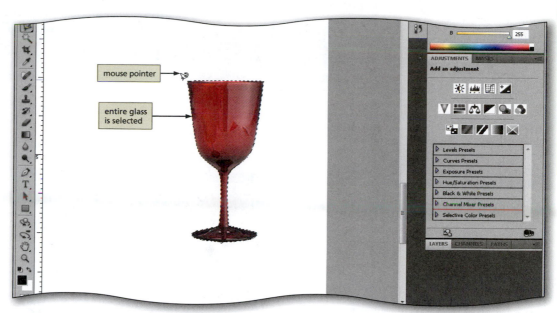

Figure 2–52

To Add to a Selection Using the Quick Selection Tool

The following steps add to the selection to include the rim of the glass.

1

- Press the z key to zoom in. Click the top of the glass several times until the magnification is 300% (Figure 2–53).

Q&A

Why does my selection marquee differ?

The marquee appears as you drag close to the glass. Depending on how close you were to the rim, and how slowly you moved the mouse pointer, your fasteners and resulting marquee might differ.

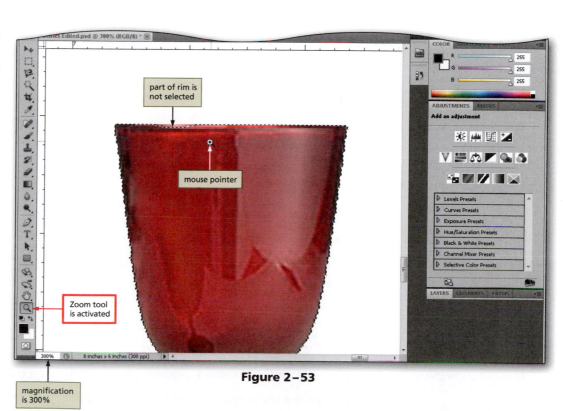

Figure 2–53

2

- Right-click the Magic Wand Tool button to display the context menu, and then click Quick Selection Tool to activate it.

- Click the 'Add to selection' button on the options bar.

- If necessary, use the LEFT BRACKET ([) key or RIGHT BRACKET (]) to either increase or decrease respectively the size of your mouse pointer, so that it more closely matches the figure.

- Drag along the rim in the area that is not inside the selection marquee to add it to the selection (Figure 2–54).

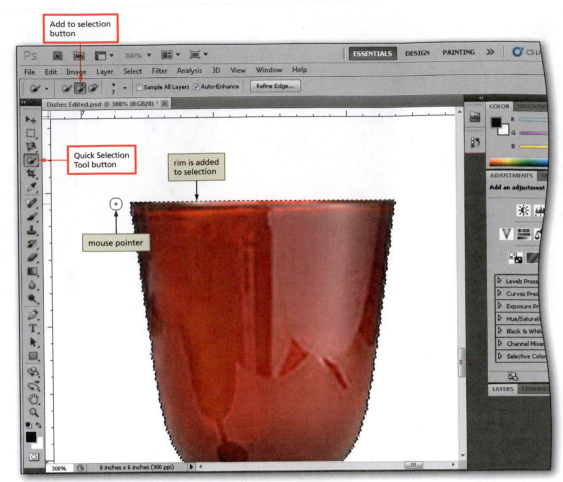

Figure 2–54

Q&A

Should the selection marquee change?

If part of the glass was not previously inside the marquee, dragging with the 'Add to selection' button should move the marquee. The change does not take place until you release the button.

3

- Zoom as necessary to look for other areas that do not fit the selection. Use the 'Add to selection' button or the 'Subtract from selection' button to refine the edge.

To Change the Magnification

The following step changes the magnification to display the entire graphic.

1 Type **25** in the magnification box on the status bar and then press the ENTER key to change the magnification to 25%.

To Create Another Guide

The following step creates a second guide to help align the glass.

1 Drag from the horizontal ruler to a location along the bottom of the tray (Figure 2–55).

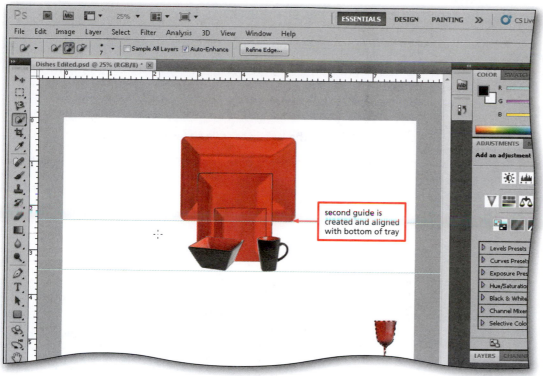

Figure 2–55

To Move a Selection Using Shortcut Keys

The following steps use shortcut keys to zoom and then move the selection.

1 Press the v key to activate the Move Tool.

2 With the glass still selected, drag the glass to a location approximately one inch to the right of the tray, snapping the bottom of the glass to the guide as shown in Figure 2–56.

Figure 2–56

To Duplicate and Scale Using the Options Bar

The following steps create a larger copy of the glass.

1 With the Move Tool still selected, ALT+drag the selection to a location slightly down and left of the original glass.

2 Press CTRL+T to display the bounding box and the Transform options bar.

3 On the options bar, type **110%** in the W box to scale the width of the glass.

4 Type **110%** in the H box to scale the height of the glass. The copy will overlap slightly (Figure 2–57).

5 On the options bar click the 'Commit transform (Return)' button to accept the transformation.

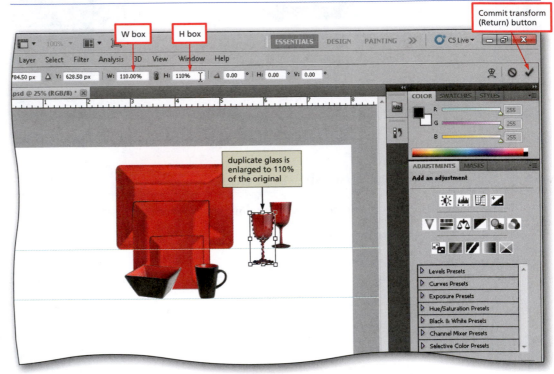

Figure 2–57

To Create and Scale Another Copy

The following steps create another copy of the glass.

1 With the Move Tool still selected, ALT+drag the selection to a location slightly down and left of the original glass. The copy will overlap slightly.

2 Press CTRL+T to display the bounding box and the Transform options bar.

3 On the option bar, type **110%** in the W box to scale the width of the glass.

4 Type **110%** in the H box to scale the height of the glass (Figure 2–58).

5 On the options bar click the 'Commit transform (Return)' button to accept the transformation.

6 Press CTRL+D to deselect.

Figure 2–58

To Save Using a Shortcut Key

You will save the image again, with the same file name, using a shortcut key.

1 Press CTRL+S to save the Dishes Edited file with the same name.

To Crop the Advertisement

Finally, you will crop the advertisement to center the dishes, including a minimal amount of border space.

1 Press the C key to activate the Crop Tool.

2 Drag from the top border to create a crop that leaves an even amount of white space on all four sides of the dishes, as shown in Figure 2–59.

3 Press the ENTER key to complete the crop.

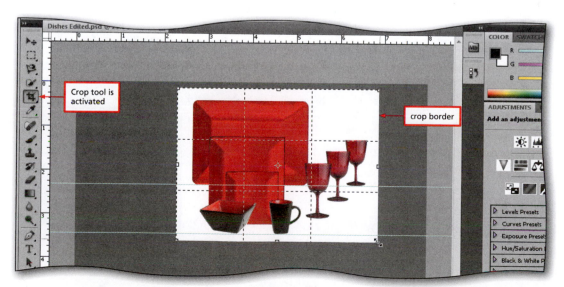

Figure 2–59

Creating PDF Files

The final step is to create a PDF file of the advertising image for document exchange. **PDF** stands for Portable Document Format, a flexible file format based on the cross-platform and cross-application PostScript imaging model. PDF files accurately display and preserve fonts, page layouts, and graphics. There are two ways to create a PDF file in Photoshop. First, you can save the file in the PDF format. Alternatively, you can use the Print command to create the PDF format, allowing you to make some changes to the settings before saving.

<table>
<tr><td>**Plan Ahead**</td><td>**Create files in portable formats.**
You might have to distribute your artwork in a variety of formats for customers, print shops, Webmasters, and as e-mail attachments. The format you choose depends on how the file will be used, but portability is always a consideration. The document might need to be used with various operating systems, monitor resolutions, computing environments, and servers.

It is a good idea to discuss with your customer the types of formats he or she might need. It usually is safe to begin work in the Photoshop PSD format and then use the Save As command or Print command to convert the files. PDF is a portable format that can be read by anyone with a free reader. The PDF format is platform and software independent. Commonly, PDF files are virus-free and safe as e-mail attachments.</td></tr>
</table>

To Save in the PDF Format

The following steps save the graphic in the PDF format for ease in distribution.

1
- Click File on the menu bar and then click Save As to display the Save As dialog box.

- Click the Format button (Save As dialog box) to display the various formats you can use to save Photoshop files (Figure 2–60).

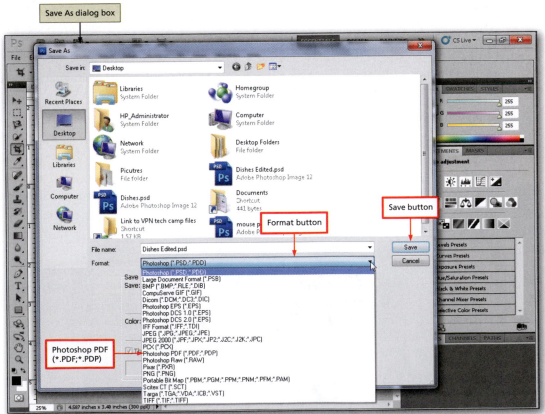

Figure 2–60

2

• Click Photoshop PDF (*.PDF;*.PDP) in the list to select the PDF format, and then click the Save button (Save As dialog box) to continue the saving process (Figure 2–61).

Figure 2–61

3

• Click the OK button (Adobe Photoshop CS5 Extended dialog box) to display the Save Adobe PDF dialog box (Figure 2–62).

Q&A

The Save PDF File As dialog box did not appear. What happened?

If you have multiple windows open on your system, the dialog box might be behind some of the other windows. In that case, minimize the other windows until the dialog box appears.

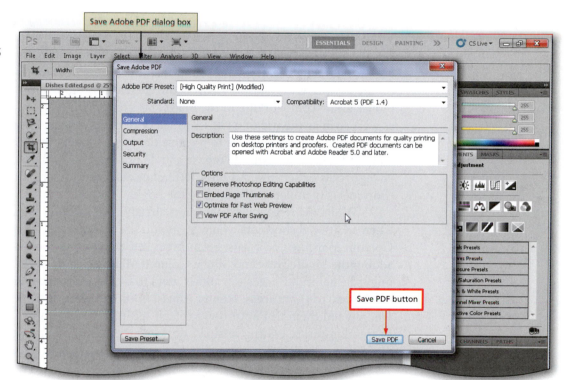

Figure 2–62

4

• Click the Save PDF button (Save Adobe PDF dialog box) to continue the saving process (Figure 2–63).

Q&A

Will the PDF version have the same name?

Yes. After you save, you will see the name Dishes Edited.pdf in the document window tab because Photoshop can edit PDF files directly. The file also can be viewed with Adobe Acrobat or any PDF reader.

Figure 2–63

5

• When Photoshop displays the Save Adobe PDF dialog box, click the Yes button to finish saving.

To Close a Photo without Closing Photoshop

Recall that when you are finished editing a photo or file, you should close it to help save system resources. You can close a photo after you have saved it and continue working in Photoshop. The following steps close the Dishes Edited.pdf file.

1 Click the Close button on the document window tab to close the Dishes Edited.pdf file.

2 If Photoshop displays a dialog box, click the No button to ignore the changes since the last time you saved the photo.

Keyboard Shortcuts

Recall that a **keyboard shortcut**, or **shortcut key**, is a way to activate menu or tool commands using the keyboard rather than the mouse. For example, pressing the **L** key on the keyboard immediately selects the current lasso tool without having to move your mouse away from working in the image. Shortcuts with two keystrokes are common as well, such as the use of CTRL+A to select an entire image. Shortcuts are useful when you do not want to take the time to traverse the menu system, or when you are making precise edits and selections with the mouse and do not want to go back to any of the panels to change tools or settings. A Quick Reference Summary describing Photoshop's keyboard shortcuts is included in the back of the book.

While many keyboard shortcuts already exist in Photoshop, there might be times when additional shortcuts would be useful. For instance, the Single Row and Single Column Marquee tools have no shortcut key. If those are tools that you use frequently, adding the Single Row and Single Column Marquee tools to the M keyboard shortcut might be helpful. Photoshop allows users to create, customize, and save keyboard shortcuts in one of three areas: menus, panels, or tools. When you create keyboard shortcuts, you can add them to Photoshop's default settings, save them in a personalized set for retrieval in future editing sessions, or delete them from your system.

Creating a Keyboard Shortcut

To create a new keyboard shortcut, Photoshop provides a dialog box interface, accessible from the Edit menu. Using that dialog box, you can select one of the three shortcut areas. Then you can choose a shortcut key or combination of keys. For menu commands, your shortcut keystrokes must include the CTRL key or a function key. When creating shortcuts for tools, you must use a single alphabetic character. To avoid conflicting duplications, Photoshop immediately warns you if you have chosen a keyboard shortcut that is used somewhere else in the program.

To Create a New Keyboard Shortcut

In the following steps, you will create a shortcut to display the Essentials workspace. While that command is accessible on the Window menu and by using the 'Show more workspaces and options' button on the Applications bar, a shortcut would save time when you need to reset the workspace.

1

- Click Edit on the menu bar to display the Edit menu (Figure 2–64).

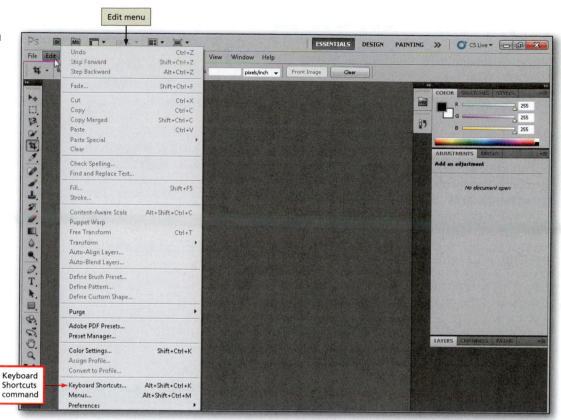

Figure 2–64

2

- Click Keyboard Shortcuts to display the Keyboard Shortcuts and Menus dialog box.

- If necessary, click the Keyboard Shortcuts tab to display its settings.

- If the Set box does not display Photoshop Defaults, click the Set box arrow (Keyboard Shortcuts and Menus dialog box) and then click Photoshop Defaults in the list.

- If the Shortcuts For box does not display Application Menus, click the Shortcuts For box arrow and then click Application Menus in the list (Figure 2–65).

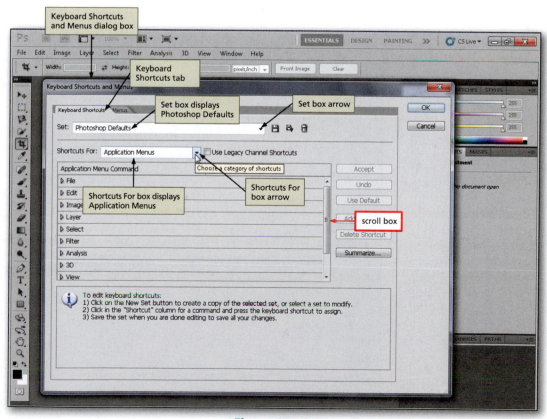

Figure 2–65

3

- In the Application Menu Command list, scroll down and then double-click Window to display the list of Window menu commands.

- Scroll down to display Workspace under the Window menu commands, and then click Essentials (Default) to display a shortcut key box (Figure 2–66).

Q&A

How are the buttons at the top of the dialog box used?

The 'Save all changes to the current set of shortcuts' button allows you to name the set for future retrieval. The 'Create a new set based on the current set of shortcuts' button creates a copy of the current keyboard shortcut settings. The 'Delete the current set of shortcuts' button deletes the set.

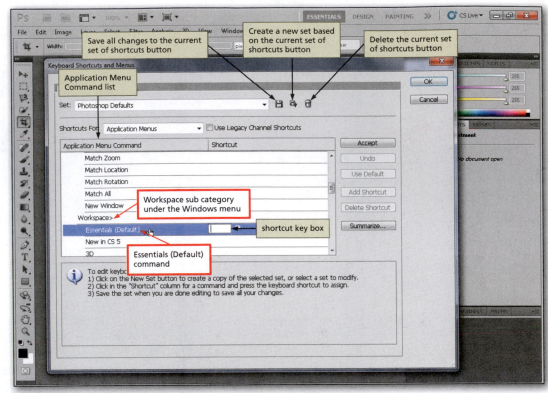

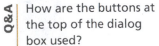

Figure 2–66

4

- Press the F12 key to enter a new short-cut keystroke for the Essentials (Default) command (Figure 2–67).

Q&A

How can I find out which shortcuts keys still are available?

When you click the Summarize button, Photoshop creates a Web page with all of the keyboard shortcuts in the set. You can save that file on your system.

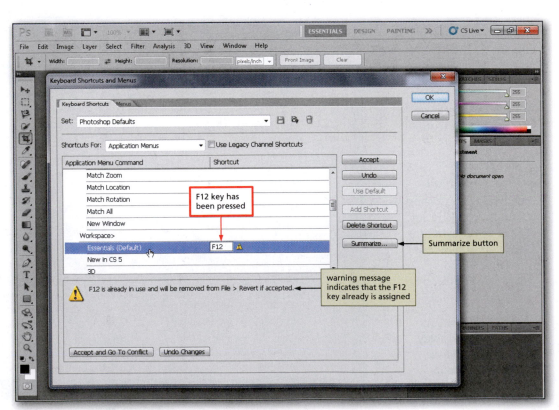

Figure 2–67

5

- Because Photoshop warns you that the F12 key already is being used as a shortcut for a different command, press CTRL+COMMA (,) to enter a new short-cut (Figure 2–68).

6

- Click the Accept button (Keyboard Shortcuts and Menus dialog box) to set the shortcut key.

- Click the OK button to close the dialog box.

Other Ways

1. Press ALT+SHIFT+CTRL+K, edit settings, click OK

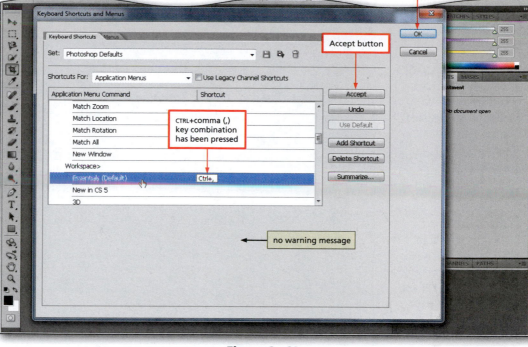

Figure 2–68

To Test a New Keyboard Shortcut

The next steps test the new keyboard shortcut.

1

- Click Design on the Application bar to change to the Design workspace.

- Click Window on the menu bar and point to Workspace to verify the shortcut key assignment (Figure 2–69).

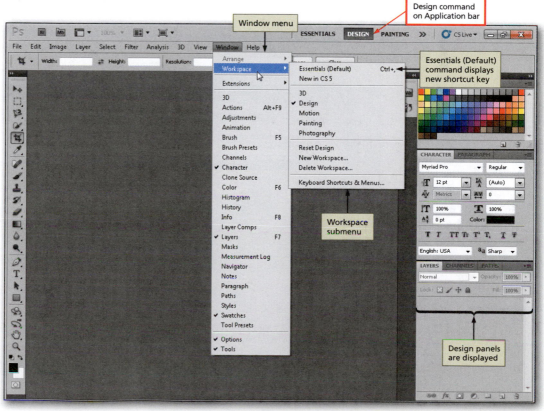

Figure 2–69

2

• Click the workspace away from the Window menu to hide the menu.

• Press CTRL+COMMA (,) to test the shortcut and display the Essentials workspace (Figure 2–70).

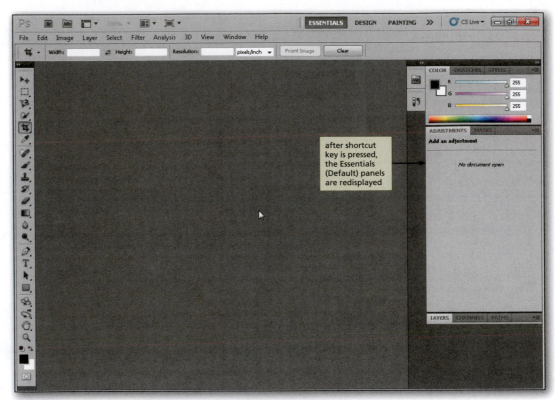

Q&A

Will the new shortcut become permanent?

The new shortcut will be saved on your system in the Photoshop Defaults (modified) set. That set will be in effect the next time you start Photoshop. If you wish to remove it, you can edit that specific shortcut, or delete the set by clicking the Delete the current set of shortcuts button.

after shortcut key is pressed, the Essentials (Default) panels are redisplayed

Figure 2–70

To Return to the Default Settings for Keyboard Shortcuts

It is a good idea, especially in a lab situation, to reset the keyboard shortcuts to their default settings. The following steps restore the default shortcut keys.

1

• Click Edit on the menu bar and then click Keyboard Shortcuts to display the Keyboard Shortcuts and Menus dialog box.

• On the Keyboards Shortcuts tab, click the Set box arrow to display the list (Figure 2–71).

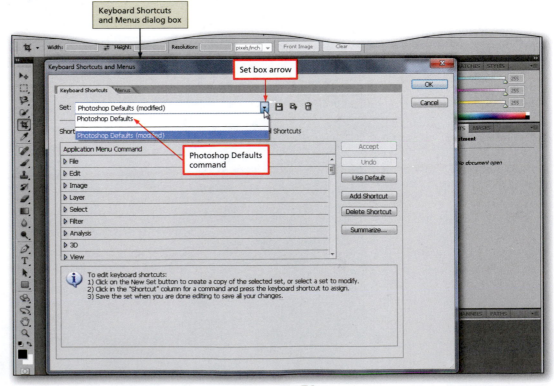

Keyboard Shortcuts and Menus dialog box

Set box arrow

Photoshop Defaults command

Figure 2–71

- Click Photoshop Defaults to choose the default settings for shortcuts. (Figure 2–72).

- When Photoshop displays a message asking if you want to save your changes, click the No button to cancel your changes.

- Click the OK button (Keyboard Shortcuts and Menus dialog box) to close the dialog box.

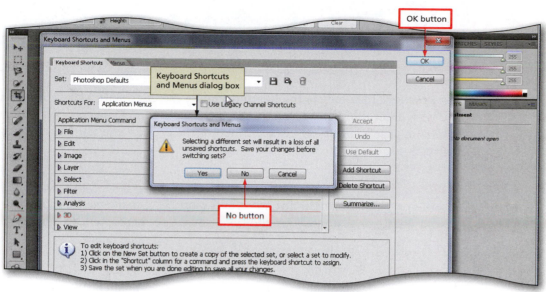

Figure 2–72

To Quit Photoshop Using a Shortcut Key

The following step quits Photoshop and returns control to Windows.

1 Press CTRL+Q to quit Photoshop.

Chapter Summary

In this chapter, you learned how to use selection tools, including the marquee tools, the lasso tools, the Quick Selection Tool, and the Magic Wand Tool. You worked with the Subtract from selection command, the Refine Edge dialog box, and the Grow command to edit the selection border. Upon completing the selection, you then learned many of the transformation commands, including rotating, scaling, and flipping. You used the Move Tool to move and copy selections. Each of the tools and commands had its own options bar with settings to control how the tool or command worked. You learned about the History panel and its states. Finally, you learned how to create and test a new keyboard shortcut.

The items listed below include all the new Photoshop skills you have learned in this chapter:

1. Use the Rectangular Marquee Tool (PS 83)
2. Use the Move Tool (PS 84)
3. Display Transformation Controls (PS 88)
4. Rotate a Selection (PS 88)
5. Use the Quick Selection Tool (PS 90)
6. Display the History Panel (PS 93)
7. Undo Changes Using the History Panel (PS 94)
8. Collapse the History Panel (PS 95)
9. Refine Edges (PS 96)
10. Duplicate the Selection (PS 98)
11. Scale a Selection (PS 99)
12. Display a Grid (PS 101)
13. Turn Off the Grid Display (PS 102)
14. Create a Guide (PS 103)
15. Select Using the Polygonal Lasso Tool (PS 105)
16. Grow the Selection (PS 107)
17. Select Using the Lasso Tool (PS 108)
18. Subtract from a Selection Using the Magic Wand Tool (PS 110)
19. Flip a Selection (PS 111)
20. Select Using the Magnetic Lasso Tool (PS 114)
21. Add to a Selection Using the Quick Selection Tool (PS 115)
22. Save in the PDF Format (PS 120)
23. Create a New Keyboard Shortcut (PS 122)
24. Test a New Keyboard Shortcut (PS 125)
25. Return to the Default Settings for Keyboard Shortcuts (PS 126)

Learn It Online

Test your knowledge of chapter content and key terms.

Instructions: To complete the Learn It Online exercises, start your browser, click the Address bar, and then enter the Web address **scsite.com/pscs5/learn**. When the Photoshop CS5 Learn It Online page is displayed, click the link for the exercise you want to complete and then read the instructions.

Chapter Reinforcement TF, MC, and SA
A series of true/false, multiple choice, and short answer questions that test your knowledge of the chapter content.

Flash Cards
An interactive learning environment where you identify chapter key terms associated with displayed definitions.

Practice Test
A series of multiple choice questions that test your knowledge of chapter content and key terms.

Who Wants To Be a Computer Genius?
An interactive game that challenges your knowledge of chapter content in the style of a television quiz show.

Wheel of Terms
An interactive game that challenges your knowledge of chapter key terms in the style of the television show *Wheel of Fortune.*

Crossword Puzzle Challenge
A crossword puzzle that challenges your knowledge of key terms presented in the chapter.

Apply Your Knowledge

Reinforce the skills and apply the concepts you learned in this chapter.

Moving and Duplicating Selections
Instructions: Start Photoshop and perform the customization steps found on pages PS 6 through PS 9. Open the Apply 2-1 Bread file in the Chapter 02 folder from the Data Files for Students and save it, in the PSD file format, as Apply 2-1 Bread Edited. You can access the Data Files for Students on the CD that accompanies this book; see the inside back cover of this book for instructions on downloading the Data Files for Students, or contact your instructor for information about accessing the required files.

You will create a grocery advertisement featuring bakery items. First, you will select individual items from within the file, and then you will transform and move them so that the finished design looks like Figure 2–73. You will place the rest of the images from back to front.

Perform the following tasks:
1. Because the checkered tablecloth is in the very back of the arrangement, you will start with it. Use the Rectangular Marquee Tool to select the checkered tablecloth.

2. Use the Move Tool to move the tablecloth to the top-center of the page. Do not deselect the tablecloth.

3. With the Move Tool still selected, press CTRL+T to display the bounding box. To distort the tablecloth and make it appear in perspective, CTRL+drag each of the lower corner sizing handles down and outward. Do not overlap any of the bread items. The result should be a trapezoid shape, as shown in Figure 2–73. If you make a mistake, press the ESC key and start again. When you are satisfied with the shape, press the ENTER key to confirm the transformation.

Figure 2–73

4. The croissant is the back-most item in the arrangement. Use the Polygonal Lasso Tool to select the croissant. (*Hint:* The croissant is the lower-right item in the Apply 2-1 Bread image.) Right-click the Quick Selection Tool button on the Tools panel, and then click Magic Wand Tool. On the options bar, click the 'Subtract from selection' button, then click the white area around the croissant to remove it.

5. Use the Move Tool to move the croissant to the upper-right portion of the tablecloth. ALT+drag a second croissant to a location below and to the left of the first, as shown in Figure 2–73. (*Hint:* Do not drag the center reference point.) Press CTRL+D to deselect it.

6. Repeat Steps 4 and 5 to select and move the French bread.

7. ALT+drag the French bread to the right to create a duplicate.

8. Select and move the remaining bread items until you are satisfied with the arrangement. For each bread item, use a selection tool that will approximate the shape of the bread. On the options bar, use the 'Add to selection' and 'Subtract from selection' buttons as necessary. Use the Magic Wand Tool to remove white space around the selection before moving it.

9. Right-click the Rectangular Marquee Tool button on the Tools panel, then click Elliptical Marquee Tool. Use the Elliptical Marquee Tool to select the Sale button. (*Hint:* Press and hold the SHIFT key as you select to maintain a perfect circle.)

10. Move the Sale button to the lower-right portion of the advertisement.

11. Use the Crop Tool to select the portion of the image to use for the final advertisement. (*Hint:* The remaining white space is unnecessary.)

12. Save the Apply 2-1 Bread Edited file, and then close Photoshop.

13. Submit the assignment in the format specified by your instructor.

Extend Your Knowledge

Extend the skills you learned in this chapter and experiment with new skills. You may need to use Help to complete the assignment.

Separating Objects from the Background

Instructions: Start Photoshop and perform the customization steps found on pages PS 6 through PS 9. Open the Extend 2-1 Flowers file in the Chapter 02 folder from the Data Files for Students and save it, in the PSD format, as Extend 2-1 Flowers Edited. You can access the Data Files for Students on the CD that accompanies this book; see the inside back cover of this book for instructions on downloading the Data Files for Students, or contact your instructor for information about accessing the required files.

The original flower image displays the flowers in their natural settings, with various colors in the background. After moving the frame and making a copy, you will select the flowers while preventing background colors from straying into the selection. Finally, you will position each flower in front of a frame as shown in Figure 2–74.

Figure 2–74

Perform the following tasks:

1. Use the Elliptical Marquee Tool to select the oval frame. (*Hint:* For more careful placement, while dragging to create the selection, you can press the SPACEBAR key to adjust the location of the drag and then release it to continue drawing the marquee.) Be careful to select only the frame, and eliminate any white around the edge of the selection using the Magic Wand Tool and the 'Subtract from selection' button.

2. Drag the selection to a location below the left side of the word, Flowers. Do not be concerned if you leave a slight shadow behind. Press CTRL+T to display the Transform options bar. Increase the selection to **110** percent in both width and height. Press the ENTER key to commit the transformation.

3. With the frame still selected, SHIFT+ALT+drag to create a duplicate and place it to the right of the original. (*Hint:* Recall that using the SHIFT key keeps the duplicate aligned with the original.)

4. Use appropriate selection tools to select the upper flower and its stem. (*Hint:* Use the Magic Wand Tool with a tolerance setting of **50** to select the contiguous pink and then add to the selection using other tools.) Click the 'Add to selection' button or the 'Intersect with selection' button to edit areas, if necessary. Do not include the background.

5. To ensure that the selection does not have any stray pixels around its border, use the Refine Edge dialog box to refine the edge by increasing the radius to .7 px.

6. As you create the selection, if necessary, press CTRL+ALT+Z to step back through the editing history and return the image to an earlier state.

7. Move the selected flower onto the left frame. Resize the flower if necessary.

8. Repeat steps 4 through 7 for the lower flower and the right frame. If you make an error, display the History panel and then click a previous state.

9. Crop the image to include only the word, Flowers, and the two framed flowers. Save the changes.

10. Use the Magic Wand Tool to select the blue color in the word, Flowers. (*Hint:* To select all of the letters, you will have to remove the check mark in the Contiguous box.) If parts of the image other than the word, Flowers, appear within the marquee, use the 'Subtract from selection' button to remove them.

11. Use Photoshop Help to investigate how to soften the edges of selections. Use the Refine Edge dialog box to soften the edges. Expand the selection and feather the edges.

12. Use Photoshop Help to investigate how to stroke a selection or layer with color. With the letters selected, use the Stroke command on the Edit menu to display the Stroke dialog box. Stroke the selection with a white color, 5 pixels wide, on the outside of the selection. If necessary, drag the Opacity slider to 100%.

13. Close the photo and close Photoshop. Send the revised photo to your instructor as an e-mail attachment.

Make It Right

Analyze a project and correct all errors and/or improve the design.

Correcting an Error in a Photo

Instructions: Start Photoshop and perform the customization steps found on pages PS 6 through PS 9. Open the Make It Right 2-1 Candles file in the Chapter 02 folder from the Data Files for Students and save it, in the PSD file format, as Make It Right 2-1 Candles Edited. You can access the Data Files for Students on the CD that accompanies this book; see the inside back cover of this book for instructions on downloading the Data Files for Students, or contact your instructor for information about accessing the required files.

Continued >

Make It Right *continued*

A gift catalog would like to advertise its selection of candles, but the photo has one leaning candle that you must fix. Zoom in on the leaning candle. Select only the candle by dragging around it with the magnetic lasso (Figure 2–75). Use other selection tools as necessary, along with the 'Add to Selection' and 'Subtract from selection' buttons to include only the candle. Refine the edge. Drag a vertical guide to the middle of the candle to use as a straight reference. Display the transformation controls and then use the mouse to rotate the candle clockwise until it is straight, then center the candle on the candle holder using the Move Tool.

Save the project again. Submit the revised document in the format specified by your instructor.

Figure 2–75

In the Lab

Design and/or create a publication using the guidelines, concepts, and skills presented in this chapter. Labs are listed in order of increasing difficulty.

Lab 1: Using the Keyboard with the Magic Wand Tool

Problem: As e-cards gain popularity, the need for good graphics also has increased. A small e-commerce site has hired you as its photo specialist to assist with images and photos used in the greeting cards provided online. Your first assignment is to provide a clean image for a card whose greeting will read, "I'm off my rocker! I forgot your birthday!" A photographer has submitted a photo of a rocker, but the layout artist needs the background removed and the rocker scaled to approximately half of its original size. The layout artist has requested a PDF of your final product. You decide to practice using the function keys to perform most of the editing tasks. The edited photo is displayed in Figure 2–76.

Instructions: Perform the following tasks:

1. Start Photoshop. Set the default workspace and reset all tools.

2. Press CTRL+O to open the Lab 2-1 Rocker file from the Chapter 02 folder of the Data Files for Students, or from a location specified by your instructor.

3. Press SHIFT+CTRL+S to display the Save As dialog box. Save the file on your storage device with the name, Lab 2-1 Rocker Edited.

4. If the photo does not appear at 16.67% magnification, press CTRL+PLUS SIGN (+) or CTRL+HYPHEN (–) to zoom in or out as necessary.

5. To remove the wallpaper:

   a. Press the w key to choose the Magic Wand Tool. If the Quick Selection Tool is the active tool, press SHIFT+W to select the Magic Wand Tool.

   b. On the options bar, click the Contiguous box so it does not display a check mark. If necessary, set the Tolerance value to 32.

   c. Click the blue wallpaper and then press CTRL+X to remove it.

6. To remove the floor:

Figure 2–76

   a. On the options bar, click the Contiguous box so it displays a check mark.

   b. Click the floor. SHIFT+click other parts of the floor to add to the selection. (*Hint*: Be sure to click the entire floor, including the spaces between the chair legs.)

   c. Use the Navigator panel to zoom as necessary, or if your computer's mouse has a wheel, ALT+wheel back and forth to zoom. Press CTRL+X to remove the floor selection.

7. To remove the baseboard:

   a. Repeat Step 6 for the baseboard.

   b. If you make an error, or some areas are deleted by mistake, click Window on the menu bar, and then click History to display the History panel. Press CTRL+ALT+Z to step backward through the states in the History panel, or click the first state in the History panel and begin again with Step 5.

8. If necessary, using the Magic Wand Tool, SHIFT+click any remaining part of the photo that is not the rocker and remove it.

9. To select only the rocker:

   a. On the Magic Wand Tool options bar, click the New selection button, if necessary, and then click to remove the check mark in the Contiguous box. Click the white area of the photo.

   b. Press SHIFT+CTRL+I to select the inverse. The rocker now should appear inside the selection marquee.

10. To scale the rocker:

    a. Press CTRL+T to free transform the rocker selection. On the options bar, drag the W scrubby slider to 50%. Drag the H scrubby slider to 50%.

    b. Press the ENTER key to commit the transformations.

    c. Press CTRL+D to deselect, if necessary.

11. Press CTRL+S to save the file with the same name. If Photoshop displays a Photoshop Format Options dialog box, click the OK button.

12. To create the PDF file:

    a. Click File on the menu bar and then click Save As to display the Save As dialog box.

    b. Click the Format button to display the various formats.

Continued >

In the Lab *continued*

    c. Click Photoshop PDF (*.PDF;*.PDP) in the list to select the PDF format, and then click the Save button to continue the saving process.

    d. Click the OK button to display the Save Adobe PDF dialog box, and then click the Save PDF button to continue the saving process.

    e. When Photoshop displays the Save Adobe PDF dialog box, click the Yes button to finish saving.

13. Quit Photoshop by pressing CTRL+Q.

14. Send the PDF file as an e-mail attachment to your instructor, or follow your instructor's directions for submitting the lab assignment.

In the Lab

Lab 2: Creating a Graphic from Back to Front

Problem: A local author has asked for your help in creating a book cover graphic about clock collecting. He has several photos of clocks that he wants placed in specific locations and sizes. The final graphic is shown in Figure 2–77.

Instructions: Perform the following tasks:

1. Start Photoshop. Set the default workspace and reset all tools.

2. Open the file, Lab 2-2 Clocks, from the Chapter 02 folder of the Data Files for Students, or from a location specified by your instructor.

3. Use the Save As command to save the file on your storage device with the name Lab 2-2 Clocks Edited.

4. To select and transform the round clock face:

    a. Use the Elliptical Marquee Tool to select the round clock face. If necessary, use the Magic Wand Tool and the 'Subtract from selection' button to remove any white from around the edge of the clock.

    b. Use the Move Tool to move it to a location in the center of the white area.

    c. Display the bounding box and enlarge the selection to fill the area. Do not let it overlap any of the other clocks. Drag a side handle to make the clock more round.

5. To select and transform the mantle clock:

    a. Use the Quick Selection Tool to select the mantle clock. Zoom as necessary. Use the Magic Wand Tool and the 'Subtract from selection' button to remove the white areas from around the selection.

    b. Use the Move Tool to move it to a location just below the round clock face and slightly to the left.

    c. Display the bounding box and enlarge the selection to match Figure 2–77.

Figure 2–77

6. To select and transform the grandfather clock:

   a. Use the Rectangular Marquee Tool to select the grandfather clock. Use the Magic Wand Tool and the 'Subtract from selection' button to remove the white areas from around the selection.

   b. Use the Move Tool to move it to a location in front of, and on the right side of the round clock face.

   c. Display the bounding box and enlarge the selection to match Figure 2–77.

7. To select and transform the wall clock:

   a. Use the Lasso Tool to select the wall clock. Zoom as necessary. Use the Magic Wand Tool and the 'Subtract from selection' button to remove any white from around the edge of the clock.

   b. Use the Move Tool to move it to a location in the upper-left corner of the scene, as shown in Figure 2–77.

   c. Display the bounding box and enlarge the selection, if necessary.

8. Submit the document, shown in Figure 2–77, in the format specified by your instructor.

In the Lab

Lab 3: Creating a Money Graphic using Transformations

Problem: Your local bank is starting an initiative to encourage children to open a savings account using their loose change. The bank would like a before and after picture showing how money can grow with interest.

Instructions: Perform the following tasks:

Start Photoshop. Set the default workspace and reset all tools. Open the file, Lab 2-3 Coins, from the Chapter 02 folder of the Data Files for Students, or from a location specified by your instructor. Save the file on your storage device with the name Lab 2-3 Coins Edited.

Use the Elliptical Marquee Tool to select the quarter. (*Hint:* While dragging, if your selection marquee does not match the quarter exactly, press and hold the SPACEBAR key to move the selection.) Once the quarter is selected, ALT+drag to create several duplicate copies. Use Figure 2–78 as a guide. As you create the duplicates, press CTRL+T to display the transformation controls, and use the context menu commands to distort, rotate 90° CW, and apply perspective. Use the Magnetic Lasso Tool to select the dime. ALT+drag to create several duplicate copies. As you create the duplicates, press CTRL+T to display the transformation controls. Use the mouse to rotate, move, and drag a corner to create a slight distortion.

Figure 2–78

Continued >

In the Lab *continued*

Use the Quick Selection Tool to select the nickel. ALT+drag to create several duplicate copies. As you create the duplicates, press CTRL+T to display the transformation controls. Flip, rotate and skew some of the copies. Use the Magic Wand Tool to select the penny. Create several copies and apply transformations of your choosing. Save the file again, and submit it in the format specified by your instructor.

Cases and Places

Apply your creative thinking and problem-solving skills to design and implement a solution.

1: Creating a Poster for the Computer Lab

Academic

The computer lab at your school wants a poster reminding students to save their work often. The department chair has asked you to create a graphic of a computer mouse that seems to be eating data. He has taken a picture of a mouse from the lab and started the poster for you. A file named Case 2-1 Poster is located in the Chapter 02 folder of the Data Files for Students. Start Photoshop and use the selection tools to select the mouse. Flip the mouse horizontally. Then, using the 'Subtract from selection' button, remove the white part around the selection. Also, remove the dark gray bottom portion of the mouse from the selection. With the top portion of the mouse selected, warp the selection up and away from the bottom part of the mouse to simulate an open mouth. Move the selection close to the 0 and 1 data pattern. Save a copy of the poster as a PDF and send it as an e-mail attachment to your instructor.

2: Creating a New Shortcut

Personal

You have decided to create a new keyboard shortcut to reset all tools, rather than having to move the mouse to the options bar, right-click, and then choose to reset all tools. Because other family members work on your computer system, you would like to save the new shortcut in a separate set for your personal use. You also would like to see a complete listing of the Photoshop shortcuts for your system. Access the Keyboard Shortcuts and Menus dialog box. Click the Shortcuts For box arrow and then click Panel Menus in the list. Scroll down and double-click Tool Presets, and then click Reset All Tools in the list. Enter the shortcut, CTRL+SLASH (/). Click the 'Create a new set based on the current set of shortcuts' button and save the shortcuts with your name. Click the Summarize button and save the summary as, My Shortcut Summary. When the summary is displayed in the browser, print a copy for your records.

3: Applying Transformations to Indicate Motion

Professional

Hobby Express, a store that specializes in model trains and remote control toys, wants a new logo. They would like to illustrate the concept of a train engine racing to the store. The picture will appear on their letterhead, business cards, and advertising pieces. They would like a digital file so they can use the logo for other graphic purposes. Open the file Case 2-3 Engine and save it on your storage device. Use the Magic Wand Tool and the 'Add to selection' button to select the sky and the grass. Press the DELETE key. When Photoshop displays a Fill dialog box, verify that the Opacity is set to 100%, and then click the OK button. On the Select menu, click Inverse. Display the bounding box. Right-click the selection and then click Warp. When Photoshop displays the warp grid, locate the upper-left warp point that appears as a gray circle on the grid (not the square sizing-handle). Drag the warp point to the left until the smokestack bends slightly. Experiment with the Skew, Perspective, and Distort commands to make the engine look as if it were moving. The front of the engine should appear closer than the rear. The smokestack should curve backward to simulate motion. Save the photo again and print a copy for your instructor.

3 | Working with Layers

Objectives

You will have mastered the material in this chapter when you can:

- Use the Layers panel and change options
- Use the Layer via Cut command
- Set layer properties
- Hide, view, and rearrange layers
- Arrange and consolidate document windows
- Create a new layer from another image or selection
- Resize a layer

- Use the Eraser, Magic Eraser, and Background Eraser Tools
- Create layer masks
- Make level adjustments and opacity changes
- Apply adjustments using the Adjustments panel
- Create a layer style
- Use the Clone Stamp Tool
- Flatten a composite image

3 | Working with Layers

Introduction

Whether it is adding a new person to a photograph, combining artistic effects from different genres, or creating 3D animation, the concept of layers in Photoshop allows you to work on one element of an image without disturbing the others. A layer is an image superimposed or separated from other parts of the photograph. You might think of layers as sheets of clear film stacked one on top of one another. You can see through transparent areas of a layer to the layers below. The nontransparent, or opaque, areas of a layer are solid and obscure lower layers. You can change the composition of an image by changing the order and attributes of layers. In addition, special features, such as adjustment layers, layer masks, fill layers, and layer styles, allow you to create sophisticated effects.

Another tool that graphic designers use when they want to recreate a portion of another photo is the Clone Stamp Tool. As you will learn in this chapter, the Clone Stamp Tool takes a sample of an image and then applies, as you draw, an exact copy of that image to your document.

Graphic designers use layers and clones along with other tools in Photoshop to create **composite** images that combine or merge multiple images and drawings to create a new image, also referred to as a **montage**. Composite images illustrate the power of Photoshop to prepare documents for businesses, advertising, marketing, and media artwork. Composite images, such as navigation bars, can be created in Photoshop and used on the Web along with layered buttons, graphics, and background images.

Project — Room Furnishing

Chapter 3 uses Photoshop to create a composite image from several photographs by using layers. Specifically, it begins with a photo of an empty room and creates a composite image by inserting layers of furniture, a plant, a painting, and other decorative pieces to create a complete room design (Figure 3–1). The enhancements will show how the room will look when furnished. Wood flooring will replace the carpeting; a sofa, lamp, table, and other decorations will be added. Finally, adjustment layers will give the room eye appeal.

ile Edit Image Layer Select Filter Analysis 3D View Window Help

Figure 3–1 (a)

Figure 3–1 (b)

Overview

As you read this chapter, you will learn how to create the composite room shown in Figure 3–1 by performing these general tasks:

- Create a layer using the Layer via Cut command.
- Insert layers from new images.
- Use the eraser tools.
- Add a layer mask.
- Create layer adjustments and layer masks.
- Apply layer styles.
- Clone from one image to another.
- Flatten the image.
- Save the photo with and without layers.

Plan Ahead

General Project Guidelines

When editing a photo, the actions you perform and decisions you make will affect the appearance and characteristics of the finished product. As you edit a photo, such as the one shown in Figure 3–1 on the previous page, you should follow these general guidelines:

1. **Gather your photos and plan your layers.** The graphics you choose should convey the overall message of your composite image. Choose high-quality photos with similar lighting characteristics. Create an ordered list of the layers you plan to include. Select images that are consistent with the visual effect you want to achieve as well as with customer requirements.

2. **Create layer adjustments.** Fine-tune your layers by creating layer adjustments. Look at each layer and evaluate how it fits into the background scene. Experiment with different adjustment tools until the layer looks just right. Decide whether to use destructive or nondestructive edits. Keep in mind the standard tonal dimensions of brightness, saturation, and hue.

3. **Edit layer styles.** Add variety to your layers by including layer styles such as shadow, glow, emboss, bevel, overlay, and stroke. Make sure the layer style does not overwhelm the overall image or detract from previous layer adjustments.

When necessary, more specific details concerning the above guidelines are presented at appropriate points in the chapter. The chapter also will identify the actions performed and decisions made regarding these guidelines during the creation of the edited photo shown in Figure 3–1.

Creating a Composite

Creating a composite with visual layers is a powerful effect. Photographers sometimes try to achieve the effect by using a sharp focus on objects in the foreground against an out-of-focus background. Others stage their photos with three layers of visual action. For example, at a baseball game, a person in the stands (foreground) may be observing a close call at first base (middle ground), while outfielders watch from afar (background). When those kinds of photographic techniques cannot be achieved, graphic artists use **composition techniques**, the layering of images and actions. Not only can you make realistic changes to parts of a photo, but you can add additional images and control their placement, blending, and special effects. In addition, you can make changes to a layer, independent of the layer itself, which is extremely helpful in composite production.

Simple layers may incorporate new objects or additional people. Layer effects create adjustments, add blending modes, or edit the coloring, fill, and opacity of the layer. Masks conceal or reveal part of a layer. All of the layering techniques are **nondestructive**, which means that no pixels are changed in the process; the effect is applied over the image or layer to create the change.

When an image duplication is required and layering a new copy does not achieve the required effect, some graphic artists **clone**, or reproduce, an image by painting a copy into the scene. As with masks, cloning allows you to control exactly how much of the image you want to use — even down to the smallest pixel. You also can use cloning to remove minor imperfections in a photo or to clone over intricate elements that do not fit into the picture.

The steps in this chapter create a composite image with layers; layer effects; and adjustments, masks, and cloning.

To Start Photoshop

If you are using a computer to step through the project in this chapter, and you want your screen to match the figures in this book, you should change your screen's resolution to 1024 × 768. For information about how to change the screen resolution, read Appendix C.

The following steps, which assume Windows 7 is running, start Photoshop based on a typical installation. You may need to ask your instructor how to start Photoshop for your computer.

1 Click the Start button on the Windows 7 taskbar to display the Start menu.

2 Type `Photoshop CS5` as the search text in the 'Search programs and files' text box, and watch the search results appear on the Start menu.

3 Click Adobe Photoshop CS5 in the search results on the Start menu to start Photoshop.

4 After a few moments, when the Photoshop window is displayed, if the window is not maximized, click the Maximize button on the title bar to maximize the window.

To Reset the Workspace

As discussed in Chapter 1, it is helpful to reset the workspace so that the tools and panels appear in their default positions. The following steps select the Essentials workspace.

1 Click the 'Show more workspaces and options' button on the Application bar to display the names of saved workspaces and then, if necessary, click Essentials to select the default workspace panels.

2 Click the 'Show more workspaces and options' button again to display the list and then click Reset Essentials to restore the workspace to its default settings and reposition any panels that may have been moved.

To Reset the Tools and the Options Bar

Recall that the Tools panel and the options bar retain their settings from previous Photoshop sessions. The following steps select the Rectangular Marquee Tool and reset all tool settings in the options bar.

1 If the tools in the Tools panel appear in two columns, click the double arrow at the top of the Tools panel.

2 If necessary, click the Rectangular Marquee Tool button on the Tools panel to select it.

3 Right-click the Rectangular Marquee Tool icon on the options bar to display the context menu and then click Reset All Tools. When Photoshop displays a confirmation dialog box, click the OK button to restore the tools to their default settings.

To Reset the Default Colors

Recall that Photoshop retains the foreground and background colors from session to session. Your colors might not display black over white on the Tools panel. The following step resets the default colors.

1 Press the D key to reset the default foreground and background colors.

To Open a Photo

To open a photo in Photoshop, it must be stored as a digital file on your computer or on an external storage device. The photos used in this book are stored in the Data Files for Students. You can access the Data Files for Students on the CD that accompanies this book. See the inside back cover of this book for instructions on downloading the Data Files for Students, or contact your instructor for information about accessing the required files.

The following steps open the file, Room, from a CD located in drive E.

1 Insert the CD that accompanies this book into your CD drive. After a few seconds, if Windows displays a dialog box, click its Close button.

2 With the Photoshop window open, click File on the menu bar, and then click Open to display the Open dialog box.

3 In the Open dialog box, click the Look in box arrow to display the list of available locations, and then click drive E or the drive associated with your CD.

4 Double-click the Chapter 03 folder to open it, and then double-click the file, Room, to open it.

5 When Photoshop displays the image in the document window, double-click the magnification box on the document window status bar, type 45, and then press the ENTER key to change the magnification (Figure 3–2).

Figure 3–2

To View Rulers

The following steps display the rulers in the document window to facilitate making precise measurements.

1 If the rulers are not shown on the top and left sides of the document window, press CTRL+R to display the rulers in the workspace.

2 If necessary, right-click the horizontal ruler and then click Inches on the context menu to display the rulers in inches.

To Save a Photo

Even though you have yet to edit the photo, it is a good practice to save the file on your personal storage device early in the process. The following steps save the photo with the name Room Edited.

1 With your USB flash drive connected to one of the computer's USB ports, click File on the menu bar to display the File menu and then click Save As to display the Save As dialog box.

2 In the File name text box, type `Room Edited` to rename the file. Do not press the ENTER key after typing the file name.

3 Click the Save in box arrow and then click UDISK 2.0 (F:), or the location associated with your USB flash drive, in the list, if necessary.

4 Click the Save button in the Save As dialog box to save the file.

Creating a Composite Image Using Layers

Photoshop has many tools to help create composite images, photomontages, and collages. A composite, or composite image, is one that combines multiple photographs or images to display in a single combined file. Graphic artists use the newer term, **photomontage**, to refer to both the process and the result of creating a composite from photos.

One of the most powerful tools in Photoshop is layering. A **layer** is a section within a Photoshop document that you can manipulate independently from the rest of the document. Layers can be stacked one on top of the other, resembling sheets of clear film, to form a composite image.

Gather your photos and plan your layers.
One of the keys to successful image compositions is finding the best source material with similar lighting situations and tonal qualities. Choose high-quality photos and images that convey your overall message. Make sure you have permission to use the images if they are not original photographs taken by you or provided to you by a colleague or client. Obtain several versions of the same photo, if possible, including photos from different angles and with different lighting situations. Make two copies of each photo and store one as a backup. Crop unwanted portions of the photos before adding them as new layers.

Plan Ahead

Layer Comps
Graphic artists often create multiple versions, or compositions, of their work. A **layer comp** is a single view of the page layout with specific visible layers and attributes. You can use layer comps to demo versions of your composition to customers or colleagues, or simply to jump back and forth between different views and layers of your document. Similar to the History panel's snapshot, a layer comp takes a picture of the composite, using the Layers panel to show a particular stage of development.

Layers have been used by business and industry for years. Cartoonists create layers of physical transparencies to help with animation. The medical field uses overlays to illustrate anatomical features. Virtual simulations use layers to display processes. With Photoshop, layers are easy to create and export for these kinds of applications.

Recall that you used selections in Chapter 2 to move, copy, transform, and delete portions of a photo. Layers can perform all of the same functions performed by selecting, while providing added features. The most powerful feature of layers is the ability to revisit a portion of the image to make further changes, even after deselecting. Layers can be created, copied, deleted, displayed, hidden, merged, locked, grouped, repositioned, and flattened. Layers can be composed of images, patterns, text, shapes, colors, or filters. You can use layers to apply special effects, correct or colorize pictures, repair damaged photos, or import text elements. In previous chapters, you worked with images in a flat, single layer called the **Background layer**. In this chapter, you will create, name, and manipulate multiple layers on top of the Background layer.

Many layer manipulations are performed using the **Layers panel**, which lists all the layers, groups, and layer effects in an image (Figure 3–3). Each time you insert a layer onto an image, the new layer is added to the top of the panel. The default display of a layer on the Layers panel includes a visibility icon, a thumbnail of the layer, and the layer's name. To the right of the layer's name, a locking icon or other manipulations might appear.

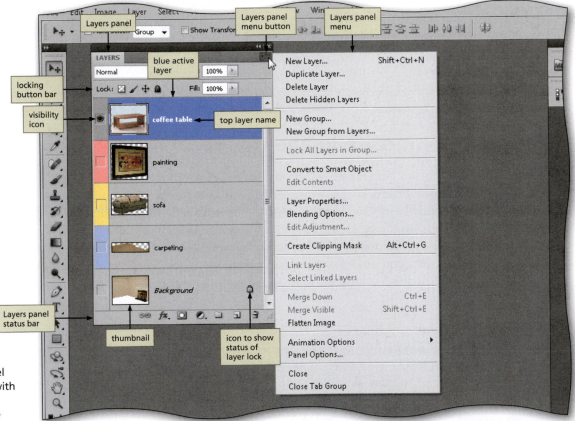

Figure 3–3

Layer Comps Panel
The Layer Comps panel includes a status bar with buttons to move back and forth through the comps, to update comps from the current view, to create them, and to delete them. The Layer Comps menu has some of those same commands, as well as others to duplicate a layer comp and set its properties.

Photoshop allows you to lock three different components of layers. The 'Lock transparent pixels' button confines editing to opaque layer portions. The 'Lock image pixels' button prevents modification of the layer's pixels using paint tools. The Lock position button prevents the layer from being moved. The Lock all button enables all of the three ways of locking the layer. A lock icon appears to the right of the name on the Layers panel on locked layers.

The Layers panel is used in several different manners: to show and hide layers, to create new layers, and to work with groups of layers. You can access additional commands and attributes by clicking the Layers panel menu button or by right-clicking a layer. The Layers panel defines how layers interact. As you use the buttons and boxes on the Layers panel, each will be explained.

While Photoshop allows background editing, as you have done in previous chapters, the Background layer cannot be moved, nor can its transparency be changed. In other words, the Background layer fills the document window, and there is no layer behind the background. Partially locked by default, the Background layer displays a hollow lock (Figure 3–3). If you want to convert the Background layer into a fully editable layer, double-click the layer on the Layers panel, and then click the OK button in the New Layer dialog box.

When working with layers, it is important to make sure you know which layer you are editing by looking at the active layer on the Layers panel or by looking at the layer name, appended to the file name on the document window tab. Many other layer commands appear on the Layer menu, including making adjustments to the layer, creating layer masks, grouping layers, and other editing and placement commands.

BTW

Layer Comps vs. History Snapshots
Layer comps include the visibility, position, and appearance of layers, not the edited steps. In addition, layer comps are saved with the document, whereas History panel snapshots are not. You can export layer comps to separate graphic or PDF files for easy distribution.

To Change Layers Panel Options

The Panel Options command, accessible from the Layers panel menu, allows you to change the view and size of the thumbnail related to each layer. A thumbnail displays a small visual preview of the layer on the Layers panel. The Panel Options dialog box allows you to choose small, medium, large, or no thumbnails. The following steps select a medium-sized thumbnail of each layer.

1

- Click the Layers panel menu button to display the Layers panel menu (Figure 3–4).

Q&A

Do I have to display thumbnails?

No, but displaying thumbnails of each layer allows you to see easily what the layer looks like and helps you to be more efficient when editing a layer. To improve performance and save monitor space, however, some Photoshop users choose not to display thumbnails.

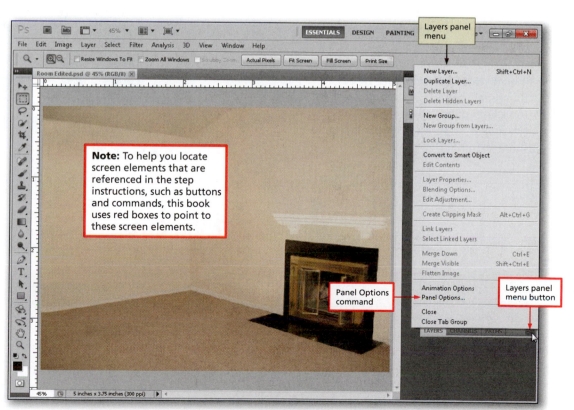

Figure 3–4

2

- Click Panel Options on the menu to display the Layers Panel Options dialog box.

- Click the medium-sized thumbnail to select it.

- Click the Layer Bounds option button, if necessary, to select it and change the look and feel of the Layers panel (Figure 3–5).

Q&A

How does the Layer Bounds option change the interface?

The Layer Bounds option causes the Layers panel to display only the layer in the thumbnail, not the entire image.

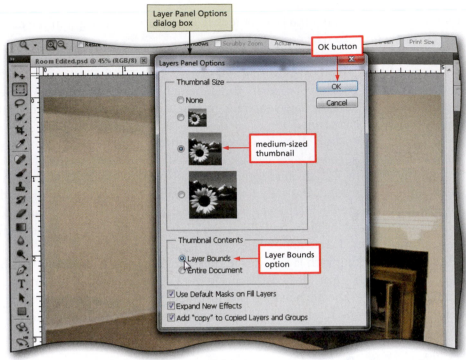

Figure 3–5

3

- Click the Layers panel tab to expand the panel.

- Click the OK button to close the Layers Panel Options dialog box (Figure 3–6).

Q&A

Should I see a difference on the Layers panel?

Unless a previous user had already changed it, the size of the thumbnail should have changed on the Layers panel. Layer bounds will not appear until you create a layer other than the Background layer.

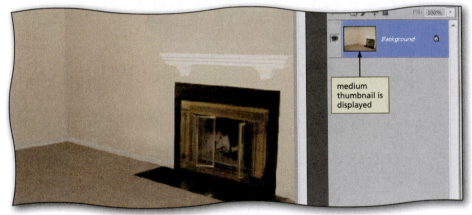

Figure 3–6

Creating a Layer Via Cut

There are several ways to create a new layer. You can:

- isolate a portion of the image and then cut or make a layer copy
- create a new layer by copying from a different image
- duplicate a layer that already exists
- create a new, blank layer on which you can draw or create text

When you add a layer to an image, a new layer appears above, or on top of, the currently selected layer, creating a **stacking order**. By default, Photoshop names and numbers layers sequentially; however, you can rearrange the stacking order to change the appearance of the image. The final appearance of an edited Photoshop document is a view of the layer stack from the top down.

To Create a Layer Via Cut

The following steps create a new layer that includes only the carpeting on the floor. You will use the Quick Selection Tool to select the area and then use the Layer via Cut command to isolate the floor from the rest of the photo, creating a new layer.

1

- On the Tools panel, select the Quick Selection Tool.

- If necessary, click the New selection button on the options bar to start a new selection.

- In the photo, drag slowly from the upper-left corner of the carpeting to the lower-right corner of the photo to select only the carpeting (Figure 3–7).

Q&A
Why did Photoshop change to the 'Add to selection' button on the options bar?

Once you create a New selection, the most common task is to add more to the selection, so Photoshop selects that button automatically. If you want to start over, you can select the New selection button again.

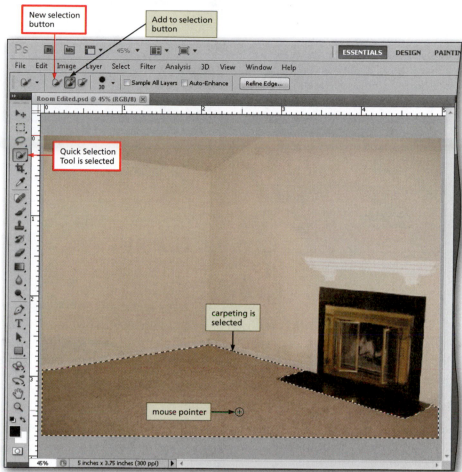

Figure 3–7

2

- Right-click the selection to display the context menu (Figure 3–8).

Q&A
Could I use the New layer command?

No. The New layer command creates a blank layer.

Figure 3–8

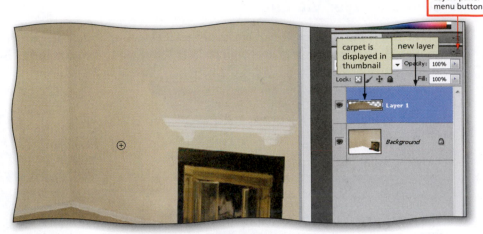

3

- Click Layer via Cut on the context menu to create the new layer (Figure 3–9).

Q&A What is the difference between Layer via Cut and Layer via Copy?

The Layer via Cut command removes the selection from the background. The Layer via Copy command creates a copy on the Layers panel and leaves the original selection intact. Future edits to the Background, such as changing the color or lighting, will not affect a cut layer.

Figure 3–9

Other Ways

1. Create selection, on Layer menu, point to New, click Layer via Cut

2. Create selection, press SHIFT+CTRL+J

To Name and Color a Layer

It is a good practice to give each layer a unique name so you can identify it more easily. The name of the active layer appears on the Layers panel and on the title bar of the document window. Photoshop allows you to give each layer its own color identification as well. The following steps name and color a layer using the Layer Properties dialog box.

1

- Click the Layers panel menu button (shown in Figure 3–9) to display the menu.

- Click Layer Properties to display the Layer Properties dialog box.

- Type **carpeting** in the Name box to name the layer, carpeting.

- Click the Color box arrow to display the list of identification colors (Figure 3–10).

 Experiment

- One at a time, click each of the colors and watch the changes on the Layers panel.

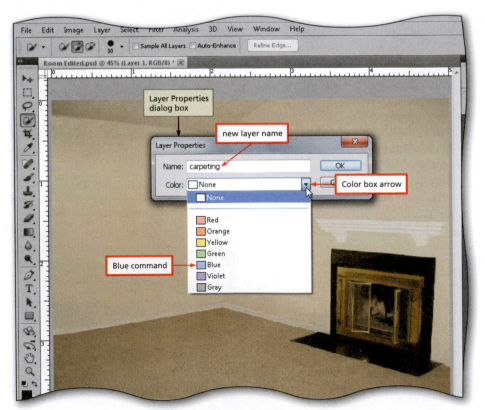

Figure 3–10

● Click Blue in the list to choose a blue identification color (Figure 3–11).

Figure 3–11

● Click the OK button to apply the new settings on the Layers panel (Figure 3–12).

Other Ways

1. Right-click layer, click Layer Properties, type new name, choose new color, click OK

2. To name layer, on Layers panel, double-click layer name, type new name, press ENTER

3. To color layer, on Layers panel, right-click visibility area, click color

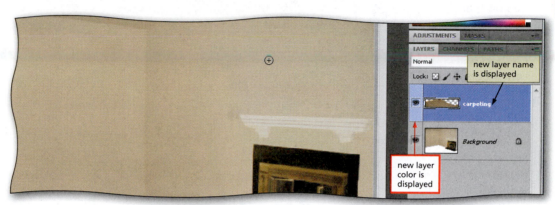

Figure 3–12

To Hide and Show a Layer

Sometimes you want to hide a layer to view other layers to make editing decisions. The following steps hide and show the Background layer.

● Click the 'Indicates layer visibility' button to the left of the Background layer to hide the layer in the document window and to remove the visibility icon (Figure 3–13).

What is the checkerboard effect in the carpeting layer?

The checkerboard effect represents blank portions of the document window that are transparent.

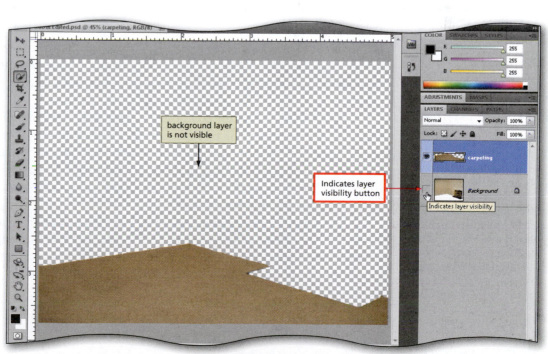

Figure 3–13

2

● Click the 'Indicates layer visibility' button again to show the Background layer in the document window and display the visibility icon (Figure 3–14).

Q&A

What is the white area on the Background layer thumbnail?

When you cut or delete from a locked layer such as the Background layer, the default background color shows through; in this case, it is the default white color. Because other layers will eclipse the white, you do not have to remove it.

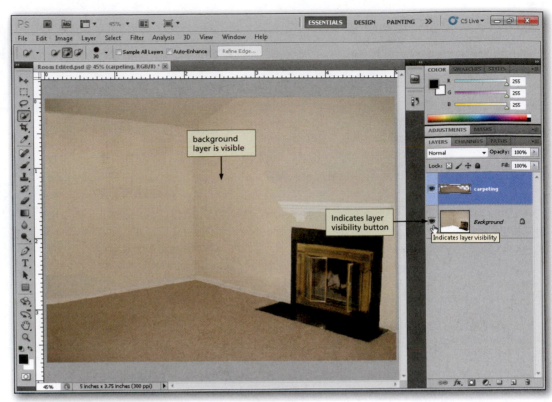

Figure 3–14

Other Ways

1. Right-click visibility icon, click Hide this layer or Show this layer

2. On Layer menu, click Hide Layers or Show Layers

Creating a Layer from Another Image

When you create composite images, you might want to create layers from other images. It is important to choose images that closely match or complement color, lighting, size, and perspective if you want your image to look natural. While you can adjust disparate images to improve how well they match, it is easier to start with as close a match as possible, ideally with similar lighting situations and tonal qualities.

Many sources exist for composite images and they come in many different file types and sizes. For example, you can use your own digital photos, scanned images, images from royalty-free Web sites, or you can draw your own. If you use a photo or image from the Web, make sure you have legal rights to use the image. Legal rights include permission from the photographer or artist to use the image, or purchasing these rights, through a contract, from an online store.

The basic process of creating a new layer from another image involves opening a second image, selecting the area you wish to use, and then moving it to the original photo in a drag-and-drop, or cut-and-paste, fashion. Once the layer exists in the destination photo, you might need to do some editing to remove portions of the layer, to resize it, or to make tonal adjustments.

BTW

Creating Layer Groups
Layer groups help you manage and organize layers in a logical manner. To create a layer group, click the Create New Group button on the Layers panel. A new layer will appear with a folder icon. You then can drag layers into the folder or use the Layers panel menu to insert a new layer. You can apply attributes and masks to the entire group.

To Open a Second Image

To add a sofa as a layer to the Room Edited image, you will need to open a new file, Sofa, from the Data Files for Students, or from a location specified by your instructor. The following steps open the Sofa file, which is stored in the PSD format.

1 Press CTRL+O to display the Open dialog box.

2 In the Open dialog box, if necessary, click the Look in box arrow, and then navigate to the Chapter 03 folder of the Data Files for Students, or a location specified by your instructor.

3 Double-click the file named Sofa to open it (Figure 3–15).

Figure 3–15

Displaying Multiple Files

Photoshop has more than 25 different ways to arrange document windows when more than one file is open. You also can create a custom workspace by moving and manipulating document windows manually.

For example, you might want to display two document windows, horizontally or vertically, in order to drag and drop from one image to another. You might want to compare different versions or views of photos beside each other in the document window. Or, when creating a panorama, you might want to preview how certain photos will look side by side.

When you are finished viewing multiple document windows in the workspace, you can **consolidate**, or view only one window at a time.

To Arrange the Document Windows

The following steps display the Room Edited and Sofa windows beside each other using the Arrange Documents button on the Application bar.

1
- On the Application bar, click the Arrange Documents button to display its list (Figure 3–16).

Q&A Why are some of the arrangements grayed out?

Because you have only two document windows open, the only arrangements enabled are the ones that display two windows.

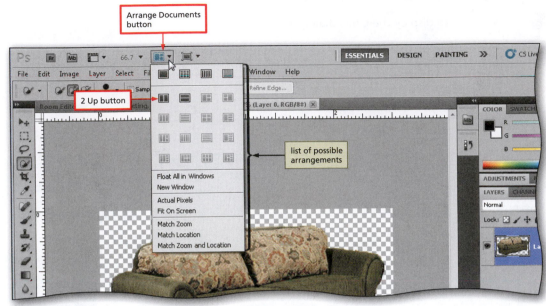

Figure 3–16

2
- Click the first 2 Up button in the list to display the windows beside each other (Figure 3–17).

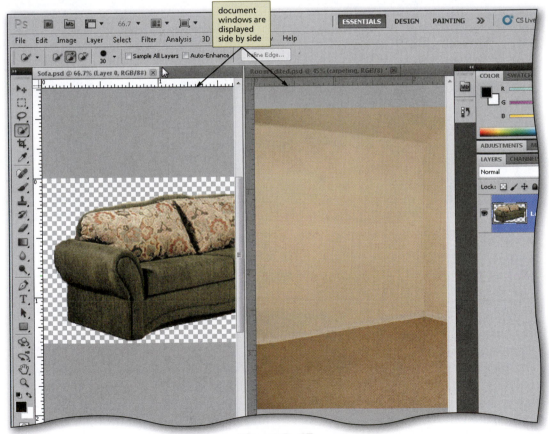

Figure 3–17

Other Ways

1. On Window menu, click Arrange, click Tile

To Create a Layer by Dragging an Entire Image

When you drag a selection from one document window to the other, Photoshop creates a new layer in the destination document window, on top of the other layers. If you want to include the entire image from the source window, use the Move Tool to drag from any location in the source window to the destination window. Dragging between document windows is an automatic duplication rather than a true move. The original, source image remains unchanged.

The following step moves the entire image from the source window, Sofa, to the destination window, Room Edited.

1

● Press the v key to activate the Move Tool.

● Drag the sofa image into the Room Edited window and drop it in the room (Figure 3–18).

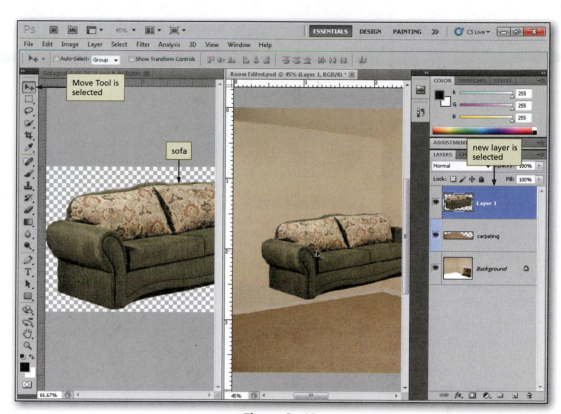

Figure 3–18

To Close the Sofa Document Window

Because you are finished with the Sofa image, the following step closes the Sofa window.

1 Click the Close button on the Sofa document window tab. If Photoshop asks you to save the file, click the No button.

BTW

The Layers Panel Context Menus
The Layers panel has many ways to work with layers. For example, right-clicking the layer name displays a different context menu from the one you see when right-clicking the thumbnail. Double-clicking the layer name allows you to rename the layer; double-clicking the thumbnail opens the Layer Style dialog box.

To Position a Layer

The following step drags the sofa to a new location.

1
- With the new layer still selected on the Layers panel, and the Move Tool still selected on the Tools panel, drag the sofa to a position along the left wall, on the floor (Figure 3–19).

Q&A

Is it acceptable for some of the sofa to disappear off the edge of the document window?

Yes. Your goal is to make it look as natural as possible, as if it is sitting on the floor.

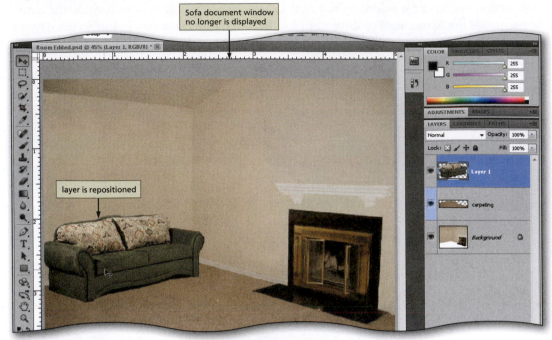

Figure 3–19

To Set Layer Properties Using the Context Menu

The following steps set the layer properties for the sofa, this time using the context menu displayed by right-clicking the layer itself.

1
- On the Layers panel, right-click the name of the layer, Layer 1, to display the context menu (Figure 3–20).

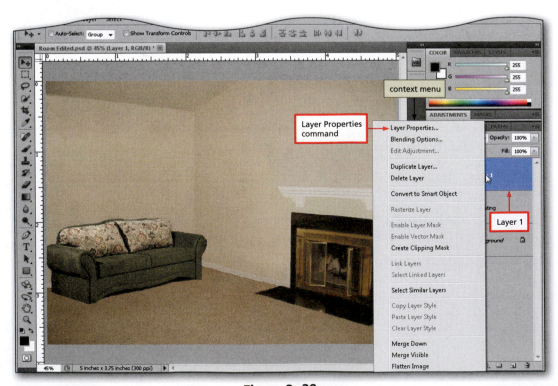

Figure 3–20

2
- Click Layer Properties on the menu to display the Layer Properties dialog box.

- Type **sofa** in the Name box to name the layer.

- Click the Color box arrow, and then click Yellow in the list to choose a yellow identification color (Figure 3–21).

3
- Click the OK button to display the new settings on the Layers panel.

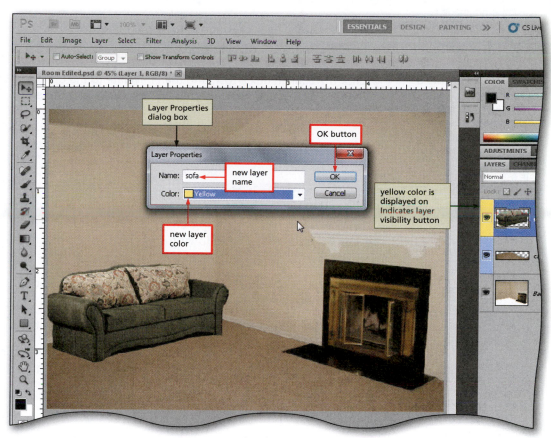

Figure 3–21

To Save the File

Because you have created layers and made changes to the image, it is a good idea to save the file again. The following step saves the file again.

1 Press CTRL+S to save the Room Edited file with the same name. If Photoshop displays a dialog box about compatibility, click the OK button.

Other Ways

1. Click Layers panel menu button, click Layer Properties, type new name, choose new color, click OK button

2. Click Layer on the menu bar, click Layer Properties, type new name, choose new color, click OK button

Break Point: If you wish to take a break, this is a good place to do so. You can quit Photoshop now. To resume at a later time, start Photoshop, open the file called Room Edited, and continue following the steps from this location forward.

Creating a Layer by Dragging a Selection

Sometimes you do not want to move an entire image from one window to another. When you want only a part of an image, you create a selection, as you learned in Chapter 2, and then move the selection to the destination window. Once the selection exists in the destination window, some editing, such as scaling, erasing, or adjusting, commonly is necessary.

BTW

JPG File Type
The Painting image is
stored as a JPG file. Recall
that JPG stands for Joint
Photographic Experts
Group and is the file
type typically generated
by digital cameras. The
JPG format supports
many different color
modes. JPG retains all
color information in an
RGB image, unlike the
GIF format.

To Open the Painting Image

The following steps open a file named Painting.

1 Press CTRL+O to display the Open dialog box.

2 Click the Look in box arrow, and then navigate to the Chapter 03 folder of the Data Files for Students, or a location specified by your instructor, if necessary.

3 Double-click the file named Painting to open it.

To Select the Painting

When adding the painting image to the Room Edited image, you will not need the surrounding wall. The following steps select the painting only, using the Rectangular Marquee Tool.

1 If necessary, right-click the current marquee tool and then click Rectangular Marquee Tool on the context menu to select it.

2 If necessary, click the New selection button on the options bar to start a new selection.

3 Drag around the painting. Avoid including the wall in the selection. If you make a mistake while selecting, press the ESC key and then begin again (Figure 3–22).

Figure 3–22

To Create a Layer by Dragging a Selection

The following steps move the selection. To facilitate dragging the selection between windows, you will view the windows above and below one another.

1

- On the Application bar, click the Arrange Documents button (shown in Figure 3–16 on page PS 152) to display its list, and then click the second 2 Up button to display the windows above and below one another (Figure 3–23).

 Experiment

- Click the Arrange Documents button and then click the Tile All Horizontally button. Open a third file and then try some of the other configurations. When you are done, close the third file. Click the Arrange Documents button and then click the second 2 Up button.

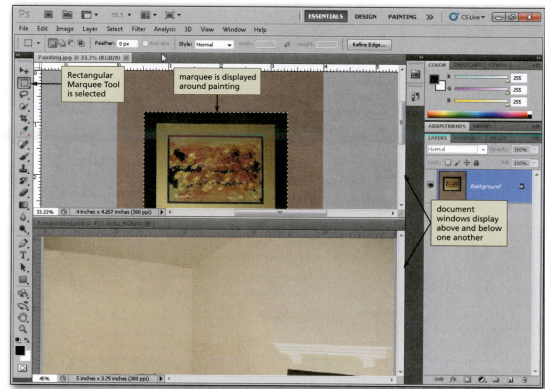

Figure 3–23

2

- Press the v key to activate the Move Tool.

- Drag the selection and drop it in the Room Edited window (Figure 3–24).

Q&A

Why is the painting so large?

The photos used in composites may come from a variety of sources and camera types, with a variety of different resolutions, and with different physical sizes. Photos generated by digital cameras, with lots of megapixels, create very large files.

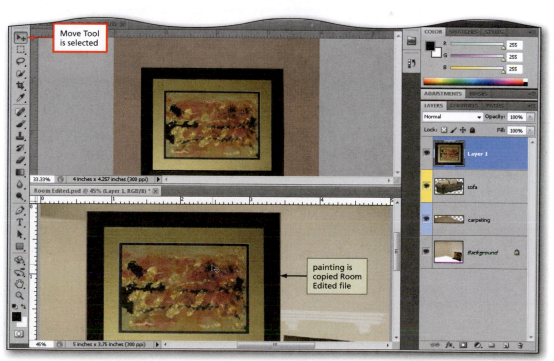

Figure 3–24

Other Ways

1. In source window, create selection, on Edit menu, click Copy, in destination window, on Edit menu, click Paste

To Close the Painting Window

The following step closes the Painting window.

1 Click the Close button on the Painting document window tab. If Photoshop displays a dialog box asking if you want to save the changes, click the No button.

To Transform the Painting

The following steps resize the layer. Also, to make the painting appear more natural in the setting, you will skew the layer using skills discussed in Chapter 2.

1 With the new layer still selected on the Layers panel, press CTRL+T to display the bounding box.

2 SHIFT+drag a corner sizing handle until the selection is approximately 50% smaller.

3 Drag the layer to a location above the sofa.

4 Right-click the selection and then click Skew on the context menu.

5 Drag the lower-left sizing handle down to skew the painting. Drag other sizing handles, if necessary, until the top of the painting appears parallel with the ceiling, as shown in Figure 3–25.

6 Press the ENTER key to commit the transformation.

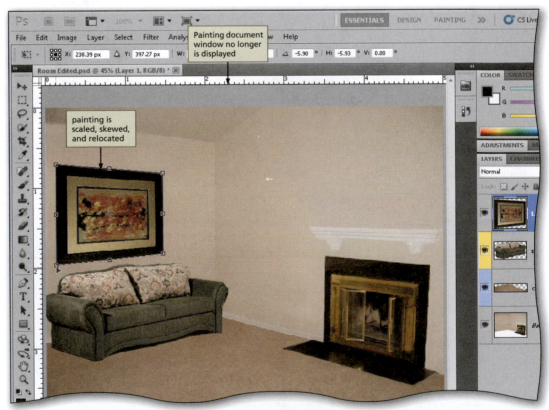

Figure 3–25

To Set the Painting Layer Properties

The following steps set the painting layer properties.

1 Right-click Layer 1 on the Layers panel. Click Layer Properties on the context menu.

2 Type `painting` in the Name box. Click the Color box arrow, and then click Red.

3 Click the OK button to apply the settings.

The Eraser Tools

In the painting layer, you eliminated the background before moving it to the composite by using a selection technique. Other times, however, a new layer still may have extra color or objects that are not appropriate for the composite image. The image might be shaped oddly, making selecting tedious, or there might be other images in the background that come along with the selection, no matter what you do. In those cases, dragging the image into a layer and then erasing part of that layer gives you more freedom and control in how the layer appears.

On the Tools panel, when you right-click the Eraser Tool button, Photoshop displays the three eraser tools. To alternate among the three eraser tools, press SHIFT+E. To access the eraser tools after using a different tool, press the E key.

The eraser tools are described in Table 3–1.

Tool	Purpose	Shortcut	Button
Table 3–1 Eraser Tools			
Eraser Tool	erases pixels beneath the cursor or brush tip	E SHIFT+E toggles through all three eraser tools	
Background Eraser Tool	erases sample color from the center of the brush	E SHIFT+E toggles through all three eraser tools	
Magic Eraser Tool	erases all similarly colored pixels	E SHIFT+E toggles through all three eraser tools	

When using the eraser tools, it is best to erase small portions at a time. That way each erasure is a separate state on the History panel. If you make mistakes, you can click earlier states on the panel. Small erasures also can be undone. To undo an erasure, press CTRL+Z, or click Edit on the menu bar, and then click Undo Eraser.

To Open the Coffee Table Image

The following step opens a file named Coffee Table in preparation for using the eraser tools.

1 Open the Coffee Table file from the Chapter 03 folder of the Data Files for Students, or a location specified by your instructor, if necessary.

PNG File Type
The Coffee Table image
is stored as a PNG file.
Recall that PNG stands for
Portable Network Graphics
and is a cross-platform
file type similar to GIF.
It differs in that you can
control the opacity of
transparent colors. PNG
files interlace, or fill in,
faster on Web pages.

To Create the Coffee Table Layer

1 On the Application bar, click the Arrange Documents button to display its list, and then click the first 2 Up button to display the windows beside each other.

2 With the Coffee Table window still active, click the Move Tool button on the Tools panel, if necessary.

3 Drag the entire coffee table image and drop it in the Room Edited window. Zoom to 33% magnification (Figure 3–26).

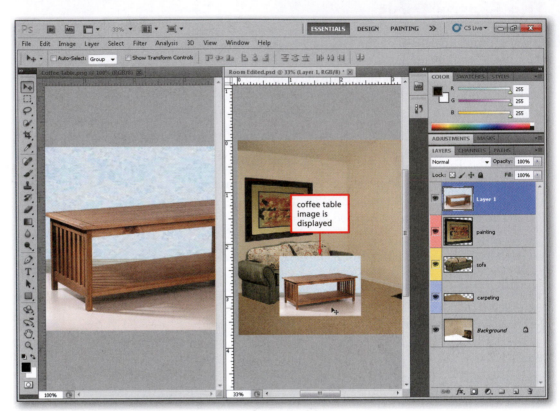

Figure 3–26

To Close the Coffee Table Window

The following step closes the original the Coffee Table window.

1 Close the Coffee Table document window. If Photoshop displays a dialog box asking if you want to save the changes, click the No button.

To Set the Layer Properties

The following steps set the layer properties.

1 Display the Layer Properties dialog box.

2 Name the layer `coffee table,` and choose a gray identification color.

3 Close the Layer Properties dialog box.

Using the Magic Eraser Tool

The Magic Eraser Tool erases all similarly colored pixels with one click. The Magic Eraser Tool options bar (Figure 3–27) gives you the choice of contiguous or non-contiguous pixels and allows you to enter a tolerance value to define the range of erasable color. A lower tolerance erases pixels within a range of color values very similar to the pixel you click. A higher tolerance erases pixels within a broader range. Recall that the Anti-alias check box creates a smooth edge that can apply to both selecting and erasing. **Opacity** refers to the level at which you can see through a color to reveal the layer beneath it. When using the eraser tools, an opacity setting of 100% completely erases pixels. A lower opacity partially erases pixels.

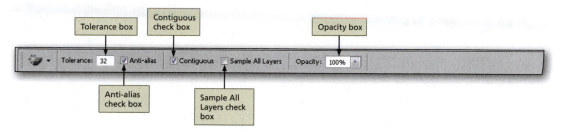

Figure 3–27

To Erase Using the Magic Eraser Tool

The following steps use the Magic Eraser Tool to remove the background from the coffee table image.

1
- Zoom to 100% magnification and scroll as necessary to view the coffee table layer.

- With the coffee table layer still selected, right-click the Eraser Tool button on the Tools panel to display the context menu (Figure 3–28).

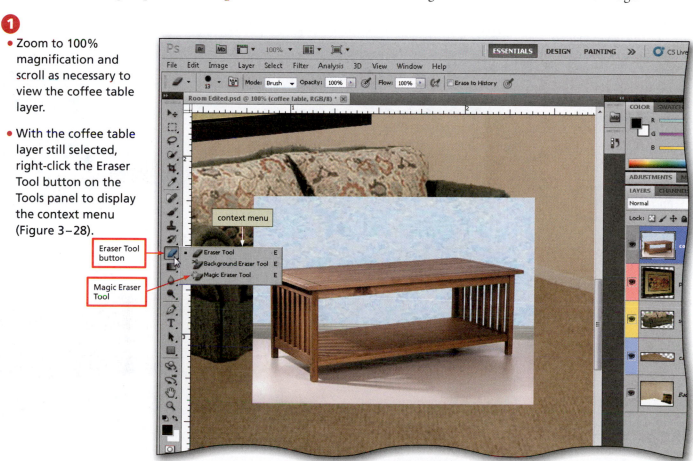

Figure 3–28

2

- Click the Magic Eraser Tool to select it.

- On the Magic Eraser options bar, type 4 0 in the Tolerance box.

- If necessary, click the Anti-alias check box to display the check mark.

- Click the Contiguous check box so it does not display a check mark (Figure 3–29).

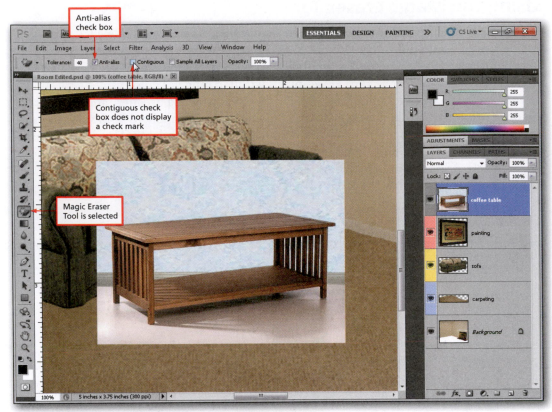

Anti-alias check box

Contiguous check box does not display a check mark

Magic Eraser Tool is selected

Figure 3–29

3

- Click the wallpaper to delete all of the blue color.

- If some blue remains in your layer, click it (Figure 3–30).

Q&A

How should I position the Magic Eraser Tool mouse pointer?

Position the center of the starburst tip over the pixel color to erase using the Magic Eraser Tool mouse pointer.

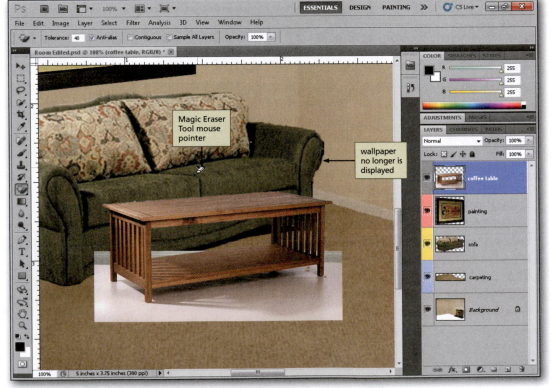

Magic Eraser Tool mouse pointer

wallpaper no longer is displayed

Figure 3–30

Other Ways

1. Press SHIFT+E until Magic Eraser Tool is selected, click document

Using the Eraser Tool

The Eraser Tool changes pixels in the image as you drag through them. On most layers, the Eraser Tool simply erases the pixels or changes them to transparent, revealing the layer beneath. On a locked layer, such as the Background layer, the Eraser Tool changes the pixels to the background color.

The Eraser Tool options bar (Figure 3–31) displays a Mode box in which you can choose one of three shapes for erasure: brush, block, and pen. The brush shape gives you the most flexibility in size, and many different brush tips are available. The default brush tip is a circle. Block mode is a hard-edged, fixed-sized square with no options for changing the opacity or flow; however, it does give you quick access to a square to erase straight lines and corners. The pencil mode is similar to the brush mode, except that the pencil does not spread as much into adjacent pixels.

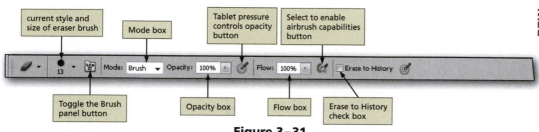

Figure 3–31

As with the Magic Eraser Tool options bar, an Opacity box allows you to specify the depth of the erasure. The Flow box specifies how quickly the erasure is performed. In addition, you can erase to a saved state or snapshot in the History panel.

As you erase with the brush shape, the RIGHT BRACKET ( ]) and LEFT BRACKET ([ ) keys increase and decrease the size of the eraser, respectively.

BTW

Hiding and Showing Multiple Layers
To view only one layer in the document window, ALT+click the visibility icon for the layer you want to view. ALT+clicking again restores the previous visibility settings. Show or hide all other layers by selecting Show/Hide all other layers from the visibility icon's context menu. To hide or view several contiguous layers, drag through the eye column.

To Display Only the Current Layer

Some users find it easier to erase in a layer when only that layer appears in the document window. The following step hides all but the current layer.

- On the Layers panel, ALT+click the coffee table layer visibility icon, so only the coffee table is displayed (Figure 3–32).

Figure 3–32

To Select the Eraser Tool and Resize the Mouse Pointer

The following steps select the Eraser Tool in preparation for erasing more of the layer.

1 Right-click the Magic Eraser Tool button on the Tools panel, and then click Eraser Tool on the context menu.

2 Move the mouse pointer into the document window.

3 If the mouse pointer is extremely small, press the RIGHT BRACKET (]) key several times to resize the eraser until the mouse pointer changes from a dot to a small circle (Figure 3–33).

Figure 3–33

To Erase Using the Eraser Tool

The following steps erase the white floor beneath the coffee table using the Eraser Tool.

1
• Drag the mouse across a portion of the floor to erase it. Do not drag across the coffee table (Figure 3–34).

Q&A
How should I position the Eraser Tool mouse pointer?

By default the Eraser Tool mouse pointer appears as a circle. When you click or drag, Photoshop erases everything within the circle. You can change the size of the mouse pointer using the bracket keys.

Figure 3–34

2

- Continue dragging to erase more of the floor and the molding, using the LEFT BRACKET ([) and RIGHT BRACKET (]) keys to change the size of your eraser. Do not erase completely along the very edge of the coffee table (Figure 3–35).

 Experiment

- Drag a short erasure over the coffee table that creates an error. Then press CTRL+Z to undo the erasure.

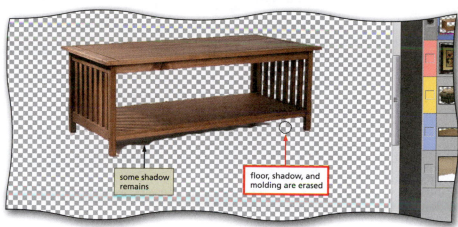

Figure 3–35

To Erase Using the Block Mouse Pointer

The following steps delete flooring and shadows that are very close to the coffee table using a block mouse pointer.

1

- Click the Mode box arrow on the options bar to display its list (Figure 3–36).

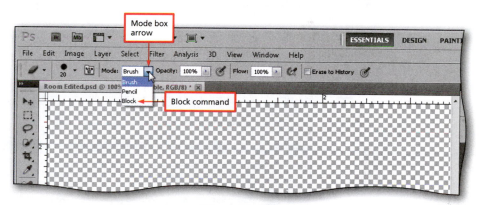

Figure 3–36

2

- Click Block to choose a block mouse pointer.

- Drag close to the coffee table to erase the rest of the flooring and shadows (Figure 3–37).

Q&A

Can I change the size of the block?

No, the block eraser mouse pointer cannot be resized. You can change the magnification, however, to help you erase smaller portions using the block.

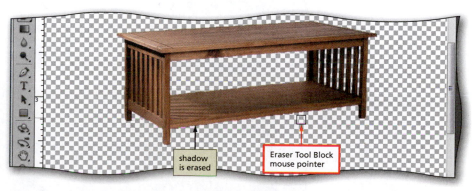

Figure 3–37

Other Ways
1. Press SHIFT+E until Eraser Tool is selected, click document

To View All Layers

The following steps show all of the layers.

1 ALT+click the coffee table visibility icon to show all of the layers.

2 If viewing all of the layers reveals other areas of the coffee table that need to be erased, drag to erase them. Zoom and scroll as necessary.

To Transform the Coffee Table Layer

The following steps transform the coffee table layer in order to make it fit the perspective of the room.

1 With the coffee table layer still selected, zoom out as necessary, and then press CTRL+T to turn on the bounding box.

2 Right-click within the bounding box to display the context menu, and then choose Perspective.

3 Drag the left-center sizing handle down to change the perspective so it resembles Figure 3–38.

4 If necessary, move the coffee table to a location in front of the sofa.

5 Press the ENTER key to confirm the transformation.

6 If necessary, zoom to 45% magnification.

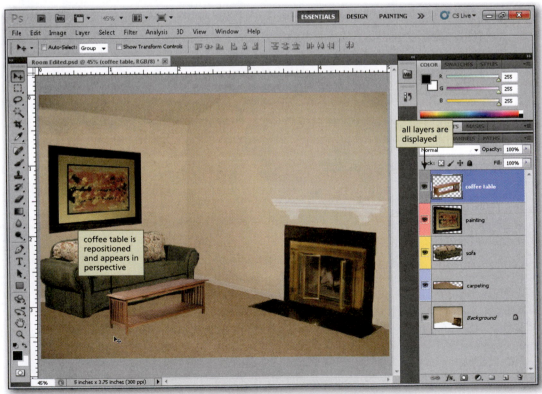

Figure 3–38

Using the Background Eraser Tool

The Background Eraser Tool erases the background while maintaining the edges of an object in the foreground, based on a set color that you choose for the background. The Background Eraser Tool samples the color in the center of the mouse pointer, called the **hot spot**. As you drag, the tool erases that color, leaving the rest of the layer as foreground. You release the mouse and drag again to sample a different color. On the Background Eraser Tool options bar (Figure 3–39) you can use the tolerance setting to control the range of colors that will be erased, sample the color selections, and adjust the sharpness of the boundaries by setting limits. The three sampling buttons on the Background Eraser Tool options bar sample in different ways. When you use the Sampling: Continuous button, it samples colors and erases continuously as you drag; the Sampling: Once button erases only the areas containing the color you first click; and the Sampling: Background Swatch button erases only areas containing the current color on the Tools panel, Color panel, or Swatches panel.

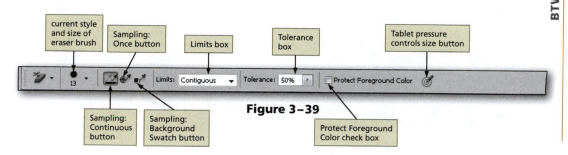

Figure 3–39

BTW

The Background Eraser Tool
The Background Eraser Tool samples the hot spot and then, as you drag, it deletes that color wherever it appears inside the brush. The Background Eraser Tool overrides the lock transparency setting of a layer.

To Open the Ivy Image

The following step opens a file named Ivy in preparation for using the Background Eraser Tool.

1 Open the Ivy file from the Chapter 03 folder of the Data Files for Students, or from a location specified by your instructor.

To Create the Ivy Layer

To create the ivy layer, you first will move the entire image into the Room Edited document window.

1 On the Application bar, click the Arrange Documents button to display its list, and then click the first 2 Up button to display the windows beside each other.

2 Activate the Move Tool.

3 Drag the ivy image and drop it in the Room Edited window.

To Close the Ivy Window

The following step closes the Ivy window because you are finished with it.

1 Close the Ivy document window. If Photoshop displays a dialog box asking if you want to save the changes, click the No button.

BTW

TIFF File Type
The Ivy file is stored as a TIF file. TIF, or TIFF, is a flexible raster image format. A raster image is a digital image represented by a matrix of pixels. TIFF stands for Tagged Image File Format and is a common file format for images acquired from scanners and screen capture programs. Because TIFF files are supported by virtually all paint, image-editing, and page-layout applications, it also is a versatile format for cross-platform applications.

To Set the Layer Properties

The following steps set the layer properties.

1 Double-click the new layer name in the Layers panel. Type **ivy** and then press the ENTER key to name the layer.

2 Right-click the 'Indicates layer visibility' button and choose the green identification color from the context menu (Figure 3–40).

Figure 3–40

To Erase Using the Background Eraser Tool

The following steps use the Background Eraser Tool to remove the paneling from behind the ivy plant. If you make a mistake while erasing, click the previous state on the History panel or press CTRL+Z and begin erasing again.

1

- With the ivy layer still selected, right-click the Eraser Tool button on the Tools panel and then click Background Eraser Tool on the context menu to select the tool.

- On the options bar, click the Sampling: Once button.

- Click the Limits box arrow to display its list (Figure 3–41).

Q&A

How should I position the Background Eraser Tool mouse pointer?

Position the center of the starburst tip over the pixel color to erase using the Magic Eraser Tool mouse pointer.

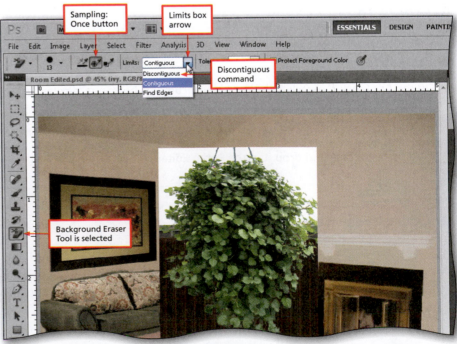

Figure 3–41

2

- Click Discontiguous to choose the setting.

- Enter 25 in the Tolerance box to lower the Tolerance setting, which will erase a more narrow range of color.

- If necessary, click to display a check mark in the Protect Foreground color check box.

- Move the mouse pointer to the document window and then press the RIGHT BRACKET (]) key several times to increase the size of the eraser, if necessary (Figure 3–42).

Q&A

What does discontiguous mean?

Discontiguous means non-contiguous, in this case pixels of the same color that are not physically located together. In the ivy layer, parts of the brown panel appear behind the ivy and are not connected color-wise to the other brown paneling.

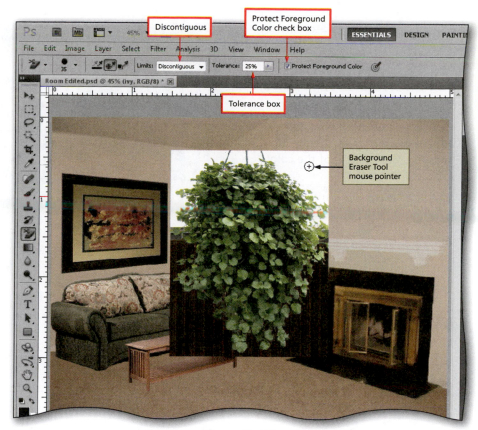

Figure 3–42

3

- Position the mouse pointer directly over a portion of the paneling.

- Click and hold the mouse button. Drag across the layer, including the ivy, to erase some of the paneling (Figure 3–43).

Q&A

What is the purpose of the Protect Foreground Color check box?

When checked, the Protect Foreground Color check box gives you even more control of the background erasing. When colors are very similar, you can ALT+click the color you want to keep, then drag the color you wish to erase.

Figure 3–43

④

- Position the mouse pointer directly over a portion of the paneling.

- Click and hold the mouse button. Drag to erase the rest of the paneling.

- If some color remains, zoom as necessary to position your mouse directly over the color. Click and drag to erase the rest of the color (Figure 3–44).

Q&A

Some of the paneling still remains. How do I delete it?

Use the Eraser Tool or the Magic Erase Tool to erase the small portions. Zoom and change the size of your mouse pointer as necessary.

all paneling is erased

Figure 3–44

Other Ways

1. Press SHIFT+E until Background Eraser Tool is selected, set options bar, click document

To Finish the Ivy Layer

The following steps erase the rest of the background.

① With the ivy layer still selected on the Layers panel, use a combination of eraser tools and techniques to erase the white portion of the layer, the hanging wires, and the chair rail molding.

② Resize the layer as necessary and move it to a location on the left side of the fireplace mantel (Figure 3–45).

background is removed and layer is scaled and repositioned

Figure 3–45

To Add a Pole Lamp to the Room

The following steps add a pole lamp layer to the room.

1 Open the file named Pole Lamp from the Chapter 03 folder of the Data Files for Students, or from a location specified by your instructor.

2 Use the techniques you have learned to create a new layer and place the pole lamp in the Room Edited document window.

3 Name the new layer `pole lamp`, and color the layer orange.

4 Close the Pole Lamp document window.

To Rearrange Layers

The following step rearranges the layers on the Layers panel, so the pole lamp appears behind the end of the sofa.

1
- Select the pole lamp layer on the Layers panel, if necessary.

- Press CTRL+LEFT BRACKET ([) several times to move the layer down and place it below the sofa layer.

- In the document window, move the pole lamp to the right end of the sofa, in the corner of the room (Figure 3–46).

🔍 **Experiment**
- Drag individual layers on the Layers panel to new locations in the stack, and watch how that changes the document window. When you are finished, rearrange the layers to appear as shown in Figure 3–46.

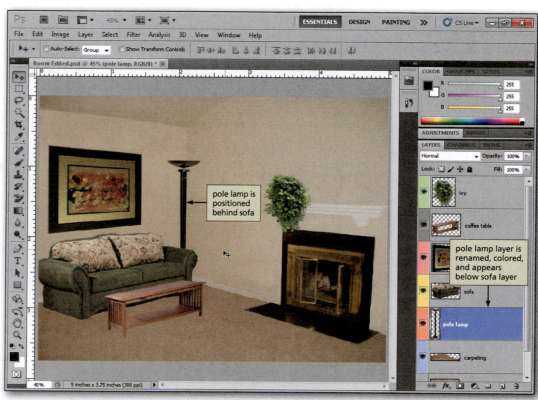

Figure 3–46

BTW

Arranging Layers
To rearrange layers, change their visibility, or better organize them, drag the layer up or down on the Layers panel. The top layer on the Layers panel appears in front of any other layers in the document window. The Layer menu also contains an Arrange submenu to help you organize your layers.

To Add Mantle Decorations to the Room

The following steps add a mantle decoration layer to the room.

1 Open the file named Mantle Decorations from the Chapter 03 folder of the Data Files for Students, or from a location specified by your instructor.

2 Use the techniques you have learned to create a new layer, edit it as necessary, and place the mantle decorations on the mantle in the Room Edited document window.

3 Name the new layer, `mantle decorations`, and color the layer violet.

4 Close the Mantle Decorations document window (Figure 3–47).

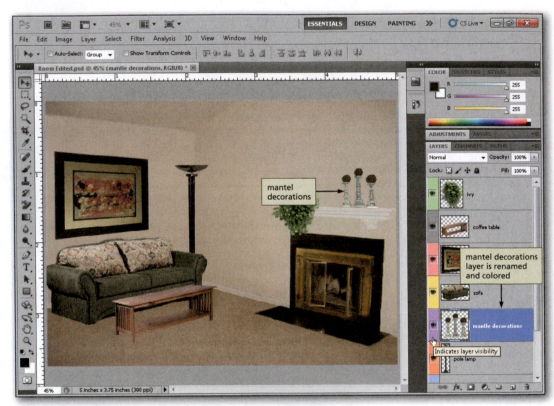

Figure 3–47

To Save the File

Many layers have been added to the composite image. The following step saves the file.

1 Save the Room Edited file with the same name.

Break Point: If you wish to take a break, this is a good place to do so. You can quit Photoshop now. To resume at a later time, start Photoshop, open the file named Room Edited and continue following the steps from this location forward.

Layer Masks

Another way to edit layers is by creating a mask. A **mask** shows or hides portions of a layer; it also can protect areas of the layer from inadvertent editing. For example, in a graphic of an exotic animal, you might want to mask all of the area except the animal, rather than permanently delete the background. Or, if you wanted to layer a musical score over the top of a piano graphic, you might mask the edges of the paper so the notes look like they blend into the piano. A mask does not alter the layer as the Eraser Tool did; it merely overlays a template to conceal a portion of the layer. That way, if you change your mind and need to display more of the layer, you can. Nothing has been erased permanently. With the Eraser Tool, you would have to delete the layer, open a backup copy, recreate the layer, and then begin to edit again. With masks, you simply edit the mask.

Photoshop provides two types of masks. **Layer masks** or **pixel masks** are resolution-dependent bitmap images, created with the painting or selection tools. **Vector masks** are resolution independent, created with a pen or shape tool. In this chapter, you will create a layer mask.

When you add a mask, a layer mask thumbnail appears on the Layers panel in **grayscale**, which means each pixel in the mask uses a single color on a scale from black to white. When selecting the layer mask thumbnail, the default colors change to white over black and the eraser tools are inactive. To mask, you paint on the layer with black. If you change your mind and want to unmask, you paint with white. Painting with gray displays various levels of transparency in the layer.

BTW

GIF File Type
The Potted Plant image is stored as GIF file. Recall that GIF stands for Graphics Interchange Format and is a cross-platform file type commonly used to display graphics and images on Web pages. It is a compressed format designed to minimize file size and electronic transfer time.

To Open the Potted Plant File

The following steps open the Potted Plant file in preparation for creating a layer mask.

1 Open the file named Potted Plant from the Chapter 03 folder of the Data Files for Students, or from a location specified by your instructor.

2 Display the windows side by side.

3 Drag the potted plant into the room. Scroll in the Room Edited document window as necessary and drag the potted plant to place it on the left side of the fireplace.

4 Name the new layer `left potted plant`, and color the layer green.

5 Because you will use the Potted Plant document window again, do not close it.

To Consolidate Windows

Sometimes, after viewing multiple document windows, you may want to view only one window, without closing the others. The steps on the next page consolidate to the Room Edited document window, while leaving the Potted Plant document window open.

1

- Right-click the tab at the top of the Room Edited document window to display the context menu (Figure 3–48)

2

- Click Consolidate All to Here to view only that document window.

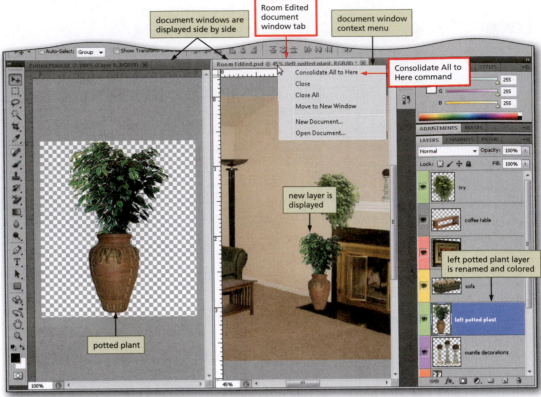

Figure 3–48

To Create a Layer Mask

The following steps mask the plant in the potted plant layer to reveal only the pot. That way, potential decorators can see what the room would look like with and without the plant.

1

- With the left potted plant layer selected, click the 'Add layer mask' button on the Layers panel status bar to create a layer mask (Figure 3–49).

Q&A

What is the new notation on the Layers panel?

Photoshop adds a layer mask thumbnail to the selected layer on the panel. The link icon **links**, or connects, the mask to the layer. A link icon appears between the layer thumbnail and the mask thumbnail. Also notice that the default colors on the Tools panel are reversed.

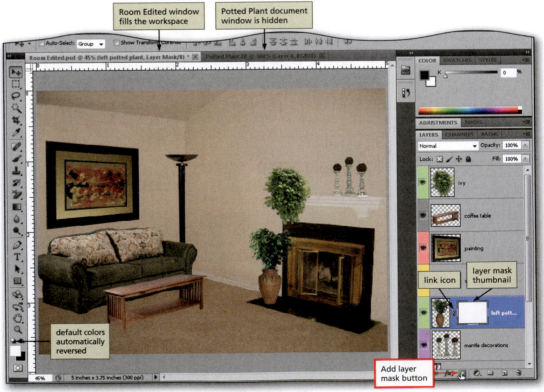

Figure 3–49

2
- If necessary, press the X key to choose black over white.
- Press the B key to activate the brush and then move the mouse pointer into the document window.
- Press the RIGHT BRACKET (]) key to increase the size of the brush's circle, as necessary.
- Drag the mouse across the plant itself. Do not drag across the pot (Figure 3–50).

Q&A

Why does the layer mask use a brush tip mouse pointer?

Layer masks use painting techniques to mask out portions of the image.

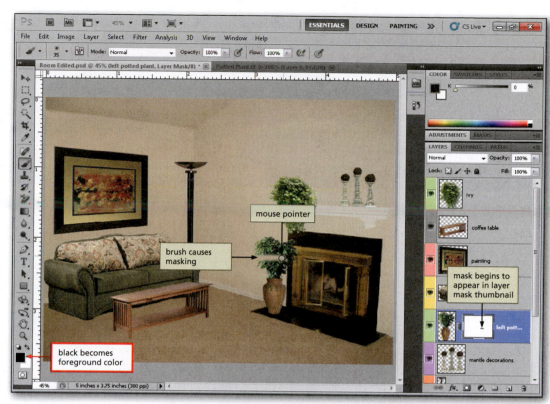

Figure 3–50

3
- Continue dragging through the layer to remove everything except the pot. Zoom the magnification and adjust the size of the brush mouse pointer as necessary (Figure 3–51).

Q&A

Why is my erasing brush fuzzy?

Your brush may be set on a soft setting that creates fuzzy or hazy erasures. To create an erasure with a more solid edge, click the Brush Preset picker on the options bar, and then drag the Hardness slider to the right.

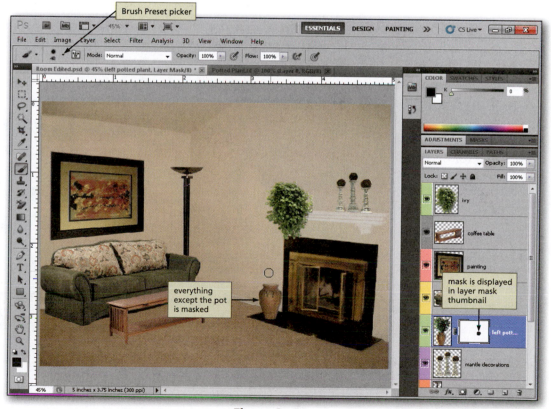

Figure 3–51

To Correct a Masking Error

The following steps create a masking error and then unmask the area by painting with white.

1
- Drag across the pot to mask a portion of the pot (Figure 3–52).

Figure 3–52

2
- Press the x key to switch the foreground and background colors so you are painting with white.

- Drag across the same portion of the pot to unmask it (Figure 3–53).

Figure 3–53

Other Ways

1. On Layer menu, point to Layer Mask, click Reveal All

The Masks Panel

The Masks panel (Figure 3–54) provides additional controls to adjust a layer mask. You can change the density of the mask to allow more or less of the masked content to show through. For example, if you wanted to create a special effects layer to show a time-line or to animate a process, you could create several layer masks with varying percentages of density. Additionally, you can create a **selection layer mask**; instead of painting in the layer mask, the selection border dictates the transparent portion of the layer. The Masks panel allows you to invert the mask in the same way you invert a selection, and allows you to feather the edges and refine the mask border.

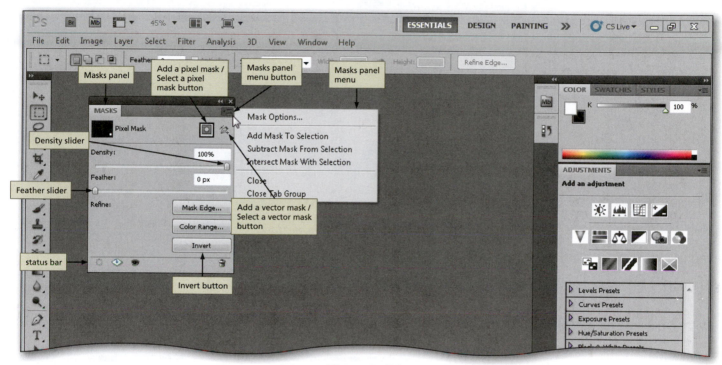

Figure 3–54

To Copy and Paste Using Shortcut Keys

The following steps copy and paste a second potted plant into the Room Edited image, creating another layer.

1 Press CTRL+TAB to view the Potted Plant document window.

2 Press CTRL+A to select the entire image.

3 Press CTRL+C to copy the image.

4 Press CTRL+TAB to view the Room Edited document window.

5 Press CTRL+V to paste the potted plant image.

6 Press the V key to activate the Move Tool and then move the second potted plant to a location on the right side of the fireplace.

7 Name the new layer `right potted plant`, and color it green.

8 Close the Potted Plant document window. If Photoshop displays a dialog box asking if you want to save the changes, click the No button.

BTW

Manipulating Masks
Once you have created a mask, you might want to perform other manipulations on the mask. For example, if you want to unlink a mask to move it independently of its layer, click the link icon on the Layers panel. To unlink a mask temporarily, SHIFT+click the link icon. If you want to mask the entire layer completely, you can ALT+click the Add layer mask button. In that case, you would paint with white in the mask to reveal portions of the mask. To make the mask permanent and reduce overall file size, apply the mask using a command on the mask's context menu.

To Display the Masks Panel

The following steps display the Masks panel.

1

• Click Window on the menu bar to display the Window menu (Figure 3–55).

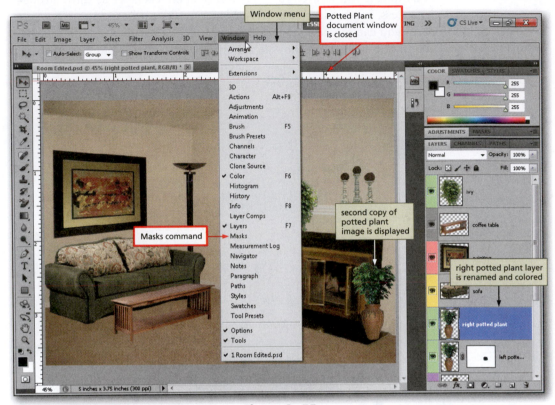

Figure 3–55

2

• Click Masks to display the Masks panel (Figure 3–56).

Figure 3–56

To Use the Masks Panel

The following step creates a selection and then use the Masks panel to edit mask properties.

- On the Tools panel, select the Rectangular Marquee Tool and create a selection around the right pot, but not the plant.

- On the Masks panel, click the 'Add a pixel mask' button to create the selection layer mask (Figure 3–57).

Experiment

- Click the Invert button to display the inverted mask. Click the Invert button again to return to the pot. Drag the Density slider to various percentages and watch the mask fade. Drag the Feather slider to various pixels and watch the edge of the mask soften and blend with less contrast.

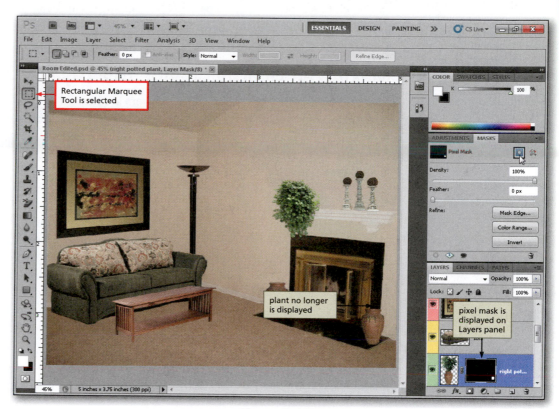

Figure 3–57

Fine-Tuning Layers

Sometimes layers need special adjustments in order to fit into their new surroundings in the document window. This fine-tuning usually involves **tonal adjustments** that affect the range of color, lighting, opacity, level, or fill; **style adjustments** such as special effects or blends; or **filter adjustments** that let you apply predetermined pictures, tiles, or patterns. With the correct adjustment, a layer seems to meld into the image, maintaining a consistency of appearance for the overall composite image.

When you do not want to alter the pixels in an image permanently, you can create an extra layer in which to make changes while preserving the original pixels. An **adjustment layer** is a new layer added to the image to affect a large-scale tonal change. You can create adjustment layers for the entire composite image or just a specific layer.

BTW

Smart Objects
You can convert a layer into a smart object, which is a nondestructive layer that does not change the original pixels. They are useful for warping, scaling, or rotating both raster and vector graphic layers. To convert a layer into a smart object, right-click the layer, and then click Convert to Smart Object on the context menu.

Plan Ahead

Create layer adjustments.
Layer adjustments allow you to fine-tune your layers. Evaluate layers to see if a change in levels, brightness, saturation, or hue would help them to fit into the background scene. Use nondestructive edits when possible, so if the client does not like the adjustment, you can remove it.

Adjustment layers have several advantages. They are nondestructive, which means you can experiment with various settings and reedit the adjustment layer at any time. Adjustment layers reduce the amount of damage you do to an image by making direct edits. You can copy adjustments to other layers and images, saving time and maintaining consistency.

If you want to make permanent tonal, style, or filter changes to the pixels themselves, you can edit the layer directly. Features such as opacity, fill, and blending modes can be changed on the Layers panel. These changes can be undone using the History panel, but become permanent when you save the image.

Making an Opacity Change to a Layer

Some adjustment tools specific to layers are located on the Layers panel. The Opacity box allows you to change the opacity or transparency of a layer. You can control exactly how solid the objects on a specific layer appear. For example, if you wanted to display an American flag superimposed over a memorial or monument, you might change the flag layer's opacity to 50 percent. The monument easily would be visible through the flag.

The Fill box changes the fill of a layer's opacity as well, but it only changes the pixels in the layer rather than changing any applied layer styles or blending modes. If you have no layer styles or blending modes, you can use either the Opacity or Fill box. When you click either the Opacity box arrow or the Fill box arrow, a slider is displayed to adjust the percentage. You also can type a percentage in either box.

The Blending mode box arrow displays a list of blending modes for the selected layer or layers. **Blending modes** define how an object interacts with other objects, such as the Background layer. You will learn more about blending modes in a later chapter.

To Make an Opacity Change to a Layer

The following step lightens the color in the ivy by lowering the opacity, to make it fit better into the room design.

1
- Zoom to display the ivy in the document window at 100% magnification.

- On the Layers panel, scroll as necessary to select the ivy layer.

- On the Layers panel, point to the word, Opacity, and then drag the scrubby slider to the left until the Opacity box displays 85% to lighten the color of the ivy (Figure 3–58).

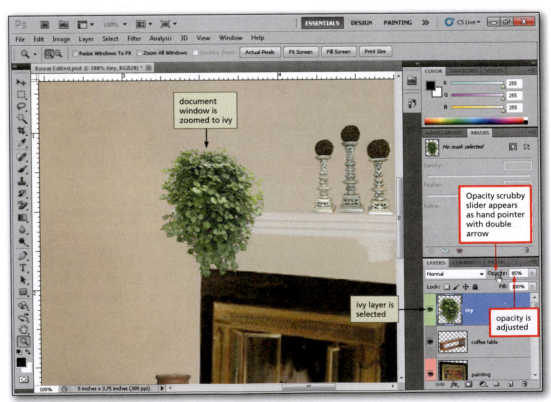

Figure 3–58

The Adjustments Panel

Other tools that nondestructively adjust image lighting and shading are located on the Adjustments panel (Figure 3–59).

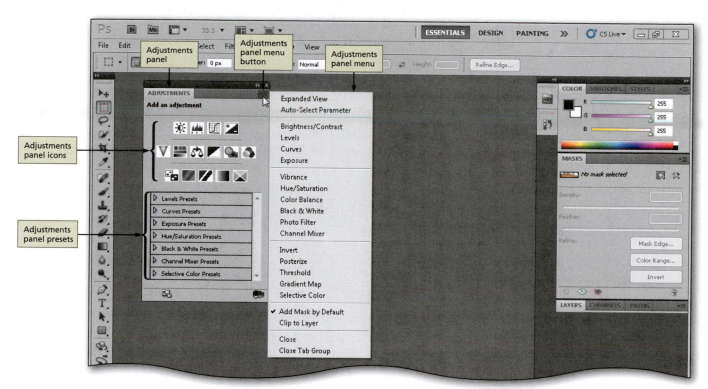

Figure 3–59

Clicking an adjustment icon or a preset displays the settings for the specific adjustment, including channel selectors, eyedroppers, sliders, and input boxes, among others. Buttons on the Adjustments panel status bar allow you to specify visibility, delete the adjustment, return to the main Adjustments panel, or create a **clip** that applies the adjustment to a layer rather than to the entire image.

Some adjustments also display their settings using a dialog box, if accessed from outside the Adjustments panel with a shortcut key or a menu command.

Table 3–2 displays a list of the adjustments available on the Adjustments panel. Many of the adjustments are available using a menu command as well.

Table 3–2 Adjustments Panel Icons			
Adjustment	**Description**	**Shortcut (if available)**	**Icon**
Brightness/Contrast	changes general brightness (shadows and highlights) and overall contrast (tonal range)		
Levels	adjusts color balance for shadows, midtones, highlights, and color channels	CTRL+L	
Curves	adjusts individual points in the tonal range of black to white	CTRL+M	
Exposure	changes exposure, which adjusts the highlights; changes offset, which darkens the shadows and midtones; changes gamma, which adjusts the midtones		
Vibrance	adjusts vibrance and color saturation settings so shifting to primary colors, or clipping, is minimized		
Hue/Saturation	changes hue, saturation, and lightness of entire image or specific colors	CTRL+U	
Color Balance	adjusts the overall midtone of colors in an image	CTRL+B	
Black & White	converts a color image to grayscale	ALT+SHIFT+CTRL+B	
Photo Filter	simulates effects of using a filter in front of a camera lens		
Channel Mixer	modifies and adjusts individual color channels		
Invert	converts every color to its inverse or opposite	CTRL+I	
Posterize	specifies the number of tonal levels in each channel		
Threshold	converts images to high-contrast black and white		
Gradient Map	maps colors to a specified gradient fill		
Selective Color	changes the mixture of colors in each of the primary color components		

While you will use some of the adjustment features in this chapter, you will learn more about these commands in future chapters.

Level Adjustments

A **level adjustment** is one way to make tonal changes to shadows, midtones, and highlights. A **shadow** is a darkened shade in an image. A **midtone**, also called **gamma**, is the midpoint gray between shadows and highlights. A **highlight** is a portion of an image that is strongly illuminated and may appear as the lightest or whitest part of the image. To change levels, Photoshop uses black, gray, and white sliders to adjust any or all of the three tonal input levels. A **histogram**, or frequency distribution bar chart, indicates the amount of color in the tonal ranges. When adjusting levels using the histogram, a general guideline is to drag the black and white (or shadow and highlight) sliders to the first indication, or outlier, of strong tonal change in the histogram. Then, experiment with the gray (or midtone) slider to change the intensity value of the middle range of gray

Level Sliders
In the Levels dialog box, the Input Level sliders on each end map the black point (on the left) and white point (on the right) to the settings of the Output sliders. The middle Input slider adjusts the gamma or midtone in the image, changing the intensity values of the middle range of gray tones without dramatically altering the highlights and shadows. As you move any of the Input Level sliders, the black point, midtone, and white point change in the Output sliders; all the remaining levels are redistributed.

tones without dramatically altering the highlights and shadows. Becoming proficient at adjusting levels takes practice. Furthermore, adjustments are subjective; the impact of some effects is a matter of opinion.

To Display the Adjustments Panel

The following step displays the Adjustments panel.

- Zoom to 45% and select the sofa layer on the Layers panel.

- Click the Adjustments panel tab to display its icons, buttons, and settings (Figure 3–60).

Q&A Why did the Layers panel collapse when I clicked the Adjustments panel?

Both the Layers panel and the Adjustments panel need a larger portion of the workspace than other panels. Photoshop automatically adjusts the size of the panel when you click the tab, to show as much of the panel as possible.

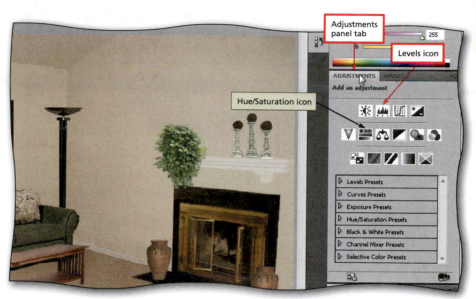

Figure 3–60

To Make a Levels Adjustment

In the sofa layer of the image, you will adjust the levels to make the layer better fit into the picture and bring out the cushion colors. The following steps make level adjustments to the sofa.

- Click the Levels icon on the Adjustments panel (shown in Figure 3–60) to display the level settings and options.

- Click the Clip to Layer button on the Adjustments panel status bar to adjust only the sofa layer (Figure 3–61).

🔍 **Experiment**

- Drag the three sliders to see how they affect the sofa layer.

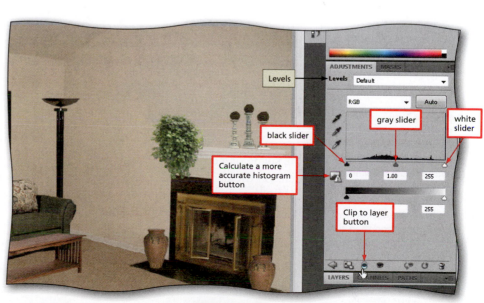

Figure 3–61

- Click the 'Calculate a more accurate histogram' button to make the level change more visible.

- In the input area, drag the white highlight slider to approximately 240, aligning it with the first visible change on the right side of the histogram.

- Drag the black shadow slider to approximately 42 to adjust the shadow input level.

- Drag the gray midtone slider to 1.20 to adjust the midtone colors (Figure 3–62).

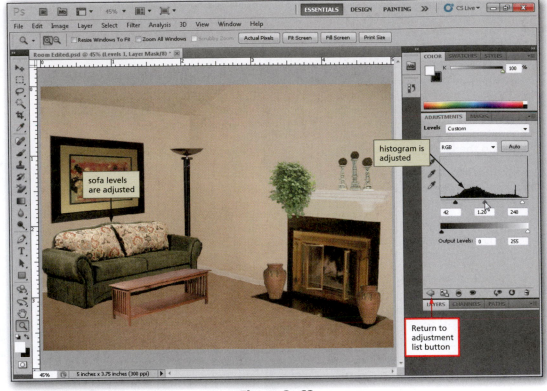

Figure 3–62

Q&A

My visible changes were at different levels. Did I do something wrong?

No, your histogram may differ, depending on your previous erasures.

- Click the 'Return to adjustment list' button to display all of the adjustment icons and settings on the Adjustments panel.

Q&A

Did the Layers panel change?

Yes, you will see an extra layer created just above the sofa layer, with a clipping symbol to imply the relationship.

Other Ways

1. Press CTRL+L, adjust levels, click OK

BTW

Other Level Adjustments

The three eyedroppers in the Levels area allow you to select the values for shadow, midtone, and highlight from the image itself. To do so, click the eyedropper and then click the location in the image that you want to use. Once selected, that color becomes the slider value.

Hue and Saturation

Another way to adjust a layer or image is to change the hue or saturation. **Hue** is the shade of a color in an image. **Saturation** is the intensity of a hue and is highly dependent on the chosen color model; but in general, pastels have low saturation, and bright colors have high saturation. You will learn more about color models and the color wheel in later chapters and by reading Appendix B.

To Adjust the Hue and Saturation

The following steps adjust the hue and saturation of the coffee table layer.

- Click the Layers panel tab to display the Layers panel, and then select the coffee table layer.

- Click the Adjustments panel tab to display the Adjustments panel, and then click the Hue/Saturation icon (shown in Figure 3–60 on page PS 183) on the Adjustments panel.

- Click the Clip to Layer button on the Adjustments panel status bar to adjust only the layer.

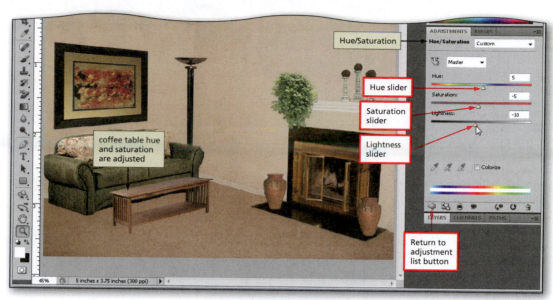

Figure 3–63

- Drag the Hue slider to +5. Drag the Saturation slider to −5. Drag the Lightness slider to −10 (Figure 3–63).

Experiment

- Drag the sliders to view the affect of hue and saturation settings to the layer. When you are done experimenting, drag the sliders to the settings listed in the step.

- Click the 'Return to adjustment list' button to display all of the adjustment icons and settings on the Adjustments panel.

Brightness and Contrast

Brightness refers to color luminance or intensity of a light source, perceived as lightness or darkness in an image. Photoshop measures brightness on a sliding scale from −150 to +150. Negative numbers move the brightness toward black. Positive numbers compress the highlights and expand the shadows. For example, the layer might be an image photographed on a cloudy day; conversely, the image might appear overexposed by having been too close to a photographer's flash. Either way, editing the brightness might enhance the image.

Contrast is the difference between the lightest and darkest tones in an image, involving mainly the midtones. When you increase contrast, the middle-to-dark areas become darker, and the middle-to-light areas become lighter. High-contrast images contain few color variations between the lightest and darkest parts of the image; low-contrast images contain more tonal gradations.

To Adjust the Brightness and Contrast

Sometimes it is easier to create a layer adjustment from the Layers panel. The following steps edit the brightness and contrast of the Background layer using the 'Create new fill or adjustment layer' button on the Layers panel.

Other Ways

1. Select layer, press CTRL+U, complete adjustments, right-click layer, click Create Clipping Mask

BTW

Layer Selection
Sometimes a menu or panel will cover the Layers panel, or a layer might be scrolled out of sight. You always can identify which layer you are working with by looking at the document window tab as shown in Figure 3–64 on the next page. The name of the current layer appears in parentheses.

1
- Display the Layers panel and scroll as necessary to select the Background layer.

- On the Layers panel, click the 'Create new fill or adjustment layer' button to display the list of adjustments (Figure 3–64).

Q&A

What is the difference between clicking the Brightness/Contrast button on the Adjustments panel and clicking the 'Create new fill or adjustment layer' button?

There is no difference when adjusting the brightness or contrast. The list of adjustments accessed from the Layers panel includes a few more settings than the Adjustments panel.

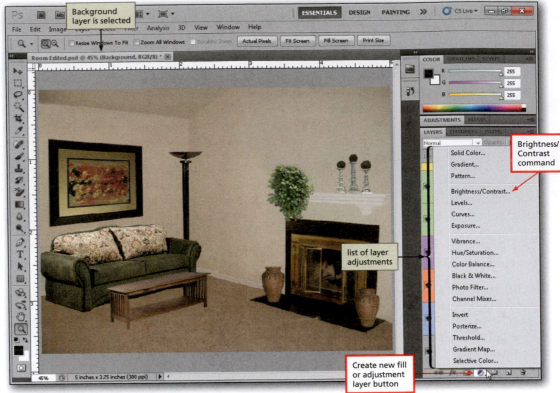

Figure 3–64

2
- Click Brightness/Contrast in the list to display the settings and access the Adjustments panel.

- Click the Clip to Layer button on the Adjustments panel status bar to adjust only the Background layer.

- Drag the Brightness slider to +10 and the Contrast slider to −10 to brighten the room (Figure 3–65).

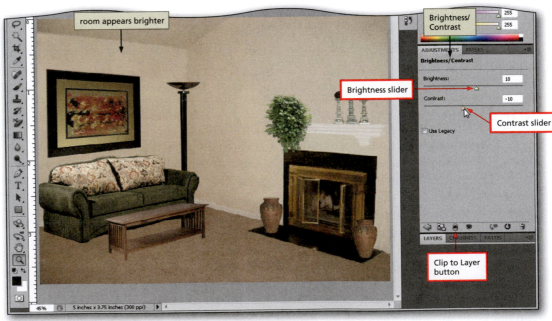

Figure 3–65

Other Ways

1. On Adjustments panel, click Brightness/Contrast icon, click third button on status bar, adjust settings

2. On Layer menu, point to New Adjustment Layer, click Brightness/Contrast, click OK, adjust settings

To View Adjustment Layers

- Display the Layers panel, and then scroll as necessary to select the coffee table layer and view the adjustment layers (Figure 3–66).

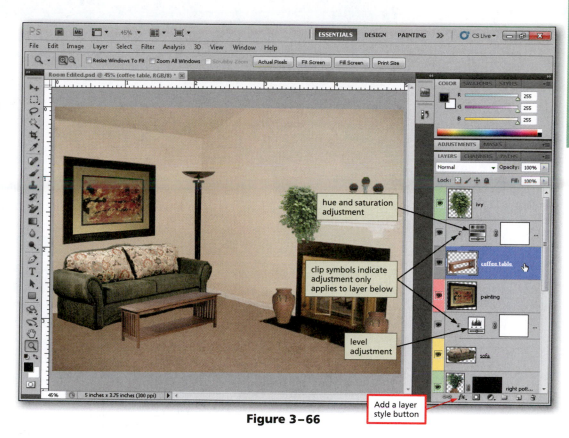

Figure 3–66

Layer Styles

Similar to a layer adjustment, a **layer style** is applied to a layer rather than changing the layer's actual pixels. Layer styles, or layer effects, affect the appearance of the layer by adding depth, shadow, shading, texture, or overlay. A layer can display multiple styles or effects.

> **Edit layer styles.**
> Layer styles add dimension, texture, and definition to your layers. Styles such as shadow, glow, emboss, bevel, overlay, and stroke commonly distinguish the layer rather than making it fit in. Choose the settings carefully and think about direction, angle, distance, and spread. Make sure the layer style does not overwhelm the overall image or detract from previous layer adjustments.

Plan Ahead

Table 3–3 lists the layer styles.

Table 3–3 Layer Styles	
Style	**Description**
Drop Shadow	creates a shadow behind the layer
Inner Shadow	creates a shadow inside the edges of the layer
Inner Glow	adds a glow around the inside edge of the layer

BTW

Copying and Moving Layer Styles
To copy a layer style, right-click the source layer and then click Copy Layer Style on the context menu. Right-click the destination layer and then click Paste Layer Style. To move a layer style, drag the fx icon from one layer to another on the Layers panel.

Table 3–3 Layer Styles (*Continued*)

Style	Description
Outer Glow	adds a glow around the outside edge of the layer
Bevel and Emboss	adds highlights and shading to a layer
Satin	applies interior shading to create a satin finish
Color Overlay	adds a color over the layer
Gradient Overlay	inserts a gradient in front of the layer
Pattern Overlay	fills the layer with a pattern
Stroke	outlines the layer with a color, gradient, or pattern

Each of the layer styles has its own set of options and properties. Table 3–4 describes some of the layer style options. The options apply to many of the styles.

Table 3–4 Layer Style Options

Option	Description
Angle	sets a degree value for the lighting angle at which the effect is applied
Anti-alias	blends the edge pixels of a contour or gloss contour
Blend Mode	determines how a layer style blends with its underlying layers
Color	assigns the color of a shadow, glow, or highlight
Contour	allows you to create rings of transparency such as gradients, fades, beveling and embossing, and sculpting
Depth	sets the depth of a bevel or pattern
Distance	specifies the offset distance for a shadow or satin effect
Fill Type	sets the content of a stroke
Global Light	allows you to set an angle to simulate the direction of the light
Gloss Contour	creates a glossy, metallic appearance on a bevel or emboss effect
Gradient	indicates the gradient of a layer effect
Highlight or Shadow Mode	specifies the blending mode of a bevel or emboss highlight or shadow
Jitter	varies the color and opacity of a gradient
Layer Knocks Out Drop Shadow	controls the drop shadow's visibility in a semitransparent layer
Noise	assigns the number of random elements in the opacity of a glow or shadow
Opacity	sets the opacity or transparency
Pattern	specifies the pattern
Position	sets the position of a stroke
Range	controls which portion or range of the glow is targeted for the contour
Size	specifies the amount of blur or the size of the shadow
Soften	blurs the results of shading to reduce unwanted artifacts
Source	specifies the source for an inner glow
Style	specifies the style of a bevel or emboss

BTW

The Angle Radius Icon
In the Layer Style dialog box, the Angle setting adjusts the direction of the layer style on a 360-degree scale: 180 degrees both clockwise and counterclockwise. In addition to entering a degree setting, the Angle radius icon (Figure 3–68) allows you to drag to the desired direction.

When a layer has a style applied to it, an fx icon appears to the right of the layer's name on the Layers panel. You can expand the icon on the Layers panel to view all of the applied effects and edit them when changing the style.

As you can tell from Table 3–3 and Table 3–4, there are a large number of layer styles and settings in Photoshop. As you use them, many of these settings will be explained in future chapters.

To Add a Layer Style

The following steps add a layer style to the ivy. You will create an inner bevel to give the ivy more depth.

1

- On the Layers panel, select the ivy layer.

- Zoom to 100% magnification.

- Click the 'Add a layer style' button (shown in Figure 3–66 on page PS 187) on the Layers panel status bar to display the menu (Figure 3–67).

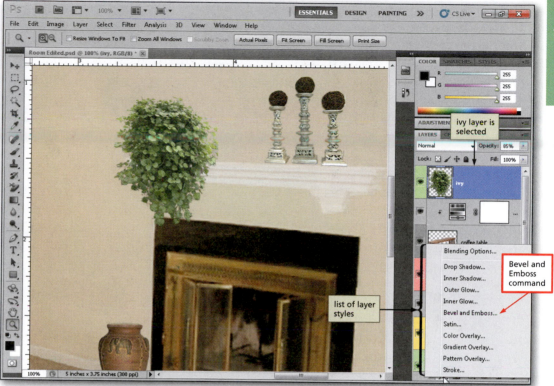

Figure 3–67

2

- Click Bevel and Emboss to display the Layer Style dialog box. If necessary, drag the title bar of the dialog box to the right, so the ivy is visible.

- In the Layer Style dialog box, enter 50 in the Depth box to decrease the strength of the shading.

- Enter 10 in the Size box and 5 in the Soften box to edit the bevel (Figure 3–68).

3

- Click the OK button to close the Layer Style dialog box.

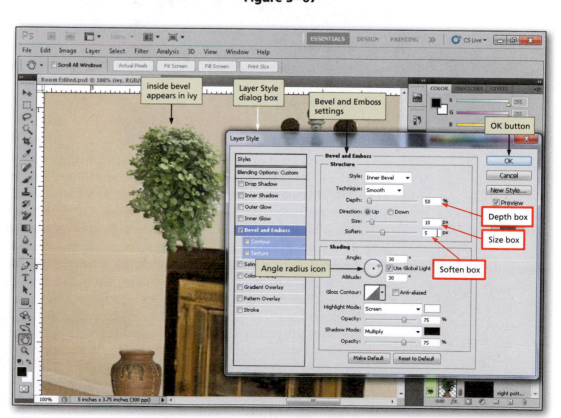

Figure 3–68

To Hide Layer Effects on the Layers Panel

The following step uses the 'Reveal layer effects in the panel' button to hide the effects on the Layers panel.

• On the Layers panel, in the ivy layer, click the 'Reveals layer effects in the panel' button to hide the added effects on the Layers panel (Figure 3–69).

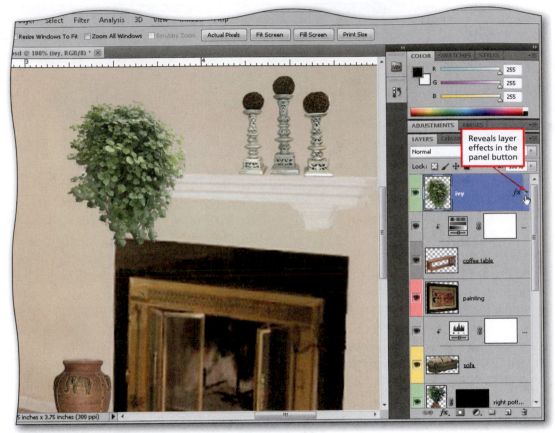

Figure 3–69

Other Ways

1. On Layer menu, point to Layer Style, click Bevel and Emboss, choose settings, click OK

The Clone Stamp Tool

The Clone Stamp Tool reproduces portions of an image, changing the pixels in a specific area. After clicking the Clone Stamp Tool button on the Tools panel, you press and hold ALT while clicking the portion of the picture that you wish to copy. Photoshop takes a **sample** of the image, remembering where you clicked. You then move the mouse pointer to the position where you wish to create the copy. As you drag with the brush, the image is applied. Each stroke of the tool paints on more of the sample. The Clone Stamp Tool is useful for duplicating specific parts of an object or correcting defects in an image. You can clone from image to image, or clone locations within the same document window.

The Clone Source panel (Figure 3–70) appears when you click Clone Source on the Window menu. The panel has options to rotate or scale the sample, or specify the size and orientation. The Clone Source panel makes it easy to create variegated patterns using multiple sources. You can create up to five different clone sources to select the one you need quickly, without re-sampling each time. For example, if you are using the Clone Stamp Tool to repair several minor imperfections in an old photo, you can select your various samples first, and then use the sources as needed. The Clone Source panel also helps you create unique clones positioned at different angles and perspectives from the original.

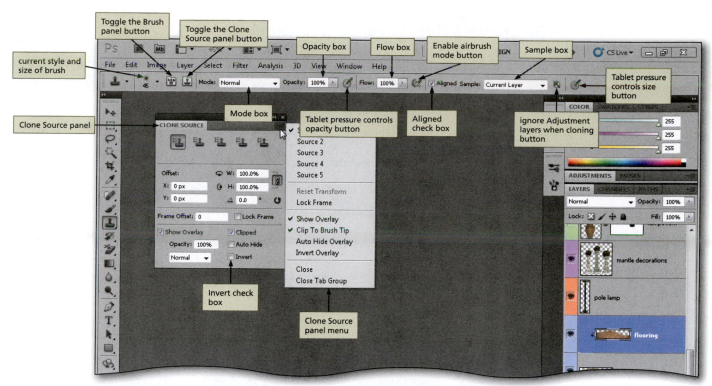

Figure 3–70

The Clone Stamp Tool options bar (Figure 3–70) displays some of the same settings that you used with layer masks, along with an Aligned check box and Sample box. When you align, the sample point is not reset if you start dragging in a new location; in other words, the sampling moves to a relative point in the original image. Otherwise, the sample point begins again as you start a new clone. The default value is to sample only the current layer or background. When you select All Layers in the Sample box, the clone displays all layers. One restriction when using the Clone Stamp Tool from one image to another is that both images have to be in the same color mode, such as RGB or CMYK. The color mode of an image appears on the document window tab. You will learn more about color modes in a later chapter.

On the Clone Stamp Tool context menu, a second kind of stamp, the Pattern Stamp Tool, allows you to paint with a pattern chosen from Photoshop's pattern library. A **pattern** is a repeated or tiled image, used to fill a layer or selection. On the Pattern Stamp Tool options bar, a Pattern Picker box arrow displays installed patterns. You can import additional patterns into the Pattern Picker box.

To Open the Flooring File and Arrange the Windows

To finish the composite image of the room, you will remove the carpet and add wood flooring to the room. The following steps open the Flooring file.

1 Open the Flooring file from the Chapter 03 folder of the Data Files for Students, or from a location specified by your instructor.

2 Arrange the windows so that windows appear one above the other and drag the border between the two document windows so more of the Room Edited window is displayed.

3 In the Room Edited window, select the carpeting layer and zoom to 45% magnification. Scroll to display the carpeting.

To Create a New Layer for the Clone

The following steps create a new flooring layer that clips to the carpeting layer.

1 ALT+click the visibility icon on the carpeting layer to display only the carpeting.

2 Press SHIFT+CTRL+N to display the New Layer dialog box.

3 Name the layer, flooring.

4 Click to display a check mark in the Use Previous Layer to Create Clipping Mask check box.

5 Choose a blue identification color. Do not change the mode or opacity (Figure 3–71).

6 Click the OK button to close the New Layer dialog box.

BTW

Deleting Layers
To delete a layer permanently, right-click the layer name and then click Delete Layer on the context menu, or activate the layer and press the DELETE key.

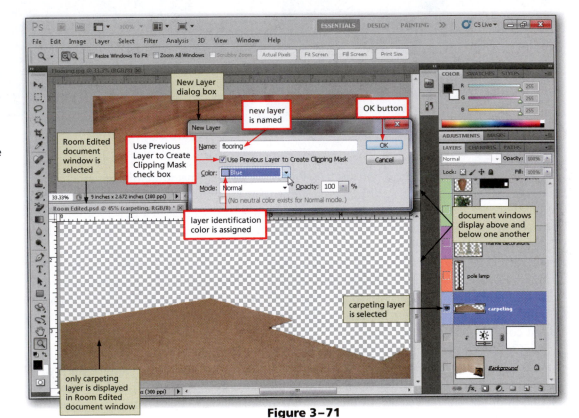

Figure 3–71

To Create a Clone

Using the Clone Stamp Tool, you will sample the Flooring image and then clone it to the carpeted area in the Room Edited image, as shown in the following steps.

As you clone the flooring, adjust the magnification of the image to view the corners and small areas clearly. If you make a mistake while cloning, press CTRL+Z to undo the most recent clone stroke or access the History panel and click a previous state. Then begin cloning again.

1

- Click the Flooring document window tab to make the window active.

- Click Window on the menu bar, and then click Clone Source to display the Clone Source panel.

- On the Clone Source panel, click the Invert box to remove its check mark, if necessary.

- On the Tools panel, right-click the Clone Stamp Tool button to display its context menu (Figure 3–72).

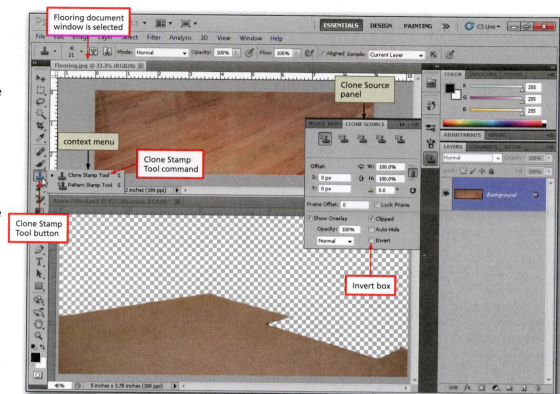

Figure 3–72

2

- Click Clone Stamp Tool on the context menu.

- On the options bar, click the Aligned check box so it displays a check mark, if necessary.

- Move the mouse pointer to the Flooring document window and ALT+click on the left edge of the flooring, approximately halfway down to sample the wood grain (Figure 3–73).

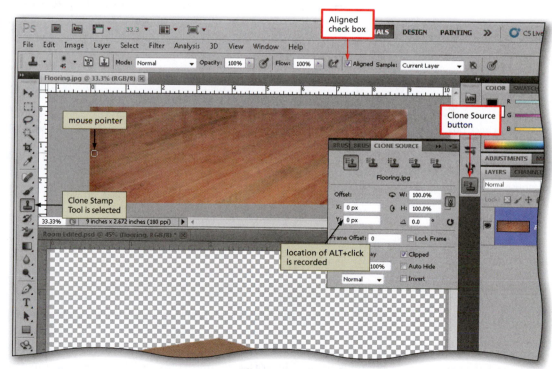

Figure 3–73

How do I know if I indicated the clone source correctly?

As you ALT+click, the Clone Stamp Tool displays a crosshair mouse pointer and the Clone Source panel displays the source of the clone.

3
- Click the Clone Source button in the vertical docking to collapse the panel.

- Click the Room Edited document window tab to make it active.

- With the flooring layer still selected, and the carpeting layer visible, move the mouse pointer into the document window.

- Working from left to right, drag to replace the carpeting. Zoom, scroll, and adjust the pointer size as necessary to fill in corners. Use short strokes, so if you make a mistake, you can press CTRL+Z to undo the error (Figure 3–74).

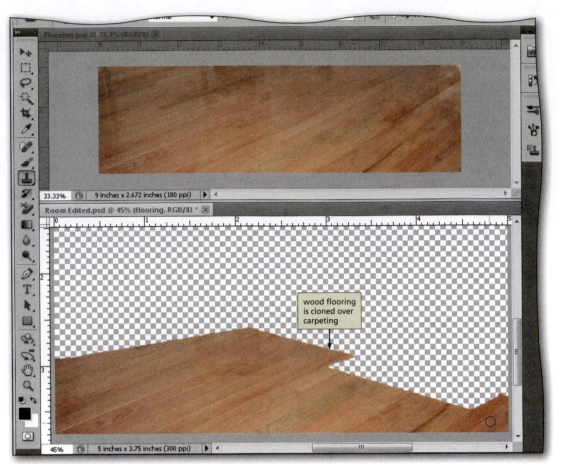

wood flooring is cloned over carpeting

Figure 3–74

Aligned Check Box
When checked, the Aligned check box allows you to use short strokes as you clone. The clone will not start over if you lift the mouse button to drag in another location. Aligning is helpful for cloning areas with a pattern.

To Close the Flooring Window

The following step closes the Flooring window and redisplays all the layers.

1 Close the Flooring document window. If Photoshop asks if you want to save changes to the document, click the No button.

2 Display all of the layers in the Room Edited document.

Flattening a Composite Image

Photoshop Help
The best way to become familiar with Photoshop Help is to use it. Appendix D includes detailed information about Photoshop Help and exercises that will help you gain confidence in using it.

When you **flatten** a composite image, Photoshop reduces the file size by merging all visible layers into the background, discarding hidden layers, and applying masks. A flattened file is easier to print, export, and display on the Web. It is a good practice, however, to save the layered version in PSD format before flattening in case you want to make further changes to the file. It is very important to remember that once a file is flattened and saved, no changes can be made to individual layers. If you flatten an image and then change your mind, if the file still is open, you can click the previous state on the History panel to restore all of the layers.

If you want to save each layer as a separate file, click File on the menu bar, point to Scripts, and then click Export Layers to Files. This script is useful if you think you might want to use your layers in other composite images.

The Layer menu has many of the same commands as the Layers panel menu. The choice of which to use is a matter of personal preference, and the location of your mouse pointer at the time. After saving the composite image, you will use the Layer menu to flatten the visible layers. Finally, you will save the flattened file in TIF format with the name, Room Complete.

To Save the Composite Image

The following steps save the Room Edited file with its layers.

1 With your USB flash drive connected to one of the computer's USB ports, click File on the menu bar and then click Save As.

2 When the Save As dialog box is displayed, type **Room Composite** in the File name text box. Do not press the ENTER key after typing the file name.

3 If necessary, click the Format box arrow and then choose Photoshop (*.PSD, *.PDD) in the list.

4 If necessary, click the Save in box arrow and then click UDISK 2.0 (F:), or the location associated with your USB flash drive, in the list.

5 Click the Save button in the Save As dialog box. If Photoshop displays an options dialog box, click the OK button.

BTW

Quick Reference
For a table that lists how to complete the tasks covered in this book using the mouse, context menu, and keyboard, see the Quick Reference Summary at the back of this book or visit the Photoshop CS5 Quick Reference Web page (scsite.com/pscs5/qr).

To Flatten a Composite Image

The following steps use the Layer menu to flatten the composite image.

1

• Click Layer on the menu bar to display the Layer menu (Figure 3–75).

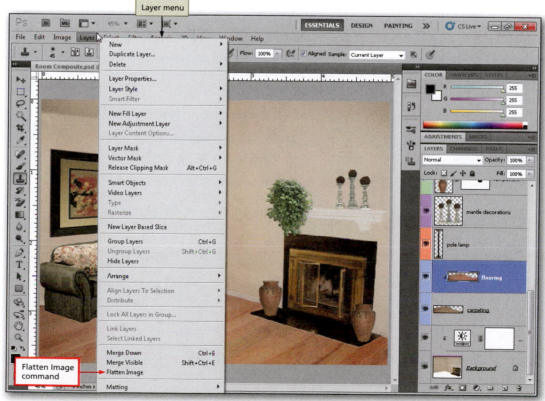

Figure 3–75

2

● Click Flatten Image on the Layer menu to flatten the layers. If Photoshop displays a confirmation dialog box, click the Yes button (Figure 3–76).

Q&A

What is the difference between flatten and merge?

The Merge command flattens specific layers together. The Flatten command uses all of the layers and merges into a Background layer.

Other Ways

1. Right-click any layer, click Flatten Image
2. Click Layers panel menu button, click Flatten Image

image appears without layers

Figure 3–76

To Save a File in the TIFF Format

The following steps save the flattened image as a TIFF file.

1 With your USB flash drive connected to one of the computer's USB ports, click File on the menu bar and then click Save As.

2 When the Save As dialog box is displayed, type `Room TIFF` in the File name text box. Do not press the ENTER key after typing the file name.

3 Click the Format box arrow and then click TIFF (*.TIF, *.TIFF) in the list.

4 Click the Save in box arrow and then click UDISK 2.0 (F:), or the location associated with your USB flash drive, in the list.

5 Click the Save button in the Save As dialog box.

6 When Photoshop displays the TIFF Options dialog box, click the OK button to finish saving the file.

To Quit Photoshop

The final step quits Photoshop.

1 Click the Close button on the right side of the Photoshop title bar. If Photoshop displays a dialog box, click the No button to ignore the changes since the last time you saved the photo.

Chapter Summary

In virtually decorating a room, you gained a broad knowledge of Photoshop's layering capabilities. First, you were introduced to the concept of layers. You created a layer via cut, a layer from another image, and a layer from a selection, using the Layers panel to set options, select, rename, color, view, and hide layers. Then you used the eraser tools to erase unneeded portions of the layer. You learned how to hide portions of layers and fine-tuned layers with layer masks, adjustments, and styles. Finally, you used the Clone Stamp Tool to add wood flooring into the composite image. The file was flattened and saved in the TIF format.

The items listed below include all the new Photoshop skills you have learned in this chapter:

1. Change Layers Panel Options (PS 145)
2. Create a Layer Via Cut (PS 147)
3. Name and Color a Layer (PS 148)
4. Hide and Show a Layer (PS 149)
5. Arrange the Document Windows (PS 152)
6. Create a Layer by Dragging an Entire Image (PS 153)
7. Position a Layer (PS 154)
8. Set Layer Properties Using the Context Menu (PS 154)
9. Create a Layer by Dragging a Selection (PS 157)
10. Erase Using the Magic Eraser Tool (PS 161)
11. Display Only the Current Layer (PS 163)
12. Erase Using the Eraser Tool (PS 164)
13. Erase Using the Block Mouse Pointer (PS 165)
14. Erase Using the Background Eraser Tool (PS 168)
15. Rearrange Layers (PS 171)
16. Consolidate Windows (PS 173)
17. Create a Layer Mask (PS 174)
18. Correct a Masking Error (PS 176)
19. Display the Masks Panel (PS 178)
20. Use the Masks Panel (PS 179)
21. Make an Opacity Change to a Layer (PS 180)
22. Display the Adjustments Panel (PS 183)
23. Make a Levels Adjustment (PS 183)
24. Adjust the Hue and Saturation (PS 185)
25. Adjust the Brightness and Contrast (PS 185)
26. View Adjustment Layers (PS 187)
27. Add a Layer Style (PS 189)
28. Hide Layer Effects on the Layers Panel (PS 190)
29. Create a Clone (PS 192)
30. Flatten a Composite Image (PS 195)

Learn It Online

Test your knowledge of chapter content and key terms.

Instructions: To complete the Learn It Online exercises, start your browser, click the Address bar, and then enter the Web address `scsite.com/pscs5/learn`. When the Photoshop CS5 Learn It Online page is displayed, click the link for the exercise you want to complete and then read the instructions.

Chapter Reinforcement TF, MC, and SA
A series of true/false, multiple choice, and short answer questions that tests your knowledge of the chapter content.

Flash Cards
An interactive learning environment where you identify chapter key terms associated with displayed definitions.

Practice Test
A series of multiple choice questions that test your knowledge of chapter content and key terms.

Who Wants To Be a Computer Genius?
An interactive game that challenges your knowledge of chapter content in the style of a television quiz show.

Wheel of Terms
An interactive game that challenges your knowledge of chapter key terms in the style of the television show *Wheel of Fortune*.

Crossword Puzzle Challenge
A crossword puzzle that challenges your knowledge of key terms presented in the chapter.

Apply Your Knowledge

Reinforce the skills and apply the concepts you learned in this chapter.

Creating Layers in a Poster

Instructions: Start Photoshop and perform the customization steps found on pages PS 6 through PS 9. Open the Apply 3-1 Storage History file from the Chapter 03 folder of the Data Files for Students. You can access the Data Files for Students on the CD that accompanies this book. See the inside back cover of this book for instructions on downloading the Data Files for Students, or contact your instructor for information about accessing the required files.

The purpose of this exercise is to create a composite poster showing the history of external storage devices by creating layers. The edited photo is displayed in Figure 3–77.

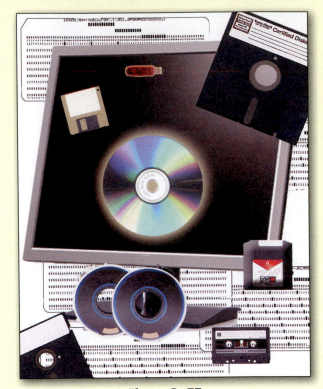

Figure 3–77

Perform the following tasks:

1. Press SHIFT+CTRL+S to open the Save As dialog box. Enter the name, **Apply 3-1 Storage History Composite**. Do not press the ENTER key. Click the Format box arrow and then select the Photoshop PSD format, if necessary. Click the Save in box arrow and then select your USB flash drive location. Click the Save button to save the file in the PSD format. Table 3–5 lists the other files, layer names, identification colors, and manipulations that you will use in this assignment.

Table 3–5 Storage Device Layers

File Name	Layer Name	Layer Color	Layer Manipulations
Apply 3-1 CD	CD	Violet	Layer Style | Outer Glow
Apply 3-1 Flash Drive	flash drive	Green	Layer Style | Inner Glow Mask lid
Apply 3-1 Zip Disk	zip disk	Orange	Layer Style | Bevel and Emboss
Apply 3-1 Tape	tape	Yellow	Adjustments | Hue 10, −10, 0
Apply 3-1 Cassette Tape	cassette tape	Yellow	Adjustments | Brightness/Contrast
Apply 3-1 Small Floppy	small floppy	Blue	erase background and rotate
Apply 3-1 Medium Floppy	medium floppy	Blue	erase background and rotate
Apply 3-1 Large Floppy	large floppy	Blue	erase background and rotate
Apply 3-1 Punched Card	punched card	Red	clone

2. To create the CD layer:

   a. Press CTRL+O to display the Open dialog box. Navigate to the Data Files for Students and then double-click the file named Apply 3-1 CD to open it.

   b. On the Photoshop Application bar, click the Arrange Documents button and click the first 2 Up button to arrange the document windows side by side.

   c. Press V to activate the Move Tool. Drag the image from the Apply 3-1 CD document window into the Apply 3-1 Storage History Composite document window. Close the Apply 3-1 CD file.

   d. Name and color the layer as directed in Table 3 – 5.

   e. Click the 'Add a layer style' button on the Layers panel status bar, and then click Outer Glow. Change the Opacity to **75%** and the Size to **150 px**. Use the default values for all other settings.

3. To create the flash drive layer:

   a. Press CTRL+O to display the Open dialog box. Navigate to the Data Files for Students and then open the file named Apply 3-1 Flash Drive.

   b. On the Photoshop Application bar, click the Arrange Documents button and click the second 2 Up button to arrange the document windows one above the other.

   c. Drag the flash drive image into the Apply 3-1 Storage History Composite document window. Close the Apply 3-1 Flash Drive file.

   d. Name and color the layer as directed in Table 3 – 5.

   e. Click the 'Add a layer style' button on the Layers panel status bar, and then click Inner Glow. Change the Opacity to **75%** and the Size to **25 px**. Use the default values for all other settings.

   f. Resize the flash drive and position it as shown in Figure 3 – 77.

   g. Click the 'Add layer mask' button. If black is not the foreground color, press the X key to exchange colors. Press the B key to access the brush and then paint over the flash drive cover to mask it.

4. To create the zip disk layer:

   a. Open the file, Apply 3-1 Zip Disk.

   b. Arrange the document windows side by side.

   c. Drag the image from the new window into the Apply 3-1 Storage History Composite document window. Close the Apply 3-1 Zip Disk file.

   d. Name and color the layer.

   e. Click the 'Add a layer style' button on the Layers panel status bar, and then click Bevel and Emboss. Click the Style box arrow and then click Inner Bevel, if necessary. Change the Size to **90 px**. Use the default values for all other settings.

   f. Position the casette tape image layer as shown in Figure 3 – 77.

5. To create the tape layer:

   a. Open the file, Apply 3-1 Tape. Select all of the image and copy.

   b. Paste the image into the Apply 3-1 Storage History Composite document window. Close the Apply 3-1 Tape file.

   c. Name and color the layer.

   d. Click Window on the menu bar and then click Adjustments to display the Adjustments panel. Click the Hue/Saturation icon to display the settings. On the panel's status bar, click the Clip to Layer button. Adjust the Hue to **10**, the Saturation to **−10** and the Lightness to **0**. Click the 'Return to adjustment list' button to redisplay the Adjustments panel.

   e. Scale and position the tape image layer as necessary.

Continued >

Apply Your Knowledge *continued*

6. To create the cassette tape layer:

   a. Open the file, Apply 3-1 Cassette Tape.

   b. Arrange the document windows and drag the image from the new window into the Apply 3-1 Storage History Composite document window. Close the Apply 3-1 Cassette Tape file.

   c. Name and color the layer.

   d. On the Adjustments panel, click the Brightness/Contrast icon and then click the Clip to Layer button. Adjust the Brightness to 35. Click the 'Return to adjustment list' button to display the Adjustments panel.

   e. Click the Adjustments button in the vertical docking to collapse the Adjustments panel.

   f. Position the layer to match Figure 3–77.

7. To create the floppy disk layers.

   a. One at a time, open each of the floppy disk files listed in Table 3–5.

   b. Copy and paste the image into the Apply 3-1 Storage History Composite document window.

   c. Name and color each layer.

   d. Use the eraser tools to erase extraneous background.

   e. Scale, position and rotate the images as shown in Figure 3–77.

8. To clone the punched card:

   a. Select the Background layer. Create a new layer by pressing CTRL+SHIFT+N. Name the layer, punched card. Do not check the Use Previous Layer to Create Clipping Mask check box. Choose a red identification color. Do not change the mode or opacity. Click the OK button to close the New Layer dialog box. Press CTRL+LEFT BRACKET ([) to move the punched card layer below the Background layer. ALT+click the visibility icon on the punched card layer to display only that layer.

   b. Open the file, Apply 3-1 Punched Card.

   c. Arrange the document windows above and below one another.

   d. Press the s key to activate the Clone Stamp Tool. On the options bar, click to display the Aligned check mark, if necessary.

   e. ALT+click in the punched card document window, close to the top-left corner.

   f. Drag in the Apply 3-1 Storage History Composite document window to create a clone.

   g. Repeat Steps e and f to create four more clones at various locations in the window. (*Hint:* in this montage, it is ok for part of a cloned image to run off the edge of the document window.)

9. Close the Apply 3-1 Punched Card window.

10. On the Layers panel of the Apply 3-1 Storage History Composite window, click the 'Indicates layer visibility' button beside each layer to display the layers.

11. Save the file again by pressing CTRL+S.

12. On the Layers panel, click the Layers panel menu button to display the menu. Click Flatten Image on the menu to flatten all of the layers.

13. Press SHIFT+CTRL+S to open the Save As dialog box. Type **Apply 3-1 Storage History Complete** in the Name box. Click the Format box arrow and then click TIFF in the list. Click the Save button. If Photoshop displays a dialog box, click the OK button.

14. Turn in a hard copy of the project to your instructor.

15. Quit Photoshop.

Extend Your Knowledge

Extend the skills you learned in this chapter and experiment with new skills. You may need to use Help to complete the assignment.

Instructions: Start Photoshop. Set the default workspace, default colors, and reset all tools. Open the file Extend 3-1 Marketing Graphic from the Chapter 03 folder of the Data Files for Students. You can access the Data Files for Students on the CD that accompanies this book. See the inside back cover of this book for instructions on downloading the Data Files for Students, or contact your instructor for information about accessing the required files.

The purpose of this exercise to create layer comps for client evaluation. The current graphic has layers for the background, inside, and outside of the box. You are to insert the trophy graphic and scale it to fit the box. Then create layer comps showing the inside and the outside. The edited photo is shown in Figure 3–78.

Perform the following tasks:

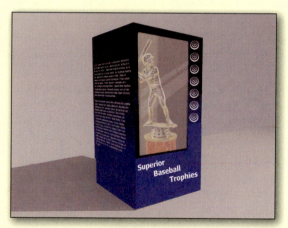

Figure 3–78

1. Save the file with the name, Extend 3-1 Marketing Graphic Composite. If necessary, click the Format box arrow and click Photoshop in the list. Browse to your USB flash drive storage device. Click the Save button. If Photoshop displays a Format Options dialog box, click the OK button.

2. Show and hide the various layers using the visibility icon to gain familiarity with the graphic.

3. Make the Background layer and inside layer visible; hide all other layers. Select the inside layer.

4. Open the file Extend 3-1 Trophy from the Chapter 03 folder of the Data Files for Students. Use the Arrange Documents button to display the windows side by side.

5. Use the Move Tool to drag the trophy from its own window into the Extend 3-1 Marketing Graphic Composite document window. Scale the trophy to fit in the box. Make the outside layer visible and make sure the trophy can be seen through the opening in the outer box. Name the layer, trophy.

6. Make the front panel layer visible and select it. Adjust the Opacity setting so the layer looks more transparent, as if it were plastic.

7. Make the gleam layer visible. Adjust the Opacity and Fill settings as necessary. Save the file.

8. Use Help to learn about Layer Comps. Also read the BTW boxes on pages PS 144 and PS 145. Open the Layer Comps panel and create the layer comps described in Table 3–6.

Table 3–6 Marketing Graphic Layer Comps	
Layer Comp Name	**Visible Layers**
Empty Box	Background, inside
Inner Box with Trophy	Background, inside, trophy
Outer Box with Trophy	Background, inside, trophy, outside, shadow
Complete Graphic	All layers

Continued >

Extend Your Knowledge *continued*

9. Save the file again.

10. For extra credit, copy the trophy layer and scale it to approximately 30 percent of its original size. In the Layers panel, move the layer above the outside layer. Position the trophy in the lower-middle portion of the box. Warp the layer to make it wrap around the corner of the box. Create a layer comp named Complete with Wrapped Logo and include all layers.

11. Submit this assignment in the format specified by your instructor.

Make It Right

Analyze a project and correct all errors and/or improve the design.

Instructions: Start Photoshop and perform the customization steps found on pages PS 6 through PS 9. Open the Make It Right 3-1 Desert file from the Chapter 03 folder of the Data Files for Students. You can access the Data Files for Students on the CD that accompanies this book. See the inside back cover of this book for instructions on downloading the Data Files for Students, or contact your instructor for information about accessing the required files.

The photo has layers that are invisible, layers that need transformation, and layers that need to be moved, trimmed, and adjusted for levels (Figure 3–79).

Save the file on your storage device in the PSD format with the name, Make It Right 3-1 Desert Composite. For each invisible layer, reveal the layer, correct any order problem by dragging the layer to an appropriate position on the Layers panel, erase or mask parts of the layer as necessary, and move the layer to a logical position.

Use the Adjustments panel and tools such as Levels, Brightness/Contrast, and Hue/Saturation to create adjustment layers. (*Hint:* Do not forget to click the Clip to Layer button on the Adjustments panel status bar, so the adjustment will apply to that layer only.) Make any other adjustments or layer style changes as you deem necessary. Save the file again and submit it in the format specified by your instructor.

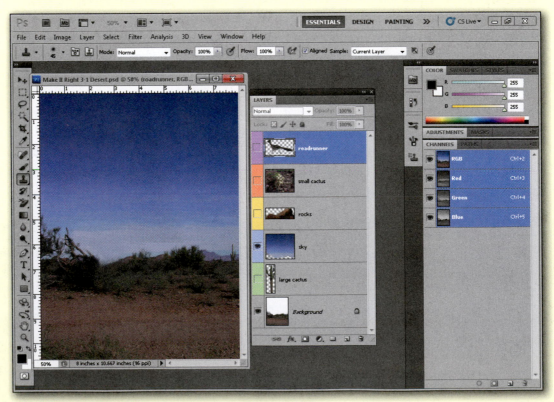

Figure 3–79

In the Lab

Design and/or create a project using the guidelines, concepts, and skills presented in this chapter. Labs are listed in order of increasing difficulty.

Lab 1: Making Level Adjustments Using Masks

Problem: A local tourist company has hired you to create its latest brochure about historic homes. You encounter a photo that is too dark to use in the brochure. You decide to try adjusting the levels to lighten the steps, grass, and shrubs in the photo and prepare it for print in the brochure. The edited photo is shown in Figure 3–80.

Instructions: Perform the following tasks:

1. Start Photoshop. Set the default work-space, default colors, and reset all tools.

2. Open the file Lab 3-1 Historic Home from the Chapter 03 folder of the Data Files for Students. You can access the Data Files for Students on the CD that accompanies this book. See the inside back cover of this book for instructions on downloading the Data Files for Students, or contact your instructor for information about accessing the required files.

Figure 3–80

3. Click the Save As command on the File menu. Type **Lab 3-1 Historic Home Composite** as the file name. Click the Format box arrow and click Photoshop in the list. Browse to your USB flash drive storage device. Click the Save button. If Photoshop displays a Format Options dialog box, click the OK button.

4. On the Tools panel, select the Quick Selection Tool. Drag very slowly to select only the house, sky, clouds, and trees. Do not include the shrubs, grounds, or steps in the selection. If necessary, use the marquee or lasso tools, adding or subtracting to the selection as necessary.

5. Click Select on the menu bar and then click Inverse to select the inverse of the house, trees, and sky, which would be the steps, shrubs, and grounds.

6. Click Layer on the menu bar, point to New, and then click Layer via Cut.

7. On the Layers panel, rename the layer, grounds. Use a green identification color.

8. With the layer selected, open the Adjustments panel and click the Levels icon. On the panel's status bar, click the Clip to Layer button. In the Input Levels area, drag the white slider to the left until the grounds are lighter and the features easily discerned.

9. Press CTRL+S to save the photo again. If Photoshop displays the Photoshop Format Options dialog box, click the OK button.

10. Flatten the image.

11. Press SHIFT+CTRL+S to access the Save As dialog box. Choose the TIFF format and name the file Lab 3-1 Historic Home Complete. If Photoshop displays a warning dialog box about layers, click the OK button.

12. Print a copy and turn it in to your instructor.

In the Lab

Lab 2: Creating a Toy Company Advertisement

Problem: You are to create a composite photo for a toy company, adding and adjusting layers, as shown in Figure 3–81.

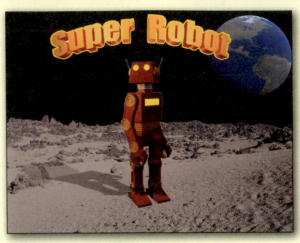

Figure 3–81

Instructions: Perform the following tasks:

1. Start Photoshop and reset the workspace, default colors, and all tools.

2. Open the Lab 3-2 Robot Background file from the Chapter 03 folder of the Data Files for Students and save it as Lab 3-2 Robot Composite. You can access the Data Files for Students on the CD that accompanies this book. See the inside back cover of this book for instructions on downloading the Data Files for Students, or contact your instructor for information about accessing the required files.

3. To clone over the shadow on the right side of the image:

   a. Select the Clone Stamp Tool. On the options bar, click the Aligned check box so it does not display a check mark.

   b. ALT+click the ground approximately one inch below the shadow to create the sample for the clone. Drag over the shadowed area, including any rocks, to create a cloned area and hide the shadow. (*Hint:* Use the left and right bracket keys to adjust the size of the mouse pointer as needed.)

4. To create a sky layer:

   a. Use the Magic Wand Tool and the 'Add to selection' button to select all of the sky.

   b. On the Layer menu, point to New, and then click Layer via Cut.

   c. On the Layers panel, double-click the layer name and type **sky** to rename the layer. Right-click the visibility icon and choose Blue in the list.

5. To add the robot body:

   a. Open the Lab 3-2 Robot Body file from the Chapter 03 folder of the Data Files for Students.

   b. On the Application bar, use the Arrange Documents button to display the windows side by side.

   c. Use the Move Tool to drag the robot body from the Lab 3-2 Robot Body document window to the Lab 3-2 Robot Composite document window. (Hint: Holding down the shift key as you drag automatically centers the image and creates a new layer.) After creating the layer, close the Lab 3-2 Robot Body document window.

   d. Name the layer, robot, and use a violet identification color.

6. Repeat Step 5 to add the shadow graphic using the file, Lab 3-2 Robot Shadow file. Position it behind the robot near the feet, as shown in Figure 3–81. Name the layer, shadow, and use a gray identification color. Close the Lab 3-2 Robot Shadow document window.

7. To move the layer behind the robot, on the Layers panel, drag the shadow layer just below the robot layer.

8. Repeat Step 3 to add the earth graphic using the file, Lab 3-2 Robot Earth file. Position it in the upper-right corner of the scene. Name the layer, earth, and use a green identification color.

9. Repeat Step 3 to add the title graphic using the file, Lab 3-2 Robot Title file. Position the words centered above the robot's head. Name the layer, title, and use a yellow identification color.

10. To create an adjustment layer and make the background appear more like a moonscape:

   a. On the Layers panel, select the Background layer.

   b. Open the Adjustments panel.

   c. Click the Hue/Saturation button to display the settings.

   d. On the Adjustments panel status bar, click the Clip to Layer button to create a new adjustment layer for the background.

   e. Change the Hue to +20 and the Saturation to –80.

   f. On the status bar, click the 'Return to adjustment list' button.

11. To create an adjustment layer and make the sky layer appear black:

   a. Select the sky layer.

   b. On the Adjustments panel, click the Brightness/Contrast button to display the controls, and then click the Clip to Layer button. Click the Use Legacy check box to select it.

   c. Drag both the Brightness and Contrast sliders to the left to create a black sky.

   d. On the Adjustments panel status bar, click the 'Return to adjustment list' button.

12. To add a layer effect to the title layer:

   a. Select the title layer.

   b. Click the 'Add a layer style' button on the Layers panel status bar, and then click Stroke to open the Layer style dialog box. (*Hint:* You may want to read about the Stroke command in Photoshop Help.) Drag the Layer Style dialog box title bar so you can view the robot and the dialog box.

   c. In the Layer Style dialog box, click the Color box to display the Select stroke color dialog box. Drag the Select stroke color dialog box title bar so you can view the robot and the dialog box, if necessary.

   d. Click one of the yellow eyes on the robot to select the yellow color. (*Hint:* The mouse pointer looks like an eyedropper when selecting a color.)

   e. Click the OK button to close the Select stroke color dialog box and then click the OK button to close the Layer Style dialog box.

13. Save the composite file again with all the layers.

14. Flatten the image.

15. Press SHIFT+CTRL+S to open the Save As dialog box. Type **Lab 3-2 Robot Complete** in the Name box. Click the Format box arrow and then click TIFF in the list. Click the Save button. If Photoshop displays a dialog box, click the OK button.

16. Quit Photoshop.

In the Lab

Lab 3: Creating a Contest Entry with Layers

Problem: You would like to enter your hamster in a creative pet photo contest. You decide to use Photoshop's layering capabilities to dress up your hamster as shown in Figure 3–82.

Figure 3–82

Instructions: Perform the following tasks:

1. Start Photoshop. Set the default workspace, default colors, and reset all tools.

2. Open the file Lab 3-3 Hamster from the Chapter 03 folder of the Data Files for Students. You can access the Data Files for Students on the CD that accompanies this book. See the inside back cover of this book for instructions on downloading the Data Files for Students, or contact your instructor for information about accessing the required files. Rename the file, Lab 3-3 Hamster Composite and save it as a PSD file on your storage device.

3. Using the file Lab 3-3 Pipe, create a new layer by dragging from one window to another. Edit the layer to remove the background and then scale and position the layer as shown in Figure 3–82. Repeat the process using the file Lab 3-3 Magnifying Glass file. Finally, use the file Lab 3-3 Hat to create a hat layer. Select the right third (back) of the hat and create a new layer via cut. Move the new layer, below the hamster layer, so that part of the hat appears behind the hamster's ear. Set layer properties to name and color each layer as desired.

4. Make any other adjustments to the layers that you feel would enhance the photo. When you are satisfied with your layers, save the image again. Flatten the image, save it as a TIFF file, named Lab 3-3 Hamster Complete, and then submit a copy to your instructor.

Cases and Places

Apply your creative thinking and problem-solving skills to design and implement a solution.

1: Cloning within the Same Document

Academic

Earlier in this chapter, a suggestion was made to create a flag with 50 percent opacity superimposed over a memorial. Open the files named Case 3-1 Memorial and Case 3-1 Flag, located in the Chapter 03 folder of the Data Files for Students. (Alternatively, locate or take a photo of a memorial in your city or a building on your campus. If necessary, obtain permission to use a digital photo or scan the image.) Arrange the windows. Select only the flag and then drag it as a new layer into the memorial photo. Resize the layer to fit across the memorial. Change the opacity to 40 percent. Make other corrections as necessary. Save the composite photo and print a copy.

2: Creating a Graphic with Opacity Changes

Personal

You recently took a photo of a deer at the local forest preserve. To make the picture more interesting, you decide to create a layer and clone the deer. Open the photo named Case 3-2 Deer, located in the Chapter 03 folder of the Data Files for Students. Click the Layer command on the menu bar, point to New, and then click Layer. Name the layer, deer. Click the Background layer, choose the Clone Stamp Tool, and take a sample of the middle of the deer. Click the new layer and clone the deer. On the Edit menu, click Free Transform and resize the cloned deer so it appears to be farther away. Flip the clone horizontally. Rename the file and save it in the TIF format on your storage device.

3: Creating a Greeting Card Graphic with Masking

Professional

You have been hired as an intern with a greeting card company. You were given several photos to use in preparing holiday cards. The photo named, Case 3-3 Santa Scene, is located in the Chapter 03 folder of the Data Files for Students. You want to use the figure of Santa Claus only, on the front of a card. Rename and save the photo in the PSD format on your USB flash drive storage device. Create a rectangular marquee selection around the figure. Use the Layer via Cut command and name the new layer, Santa. Hide the background. Create a layer mask, painting with black to display only the figure. Print with the background hidden.

4 | Drawing and Painting with Color

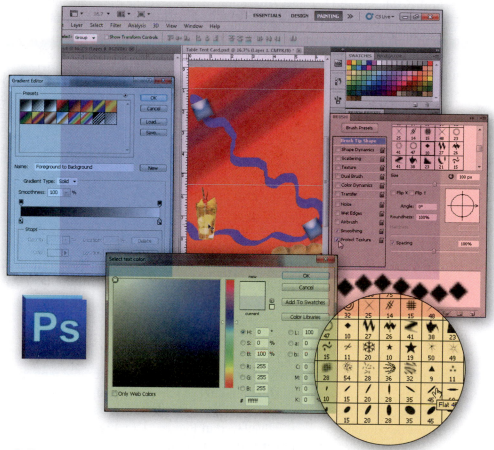

Objectives

You will have mastered the material in this chapter when you can:

- Create a Photoshop document from scratch using the Painting workspace
- Differentiate between color modes
- Apply gradients using the Gradient Tool
- Select colors using the Swatches panel
- Paint and draw using Photoshop brushes
- Adjust the hardness and diameter settings of brushes

- Load new brushes in the Brush panel
- Use the Brush Preset picker
- Differentiate among the shape tools, modes, and settings
- Create a custom shape
- Sample colors with the Eyedropper Tool
- Create text with the type tools
- Stroke text
- Rotate the canvas

4 | Drawing and Painting with Color

Introduction

In both academic and business environments, you will be called upon to create graphics from scratch using the tools and techniques available in Photoshop. While many sources of graphics, such as clip art and stock photos, are widely available, some are copyrighted, rights-controlled, or expensive to buy. Others have to be edited so extensively that it might be easier to start from scratch. Still others simply do not fit the particular circumstances for the required project. By creating an original graphic, you solve many of the problems that result when attempting to use ready-made images. If you have good artistic and drawing skills, and an input device such as a graphics tablet, the kinds of graphics you can create are unlimited.

Another way to design graphics is to start from scratch and add images that are digital photographs or scans. That way, your image has the best of both worlds — incorporating the texture and lines of drawing with the realism of actual photographs. In Photoshop, working from scratch to create an image or illustration is better when the subject is conceptual, imaginative, less formal, or open to interpretation. Beginning with a digital photo is better when the subject is living, tangible, for sale, or more formal; photography does not risk loss of meaning through interpretation. Regardless of the approach you choose, you need to know how to use the drawing and painting tools in Photoshop.

Project — Table Tent Card

Chapter 4 uses Photoshop to create a graphic for a restaurant table tent card. It constructs the gradient, text, shapes, and ribbon from scratch, while using the images of real food and drink to add a sense of reality and detail. The graphic advertises party trays and restaurant items. The completed image is displayed in Figure 4–1a. Figures 4–1b and 4–1c display the front and back of the tent card after it is folded.

(a) Tent Card Graphic

(b) Front of Folded Tent Card

(c) Back of Folded Tent Card

Figure 4–1

Overview

As you read this chapter, you will learn how to create the composite image shown in Figure 4–1 by performing these general tasks:

- Create a new file, starting with a blank canvas.
- Apply a gradient background.
- Choose colors using a variety of tools and dialog boxes.
- Use brushes to draw lines, shapes, and strokes.
- Create a realistic-looking graphic using shapes.
- Insert real images combined with drawn images.
- Create a stroke layer.

General Project Guidelines

When editing a photo, the actions you perform and decisions you make will affect the appearance and characteristics of the finished product. As you create a graphic such as the one shown in Figure 4–1 on the previous page, you should follow these general guidelines:

1. **Plan your layout and gather necessary photos.** As you plan your layout of original graphics, create the storyboard and the graphic from the back to the front. Decide on the background first, then layers, followed by foreground objects or text. The graphics you choose should convey the overall message, incorporating high-quality photos with similar lighting characteristics. Keep in mind the customer requirements. For professional-looking graphics, adhere to the general principles of alignment, contrast, repetition, and proximity.

2. **Choose colors purposefully.** Consider the cost of full color printing, paper, shelf life, and customer requirements when choosing your colors. Try to repeat colors that already exist in incorporated images. Some clients already may have colors that help brand their publications. Consult with the client and print shops for the correct color numbers and the plan for printing. Unless you want a rainbow special effect, limit your colors to two or three on a contrasting background.

3. **Design your brush strokes.** Photoshop brushes imitate the actions of artistic paintbrushes. By varying the settings, such as tip shape, hardness, and so on, you can add imaginative strokes to your work.

4. **Use predefined shapes for tangible objects.** Use shapes rather than freehand drawings when you are trying to create a graphic that represents a tangible object. Shapes allow you to maintain straight lines, even corners, constrained proportions, and even curves. Except when intentionally creating a randomized pattern, try to align shapes with something else in the graphic, or parallel to the edge of the publication.

5. **Apply effective text styles and strokes.** It is common to use text to educate and inform, but text often becomes a creative element itself in the design. The first rule of text is to choose a font that is easy to read. No matter how creative the font style is, if the customer cannot make out the words, the message fails. Avoid using more than two different fonts on the same page or graphic. As a second font, use either the same font at a different size, or a highly contrasting font. Keep similar text components in proximity of each other. For example, do not split the address, phone number, and Web page address onto different parts of the page. Use a stroke of color around the text for a more distinctive look that stands out.

When necessary, more specific details concerning the above guidelines are presented at appropriate points in the chapter. The chapter also will identify the actions performed and decisions made regarding these guidelines during the creation of the edited photo shown in Figure 4–1.

BTW

Color Modes and File Size
Because there are four colors involved in CMYK images, instead of three as in RGB images, CMYK images use 33% more file space than RGB images.

BTW

Converting Between Modes
In Photoshop, you easily can convert from one color mode to another using the Mode command on the Image menu. As you choose a new color mode, Photoshop will inform you of any problems converting the image.

Creating a New File

In this chapter, you will create a new Photoshop document starting with a blank canvas. Photoshop allows you to customize the attributes of file name, image size, resolution, color mode, and background when creating a new document image. Alternatively, Photoshop provides several groups of attributes that are preset. The new image size can be set in pixels, inches, or centimeters, among others. You can set the width and height independently. When setting the resolution of an image, you specify the number of **pixels per inch (ppi)**, or **pixels per centimeter**, on the printed page.

A **color mode**, or **color method**, determines the number of colors and combinations of colors used to display and print the image. Each color mode uses a numerical method called a **color model**, or **color space**, to describe the color. Photoshop bases its color modes on the color models that are commonly useful when publishing images.

Color modes also directly affect the file size of an image. As you will learn in this chapter, choosing a color mode determines which Photoshop tools and file formats are available.

When choosing a color mode, you must take into consideration many factors, including purpose, printing options, file size, number of colors, and layers that may be flattened in later conversions between color modes. Common color modes include RGB, CMYK, LAB, Indexed, and Grayscale, among others. See Appendix B for more details about each of the color modes.

RGB (red, green, blue) is an additive color mode because its colors are created by adding together different wavelengths of light in various intensities. Also called **24-bit color**, RGB color mode is used typically for images that are reproduced on monitors, projectors, slides, transparencies, and the Web.

CMYK (cyan, magenta, yellow, black) is a subtractive color mode because its colors are created when light strikes an object or image and the wavelengths are absorbed. Also called the **four-color process**, the CMYK color mode is used by most desktop printers and commercial printing businesses.

A **gamut**, or **color gamut**, is the range of printed or displayed colors. The color gamut on your monitor may not be the same as on your printer. For example, the RGB color mode displays a wider range of discernible colors than does CMYK. When you print an RGB image from your monitor, it must be reproduced with CMYK inks on your printer. Because the gamut of reproducible ink colors is smaller than what we see with our eyes, any color that cannot be printed is referred to as **out of gamut**. In Photoshop, you will see an out of gamut warning if you select colors that have to be converted from RGB to CMYK. If you plan to send your image to a professional print shop, be sure to get details about color modes, models, and gamuts before the image is printed.

Once you choose a color mode, you also can set a bit depth. The **bit depth**, also called **pixel depth** or **color depth**, measures how much color information is available for displaying or printing each pixel in an image. The word **bit** stands for binary digit. A bit depth of eight, means that Photoshop assigns eight binary settings for each color.

Photoshop's **color management system** (**CMS**) translates colors from the color space of one device into a device-independent color space. The process is called **color mapping**, or **gamut mapping**.

To Start Photoshop

The following steps, which assume Windows 7 is running, start Photoshop based on a typical installation.

1 Click the Start button on the Windows 7 taskbar to display the Start menu.

2 Type `Photoshop CS5` as the search text in the 'Search programs and files' text box, and watch the search results appear on the Start menu.

3 Click Adobe Photoshop CS5 in the search results on the Start menu to start Photoshop.

4 After a few moments, when the Photoshop window is displayed, if the window is not maximized, click the Maximize button on the title bar to maximize the window.

To Reset the Tools and the Options Bar

The following steps select the Rectangular Marquee Tool and reset all tool settings in the options bar.

1 If the tools in the Tools panel appear in two columns, click the double arrow at the top of the Tools panel.

BTW

LAB Color
Three basic parameters make up the LAB color mode. First, the lightness of the color is measured from 0 (indicating black) to 100 (indicating white). The second parameter represents the color's position between magenta and green — negative values indicate green, whereas positive values indicate magenta. Finally, the third parameter indicates a color's position between yellow and blue — negative values indicate blue, whereas positive values indicate yellow.

BTW

Indexed Color
When converting to Indexed color, Photoshop builds a **color lookup table** (CLUT), which stores and indexes the colors in the image. If a color in the original image does not appear in the table, Photoshop chooses the closest one, or dithers the available colors, to simulate the color. Indexed color mode therefore limits the panel of colors to reduce file size yet maintain visual quality.

BTW

Image Sizes
For very large publications, reduce the magnification to see the entire image in the document window. The larger the dimensions of your publication, the larger the file size. Photoshop imposes no limit to the size of your publication, except for its ability to fit on your storage device. System resources may be slower in larger documents.

2 If necessary, click the Rectangular Marquee Tool button on the Tools panel to select it.

3 Right-click the Rectangular Marquee Tool icon on the options bar to display the context menu, and then click Reset All Tools. When Photoshop displays a confirmation dialog box, click the OK button to restore the tools to their default settings.

To Reset the Default Colors

The following step resets the default colors.

1 Press the D key to reset the default foreground and background colors.

To Select the Painting Workspace

The Painting workspace displays the Brush Presets, Swatches, and Layers panels open and on top of their panel grouping. Later in the chapter, this workspace will be helpful when choosing brushes and colors. The following step selects the Painting workspace.

1
- Click Painting on the Application bar to choose the Painting workspace.

- If necessary, click the 'Show more workspaces and options' button and then click Reset Painting on the context menu (Figure 4–2).

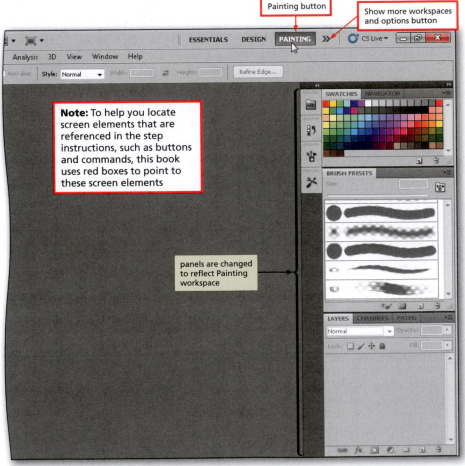

Painting button

Show more workspaces and options button

Note: To help you locate screen elements that are referenced in the step instructions, such as buttons and commands, this book uses red boxes to point to these screen elements

panels are changed to reflect Painting workspace

Figure 4–2

Other Ways
1. Click Show More Workspaces and Options button, click Painting
2. Click Window on menu bar, point to Workspace, click Painting

To Start a New Photoshop File

The table tent card will be printed on 8.5 × 11-inch paper, and then folded and trimmed to display two, 7½ × 3⅝ sides. A 1-inch fold from each end will tuck under to form the base. A resolution of 300 ppi will be used to maintain a high-quality printed image. Because the graphic will be printed, rather than used on the Web, the color mode will be CMYK and the bit depth will be 8. The background will be transparent at the beginning.

The following steps use the New command on the File menu to set the attributes for a new document image.

1
- Click File on the menu bar, and then click New to display the New dialog box (Figure 4–3).

Q&A My settings are different. Did I do something wrong?

No, your settings will differ. Photoshop imports the settings from the last copy performed on your system, in case you want to create a new file from something you copied.

Figure 4–3

2
- Type **Table Tent Card** in the Name box to name the graphic.

- If necessary, click the Preset box arrow, and then click Custom in the list.

- If necessary, click the Width unit box arrow, and then click inches in the list.

- Double-click the Width box and then type **8.5** to enter a value of 8.5 inches wide.

- Double-click the Height box and then type **11** to enter a value of 11 inches high (Figure 4–4).

Q&A What other measurement units can I use?

Photoshop allows you to choose various scales for new images, including inches, pixels, centimeters, millimeters, points, and others.

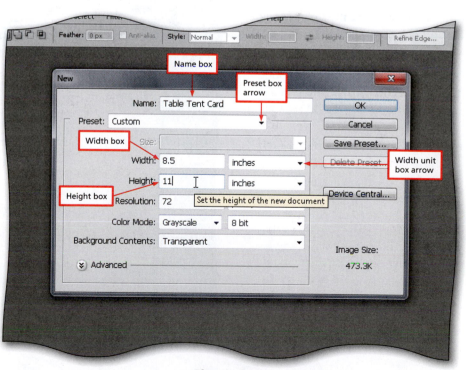

Figure 4–4

3

- Double-click the Resolution box and then type 3 0 0 to enter a value of 300 pixels per inch.

- If necessary, click the Resolution unit box arrow, and then click pixels/inch in the list.

- Click the Color Mode box arrow to display its list (Figure 4–5).

Q&A

What does the Save Preset button do?

If you find that you commonly use specific settings, you can click the Save Preset button and give your attributes a name. In future sessions, you then can choose the preset from a list.

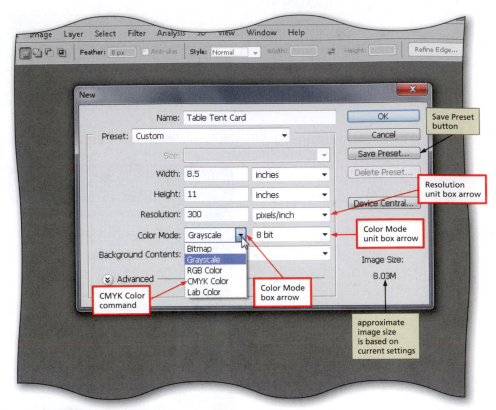

Figure 4–5

4

- Click CMYK Color in the list to choose the CMYK Color mode.

- If necessary, click the Color Mode unit box arrow and then click 8 bit in the list.

- If necessary, click the Background Contents box arrow, and then click Transparent in the list to set the color (Figure 4–6).

Q&A

What color would be displayed if I chose Background Color?

When you select Background Color in the Background Contents list, the current background color, as noted on the Tools panel, becomes the default color of the blank canvas. The other option is white.

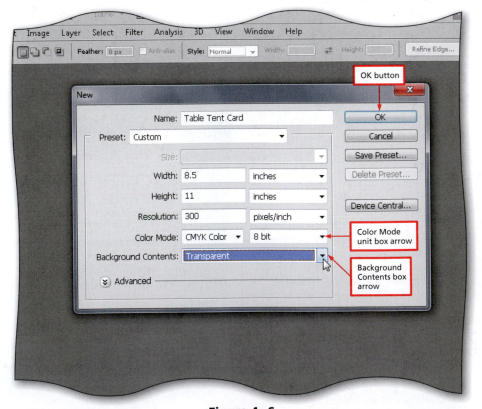

Figure 4–6

5
- Click the OK button to close the dialog box.

- On the document window status bar, double-click the magnification box, type `16.67` if necessary, and then press the ENTER key.

- If the rulers do not appear in the document window, press CTRL+R (Figure 4–7).

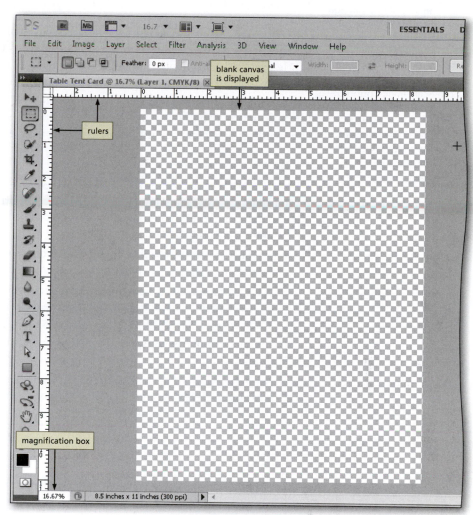

Figure 4–7

To Save a Photo

Even though the file has a name in the document window tab, it is not saved on a storage device. The next steps save the file with the name Table Tent Card.

1 With your USB flash drive connected to one of the computer's USB ports, click File on the menu bar to display the File menu and then click Save As to display the Save As dialog box.

2 If necessary, in the File name text box, type `Table Tent Card` to rename the file. Do not press the ENTER key after typing the file name.

3 Click the Save in box arrow and then click UDISK 2.0 (F:), or the location associated with your USB flash drive, in the list, if necessary.

4 Click the Save button in the Save As dialog box to save the file. If Photoshop displays a compatibility dialog box, click the OK button.

BTW

Colors on the Web
The Web typically uses a six-digit hexadecimal number to represent its color mode. Hexadecimal is a numbering system based on groups of 16, using the numbers 0 through 9 and the letters A through F. In decimal numbers, used for color modes other than the Web, three separate numbers are used for each of the 256 available colors per channel.

BTW

Grayscale Printing
Although a grayscale image on a computer screen can display up to 256 levels of gray, a printing press can reproduce only about 50 levels of gray. Therefore, a grayscale image printed with only black ink can look coarse compared to the same image printed with two to four inks, with each individual ink reproducing up to 50 levels of gray.

Gradients

A **gradient**, or **gradient fill**, is a graphic effect consisting of a smooth blend, change, or transition from one color to another. While there is potential for overuse with gradients, subtle gradients add depth and texture to a graphic or Web page. Shade-to-shade gradients sometimes seem elegant and emotive. They can emulate how light strikes real-world surfaces. Vertical gradients help the eyes to move further down the page. Graphic artists usually save bright, striped gradients for smaller portions of a page, such as a heading or when they intentionally want to overwhelm the viewer.

Plan Ahead

Plan your layout and gather necessary photos.
Recall that a storyboard is a preliminary layout sketch used to help plan graphics placement, size, perspective, and spacing. Using a storyboard allows you to create an original graphic from the back to the front.

- As you start on the graphic, fill the background with color, unless the graphic will become part of another publication.

- For busy foregrounds, keep the background simple, with perhaps one color. If text will be used, keep in mind that anything in the darker half of the color spectrum will need light text and vice versa.

- Use black backgrounds sparingly — they are most effective for starkness and special effects.

- For extra depth or perspective, consider using a gradient. A gradient can create depth, add visual interest, or highlight a portion of an image. Use colors that will match colors in your graphic or those desired by the customer. The direction of the gradient should either lead viewers toward a specific focal point or entice them to turn the page.

BTW

Gradient Tool button
If you right-click the Gradient Tool button, its context menu includes the Gradient Tool and the Paint Bucket Tool.

Typically used as a graduated blend between two colors, the direction of a gradient transition can be top to bottom, bottom to top, side to side, or a variety of other shapes and diagonals. You can apply gradients to the entire image or a selected portion of an image. Photoshop offers many preset gradient fills, or you can create your own. Gradients work best with RGB or CMYK colors. The Gradient Tool cannot be used with the Bitmap or Index color modes.

To create a gradient in a specific part of your image, you select an area of an image and then click the Gradient Tool button on the Tools panel. Otherwise the gradient will add color to the entire image.

The Gradient options bar (Figure 4–8) allows you to set the style, blending mode, and other attributes for the gradient fill.

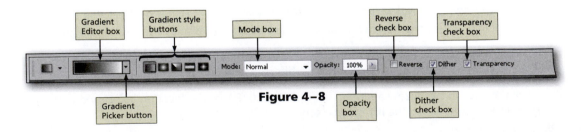

Figure 4–8

You can click the Gradient Editor box to display the Gradient Editor dialog box, or you can choose a preset gradient by clicking the Gradient picker button. The Gradient Editor dialog box, also called the Gradient Editor, allows you to define a new gradient by modifying a copy of an existing gradient or preset, or by choosing colors to create a new blend.

To the right of the Gradient picker button are the gradient styles or shades. A **gradient style** is the way the colors are arranged with regard to the reflection of light in the gradient. Table 4–1 displays the five gradient styles available.

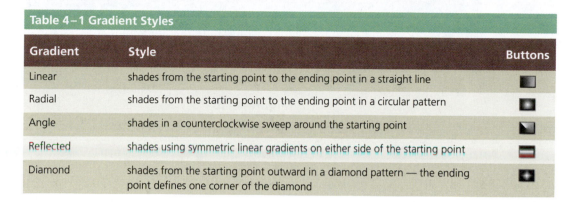

Table 4–1 Gradient Styles		
Gradient	**Style**	**Buttons**
Linear	shades from the starting point to the ending point in a straight line	
Radial	shades from the starting point to the ending point in a circular pattern	
Angle	shades in a counterclockwise sweep around the starting point	
Reflected	shades using symmetric linear gradients on either side of the starting point	
Diamond	shades from the starting point outward in a diamond pattern — the ending point defines one corner of the diamond	

On the right side of the Gradient options bar, Photoshop includes an Opacity box to set the percentage of opacity, a Reverse check box to reverse the order of colors in the gradient fill, a Dither check box to create a smoother blend with less banding, and a Transparency check box to create a transparency mask for the gradient fill.

To Select the Gradient Tool and Style

To create a gradient in the Table Tent Card image, you will select the Gradient Tool and then access the Gradient Editor from the options bar.

1

• Right-click the Gradient Tool button or the Paint Bucket Tool button on the Tools panel to display the context menu (Figure 4–9).

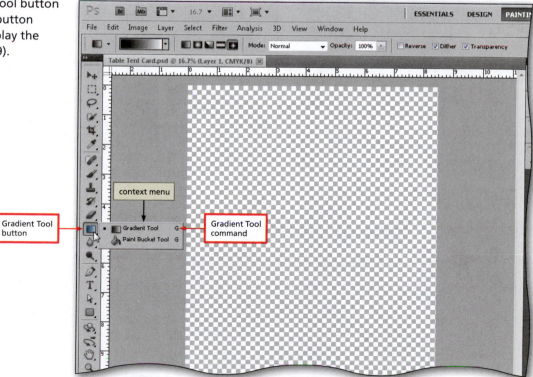

Figure 4–9

2

- Click Gradient Tool to choose the Gradient Tool and display the Gradient options bar.

- On the Gradient options bar, click the Reflected Gradient button to select the gradient style (Figure 4–10).

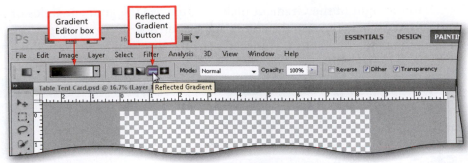

Figure 4–10

Gradient Presets

When you click the Gradient Editor box on the options bar, Photoshop displays the Gradient Editor dialog box (Figure 4–11). In the Gradient Editor dialog box, the Presets area contains a menu button. When clicked, the menu button displays choices for thumbnail size and other gradient presets. Photoshop has nine sets of additional gradients to create a wide variety of special fill effects. When you choose one of the additional sets, Photoshop will ask if you want to replace or append the new gradient set. Clicking the Reset Gradients command changes the presets back to the default list.

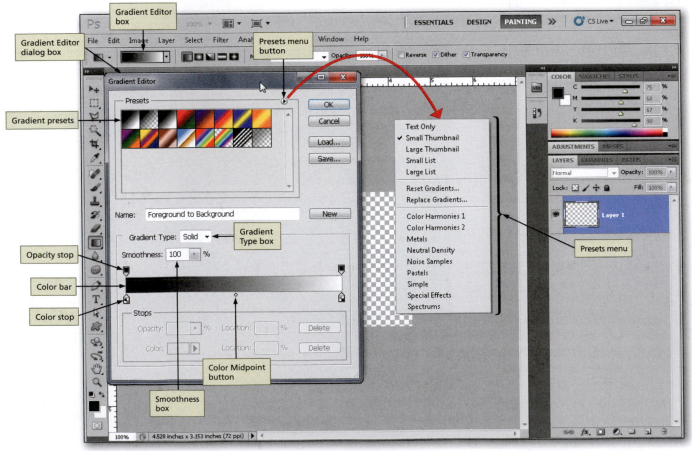

Figure 4–11

The **smoothness** setting is a percentage determining the smoothness of the transition between color bands. A setting of 100% indicates an equally weighted transition in color pixels. Using lower transition values, the gradient colors will appear more pixilated, with abrupt transitions in the color bands. This effect is more evident when creating gradients with nonadjacent colors in the color spectrum. When working with a noise gradient, the Smoothness box becomes a Roughness box that indicates how vividly the colors transition between one another.

A **solid gradient** is one that uses the color spectrum to transition the gradient from one color to another. If you choose a solid gradient, Opacity Stop buttons appear above the Color bar and Color Stop buttons appear below it. Double-clicking a Color Stop button opens the Select stop color dialog box, so you can choose a new color. If you adjust the colors, a small diamond, called the Color Midpoint button, appears below the color bar. It indicates the place in the gradient where it displays an even mix of the starting and ending colors. By placing Color Stop buttons very close together in the Gradient Editor, you can reduce the gradient effect and produce strong, distinct bands of color for exciting and creative special effects.

A **noise gradient** is a gradient that contains randomly distributed color specks within the range of colors that you specify. If you choose a noise gradient, the color bar is adjusted by dragging sliders. Noise gradients also display options for restricting color, setting the transparency, and randomizing the colors.

If the gradient you create is one that you plan to use several times, you can name it in the Name box and then click the New button to save it as a gradient file within Photoshop. In subsequent sessions, you then can load the saved gradient to use it again.

To Select a Noise Gradient Preset

The following step uses the Gradient Editor dialog box to choose a noise gradient preset for the tent card.

- Click the Gradient Editor box to display the Gradient Editor dialog box (Figure 4–12).

Experiment

- Click each of the various presets in the Gradient Editor dialog box and watch how the color settings vary. Choose a colorful gradient preset and then drag a Color Stop button below the color bar to watch the colors change.

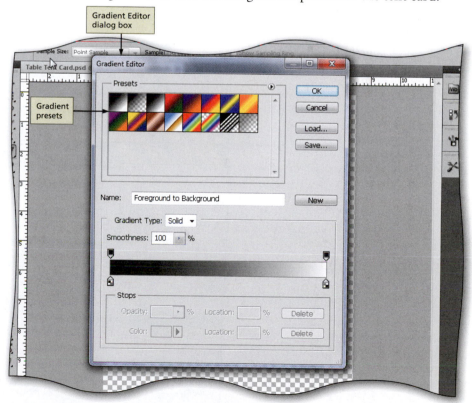

Figure 4–12

2

- In the Presets area, click the menu button to display the Presets menu (Figure 4–13).

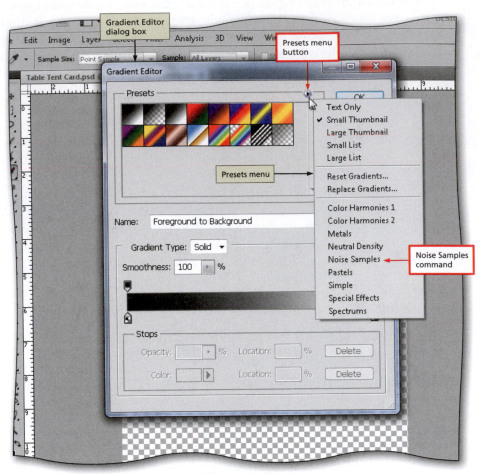

Figure 4–13

3

- Click Noise Samples to select the group of presets (Figure 4–14).

Figure 4–14

4

- Click the Append button (Gradient Editor dialog box) to append the additional presets.

- Click the Reds preset to select it (Figure 4–15).

5

- Click the OK button (Gradient Editor dialog box) to close the dialog box.

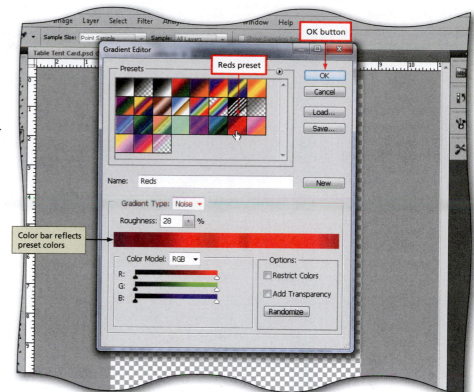

Other Ways

1. Press G, click Gradient Editor box, select preset and options, click OK button

Figure 4–15

To Edit a Solid Gradient

If you wanted to edit the colors when using a solid gradient, you would perform the following steps using the Gradient Editor dialog box.

1. On the options bar, click the Gradient Editor box to display the Gradient Editor dialog box.

2. Double-click the left Color Stop button below the gradient bar to display the 'Select stop color' dialog box. Choose a color and click the OK button ('Select stop color' dialog box).

3. Double-click the right Color Stop button below the gradient bar to display the 'Select stop color' dialog box. Choose a color and click the OK button ('Select stop color' dialog box).

4. To change the transition, drag the Color Midpoint button.

5. To add a new color, double-click a blank area below the Color bar and select a color.

6. To delete a color, click the Color Stop button, and then click the Delete button (Gradient Editor dialog box).

BTW

Gradient Directions
You can create a gradient at any straight line, angle, or position. If you start and end in the extreme corners of the frame, the gradient appears across the entire area. To leave the corners solid and start the gradient more toward the center, drag and end closer to the middle of the area. To constrain the line angle to a multiple of 45°, hold down the SHIFT key as you drag.

To Draw the Gradient

The steps on the next page create a gradient background for the table tent card. To draw or apply the gradient, you drag in the image or selected area at the point where you want the base color to begin. For linear and radial gradients, you drag in the direction of the desired transition — the rate of transition is dependent on the settings in the Gradient Editor dialog box.

1

- In the document window, drag from a location in the center of the upper-left quadrant down and right, to the center of the lower-right quadrant. Do not release the mouse button (Figure 4–16).

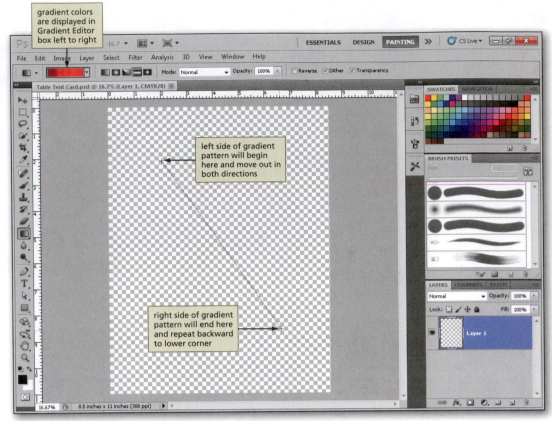

Figure 4–16

2

- Release the mouse button to apply the gradient (Figure 4–17).

 Experiment

- Click another style button on the Gradient options bar. Drag in the document window to display a different style gradient. Press CTRL+Z to return to the gradient shown in Figure 4–17.

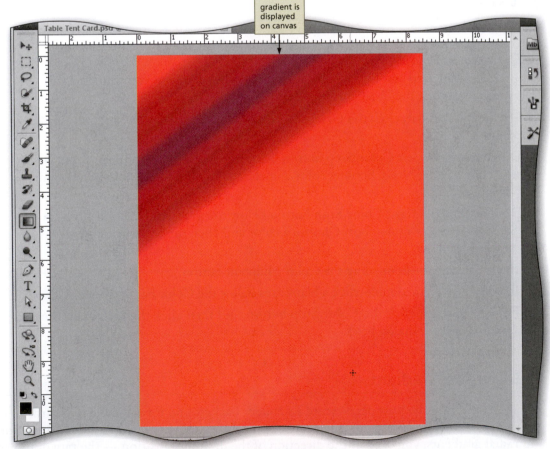

Figure 4–17

To Set Layer Properties

The following steps name the layer and set its identification color.

1 Double-click the name of the layer, Layer 1, in the Layers panel. Type `gradient background` and then press the ENTER key to replace the name.

2 Right-click the 'Indicates layer visibility' button, and then click Red in the list to change the layer's identification color (Figure 4–18).

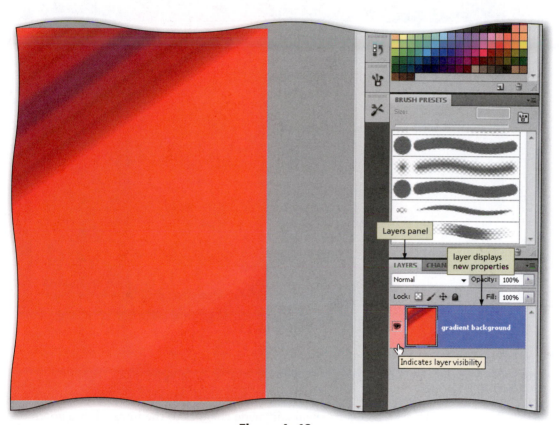

Figure 4–18

To Create Ruler Guides

The following steps create several ruler guides to help place and draw objects on the table tent card. The ruler guides indicate the fold lines on the final hard copy.

1 Drag from the horizontal ruler down to the 10-inch mark on the vertical ruler to create a ruler guide at 10 inches.

2 Drag from the horizontal ruler down to the 5.5-inch mark on the vertical ruler to create a ruler guide at 5.5 inches.

3 Drag from the horizontal ruler down to the 1-inch mark on the vertical ruler to create a ruler guide at 1 inch (Figure 4–19 on the next page).

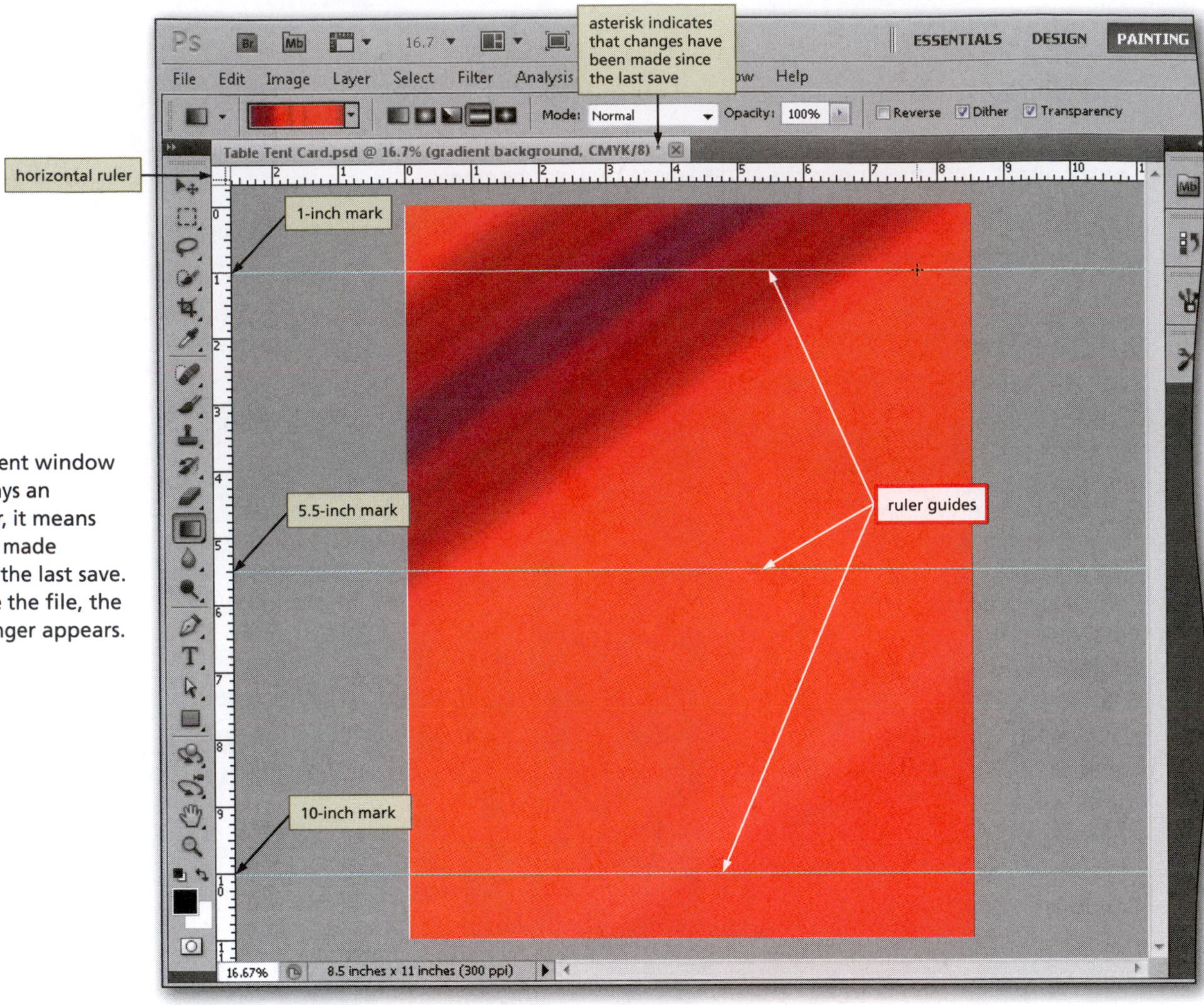

Figure 4–19

Saving Files
If your document window title bar displays an asterisk or star, it means that you have made changes since the last save. Once you save the file, the asterisk no longer appears.

To Save the File

Because you have created a gradient and made changes to the image, it is a good idea to save the file again.

1 Press CTRL+S to save the Table Tent Card file with the same name.

Break Point: If you wish to take a break, this is a good place to do so. You can quit Photoshop now. To resume at a later time, start Photoshop, open the file called Table Tent Card, and continue following the steps from this location forward.

The Swatches Panel

The Swatches panel stores colors for repeated use (Figure 4–20). You can add or delete colors from the panel or display different libraries of colors for different projects. Each color displays a tool tip. To choose a foreground color, click a color in the Swatches panel. To choose a background color, CTRL+click a color in the Swatches panel. The Swatches panel menu allows you to add more color libraries, or change the settings of the current panel.

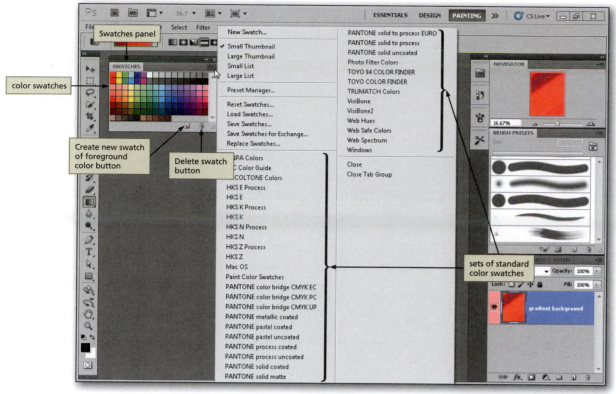

Figure 4–20

Choose colors purposefully.
Choose two or three colors that fit with your client's colors or that match a color that already exists in an image in your layout. Limiting the number of colors creates a stronger brand or identity. The main color should be the one that viewers will remember when they look away. Colors two and three should either contrast or complement the main color to balance the design. Complementary colors create gray, white, or black when mixed in proper proportions, or are found opposite one another on a standard color wheel.

Plan Ahead

To Choose a Color in the Swatches Panel

The following step chooses a foreground color in the Swatches panel.

- On the Swatches panel, in the middle of the fifth row, click the color Pure Blue Violet to change the foreground color (Figure 4–21).

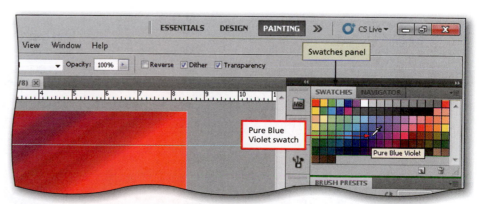

Figure 4–21

Painting with Brushes

The painting tools change the color of pixels in an image. The Pencil and Brush tools work like their traditional counterparts, applying color with strokes. The Color Replacement Tool replaces a selected color with a new color. Recall that the Gradient Tool creates blends between colors. The Paint Bucket Tool fills similarly colored areas with the foreground color. The History Brush Tool paints a copy of the selected state or snapshot into the current image window. The Art History Brush Tool paints with stylized strokes that simulate the look of different paint styles, using a selected state or snapshot. The Mixer Brush Tool simulates realistic painting techniques, such as blending canvas colors and varying paint wetness. By specifying how each tool applies or modifies the color, you can create an endless number of possibilities. You can apply color gradually, with soft or hard edges, with small or large brush tips, with various brush dynamics and blending properties, as well as by using brushes of different shapes. You even can simulate spraying paint with an airbrush.

Plan Ahead

> **Design your brush strokes.**
> When choosing a brush tip, keep in mind the basic shape of your brush strokes or marks. Use the Brush panel to choose a Brush Preset or Brush Tip shape. Then adjust settings for the beginning, middle, and end of the brush stroke. For the beginning, choose an appropriate tip, color, shape, rotation, hardness, spacing, and diameter. For the middle of the stroke, set the shape dynamics, such as pen pressure and tilt, texture, flow, brush edge, distortion, noise, and scattering. For the end of the brush stroke, set the fading.

In the next section, you first will create a new layer for the ribbon. Then, you will select the Brush Tool, choose a Brush preset, and finally draw ribbon on the new layer.

To Create a New Layer

The following steps create a new layer on which to draw the ribbon.

1 Press SHIFT+CTRL+N to create a new layer.

2 In the New Layer dialog box, type `ribbon` in the Name text box.

3 Click the Color box arrow, and then click Blue to change the layer's identification color.

4 Click the OK button to close the New Layer dialog box and display the new layer on the Layers panel (Figure 4–22).

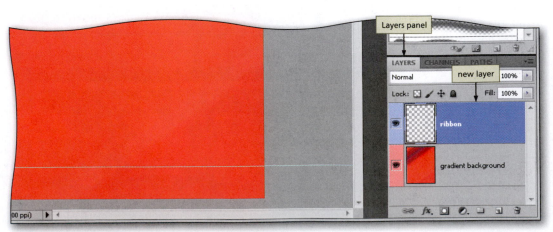

Figure 4–22

The Brush Tool

The Brush Tool paints the current foreground color on an image with strokes of color as you drag. When you click the Brush Tool button on the Tools panel, the Brush options bar appears (Figure 4–23).

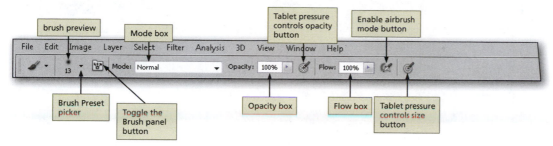

Figure 4–23

Similar to the Gradient picker, the Brush Preset picker displays the current set of brush tips and settings, such as brush size and hardness. Next to the Brush Preset picker is the Toggle the Brush panel button, which shows and hides the Brush panel. The Mode box arrow displays Brush blending modes when clicked, and the Opacity box allows you to specify the degree of transparency. Entering a value in the Flow box specifies how quickly the paint is applied. A lower number applies paint more slowly. The airbrush button enables airbrush capabilities.

Accessed from the Brush Tool's context menu, the Pencil and Color Replacement tools are related closely to the Brush Tool. The only difference between the Pencil and Brush tools is that the Brush Tool paints with an anti-aliased or smooth edge, and the Pencil Tool draws with an aliased or rough edge. The Color Replacement Tool replaces specific colors when you paint over a targeted color with a corrective color. The Color Replacement Tool does not work with Bitmap or Indexed color modes.

To Select the Brush Tool

The following steps select the Brush Tool on the Tools panel.

1

- Right-click the current brush tool on the Tools panel to display the context menu (Figure 4–24).

Q&A

What is the difference between the Brush Tool and the Pencil Tool?

The Brush Tool paints brush strokes. The Pencil Tool paints hard-edged strokes.

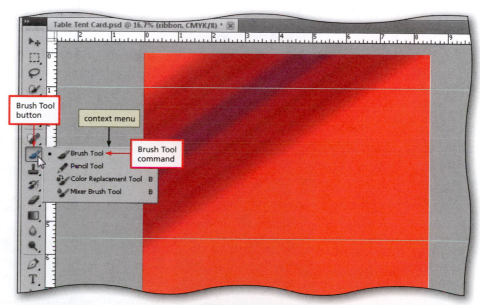

Figure 4–24

2

• Click Brush Tool in the list to select it and to display the Brush options bar (Figure 4–25).

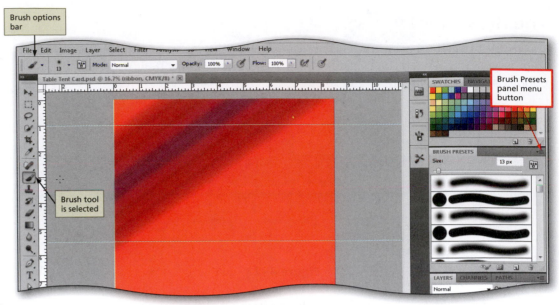

Figure 4–25

Brush Presets

BTW

Brush Preset Previews
When you click the Brush Preset picker button, your previews might appear as thumbnails, as lists, or as text only. You can choose the preview style on the Brush Presets panel menu.

You may choose from 54 standard brushes when you first start using the Brush Tool. These brushes appear when you click the Brush Preset picker on the options bar; they also appear on the Brush Presets panel. The Brush Presets panel (Figure 4–26) may display the brush options as strokes or brush tips. Buttons on the panel help you set the size of the brush, create new brushes, and perform other functions. The Brush Presets panel menu allows you to display other libraries of brush presets.

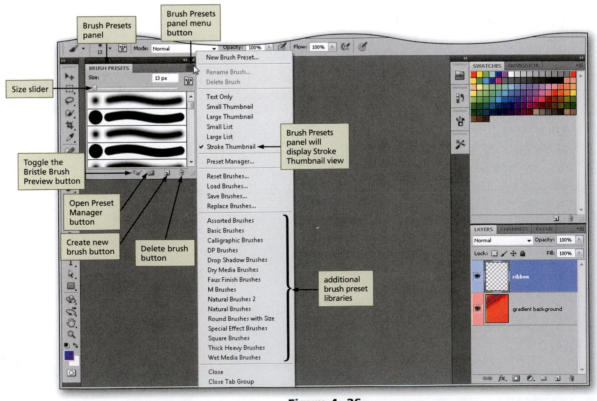

Figure 4–26

To Append Brush Presets

The following steps append two libraries of brush presets to the default list.

• Click the Brush Presets panel menu button (shown in Figure 4–25) to display the menu (Figure 4–27).

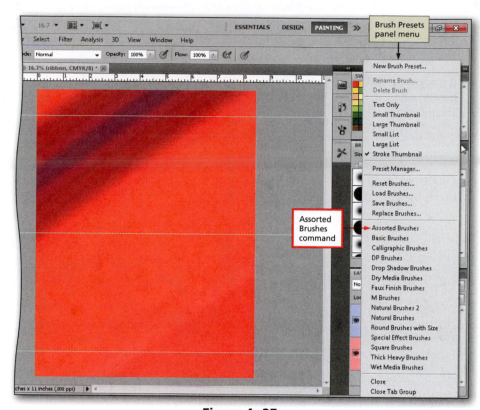

Figure 4–27

• Click Assorted Brushes to choose the library of presets (Figure 4–28).

• When Photoshop asks if you wish to replace the current brushes, click the Append button (Adobe Photoshop CS5 dialog box).

• Repeat Steps 1 through 3 to append the Calligraphic Brushes.

Figure 4–28

Other Ways

1. Click Brush Preset picker, click menu button, click desired set of brush presets

To Select a Brush Using the Brush Preset Picker

The following step selects a brush from the Brush Preset picker.

1

- On the Brush options bar, click the Brush Preset picker to display the Brush Preset picker panel.

- If necessary, click the panel menu button and then click Small Thumbnail.

- Scroll to the lower portion of the brush tip previews.

- Click the Flat 45 px brush to select it (Figure 4–29).

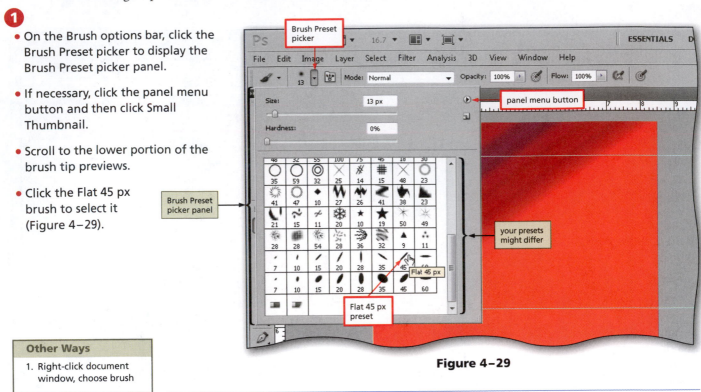

Figure 4–29

Other Ways

1. Right-click document window, choose brush

To Change the Size and Hardness of the Brush

You can change the size and hardness of the brush using the Brush preset picker. The brush **size** is the diameter of the brush tip measured in pixels. **Hardness** is a percentage value indicating how solid the edge of the brush stoke appears.

1

- Drag the Size slider to 150 pixels.

- If necessary, drag the Hardness slider to 100% (Figure 4–30).

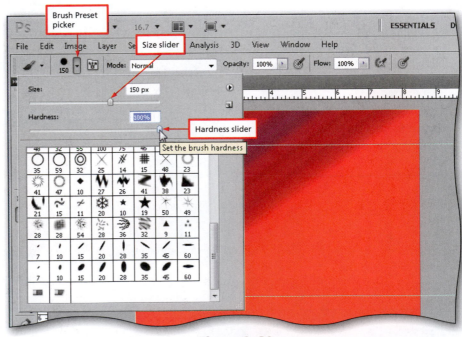

Other Ways

1. To change brush size, drag Size slider on Brush Preset panel

Figure 4–30

To Hide the Brush Preset Picker Panel

The following step hides the Brush Preset picker panel.

1 Click the Brush Preset picker again to hide the panel.

To Draw Using the Brush Tool

The following step uses the Brush Tool to draw the ribbon. If you create a brush stroke that is incorrect, press CTRL+Z and draw again. As you draw with the Brush Tool, the strokes appear with the settings of the chosen brush in the selected foreground color.

1

• With the ribbon layer still selected, position the mouse pointer at the left margin, just below the 1-inch ruler guide.

• Drag a wavy line similar to the one in Figure 4–31 to create a ribbon effect. As you drag, change direction sharply to simulate a ribbon curl.

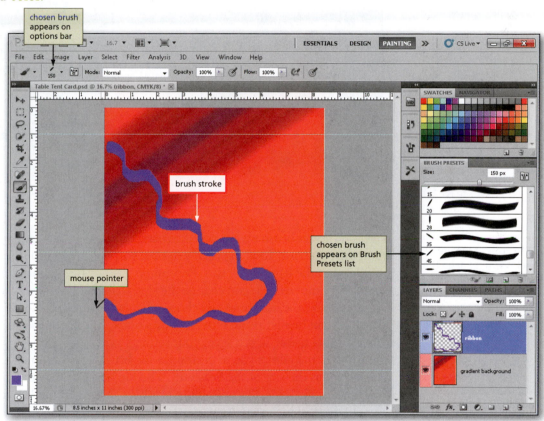

Figure 4–31

The Brush Panel

Recall that clicking the Brush Picker button displays a small panel with presets, diameter, and hardness settings. The Brush panel (Figure 4–32 on the next page) displays even more settings, including brush tips, painting characteristics, angles, and spacing, among others. To display the Brush panel, you can click the Toggle the Brush panel button on the Brush options bar (shown in Figure 4–23 on page PS 229), click Brush on the Window menu, or press the F5 key. Once the Brush panel is open, you can click the Brush panel menu button to display a list of available commands, thumbnail sizes, and sets of brushes that can replaced or be appended to the current list.

BTW

Graphics Tablet
Dragging, without using the SHIFT key, creates strokes of color that may include corners, curves, and arcs. Graphic designers who create many freehand brush strokes sometimes use a graphics tablet, which is an input device that uses a stylus, or specialized mouse, to draw on a tablet surface.

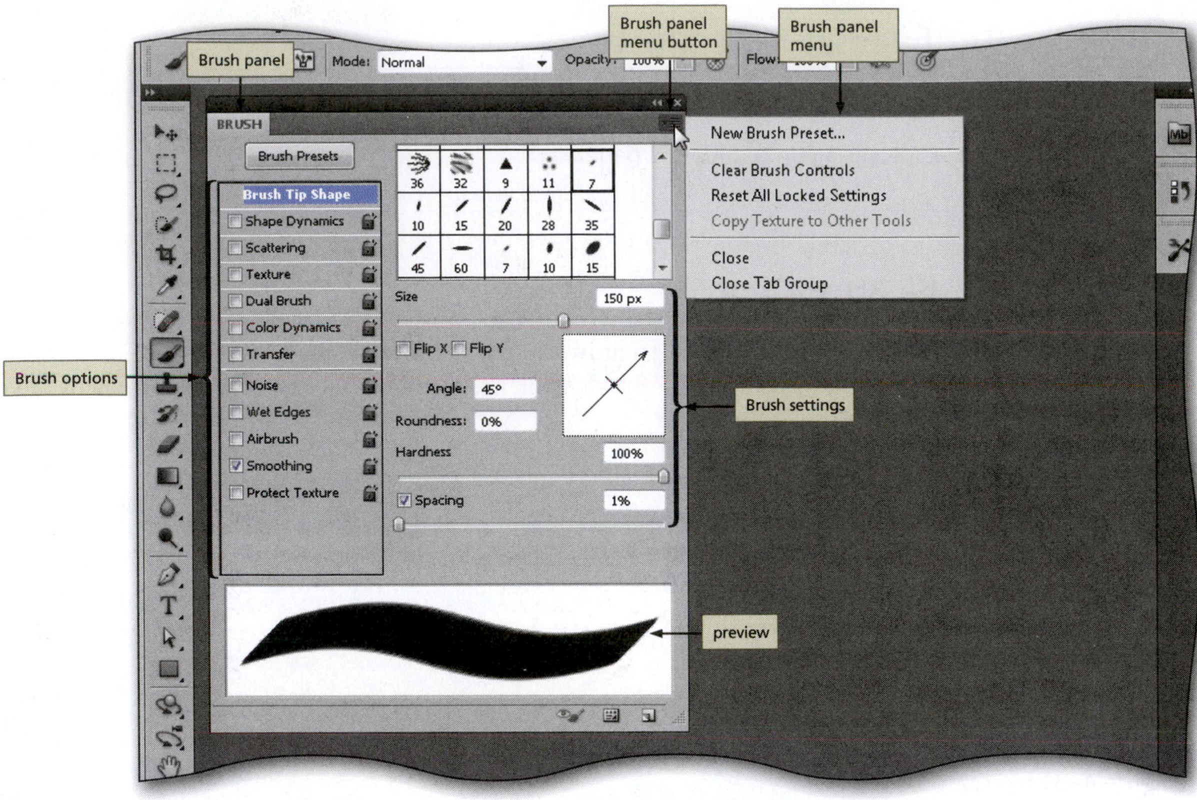

Figure 4–32

BTW

The Preset Manager

The Preset Manager helps you manage the libraries of preset brushes, gradients, styles, custom shapes, patterns, and other tools. Use it to change the current set of preset items or create new libraries. The Preset Manager lists new presets all in one place for easy access. To use the Preset Manager, click Preset Manager on the Edit menu.

Choosing Brushes

Sometimes it is confusing whether to use the Brush Preset picker, the Brush panel, or the Brush Presets panel to choose a brush. Normally, you should choose the tool that is closer to your current location. However, if you want to customize the brush, use the Brush panel.

A preset brush tip has specific characteristics such as size, shape, and hardness. When you use the Brush Tool, the tip creates the shape that paints in the document window. In addition to the basic brush tips, Photoshop has 11 other libraries of brush tips that you can append to the panel. If you change the size, shape, or hardness of a preset brush, the change is temporary; the next time you choose that brush, it reverts to its original settings. If you use a certain brush tip and characteristics often, you might use the Save command on the Brush panel menu, which saves your settings as a preset. The Brush panel displays the preset brush tips, and allows you to customize the brush. For example, you can set the diameter, which scales the size of the brush tip. The flip boxes change the direction of the brush tip on the specified axis. For example, a brush tip that displays a leaf image with the stem down would display the leaf with the stem up if the Flip X check box were checked. The Angle box allows you to enter degrees of flat rotation. Positive numbers rotate the brush tip counterclockwise; negative numbers rotate the brush tip clockwise. For example, a brush tip of a raindrop with the pointed end straight up would point left if rotated 90 degrees.

The Roundness percentage specifies the ratio between the brush's short and long axes. Adjusting the roundness makes the brush tip appear to rotate on its vertical axis in a 3D fashion. A value of 100% indicates a full view or circular brush tip. A value of 0% indicates a sideways view or linear brush tip. Values between 0% and 100% represent partial view or elliptical brush tips. For example, a star brush tip set at 50% roundness creates a star that tips backward from the top.

The Spacing slider controls the distance between the brush marks in a stroke. The lower the percentage, the closer together the brush tips are within the stroke. For example, a snowflake brush tip set at 1% spacing would display a snowflake shape connected to another snowflake shape. Higher percentages — up to 1000% — space the brush tips farther apart as you drag. For example, a spacing value of 200% would create snowflakes all across the brush stroke with some space in between each one. When the Spacing check box is deselected, the speed of the cursor determines the spacing.

Solid brush tips have a hardness setting that indicates the amount of anti-aliasing for the Brush Tool. The higher the percentage, the cleaner the edge appears.

To Display the Brush Panel

The following step displays the Brush panel.

1

• Click the Brush button on the vertical docking of collapsed panels to display the Brush panel (Figure 4–33).

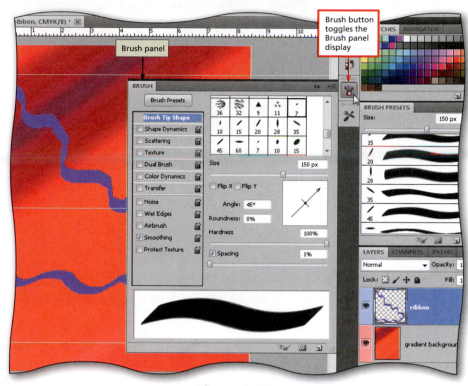

Figure 4–33

Brush Options

When you choose a Brush option, settings specific to that dynamic appear on the Brush panel. Table 4–2 displays some of the brush options not previously mentioned, along with their settings and descriptions.

BTW | **Brush Sets**
Sometimes you might want a unique or distinctive brush that is not among the many brush tips available in Photoshop. In that case, you can purchase the design or create it from scratch. Brush tip files have the extension abr and are available for purchase on the Web.

Table 4–2 Brush Shape Options

Option	Setting	Description
Shape Dynamics	Jitter	specifies how the size, angle, or roundness of brush marks vary in a stroke
	Fade	fades the size of brush marks between the initial diameter and the minimum diameter in the specified number of steps
	Pen Pressure, Pen Tilt, Stylus Wheel, Rotation	available only with graphic tablets — varies the size of brush marks between the initial diameter and the minimum diameter based on the pen pressure, pen tilt, position of the pen thumbwheel, or rotation of the pen
Scattering	Scatter	specifies how brush marks are distributed in a stroke — if Both Axes is selected, brush marks are distributed in a radial direction; if Both Axes is deselected, brush marks are distributed perpendicular to the stroke path
	Count	specifies the number of brush marks applied at each spacing interval

Table 4–2 Brush Shape Options *(Continued)*

Option	Setting	Description
Texture	Invert	used for patterns — inverts the high and low points in the texture based on the tones in the pattern
	Scale	specifies the scale of the pattern
	Depth	specifies how deeply the paint penetrates into the texture
Dual Brush	Mode	sets a blending mode to use when combining brush marks from the primary tip and the dual tip
Color Dynamics	Hue, Saturation, Brightness, Purity	specifies a percentage by which the hue, saturation, or brightness of the paint can vary in a stroke
Transfer	Opacity Jitter and Control	specifies how the opacity of paint varies in a brush stroke
	Flow Jitter and Control	specifies how the flow of paint varies in a brush stroke
Noise		adds additional randomness to individual brush tips
Wet Edges		causes paint to build up along the edges of the brush stroke, creating a watercolor effect
Airbrush		applies gradual tones to an image, simulating traditional airbrush techniques
Smoothing		produces smoother curves in brush strokes
Protect Texture		applies the same pattern and scale to all brush presets that have a texture

BTW

The Restore Sample Size Button
When selecting brush tip shapes on the Brush panel, if you change the diameter of a brush tip, Photoshop might display a Restore Sample Size button. The Restore Sample Size button allows you to reset the brush tip back to its default size.

To Set Brush Options

The following steps choose a brush tip and set the brush options.

1
- If necessary, on the left side of the Brush panel, click Brush Tip Shape to display the presets.
- Scroll as necessary and click the Diamond preset (Figure 4–34).

🔍 **Experiment**
- Drag the angle radius to rotate the diamond preset and watch how the preview changes. When you are finished, type 0 in the Angle box.

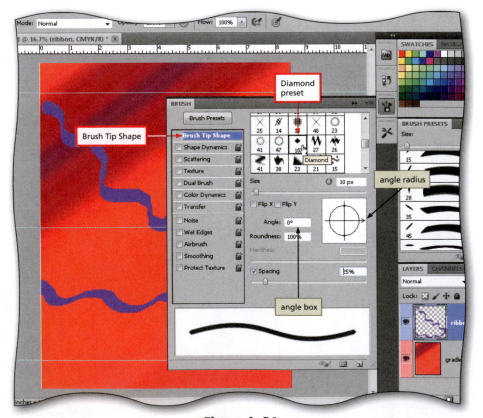

Figure 4–34

2

- Drag the Size slider to 100 pixels.

- Drag the Spacing slider to 100 percent (Figure 4–35).

🔍 **Experiment**

- One at a time, click each of the check boxes on the left side of the panel and experiment with dragging the settings to watch how the preview changes. When you are finished, remove the check mark from each of the check boxes.

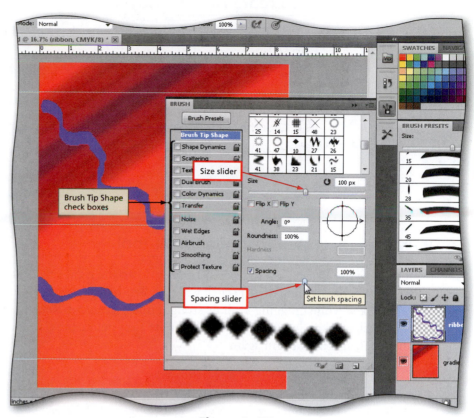

Figure 4–35

3

- If necessary, click to display a check mark in the Smoothing check box to produce smoother curves in brush strokes.

- Click to display a check mark in the Protect Texture check box to preserve the texture pattern when applying brush presets (Figure 4–36).

4

- Press the F5 key to minimize the Brush panel.

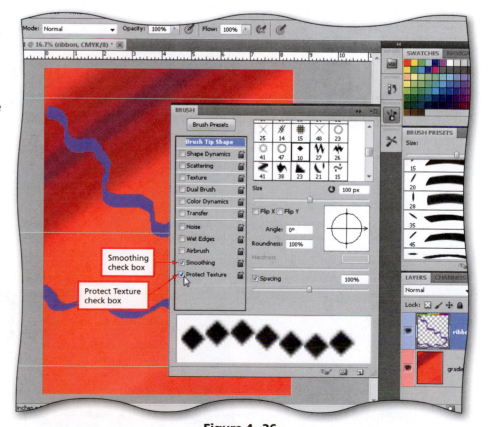

Figure 4–36

To Create Another Layer

The following steps create a new layer on which to draw using the diamond brush tip.

1 Press SHIFT+CTRL+N to create a new layer.

2 In the New Layer dialog box, type **diamond stripe** in the Name text box.

3 Click the Color box arrow and then click Blue to change the layer's identification color.

4 Click the OK button to close the New Layer dialog box and to display the new layer on the Layers panel.

To Draw Straight Lines with the Brush Tool

You will use the Brush Tool to draw diamonds down the right side of the image. To draw straight lines with exact corners you will click and SHIFT+click with the Brush Tool, which connects the color. Alternatively, you can press the SHIFT key while dragging to draw straight lines, freehand. Remember that if you make a mistake while creating the brush strokes, you can click Undo on the Edit menu, press CTRL+Z to undo, or click a previous state in the History panel, and then begin again.

- With the diamond stripe layer still selected, click the upper-right corner of the document window.

- Move rather than drag, the mouse pointer to the lower-right corner of the document window (Figure 4–37).

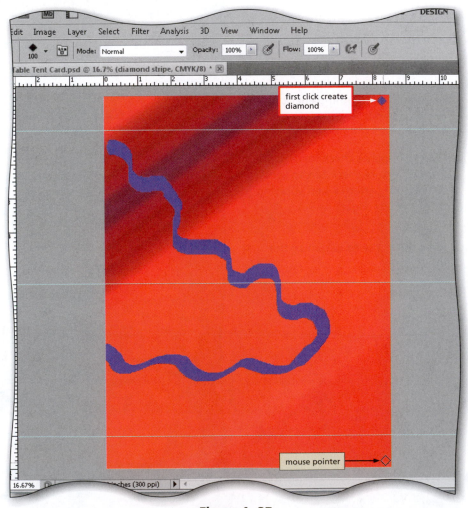

Figure 4–37

2
- SHIFT+click to connect the two locations with a brush stroke (Figure 4–38).

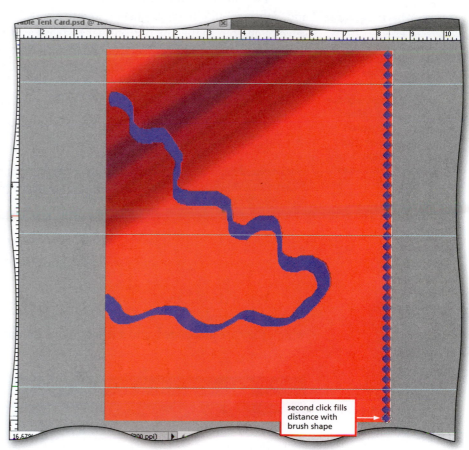

second click fills distance with brush shape

Figure 4–38

Shapes

One of the more creative uses for Photoshop is drawing shapes. A **shape** is a specific figure or form that can be drawn or inserted into an image. A shape is usually a **vector object** or **vector shape**, which means it does not lose its sharp lines or anti-aliasing if it is resized or reshaped. A vector object is made up of lines and curves defined by mathematical vectors or formulas. Photoshop provides six standard shapes, a variety of custom shapes, and the ability to create new shapes using a path. A path is a special kind of vector shape that you will learn about in a later chapter.

BTW

Shapes
Additional shapes can be appended using the Shape picker menu button, providing access to shapes ranging from arrows and shields to musical notes, thought bubbles, and more.

Use predefined shapes for tangible objects.
If your goal is to create a graphic that the viewer will recognize right away, start with a predefined shape. This approach is a necessity if you do not have a drawing tablet or if your artistic skills are limited. Shapes allow you to maintain straight lines, even corners, constrained proportions, and consistent curves. To create unique graphics, shapes can be scaled, distorted, skewed, warped, shadowed, and combined in many ways. Using shapes does not limit your creativity, however. Try experimenting with combinations and transformations of shapes to create graphics with perspective, horizon lines, and alignment.

Plan Ahead

BTW

Shape Modes

Photoshop has three shape modes: shape layers, paths, and fill pixels, which are accessible through the options bar. A shape layer is a vector object that occupies its own layer. Because shape layers are moved, resized, aligned, and distributed easily, they are useful for creating Web graphics. You can draw multiple shapes on a single layer.

The Shape Tool options bar (Figure 4–39) contains buttons to choose shapes; to add, subtract, and intersect shapes; and to choose shape styles, modes, and colors. If you select a custom shape, the options bar displays a Shape box with a Custom Shape picker button, which lets you choose from a panel of customized shapes. Besides the traditional shapes of lines, rectangles, and an ellipse, you can create freeform shapes, equilateral polygons, rounded rectangles and custom shapes.

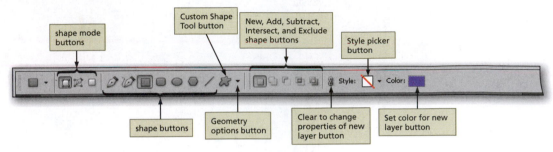

Figure 4–39

When clicked, the Geometry options button displays context-sensitive settings for each of the shapes. Table 4–3 displays the geometry options, the shape or shapes with which they are associated, and a description of their functions.

BTW

Resizing Shapes

To resize a shape, press CTRL+T to display the shape's bounding box. Resize the shape by dragging the sizing handles, then press the ENTER key.

Table 4–3 Geometry Options for Shapes

Options	Applicable Shape(s)	Description
Arrowheads, Width, Length, Concavity	Line	adds arrowheads to a line, specifies the proportions of the arrowhead as a percentage of the line width, specifies concavity value defining the amount of curvature on the widest part of the arrowhead
Circle	Ellipse	constrains to a circle
Curve Fit	Freeform Pen	controls how sensitive the final path is to the movement of the mouse or stylus based on a value between 0.5 and 10.0 pixels — a higher value creates a simpler path with fewer anchor points
Proportional or Define Proportions	Rectangle, Rounded Rectangle, Ellipse, Custom Shape	renders proportional shape based on the values you enter in the W (width) and H (height) boxes
Defined Size	Custom Shape	renders a custom shape based on the size specifications
Fixed Size	Rectangle, Rounded Rectangle, Ellipse, Custom Shape	renders a fixed size based on the values you enter in the W (width) and H (height) text boxes
From Center	Rectangle, Rounded Rectangle, Ellipse Custom Shape	renders the shape from the center
Magnetic	Freeform Pen	draws a path that snaps to the edges of defined areas, allowing the user to define the range and sensitivity of the snapping behavior, as well as the complexity of the resulting path
Pen Pressure	Freeform Pen	when working with a stylus tablet, an increase in pen pressure causes the width to decrease
Radius	Rounded Rectangle, Polygon	for rounded rectangles, specifies the corner radius; for polygons, specifies the distance from the center of a polygon to the outer points
Rubber Band	Pen	previews path segments as you draw
Sides	Polygon	specifies the number of sides in a polygon
Smooth Corners or Smooth Indents	Polygon	renders the shape with smooth corners or indents

BTW

The Polygon Shape

You can specify the number of sides a polygon shape has. For example, to create a triangle, enter 3 in the Sides box on the options bar. If you click the Geometry options button, you can change the polygon to a star. The number of sides then becomes the number of points on the star.

Table 4–3 Geometry Options for Shapes *(Continued)*

Options	Applicable Shape(s)	Description
Snap to Pixels	Rectangle, Rounded Rectangle	snaps edges of a rectangle or rounded rectangle to the pixel boundaries
Square	Rectangle, Rounded Rectangle	constrains to a square
Star	Polygon	creates a star from the specified radius — a 50% setting creates points that are half the total radius of the star; a larger value creates sharper, thinner points; a smaller value creates fuller points
Unconstrained	Rectangle, Rounded Rectangle, Ellipse, Custom Shape	does not constrain shapes

To Create a Shape

The following steps draw a diamond shape on the table tent card.

- Right-click the current shape tool to display the context menu (Figure 4–40).

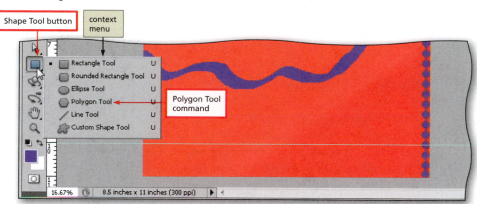

Figure 4–40

- Click Polygon Tool to select it.
- On the options bar, click the Shape layers button and then type 4 in the Sides box.
- Click the Style picker to display its settings (Figure 4–41).

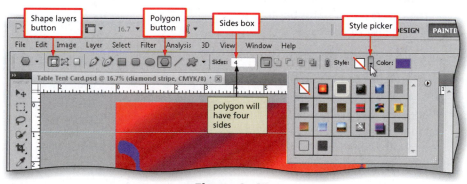

Figure 4–41

- Click the Blue Glass (Button) preset to select it (Figure 4–42).

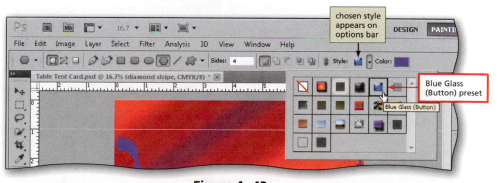

Figure 4–42

4
- In the document window, click the upper-left part of the ribbon. Drag straight down and then slightly left to create a 1-inch diamond shape, as shown in Figure 4–43.

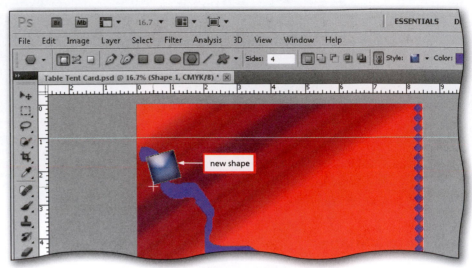

new shape

Figure 4–43

To Add a Drop Shadow

A **drop shadow** is a gray border that appears along one or two sides of an image to create the illusion of light shining on the object. A drop shadow adds to the three-dimensional effect by creating depth and giving the impression that the object is raised above the background. The following steps add a drop shadow to the diamond shape, using the Layer Style dialog box.

1
- With the Shape 1 layer still selected, click the 'Add a layer style' button on the Layers panel status bar to display the list of layer styles.

- Click Drop Shadow to display the Layer Style dialog box (Figure 4–44).

Q&A

Why are some layer style settings already selected?

The Blue Glass (Button) style applied several layer styles for you.

Layer Style dialog box

Drop Shadow option

Figure 4–44

Add a layer style button

2

- Drag the Opacity slider to 17% to create a shadow that is 17 percent transparent.

- If necessary, click to remove the check mark in the Use Global Light check box.

- Type **132** in the Angle box.

- Type **45** in the Distance box to specify the offset distance for the shadow.

- Type **30** in the Spread box to change the size of the layer mask.

- Type **40** in the Size box to set the size of the shadow (Figure 4–45).

Experiment

- Practice adjusting the shadow by dragging the distance, spread, and size sliders. Watch the changes in the preview (Layer Style dialog box) When you are finished, return the three settings to 45, 30, and 40 respectively.

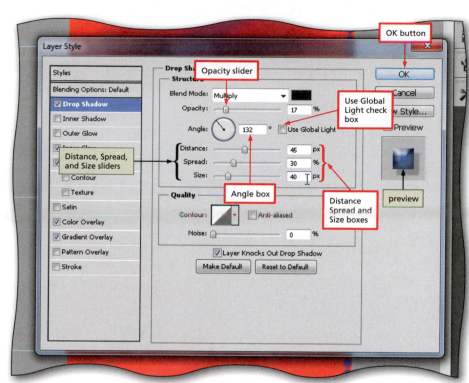

Figure 4–45

3

- Click the OK button (Layer Style dialog box) to close the Layer Style dialog box and apply the drop shadow to the shape (Figure 4–46).

Q&A

Could I have dragged the Angle radius itself, instead of typing in the Angle box?

Yes, in any panel or dialog box that an Angle radius appears, you can drag the radius clockwise or counterclockwise to adjust the angle by how it looks, rather than by entering a number.

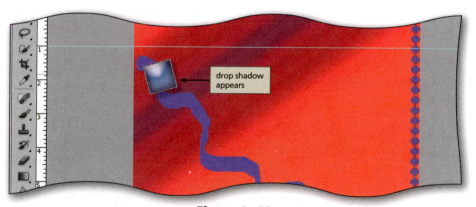

Figure 4–46

To Set Layer Properties

The following steps name the diamond layer and set its identification color.

1 Double-click the name, Shape 1, in the Layers panel. Type **diamond** to replace the name and press the ENTER key.

2 Right-click the visibility icon, and then click Yellow in the list to change the layer's identification color.

To Duplicate and Rotate a Shape Layer

The following steps duplicate the diamond layer and edit its placement, adding a new graphical element to the table tent card.

1
- Right-click the diamond layer on the Layers panel to display the context menu (Figure 4–47).

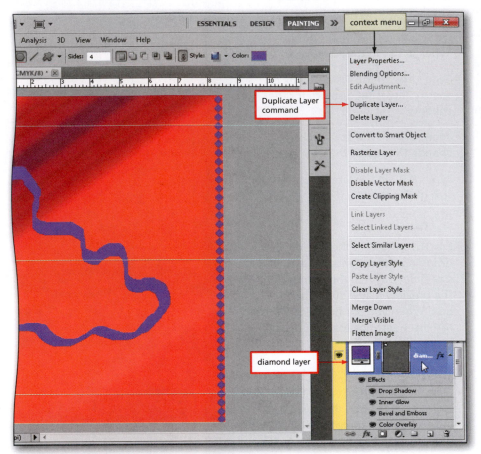

Figure 4–47

2
- Click Duplicate Layer to display the Duplicate Layer dialog box (Figure 4–48).

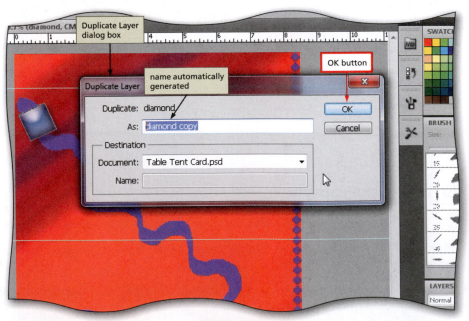

Figure 4–48

3

- Click the OK button (Duplicate Layer dialog box) to name the new layer with the default name.

- Press the v key to access the Move Tool.

- Drag down and to the right, to place the duplicate copy on the lower portion of the ribbon, as shown in Figure 4–49.

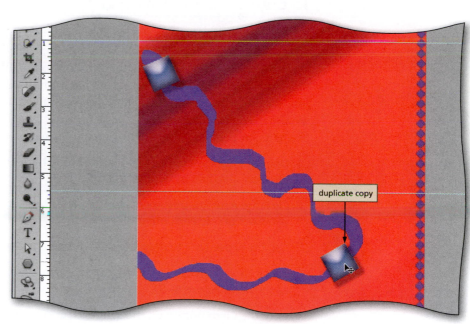

duplicate copy

Figure 4–49

Shape Picker

The Shapes option bar has a Custom Shape tool that provides access to a wide variety of shapes. Figure 4–50 displays some of the shapes you can choose by clicking the Custom Shape picker. The Custom Shape picker menu button displays several libraries of shapes that you can append to the list of presets.

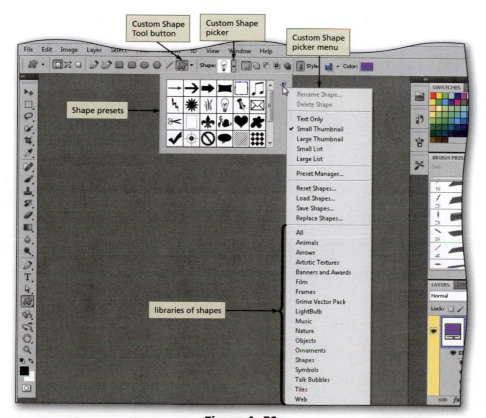

Figure 4–50

To Create the Sandwich Layer

Now you must add a sandwich and drink to the table tent card, by dragging from one window to another. The following steps open the file, Sandwich, arrange the document windows, and drag a copy from one window to the other, to add the sandwich to the table tent card. You will open the Sandwich file from the Chapter 04 folder of the Data Files for Students. You can access the Data Files for Students on the CD that accompanies this book; see the inside back cover of this book for instructions on downloading the Data Files for Students, or contact your instructor for information about accessing the required files.

1 Open the Sandwich file from the Chapter 04 folder of the Data Files for Students, or a location specified by your instructor.

2 Click the Arrange Documents button, and then click the first 2 Up button to display the windows beside each other.

3 Use the Move Tool to drag the sandwich image and drop it in the Table Tent Card window.

4 In the Table Tent Card window, drag the sandwich to a location below the second diamond, as shown in Figure 4–51.

5 Click the Close button on the Sandwich document window title bar. If Photoshop displays a dialog box asking if you want to save the changes, click the No button.

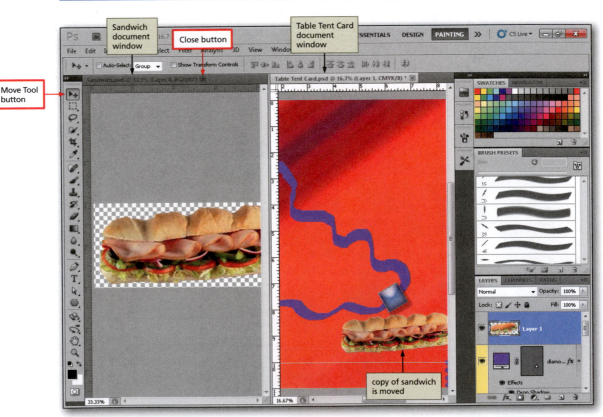

Figure 4–51

To Set Layer Properties

The following steps name the layer and set its identification color.

1 Rename the new layer, sandwich.

2 Change the layer's identification color to green.

To Create the Lemonade Layer

The following steps open the file, Lemonade, arrange the document windows, and drag a copy from one window to the other to add the glass of lemonade.

1 Open the Lemonade file from the Chapter 04 folder of the Data Files for Students, or a location specified by your instructor.

2 Click the Arrange Documents button, and then click the first 2 Up button to display the windows beside each other.

3 Use the Move Tool to drag the lemonade image and drop it in the Table Tent Card window.

4 In the Table Tent Card window, place the lemonade on the left side of the window, as shown in Figure 4–52. Ensure that the lemonade, including the straw, is below the 5.5-inch guide so that the straw does not extend onto the other side of the table tent when you print and fold the image (later in this chapter).

5 Close the Lemonade document window. If Photoshop displays a dialog box asking if you want to save the changes, click the No button.

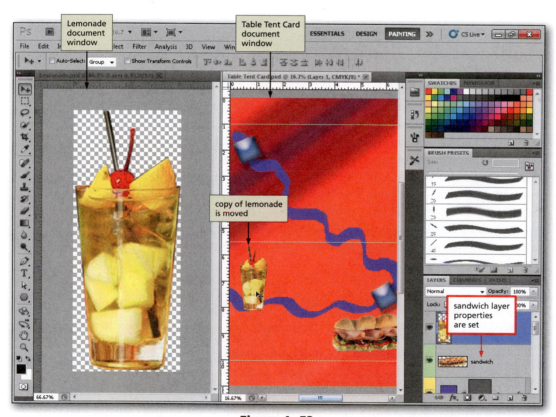

Figure 4–52

To Set Layer Properties

BTW

Color Sampler Tool
If you right-click the
Eyedropper Tool button on
the Tools panel, you can
choose the Color Sampler
tool from the context
menu. Clicking with the
Color Sampler tool displays
the color mode values in
the Info panel. You can
click to select up to four
color samples per image.

The following steps name the layer and set its identification color.

1 Rename the new layer, lemonade.

2 Change the layer's identification color to green.

To Save the File

Because you have added new images, you should save the file again.

1 Press CTRL+S to save the Table Tent Card file with the same name.

Break Point: If you wish to take a break, this is a good place to do so. You can quit Photoshop now. To resume at a later time, start Photoshop, open the file called Table Tent Card, and continue following the steps from this location forward.

Sampling Colors

BTW

Info Panel
The Info panel displays
information about the
color values beneath
the mouse pointer and
other useful information
depending on the tool
that you use. For example,
the Info panel can tell you
if the color you are using
will not print in certain
color modes. To view the
Info panel, click Info on
the Window menu, or
press the F8 key.

The Eyedropper Tool samples an existing color in a graphic or panel to assign a new foreground or background color. When you click a color using the Eyedropper Tool, Photoshop sets a new foreground color in the Tools panel and Color panel. When you ALT+click a color, Photoshop sets a new background color.

The Eyedropper options bar (Figure 4–53) allows you to change the sample size and create a color sample from the active image or from anywhere else in the Photoshop window. The Sample Size box list contains several choices. The default size, Point Sample, samples the precise color of the pixel you click. The other sample sizes, such as 3 by 3 Average and 5 by 5 Average, sample the color of the pixel where you click along with the surrounding pixels; Photoshop then calculates an average color value of the area.

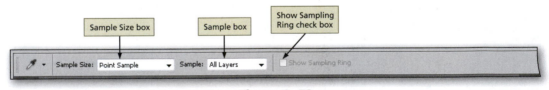

Figure 4–53

Sampling a color ensures that you will match the color without having to reenter color values on the Color panel.

To Use the Eyedropper Tool

The following steps select the Eyedropper Tool and then sample a light blue/gray color from the diamond shape to use as a stroke color for the ribbon. Using a color from the diamond maintains color consistency in all parts of the table tent card.

1

- On the Tools panel, right-click the Eyedropper Tool button to display its context menu (Figure 4–54).

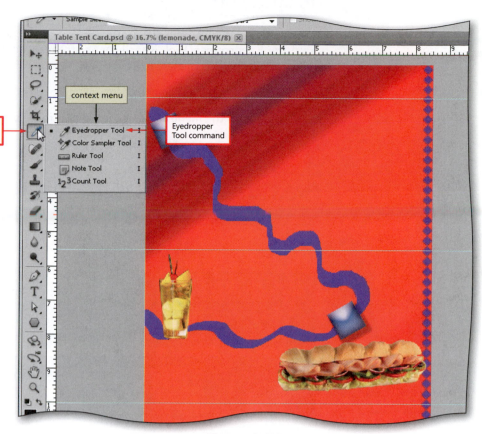

Figure 4–54

2

- Click Eyedropper Tool to select it.

- Move the mouse pointer into the document window and then click the light blue/gray color in the diamond to set the foreground color (Figure 4–55).

Q&A

Why did my Eyedropper Tool set the background color instead of the foreground color?

It is possible that someone has reversed your foreground and background colors. To fix the problem, press the F6 key to display the Color panel and then click the 'Set foreground color' button that appears as a square color swatch on the left side of the panel.

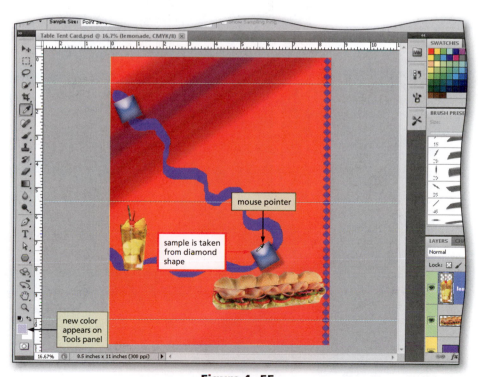

Figure 4–55

Other Ways

1. Press I, click color

To Stroke the Ribbon

The following steps stroke the ribbon with the light blue/gray color selected with the Eyedropper Tool. Recall that a stroke is a colored outline added to the edge of a selection, layer, or the entire graphic.

1 Click the ribbon layer on the Layers panel to select it.

2 Click Edit on the menu bar and then click Stroke to display the Stroke dialog box.

3 Type **3 px** in the Width box.

4 Click the Outside option button.

5 Click the OK button (Stroke dialog box) to apply the stroke (Figure 4–56).

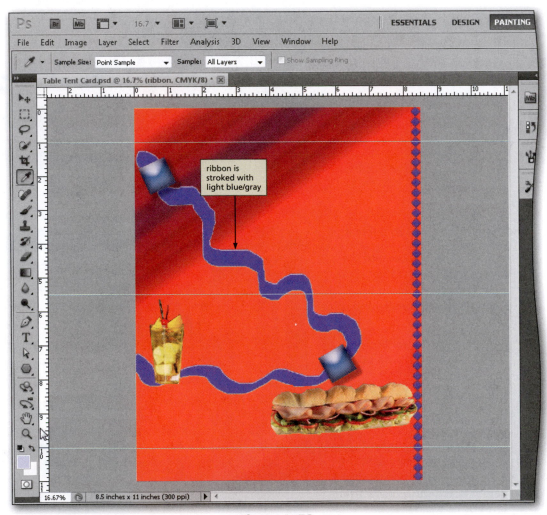

Figure 4–56

Inserting Text

The next steps use a type tool to create text for the table tent card. On the Tools panel, the default type tool is the Horizontal Type Tool. When you right-click the tool button, Photoshop displays the Vertical Type Tool, the Horizontal Type Mask Tool, and the Vertical Type Mask Tool on the context menu. When you use the Horizontal or Vertical Type tools, Photoshop automatically creates a new layer in the Layers panel. The mask tools create a selection in the shape of the text on the current layer rather than creating a new layer.

Apply effective text styles and strokes.
A font or typeface defines the appearance and shape of the letters, numbers, and special characters used in text. The fonts you use create the look, feel, and style of your graphic publications.

- For a more historical, retro, formal, or literary look and feel, use a serif font. Serif means flourish, and indicates that the letters will contain small intersecting lines, sometimes called appendages, at the end of characters.

- For a more modern feel, use sans-serif, which means without flourish, and displays in block-like letters without appendages.

- Use strokes or outlines around the lettering when the text has high priority in the graphic, and you want a distinctive look. White strokes make dark text stand out; conversely, black strokes around light-colored text help delineate the text and make it stand out.

The options bar for the type tools (Figure 4–57) includes boxes and buttons typical of those found in a word processing toolbar, including font family, font style, font size, and justification. An additional box controls the anti-aliasing. A Create warped text button allows you to create text in specialized formations, similar to the WordArt tool in Microsoft Word. On the right side of the options bar are buttons to cancel and commit editing changes. In a future chapter, you will learn about the Character and Paragraph panels that provide additional tools for manipulating text.

BTW

Adjusting Text
To adjust the size of the text bounding box, drag the sizing handles. Later, if you need to edit the text, you select the layer and select the type tool. The mouse pointer then becomes a cursor when positioned over the text.

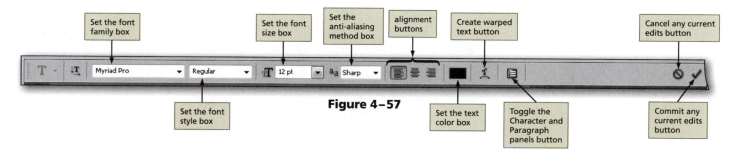

Figure 4–57

Set the font family box

Set the font style box

Set the font size box

Set the anti-aliasing method box

alignment buttons

Create warped text button

Set the text color box

Toggle the Character and Paragraph panels button

Cancel any current edits button

Commit any current edits button

BTW

Quick Reference
For a table that lists how to complete the tasks covered in this book using the mouse, context menu, and keyboard, see the Quick Reference Summary at the back of this book or visit the Photoshop CS5 Quick Reference Web page (scsite.com/pscs5/qr).

To Select the Horizontal Type Tool

The following steps select the Horizontal Type Tool on the Tools panel.

1
- Right-click the current type tool on the Tools panel to display the context menu (Figure 4–58).

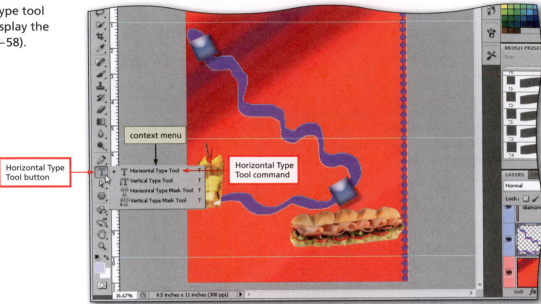

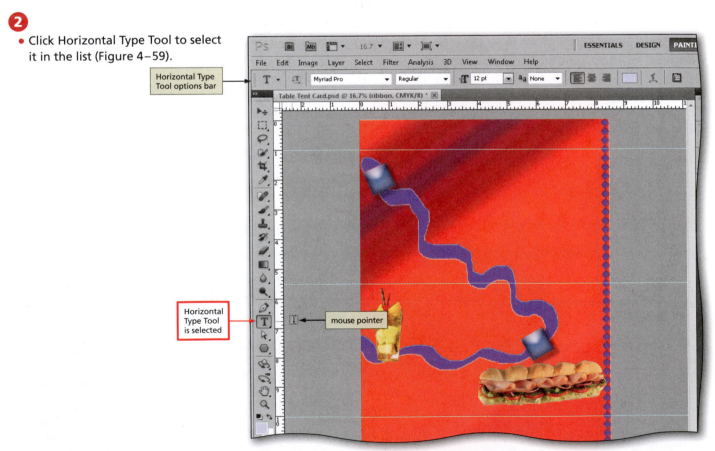

Figure 4–58

2
- Click Horizontal Type Tool to select it in the list (Figure 4–59).

Figure 4–59

To Set Font Options

The following steps select font settings on the options bar. In addition to the font and alignment options, when you click the color box, Photoshop uses color picker tools, such as a color field and color model boxes, to help you select the text color.

1
- On the options bar, click the 'Set the font family' box arrow to display the list of font families (Figure 4–60).

Q&A

What is the notation that appears to the left of the font name?

TT stands for True Type, which is a scalable font whose general shape or outline is geometrically defined, thus providing a close match between screen and printer. The O stands for Open Type, which is a cross-platform font that supports an expanded character set for linguistic support and typography.

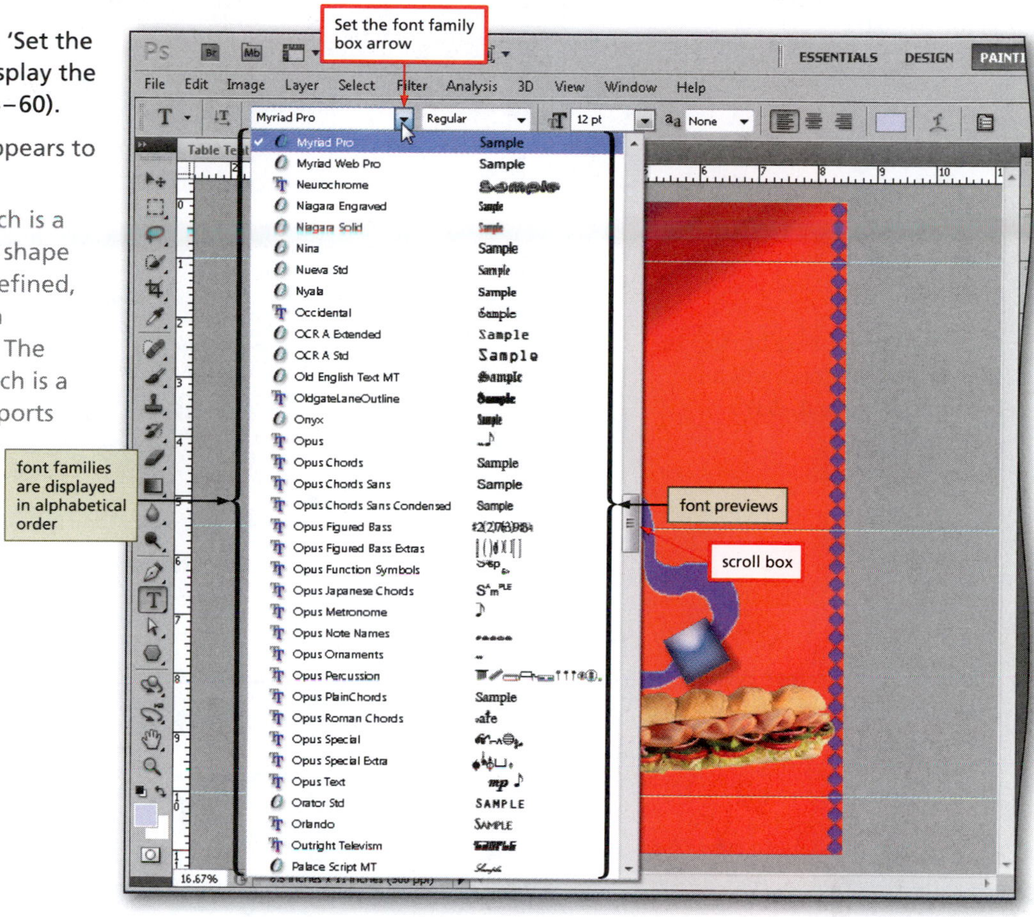

Figure 4–60

2
- Scroll as necessary, and then click Rockwell Extra Bold or a similar font in the list.
- Click the 'Set the font size' box arrow to display the list of font sizes (Figure 4–61).

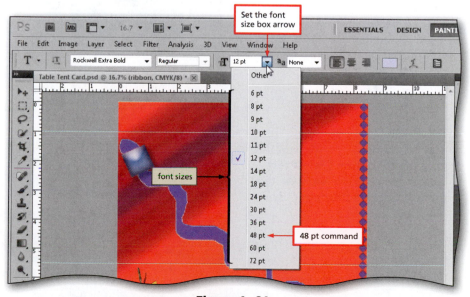

Figure 4–61

- Click 48 pt to choose a font size of 48.

- Click the 'Set the anti-aliasing method' box arrow to display the various anti-aliasing methods (Figure 4–62).

Figure 4–62

④

- Click Smooth to set the anti-aliasing method.

- Click the Center text button to specify that the text will be centered (Figure 4–63).

Figure 4–63

⑤

- Click the 'Set the text color' box to open the 'Select text color' dialog box.

- Click a white color in the upper-left corner of the color field (Figure 4–64).

Q&A What do the numerical boxes indicate?

Each color mode uses a numerical method called a color model, or color space, to describe the color. Some companies use specific numbers to create exact colors for branding purposes.

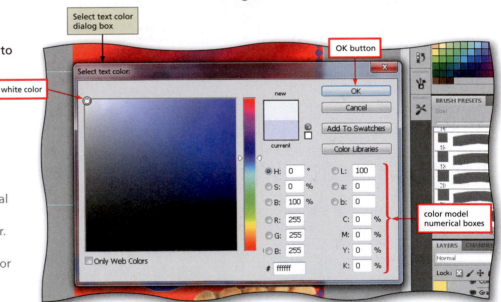

Figure 4–64

- Click the OK button ('Select text color' dialog box) to apply white as the text color on the options bar (Figure 4–65).

Figure 4–65

To Insert Text

With the type tool selected, you drag a bounding box in the document window to create a place to insert text. The mouse pointer changes to a small, open book outline. After typing the text, use the Commit any current edits button to complete the entry. Then, if the size of the bounding box needs to be adjusted, you can drag the sizing handles. Later, if you need to edit the text, you select the layer and select the type tool. The mouse pointer then becomes a cursor or insertion point when positioned over the text.

The following steps enter text on the table tent card.

1

- On the Layers panel, click the lemonade layer so that the new text layer will appear on top of, or in front of, all other layers.

- With the Horizontal Type Tool still selected, drag a bounding box beginning just below the 5.5-inch ruler guide and just right of the lemonade. Continue dragging until the box is approximately 4 inches wide and 2.5 inches tall, as shown in Figure 4–66.

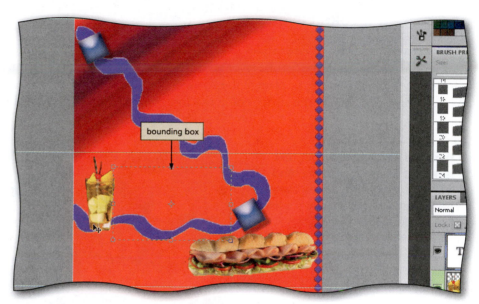

Figure 4–66

2

- Type **Big** and then press the ENTER key.

- Type **Diamond** and then press the ENTER key.

- Type **Subs** to complete the text (Figure 4–67).

Q&A Can I make changes and corrections to the text?

Yes, you can click anywhere in the text box, use the ARROW keys, the BACKSPACE key, and the DELETE key just as you do in word processing. If your bounding box is too small, you can drag the sizing handles.

3

- On the options bar, click the 'Commit any current edits' button to finish the new layer. If necessary, press the V key to access the Move Tool and then reposition the text layer in the document window.

Figure 4–67

To Set Layer Properties

The following step sets the identification color for the new text layer. While you can rename text layers, Photoshop uses the words of the text as the layer name, by default.

1 Right-click the 'Indicates layer visibility' button for the new text layer, and then click Gray in the list to change the layer's identification color.

To Create a Stroke Layer

Recall that you used layer styles to create a shadow and bevel in Chapter 3. You also stroked the ribbon using the Edit menu. By using the Stroke layer style, you can keep the stroke separate from the rest of the layer, which allows you to copy, remove, or change the stroke. The following steps create a stroke layer on the table tent card text. If you do not change the stroke color, the foreground color, in this case black, is used.

1

• With the Big Diamond Subs text layer still selected, click the 'Add a layer style' button on the Layers panel status bar to display the list of layer styles (Figure 4–68).

Figure 4–68

2

• Click Stroke to display the Layer Style dialog box.

• Drag the Size slider to 10 pixels to increase the size of the stroke (Figure 4–69).

 Experiment

• Drag the Size slider to various sizes and watch how it affects the text. Drag the opacity slider to various settings and watch the transparency of the stroke change. Reset the Size back to 10 pixels and the Opacity to 100% when you are finished.

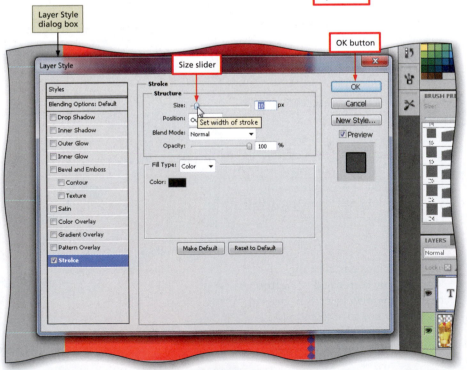

Figure 4–69

3
- Click the OK button (Layer Style dialog box) to apply the stroke (Figure 4–70).

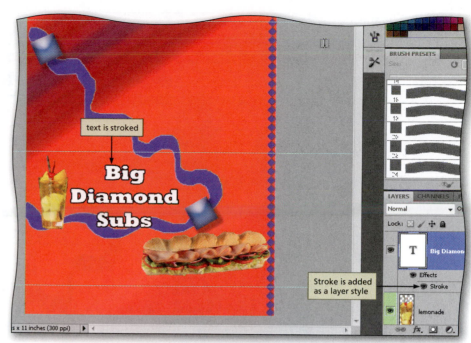

Figure 4–70

To Rotate the Canvas

Because the table tent card will be folded, additional text and graphics need to be facing the top. It is easier to rotate the entire page than to edit text and graphics upside down. The following steps rotate the canvas.

1
- Click Image on the menu bar and then point to Image Rotation to display its submenu (Figure 4–71).

Figure 4–71

• Click 180° on the Image Rotation submenu to rotate the image (Figure 4–72).

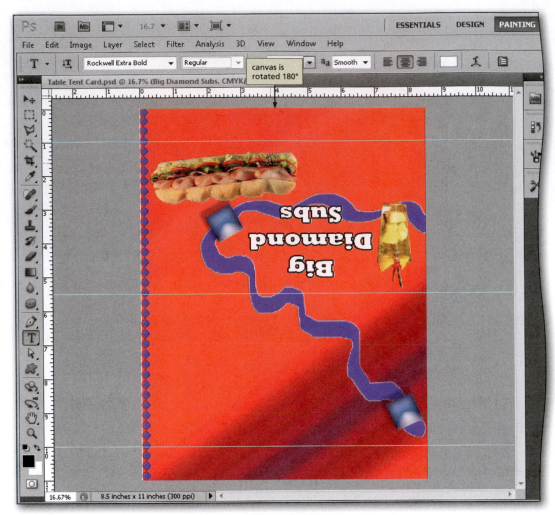

Figure 4–72

To Insert Another Graphic

The following steps open the file, Party Tray, and add the party tray to the table tent card image.

1 Open the Party Tray file from the Chapter 04 folder of the Data Files for Students, or a location specified by your instructor.

2 Click the Arrange Documents button, and then click the first 2 Up button to display the windows beside each other.

3 Use the Move Tool to drag the party tray image and drop it in the Table Tent Card window.

4 In the Table Tent Card window, drag the party tray to the left side of the canvas, just above the 10-inch ruler guide (Figure 4–73).

5 Click the Close button on the Party Tray document window title bar. If Photoshop displays a dialog box asking if you want to save the changes, click the No button.

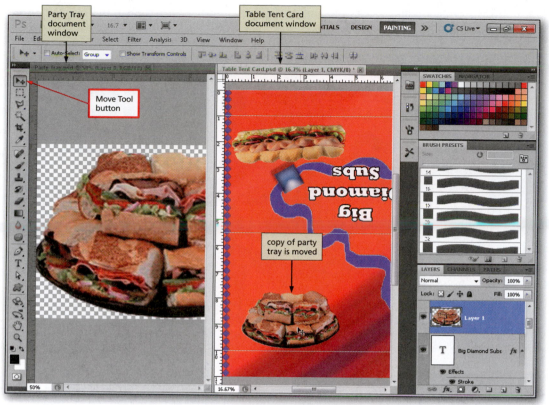

Figure 4–73

To Set Layer Properties

The following steps name the layer and set its identification color.

1 Rename the new layer, party tray.

2 Change the layer's identification color to violet.

To Insert More Text

The following steps create more text for the table tent card.

1 Select the Horizontal Type Tool on the Tools panel.

2 In the document window, drag a bounding box beginning at a location 3.5 inches from the left margin and 6.5 inches from the top margin. Continue dragging down and right to create a box approximately 4.5 inches wide and 4 inches tall.

3 Type `Order a party tray…` and then press the ENTER key.

4 Type `today!` to complete the text.

5 On the options bar, click the 'Commit any current edits' button to complete the entry and create the new layer. If necessary, press the V key to access the Move Tool, and then reposition the text layer in the document window.

6 On the Layers panel, click the 'Add a layer style' button and then click Stroke. When Photoshop displays the Layer Style dialog box, if necessary, change the stroke size to 10 px, otherwise, click the OK button to accept the previous stroke settings.

BTW

Photoshop Help
The best way to become familiar with Photoshop Help is to use it. Appendix D includes detailed information about Photoshop Help and exercises that will help you gain confidence in using it.

7 Right-click the visibility icon for the new text layer, and then click Gray in the list to change the layer's identification color (Figure 4–74).

Figure 4–74

To Save the File

The table tent card is complete. You will save the file with the name Table Tent Card with Layers in the PSD format.

1 Press SHIFT+CTRL+S and save the file with the name, Table Tent Card with Layers.

To Flatten and Save the File

The following steps flatten the image and save it as a TIFF file.

1 On the Layer menu, click the Flatten Image command.

2 Press SHIFT+CTRL+S and save the file with the name Table Tent Card for Printing, in the TIFF format. When Photoshop displays the TIFF Options dialog box, click the OK button to finish saving the file.

To Print the Table Tent Card

1 Prepare the printer according to the printer instructions.

2 Click File on the menu bar, and then click Print to display the Print dialog box.

3 If necessary, click the Printer box arrow and then select your printer from the list. Do not change any other settings.

4 In the Print dialog box, click the Print button to start the printing process. If your system displays a second Print dialog box or a Print Settings dialog box, unique to your printer, click its Print button.

5 When the printer stops, retrieve the hard copy of the image. Fold the tent card in the middle and then again at 1 inch from each end (Figure 4–75).

(a) Front of Tent Card

(b) Back of Tent Card

Figure 4–75

To Close the Document Window and Quit Photoshop

The final step is to close the document window and quit Photoshop.

1 Click the Close button on the Application bar to close the document window and quit Photoshop.

Chapter Summary

You used many tools and panels to create the table tent card in this chapter. You started a new file from scratch and used the Gradient Tool to create a colorful background. You selected a brush and drew a ribbon, and then used a different brush tip to draw diamonds down the side of the tent card. You created a shape and added a drop shadow for the diamond. You added images of a sandwich, lemonade, and a party tray. You used the Horizontal Type Tool to add text, and then you stroked the text. You rotated the image to allow for a two-sided card. Finally, you flattened the image and saved the file.

The items listed below include all the new Photoshop skills you have learned in this chapter:

1. Select the Painting Workspace (PS 214)
2. Start a New Photoshop File (PS 215)
3. Select the Gradient Tool and Style (PS 219)
4. Select a Noise Gradient Preset (PS 221)
5. Edit a Solid Gradient (PS 223)
6. Draw the Gradient (PS 223)
7. Choose a Color in the Swatches Panel (PS 227)
8. Select the Brush Tool (PS 229)
9. Append Brush Presets (PS 231)
10. Select a Brush Using the Brush Preset Picker (PS 232)
11. Change the Size and Hardness of the Brush (PS 232)
12. Draw Using the Brush Tool (PS 233)
13. Display the Brush Panel (PS 235)
14. Set Brush Options (PS 236)
15. Draw Straight Lines with the Brush Tool (PS 238)
16. Create a Shape (PS 241)
17. Add a Drop Shadow (PS 242)
18. Duplicate and Rotate a Shape Layer (PS 244)
19. Use the Eyedropper Tool (PS 248)
20. Select the Horizontal Type Tool (PS 252)
21. Set Font Options (PS 253)
22. Insert Text (PS 255)
23. Create a Stroke Layer (PS 256)
24. Rotate the Canvas (PS 257)

Learn It Online

Test your knowledge of chapter content and key terms.

Instructions: To complete the Learn It Online exercises, start your browser, click the Address bar, and then enter the Web address **scsite.com/pscs5/learn**. When the Photoshop CS5 Learn It Online page is displayed, click the link for the exercise you want to complete and then read the instructions.

Chapter Reinforcement TF, MC, and SA

A series of true/false, multiple choice, and short answer questions that tests your knowledge of the chapter content.

Flash Cards

An interactive learning environment where you identify chapter key terms associated with displayed definitions.

Practice Test

A series of multiple choice questions that test your knowledge of chapter content and key terms.

Who Wants To Be a Computer Genius?

An interactive game that challenges your knowledge of chapter content in the style of a television quiz show.

Wheel of Terms

An interactive game that challenges your knowledge of chapter key terms in the style of the television show *Wheel of Fortune*.

Crossword Puzzle Challenge

A crossword puzzle that challenges your knowledge of key terms presented in the chapter.

Apply Your Knowledge

Reinforce the skills and apply the concepts you learned in this chapter.

Creating a Book Cover

Instructions: Start Photoshop and perform the customization steps found on pages PS 6 through PS 9. Open the Apply 4-1 Book Cover file from the Chapter 04 folder of the Data Files for Students. You can access the Data Files for Students on the CD that accompanies this book; see the inside back cover of this book for instructions on downloading the Data Files for Students, or contact your instructor for information about accessing the required files.

The purpose of this exercise is to create a composite photo by adding a gradient and custom shape to create a graphic similar to the one shown in Figure 4–76.

Figure 4–76

Perform the following tasks:

1. Use the Save As command to save the image on your USB flash drive as a PSD file, with the file name Apply 4-1 Book Cover Edited. Hide the text layers.

2. Select the Gradient Tool. On the options bar, click the Gradient Editor box. If necessary, click the Foreground to Background preset. Double-click the left Color Stop button to display the 'Select stop color' dialog box. Click a yellow color on the color bar and then click the OK button ('Select color stop' dialog box). Repeat the process to select a light orange or peach color for the right Color Stop button. If other Color Stop buttons appear, click them, and then click the Delete button in the Gradient Editor dialog box. When you are finished, click the OK button (Gradient Editor dialog box).

3. In the document window, drag from the upper-left to the lower-right to create the gradient.

4. Open the file named Apply 4-1 Rose from the Chapter 04 folder of the Data Files for Students. Use the Arrange Documents button to display the windows side by side. Use the Move Tool to drag the rose into the Apply 4-1 Book Cover Edited document window. Close the Apply 4-1 Rose document window. If necessary, press CTRL+T, and then scale the rose to match the size in Figure 4–76 and reposition it. Press the ENTER key to commit the transformation. Name the layer, rose.

5. Use the Magic Eraser Tool to erase the black background from the rose layer.

6. On the Tools panel, click the current shape tool. On the Shape options bar, click the Custom Shape Tool button. Click the Custom shape picker. When the panel appears, click the menu button. Click Nature in the list. Append the shapes. Scroll as necessary, and then click the Raindrop shape.

Continued >

Apply Your Knowledge *continued*

7. On the Tools panel, click the 'Set foreground color' button to access the Color Picker (Foreground Color) dialog box. Click in the color slider to choose blue, and then click a light blue in the color field. Click the OK button.

8. Drag in the document window several times, with varying lengths, to create the raindrops similar to those shown in Figure 4–76 on the previous page. Each raindrop will create its own layer.

9. Click the visibility icon next to both text layers.

10. Save the file again, and then flatten the image.

11. Save the flattened file with the name Apply 4-1 Book Cover Complete in the TIFF format. Submit the file in the format specified by your instructor.

Extend Your Knowledge

Extend the skills you learned in this chapter and experiment with new skills. You may need to use Help to complete the assignment.

Creating a Promotional Movie Poster

Instructions: Start Photoshop and perform the customization steps found on pages PS 6 through PS 9. Open the Extend 4-1 Movie Poster file from the Chapter 04 folder of the Data Files for Students. You can access the Data Files for Students on the CD that accompanies this book; see the inside back cover of this book for instruction on downloading the Data Files for Students, or contact your instructor for information about accessing the required files. The purpose of this exercise is to create a composite image with various components, similar to Figure 4–77, and to create both a PSD and TIFF version of the final composition.

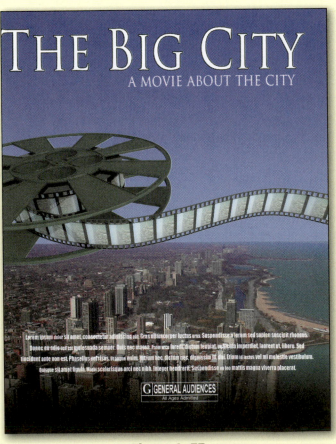

Figure 4–77

1. Save the image on your USB flash drive as a PSD file, with the file name Extend 4-1 Movie Poster Edited.

2. To create a gradient at the top of the photo:

   a. Create a new layer named, sky.

   b. With the new layer selected, use the Rectangular Marquee Tool to create a selection that includes the top half of the canvas, down to the horizon line in the photo.

   c. Select the Gradient Tool and its Linear Gradient style. Click the Gradient Editor box to display the Gradient Editor dialog box. Click the left stop button and sample a dark blue in the photo. Click the right stop button and sample a light blue from the photo. (*Hint*: You may have to drag the dialog boxes out of the way to sample the colors.) Close the Gradient Editor dialog box.

   d. SHIFT+drag from the top of the selection to the bottom of the section to create a linear gradient. If necessary, press CTRL+D to deselect.

3. To create a gradient at the bottom of the photo:

   a. Create a new layer and name it footer.

   b. With the new layer selected, use the Rectangular Marquee Tool to create a selection that includes the bottom two inches of the photo.

   c. Select the Gradient Tool and its Linear Gradient style. Click the Gradient Editor box to display the Gradient Editor. Choose the second preset, named Foreground to Transparent. Close the Gradient Editor dialog box.

   d. Press the D key to reset the foreground and background colors.

   e. SHIFT+drag from the bottom of the selection to the top of the section to create a linear gradient. If necessary, press CTRL+D to deselect.

4. To insert placeholder text:

   a. Open the Extend 4-1 Movie Text file and arrange the two document windows side by side.

   b. Use the Move Tool to drag the text into the Extend 4-1 Movie Poster Edited file and position it in the lower part of the photo as shown in Figure 4–77.

   c. Close the Extend 4-1 Movie Text file.

5. To insert movie rating text:

   a. Open the Extend 4-1 Movie Rating file and arrange the two document windows side by side.

   b. Use the Move Tool to drag the rating into the Extend 4-1 Movie Poster Edited file and position it below the placeholder text as shown in Figure 4–77.

   c. Close the Extend 4-1 Movie Rating file.

6. To create movie title text:

   a. Select the Horizontal Type Tool. Choose a serif font similar to Trajan Pro or Garamond. Set the font size to 100 and select a light shade for the color. Drag a text box across the top of the canvas. Type `The Big City` in the text box. Click the 'Commit any current edits' button on the options bar.

   b. On the Layers panel, use the 'Add a layer style' button to add a stroke to the title using a dark gray color sampled from the photo.

7. To create movie subtitle text:

   a. Using the Horizontal Type Tool again, with the same font, set the font size to 30. Drag a text box below the title and to the right. Type `A MOVIE ABOUT THE CITY` in the text box. Click the 'Commit any current edits' button on the options bar.

8. To add the movie reel image:

   a. Use Photoshop Help to read about the Place command. Click File on the menu bar, and then click Place. Browse to the file named Extend 4-1 Movie Reel and select it. Click the Place button and then position the movie reel image as shown in Figure 4–77. Press the ENTER key to finish the place.

Continued >

Extend Your Knowledge *continued*

9. Save the file again and then flatten the image.

10. Press SHIFT+CTRL+S to open the Save As dialog box. Type **Extend 4-1 Movie Poster Complete** in the Name box. Click the Format box arrow and then click TIFF in the list. Click the Save button. When Photoshop displays the TIFF Options dialog box, click the OK button to finish saving the file.

11. Submit the file in the format specified by your instructor.

Make It Right

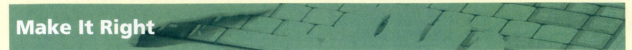

Analyze a project and correct all errors and/or improve the design.

Correcting a Cell Phone Ad

Instructions: Start Photoshop and perform the customization steps found on pages PS 6 through PS 9. Open the Make It Right 4-1 Cell Phone file from the Chapter 04 folder of the Data Files for Students. You can access the Data Files for Students on the CD that accompanies this book; see the inside back cover of this book for instructions on downloading the Data Files for Students, or contact your instructor for information about accessing the required files.

The file contains an ad for the Super Chrome 2000 cell phone (Figure 4–78). The client thinks that it is too bland. You are to improve the look of the ad with gradients and brushes.

Figure 4–78

1. On the background layer, create a radial gradient with shades of purple, from the middle of the cell phone to the lower-left corner of the image, so the radial appears around the cell phone.

2. On the green layer, draw a radial gradient with shades of green from left to right.

3. On the blue layer, draw a radial gradient with shades of blue from the middle to the bottom.

4. On the Layers panel, click the super chrome layer, and then CTRL+click the super chrome layer thumbnail to select its content. Apply the Chrome preset gradient in a linear style from top to bottom.

5. Repeat Step 4 for the 2000 layer.

6. For a final touch, use the 'Add a layer style' button to add a bevel and a drop shadow to help set the text layers apart from the blue background. Use the default settings for both layer styles.

7. Save the file as Make It Right 4-1 Cell Phone Edited.

In the Lab

Design and/or create a publication using the guidelines, concepts, and skills presented in this chapter. Labs are listed in order of increasing difficulty.

Lab 1: Creating an Advertisement Using Gradients and Shapes

Problem: Your uncle owns a small golf course on the edge of town. He has heard you are studying Photoshop, and he would like you to create an advertisement for him. He plans to place the color ad in a regional golfing magazine; therefore, he wants a high resolution, CMYK file to submit to the publisher. He has a file with the appropriate text copy, an image of a golf ball, and an image of a golfer. You need to put it all together, adding a gradient background and inserting a shape. A sample solution is shown in Figure 4–79.

Figure 4–79

Continued >

In the Lab *continued*

Instructions: Perform the following tasks:

1. Start Photoshop. Set the default workspace, default colors, and reset all tools. Open the file Lab 4-1 Golf Outing from the Chapter 04 folder of the Data Files for Students. You can access the Data Files for Students on the CD that accompanies this book; see the inside back cover of this book for instructions on downloading the Data Files for Students, or contact your instructor for information about accessing the required files.

2. Click the Save As command on the File menu. Browse to your USB flash drive storage device. Click the Save button. If Photoshop displays a format Options dialog box, click the OK button.

3. In the Layers panel, click the visibility icons to hide all text layers. Click the Background layer to select it, if necessary.

4. Press the G key to activate the Gradient Tool. If the Paint Bucket Tool is active, press SHIFT+G to toggle to the Gradient Tool.

5. On the Gradient options bar, click the Linear Gradient button and then click the Gradient Editor box. When Photoshop displays the Gradient Editor dialog box, click the Foreground to Background preset. Click the Gradient Type box arrow and then click Solid. Double-click the Smoothness box and then type 100.

6. Below the color bar, double-click the left Color Stop button. When the 'Select stop color' dialog box is displayed, click light blue in the color panel. Click the OK button.

7. Below the color bar, double-click the right Color Stop button. When the 'Select stop color' dialog box is displayed, click light yellow in the color panel. Click the OK button.

8. Below the center of the color bar, double-click to create a new Color Stop button. When the 'Select stop color' dialog box is displayed, choose a light orange color. Click the OK button.

9. Drag the orange Color Stop button slightly to the right until the gradient smoothly transitions from one color to another, similar to that shown in Figure 4–79 on the previous page. Adjust any Color Midpoint diamonds as necessary.

10. Click the OK button in the Gradient Editor dialog box. Draw a gradient by dragging from the upper-right corner of the page in the document window to the lower-left corner. (*Hint:* If you do not like the result and want to redo the gradient, press CTRL+Z to undo the step and then repeat Steps 6 through 10.)

11. In the Layers panel, display the text layers.

12. Press CTRL+O and then navigate to the file named Lab 4-1 Golfer. Open the file.

13. Use the Arrange Documents button to display the windows side by side. In the Lab 4-1 Golfer document window, press CTRL+A to select the entire image. Use the Move Tool to drag the image to the Lab 4-1 Golf Outing document window. Position the golfer as shown in Figure 4–79.

14. Close the Lab 4-1 Golfer document window. In the Layers panel, rename the new layer, golfer.

15. Press CTRL+O and then navigate to the file named Lab 4-1 Golf Ball. Open the file.

16. In the Lab 4-1 Golf Ball document window, press CTRL+A to select the entire image. Press CTRL+C to copy the image. Select the Lab 4-1 Golf Outing document window and then press CTRL+V to paste the image. Close the Lab 4-1 Golf Ball document window. Position the golf ball as shown in Figure 4–79.

17. Increase the magnification as necessary in the Lab 4-1 Golf Outing document window. Press the E key to access the current Eraser Tool. Use the Magic Eraser Tool to erase the blue areas around the golf ball.

18. Resize the golf ball to make it smaller by pressing CTRL+T to display the bounding box. SHIFT+drag a corner sizing handle and then press the ENTER key. Rename the new layer, golf ball.

19. Press the U key to access the shape tools. On the Shape options bar, click the Shape layers button to select it, if necessary. Click the Custom Shape Tool button.

20. On the Shape options bar, click the Custom Shape picker. When the pop-up panel is displayed, click the menu button and then click Web in the list. When Photoshop asks if you want to replace or append the shapes, click the Append button. When the new shapes are displayed, scroll as necessary and double-click the Time shape.

21. On the Shape options bar, click the Color box. When the Color Picker dialog box is displayed, select a Light Gray color. Click the OK button.

22. In the document window, SHIFT+drag to create a clock in the lower-right portion of the image, similar to the one shown in Figure 4–79 on page PS 267. On the Layers panel, drag the Opacity slider to make the appearance of the clock more subtle. Rename the layer, clock. A border may appear around the edges of the clock. It will disappear when you flatten the image.

23. On the File menu, click Save.

24. On the Layer menu, click Flatten Image. Save the flattened image as **Lab 4-1 Golf Outing Complete** in the TIFF format.

25. Quit Photoshop. E-mail the file as an attachment to your instructor.

In the Lab

Lab 2: Creating a Web Graphic from Scratch

Problem: The planetarium is holding a contest to choose a Web graphic to advertise its new exhibit. The winning promotional piece will represent themes related to the search for life in deep space. The winner of the contest will receive $500 and a family membership to the planetarium. You decide to enter. Using a gradient, a shape, and brush strokes, you create a piece that symbolizes the planets, the sky, motion, searching, and life. A sample image is displayed in Figure 4–80.

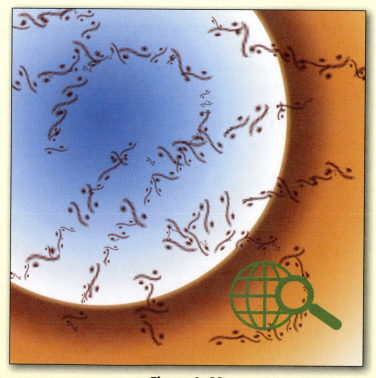

Figure 4–80

Continued >

In the Lab *continued*

Instructions: Perform the following tasks:

1. Start Photoshop. Set the default workspace and reset all tools.

2. Click New on the File menu. When the New dialog box is displayed, use the following settings:

   Name: Lab 4-2 Planetarium Graphic

   Width: 8 inches

   Height: 8 inches

   Resolution: 300 pixels/inch

   Color Mode: RGB Color, 8 bit

   Background Contents: White

3. Save the file on your storage device in the PSD format.

4. Select the Gradient Tool. On the Gradient options bar, click the Gradient Editor box arrow and then double-click the Chrome gradient.

5. On the options bar, click the Radial Gradient button, and then drag from the upper-left corner to the lower-right corner.

6. Select the Eyedropper Tool and sample the darkest brown color in the Chrome gradient. In the Color panel, if a warning triangle is displayed, click the square next to it to select a gamut color.

7. Select the Brush Tool. Click the Brush Presets picker on the options bar and then click the panel menu button. On the panel menu, click Assorted Brushes and append the brushes.

8. Display the Brush panel. Click the Brush Tip Shape button. Scroll as necessary and then click the Ornament 7 size 15 brush tip. Click the Shape Dynamics check box so it displays a check mark. Set the Diameter to 200 pixels, and the Spacing to 150%. Press the F5 key to return the Brush panel to the dock of collapsed panels. Drag with short strokes, randomly in the image and at different angles. Your design does not have to match the one in Figure 4–80 on the previous page.

9. Click the 'Set foreground color' button on the Tools panel. When Photoshop displays the Color Picker (Foreground Color) dialog box, click the Only Web Colors check box so it displays a check mark. Click green in the color slider and then click an appropriate green color in the color field. Click the OK button.

10. Select the Shape Tool. On the Shape options bar, click the Shape layers button. Click the Custom Shape Tool button. Click the Custom Shape picker, and then click the panel menu button. On the menu, click Web. When Photoshop asks if you want to replace or append, click the Append button. Scroll as necessary and then select the World Wide Web Search shape.

11. In the document window, SHIFT+drag to add the shape in the lower-right corner. Adjust the position if necessary.

12. Assign an appropriate name and identification color to the new layer you created.

13. Save the file again and then flatten the image.

14. Press SHIFT+CTRL+S to access the Save As dialog box. In the File name box, type **Lab 4-2 Planetarium Graphic Complete** as the name. Save the file using the TIFF format.

15. For extra credit, create a simple Web page and display your image. Send your instructor a copy of the image as an e-mail attachment or send the URL.

In the Lab

Lab 3: Creating a Flyer

Problem: A local bowling alley has asked you to create a simple image with the words, Bowl-O-Rama above a colorful bowling ball. The address should appear below the bowling ball. A sample image is displayed in Figure 4–81.

Instructions: Perform the following tasks: Start Photoshop. Set the default workspace and reset all tools. Create a new Photoshop file named Lab 4-3 Bowling Flyer and save it to your USB flash drive storage device. The new file should be approximately 8.5 inches wide by 5.5 inches high. Set the resolution to 150 and use RGB, 8 bit for the color mode.

Create a background layer containing a radial gradient with shades of purple. Drag in the canvas from the middle to the upper-right corner. Create a selection that includes the lower half of the canvas and create a second linear gradient as shown in Figure 4–81. (*Hint:* The Reverse check box on the options bar should not display a check mark.) Create a new layer named shadow and draw a large circle in the middle of the canvas. (*Hint:* Use the Elliptical Marquee Tool and the SHIFT key.) Add a radial gradient using the Foreground to Transparent preset, set the foreground color to black, and then drag from the middle to the edge of the selection.

In a new layer, use a Shape Tool to create the bowling ball. (*Hint:* On the options bar, click the Style picker and then click the Nebula preset.) Adjust the opacity of the bowling ball. Create the finger holes on the bowling ball. (*Hint:* Reset the default colors to black over white.) Add the Pattern Overlay layer style to the ball layer, and use the Tie Dye pattern.

Create the upper text using the appropriate tool, a typeface similar to Cooper Std, and a large size font. (*Hint:* Warp the text using the Arc style from within the Warp Text dialog box.) Add the lower text. Create the stars in their own layer using an appropriate brush to make a star pattern randomly across the top of the background.

Save the image again, flatten it, and then save it in the TIFF format with the file name, Lab 4-3 Bowling Flyer Complete. Submit it in the format specified by your instructor.

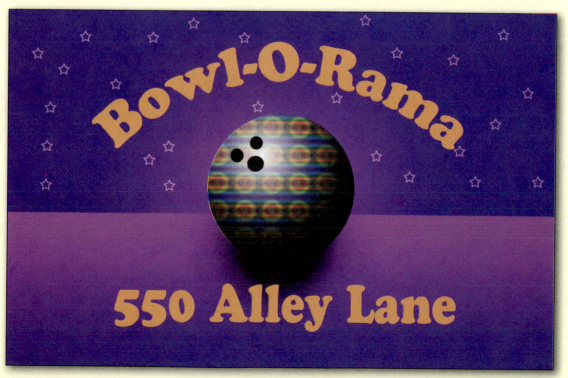

Figure 4–81

Cases and Places

Apply your creative thinking and problem-solving skills to design and implement a solution.

Note: To complete these assignments, you may be required to use the Data Files for Students. See the inside back cover of this book for instructions on downloading the Data Files for Students, or contact your instructor for information about accessing the required files.

1: Create a Sign with Shapes

Academic

Create a sign to place on the paper recycling box in your computer lab. Start with a blank page that is 8.5 × 11 inches. Choose a shape tool and then click the Custom Shape Tool button on the Shape options bar. Click the Shape box. When the shapes are displayed, click Shape Preset picker menu button and then click Symbols in the list. Click to Append the Symbols to the current set. Scroll to display the recycling logo and click it. Drag to create a recycling logo that fills the page, leaving a 1-inch margin on each side. Select a dark blue color from the Swatches panel and then use the Paint Bucket Tool to color the logo. If you are asked to rasterize the layer, click the OK button. Find a graphic of a piece of paper with something printed on it. Drag a copy to the middle of the recycling logo. Print the sign on a color printer.

2: Color a Photo

Personal

Scan in a black-and-white photo and open it in Photoshop. Print a copy of the photo. Use the Magic Wand Tool to select portions of clothing, buildings, sky, grass, or walls. Double-click the 'Set foreground color' button on the Tools panel, and then select a color using the Color Picker (Foreground Color) dialog box. Use the Paint Bucket Tool to fill the selections with color. Save the colorized version of the photo with a different name. Print the colorized version. Turn in both the before and after printouts to your instructor.

3: Create a Special Effects Storyboard

Professional

You are in charge of special effects for a small movie production company. You need to plan a storyboard of special effects for an upcoming action movie. Decide on a theme for your movie. Create a new document that is 11 × 8.5 inches. Copy several digital or electronic images onto your blank canvas. Use painting and drawing tools to add at least four of the following special effects to each of the real images: flames, lightning bolts, explosions, tattoos, jet streams, rocket flares, spider webs, sunbursts, or some other effect of your choosing. Save the file and submit it as directed by your instructor.

5 | Enhancing and Repairing Photos

Objectives

You will have mastered the material in this chapter when you can:

- Discuss technical tips for digital cameras and scanners

- Convert an image to Grayscale mode

- Create new layers for editing and viewing corrections

- Apply blending modes

- Fill using Content-Aware

- Repair documents with aging damage

- Make level corrections for contrast

- Sharpen images with the Unsharp Mask

- Correct damage using the healing tools

- Retouch images using the Patch Tool

- Correct red eye

- Use the Dodge and Burn Tools

- Remove or correct angle and perspective distortions

- Enhance a photo using the Smudge Tool

5 | Enhancing and Repairing Photos

Introduction

Repairing and enhancing photos is an important skill for people such as graphic designers, restoration experts, and professional photographers. It is a useful skill for the amateur photographer as well. Many families have old photographs that have been damaged over time, and most people have taken a red-eye photo, a photo that is too light or dark, or one in which the subject is tilted. Freelance photographers, genealogists, family historians, and proud parents all use Photoshop to restore, correct, and improve their photographs.

It is impossible to make every photo look perfect — even with graphic-editing software. Graphics-related professionals know that a camera lacks the flexibility to rival reality — the tonal range of color is too small. Digital cameras or digital creations cannot reproduce the large number of spectrum colors visible to the human eye. Therefore, enhancing and repairing photos is both an art and a science. Using the digital tools available in Photoshop, you can employ technology to make reparative and restorative changes. Artistically, you need strong color and design sensibility.

Restoring original documents is a highly skilled art. It takes education, research, and years of practice. When dealing with documents of great value, or when dealing with materials in advanced stages of deterioration, you should consult a professional conservator or restoration service. Many restorers, however, choose to renovate original documents using digital copies. If the document can be scanned or photographed, the original does not have to be disturbed. Photoshop has many tools to help repair and enhance documents.

Project — Enhancing and Repairing Photos

Chapter 5 uses Photoshop to enhance and repair several photographs and documents. A yellowed and torn piece of sheet music needs to be repaired for easier reading. A picture of a waterfall has a missing corner. An old photo of a child contains wrinkles and defects. A photo of a graduate needs to be enhanced by lightening the image. A photo of a building needs a perspective correction. A picture of some children needs to have the red eye removed. Finally, another photo is enhanced artistically. The before and after photos are illustrated in Figure 5 – 1.

Figure 5–1

Overview

As you read this chapter, you will learn how to enhance and repair the images shown in Figure 5–1 on the previous page by performing these general tasks:

- Remove yellowing.
- Apply blending modes.
- Sharpen images.
- Fix dark spots in a photo.
- Restore missing portions of a document.
- Repair tears and blemishes.
- Correct red eye.
- Create a vignette.
- Correct lens errors and distortions.
- Use smudging for artistic effect.

Plan Ahead

General Project Guidelines

When editing a photo, the actions you perform and decisions you make will affect the appearance and characteristics of the finished product. As you edit photos, such as the ones shown in Figure 5–1 on the previous page, you should follow these general guidelines:

1. **Create a high-resolution digital image.** When repairing a printed photo or document, the scanning technique is the most important step in enhancing and repairing the image. Scan using the highest resolution possible with the correct settings. Other image sources may include digital cameras and graphics from the Web. Always work on a copy of the original scan, or create a corrections layer.

2. **Sharpen images and retouch as necessary.** Sharpening images that have been scanned creates more defined edges and improves the overall look of the image. Retouching includes erasing, cloning, and correcting light and dark spots.

3. **Heal specific defects.** Remove defects, such as yellowing, blemishes, tears, and red eye, to improve legibility and clarity. Restoration professionals attempt to recreate the original look and feel of old documents and photos.

4. **Correct lens errors.** The final touch is to correct any lens errors. You can correct distortion, angles, blurs, vignetting, perspective errors, keystone distortions, barrel distortions, chromatic aberrations, and scaling.

When necessary, more specific details concerning the above guidelines are presented at appropriate points in the chapter. The chapter also will identify the actions performed and decisions made regarding these guidelines during the creation of the edited photos shown in Figure 5–1.

Gathering Images

Recall that a variety of pictures and documents can be imported into Photoshop in different ways. Pictures taken using old photograph-generating devices, such as tintypes, daguerreotypes, and stereographic cameras, as well as those taken with film and instant print cameras, must be scanned using a digital scanner. Many photo-processing services will digitize any type of film onto a photo CD or DVD. Modern digital cameras use simple software to transfer pictures directly into computer systems. Documents and personal papers can be scanned in as images; or, if they are typewritten and easily legible, some scanners can produce digital text files. However, no matter how you generate the image, creating a high quality, high-resolution copy is an important step in enhancing and repairing photos and documents.

**Plan
Ahead**

Create a high-resolution digital image.
You may acquire images from a variety of sources:

- Scanners: Considerations that affect the outcome of a scanned image include color, size, and resolution settings of the scanner and the desired file type. When converting an original image to a digital copy, some loss of resolution is inevitable, so you should try to minimize that loss by using correct scanner settings.

- Digital cameras and cell phones: Images can be transferred directly from a digital camera's storage medium to a file or imported into Photoshop, avoiding any loss of resolution. Use the highest possible image file settings. Cell phone images can be sent electronically as well.

- Web: Images downloaded from the Web or sent by e-mail sometimes need enhancement or repair. Make sure you have the legal rights to use the image.

Scanners

A scanner is a peripheral hardware device that scans photos, documents, or even 3D objects, in an optical manner, converting the result to a digital image. Table 5–1 displays some simple tips about using digital scanners that will produce better results. In addition, you should review your scanner documentation carefully.

Table 5–1 Scanner Tips	
Issue	**Tip**
File Type and Mode	Most scanners have a setting related to the type of file you are selecting. Scanners make automatic anti-aliasing adjustments and tonal changes based on the file type you choose. Use the closest possible settings to your original. For example, if you have a text-only document, do not use a setting related to color photos; use the black-and-white or grayscale setting.
Multiple Scans	Do not assume that your first scan is the one you will use. Try scanning with various file types, settings, and at different sizes. Look at a black-and-white scan even if color was your first choice. Keep in mind your final use of the image.
Placement	Place the photo in the upper-left corner of the scanner bed. Align the long side of the original with the long side of the scanner. Use the scanner's preview capability so that the scanner will determine the size and location of the photograph. Use scanner settings to select the exact size rather than the entire scanner bed when possible. After a preview scan, if available, a scaling feature, such as Scale to Fit page, will produce a bigger copy.
Quality	Always choose the best resolution when scanning an image for use in Photoshop, keeping in mind that an image with higher resolution requires more disk space to store and may be slower to edit and print. Image resolution is a compromise between image quality and file size.
Resolution	The scanner's resolution is a measure of how many dots per inch are scanned. Higher-resolution images can reproduce greater detail and subtler color transitions than lower-resolution images because of the density of the pixels in the images. High-quality images often look good at any print size.
Shading	To maintain the background shading, especially in color, select a setting related to text with pictures rather than just text. A text-only setting can create a picture area that appears as a solid black rectangle.
Size	Use the largest original you can. For instance, an 8 x 10-inch photo will produce a higher quality 24-inch poster than a 4 x 6-inch photo. Only use a reduced or enlarged setting when absolutely necessary. Keep in mind that when you print a copy, most printers need at least 1/4-inch margin. A printed copy produced from a scan may lose its edges if the original is the exact size as the paper.
Text	Most scanners have a text or drawing setting, which is appropriate only if your original document contains only black-and-white areas, text, or other solid areas, such as signatures, clip art, line drawings, maps, or blueprints. If you use this setting for a photograph or picture that also contains gray areas, the result may be unsatisfactory.
Tone	If the copy appears too light or too dark, or just appears as solid black, make sure that you have selected the correct file type for the original you are using. Look for darken and lighten settings that might be adjusted.

BTW

Image Resolution
Image resolution is a compromise between image quality and file size. Resolution is measured by the number of dots per linear inch on a hard copy, or the number of pixels across and down on a display screen. A digital image's file size is proportional to its resolution. In other words, if you increase the resolution, the file size increases. And, if you decrease the resolution, the file size decreases. You should try to optimize images to produce the highest quality image at the lowest file size, making sure that you find a good compromise.

Camera Raw Files
Working with camera raw files allows maximum control for settings such as white balance, tonal range, contrast, color saturation, and sharpening, similar to how photo processors try to fix photos taken by traditional film, reprocessing the negative with different shades and tints. Photoshop displays a special dialog box when working with camera raw photos.

Digital Cameras

The advent of digital cameras and cell phones with cameras has reduced dramatically the need for the intermediate step of scanning. Images can be transferred directly from the camera's storage medium to a file or imported directly into Photoshop. A digital camera's resolution is measured in megapixels, or millions of dots per inch. It is not uncommon for a digital camera to create photos with eight or more megapixels. Figure 5–2a displays a photo taken at 8 megapixels. Figure 5–2b displays the same image taken at 2 megapixels. Notice the finer details and brighter colors produced by more megapixels. Certain digital cameras export images using Windows Image Acquisition (WIA) support. When you use WIA, Photoshop works with Windows and your digital camera or scanner software to import images directly into Photoshop.

(a) 8 megapixels

(b) 2 megapixels

Figure 5–2

Table 5–2 displays some simple tips about digital cameras that will produce better results when working with Photoshop. Again, carefully review your camera's documentation.

Table 5–2 Digital Camera Tips

Issue	Tip
File Type	If possible, set the camera to save files in its own raw file format. The Adobe Web site has a list of cameras supported by Photoshop.
Quality	Use high-capacity memory cards and higher megapixel counts to take more images at a much higher resolution. Use the highest quality compression setting as well.
Storage	Copy images from the camera to a storage device before editing them in Photoshop. Adobe Bridge can read from most media cards, or you can use the software that comes with your camera.
Lighting and Speed	Experiment with the correlation between light and shutter speeds. Most of the newer digital cameras can take many pictures in a short amount of time, avoiding the shutter lag problem — the delay that occurs between pressing the shutter release button and the actual moment the picture is taken.

Table 5–2 Digital Camera Tips (*continued*)

Issue	Tip
Balance	Changing your white balance setting from auto to cloudy when shooting outdoors creates a filtered, richer color, increasing the reds and yellows.
Filters	If possible, use a polarizing filter for landscapes and outdoor shooting. It reduces glare and unwanted reflections. Polarized shots have richer, more saturated colors, especially in the sky. You also can use sunglasses in front of the lens to reduce glare. When shooting through glass, use an infinity focus setting.
Flash	When shooting pictures of people or detailed subjects, use the flash — even outdoors. If available, use the camera's fill flash or flash on mode. That way, the camera exposes the background first and then adds just enough light to illuminate your subject. Keep in mind that most flash mechanisms only have a range of approximately 10 feet.
Settings	When possible, use a plain background, look at your subject in a straight, level manner, and move in as close as possible. Consider the rule of thirds when taking photographs. For busy backgrounds, if your camera has a focus lock feature, center the subject and push the shutter button halfway down to focus on the subject. Then move the camera horizontally or vertically away from the center before pressing the shutter button all the way down.
Motion	For moving objects, use a fast shutter speed.

Web Graphics

A vast source of images and documents can be found on the Web. The advantage in using Web graphics is the fact that the pictures and documents already are digitized, so you do not have to manipulate or scan them; neither do you lose any resolution when transferring them to your computer system. The disadvantage of using Web graphics is in ownership. You must obtain permission to use images you download from the Web unless the image is free and unrestricted. You need to scrutinize carefully any Web sites that advertise free graphics. Some cannot be used for business purposes, for reproductions, or for resale. Some illegitimate sites that advertise free downloads also may embed spyware on your system.

Starting and Customizing Photoshop

The following steps start Photoshop and reset the default workspace, tools, colors, and Layers panel options.

To Start Photoshop

The following steps, which assume Windows 7 is running, start Photoshop based on a typical installation. You may need to ask your instructor how to start Photoshop for your computer.

1 Click the Start button on the Windows 7 taskbar to display the Start menu.

2 Type `Photoshop CS5` as the search text in the 'Search programs and files' text box, and watch the search results appear on the Start menu.

3 Click Adobe Photoshop CS5 in the search results on the Start menu to start Photoshop.

4 After a few moments, when the Photoshop window is displayed, if the window is not maximized, click the Maximize button on the title bar to maximize the window.

Duplicate Layer vs. Layer From Background

The Duplicate Layer command creates a copy of the background on a new layer in the Layers panel. The Layer From Background command changes the Background layer itself, unlocking it for additional kinds of editing such as the application of blending modes and erasing to transparency.

To Reset the Workspace

As discussed in Chapter 1, it is helpful to reset the workspace so that the tools and panels appear in their default positions. The following steps select and reset the Essentials workspace.

1 Click the 'Show more workspaces and options' button on the Application bar to display the names of saved workspaces and then, if necessary, click Essentials to select the default workspace panels.

2 Click the 'Show more workspaces and options' button again to display the list and then click Reset Essentials to restore the workspace to its default settings and reposition any panels that may have been moved.

Correcting Corrections

If you find you have made a poor correction in an image, you have two choices. You can open the History panel and click a state before the error; or, you can start over with your original. It is not a good idea to try to correct a correction. Always revert back to a clean copy. Save versions of your corrections along the way.

To Reset the Tools and the Options Bar

Recall that the Tools panel and the options bar retain their settings from previous Photoshop sessions. The following steps select the Rectangular Marquee Tool and reset all tool settings in the options bar.

1 If the tools in the Tools panel appear in two columns, click the double arrow at the top of the Tools panel.

2 If necessary, click the Rectangular Marquee Tool button on the Tools panel to select it.

3 Right-click the Rectangular Marquee Tool icon on the options bar to display the context menu and then click Reset All Tools. When Photoshop displays a confirmation dialog box, click the OK button to restore the tools to their default settings.

Converting to Black and White

Photoshop has many ways to convert color images to black and white, including images modes, adjustment layers, and blending modes. You will learn more about converting images to black and white in a later chapter.

To Reset the Default Colors

Recall that Photoshop retains the foreground and background colors from session to session. Your colors might not display black over white on the Tools panel. The following step resets the default colors.

1 Press the D key to reset the default foreground and background colors.

Restoring Documents

Antique documents, such as licenses, records, letters, and other forms of paper, have some unique aging features that photographs typically do not have. Common document paper is an organic substance composed of cellulose plant fibers that will deteriorate faster than professional photo paper. While some paper used before the year 1900 was very strong and durable, much of it was not. Rapid deterioration results from the use of production acids that break down the fibers, weakening the paper. Acid deterioration commonly is accompanied by a yellow discoloration due to the alum-resin sizing agents. High temperatures and moisture compound the problem. Even now, unless the paper is designated as acid-free, archival quality, or permanent, its expected useful life is less than 50 years.

Other types of damage include dry and brittle creases caused by folding or rolling documents; brown spots due to water stains or fungus, called **foxing**; brown edges due to airborne pollutants; the fading of colors due to light damage; as well as mold, bacteria, improper storage, and deterioration caused by animal or insect damage. Handwritten portions of documents are particularly vulnerable. Ink and pencil exposed to significant amounts of sunlight can fade dramatically.

Repairing damage using the Photoshop restoration tools can require some trial and error. Many of the tools work in similar ways, and you might find it more intuitive to use one tool rather than another. It also is possible that in correcting one error, you create another. In this case, use CTRL+Z to undo the last step, or work your way back through the History panel. The effectiveness or obviousness of a repair is subjective, so be willing to experiment to achieve the desired results. The more you work with the Photoshop repair tools, the more proficient you will be with them.

To Open the Sheet Music File

The first image you will edit is the yellowed sheet music. The sheet music has discoloration, foxing, torn edges, and fading. To repair the photo, several restorative techniques will be employed. The following step opens the scanned image from the Data Files for Students. See the inside back cover of this book for instructions on downloading the Data Files for Students, or contact your instructor for information about accessing the required files.

1 Open the Sheet Music file from the Chapter 05 folder of the Data Files for Students, or a location specified by your instructor (Figure 5–3).

BTW

Photo Fading
Exposure to light is the main factor causing printed photos to fade. Humidity, temperature, and ozone levels also can cause photos to fade. The better the quality of the ink and paper you use, the less tendency it has to fade.

BTW

Layers and the Grayscale Mode
The Grayscale mode conversion only works on a flat file — an image file with no layers. Thus, in the Sheet Music file, you do not create an edits layer. Always work from a copy of the original file. If you make errors and want to start over, you can download the file again, from the Data Files for Students.

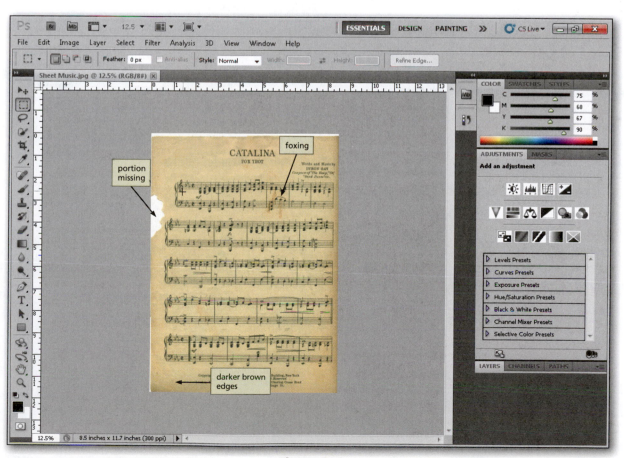

Figure 5–3

To Save the Sheet Music File in the PSD Format

The following steps save the file in the PSD format.

1 With your USB flash drive connected to one of the computer's USB ports, click File on the menu bar to display the File menu and then click Save As to display the Save As dialog box.

2 In the File name text box, type `Sheet Music Repaired` to rename the file. Do not press the ENTER key after typing the file name.

3 Click the Save in box arrow, and then click UDISK 2.0 (F:), or the location associated with your USB flash drive, in the list. If you want to create a folder for the photos in Chapter 5, click the Create New Folder button. Then when the new folder is displayed, type a chapter name, such as Chapter 05, and press the ENTER key.

4 Click the Format button to display the list of available file formats and then click Photoshop (*.PSD, *.PDD) in the list, if necessary.

5 Click the Save button in the Save As dialog box to save the file. If Photoshop displays a dialog box, click the OK button.

Correct Yellowed Portions of a Document

The following steps begin the document repair by removing all yellow and brown from the image by converting it to Grayscale mode. When Photoshop converts an image with color to grayscale, it discards all color information in the original image. The luminosity of the original pixels is represented by shades of gray in the converted pixels.

1
- Click Image on the menu bar, then point to Mode to display the Mode submenu (Figure 5–4).

Q&A Should I make these changes on a duplicate layer?

The process of converting to Grayscale mode changes all layers. If you had a duplicate layer for corrections, Photoshop would require you to merge before converting to grayscale.

Experiment
- Click various color modes and watch how the image changes. Press CTRL+Z to undo each one.

Figure 5–4

2

- Click Grayscale to remove all color. If Photoshop asks if you want to discard all color information, click the Discard button (Figure 5–5).

Q&A Is this a destructive process?

Yes; however, you can reopen the original file from the Data Files for Students should you need it.

Figure 5–5

To Create a Layer from a Background

The Background layer is locked for direct editing. The following steps change the Background layer into a fully editable layer.

- Click the Layers panel tab to display the Layers panel.

- Right-click the Background layer to display the context menu (Figure 5–6).

Figure 5–6

2

- Click Layer From Background to display the New Layer dialog box.

- Type **corrections** in the Name box (Figure 5–7).

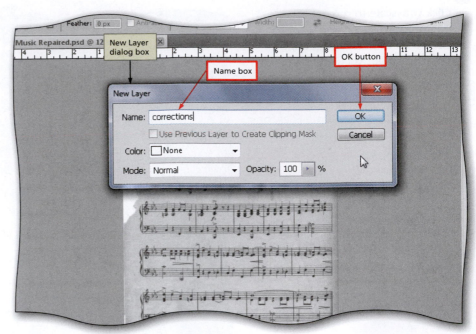

Figure 5–7

3

- Click the OK button (New Layer dialog box) to create the layer (Figure 5–8).

Figure 5–8

Other Ways

1. Double-click Background layer, enter new name (New Layer dialog box), click OK button

2. On Layer menu, point to New, click Layer From Background, enter new name (New Layer dialog box), click OK button

To Create a New Adjustment Layer

The following steps create an adjustment layer and edit the levels. Recall that a level adjustment is one way to make tonal changes to shadows, midtones, and highlights.

1
- Click the 'Create new fill or adjustment layer' button on the Layers panel status bar to display the list of adjustment layers (Figure 5–9).

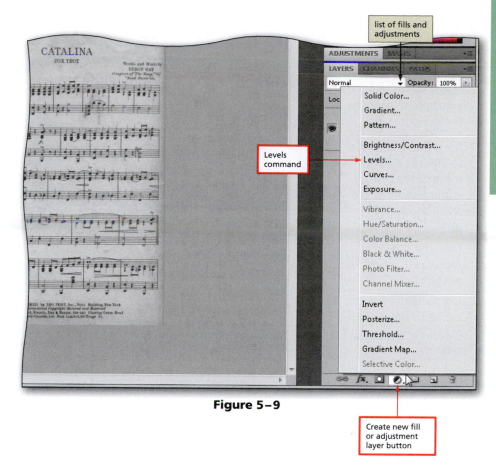

list of fills and adjustments

Levels command

Figure 5–9

Create new fill or adjustment layer button

2
- Click Levels to display Levels on the Adjustments panel (Figure 5–10).

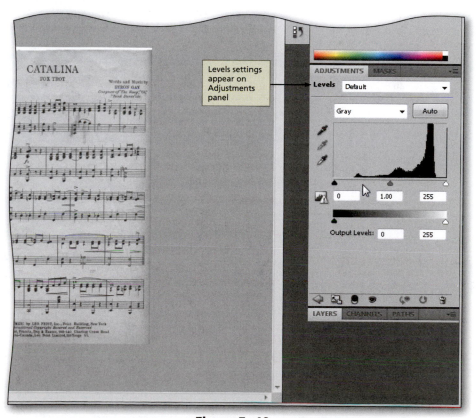

Levels settings appear on Adjustments panel

Figure 5–10

3
- Click the 'Clip to layer' button on the Adjustments panel status bar to apply the adjustment layer to the current layer.

- Drag the white slider to 200 to remove some of the gray edges (Figure 5–11).

Q&A
Does it make any difference whether I use the slider or type the numbers in the box?

No. Sometimes it is easier to enter exact measurements by typing.

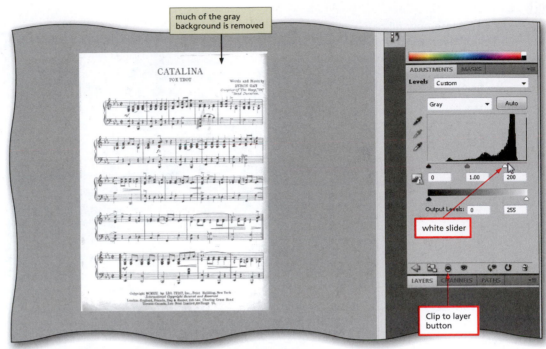

much of the gray background is removed

white slider

Clip to layer button

Figure 5–11

4
- Click the Layers panel tab to display the new adjustment layer (Figure 5–12).

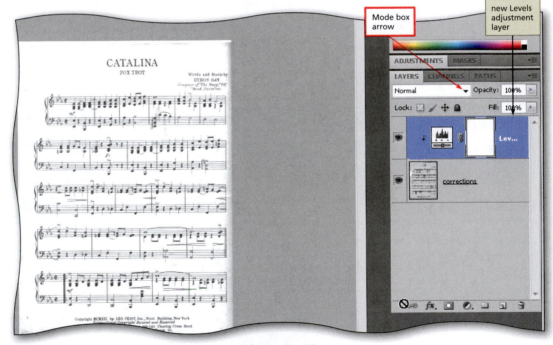

Mode box arrow

new Levels adjustment layer

Figure 5–12

Other Ways
1. On Layer menu, point to New Adjustment Layer, click Levels, click OK button (Levels dialog box)

Tonal Range
Most images look best when they utilize the full tonal range of dark to light that can be displayed on the screen or in print. Make sure the histogram extends all the way from black to white. Images that do not extend to fill the entire tonal range often look washed out.

Blending Modes

Blending modes define how an object interacts with other objects, specifically with respect to tonal adjustments. In previous chapters you used a blending mode, such as opacity, to edit a layer's transparency. The Mode box appears in the options bar of many tools, as well as on several panels in Photoshop. Typically, it displays a list of blending modes to change how pixels in the image are affected by a color. The default blending mode is Normal, which sometimes is called the **threshold**. Each blending mode works differently depending on the tool. For example, if you select the Gradient Tool, the blending mode changes how the gradient recolors the pixels as the colors change from one shade to another. The combination of these blending modes with the other settings on the options bar creates an almost infinite number of possibilities.

Experimenting with the blending modes can give you a better feel for how they work. Photoshop Help has sample images of each of the blending modes. Table 5–3 describes some of the blending modes. As you look through the list, keep in mind that the **base color** is the original color in the image. The **blend color** is the color being applied with the painting or editing tool. The **result color** is the color resulting from the blend. Not all of the blending modes appear in every Mode list.

BTW

Blending Modes
Not all modes are available to every color event. The burn-based or darkening blending modes are more appropriate for applying a gradient over another image or layer. Other blending modes result in solid white or black unless the opacity setting is changed. The dodge-based or lighten blending modes — hard, vivid, and linear — react differently for colors on either side of the 50% gray threshold.

Table 5–3 Blending Modes

Blending Mode	Description
Normal	paints each pixel to make it the result color
Dissolve	used in conjunction with opacity to paint each pixel randomly with the result color
Behind	paints each pixel in the transparent part of a layer — the Transparency check box must be deselected
Darken	the result color becomes the darker of either the base or blend color — pixels lighter than the blend color are replaced, and pixels darker than the blend color do not change
Multiply	multiplies the base color by the blend color, resulting in a darker color
Color Burn	darkens the base color to reflect the blend color by increasing the contrast
Linear Burn	darkens the base color to reflect the blend color by decreasing the brightness
Darker Color	the result color is the lower value of the base or blend colors
Lighten	the result color becomes the lighter of either the base or blend color — pixels darker than the blend color are replaced, and pixels lighter than the blend color do not change
Screen	multiplies the inverse of the blend and base colors, resulting in a lighter color
Color Dodge	brightens the base color to reflect the blend color by decreasing the contrast
Linear Dodge (Add)	brightens the base color to reflect the blend color by increasing the brightness
Lighter Color	the result color is the higher value of the base or blend colors
Overlay	preserves the highlights and shadows of the base color as it is mixed with the blend color to reflect the lightness or darkness of the base color
Soft Light	darkens or lightens the colors depending on the blend color — the effect is similar to shining a diffused spotlight on the image
Hard Light	multiplies or screens the colors depending on the blend color — the effect is similar to shining a harsh spotlight on the image
Vivid Light	burns or dodges the colors by increasing or decreasing the contrast depending on the blend color
Linear Light	burns or dodges the colors by decreasing or increasing the brightness depending on the blend color
Pin Light	replaces the colors depending on the blend color, creating a special effect
Hard Mix	changes all pixels to primary colors by adjusting the RGB values
Difference	looks at the color information in each channel and subtracts either the blend color from the base color, or the base color from the blend color, depending on which has the greater brightness value; blending with white inverts the base color values; blending with black produces no change
Exclusion	creates an effect similar to, but lower in contrast than, the Difference blending mode
Hue	creates a result color with the luminance and saturation of the base color, and the hue of the blend color
Saturation	creates a result color with the luminance and hue of the base color, and the saturation of the blend color
Color	creates a result color with the luminance of the base color, and the hue and saturation of the blend color
Luminosity	creates a result color with the hue and saturation of the base color and the luminance of the blend color

To Apply the Blending Mode

The following steps apply the blending mode.

1

● Click the Mode box arrow (shown in Figure 5–12 on page PS 286) on the Layers panel to display the list of blending modes (Figure 5–13).

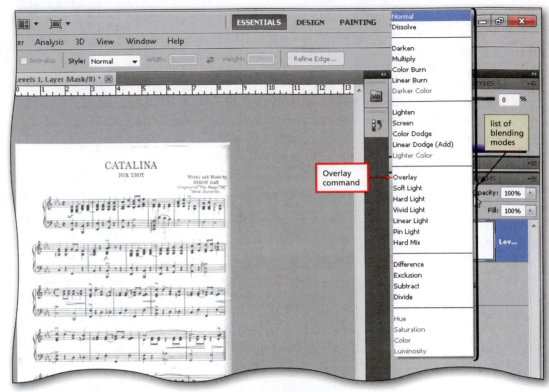

Figure 5–13

2

● Click Overlay to set the layer's blending mode to Overlay (Figure 5–14).

Q&A

Why did I choose the Overlay blending mode?

The Overlay blending mode multiplies dark areas and screens light areas at the same time, boosting the contrast in an image.

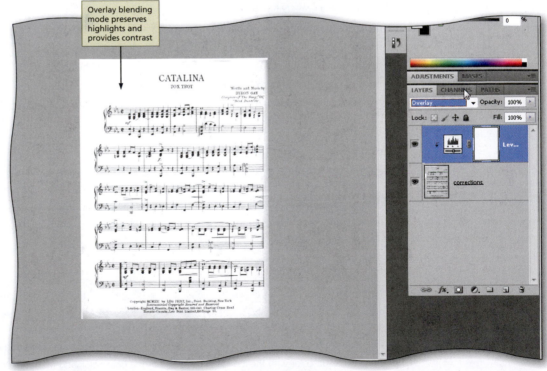

Figure 5–14

Sharpening Images

The Unsharp Mask is a filter used to sharpen images. When you **sharpen**, you emphasize the transitions between light and dark objects in your image. The Unsharp Mask works by evaluating the contrast between adjacent pixels and increasing that contrast based on your settings. While Photoshop has a Sharpen command and a Sharpen More command, the Unsharp Mask command is more versatile because it allows you to sharpen with more precision, including settings for amount, radius, and threshold. The way you adjust these settings depends primarily on the image content and secondarily on the resolution and output purpose. Close subjects with soft details need adjusting in different ways from distant subjects with fine details. While changing these settings is somewhat subjective and depends on your point of view, there are some general guidelines, as discussed in the following paragraphs.

BTW

Blending Modes and Photo Exposure
The Multiply blending mode darkens images and is used to restore shadows and fix overexposed photos. The Screen blending mode lightens images and is used for brightening highlights and fixing underexposed photos.

Sharpen images and retouch as necessary.
Sharpening enhances the edges of all objects in an image. Here are a few tips when sharpening:

- **Use a copy of the digital file or create a corrections layer.** Using a copy gives you the flexibility of making changes later. In color images, set the blending mode of the layer to Luminosity to prevent color shifts along edges.

- **Make other edits first.** If you need to make other edits, such as reducing image noise, do so before sharpening.

- **Sharpen your image multiple times in small amounts.** Sharpen to correct capture blur, then sharpen after colorization and resizing.

- **Adjust sharpening to fit the output media.** If you have a Background layer, compare it against the corrections layer as you sharpen.

Plan Ahead

The Amount value specifies how much of the sharpening effect to apply to the image. By dragging the slider or entering an amount, you can preview the results. It is a good practice to keep the amount below 300. More than that tends to create a halo effect.

The Radius setting specifies the width of the sharpened edge, measured in pixels. Larger values will sharpen surrounding pixels. A good rule is to start with a radius value of 2, and then reduce the radius if the image has fine, crisp details. Raise it if the image has soft details.

The Threshold setting specifies how different the sharpened pixels must be from the surrounding area before they are considered edge pixels and sharpened by the filter. For example, a threshold of 4 affects all pixels that have tonal values that differ by a value of 4 or more. A value of 0 sharpens all pixels in the image.

Many graphic artists set the radius first, the threshold second, and then the amount. That way, the width and edge are specified before the sharpening effect is applied, allowing the amount value to be more flexible. Additionally, sharpening at magnifications from 50% to 100% gives you a better feel for the final result.

BTW

Color Photos
Moving the Levels sliders to the edge of the histogram can clip the subtle shadows and highlights in a color photo, causing the image to lose its soft light or mood. Color photos are more prone to user levels errors than are black-and-white images.

BTW

Unsharp Mask Preview
As you try different settings, toggle the Preview check box off and on to see how your changes affect the image in the image window. If your image is large, using the display in the dialog box can be more efficient because only a small area is redrawn.

To Apply the Unsharp Mask Filter

The following steps apply the Unsharp Mask filter to improve the appearance of the sheet music.

1
- Click the corrections layer on the Layers panel to select it.

- Click Filter on the menu bar and then point to Sharpen to display the Sharpen submenu (Figure 5–15).

 Q&A
Could I use the Sharpen Tool on the Tools Panel?

Yes, but for entire images, the Unsharp Mask filter will display a dialog box with a preview to help you choose settings.

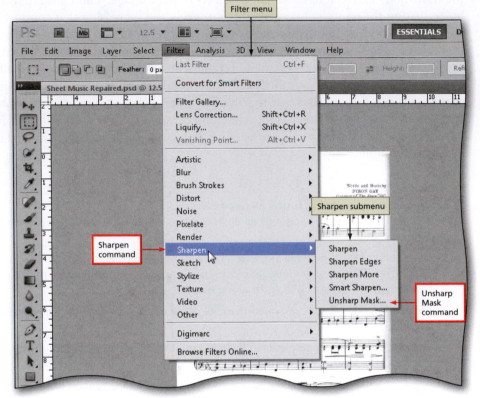

Figure 5–15

2
- Click Unsharp Mask to display the Unsharp Mask dialog box.

- Type **4** in the Radius box to specify a width of 4 pixels.

- Type **30** in the Threshold box to specify how different the pixels must be from their surroundings in order to become an edge.

- Drag the Amount slider until the image appears sharper, but not oddly pixilated (Figure 5–16).

Q&A
How does the Amount slider work?

The amount slider increases the contrast between pixels, like a volume control. Photoshop recommends 100% or more for high-resolution images.

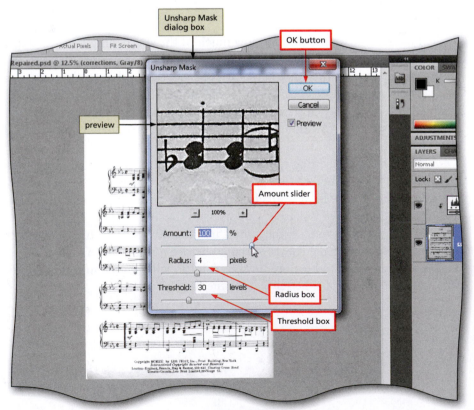

Figure 5–16

3

- Click the OK button to close the Unsharp Mask dialog box (Figure 5–17).

Figure 5–17

To Lock Transparent Pixels

The following step locks the image so that erasing any dark spots will result in a white area rather than a transparent area.

1

- Click the 'Lock transparent pixels' button on the Layers panel to lock the pixels (Figure 5–18).

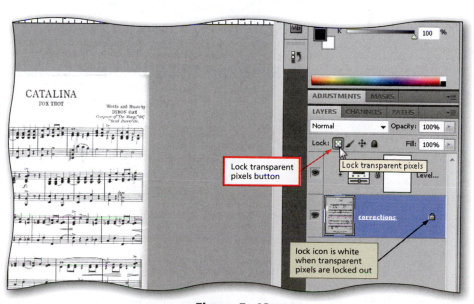

Figure 5–18

To Use the Eraser Tool

Finally, the following steps clean the dark spots in the document using the Eraser Tool.

1 On the Tools panel, right-click the current eraser tool, and then click Eraser Tool to select it.

2 Use the LEFT BRACKET ([ ) or RIGHT BRACKET ( ]) keys to adjust the size of the eraser brush. With short strokes, drag through remaining gray areas that are not part of the music itself. If you make a mistake, press CTRL+Z. Zoom and scroll as necessary.

3 When you are finished, zoom out to display the entire document (Figure 5–19).

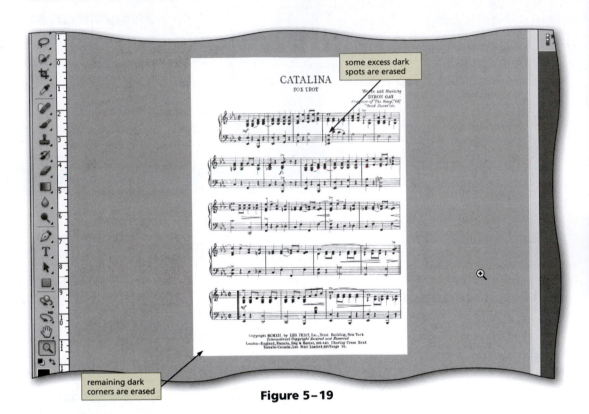

Figure 5–19

To Save and Close the Sheet Music Repaired File

The following steps save the file again and close it.

1 Press CTRL+S to save the file again. If Photoshop displays a confirmation dialog box, click the OK button.

2 Press CTRL+W to close the file without quitting Photoshop.

Content-Aware

Content-Aware is a new, texture synthesis technology included in Photoshop CS5. Using mathematical algorithms, Content-Aware fills the selection with similar nearby content to replicate a portion of an image. By sampling image data from around the area to patch, Content-Aware reconstructs a texture based on the sampled data in order to replicate the area. Texture synthesis is used in computer graphics, digital image editing, 3D computer graphics, and post-production of films.

You can use Content-Aware to fill in portions of an image that are missing, either because the photo was damaged or because the original photo contained an error; or, you can remove portions of an image such as a spot on a camera lens or an object that should not be in the scene.

<table>
<tr><td>

Heal specific defects.
Defects in photos and documents that are not related to user or lens errors may include the following:

- physical tears, ragged edges, or missing portions
- fading due to exposure to light
- light or dark spots due to aging
- creasing due to folding
- natural aging of paper

It is helpful to make a list of the specific repairs you plan to apply. Create a corrections layer so you can use portions, textures, and colors from the original document for the repairs. Repair smaller areas first. Consider making separate layers for each large repair. Do not be afraid to experiment until the repair is perfect.

</td><td>

Plan Ahead

</td></tr>
</table>

To Open the Falls File

The following step opens a scanned image with a missing corner from the Data Files for Students.

1 Open the Falls file from the Chapter 05 folder of the Data Files for Students, or a location specified by your instructor (Figure 5–20).

Falls image

corner is missing

Figure 5–20

To Save the Falls File in the PSD Format

The following steps save the file in the PSD format.

1 Press SHIFT+CTRL+S to open the Save As dialog box and then navigate to your preferred storage location.

2 In the File name text box, type **Falls Repaired** to rename the file. Do not press the ENTER key after typing the file name.

3 Click the Format button to display the list of available file formats and then click Photoshop (*.PSD, *.PDD) in the list, if necessary.

4 Click the Save button (Save As dialog box) to save the file. If Photoshop displays a confirmation dialog box, click the OK button.

To Create an Edits Layer in the Falls Repaired File

It is a good idea to create a second layer on which you make your corrections. That way, you can immediately look back and see your edits. The following steps duplicate the Background layer.

1 If necessary, click the Layers tab to expand the Layers panel.

2 On the Layers panel, right-click the Background layer and then click Duplicate Layer on the context menu.

3 When Photoshop displays the Duplicate Layer dialog box, type **edits** in the As box and then click the OK button (Duplicate Layer dialog box) to create the edits layer.

4 Click the visibility icon on the Background layer so it is hidden.

5 Select the visible edits layer.

To Fill with Content-Aware

The following steps reproduce a missing portion of an image, using Content-Aware to fill.

1

- Right-click the Quick Selection Tool button on the Tools Panel and then click Magic Wand Tool on the context menu.

- Click the missing corner area of the image to select it (Figure 5–21).

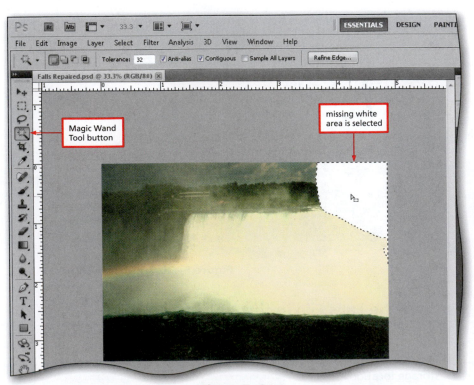

Magic Wand Tool button

missing white area is selected

Figure 5–21

• Click Edit on the menu bar and then click Fill to display the Fill dialog box.

• Click the Use box arrow (Fill dialog box) to display the list (Figure 5–22).

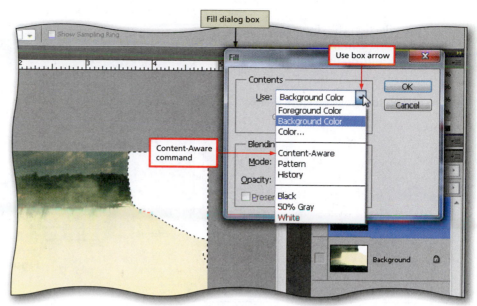

Figure 5–22

• If necessary, click Content-Aware in the list.

• Click the OK button (Fill dialog box) to fill the selection.

• Press CTRL+D to deselect (Figure 5–23).

Figure 5–23

4

• Select the Rectangular Marquee Tool and then drag a rectangle around any seam that appears around the correction (Figure 5–24).

Figure 5–24

5

- With the selection still displayed, click Fill on the Edit menu, and then click the OK button (Fill dialog box) to fill the area using Content-Aware.

- Press CTRL+D to deselect (Figure 5–25).

seam disappears

Figure 5–25

BTW

Content-Aware Fill
Many users find it easier to use the DELETE key to access Content-Aware. When working with the locked Background layer, the DELETE key does not immediately delete a selection to transparency; rather, Photoshop offers to fill the selection with a color or with Content-Aware texture. If you are not on the Background layer, you must use the Fill command on the Edit menu.

To Save and Close the Falls Repaired File

The following steps save the file and close it.

1 Press CTRL+S to save the file again. If Photoshop displays a confirmation dialog box, click the OK button.

2 Press CTRL+W to close the file without quitting Photoshop.

Retouching Tools

Sometimes photos are damaged or worn from excessive use, age, physical damage, or improper storage. Photoshop has several **retouching tools** that help you touch up spots, tears, wrinkles, and scratches. The retouching tools are organized in the middle of the Tools panel. Table 5–4 lists some of the tools and their usage. Each of the retouching tools will be explained further as it is used.

Table 5–4 Retouching Tools		
Tool	**Use**	**Button**
Blur Tool	blurs small portions of the image	◌
Burn Tool	darkens areas in an image	◉
Dodge Tool	lightens areas in an image	🔍
Healing Brush Tool	removes and repairs imperfections by first taking a sample from another place in the image and then painting to match the texture, lighting, transparency, and shading of the sampled pixels to the pixels being healed	✐
Patch Tool	repairs imperfections in a selected area of an image by copying a sample or pattern taken from another part of the image — commonly used for larger areas and does not allow brush size selection as with the Healing Brush Tool	▦
Red Eye Tool	removes the red tint from all contiguous cells	⁺◉
Sharpen Tool	sharpens small portions of an image	△

Table 5–4 Retouching Tools (continued)

Tool	Use	Button
Smudge Tool	simulates the effect you see when you drag a finger through wet paint	
Sponge Tool	changes the color saturation of an area	
Spot Healing Brush Tool	removes blemishes and imperfections by sampling pixels around the spot and then paints with matching texture, lighting, transparency, and shading	

To Open the Child Image

The following step opens the Child image from the Data Files for Students.

1 Open the file named Child from the Chapter 05 folder of the Data Files for Students, or from a location specified by your instructor.

To Save the Child File in the PSD Format

The following step saves the file in the PSD format.

1 Use the Save As dialog box to save the file on your preferred storage device in the PSD format using the name, Child Repaired.

To Create a Corrections Layer and Crop

The following steps create a duplicate layer for corrections.

1 Right-click the Background layer on the Layers panel to display its context menu, and then click Duplicate Layer to display the Duplicate Layer dialog box.

2 Type `corrections` in the As box (Duplicate Layer dialog box) to name the layer.

3 Click the OK button (Duplicate Layer dialog box) to create the layer.

4 To remove the excess border, click the Crop Tool button on the Tools panel and then, in the photo itself, drag from the upper-left corner to the lower-right corner. Press the ENTER key to crop the image (Figure 5–26).

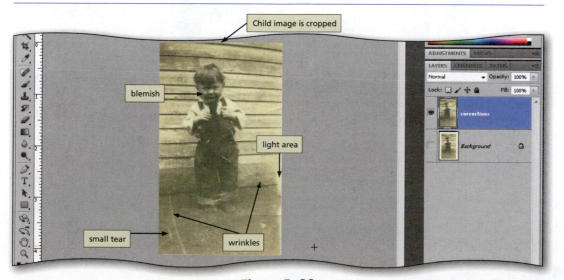

Figure 5–26

The Spot Healing Brush Tool

The Spot Healing Brush Tool removes blemishes and imperfections by sampling pixels around the spot. Photoshop then paints in the image with matching texture, lighting, transparency, and shading. Recall that sampling occurs when Photoshop stores the pixel values of a selected spot or area. The Spot Healing Brush Tool options bar contains settings for the blending mode of the repair and the sampling methods (Figure 5–27).

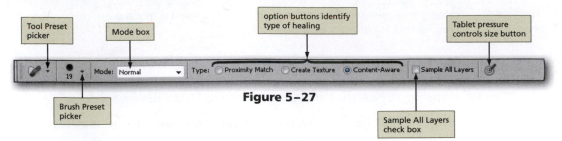

Figure 5–27

To Repair Damage with the Spot Healing Brush Tool

The following steps use the Spot Healing Brush Tool to fix several small damaged spots. When using the Spot Healing Brush Tool, it is important to use the smallest possible brush tip so that the sample comes from the area directly adjacent to the imperfection.

1
- Zoom in on the child's face and head.

- Right-click the current healing tool on the Tools panel (Figure 5–28).

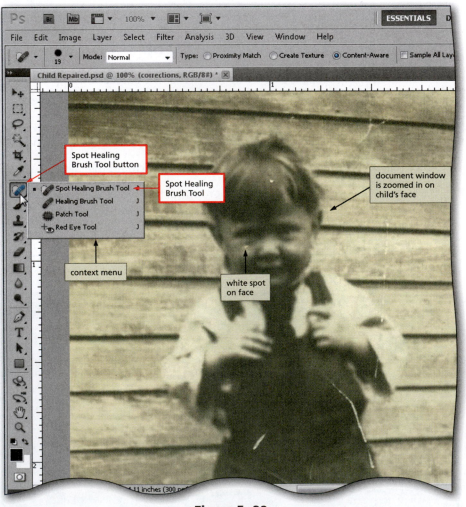

Figure 5–28

2

- Click Spot Healing Brush Tool in the list to select it.

- If necessary on the options bar, click the Mode box arrow, and then click Normal.

- Click the Proximity Match option button, if necessary, to select it.

- Move the mouse pointer into the document window and point to the white spot on the face. Press the LEFT BRACKET ([) key or the RIGHT BRACKET (]) key until the brush tip is just slightly larger than the spot (Figure 5–29).

  What is a proximity match?

A proximity match uses pixels around the edge of the selection to define the repair.

Figure 5–29

3

- Click the spot and then move the mouse pointer away to view the results (Figure 5–30).

  Why does my correction look different?

The size or position of your mouse pointer may have been different, or the color settings on your monitor may be slightly different. If you do not like the result, press CTRL+Z and then try it again.

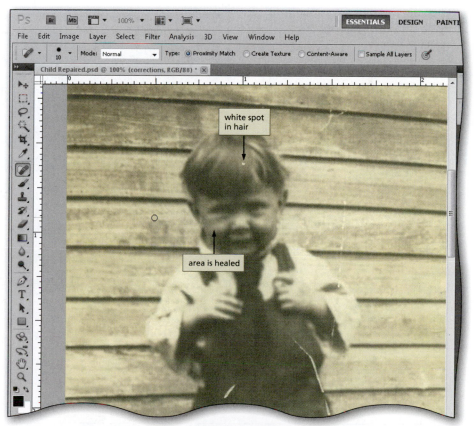

Figure 5–30

4
- Click the Create Texture option button on the options bar to select it.

- Point to the white spot in the child's hair and adjust the size of the brush as necessary.

- Click the spot on the child's hair, and then move the mouse pointer away to view the results (Figure 5–31).

Q&A How does the Create Texture option button work?

Uses pixels in the selection to create a texture. If the texture doesn't work, try dragging through the area a second time.

 Experiment

- Try fixing a large spot in the photo. Notice that the larger the correction, the poorer the quality, as the Spot Healing brush is better suited for small imperfections. Press CTRL+Z to undo the unwanted correction.

Figure 5–31

5
- Zoom to 100% and scroll to the lower-left portion of the image.

- Click the Content-Aware option button on the options bar to select it.

- Adjust the size of the mouse pointer as necessary, drag over the long wrinkle that runs across the building and onto the ground (Figure 5–32).

Q&A How does the Content-Aware option button work?

The Content-Aware option button works in the same way as it did when you used the Fill command. It compares nearby image content to fill the selection, maintaining key details such as shadows and object edges.

Q&A What if I make a repair that does not look good?

You can press CTRL+Z to undo your most recent repair. Pressing CTRL+ALT+Z steps back through your recent steps. Or, you can display the History panel and click a previous state. Then, you can try the repair again.

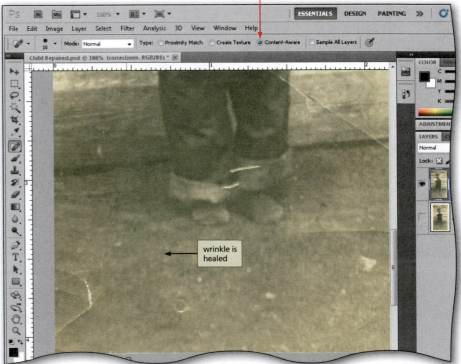

Figure 5–32

Other Ways

1. Press J or SHIFT+J, adjust brush size, click imperfection

The Healing Brush Tool

The Healing Brush Tool is better suited for larger areas such as tears or wrinkles. While the Spot Healing Brush Tool samples the surrounding pixels automatically, the Healing Brush Tool requires you to choose the sampled (source) area, as you did with the Clone Tool. When using the Healing Brush Tool, the Brush Preset picker allows you to set specific characteristics of the brush, including the use of a tablet pen. The Mode box allows you to choose one of several blending modes, or choose to replace the pixels to preserve the grain and texture at the edges of the brush stroke. Additionally, the Healing Brush Tool options bar has an Aligned setting to sample pixels continuously without losing the current sampling point, even if you release the mouse button (Figure 5–33).

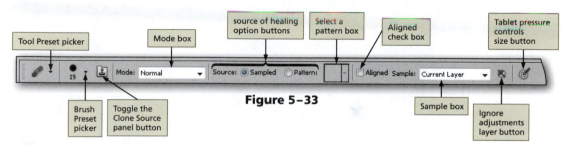

Figure 5–33

To Sample and Paint with the Healing Brush Tool

The following steps use the Healing Brush Tool to fix the damage in the lower-left corner of the photo.

1

- Right-click the Spot Healing Brush Tool button to display the context menu and then click Healing Brush Tool in the list.

- If necessary, click the Sampled option button on the options bar to select it.

- Click the Aligned check box so it displays a check mark.

- Click the Brush Preset picker on the options bar to display the settings.

- If necessary, drag the Size slider to 19.

- At the bottom of the panel, click the Size box arrow, and then click Off in the list (Figure 5–34).

Q&A

Why should I turn the size off?

The Size box allows you to specify if you will be using pen pressure or the stylus wheel to change the size of the healing brush mouse pointer. Because you changed the diameter of the brush size manually, you do not have to rely on the other methods.

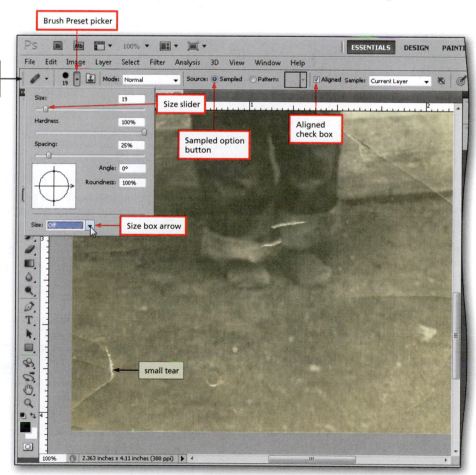

Figure 5–34

2

• To sample the pixels, ALT+click to the right of the small tear.

• Drag across the tear to repair the damage (Figure 5–35).

Q&A

What is the difference between the Healing Brush Tool and the Clone Tool?

The Healing Brush Tool does not create an exact copy. It samples the texture, color, and grain of the source and then applies that to the destination, matching the destination's surrounding pixels as much as possible.

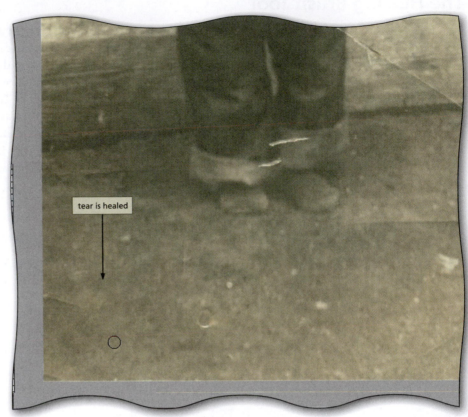

tear is healed

Figure 5–35

Other Ways

1. Press J or SHIFT+J, ALT+click sample, drag flawed areas

BTW

The Replace Blending Mode
The healing brush tools can access the Replace blending modes. The Replace blending mode preserves noise, film grain, and texture at the edges of the brush stroke when using a soft edge brush.

The Patch Tool

The Patch Tool lets you repair imperfections within a selected area using pixels from another area or by using a pattern. The Patch Tool is more than just a copy-and-paste mechanism, however. Like the Healing Brush Tool, the Patch Tool matches the texture, shading, and lighting of the pixels. When repairing with pixels from the image, select a small area to produce the best results. The Patch Tool can sample pixels from the same image, from a different image, or from a chosen pattern. The Patch Tool options bar displays settings for the source and destination of the patch, as well as options to adjust the selection or use a pattern to make the patch repair (Figure 5–36).

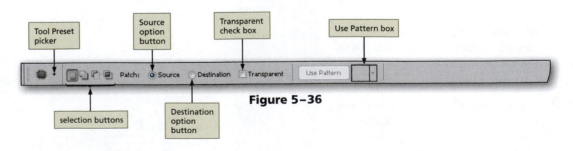

Tool Preset picker

Source option button

Transparent check box

Use Pattern box

selection buttons

Destination option button

Figure 5–36

To Patch Areas

The following steps use the Patch Tool to patch the wrinkle in the lower-right corner of the photo.

1

- Scroll to the lower-right portion of the photo.

- Right-click the Healing Brush Tool button and then click Patch Tool in the list.

- If necessary, click the Source option button on the Patch Tool options bar to select it.

- Move the mouse pointer to an area below the wrinkle (Figure 5–37).

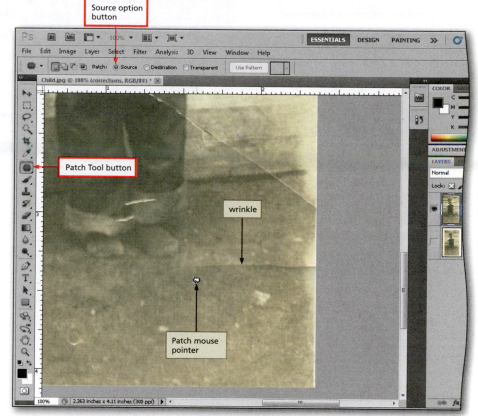

Figure 5–37

2

- Draw a rectangular area below the wrinkle. Avoid any other damaged areas (Figure 5–38).

Q&A

Do I have to click Source first, before I draw the marquee?

Actually, you can do it either way — draw the marquee first and then click Source, or vice versa.

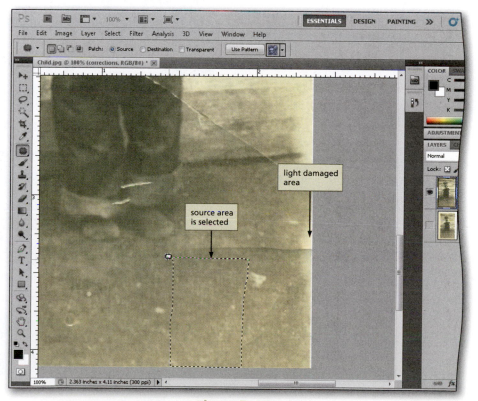

Figure 5–38

3

- On the Patch options bar, click the Destination option button.

- Drag the selection to cover part of the wrinkle and repair it.

- Drag the selection again to cover other damaged areas in the lower-right portion of the photo.

- Press CTRL+D to remove the selection and display the patch (Figure 5–39).

Q&A

What is the difference between the Patch Tool and the Healing Brush Tool?

They are very similar, but the Patch Tool is intended for larger areas of correction. Both tools apply tonal characteristics of the sampled source to the area of the flaw.

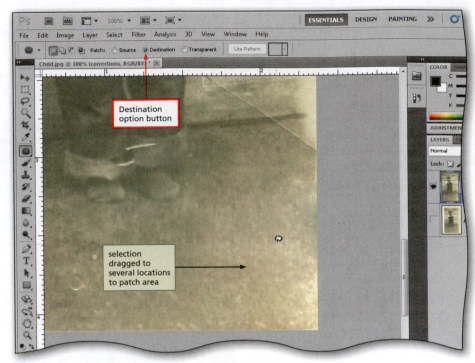

Figure 5–39

Other Ways

1. Press J or SHIFT+J, click Source, drag area, click Destination, drag area

To Repair Other Damage

The following steps repair other damaged areas in the photo. If you make a repair that does not look good, press CTRL+Z, and then try again. Zoom and scroll as necessary.

1 Use a combination of healing brushes and options bar settings to repair any other damaged areas in the photo.

2 Zoom out to display the entire photo (Figure 5–40).

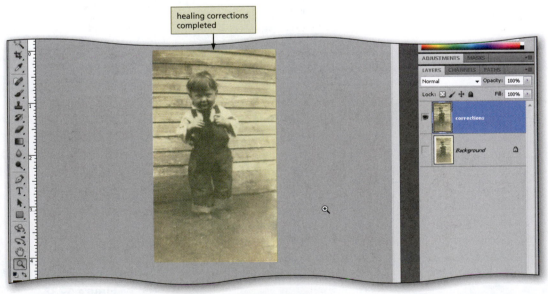

Figure 5–40

To View the Corrections

The following step compares the original layer with the corrections layer.

- On the Layers panel, click the visibility icon on the Background layer to make it visible, if necessary.

- Click the visibility icon on the corrections layer to hide it and view the original image before corrections (Figure 5–41).

- Click the visibility icon on the corrections layer again to view the corrections.

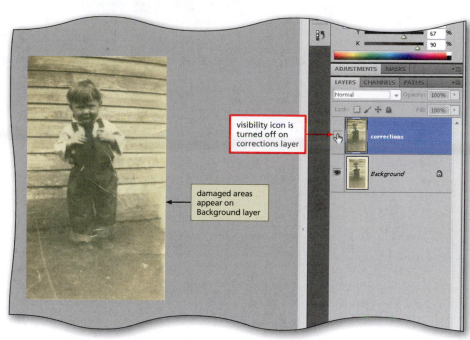

visibility icon is turned off on corrections layer

damaged areas appear on Background layer

Figure 5–41

To Save and Close the Child Repaired File

The following steps save the file again and close it.

1 Press CTRL+S to save the file again. If Photoshop displays a confirmation dialog box, click the OK button.

2 Press CTRL+W to close the file without quitting Photoshop.

The Red Eye Tool

In photographs, **red eye** is when the pupils of the subject's eyes appear red. Red eye is caused in flash photography where the flash of a camera is bright enough to cause a reflection off the retina. The red color comes from the blood vessels in the eye. Red eye can be avoided by moving the flash farther away from the lens or by using a more modern camera that has a red-eye reduction feature. In those cameras, the flash goes off twice — once before the picture is taken and then again to take the picture. The first flash causes the pupils to contract, which significantly reduces red eye.

Red eye can be corrected in Photoshop using a specialized tool designed specifically for this problem. The Red Eye Tool removes red eye in flash photos by recoloring all contiguous red pixels. The Red Eye options bar has settings to change the pupil size and the darken amount. The Red Eye Tool can be used only on photos in the RGB and Lab color formats. It does not work with CMYK color mode.

BTW

TIFs and JPGs
Some file resolution is lost through compression when saving JPG edits in Photoshop. Saving JPG files in the TIF format allows for the exchange of files between applications and across computer platforms. TIF is a flexible format supported by virtually all paint, image editing, and page layout applications. However, TIF files are larger in size.

The Red Eye Tool options bar displays options for the pupil size and percentage of darkening (Figure 5–42). The labels are scrubby sliders.

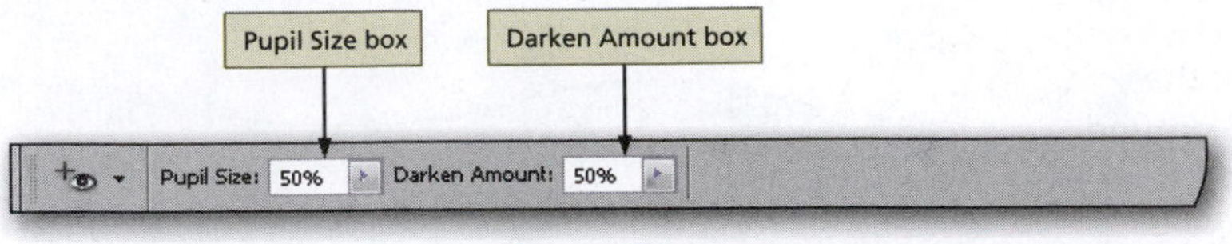

Figure 5–42

To Open the Girls Image

The next photo is of some children that was taken with an older camera that generated red eye. The following step opens a file named Girls.

1 Open the file named Girls from the Chapter 05 folder of the Data Files for Students, or from a location specified by your instructor.

To Save the Girls File in the PSD Format

The following step saves the file in the PSD format.

1 Use the Save As dialog box to save the file on your preferred storage device in the PSD format using the name, Girls Repaired.

To Create an Edits Layer in the Girls Repaired File

The following steps create an edits layer.

1 If necessary, click the Layers tab to expand the Layers panel.

2 On the Layers panel, right-click the Background layer and then click Duplicate Layer on the context menu.

3 When Photoshop displays the Duplicate Layer dialog box, type `edits` in the As box and then click the OK button (Duplicate Layer dialog box) to create the edits layer.

4 Click the visibility icon on the Background layer so it is hidden.

5 Select the visible edits layer, if necessary.

6 Zoom to 100% magnification and scroll to display the red-eye problem (Figure 5–43).

BTW

Photoshop Help
The best way to become familiar with Photoshop Help is to use it. Appendix D includes detailed information about Photoshop Help and exercises that will help you gain confidence in using it.

BTW

Quick Reference
For a table that lists how to complete the tasks covered in this book using the mouse, menu, context menu, and keyboard, see the Quick Reference Summary at the back of this book or visit the Photoshop CS5 Quick Reference Web page (scsite.com/pscs5/qr).

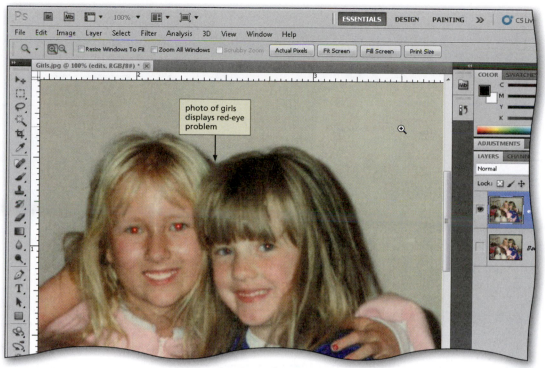

photo of girls
displays red-eye
problem

Figure 5–43

To Correct Red Eye

The following steps remove the red eye from the photo.

1

- On the Tools panel, right-click the current healing tool button and then click Red Eye Tool in the list.

- On the options bar, drag the Darken Amount scrubby slider to 25%.

- Move the mouse pointer to the girl's eye on the left to display the Red Eye Tool mouse pointer (Figure 5–44).

Q&A

How does the Darken Amount setting affect the image?

Setting a very low Darken Amount value will make only small changes of color to the eye; conversely, a large value will darken the eye dramatically.

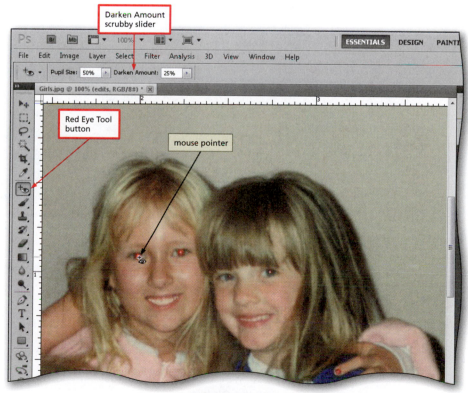

Darken Amount
scrubby slider

Red Eye Tool
button

mouse pointer

Figure 5–44

2

• Click the red portion of the eye to remove the red eye. Move the mouse pointer to view the result (Figure 5–45).

Figure 5–45

3

• Click each of the other eyes to fix the red-eye problem (Figure 5–46).

Figure 5–46

Other Ways

1. Press SHIFT+J until Red Eye Tool is active, click red eye

To Save and Close the Girls Repaired File

The following steps save the file again and close it.

1 Press CTRL+S to save the file again. If Photoshop displays a confirmation dialog box, click the OK button.

2 Press CTRL+W to close the file without quitting Photoshop.

The Dodge, Burn, and Sponge Tools

The Dodge Tool is used to lighten areas of an image. The Burn Tool does just the opposite; it darkens areas of an image. Both tools are based on a technique of traditional photography, regulating exposure on specific areas of a print. Photographers reduce exposure to lighten an isolated area on the print, which is called **dodging**. Increasing the exposure to darken areas on a print is called **burning**. Another tool, the Sponge Tool, subtly changes the color saturation of an area, increasing or decreasing the amount of color by a flow percentage.

An Exposure box on the options bar allows you to specify a percentage of dodging or burning. The default value is 50%. A higher percentage in the Exposure box increases the effect (for example, while using the Dodge Tool, a higher exposure results in greater lightening of the image), while a lower percentage reduces it (Figure 5–47). The Dodge, Burn, and Sponge Tools have similar options bars.

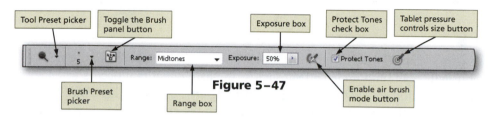

Tool Preset picker

Toggle the Brush panel button

Exposure box

Protect Tones check box

Tablet pressure controls size button

Brush Preset picker

Range box

Enable air brush mode button

Figure 5–47

Sponge Tool in Grayscale Mode
In Grayscale mode, the tool increases or decreases contrast by moving gray levels away from or toward the middle gray.

To Open the Graduation Photo

The next photo to repair is a graduation photo that is too dark to make out facial features.

1 Open the file named Graduation from the Chapter 05 folder of the Data Files for Students, or from a location specified by your instructor (Figure 5–48).

Graduation image is very dark

Figure 5–48

To Save the Graduation File in the PSD Format

The following step saves the file in the PSD format.

1 Use the Save As dialog box to save the file on your preferred storage device in the PSD format using the name, Graduation Vignette.

To Create an Edits Layer in the Graduation Vignette File

The following steps create an edits layer.

1 If necessary, click the Layers tab to expand the Layers panel.

2 On the Layers panel, right-click the Background layer and then click Duplicate Layer on the context menu.

3 When Photoshop displays the Duplicate Layer dialog box, type `edits` in the As box and then click the OK button (Duplicate Layer dialog box) to create the edits layer.

4 Click the visibility icon on the Background layer so it is hidden.

5 Select the visible edits layer, if necessary.

Vignetting

Vignetting is a change of an image's brightness at the edges compared to the center. Vignetting usually is an unintended effect, such as the halo effect that occurs when photographing a projection screen or other light source against a dark background, but sometimes it is used as a creative effect to draw attention to the center of the image. Special camera filters and post-processing procedures can create a vignette, but you also can create it using Photoshop.

To Create an Oval for the Vignette

The following steps create an oval in preparation for creating the vignette.

1 Right-click the current marquee tool button and then click Elliptical Marquee Tool on the context menu.

2 Drag an oval over the center portion of the image, approximately 7 inches long. While dragging, press and hold the SPACEBAR key to reposition the marquee (Figure 5–49).

BTW

Colorization of Old Photos
Before the advent of color film, black and white photos were often colorized by painting directly on the photographic prints with special paints or inks. The original photo of the Graduation was hand tinted with blue sky.

BTW

Exposure
Exposure refers to the amount of light allowed in during the process of taking a photograph. If exposed too long, the photograph will be washed out. If exposed too short, the photograph will appear too dark. A light meter can be used to measure the light and set an ideal exposure rate.

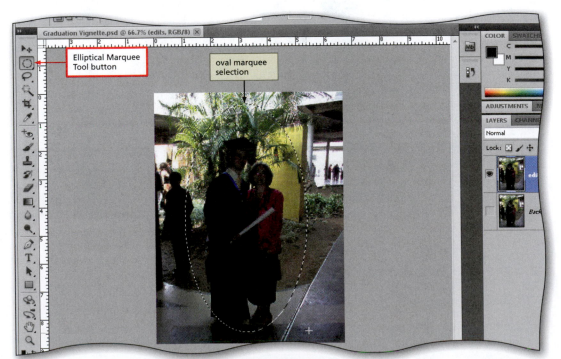

Figure 5–49

To Lighten Using the Dodge Tool

The following steps use the Dodge Tool to lighten the oval, creating the vignette effect, and enhancing the details in the features.

1

- Right-click the Dodge Tool button to display the context menu (Figure 5–50).

Dodge Tool button

Dodge Tool

context menu

Figure 5–50

2

- Click Dodge Tool on the context menu to select it.

- Use the RIGHT BRACKET (]) key to increase the size of the brush tip so that it is just larger than the selection.

- Click several times to dodge the image, enhancing the details of the photo (Figure 5–51).

Q&A

Why should I increase the size of the brush to cover the selection?

If your brush is bigger than the selection, clicking once changes the entire selection evenly and does not change the non-selected area.

brush is resized to be larger than selection marquee

area inside selection marquee is lightened

Figure 5–51

Other Ways

1. Press O or SHIFT+O, adjust brush size, click imperfection

To Select the Inverse

The following step selects the inverse of the current selection.

1 Click Select on the menu bar and then click Inverse on the Select menu to select the inverse of the current selection.

To Darken Using the Burn Tool

The following steps darken the outer edges of the photo to increase the contrast.

1

- Right-click the Dodge Tool button and then click Burn Tool to select it.

- Use the RIGHT BRACKET (]) key to increase the size of the brush tip so that it is just larger than the selection, in this case, the entire image.

- Click several times to burn the image, enhancing the contrast of the photo (Figure 5–52).

🔎 Experiment

- Right-click the Burn Tool button on the Tools panel, and then select the Sponge Tool. On the options bar, change the Mode to Saturate and the Flow to 100%. Drag across the bright yellow wall in the background to see how the Sponge Tool works. Press CTRL+Z to undo the sponge.

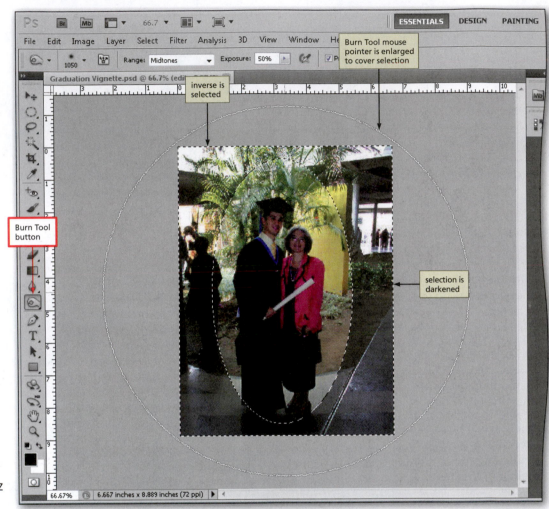

Figure 5–52

2

- Deselect to view the changes.

Other Ways

1. Press O or SHIFT+O, adjust brush size, click imperfection

To Save and Close the Graduation Vignette File

The following steps save and close the Graduation Vignette file.

1 Press CTRL+S to save the file again.

2 Press CTRL+W to close the file without quitting Photoshop.

Lens Correction Tools

Many kinds of photographic errors can be corrected in Photoshop. The most common mistakes include lens flaws, focus errors, distortions, unintended angle errors, and perspective errors. Every photographer has made an error from time to time.

**Plan
Ahead**

> **Correct lens errors.**
> While modern digital cameras help you correct many user and lighting errors, some **lens correction** is necessary from time to time. If you have a photo that has lens errors, correct these errors after making any color, sharpening, cropping, or healing corrections.

The next series of steps uses the Lens Correction filter to fix some of the lens flaws, distortions, and errors in the Building photo. You can try different settings before committing them permanently to the image. Table 5–5 describes some typical errors and correction methods using the Lens Correction filter.

Table 5–5 Kinds of Distortions

Type of Error	Description	Correction Method
Angle Error	an image is crooked or tilted in the photograph	rotate image
Barrel Distortion	a lens defect that causes straight lines to bow out toward the edges of the image	decrease the barrel effect by negatively removing distortion
Chromatic Aberration	appears as a color fringe along the edges of objects caused by the lens focusing on different colors of light	increase or decrease the red/cyan fringe or blue/yellow fringe in different planes
Keystone Distortion	wider top or bottom effect that occurs when an object is photographed from an angle or perspective	correct vertical and/or horizontal perspective error
Pincushion Distortion	a lens defect that causes straight lines to bend inward	decrease the pincushion effect by positively removing distortion
Vignette Distortion	a defect where the edges, especially the corners, of an image are darker than the center	lighten or darken the amount of color at the four corners based on a midpoint in the image

You also can use the Lens Correction filter to rotate an image or fix image perspective caused by vertical or horizontal camera tilt. The filter's image grid makes these adjustments more easily and more accurately than using the Transform command.

Angle and Perspective Errors

While the Crop Tool and warp grids can be used to transform and correct the perspective in an image, the Lens Correction dialog box has the added advantages of allowing very precise measurements and other ways to correct errors. This is useful particularly when working with photos that contain keystone distortion. Keystone distortion in perspective occurs when an object is photographed from an angle. For example, if you take a picture of a tall building from ground level, the edges of the building appear closer to each other at the top than they do at the bottom. Keystone distortions can be corrected by changing the vertical or horizontal perspective in the photo. Angle errors occur when the camera is tilted to the left or right, making objects in the photo appear slanted.

After correcting keystone and angle errors, it is sometimes necessary to scale the image to regain any edges that were clipped by the correction. You also might need to fill in transparent edges created by changing the angle. The Lens Correction dialog box (Figure 5–53 on the next page) has boxes, sliders, and buttons for correcting the distortions and repairing collateral damage created by the correction.

BTW

Extending Edges
Because angle distortion corrections sometimes create transparent areas along the edge of the photo. In those cases, extend the edges after the lens correction for an image with square corners. See Figure 5–58 on page PS 317. The extension might not look good temporarily, but filling in the transparent areas allows you to crop to the maximum usable area.

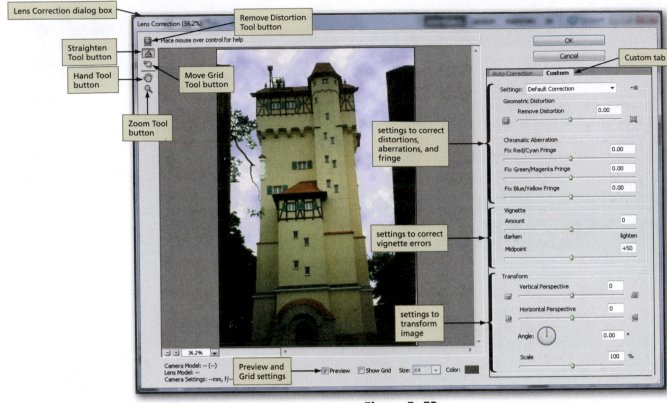

Figure 5–53

To Open the Building Image File

The following steps open the image file named Building.

1 Open the file named Building from the Chapter 05 folder of the Data Files for Students, or from a location specified by your instructor.

2 Use the Zoom Tool to zoom to 33% magnification, if necessary (Figure 5–54).

BTW

Focal Length
Some camera lenses cause defects because of the focal length or the f-stop used. You can set the Photoshop Lens Correction filter with settings based on the camera, lens, and focal length used to take the image.

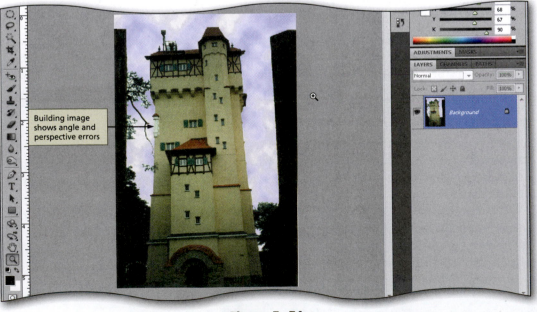

Figure 5–54

To Save the Building File in the PSD Format

The following step saves the file in the PSD format.

1 Use the Save As dialog box to save the file on your preferred storage device in the PSD format using the name, Building Repaired.

To Create an Edits Layer in the Building Repaired File

The following steps create an edits layer.

1 If necessary, click the Layers tab to expand the Layers panel.

2 On the Layers panel, right-click the Background layer and then click Duplicate Layer on the context menu.

3 When Photoshop displays the Duplicate Layer dialog box, type **edits** in the As box and then click the OK button (Duplicate Layer dialog box) to create the edits layer.

4 Click the visibility icon on the Background layer so it is hidden.

5 Select the visible edits layer, if necessary.

To Display the Lens Correction Dialog Box

The following steps display the Lens Correction dialog box.

1
- Click Filter on the menu bar to display the Filter menu (Figure 5–55).

Figure 5–55

② Click Lens Correction on the Filter menu to display the Lens Correction dialog box (Figure 5–56).

🔍 **Experiment**

● Click the Show Grid check box to obtain a visual cue on how much correction you will need to apply. Click the Move Grid Tool button and move the grid so a corner aligns with the top corner of the building. When you are finished evaluating the distortion, click the Show Grid check box again to turn off the grid.

Lens Correction dialog box

Figure 5–56

Other Ways

1. Press SHIFT+CTRL+R

To Straighten the Photo

To straighten the photo, the following steps use the Straighten Tool.

① ● Click the Straighten Tool button (Lens Correction dialog box) to select it.

● Drag horizontally across something in the photo that should be straight, such as the bottom of the roof. Do not release the mouse button so you can see the line and readjust as necessary (Figure 5–57).

Q&A What if my adjustment causes part of my image to disappear?

If that happens, click the Cancel button and open the Lens Correction dialog box again. Drag shorter strokes. You do not have to drag across the entire image to straighten it.

Straighten Tool button

mouse pointer

line is drawn across an area that should be straight

Figure 5–57

2

• Release the mouse button to straighten the photo horizontally.

• Drag vertically across something in the photo that should be straight, such as the decorative strips just below the roof, to straighten the photo vertically (Figure 5–58).

Experiment

• Drag at different angles and watch the image change. When you are finished, drag in the image in a straight line, left to right and top to bottom.

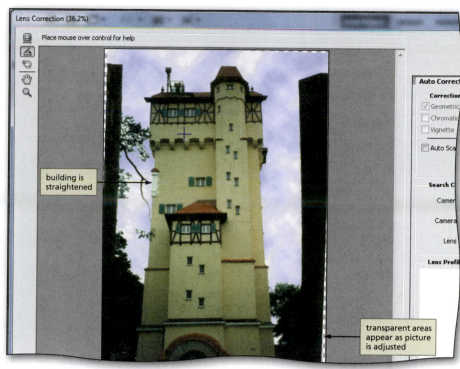

building is straightened

transparent areas appear as picture is adjusted

Figure 5–58

Other Ways

1. Click Custom tab (Lens Correction dialog bog), drag Angle icon

To Extend the Edges

When you alter the angle or perspective of a photo using the Lens Correction dialog box, you commonly move the edges of the photo, leaving transparency along the edge of the original rectangular shape of the image. Photoshop will use content-aware technology to try to fill in those transparent areas. The following steps extend the edges to fill in the transparency.

1

• If necessary, click the Zoom out button until the entire photo is displayed in the preview area.

• Click the Edge button to display a list of tools to manage the edges of the photo after straightening (Figure 5–59).

Experiment

• One at a time, select each of the choices in the list and watch how Photoshop fills in the edges of your image. When you are done, click the Edge button again.

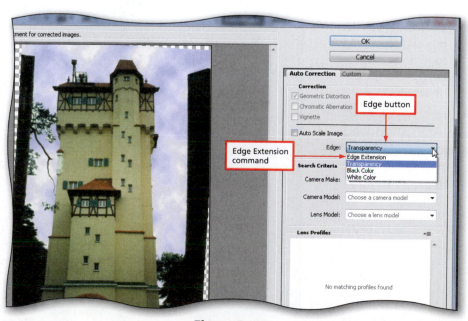

Edge button

Edge Extension command

Figure 5–59

2
- Click Edge Extension to fill the transparent edges. Depending on the amount of experimentation you did with straightening and perspective, the width of your extension may vary (Figure 5–60).

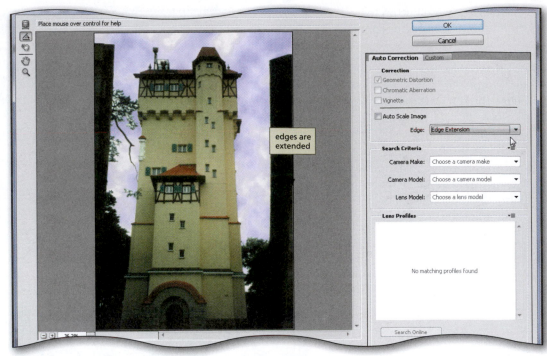

Figure 5–60

To Correct Perspective Errors

The following steps correct perspective errors and keystone distortion in the photo.

1
- Click the Custom tab (Lens Correction dialog box) to display the correction settings.

- Double-click the Vertical Perspective box and type -28 to remove the keystone distortion (Figure 5–61).

Q&A

How do negative values affect the vertical perspective?

A negative value in the Vertical Perspective box brings the top of the picture closer, such as when shooting up from the base of a tall building.

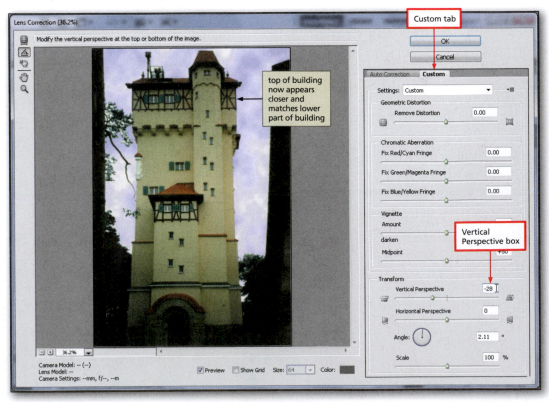

Figure 5–61

2
- Double-click the Horizontal Perspective box. Type - 5 to adjust the slight left-to-right distortion (Figure 5–62).

Q&A

Some of my building is not in the picture. What should I do?

You may have overadjusted the perspective. For example, if the top of the building is missing, increase the vertical perspective in small increments until you can see the top of the building.

3
- Click the OK button to close the Lens Correction dialog box.

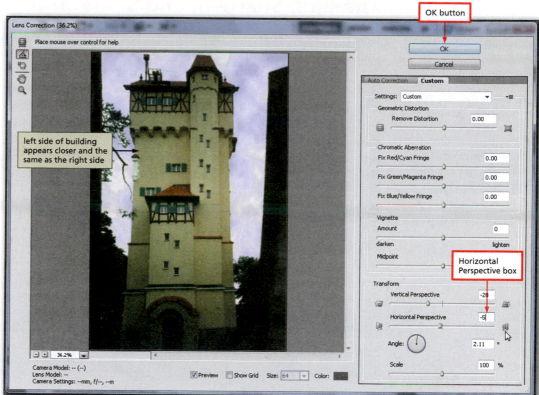

Figure 5–62

Other Ways

1. Drag perspective slider (Lens Correction dialog box)

To Crop the Image

With the image distortion corrected, the following steps crop the edited image to remove any edge extension and to focus attention on the center building.

1 Press the c key to access the Crop Tool.

2 Drag from the upper-left corner of the sky, down and to the right to include all of the photo that is in focus.

3 Press the ENTER key to crop the image (Figure 5–63).

To Save and Close the Building Repaired File

The following steps save and close the Building Repaired file.

1 Press CTRL+S to save the file again. If Photoshop displays a confirmation dialog box, click the OK button.

2 Press CTRL+W to close the file without quitting Photoshop.

Figure 5–63

BTW

Vanishing Point
For photographs with several planes and angles, correcting perspective errors can be tricky. On the Filter menu, the Vanishing Point command lets you specify the planes in the photo. Photoshop remembers the perspective of the plane, resulting in properly scaled and oriented, more realistic-looking pictures.

The Blur, Sharpen, and Smudge Tools

A final set of tools used to help enhance, restore, and create special effects include the Blur, Sharpen, and Smudge Tools.

The Blur Tool softens hard edges or reduces detail in an image when you drag in the selection or image, by decreasing the color contrast between consecutive pixels. The Blur Tool is used for very subtle changes in small areas. If you are working on a high-resolution image, then the effect of the Blur Tool can be very slight; zooming in on a portion of the photo helps you notice the effect. The options bar includes settings for brush size, mode, and strength. The Sharpen Tool is the opposite of the Blur Tool. It increases contrast along edges to add sharpness. The more you paint over an area with the tool, the greater the sharpen effect. The Smudge Tool simulates the effect you see when you drag a finger through wet paint. The tool picks up color where the stroke begins and pushes it in the direction you drag. The effect is much like finger painting.

The Blur, Sharpen, and Smudge Tools have similar options bars (Figure 5–64).

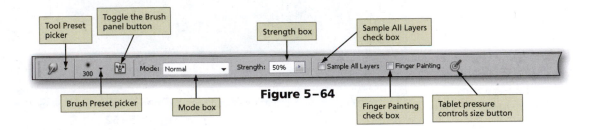

Figure 5–64

BTW

Sharpen Tool
While the Sharpen filter's Unsharp Mask provides an overall sharpening of the focus in an image, the Sharpen Tool works more like the Blur Tool — the effect is more apparent when you zoom in and use it with small portions of the image. The options bar includes settings for brush size, mode, and strength.

To Open the Garden Image

The following step opens the Garden image in preparation for using the Smudge Tool.

1 Open the file named Garden from the Chapter 05 folder of the Data Files for Students, or from a location specified by your instructor.

To Save the Garden File

The following step saves the file in the PSD format.

1 Use the Save As dialog box to save the file on your preferred storage device in the PSD format using the name, Garden Repaired.

To Create an Edits Layer in the Garden Repaired File

The following steps create an edits layer.

1 If necessary, click the Layers tab to expand the Layers panel.

2 On the Layers panel, right-click the Background layer and then click Duplicate Layer on the context menu.

3 When Photoshop displays the Duplicate Layer dialog box, type `edits` in the As box and then click the OK button (Duplicate Layer dialog box) to create the edits layer.

4 Click the visibility icon on the Background layer so it is hidden.

5 Select the visible edits layer, if necessary.

To Smudge

The following steps use the Smudge Tool to create an artistic swirl in the Garden image.

1
• On the Tools panel, right-click the Blur Tool button to display the context menu (Figure 5–65).

2
• Click Smudge Tool to select it.

• Press the RIGHT BRACKET (]) key to increase the size of the brush until the options bar displays 300 for the brush size.

Figure 5–65

3
• Slowly drag a large S-shape over the image to create a smudge. The smudge will take several moments to appear (Figure 5–66).

Q&A

How do I use the Smudge Tool's options bar?

The Smudge Tool's Strength setting modifies the power of the smudge. Setting the Strength to 100% erases nearly all of the existing color. A Strength setting of 15% will give the appearance of trying to smudge dried paint. The Finger Painting check box mimics dipping your finger in the paint color before performing the smudge.

Figure 5–66

To Save the Garden Repaired File and Quit Photoshop

The final steps are to save the Garden Repaired file and quit Photoshop.

1 Press CTRL+S to save the file again. If Photoshop displays a confirmation dialog box, click the OK button.

2 Press CTRL+Q to quit Photoshop.

Chapter Summary

To repair and enhance photos, you used healing tools, tools that repaired damage, tools to straighten and align, and tools to create an artistic effect. You first removed yellowing from a document, and used the Unsharp Mask dialog box to bring it into better focus. You used Content-Aware to fill in a missing portion of a picture. You then repaired scratches and damage to a black-and-white photo. You removed the red eye from a color photo of some children. Next, you repaired poor lighting in a graduation picture and added a vignetting effect. You opened a building photo that had keystone and angle distortion, which you corrected using the Lens Correction dialog box. Finally, you used the Smudge Tool to enhance the photo artistically.

The items listed below include all the new Photoshop skills you have learned in this chapter:

1. Correct Yellowed Portions of a Document (PS 282)
2. Create a Layer from a Background (PS 283)
3. Create a New Adjustment Layer (PS 284)
4. Apply the Blending Mode (PS 288)
5. Apply the Unsharp Mask Filter (PS 290)
6. Lock Transparent Pixels (PS 291)
7. Fill with Content-Aware (PS 294)
8. Repair Damage with the Spot Healing Brush Tool (PS 298)
9. Sample and Paint with the Healing Brush Tool (PS 301)
10. Patch Areas (PS 303)
11. View the Corrections (PS 305)
12. Correct Red Eye (PS 307)
13. Lighten Using the Dodge Tool (PS 311)
14. Darken Using the Burn Tool (PS 312)
15. Display the Lens Correction Dialog Box (PS 315)
16. Straighten the Photo (PS 316)
17. Extend the Edges (PS 317)
18. Correct Perspective Errors (PS 318)
19. Smudge (PS 321)

Learn It Online

Test your knowledge of chapter content and key terms.

Instructions: To complete the Learn It Online exercises, start your browser, click the Address bar, and then enter the Web address **scsite.com/pscs5/learn**. When the Photoshop CS5 Learn It Online page is displayed, click the link for the exercise you want to complete and then read the instructions.

Chapter Reinforcement TF, MC, and SA

A series of true/false, multiple choice, and short answer questions that test your knowledge of the chapter content.

Flash Cards

An interactive learning environment where you identify chapter key terms associated with displayed definitions.

Practice Test

A series of multiple choice questions that test your knowledge of chapter content and key terms.

Who Wants To Be a Computer Genius?

An interactive game that challenges your knowledge of chapter content in the style of a television quiz show.

Wheel of Terms

An interactive game that challenges your knowledge of chapter key terms in the style of the television show *Wheel of Fortune*.

Crossword Puzzle Challenge

A crossword puzzle that challenges your knowledge of key terms presented in the chapter.

Apply Your Knowledge

Reinforce the skills and apply the concepts you learned in this chapter.

Enhancing a Photo for the Web

Instructions: Start Photoshop and perform the customization steps found on pages PS 6 through PS 9. Open the Apply 5-1 Antique file from the Chapter 05 folder of the Data Files for Students. You can access the Data Files for Students on the CD that accompanies this book. See the inside back cover of this book for instructions on downloading the Data Files for Students, or contact your instructor for information about accessing the required files.

Figure 5–67

The purpose of this exercise is to repair a photo of an antique typewriter and enhance it for use on an auction Web site. The edited photo is shown in Figure 5–67.

1. Use the Save As command to save the image on your USB flash drive as a PSD file with the file name, Apply 5-1 Antique Enhanced.

2. In the Layers panel, right-click the Background layer and then click Duplicate Layer on the shortcut menu.

3. In the Duplicate Layer dialog box, type **Corrections** in the As box, and then click the OK button.

4. With the Corrections layer selected, click Filter on the menu bar, and then click Lens Correction.

5. When the Lens Correction dialog box is displayed, edit the following settings:

   a. To adjust the barrel distortion, type **15** in the Remove Distortion box.

   b. To straighten the photo, type **1.85** in the Angle box.

   c. To correct the keystone distortion, type **50** in the Vertical Perspective box.

6. Click the OK button in the Lens Correction dialog box.

7. Click Filter on the menu bar, point to Sharpen, and then click Unsharp Mask. When the Unsharp Mask dialog box is displayed, edit the following settings:

   a. Type **4** in the Threshold box.

   b. Type **1** in the Radius box.

   c. Type **50** in the Amount box.

8. Click the OK button in the Unsharp Mask dialog box.

9. On the Tools panel, right-click the current healing tool button and then click Spot Healing Brush Tool in the list. Use the Spot Healing Brush Tool to correct the damaged area on the wall to the right of the typewriter. Zoom as needed. (*Hint:* Remember to adjust the brush size to be only slightly larger than the damaged area.)

10. Experiment with the healing tools to correct flaws in the white baseboard and remove the small red ball to the left of the table.

11. Right-click the Spot Healing Brush Tool and then click Healing Brush Tool in the list. On the options bar, click the Mode box arrow and then click Replace.

12. ALT+click a light area in the floor and then, using short strokes, drag through the darker areas in the floor. Resample as necessary.

13. To remove the electrical cord in the photo:

   a. Click the Clone Stamp Tool.

Continued >

Apply Your Knowledge *continued*

    b. ALT+click the floor at the bottom of the photo just inside the left leg of the table. Drag from left to right through the parts of the electrical cord that are visible on the floor.

    c. ALT+click below the table at the top of the baseboard, close to the left leg of the table. Drag from left to right through the parts of the electrical cord and outlet that are visible on the baseboard.

14. Press CTRL+S to save the file again. If Photoshop displays an options dialog box, click the OK button.

15. Click File on the menu bar and then click the Save for Web & Devices command. When the Save for Web & Devices dialog box is displayed, click the 4-Up tab, if necessary, and then click the best preview for your system. Click the Save button. When the Save Optimized As dialog box is displayed, save the image on your USB flash drive. Photoshop will fill in the name, Apply-5-1-Antique-Enhanced, and the file type for you.

16. Submit this assignment in the format specified by your instructor.

Extend Your Knowledge

Extend the skills you learned in this chapter and experiment with new skills. You may need to use Help to complete the assignment.

Creating a Moving Automobile Photo

Instructions: Start Photoshop and perform the customization steps found on pages PS 6 through PS 9. Open the Extend 5-1 Auto file from the Chapter 05 folder of the Data Files for Students. See the inside back cover of this book for instructions on downloading the Data Files for Students, or contact your instructor for information on accessing the required files. The purpose of this exercise is to edit a photograph of a parked automobile and make it look like it is in motion, creating both PSD and TIF versions of the final image. Many times, it is impossible to take an action photo of an automobile or other subject traveling at a high speed. This technique will illustrate how to take an existing still photo and make it appear to be moving, as in Figure 5–68.

Figure 5–68

Perform the following tasks:

1. Save the image on your USB flash drive as a PSD file, with the file name Extend 5-1 Auto Complete.

2. To separate the foreground from the background:

    a. Create a selection marquee around the entire car to separate it from the background.

    b. Press CTRL+J or use the Layer via Copy command to place a copy of the automobile on a new layer and assign the layer an appropriate name.

3. To create an illusion of speed in the background:

    a. Select the Background layer. Click Filter on the menu bar, point to Blur and then click Motion Blur to display the Motion Blur dialog box. (*Hint:* You might want to read about Blur filters in Photoshop Help.)

    b. When the Motion Blur dialog box appears, experiment with the Angle and Distance settings until you are satisfied with the results. Close the Motion Blur dialog box.

4. To create the illusion of wheel spin:

   a. Select the automobile layer and then create a selection marquee around the front wheel.

   b. Add a RADIAL BLUR to the wheel by clicking Filter on the menu bar. Click Blur on the Filter submenu, and then click Radial Blur to display the Radial Blur dialog box. Select the Spin Blur method. Set the Amount to 50. Click the OK button to close the Radial Blur dialog box and then deselect the wheel.

   c. Select the back wheel and then apply the same Radial Blur setting used for the front wheel by pressing CTRL+F to repeat the filter. Deselect the back wheel.

5. To tint the windshield and side windows:

   a. With the automobile layer still active, create a selection marquee around the windshield. Use the 'Add to selection' button to add the side windows to the selection.

   b. Press CTRL+J or use the Layer via Copy command to create a new layer. Assign the layer an appropriate name.

   c. Press CTRL+L to display the Levels dialog box.

   d. Drag the white Output Levels slider to the left until the windows look tinted.

   e. Click OK to close the dialog box.

6. Save the file again. If Photoshop displays a dialog box, click the OK button. Flatten the image.

7. Save the image as Extend 5-1 Auto Complete in the TIFF format. If Photoshop displays a dialog box, click the OK button.

8. Submit the assignment in the format specified by your instructor.

9. Quit Photoshop.

Make It Right

Analyze a project and correct all errors and/or improve the design.

Restoring a Historical Document

Instructions: Start Photoshop and perform the customization steps found on pages PS 6 through PS 9. Open the Make It Right 5-1 Letter file from the Chapter 05 folder of the Data Files for Students. See the inside back cover of this book for instructions on downloading the Data Files for Students, or contact your instructor for information on accessing the required files.

Members of the local historical society started working on repairing the Civil War letter, shown in Figure 5–69, but ran out of time after they created the various correction layers. They did not realize that converting to grayscale would merge their layers. They would like you to finish the job.

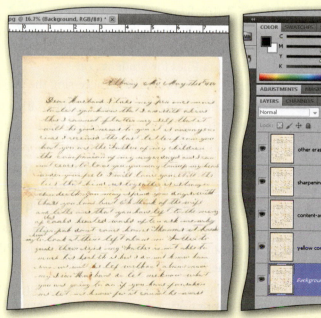

Figure 5–69

Continued >

Make It Right *continued*

Perform the following tasks:
Using the techniques you learned in the chapter, make the following corrections:

1. Convert to grayscale, merging the layers.

2. Create a Layer From Background, named corrections.

3. Create a new adjustment layer with levels.

4. Apply the Overlay blending mode.

5. Apply the Unsharp Mask Filter.

6. Lock transparent pixels and erase any other extraneous marks.

7. Flatten the image.

8. Save the file with the name, Make It Right 5-1 Letter Repaired, in the PSD format.

In the Lab

Design and/or create a document using the guidelines, concepts, and skills presented in this chapter. Labs are listed in order of increasing difficulty.

Lab 1: Repairing Blemishes and Red Eye

Problem: You would like to fix a photo of your nephew and print several copies. The photo has several lens flares, blemishes, and a red-eye problem. The repaired photo is shown in Figure 5–70.

Figure 5–70

Instructions: Perform the following tasks:

1. Start Photoshop. Set the Default Workspace and then reset all tools. Reset the previews in the Layers panel and then reset the default colors.

2. Open the file Lab 5-1 Boy from the Chapter 05 folder of the Data Files for Students. See the inside back cover of this book for instructions on downloading the Data Files for Students, or contact your instructor for information on accessing the required files.

3. Click the Save As command on the File menu. Type **Lab 5-1 Boy Repaired** as the file name. Save the file in the PSD format on your USB flash drive.

4. Duplicate the Background layer and name it, corrections. Hide the Background layer.

5. Select the Spot Healing Brush Tool. On the options bar, click Proximity Match. Change the size of the brush to be slightly larger than the blemish. Fix the small blemishes on the boy's forehead.

6. Use the healing tools to fix reflections from the flash. If you make a bad correction, press CTRL+Z and then decrease your brush size before trying again.

7. Select the Red Eye Tool. On the options bar, change the Pupil Size to 40%. Change the Darken Amount to 45%. In the image, click each eye.

8. Make any other adjustments you feel are necessary. Turn off and on the visibility of the corrections and Background layers to notice the difference between the original and the corrections.

9. Save the image again. Flatten the layers. If Photoshop displays a dialog box asking to discard hidden layers, click the OK button. Save the image with the file name Lab 5-1 Boy Final in the TIFF format, and then print a copy for your instructor.

In the Lab

Lab 2: Altering a Building Photo

Problem: A local apartment complex needs to create a flyer to publicize improvements that have been made to one of the units. The only photo available shows a building with graffiti. To make matters worse, this photo shows an old apartment building with only three windows, and all the new ones have four. You will need to lighten the photo, clean up the graffiti from the bricks, and make another window. Because the photo is at an angle, the Clone Stamp Tool will not work very well; thus, you will use the Vanishing Point filter. After your edits, the photo should appear as shown in Figure 5–71.

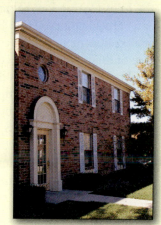

Figure 5–71

Instructions: Perform the following tasks:

1. Start Photoshop. Set the Default Workspace and then reset all tools. Reset the previews in the Layers panel and then reset the default colors.

2. Open the Lab 5-2 Graffiti file from the Chapter 05 folder of the Data Files for Students.

3. Save the file on your USB flash drive as Lab 5-2 Graffiti Repaired in the PSD format.

4. Create a corrections layer and fix the levels in the photograph. In the Levels dialog box, drag the black, midtone, and white Input Levels sliders to 14, 1.45, and 238, respectively. Close the Levels dialog box.

5. To create a correction that is in perspective, click Filter on the menu bar, and then click Vanishing Point to display the Vanishing Point dialog box. (*Hint:* Read the BTW information about the Vanishing Point filter on page PS 320.)

6. Press the z key to access the Zoom Tool and then ALT+click to zoom out. If necessary, click the Edit Plane Tool. Drag the corners of the grid to align with the corners of the building.

7. Press the s key to access the Stamp Tool, which acts as a perspective-oriented Clone Tool. On the options bar, change the Diameter to 200, the Hardness to 50, and the Opacity to 100.

8. Using the cloning techniques you learned in Chapter 3, ALT+click to establish a clone source point and slowly paint over the graffiti, resampling as necessary. If you make an error, close the dialog box and start again with Step 5.

9. Press the M key to switch to the Marquee Tool. Drag a marquee selection around the upper window. ALT+drag a copy of the window to the newly repaired blank area.

10. Close the Vanishing Point dialog box and save the image again.

11. Flatten the layers. Save a copy of the image as Lab 5-2 Graffiti for Print in the EPS format. If Photoshop displays a dialog box about saving options, click the OK button. Submit the assignment in the format specified by your instructor.

In the Lab

Lab 3: Fixing Distortions

Problem: A church in your area would like a photo that they can use on brochures and on the Web, but the photo they sent you was slightly out of perspective and slanted. There were signs and cars in the photo that should be removed. After your repairs, the photo should appear as shown in Figure 5–72 on the next page.

Instructions: Perform the following tasks:
Start Photoshop and perform the customization steps found on pages PS 7 through PS 9. Open the file Lab 5-3 Church and save it as Lab 5-3 Church Repaired.psd on your storage device.

Continued >

In the Lab *continued*

Duplicate the Background layer and name it, corrections. With the corrections layer selected, open the Lens Correction dialog box and adjust the horizontal and vertical angles. (*Hint:* Because the picture was taken at a significant angle, the correction will not make the face of the building perfectly flat.) Use the Straighten Tool button to straighten the photo using the base of the church where it touches the ground. Change the edge to Edge Extension. Use Content-Aware to remove the cars from the photo. Use the Spot Healing Brush Tool with Content-Aware to remove the signs and poles. Do not remove the small poles along the sidewalk. Crop the photo as necessary. Save the image again.

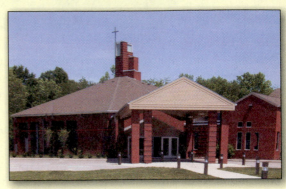

Figure 5–72

Cases and Places

Apply your creative thinking and problem solving skills to design and implement a solution.

Note: To complete these assignments, you may be required to use the Data Files for Students. See the inside back cover of this book for instructions on downloading the Data Files for Students, or contact your instructor for information about accessing the required files.

1: Create a Clean Photo for a Slide Show

Academic

On a recent vacation, you took pictures in Washington, D.C. You want to use a photo of the Lincoln memorial for your history class, but the picture you took has some people in the photo. Open the Case 5-1 Lincoln Memorial file that is located in the Chapter 05 folder of the Data Files for Students. Use content-aware techniques to remove the people from the image. Use one of the healing brushes to remove the shadows on the floor. Create evenly spaced chain link poles using Content-Aware to remove poles, or the Clone Tool to create them. Save the file as Case 5-1 Lincoln Memorial Edited.

2: Repair Tears and Sharpen

Personal

Your grandmother's favorite photo of your mother has a tear on the edge. You decide to fix it for her. Start Photoshop and then reset all the defaults. Open the Case 5-2 Girl With Carriage photo that is located in the Chapter 05 folder of the Data Files for Students. Use the Polygonal Lasso Tool to outline the torn corner. On the Layer menu, point to New and then click Layer via Cut. Hide the Background layer. Select the new layer. Delete any white that appears in the new layer. Redisplay the background image and move the layer closer to the rest of the picture. When you have the best match (the tear will not fit exactly), flatten the image. Use the Healing Brush Tool to repair any remnants of the tear. Use the Unsharp Mask dialog box to sharpen the image. Crop the original white border. Save the photo in the PSD format with the name Case 5-2 Girl With Carriage Repaired.

3: Creating a Signature File

Professional

You need to create a signature to place on various electronic documents including PDF files. Sign your name on a piece of paper and scan it using a high resolution of black and white (or use the Case 5-3 Signature file included in the Chapter 05 folder of the Data Files for Students). Create a Layer From Background. Remove any white and extraneous marks. Lock the layer for transparency. Use the Burn Tool to darken the signature. Save the file with the name, Case 5-3 Signature Transparent.

6 | Applying Filters and Patterns

Objectives

You will have mastered the material in this chapter when you can:

- Select colors using the Color panel
- Apply color with the Paint Bucket Tool
- Discuss and use rendering filters such as Lighting Effects
- Use the Puppet Warp Tool
- Describe the categories of filters in Photoshop
- Use the Filter Gallery to create special effects

- Retouch images with the Liquify Filter
- Create Smart objects
- Define, use, and delete a new pattern
- Adjust type
- Explain the terms knockout, trapping, surprinting, and misregistration
- Convert to CMYK
- Print a hard proof

6 | Applying Filters and Patterns

Introduction

Special effects or visual effects are commonplace, and because computers facilitate nearly all commercial graphics and animation, many clients and customers expect to see effects in their creative designs. Effects that seemed rare and cutting-edge 20 years ago are now the norm. Special effects visually spice up static graphics with distortions, blurs, contour alterations, color manipulations, and applied overlays. Imaginative visual effects create a customized, attention-grabbing appearance, and are used in everything from DVD liners to branding logos to billboards. Most people subconsciously expect to see fancy, stimulating graphics in every advertisement; indeed, when a special effect is not present, some may interpret the graphic as retro or even boring.

The entertainment industry has led the way with artistic rendering and advanced animation techniques. Specialized graphic manipulations are saved and sold as downloadable filters for most popular graphic editing software packages. Filters are the most common way to create special effects in Photoshop. In fact, entire books have been written about the vast number of filters included in the Photoshop installation, along with the thousands of filters that can be added. Filters have the capability to mimic many traditional forms of art such as pastels, line drawings, or watercolors. You can blend, blur, or warp graphics in every way imaginable, allowing you to enliven commercial artwork in-house with relative ease.

In this chapter, as you learn about filters and patterns, you might find the many options and settings to be overwhelming at first. It is easy to become carried away when applying filters. Your goal will be a subtle, judicious, and purposeful use of filters to enhance the meaning of the digital image.

BTW

Spot Colors
Occasionally design specialists add a fifth color to match an exact brand color or to add a specialized finish or sheen, such as a metallic look. Adding a fifth spot color is more expensive but is sometimes preferable.

Project — Creating a Poster

Chapter 6 uses Photoshop to create a poster for sale in a beach store. The poster incorporates graphics, color, lighting, and patterns. Photoshop filters are applied to the various seashells. A special spotlight filter highlights from the bottom to the top of the poster. A pattern created from a shell graphic appears horizontally across the lower portion of the poster. The completed image appears in Figure 6–1. Nearly all posters, magazines, and catalogs on the market today are full-color and are printed using a four-color process (CMYK), providing bright color shades and an eye-catching look. Recall that CMYK is an acronym for the four-color process used in printing, Cyan, Magenta, Yellow, and Black. You will use colors from the CMYK color mode. However, more filter effects are available for RGB images, so you will design the image in RGB and later convert it to CMYK.

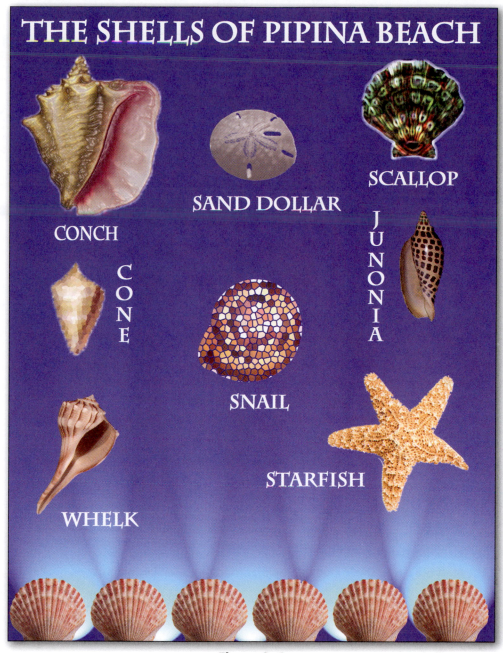

Figure 6–1

Overview

As you read this chapter, you will learn how to create the poster shown in Figure 6–1 by performing these general tasks:

- Fill a background with color.
- Create lighting effects.
- Fix an image using the Liquify filter.
- Apply filters using the Filter Gallery.
- Create and use a pattern.
- Convert color modes and print a hard proof.

<table>
<tr><td>

Plan Ahead

</td><td>

General Project Guidelines

When editing a photo, the actions you perform and decisions you make will affect the appearance and characteristics of the finished product. As you create a graphic, such as the ones shown in Figure 6–1 on the previous page, you should follow these general guidelines:

1. **Plan your use of filters.** Think about your purpose in using filters. Is it for correction or decoration? Are you trying to create a special effect, or does the filter enhance the message being conveyed by the image? Decide if a filter is appropriate for the entire image or just a portion. As with all types of projects, if you are working on a business photo, consult with the client, and offer him or her many examples or layer comps.

2. **Use type wisely.** When using large text, pay close attention to formatting type styles, spacing, and character effects such as kerning, tracking, leading, and baseline shift. Use a stroke of color around the text for a more distinctive look. Apply overlays to prevent misregistration.

3. **Avoid color printing problems.** In commercial printing, the speed of the printer and possible shifts in the paper might make some colors run together, creating spreads of blended color; or the printer might miss small areas between very close objects or layers. Use knockout techniques and correct alignment to avoid color printing problems.

4. **Consult with printing professionals.** As design specialists create and modify artwork, they routinely consult with printing professionals to help plan the best method to produce projects. Print professionals can provide information on paper, color management systems, file transfer, output devices, and the way those devices interpret and process color and type information.

</td></tr>
</table>

Starting and Customizing Photoshop

The following steps start Photoshop and reset the default workspace, tools, and colors.

To Start Photoshop

The following steps, which assume Windows 7 is running, start Photoshop based on a typical installation.

1 Click the Start button on the Windows 7 taskbar to display the Start menu.

2 Type **Photoshop CS5** as the search text in the 'Search programs and files' text box, and watch the search results appear on the Start menu.

3 Click Adobe Photoshop CS5 in the search results on the Start menu to start Photoshop.

4 After a few moments, when the Photoshop window is displayed, if the window is not maximized, click the Maximize button on the title bar to maximize the window.

To Reset the Workspace

As discussed in Chapter 1, it is helpful to reset the workspace so that the tools and panels appear in their default positions. The following steps select the Essentials workspace.

1 Click the 'Show more workspaces and options' button on the Application bar to display the names of saved workspaces and then, if necessary, click Essentials to select the default workspace panels.

2 Click the 'Show more workspaces and options' button again to display the list and then click Reset Essentials to restore the workspace to its default settings and reposition any panels that may have been moved.

To Reset the Tools and the Options Bar

The following steps select the Rectangular Marquee Tool and reset all tool settings in the options bar.

1 If the tools in the Tools panel appear in two columns, click the double arrow at the top of the Tools panel.

2 If necessary, click the Rectangular Marquee Tool button on the Tools panel to select it.

3 Right-click the Rectangular Marquee Tool icon on the options bar to display the context menu, and then click Reset All Tools. When Photoshop displays a confirmation dialog box, click the OK button to restore the tools to their default settings.

To Reset the Default Colors

The following step resets the default colors.

1 Press the D key to reset the default foreground and background colors.

To Open a Photo

To open a photo in Photoshop, it must be stored as a digital file on your computer or on an external storage device. The photos used in this book are stored in the Data Files for Students. You can access the Data Files for Students on the CD that accompanies this book. See the inside back cover of this book for instructions on downloading the Data Files for Students, or contact your instructor for information about accessing the required files.

The following steps open the file, Seashells, from a CD located in drive E. This file is an RGB file with many layers.

1 Insert the CD that accompanies this book into your CD drive. After a few seconds, if Windows displays a dialog box, click its Close button.

2 Click File on the menu bar, and then click Open to display the Open dialog box.

3 In the Open dialog box, click the Look in box arrow to display the list of available locations, and then click drive E or the drive associated with the Data Files for Students.

4 Double-click the Chapter 06 folder to open it, and then double-click the file, Seashells, to open it (Figure 6–2 on the next page).

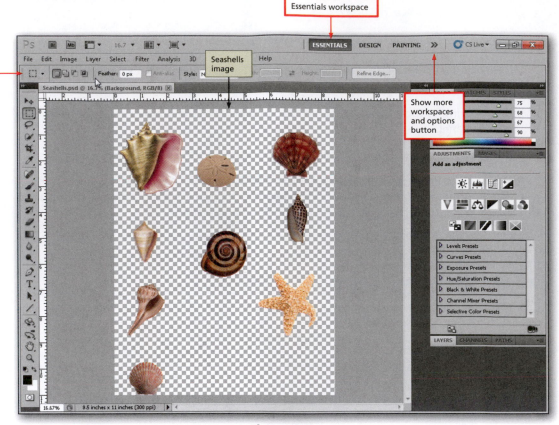

Figure 6–2

To Save the File with a New Name

The following steps save the file on a storage device using the Save As command.

1 With your USB flash drive connected to one of the computer's USB ports, press SHIFT+CTRL+S to display the Save As dialog box.

2 Type `Seashells Edited` in the Name box.

3 Click the Save in box arrow and then click UDISK 2.0 (F:), or the location associated with your USB flash drive, in the list. If you want to create a folder for the photos in Chapter 6, click the Create New Folder button. Then when the new folder is displayed, type a chapter name, such as Chapter 06, and press the ENTER key.

4 If necessary, click the Format button to display the list of available file formats, and then click Photoshop (*.PSD; *.PDD) in the list.

5 Click the Save button in the Save As dialog box to save the file.

The Color Panel

Photoshop has many different ways to select or specify colors for use in the document window. You specify colors when you use paint, gradient, or fill tools. Previously you used the Color picker dialog box and the Swatches panel to choose colors. Some other ways include using the Color panel, the Color Sampler Tool, and the Info panel.

A convenient way to select and edit colors is to use the Color panel (Figure 6–3), which displays numeric color values for the current foreground and background colors. Using the sliders in the Color panel, you can edit the foreground and background colors using different color modes. Recall that a color value is a numeric representation of the color mode. Photoshop uses the foreground color to paint and fill selections and to create text. The background color commonly is used with fills and masks. Some special effects filters also use the foreground and background colors. You can click in the color ramp, located at the bottom of the Color panel, to choose a color from the entire color spectrum. The Color panel menu allows you to change the color mode, change the displayed sliders, copy the color, or close the panel. To choose a foreground color, click a color in the Color panel. To choose a background color, ALT+click a color in the Color panel.

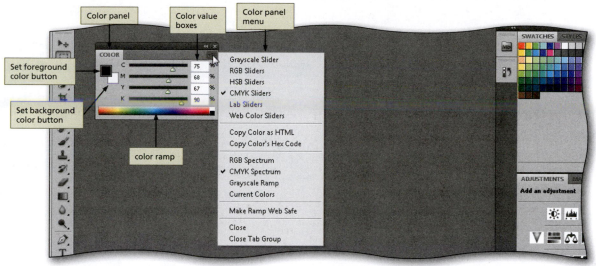

Figure 6–3

To Hide Layers

The following steps hide all of the layers except the Background layer in preparation for using the Color panel.

1 Click the Layers panel tab to display the Layers panel.

2 If necessary, scroll in the Layers panel to display the Background layer and select it.

3 ALT+click the visibility icon on the Background layer to hide the other layers (Figure 6–4).

BTW

Layer Transparency
On the Layers panel, if your layers display a solid background, the Transparency Grid setting has been set to None. To display a checkerboard instead of a solid background, click Edit on the menu bar, point to Preferences, and then click Transparency & Gamut in the Preferences dialog box. Then, adjust the Grid Size and Grid Colors.

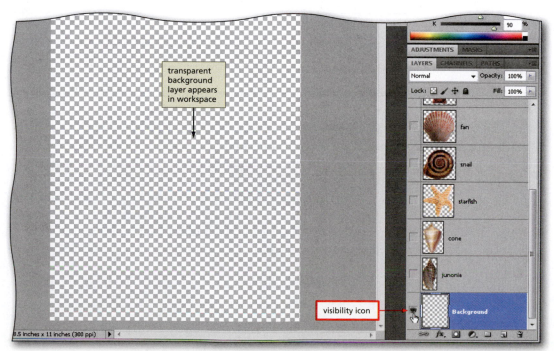

Figure 6–4

To Select a Color Using the Color Panel

The following steps edit the Background layer, changing it from transparent to navy blue. You will choose the color from the Color panel and then apply it with the Paint Bucket Tool.

Recall that you are working with a file that uses the RGB color mode because more filter effects are available for RGB images and you plan to use filters. However, the final version will be converted to the CMYK color mode for printing; therefore, you will choose colors that will be compatible with CMYK.

- Move the mouse pointer into the Color panel and position it over the color ramp to display the Eyedropper mouse pointer (Figure 6–5).

Q&A

Why do my colors look different?

Someone may have changed the colors or the color mode in the Color panel. To reset the colors, press the D key. To reset the color mode, click the Color panel menu button, and then click CMYK Sliders in the list.

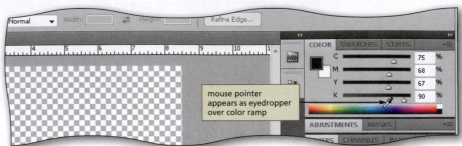

Figure 6–5

- Click a dark blue color to select it as the foreground color (Figure 6–6).

Q&A

Could I enter the color numbers rather than use the color ramp?

Yes, if you want your color to match the figures in this chapter exactly, you can enter 100 in the C box, 90 in the M box, and 0 in both the Y and K boxes.

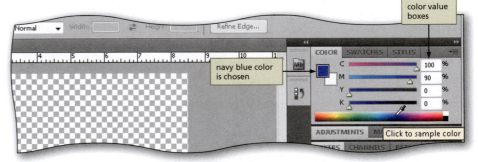

Figure 6–6

Info Panel
When you want more information about a specific color in your document, use the **Info panel** to show the color values beneath the mouse pointer. The Info panel also shows information and suggestions about using the currently selected tool.

The Paint Bucket Tool

The Paint Bucket Tool fills adjacent, similar pixels with color. To use the Paint Bucket Tool, you select it on the Tools panel, and then click in the document window. Recall that the Paint Bucket Tool appears on the same context menu as the Gradient Tool. The Paint Bucket options bar displays choices for fine-tuning the use of the Paint Bucket Tool (Figure 6–7). By default, the Paint Bucket Tool uses the foreground color as its fill color, but you also can choose from a predefined pattern when filling. The Fill, Mode, Opacity, and Tolerance boxes work the same way as they do for the Magic Wand Tool and the eraser tools. Recall that higher tolerance values fill a wider range of colors. The Contiguous check box allows you to fill all adjacent pixels of the same color within the tolerance. To fill pixels based on the merged color data from all visible layers, select the All Layers check box.

The Paint Bucket Tool mouse pointer displays a paint bucket. The tip of the paint coming out of the bucket is the fill location.

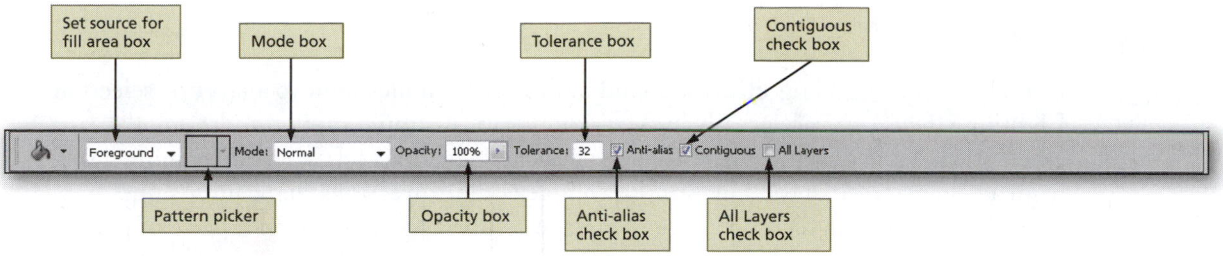

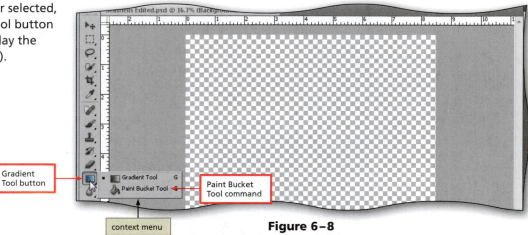

Figure 6–7

To Use the Paint Bucket Tool

The following steps use the Paint Bucket Tool to color the Background layer.

1

• With the Background layer selected, right-click the Gradient Tool button on the Tools panel to display the context menu (Figure 6–8).

Figure 6–8

2

• Click the Paint Bucket Tool to select it.

• Click the canvas to color the Background layer with the selected color from the Color panel (Figure 6–9).

How does the Paint Bucket Tool determine which part of the image to color?

If the Contiguous check box is selected, the Paint Bucket Tool fills all pixels of the same color that are connected to the position of the click. If the Contiguous check box is not selected, all pixels of the same color are filled in.

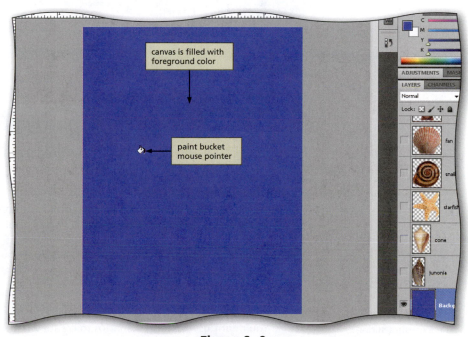

Figure 6–9

Other Ways

1. Press SHIFT+G, click document window

BTW

Gloss
The Gloss slider (Lighting Effects dialog box) determines how much the surface reflects the light. Matte is a low reflection, indicated as a negative number. Shiny is a higher reflection, indicated as a positive number.

Lighting Effects

In Photoshop, a **lighting effect** is a kind of filter that applies light to a layer or selection. Lighting effects can vary greatly in their complexity. A simple spotlight filter might cast an elliptical beam of light, whereas a directional effect could act as a beam shining light from a distance — like the sun. A more complex omni-directional light filter shines light in all directions from directly above the image — like a light bulb over a piece of paper. The Lighting Effects dialog box contains numerous settings to create a wide variety of lighting effects (Figure 6–10). **Lighting styles** have to do with the number of light sources in the lighting effect, and their individual color, intensity, direction, and focus. A **light type** specifies the direction and distance of the perceived light. Properties such as Gloss, Material Exposure, and Ambience affect the reflection and quantity of the perceived light source.

BTW

Material
The Material slider (Lighting Effects dialog box) determines which is more reflective: the light, or the object on which the light is cast. Plastic reflects the light's color; Metallic reflects the object's color.

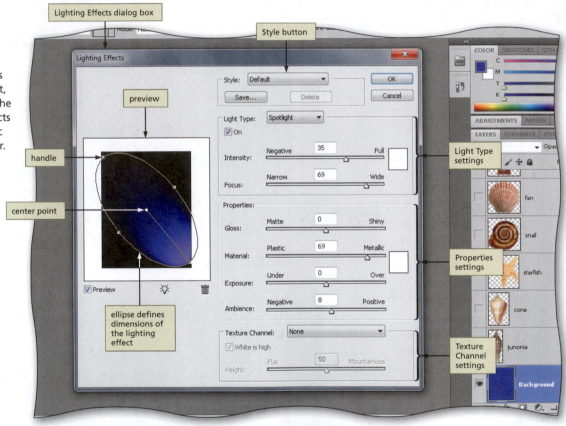

Figure 6–10

Plan
Ahead

Plan your use of filters.
Some filters in Photoshop help you perform restorations on your photos. Others alter color to create sophisticated renderings or to distort pixels purposefully. The possibilities are endless. It is a good idea to look through the lists of filters in this chapter or use Photoshop Help to become familiar with what is available. Remember: the purpose of the photo should guide your decisions on when or if to use filters.

- For example, you might use a filter to simulate the appearance of stained glass or texture paintings to portray a sophisticated artistic tone.
- You might use lighting scenarios to create what-if images.
- You might want to use a water filter on a picture of water.
- A popular trend uses filters to create **photomosaics**, or recognizable pictures made up of many smaller pictures.

BTW

Exposure
The Exposure slider (Lighting Effects dialog box) increases or decreases the total amount of light to fall on the canvas.

(continued)

(continued)

> Most filters can be applied either to the entire image or to a specific layer, channel, or selection. Filters can be used for correction or decoration, but should always be applied to a non-destructive layer with correct labeling or by creating a smart object layer.

**Plan
Ahead**

The Lighting Effects dialog box has a preview that lets you change the direction and angle of the light by dragging the handles that define the edges of an ellipse. The Color box changes the color of the light. A Texture Channel setting allows you to specify which channel to render. If you choose none, the lighting effect is applied to all channels. A center point positioned over the background rectangle preview allows you to set the direction of the light source graphically.

To Create a Duplicate Layer

Because filters are destructive to the layer on which they are applied, a duplicate layer is necessary; the following steps create a duplicate layer for the first filter effect.

BTW

**Changing Spotlight
Color**
To change the color of
the spotlight, click the
color box in the Light
Type area (Lighting Effects
dialog box) and use the
Color Picker dialog box to
choose a color.

1 Right-click the Background layer to display the context menu.

2 Click Duplicate Layer on the context menu to open the Duplicate Layer dialog box.

3 Type **lighting effects** in the As box (Duplicate Layer dialog box), and then click the OK button to create the new layer.

To Choose a Lighting Effects Style

For the Seashell poster, you will use a lighting style called Five Lights up. The following steps open the Lighting Effects dialog box and choose a style.

1
- With the lighting effects layer selected, click Filter on the menu bar to display the Filter menu.

- Point to Render on the Filter menu to display the Render submenu (Figure 6–11).

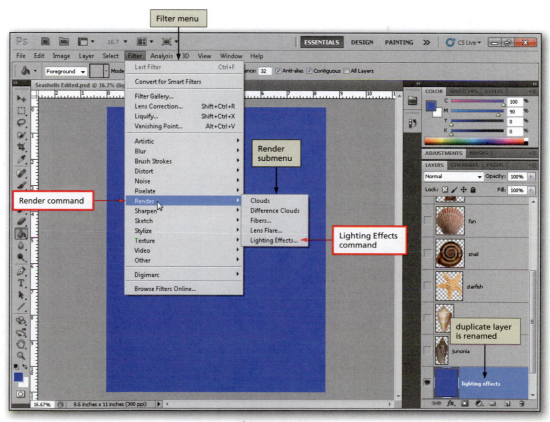

Figure 6–11

2

- Click Lighting Effects to display the Lighting Effects dialog box (Figure 6–12).

Q&A

What is the default setting for lighting effects?

Photoshop creates a single, white, elliptical beam of light that generally fills the layer or selection as shown in the preview. The light focuses from the center point of the preview circle outward along the radius. The brightest spot occurs on the edge of the preview circle.

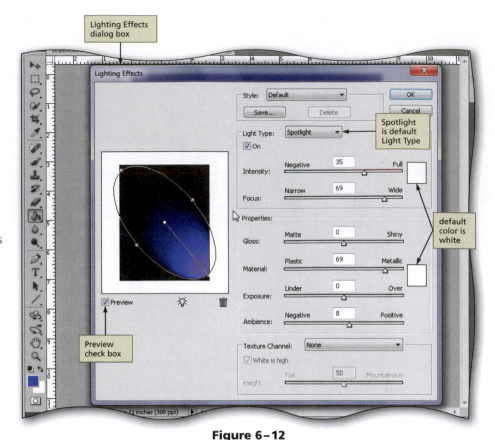

Figure 6–12

3

- Click the Style button (Lighting Effects dialog box) to display the list of styles (Figure 6–13).

 **Experiment**

- One at a time, click each of the lighting effects and watch how the preview changes.

Figure 6–13

4

- Click Five Lights Up to choose the lighting effects style (Figure 6–14).

Q&A

What are the small squares that appear at four places around the preview circle?

They are handles. You can drag them to change the size of the preview circle or to rotate the direction of the light.

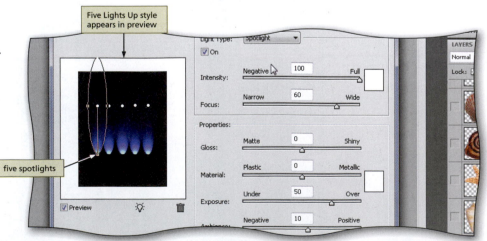

Figure 6–14

To Edit Spotlight Properties

The following step edits the ambience for the spotlights. Changing a property setting on one of the five spotlights changes them all.

1

• In the Properties area (Lighting Effects dialog box), drag the Ambience slider to 35 (Figure 6–15).

Q&A How does the Ambience slider affect the spotlight?

The Ambience slider (Lighting Effects dialog box) diffuses the light as if it were combined with another light in a room, such as sunlight or fluorescent light. A setting of 35 diffuses the light slightly so other parts of the poster will have some lighting rather than display black.

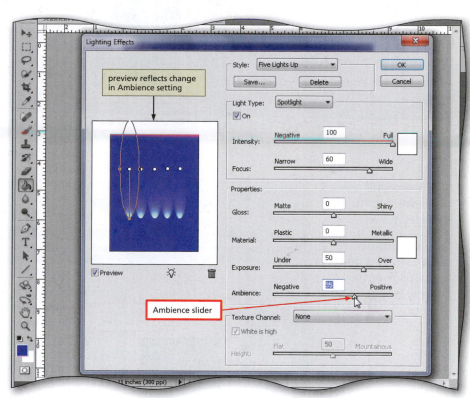

Figure 6–15

To Position the Spotlights

The following steps position the spotlights.

1

• With the first spotlight selected as shown by the preview circle, drag the center point to the left edge of the preview.

• Drag the bottom handle down to the bottom edge of the preview and slightly right as shown in Figure 6–16.

Q&A What does the Intensity slider do?

The Intensity slider increases or decreases the size of the bright spot at the end of the beam of light.

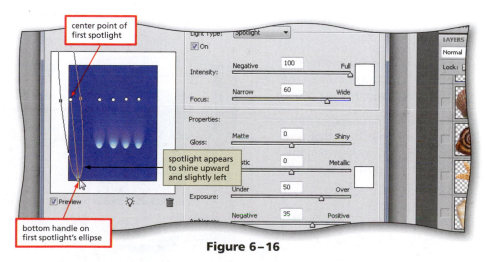

Figure 6–16

2

- Click the center point of the fifth spotlight to select it.

- Drag it to the right edge of the preview.

- Drag the bottom handle down to the bottom edge of the preview and slightly left as shown in Figure 6–17.

Q&A

What does the Focus slider do?

The Focus slider increases or decreases the length of the beam.

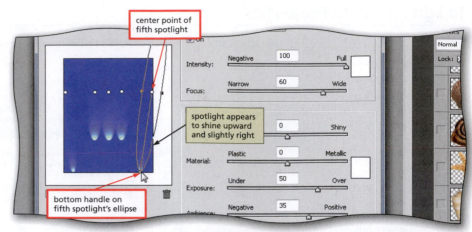

Figure 6–17

3

- Click the center point of the third spotlight to select it.

- Drag the bottom handle straight down to the edge of the preview (Figure 6–18).

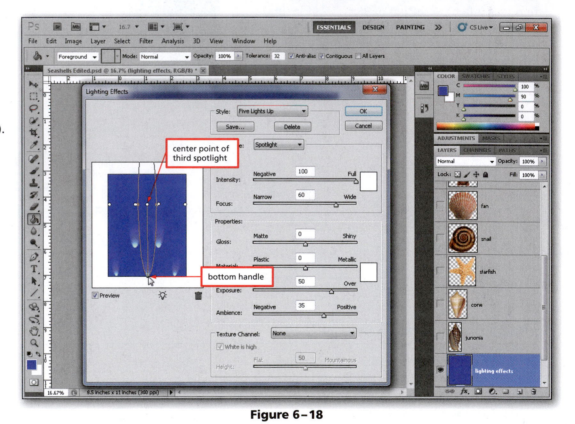

Figure 6–18

4

- Position the second and fourth spotlights halfway between the others, by dragging their centers.

- Drag the bottom handles of the second and fourth spotlights to positions halfway between the others at the bottom of the preview (Figure 6–19).

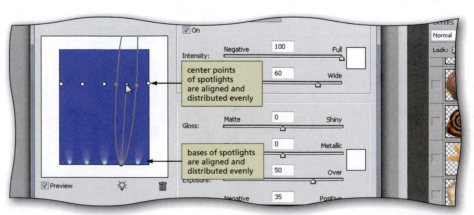

Figure 6–19

To Widen the Spotlights

The following steps widen the spotlights. To select a spotlight, you click its center point in the preview. To adjust the width of a spotlight, you drag the side handles.

1
- One at a time, select each spotlight by clicking its center. Drag the side handles outward to meet the adjacent spotlight centers (Figure 6–20).

Q&A
Can I go back and change a spotlight after I have edited it in the preview?

Yes. Select the spotlight by clicking its center point and then drag the handles until you like the way it looks.

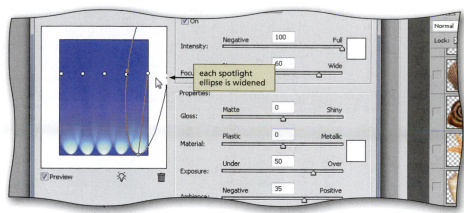

Figure 6–20

 Experiment
- Try SHIFT+dragging the handles to see how it affects the spotlight.

2
- Click the OK button (Lighting Effects dialog box) to apply the spotlights (Figure 6–21).

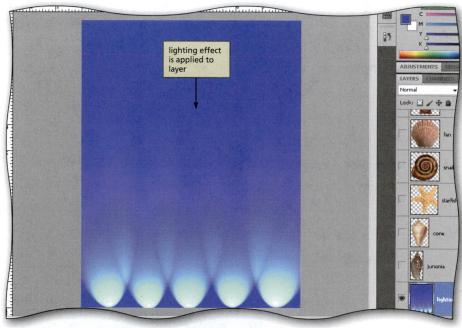

Figure 6–21

To Save the File

Because you have created lighting effects and made changes to the image, it is a good idea to save the file again in the following step.

1 Press CTRL+S to save the Seashell Edited file with the same name.

Break Point: If you wish to take a break, this is a good place to do so. You can quit Photoshop now. To resume at a later time, start Photoshop, open the file called Seashells Edited, and continue following the steps from this location forward.

Puppet Warp

Puppet Warp provides a visual mesh that allows you to distort or fix specific image areas, while leaving other areas intact. The Puppet Warp Tool especially is useful when portions of an image are crooked or need repositioning. Puppet Warp lets you click visual pins along a mesh overlay as points at which to apply the transformation; it offers more fine tuning than does the Warp transformation command with its 12 handles. The Puppet Warp options bar (Figure 6–22) contains boxes and buttons to adjust the Puppet Warp. The Mode determines the overall elasticity of the mesh. The Density determines the spacing of mesh points. The Expansion setting expands or contracts the outer edge of the mesh. The Pin depth buttons allow you to apply the pin to overlapping layers.

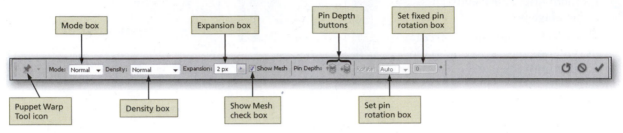

Figure 6–22

To Duplicate the Starfish Layer

The following steps create a duplicate layer for the starfish layer in preparation for the puppet warp.

1 On the Layers panel, scroll as necessary to display the starfish layer.

2 Right-click the starfish layer and then click Duplicate Layer on the context menu to open the Duplicate Layer dialog box.

3 Click the OK button (Duplicate Layer dialog box) to create the new layer.

4 Click the visibility icon on the starfish copy layer to make it visible (Figure 6–23).

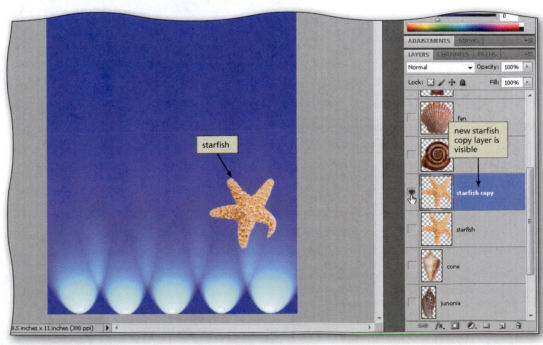

Figure 6–23

To Apply a Puppet Warp

The following steps apply a puppet warp to straighten one of the arms on the starfish.

1

- With the starfish copy layer still selected, click Edit on the menu bar to display the Edit menu.

- Click Puppet Warp on the Edit menu to display the Puppet Warp options bar.

- If necessary, on the options bar, click the Show Mesh check box to turn off the mesh.

- In the document window, click the center of the starfish to add a pin.

- Click the starfish at a position approximately halfway between the center point and the bend in the starfish's arm.

- Click to add a third pin at the end of the curved arm (Figure 6–24).

 Q&A How do I know which pin I am working with?

The selected pin will contain a black dot similar to a radio button selection.

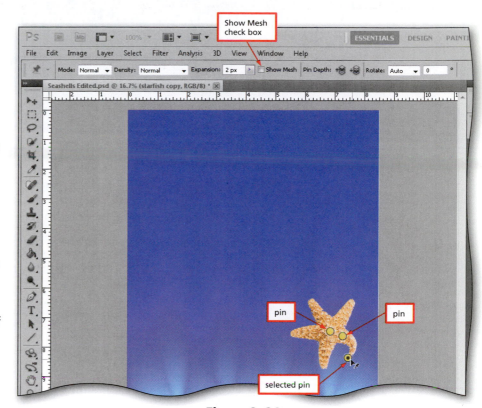

Figure 6–24

2

- Drag the selected pin to straighten the arm (Figure 6–25).

Q&A How do I delete a pin?

Select the pin by clicking it and then press the DELETE key. Or ALT+click non-selected pins. To remove all pins, click the 'Remove all pins' button on the options bar.

Figure 6–25

• Click the Commit Puppet Warp (Return) button to finish the puppet warp (Figure 6–26).

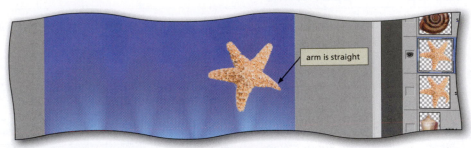

arm is straight

Figure 6–26

To Rename the Starfish Copy Layer

The following steps rename the layer to reflect the filter settings.

1. On the Layers panel, double-click the name, starfish copy, to select it.

2. Type `puppet warp` and press the ENTER key to rename the layer with a name that reflects the editing.

Filters

A **filter** is a special effect that changes the look of your image or selection by altering the pixels either via their physical location or via a color change. Filters can mimic traditional photographic filters, which are pieces of colored glass or gelatin placed over the lens to change the photo's appearance, or they can be more complex, creating advanced artistic effects. Figure 6–27 displays an original photo and five applied filters.

original image

Sketch Photocopy filter

Brush Strokes Accented Edges filter

Sketch Waterpaper filter

Artistic Plastic Wrap filter

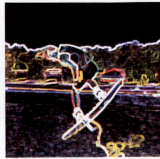

Stylize Glowing Edges filter

Figure 6–27

You already have used filters in previous chapters when you corrected perspective, reduced noise and used the Unsharp Mask command. In this chapter, you will use new filters to change the appearance of the graphics on the poster.

Photoshop categorizes filters into groups: Artistic, Blur, Brush Strokes, Distort, Pixelate, Sketch, Stylize, and Texture, among others. Three special filters are Lens Correction, Liquify, and Vanishing Point. Although you will not use all of the filter categories in the poster for this chapter, the following sections provide a general description of each category and a table of specific filters and their adjustable settings.

Artistic Filters

The Artistic filters (Table 6–1) create painting and artistic effects, adding a certain amount of texture, dimension, and abstraction to an image. The Artistic filters replicate traditional media effects such as grain patterns, oils, watercolors, charcoals, pastels, line drawings, neon shading, and sponges. Artistic filters are used in typography, commercial art, and personal art expression.

BTW

Installing Filters
To install a filter, you simply copy it into the Filters folder, usually located in C:\Program Files\Adobe\Adobe Photoshop CS5\Plug-ins\Filters.

Table 6–1 Artistic Filters

Artistic Filters	Description	Adjustable Settings
Colored Pencil	redraws to simulate colored pencils on a solid background to create a crosshatched effect	Pencil Width, Stroke Pressure, Paper Brightness
Cutout	redraws to simulate roughly cut pieces of colored paper such as a collage or a screen print	Number of Levels, Edge Simplicity, Edge Fidelity
Dry Brush	uses a dry brush technique on all edges and reduces the range of color	Brush Size, Brush Detail, Texture
Film Grain	applies a film grain pattern to shadow tones and midtones with a smoother pattern to lighter areas; helps to unify diverse elements in an image	Grain, Highlight, Area Intensity
Fresco	repaints using coarse, short, and rounded daubs	Brush Size, Brush Detail, Texture
Neon Glow	inserts various types of glows to objects in the image	Glow Size, Glow Brightness, Glow Color
Paint Daubs	redraws to simulate an oil painting	Brush Size, Sharpness, Brush Type
Palette Knife	reduces detail to simulate a thinly painted canvas, revealing underlying textures	Stroke Size, Stroke Detail, Softness
Plastic Wrap	redraws the image as if it were coated in shiny plastic	Highlight, Strength Detail, Smoothness
Poster Edges	reduces the number of colors in an image and draws black lines on edges	Edge Thickness, Edge Intensity, Posterization
Rough Pastels	applies strokes of chalk, pastel-like color on a textured background; appears thicker in brighter colors	Stroke Length, Stroke Detail, Texture, Scaling, Relief, Light, Invert
Smudge Stick	uses short diagonal strokes to smudge or smear darker parts of the image; lighter areas become brighter with a spotty texture and less detail	Stroke Length, Highlight Area, Intensity
Sponge	creates textured areas of contrasting color that simulate the effect of sponge painting	Brush Size, Definition, Smoothness
Underpainting	creates a textured background and then paints the image over the background to create a paler, softer version; commonly used in conjunction with other filters	Brush Size, Texture Coverage, Texture, Scaling, Relief, Light, Invert
Watercolor	creates a watercolor style that flattens yet brightens color; the greater the detail, the more realistic the image will appear	Brush Detail, Shadow Intensity, Texture

Blur Filters

The Blur filters (Table 6–2) soften or smooth an image by locating defined edges, lines, and shadows, adding together the color value, and then averaging the pixels to create a new value. Blur filters commonly are used to **retouch** or improve an image by adding details, smoothing the appearance, or removing flaws. Most of the Blur filters allow you to specify the radius of affected pixels. You can blur the background to draw attention to foreground objects, create dreamlike scenes and portraits, or add visual movement to an image.

Table 6–2 Blur Filters		
Blur Filter	**Description**	**Adjustable Settings**
Average	creates a smooth look by averaging the pixels in the entire selection or image to create a new replacement color	None
Blur, Blur More	eliminates extraneous noise in areas with strong color transitions by averaging pixels	None
Box Blur	averages the pixel color values of all neighboring pixels to create special effects; the larger the radius setting, the greater the blur	Radius
Gaussian Blur	blurs using a weighted average to add low-frequency detail that produces a hazy effect	Radius
Lens Blur	applies a blur with a narrower depth of field so that some objects in the image stay in focus and others are blurred	Depth Map, Iris, Special Highlights, Noise, Distribution, Monochromatic
Motion Blur	blurs in a specified direction and at a specified intensity or distance	Angle, Distance
Radial Blur	simulates the blur of a zooming or rotating camera	Amount, Blur Method, Quality
Shape Blur	blurs in a specified pattern or shape	Radius, Shape
Smart Blur	blurs with precise settings	Radius, Threshold, Quality, Mode
Surface Blur	blurs an image while preserving edges	Radius, Threshold

Brush Strokes Filters

The Brush Strokes filters (Table 6–3) paint with an artistic impression using different brush and ink stroke effects. Many of the Brush Strokes filters allow you to set smoothness, sharpness, and intensity. Graphic artists use the Brush Strokes filters to achieve natural or traditional media effects.

Table 6–3 Brush Strokes Filters		
Brush Strokes Filter	**Description**	**Adjustable Settings**
Accented Edges	accentuates edges based on a brightness control	Edge Width, Edge Brightness, Smoothness
Angled Strokes	creates brush strokes at opposite angles	Direction Balance, Stroke Length, Sharpness
Crosshatch	preserves details while adding pencil hatching texture	Stroke Length, Sharpness, Strength
Dark Strokes	paints dark areas with short, dark strokes and light areas with long, white strokes	Balance, Black Intensity, White Intensity
Ink Outlines	redraws with fine narrow lines, creating a strong edge effect similar to an ink outline	Stroke Length, Dark Intensity, Light Intensity

Table 6–3 Brush Strokes Filters (Continued)

Brush Strokes Filter	Description	Adjustable Settings
Spatter	simulates an airbrush, creating an exaggerated spatter and ripple effect	Spray Radius, Smoothness
Sprayed Strokes	repaints using dominant colors, with angled, sprayed strokes in specific directions	Stroke Length, Spray Radius, Stroke Direction
Sumi-e	creates soft, blurred edges with full ink blacks and uses a saturated brush style similar to Japanese rice paper painting	Stroke Width, Stroke Pressure, Contrast

Distort Filters

The Distort filters (Table 6–4) reshape images not by recoloring pixels, but by moving pixels in a geometric fashion to create 3D and reshaping effects. Some of the distort filters purposefully add noise or altering effects to the image, while others correct the same kinds of problems. Recall using the Lens Correction filter in a previous chapter to correct perspective, keystone, and barrel distortions. Distortion used in advertising adds an emotional, comical, or exaggerated dimension for product recognition, or to express shape, size, and spatial relations.

Table 6–4 Distort Filters

Distort Filter	Description	Adjustable Settings
Diffuse Glow	a soft diffusion filter that adds see-through white noise; glow fades from the center	Graininess, Glow Amount, Clear Amount
Displace	distorts using a displacement map	Horizontal Scale, Vertical Scale, Displacement Map, Undefined Areas
Glass	distorts as if viewed through glass	Distortion, Smoothness, Texture, Scaling, Invert
Ocean Ripple	ripples the surface randomly as if underwater	Ripple Size, Ripple Magnitude
Pinch	squeezes from the center	Amount
Polar Coordinates	toggles between rectangular and polar coordinates simulating a mirrored cylinder	Rectangular to Polar, Polar to Rectangular
Ripple	redraws with ripples	Amount, Size
Shear	distorts or warps along a line	Undefined Areas
Spherize	creates a spherical distortion	Amount, Mode
Twirl	rotates, creating a twirl pattern	Angle
Wave	precisely redraws with ripples	Number of Generators, Wavelength, Amplitude, Scale Type, Undefined Areas
ZigZag	distorts radially, with reversals from center	Amount, Ridges, Style

Noise Filters

Noise is a term that refers to hazy, grainy, or extraneous pixels as well as flecks of random color distributed through a background. Noise also can refer to variation in brightness or color information. The Noise filters (Table 6–5 on the next page) add or remove noise and help blend a selection into the surrounding pixels. Noise filters can create unusual textures or remove problem areas such as dust and scratches.

Table 6–5 Noise Filters

Noise Filter	Description	Adjustable Settings
Add Noise	applies random pixels to an image, simulating the effect of high-speed film photography	Amount, Distribution, Monochromatic
Despeckle	detects edges of color in an image and blurs all of the selection except those edges	None
Dust & Scratches	reduces noise by changing dissimilar pixels	Radius, Threshold
Median	reduces noise by blending the brightness of pixels within a selection; useful for eliminating or reducing the effect of motion on an image	Radius
Reduce Noise	reduces noise while preserving edges based on user settings	Strength, Preserve Details, Reduce Color Noise, Sharpen Details, Remove JPEG Artifact

BTW

Combining Filters
Many interesting effects can be created when combining filters as well as applying them more than once. The only restrictions are that filters cannot be applied to Bitmap or Index color images, and some filters will only work on 8-bit or RGB images.

Pixelate Filters

The Pixelate filters (Table 6–6) redraw an image or selection by joining, grouping, or clustering pixels of similar color values into cells defined by the tolerance settings. The cells become blocks, rectangles, circles, or dots of color, creating the impression of looking at an image through a magnifying glass. Many of the Pixelate filters replicate artistic movement styles such as pointillism, divisionism, or stippling.

Table 6–6 Pixelate Filters

Pixelate Filter	Description	Adjustable Settings
Color Halftone	replaces rectangular areas with circles of halftone screening on each color channel	Max. Radius, Screen Angles (Degrees)
Crystallize	creates a solid color polygon shape by clustering pixels	Cell Size
Facet	creates solid color by clustering similarly colored pixels; commonly used to remove color noise and specks	None
Fragment	draws four copies of pixels and then averages the values and offsets them, creating a hazy blur	None
Mezzotint	randomizes black-and-white or color areas, creating pixilation according to the chosen type	Type
Mosaic	creates solid-colored, square blocks based on original pixel colors	Cell Size
Pointillize	randomizes foreground colors and creates dots similar to pointillism; background simulates a canvas texture	Cell Size

Render Filters

In publishing, graphic design, and image editing, the term **render** simply means to create an artistic change. In Photoshop, rendering creates a drawing or painting represented by discrete pixels, especially in perspective. The Render filters (Table 6–7) create cloud patterns, texture fills, 3D shapes, refraction patterns, and simulated light reflections in an image. During rendering, Photoshop replaces image data on the active layer, so it is best to use the commands on layer copies rather than on the original.

Table 6–7 Render Filters

Render Filter	Description	Adjustable Settings
Clouds	creates a soft cloud pattern using random values that vary between the foreground and the background colors	None
Difference Clouds	same as Clouds filter except the filter blends with existing pixels	None
Fibers	generates the look of woven fibers using the foreground and background colors	Variance, Strength
Lens Flare	simulates camera lens refraction caused from bright lights	Brightness, Lens Type
Lighting Effects	produces various lighting effects using settings	Style, Light Type, Properties, Texture Channel

Sharpen Filters

Recall that sharpening means to emphasize the transitions between light and dark objects in your image. The Sharpen filters (Table 6–8) focus blurred images by increasing the contrast of adjacent pixels.

Table 6–8 Sharpen Filters

Sharpen Filter	Description	Adjustable Settings
Sharpen	focuses a selection to improve its clarity	None
Sharpen Edges	sharpens edges but preserves smoothness of the image	None
Sharpen More	applies a stronger sharpening effect than the Sharpen filter	None
Smart Sharpen	sharpens the parts of the image where significant color changes occur, with more control using the settings	Sharpen, Shadow, Highlight
Unsharp Mask	adjusts the contrast of edge detail, producing lighter and darker edges	Amount, Radius, Threshold

Sketch Filters

The Sketch filters (Table 6–9) add texture and changes in color, creating artistic 3D effects and hand-drawn looks. Many of the filters mimic sketch media used for loosely executed freehand drawing, not intended as a finished work. The Sketch filters use many techniques including overlapping lines, dry media imitation, pencil, pen, and watercolor simulations. Most of the Sketch filters convert the image to black and white; however, they can be applied to individual channels to create interesting color combinations.

BTW

Add-On Filters
A large number of filter plug-ins are available to add to your installation of Photoshop. These aftermarket filters add more power and features to Photoshop. Add-on filters can be purchased or downloaded as shareware from reputable Web sites.

Table 6–9 Sketch Filters

Sketch Filter	Description	Adjustable Settings
Bas Relief	accents surface variations with carving-like strokes; dark areas use the foreground color, and light areas use the background color	Detail, Smoothness, Light
Chalk & Charcoal	simulates a coarse chalk sketch with black diagonal charcoal lines in the foreground	Charcoal Area, Chalk Area, Stroke Pressure

Table 6–9 Sketch Filters (Continued)

Sketch Filter	Description	Adjustable Settings
Charcoal	redraws with a smudged, posterized effect using diagonal strokes; a charcoal color is used on the foreground, while the background simulates paper	Charcoal Thickness, Detail, Light/Dark Balance
Chrome	creates a polished chrome surface	Detail, Smoothness
Conté Crayon	simulates the Conté style with textured crayon-like, chalk strokes	Foreground Level, Background Level, Texture, Scaling, Relief, Light, Invert,
Graphic Pen	redraws using thin, linear ink strokes for the foreground color, and uses background color to simulate paper	Stroke Length, Light/Dark Balance, Stroke Direction
Halftone Pattern	a halftone screen effect that maintains a continuous range of tones, consisting of dots that control how much ink is deposited at a specific location	Size, Contrast, Pattern Type
Note Paper	replicates handmade paper with dark areas masked out to reveal background colors	Image Balance, Graininess, Relief
Photocopy	creates a photocopy effect	Detail, Darkness
Plaster	simulates molded plaster, with dark areas raised, and light areas recessed	Image Balance, Smoothness, Light
Reticulation	distorts similar to film emulsion patterns in negatives caused by extreme changes of temperature or acidity and alkalinity during processing	Density, Foreground Level, Background Level
Stamp	simulates a rubber or wooden stamp version	Light/Dark Balance, Smoothness
Torn Edges	redraws to look like ragged, torn pieces of paper	Image Balance, Smoothness, Contrast
Water Paper	daubs with color imitating fibrous, damp paper	Fiber Length, Brightness, Contrast

BTW

Filters and Printing
If you plan to print to a grayscale printer, convert a copy of the image to grayscale before applying filters to increase performance of Photoshop. However, applying a filter to a color image, and then converting to grayscale, may not have the same effect as applying the filter to a grayscale version of the image.

Stylize Filters

The Stylize filters (Table 6–10) displace pixels and heighten contrast, producing an impressionistic, painting-like effect. Graphic artists use Stylize filters to create unique and interesting effects and accents to artwork. Several of the Stylize filters accent edges of contrast, which then can be inverted to highlight the image inside the outlines.

Table 6–10 Stylize Filters

Stylize Filter	Description	Adjustable Settings
Diffuse	softens focus by rearranging pixels randomly or by dark and light settings	Mode
Emboss	converts fill color to gray and traces the edges to create raised or stamped effects	Angle, Height, Amount
Extrude	adds a 3D texture based on specific settings	Type, Size, Depth
Find Edges	outlines edges with dark lines against a white background for a thickly outlined, coloring book effect	None
Glowing Edges	adds a neon glow to edges	Edge Width, Edge Brightness, Smoothness
Solarize	creates a photographic light exposure tint	None
Tiles	creates a series of offset blocks with tiled edges	Number Of Tiles, Maximum Offset, Fill Empty Area With
Trace Contour	outlines transition areas in each channel, creating a contour map effect	Level, Edge
Wind	redraws using small horizontal lines to create a windblown effect	Method, Direction

Texture Filters

The Texture filters (Table 6–11) add substance or depth to an image by simulating a texture or organic representation. Graphic artists use the Texture filters to add a 3D effect or to apply a segmented style to photos.

Table 6–11 Texture Filters		
Texture Filter	**Description**	**Adjustable Settings**
Craquelure	creates an embossing effect with a network of cracks on a plaster-like background	Crack Spacing, Crack Depth, Crack Brightness
Grain	simulates different types of graininess	Intensity, Contrast, Grain Type
Mosaic Tiles	creates small tiles with grout	Tile Size, Grout Width, Lighten Grout
Patchwork	redraws with randomly filled squares replicating highlights and shadows	Square Size, Relief
Stained Glass	repaints using random, five-sided, polygonal shapes to emulate stained glass	Cell Size, Border Thickness, Light Intensity
Texturizer	applies selected texture with settings	Texture, Scaling, Relief, Light, Invert

The Filter Gallery

Photoshop filters are grouped by category on the Filter menu. You can choose a specific filter on one of the submenus, or you can click the Filter Gallery command and make your choice in the resulting dialog box. The **Filter Gallery** lets you apply filters cumulatively and apply individual filters more than once for a more intense effect. With thumbnail examples organized into folders, the Filter Gallery previews the effect of the filter on your image. You can use the Filter Gallery to make appropriate choices, rearrange filters, and change individual settings to achieve the desired special effect.

Not all filters are included in the Filter Gallery. Those filters with adjustable settings that are not in the gallery itself present their own preview when selected from the menu system. Photoshop Help also has many visual examples of the various filters.

Some artists rename filtered layers with both the name of the filter and the numerical settings. For example, if your edits layer employs the Plastic Wrap filter, you might assign a name, such as, edits plastic wrap 8–8-11, so you could remember the filter and settings you used.

Applying Filters

In the following steps, you will apply a different filter to seven of the seashell layers. First, you will create a filter layer and apply the filter the using the Filter Gallery. Then you will apply a filter that is not part of the Filter Gallery. Finally, you will create smart object layers, and apply filters.

To Duplicate the Snail Layer

The following steps create a duplicate layer for the snail layer.

1 On the Layers panel, scroll as necessary to display the snail layer.

2 Right-click the snail layer, and then click Duplicate Layer on the context menu to open the Duplicate Layer dialog box.

3 Click the OK button (Duplicate Layer dialog box) to create the new layer.

4 Click the visibility icon on the snail copy layer to make it visible.

BTW

Filter Gallery Settings
Filter Gallery settings carry over each time you use the filter gallery. When you choose a new filter, the previous one is replaced. However, if more than one filter appears in the list of filter effects, and you do not want to use the filters, click the 'Delete effect layer' button.

BTW

Filter Gallery Lists
The drop-down list in the Filter Gallery lists all of the filters in the gallery in alphabetical order, which is useful if you cannot remember the category. In the lower-right portion of the Filter Gallery, each new layer is added to the top of the 'List of filter effects to apply or arrange' area.

To Use the Filter Gallery

Using the Filter Gallery, the following steps apply a Texture filter named Stained Glass to the snail copy layer creating a stained glass effect that highlights the rings of the snail shell.

1
- With the snail copy layer selected, click Filter on the menu bar to display the Filter menu.
- Click Filter Gallery on the Filter menu to display the Accented Edges dialog box.
- Click the Zoom box arrow at the bottom of the preview area to display its list (Figure 6–28).

Q&A

What do the minus and plus buttons do?

They decrease and increase the magnification, respectively. You also can drag in the preview area to reposition the layer. A hand icon appears as you drag.

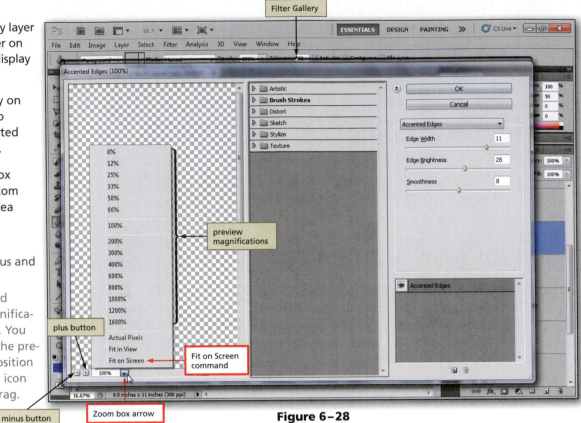

Figure 6–28

2
- Click Fit on Screen to maximize the dialog box and to cause the entire layer to appear in the preview area (Figure 6–29).

Q&A

What does the Fit in View option do?

The Fit in View option causes the entire layer to appear in the preview area, but does not maximize the dialog box.

Experiment
- Click each of the filter folders in the list to view the various filters. When you are finished, click the folders again to close them.

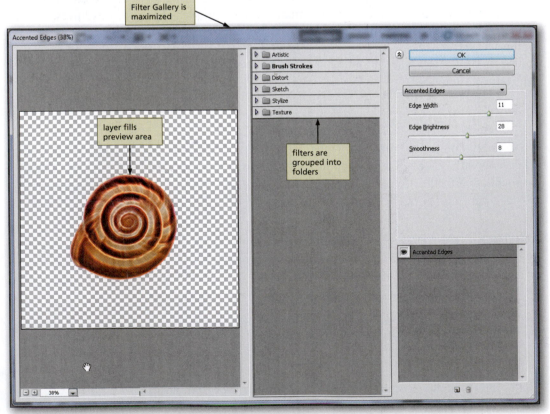

Figure 6–29

3
- Click the Texture folder in the list of filter categories and then click Stained Glass to choose the filter.

- Drag the Cell Size slider to 15; drag the Border thickness slider to 8; and then drag the Light Intensity slider to 5 to adjust the settings (Figure 6–30).

Q&A

What is the purpose of the buttons below the 'List of filter effects to apply or arrange' area?

The 'New effect layer' button allows you to apply multiple filters to the same image by clicking the button between each filter choice that you apply. The 'Delete effect layer' button allows you to delete a layer if there are multiple layers in the list.

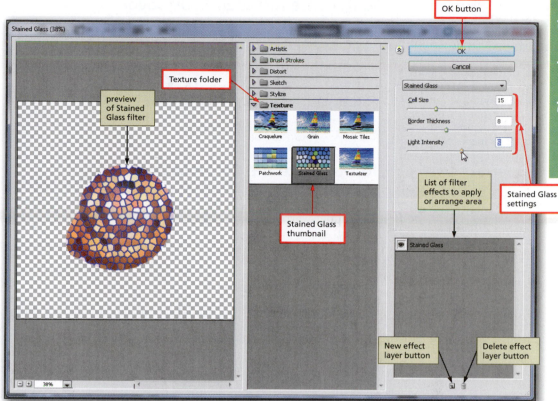

Figure 6–30

4
- Click the OK button to close the filter's dialog box and apply the filter to the layer (Figure 6–31).

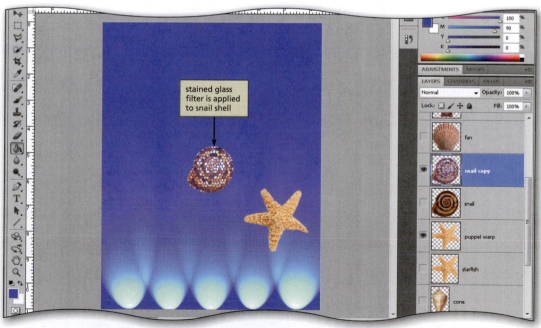

Figure 6–31

Other Ways

1. On Filter menu, point to Texture, click Stained Glass, apply settings, click OK button

Stained Glass Filter Settings
The Stained Glass filter repaints the image as single-colored adjacent pentagon and hexagon cells outlined in the foreground color. The Cell Size and Border Thickness settings adjust the sizes of the cells (panes of glass) and the border (grout) between panes. The Light Intensity setting measures how much light seems to shine through from the back of the image (through the window).

To Rename the Snail Copy Layer

The following steps rename the layer to reflect the filter settings.

1 On the Layers panel, double-click the name, snail copy, to select it.

2 Type `stained glass 15-8-5` and press the ENTER key to rename the layer with a name that reflects the filter settings.

To Duplicate the Conch Layer

The following steps create a duplicate layer for the conch layer in preparation for the puppet warp.

1 On the Layers panel, scroll as necessary to display the conch layer.

2 Right-click the conch layer and then click Duplicate Layer on the context menu to open the Duplicate Layer dialog box.

3 Click the OK button (Duplicate Layer dialog box) to create the new layer.

4 Click the visibility icon on the conch copy layer to make it visible.

To Choose a Filter from the Menu System

Using the Filter Gallery, the following steps apply an Artistic filter named Plastic Wrap to the conch copy layer. The Plastic Wrap filter redraws the image to look as if it were covered in plastic wrap. You will use the Photoshop menu to go directly to the filter preview, rather than opening the Filter Gallery first.

1
• With the conch copy layer selected, click Filter on the menu bar, and then point to Artistic to display the list of Artistic filters (Figure 6–32).

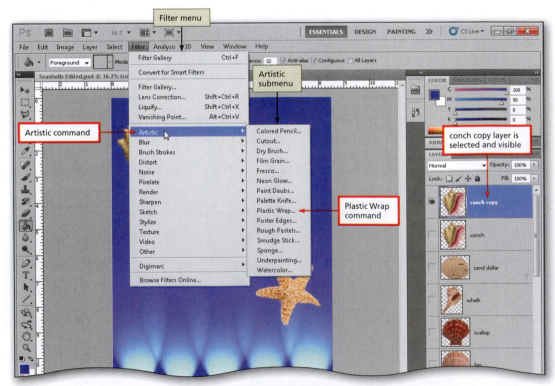

Figure 6–32

②

- Click Plastic Wrap to open the Filter Gallery with the filter already selected.

- If necessary, adjust the size of the preview using the zoom buttons or Zoom box.

- Drag the Highlight Strength slider to 15; drag the Detail slider to 9; and then drag the Smoothness slider to 7 to adjust the settings (Figure 6–33).

 Experiment

- Drag the three sliders back and forth to see how they change the layer. Reset them to 15, 9, and 7 when you finish experimenting.

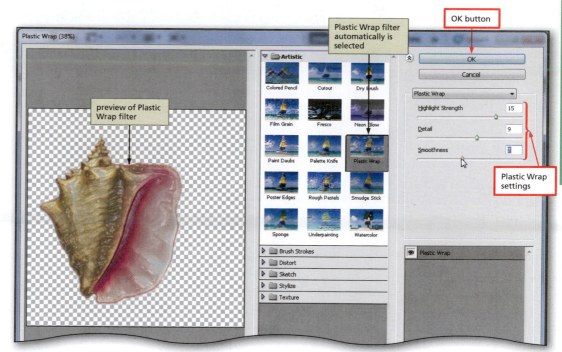

Figure 6–33

③

- Click the OK button to apply the Plastic Wrap filter to the conch layer.

To Rename the Conch Copy Layer

The following steps rename the layer to reflect the filter settings.

① On the Layers panel, double-click the name, conch copy, to select it.

② Type `plastic wrap 15-9-7` and press the ENTER key to rename the layer with a name that reflects the filter settings.

The Liquify Filter

The Liquify filter lets you push, pull, rotate, reflect, pucker, and bloat any area of an image. The distortions you create can be subtle or dramatic, which makes the Liquify command a powerful tool for retouching images as well as for creating artistic effects. The Liquify filter is not a part of the Filter Gallery. Like the Lens Correction filter that you used in Chapter 5, the Liquify filter has its own dialog box and tools panel. Table 6–12 on the next page displays some of the Liquify dialog box tools. Other settings edit the brush, reconstruct the image, set the mask, and change the view.

Other Ways

1. On Filter menu, click Filter Gallery, click Plastic Wrap, adjust settings, click OK

BTW

Plastic Wrap Filter Settings
The Plastic Wrap filter redraws the image with a Highlight Strength setting that controls the brightness of the highlights in the plastic wrap. The Detail setting changes the frequency of the bubbles in the plastic wrap — larger numbers create more bubbles. The Smoothness setting changes the contrast between the top of the bubble and the bottom of the bubble. The larger the value, the more the highlights and contrast are blurred.

Table 6–12 Liquify Filter Tools

Liquify Filter	Description	Shortcut Key	Button
Forward Warp	pushes the pixels of the image forward as you drag	W	
Reconstruct	reconstructs areas of the previously distorted image as you drag	R	
Twirl	rotates pixels clockwise as you click or drag, or counterclockwise, as you ALT+click or ALT+drag	C	
Pucker	moves pixels toward the center of the brush area as you click or drag	S	
Bloat	moves pixels away from the center of the brush area as you click or drag	B	
Push	moves pixels to the left as you drag up, to the right as you drag down, increases size as you drag clockwise, or decreases size as you drag counterclockwise	O	
Mirror	creates a mirrored image by creating new pixels perpendicular to the direction of the drag	M	
Turbulence	scrambles the pixels smoothly as you drag	T	
Freeze Mask	creates a protected area as you drag to prevent any change as you work with other filters	F	
Thaw Mask	unprotects the area, so other filters can apply	D	
Hand	moves the preview area as you drag	H	
Zoom	zooms in as you click, zooms out as you ALT+click	Z	

To Duplicate the Whelk Layer

The following steps create a duplicate layer for the whelk layer.

1 On the Layers panel, scroll as necessary to display the whelk layer.

2 Right-click the whelk layer and then click Duplicate Layer on the context menu to open the Duplicate Layer dialog box.

3 Click the OK button (Duplicate Layer dialog box) to create the new layer.

4 Click the visibility icon on the whelk copy layer to make it visible.

To Apply the Liquify Filter

The following steps use the Liquify filter and its Forward Warp Tool to retouch the whelk seashell, filling in a missing portion of the shell.

1

• With the whelk copy layer selected on the Layers panel, click Filter on the menu bar and then click Liquify to display the Liquify dialog box (Figure 6–34).

Experiment

• Click the Mask All button to view the mask that covers the entire layer to protect it from editing. Click the None button to remove the mask.

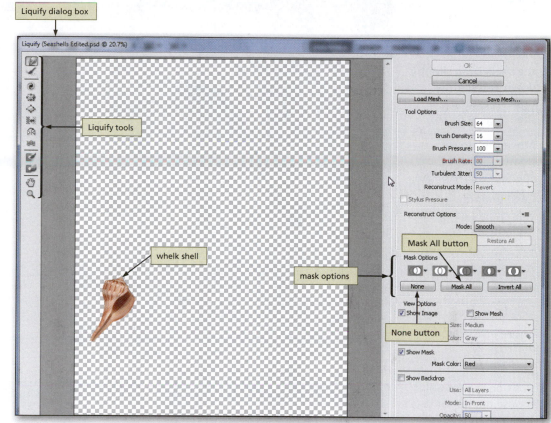

Figure 6–34

2

• Click the Zoom Tool button on the Liquify toolbar to select it and then click the preview area three times to zoom in.

• If necessary, click the Hand Tool button on the Liquify toolbar to select it, and then drag right in the preview area to view the whelk shell (Figure 6–35).

Experiment

• Click other buttons on the Liquify toolbar and then drag in the preview area to watch the effect. After each drag, press CTRL+Z to undo the change.

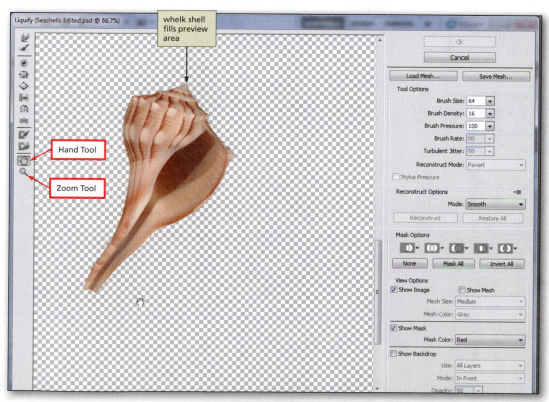

Figure 6–35

3

- Click the Forward Warp Tool button to select it.

- Position the crosshair mouse pointer at the lower-left corner of the shell. Drag slightly down and slightly right to extend the shell (Figure 6–36).

- Move the mouse pointer to view the change (Figure 6–36).

Q&A

Can I undo the changes if I do not like the outcome?

Yes. Press CTRL+ALT+Z to move backward through your keystrokes, or you can click the 'Reconstruct entire image' button.

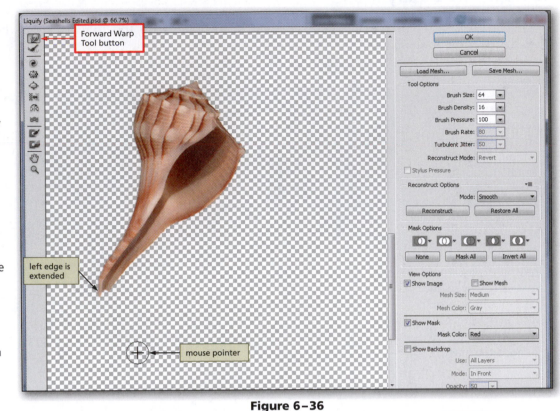

Figure 6–36

4

- Position the crosshair mouse pointer at the lower-right corner of the shell, and then drag down and slightly right to extend the shell and create an end point.

- Move the mouse pointer to view the change (Figure 6–37).

Q&A

What do the Reconstruct options do?

After you make an edit to the preview, the Reconstruct options become enabled. Choose a mode and then click the Reconstruct button to reconstruct the most recent change, or click the Reconstruct All button to return the image to its original state.

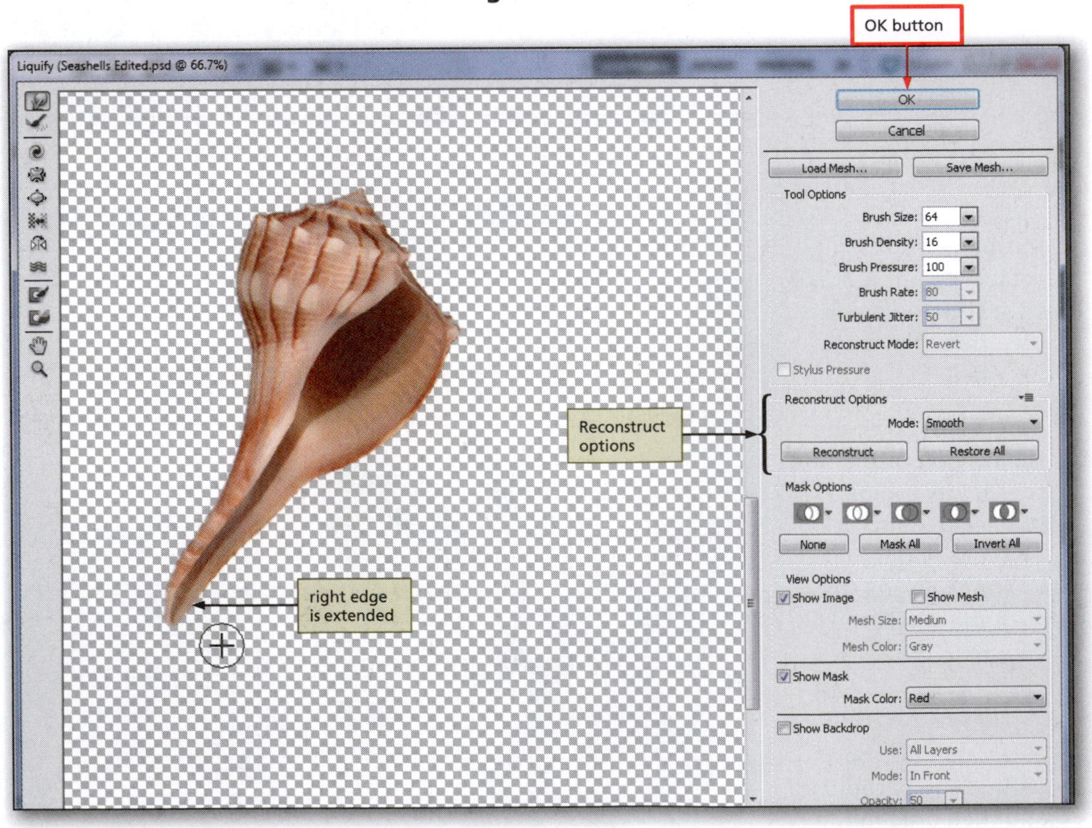

Figure 6–37

5

- Click the OK button (Liquify dialog box) to apply the filter.

Other Ways

1. Press SHIFT+CTRL+X, adjust settings, click OK button (Liquify dialog box)

To Rename the Whelk Copy Layer

The following steps rename the layer to reflect the filter settings.

1 On the Layers panel, double-click the name, whelk copy, to select it.

2 Type `liquify forward warp` and press the ENTER key to rename the layer with a name that reflects the filter settings.

Liquify Filter Editing
When using tools in the Liquify Filter dialog box, such as the Forward Warp, you can change the size of the mouse pointer by using the LEFT BRACKET ([) or RIGHT BRACKET (]) keys. You also can use the Brush Size box on the right side of the dialog box to adjust the size of the brush.

To Save the File

After adding many layers and applied filters, it is a good time to save the file again, as in the following step.

1 Press CTRL+S.

Break Point: If you wish to take a break, this is a good place to do so. You can quit Photoshop now. To resume at a later time, start Photoshop, open the file called Seashells Edited, and continue following the steps from this location forward.

Smart Objects

By default, filters change the pixels in a layer and therefore are destructive; however, you can use the Convert for Smart Filters command to convert your layers into smart objects that allow you to change filters without disturbing the original layer. **Smart objects** are layers that preserve the source content of an image with all its original characteristics, separately from any filters, edits, or styles. Smart objects enable you to perform nondestructive editing to the layer. A filter added to a smart object is called a **smart filter**. Smart filters add to the size of the file on your storage device but offer the convenience of keeping the pixels in the original layer, and adjusting or deleting filters. Smart filters also retain the name of the filter used and its filter settings, even when those may have been reset by you or another user. A smart filter, therefore, is an alternative to creating a copy of the layer on which to apply filters, and renaming it to include the filter name and settings.

Glowing Edges Filter Settings
When using the Glowing Edges filter, Photoshop looks for strong color change to define an edge. The Edge Width setting increases or decreases the thickness of the edge lines. The Edge Brightness setting adjusts the contrast between the edges and the background. Finally, the Smoothness setting softens the color change between the edges and the background.

To Create a Smart Object

The following step uses the Convert for Smart Filters command to convert a layer to a smart object. Because a smart filter can be edited independently from the layer, there is no need to create a duplicate layer.

1
- On the Layers panel, select the scallop layer and click its visibility icon to make the layer visible.
- Click Filter on the menu bar to display the Filter menu.
- Click Convert for Smart Filters to create an adjustable smart filter. If Photoshop displays a dialog box, click the OK button to create the smart filter (Figure 6–38).

Q&A What changed on the Layers panel?

The thumbnail now displays a smart object notation.

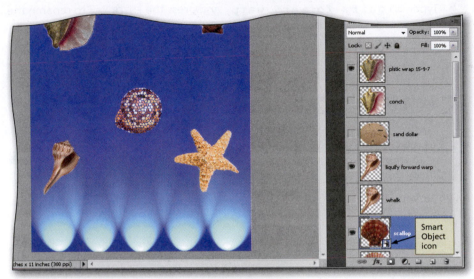

Figure 6–38

Other Ways

1. Right-click layer, click Convert to Smart Object

To Apply a Smart Filter

You will apply a Stylize filter named Glowing Edges as a smart filter to the scallop layer in the following steps. The Glowing Edges filter adds a neon glow to obvious edges in the images.

1
- With the scallop layer selected, click Filter on the menu bar, and then click Filter Gallery to display the Filter Gallery. Adjust the size of the preview using the zoom buttons.
- Click the Stylize folder in the list, and then click the Glowing Edges thumbnail.
- Type 9 in the Edge Width box, 8 in the Edge Brightness box, and 11 in the Smoothness box to adjust the settings (Figure 6–39).

Figure 6–39

Q&A Do I need to rename this layer as I did with the other filters?

No, the filter settings on a smart filter will appear automatically.

2

- Click the OK button to apply the filter.

- If necessary, scroll down in the Layers panel to view the Smart Filter (Figure 6–40).

Q&A What changed on the Layers panel?

The filter settings now are displayed as a smart filter with visibility icons and a button for editing the filter settings.

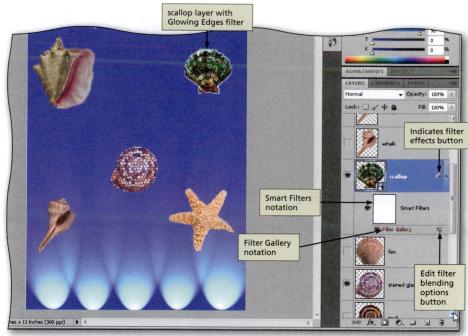

scallop layer with Glowing Edges filter

Indicates filter effects button

Smart Filters notation

Filter Gallery notation

Edit filter blending options button

Other Ways

1. On Filter menu, point to Stylize, click Glowing Edges, adjust settings, click OK button

Figure 6–40

To Choose a Filter from the Filter Gallery List

The following steps choose the Angled Strokes filter from the list in the Filter Gallery, and then apply it to the junonia layer to add some depth and texture to the shell.

1

- On the Layers panel, click the visibility icon on the junonia layer so the layer appears in the document window.

- Right-click the junonia layer, and then click Convert to Smart Object to create the smart object.

- Click Filter on the menu bar, and then click Filter Gallery to display the Filter Gallery. Adjust the size of the preview using the zoom buttons.

- Click the Filter List button on the right side of the dialog box to display the alphabetical list of filters (Figure 6–41).

Q&A Does the list contain all of the filters in Photoshop?

No, it only contains the filters that are editable using the Filter Gallery. The filters that have their own editing dialog boxes are not in this list.

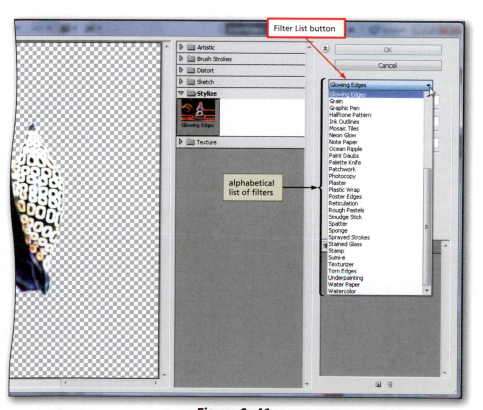

Filter List button

alphabetical list of filters

Figure 6–41

2

- Scroll as necessary, and then click Angled Strokes in the list.

- Type **2 3** in the Direction Balance box, **7** in the Stroke Length box, and **6** in the Sharpness box (Figure 6–42).

Experiment

- Click the visibility icon beside the filter name in the 'List of filter effects to apply or arrange' area to turn off the filter and view the shell without the filter. Click the visibility icon again to display the filter in the preview.

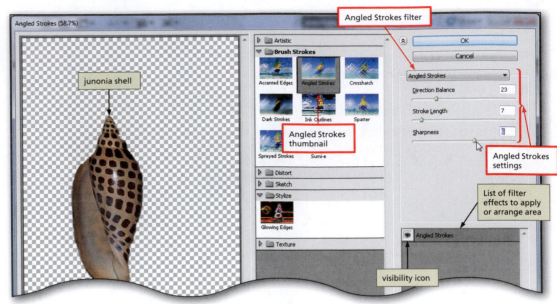

Figure 6–42

To Apply a Second Filter

Combining filters may create special effects. Be cautious, however, when applying multiple filters because this effect is easy to overdo. The following steps add a second filter to the junonia layer, the Diffuse Glow in the Distort group.

1

- Click the 'New effect layer' button to create a second layer effect.

- In the list of filter folders, click Distort, and then click Diffuse Glow.

- Type **6** in the Graininess box, **7** in the Glow Amount box, and **15** in the Clear Amount box (Figure 6–43).

Q&A

What is the purpose of the 'List of filter effects to apply or arrange' area?

When using more than one filter, you can drag filters up or down to rearrange them. Each filter has a visibility icon so you can see how the layer looks with and without the applied filter.

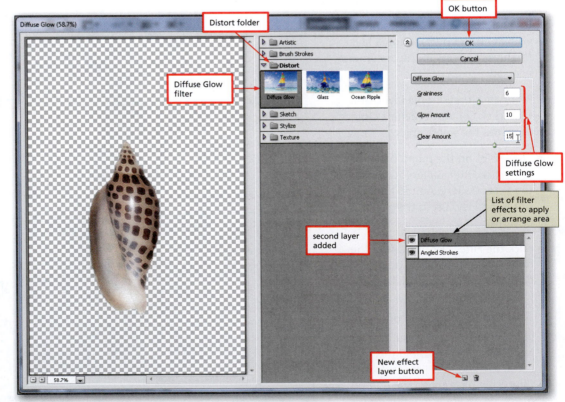

Figure 6–43

❷
- Click the OK button to apply both of the filters.

To Apply a Sketch Filter

The following steps apply the Sketch filter named Chalk & Charcoal to the sand dollar layer. The filter redraws the image with chalk and charcoal diagonal lines, using the foreground color.

① On the Layers panel, display the sand dollar layer.

② Convert the layer to a smart object.

③ Access the Filter Gallery.

④ Open the Sketch folder, and then click the Chalk & Charcoal thumbnail.

⑤ Type **6** in the Charcoal Area box, **6** in the Chalk Area box, and **2** in the Stroke Pressure box (Figure 6–44).

⑥ Click the OK button to apply the filter.

Chalk and Charcoal Filter Settings
The Charcoal Area and Chalk Area settings allow you to balance the portion of the image that is redrawn using each of the mediums. The Stroke Pressure setting controls the contrast between the two.

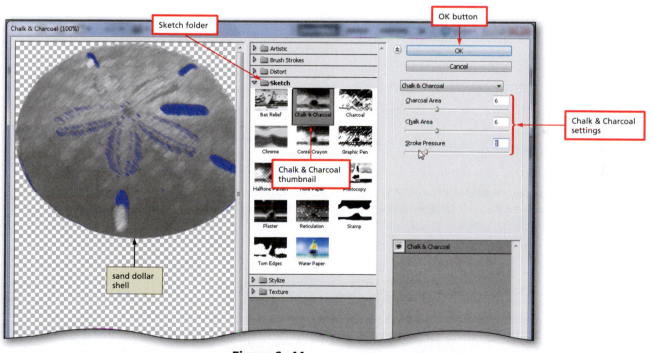

Figure 6–44

To Apply a Crystallize Smart Filter

The Pixelate filters have their own dialog boxes and are not a part of the Filter Gallery. Each of the Pixelate filters combines pixels of similar colors into cells creating an impression of a magnified pixel image, as if you are looking at a digital image through a magnifying glass. The pixelate filters differ in the ways that they cluster or clump similarly colored pixels. For example, the Mosaic filter clusters pixels into square blocks, while the Crystallize filter creates polygon shapes. Pixelate filters often are used in advertising that relates to digital products. The following steps apply a Pixelate filter named Crystallize.

1

- On the Layers panel, scroll as necessary and display the cone layer.

- Convert the layer to a smart object.

- Click Filter on the menu bar, and then point to Pixelate to display the submenu.

- Click Crystallize to display the Crystallize dialog box.

- Zoom to display the cone shell.

- Drag the Cell Size slider to 25 to set the pixilation cell size (Figure 6–45).

 **Experiment**

- Experiment by dragging the slider to increase and decrease cell size.

2

- Click the OK button to apply the filter.

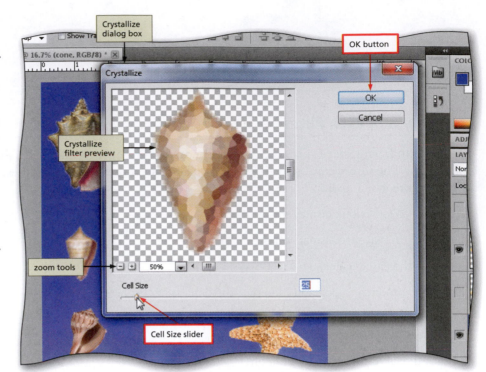

Figure 6–45

Crystallize Filter Settings

This Crystallize filter combines pixels of the same color in rectangle-shaped cells. Its only adjustable setting is the Cell size, used to create either a more detailed or a more blurred images.

To Save the File Again

Because you have applied several filters and made changes to the image, it is a good idea to save the file again.

1 Press CTRL+S to save the Seashell Edited file with the same name.

Break Point: If you wish to take a break, this is a good place to do so. You can quit Photoshop now. To resume at a later time, start Photoshop, open the file called Seashells Edited, and continue following the steps from this location forward.

Filters and RAM

Some filter effects can be memory-intensive, especially when applied to a high-resolution image. To improve performance try one of the following: apply filters on a smaller portion of the image, apply the filter in an individual channel, turn off the thumbnail display on the Layers panel, allocate more RAM to Photoshop, exit other applications to make more memory available to Photoshop, or try changing settings to improve the speed of memory-intensive filters.

Purging

Sometimes when working with many layers and filters, your computer may start to slow down. It is possible that Photoshop needs more random access memory (RAM) to operate more efficiently. While there are several ways to free more RAM, the Purge command helps by eliminating the layers and Clipboard, which are memory intensive and stored in the computer's cache. The purge operation cannot be undone, so you must be certain that you will not need to go back through the history and your stored steps.

TO PURGE

If you wanted to purge the system, you would perform the following steps.

1. Click Edit on the menu bar to display the Edit menu, and then point to Purge to display the Purge submenu.

2. Click All on the Purge submenu to purge all the cached settings. If Photoshop displays a dialog box, click the OK button.

Patterns

A **pattern** is an image that is tiled, or repeated, to fill a selection or a layer. Photoshop has libraries of preset patterns that can be loaded and used in any document, but by default, two patterns appear in the Pattern picker box, including Bubbles and Tie Dye. You can access the Pattern picker box from the Layer Style dialog box or from the options bar associated with the Paint Bucket Tool, the Pattern Stamp Tool, the Healing Brush Tool, or the Patch Tool. Commands on the Pattern picker box menu allow users to load, save, and manage pattern libraries. Recall that libraries associated with many kinds of presets — including gradients, brushes, styles, and custom shapes — also can be managed using the Preset Manager command on the Edit menu.

In Photoshop, you can use one of the preset patterns, or you can create your own patterns and save them for use with different tools and commands. Photoshop gives you the ability to create a specific pattern, either from scratch or from another image. Patterns must be rectangular (or square) in shape. Alternatively, you can use the Pattern Maker filter that generates a random pattern based on a selection or image.

To Define a Pattern

You will use the fan seashell to create a pattern using the Define Pattern command in the following steps.

- On the Layers panel, ALT+click the fan layer's visibility icon to display it by itself in the document window.

- On the Tools panel, right-click the current marquee tool button and then click Rectangular Marquee Tool in the list.

- Drag to form a selection rectangle around the fan shell (Figure 6–46).

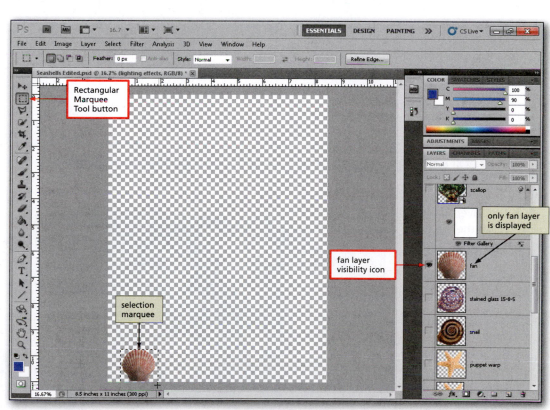

Figure 6–46

2

- Click Edit on the menu bar to display the menu.

- Click Define Pattern to display the Pattern Name dialog box.

- Type `seashell` in the Name box to name the pattern (Figure 6–47).

3

- Click the OK button to close the Pattern Name dialog box and designate the fan shell as a new pattern.

- Press CTRL+D to deselect.

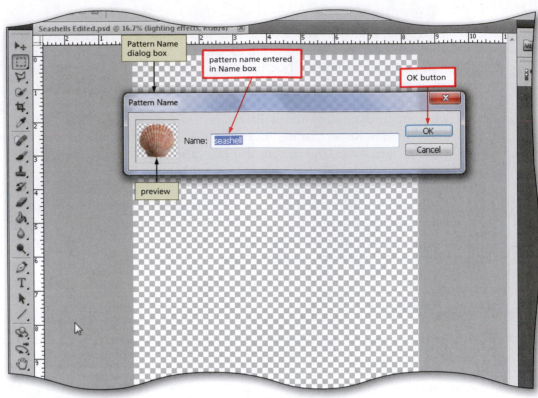

Figure 6–47

To Use a Pattern

The next steps apply the new pattern along the lower portion of the poster.

1

- On the Layers panel, ALT+click the fan layer again and then scroll as necessary to select the lighting effects layer.

- Press SHIFT+CTRL+N to create a new layer and name it, pattern.

- Use the Rectangular Marquee Tool to drag a selection rectangle along the bottom of the document window, approximately 1 inch tall (Figure 6–48).

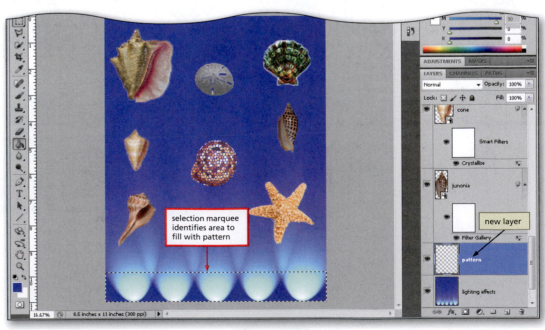

Figure 6–48

2

- Press the G key to access the Paint Bucket Tool.

- On the options bar, click the 'Set source for fill area' box arrow, and then click Pattern in the list.

- Click the Pattern picker box to display the patterns (Figure 6–49).

Q&A My patterns look different. Did I do something wrong?

Your patterns may vary. If you point to the newly defined pattern, Photoshop displays the name in a tool tip.

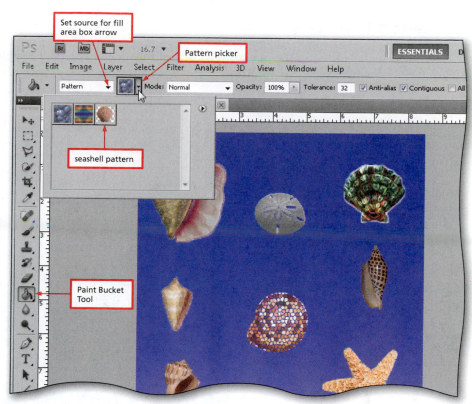

Figure 6–49

3

- Click the seashell pattern, and then click in the selection rectangle to fill the selection with the pattern.

- Press CTRL+D to deselect (Figure 6–50).

Q&A My seashell pattern is cut off vertically. How can I fix that?

Press ALT+CTRL+Z several times to undo the steps. Deselect if necessary. Create a new rectangular marquee selection that is slightly shorter than the previous selection. Repeat Steps 2 and 3.

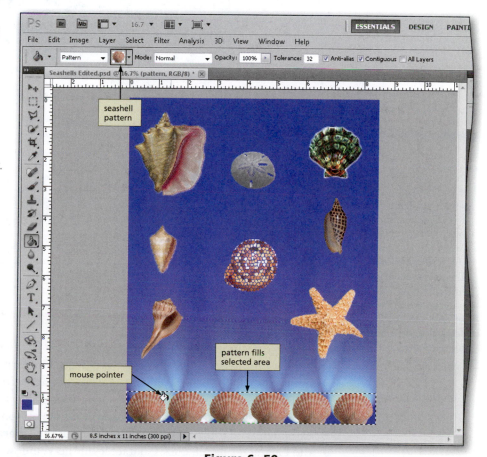

Figure 6–50

To Delete a Pattern

Unless you plan to use the new pattern in multiple documents, it is a good practice to delete your patterns — especially in lab situations. The following step deletes a pattern.

1

- Press the G key to select the Paint Bucket Tool, if necessary. On the options bar, click the Pattern picker box again.

- Right-click the seashell pattern to display its context menu (Figure 6–51).

- Click Delete Pattern on the context menu to delete the pattern.

- Click the Pattern picker box again so the panel no longer appears.

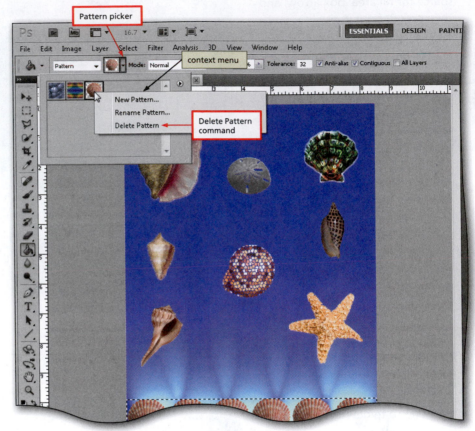

Figure 6–51

Editing Filters
If you are using smart filters, they appear in the Layers panel as a layer effect. To edit a smart filter, double-click the filter name on the Layers panel. When using multiple smart filters, you can move them up or down to apply in sequence, over or under one another.

To Save Again

The following step saves the file.

 Press CTRL+S to save the file again.

Adjusting Type

Graphic designers use the term, **type**, to refer to the mathematically defined shapes of letters, numbers, and symbols in a typeface. The terms, type, text, and copy have become interchangeable with the advent of desktop publishing; however, Photoshop uses the word, type, when referring to the various tools that manipulate text. Besides the basic text and style buttons and boxes shown on the options bar, Photoshop provides a set of extended type tools and character effects in the Character panel (Figure 6–52). To access the Character panel, click Character on the Window menu. Included in the Character panel are some of the same tools that are contained on the options bar with the addition of scaling, tracking, kerning, leading, and baseline shift.

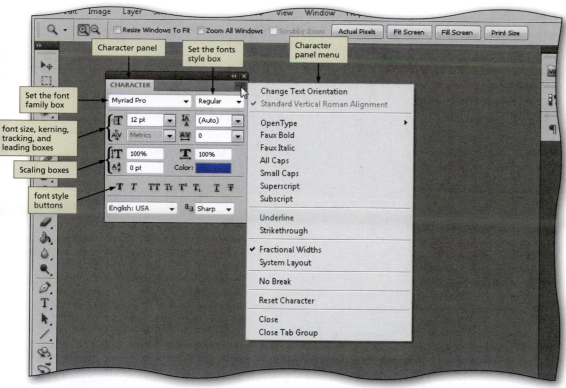

Figure 6–52

Scaling, the process of shrinking or stretching text, changes the width of individual characters. **Tracking**, on the other hand, refers to the adjustment of the general spacing between characters. Tracking text compensates for the spacing irregularities caused when you make text much bigger or much smaller. For example, smaller type is easier to read when it has been tracked loosely. Tracking both maintains the original height and width of the characters and overrides adjustments made by justification or bounding box changes.

Use type wisely.
Make purposeful decisions about your type styles and typefaces, including the font family, font size, font style, direction, color, spacing, character effects, and stroking.

- When combining font families on the same page, chose fonts that strongly contrast in style, weight, and form. For example, if one typeface is tall and thin, choose a contrasting one that is short and thick — and vice versa.

- Be consistent about using the same font style for similar purposes, such as bold for emphasis.

- Look for the stress or slant where the typeface displays wider vs. thinner lines within the same letter, or serifs on lowercase letters.

- Examine text for places where kerning, tracking, or leading might create increased legibility or contrast.

- Use a stroke of color around the text for a more distinctive look that stands out.

- Apply overlays to prevent misregistration.

Plan Ahead

BTW

Kerning
The term, kerning, comes from the pre-computer era, when individual type characters were made from metals, including lead. Bits of lead were shaved off wider characters, thus allowing the smaller character to be moved underneath the larger one. The resulting overhang was called a kern.

Kerning is a special form of tracking related to pairs of adjacent characters that can appear too far apart. For instance, certain letters such as T, V, W, and Y often need kerning when they are preceded or followed by a, e, i, o, or u. The word, Tom, typed in a large font might create too much space between the letters T and o. Clicking between the letters and then adjusting the kerning would make the word more readable.

BTW

Typeface
Many of the terms used when working with type tools come from the field of typesetting. Typeface, the design of the individual characters, now commonly is synonymous with the word, font. Typefaces are available in more than one format. The most common formats are TrueType, Type 1 or PostScript, OpenType, and New CID, a format developed to support non-English characters.

Leading, also called line spacing, refers to the amount of vertical spacing between lines of type, referring to the pre-computer practice of adding lead to create space between lines of metal type characters.

Baseline shift controls the distance of type from its original baseline, either raising or lowering the selected type. Shifting the baseline is especially useful when using superscripts, subscripts, and fractions.

Font style buttons and language buttons are displayed in the lower portion of the Character panel. The Character panel menu button displays many of the same commands and provides the capability to reset all value boxes so fractional settings can be used.

The Paragraph panel (Figure 6–53) contains buttons to change the formatting of columns and paragraphs, also called text blocks. To access the Paragraph panel, click Paragraph on the Window menu. Unique to the Paragraph panel are settings to change the justification for paragraphs, indenting margins and first lines, and changing the spacing above and below paragraphs. The panel's menu button displays other commands to change settings, including access to the Hyphenation dialog box where you specify how and when hyphenation occurs.

BTW

Typography
Recall from Appendix B that font family, style, classification, and color all play important roles in typography. These choices set the tone for a layout. Readability is determined by font, point size, line space, line length, and style, such as italics or all caps.

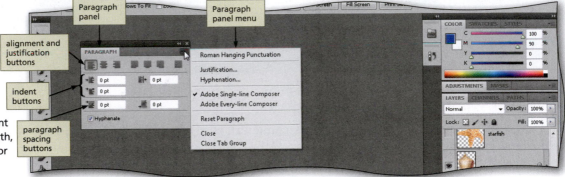

Figure 6–53

BTW

Type Professions
The art of designing typefaces is called type design. **Type designers** work for software companies and graphic design firms, and sometimes freelance as calligraphers and artists. **Typographers** are responsible for designing the layout of the printed word and blocks of text on a page. Because the chosen font contributes significantly to an overall layout, typographers have in-depth knowledge and understanding about the intricacies in which typefaces are utilized to convey particular messages.

To Insert the Title Text

The title text will use the Charlemagne Std font to emulate the idea of curled shells and water. When printed, the text will not be produced as white ink printed over the top of the blue background; rather, the blue color will not print in those areas so the white paper will show through. You will learn more about these kinds of knockouts later in the chapter.

1 On the Layers panel, select the lighting effects layer.

2 Press the T key to access the type tools. If the Horizontal Type Tool is not displayed on the Tools panel, right-click the current type tool button, and then click Horizontal Type Tool in the list.

3 On the options bar, click the 'Set the font family' box arrow and then choose the Charlemagne Std font or a similar font.

4 Set the font size to 36. Click the Center text button and change the color to white, if necessary.

5 Drag a box close to the top of the poster, approximately .75 inches tall and stretching from edge to edge. The box may overlap the shells slightly.

6 Type **The Shells of Pipina Beach** in the bounding box to display the new text and create the type layer (Figure 6–54).

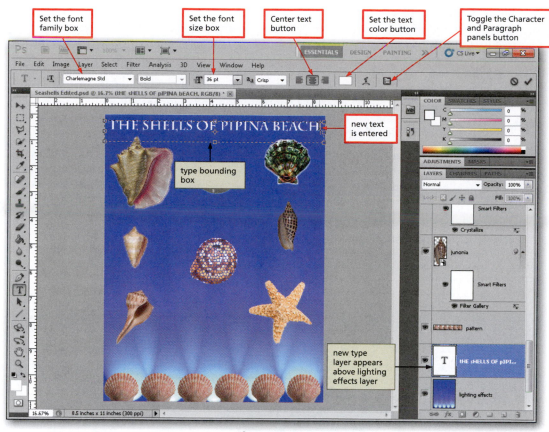

Set the font family box

Set the font size box

Center text button

Set the text color button

Toggle the Character and Paragraph panels button

new text is entered

type bounding box

new type layer appears above lighting effects layer

Figure 6–54

BTW

Faux Bold

Faux Bold creates a heavier character when the font you have chosen does not contain a bold stylistic set. Be sure to check with your printing professional about using Faux Bold characters. You cannot warp text that has the Faux Bold attribute.

BTW

Tracking

A negative entry in the tracking box moves the selected letters closer together. A positive number moves the selected letters farther apart.

To Set the Tracking

The following steps set the tracking. You also will change the font size and make the text bold.

- With the type layer and Horizontal Type Tool still selected, press CTRL+A to select all of the text.

- On the options bar, click the Toggle the Character and Paragraph panels button to show the panels.

- Double-click the 'Set the tracking for the selected characters' box and then type −40 to display the characters closer together.

- Click the Faux Bold button (Figure 6–55).

Toggle the Character and Paragraph panels button

Character panel

text is selected

Set the tracking for the selected characters box

Faux Bold button

Figure 6–55

- On the options bar, click the 'Commit any current edits' button. If necessary, move the text box in the document window to adjust its placement.

- Click the Toggle the Character and Paragraph panels button to hide the panel.

To Insert More Text

The following steps insert more text to create labels for each of the shells in the poster.

1 Press the T key to activate the Horizontal Type Tool. In the document window, drag a box below the conch shell, approximately 2.5 inches wide and .5 inches tall.

2 Enter `24 pt` in the 'Set the font size' box.

3 Type `conch` in the type bounding box to enter the text. On the options bar, click the 'Commit any current edits' button.

4 If necessary, press the V key to access the Move Tool and drag the label to a better position.

5 Repeat steps 1 through 4 for each of the other shells. Use the Vertical Type Tool for the cone and junonia shells (Figure 6–56).

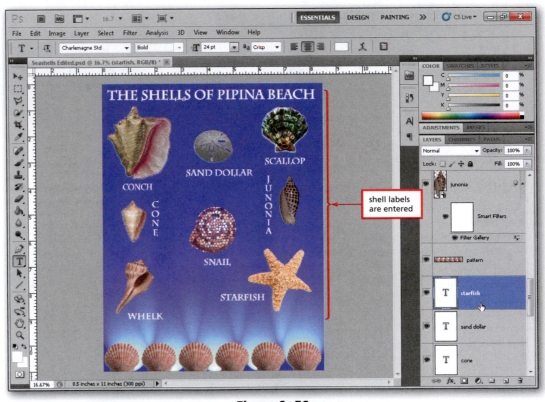

Figure 6–56

To Save the File with Layers

Before converting the image to CMYK and flattening the layers, you should save the file again. Because there are so many layers, the save process may take several minutes.

1 Press SHIFT+CTRL+S to open the Save As dialog box.

2 Type `Seashell Poster with Layers` in the File name text box.

3 Click the Save button. If Photoshop displays a Photoshop Format Options warning message box, click the OK button.

BTW

Color Modes and File Size
Because there are four colors involved in CMYK images, instead of three as in RGB images, CMYK images use 33% more file space than RGB images.

Knockouts and Trapping

In most printing media, when two objects of different colors overlap, they create a **knockout** — the inks will not print on top of each other. At the point where the top layer overlaps the bottom one, the bottom one is not printed at all. In Photoshop, the Flatten Layers command automatically saves only the topmost color in overlapped layers, which creates the knockout for you. Sometimes that is not enough to prevent all of the problems caused by overlapping colors, however.

BTW

Photoshop Help
The best way to become familiar with Photoshop Help is to use it. Appendix D includes detailed information about Photoshop Help and exercises that will help you gain confidence in using it.

Avoid color printing problems.
As you plan your graphic designs, consider the following ways to avoid color printing problems.

- Avoid putting colored objects too close together. Leave some white space between objects in your design or use black trim to stroke objects that overlap, or meet, with black outlines.

- Use common process colors when colors must touch each other.

- For contiguous colors, use colors within 20 percent of each other in the CMYK color spectrum.

- Overprint black text using an overlay blending mode on type layers to cancel the knockout and force black ink to print on the background color.

Plan Ahead

BTW

Quick Reference
For a table that lists how to complete the tasks covered in this book using the mouse, context menu, and keyboard, see the Quick Reference Summary at the back of this book or visit the Photoshop CS5 Quick Reference Web page(scsite.com/pscs5/qr).

When you print a hard copy using a desktop printer, the color is applied all at once; each color normally is printed where you expect it to be. In commercial printing, the printing device makes multiple passes over the paper. The speed of the printer and possible shifts in the paper might cause some colors to run together, creating spreads of blended color, or the printer may leave small missed areas between very close objects or layers (Figure 6–57). Service bureaus use the term **misregistration** to describe those gaps in printing that are out of the printer's register or alignment.

Figure 6–57

Trapping is the prepress activity of calculating an intentional compensation for the misregistration. Photoshop's automatic settings use industry standard rules when applying a trap:

- White is knocked out automatically.
- All colors spread under black.
- Lighter colors spread under darker colors.
- Yellow spreads under cyan, magenta, and black.
- Pure cyan and pure magenta spread under each other equally.

Chokes and spreads are both methods of trapping. **Chokes** intentionally shrink an image to eliminate overprinting, and **spreads** intentionally overlap images to avoid gaps in the ink coverage where the base paper might show through.

When you cannot avoid placing colors close together, intentionally printing one layer of ink on top of another is called **overprinting**, or **surprinting**. Most service bureaus determine if trapping is needed in the overprinting process and can perform that prepress activity for you. It is not recommended you do this yourself, but if you need or want to do it, you will have to enter values in the Trap dialog box. The Trap command is on the Image menu. A service bureau understands its printing process best and is the ideal source for correctly gauging these values.

White text will not cause a problem because it will be knocked out to the paper color.

To Convert to the CMYK Color Mode

The next step is to convert the image to CMYK and merge the layers. Recall that the color mode is changed using the Image menu. CMYK is the correct color mode for professional print jobs.

1 On the Image menu, point to Mode, and then click CMYK Color.

2 When Photoshop displays a warning message about rasterizing the image, click the Rasterize button. If Photoshop displays a warning message about merging layers, click the Merge button. If Photoshop displays a dialog box about conversion profiles, click the OK button.

Proofs

A **proof** is a copy of a document that you can examine to check color, layout, spelling, and other details before printing the final copy. A **hard proof** simulates what your final output will look like on a printing press. Sometimes called a proof print, or a match print, a hard proof is produced on an output device that is less expensive to operate than a printing press. Some ink-jet printers have the resolution necessary to produce inexpensive prints that can be used as hard proofs. Hard proofs need to fit on the page of the proof printer, so it sometimes is necessary to scale the proof. Alternatively, if you need to see a full-size proof, you may be able to tile or poster-print the image, printing smaller portions of the image, each on its own sheet of paper, but at actual size. Be careful about judging color with a desktop printer. Less-expensive printers sometimes produce output that does not represent the screen color accurately. For example, lower quality printers can produce a blue hue that appears slightly purple; red hues sometimes appear orange. Users should be aware that the use of inferior printers for printing proofs could result in somewhat false or misleading output — sometimes indicating a problem where none exists. Ask your service bureau about color matching.

Consult with printing professionals.
Printing professionals can help you make decisions about paper, color, type, surprinting, trapping, knockouts, and misregistration. Some print shops provide professional proofreading, prepress activities, digital proofing, die-cutting, typesetting, binding, and a variety of other services. Digital typesetters, lithographers, and machine operators are the best source of information because they know the machinery, color management systems, and font libraries.

Plan Ahead

While a hard proof is a printed copy, a **soft proof** is a copy you look at on the screen. Soft proofs can be as simple as a preview, or more complex when color adjustments and monitor calibrations take place.

To Print a Hard Proof

The next series of steps prints a hard proof that resembles what a final copy of the poster should look like. Settings in the Print Preview dialog box are adjusted to match professional print settings. Your result will be printer dependent. Some printers handle color matching and overlays better than others do. See your instructor for exact settings.

1
- On the View menu, point to Proof Setup to display the submenu (Figure 6–58).

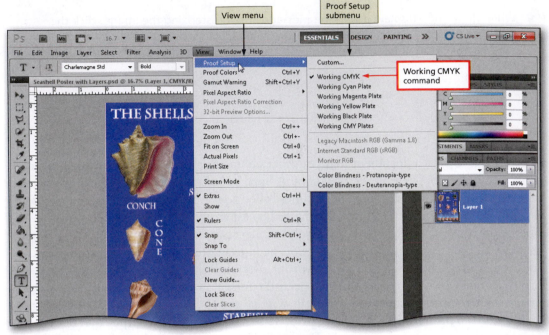

Figure 6–58

2
- If the Working CMYK command does not display a check mark, click it.

- Click the document window to close the menu if necessary.

- Press CTRL+P to display the Print dialog box.

- Click the Scale to Fit Media check box to select it.

- In the Color Management area, click the Proof option button.

- Click the Color Handling box arrow to display the choices (Figure 6–59).

Q&A What is the purpose of the Proof option button?

Choosing to print a proof will cause your printer to emulate how the document will print using another printer or printing press.

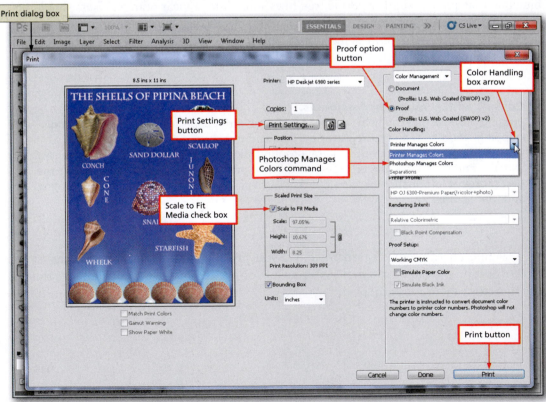

Figure 6–59

3

- Click Photoshop Manages Colors to select it.

- Click the Print Settings button to display your printer's Print dialog box.

- Look through the tabs or settings for a Color, Properties, or Preferences button. Turn off color management or set the printer to Application-Managed Colors if possible, so the printer profile settings do not interfere with the CMYK process color printing.

- Click the OK or Print button in your printer's Print dialog box. If Photoshop displays a warning message about the printer's printable area, click the Proceed button. If your printer displays a second dialog box, click its Print button. Retrieve the printout as shown in Figure 6–60.

Q&A

How will Photoshop manage colors?

Photoshop will manage any necessary conversions of color numbers between your document and the chosen printer.

Figure 6–60

To Save the File and Quit Photoshop

The poster is complete. The final steps are to save the file and quit Photoshop.

1 Press SHIFT+CTRL+S to open the Save As dialog box.

2 Type `Seashell Poster CMYK` in the File name text box.

3 Click the Save button. If Photoshop displays an options dialog box, click the OK button.

4 Click the Close button on the Photoshop Application bar. If Photoshop prompts you to save the changes, click the No button.

Chapter Summary

In this chapter, you created a poster using a variety of filters and effects. After filling the Background layer with the chosen color, you created a lighting effect. You fixed images using the Puppet Warp Tool and the Liquify filter. You learned that Photoshop contains a large number of filters that can be combined and edited to produce an endless number of special effects. Some of the filters manipulate the pixels geometrically, while others change the color. Filters that specialize in strokes and edges analyze the image to produce effects only in certain areas. After the filters were applied, you defined a new pattern to create a seashell pattern across the poster. You created headline text that will knockout to the white page. Finally, you learned about misregistration, potential printing problems associated with objects being close to one another, and the value of consulting with a print service bureau to obtain information about printing details. With the poster complete, you converted it to CMYK, flattening the image, and printed a hard proof.

The items listed below include all the new Photoshop skills you have learned in this chapter:

1. Select a Color Using the Color Panel (PS 336)
2. Use the Paint Bucket Tool (PS 337)
3. Choose a Lighting Effects Style (PS 339)
4. Edit Spotlight Properties (PS 341)
5. Position the Spotlights (PS 341)
6. Widen the Spotlights (PS 343)
7. Apply a Puppet Warp (PS 345)
8. Use the Filter Gallery (PS 354)
9. Choose a Filter from the Menu System (PS 356)
10. Apply the Liquify Filter (PS 359)
11. Create a Smart Object (PS 362)
12. Apply a Smart Filter (PS 362)
13. Choose a Filter from the Filter Gallery List (PS 363)
14. Apply a Second Filter (PS 364)
15. Apply a Crystallize Smart Filter (PS 365)
16. Purge (PS 366)
17. Define a Pattern (PS 367)
18. Use a Pattern (PS 368)
19. Delete a Pattern (PS 370)
20. Set the Tracking (PS 373)
21. Print a Hard Proof (PS 378)

Learn It Online

Test your knowledge of chapter content and key terms.

Instructions: To complete the Learn It Online exercises, start your browser, click the Address bar, and then enter the Web address `scsite.com/pscs5/learn`. When the Photoshop CS5 Learn It Online page is displayed, click the link for the exercise you want to complete and then read the instructions.

Chapter Reinforcement TF, MC, and SA
A series of true/false, multiple choice, and short answer questions that tests your knowledge of the chapter content.

Flash Cards
An interactive learning environment where you identify chapter key terms associated with displayed definitions.

Practice Test
A series of multiple choice questions that test your knowledge of chapter content and key terms.

Who Wants To Be a Computer Genius?
An interactive game that challenges your knowledge of chapter content in the style of a television quiz show.

Wheel of Terms
An interactive game that challenges your knowledge of chapter key terms in the style of the television show *Wheel of Fortune*.

Crossword Puzzle Challenge
A crossword puzzle that challenges your knowledge of key terms presented in the chapter.

Apply Your Knowledge

Reinforce the skills and apply the concepts you learned in this chapter.

Creating a Digital Painting

Instructions: Start Photoshop and perform the customization steps found on pages PS 6 through PS 9. Open the Apply 6-1 Garden file from the Chapter 06 folder of the Data Files for Students. You can access the Data Files for Students on the CD that accompanies this book. See the inside back cover of this book for instructions on downloading the Data Files for Students, or contact your instructor for information about accessing the required files. You will edit the file to create a digital painting from a digital photograph of a garden by increasing the saturation of color, adjusting the lighting, and then adding filters to create the painting shown in Figure 6–61.

Figure 6–61

Continued >

Apply Your Knowledge *continued*

Perform the following tasks:

1. Save the image on your USB flash drive as a PSD file, with the file name Apply 6-1 Garden Painting.

2. On the Layers panel, right-click the Background layer and then click Duplicate Layer. Name the new layer, edits. Select only the edits layer, and hide the Background layer by clicking its visibility icon.

3. To increase the saturation of the colors, click Layer on the menu bar, point to New Adjustment Layer, and then click Hue/Saturation. When Photoshop displays the New Layer dialog box, click the OK button. On the Adjustments panel, click the Master box arrow, and then select Reds. Enter a saturation of 50. Similarly, select Yellows and enter a saturation of 60. Select Blues and enter a saturation of 73. On the Adjustments panel status bar, click the 'Clip to layer' button.

4. On the Layers panel, select the edits layer. On the Filter menu, click Filter Gallery. In the lower-right portion of the Filter Gallery, locate the filter list. If more than one filter appears, click the 'Delete effect layer' button until only one filter is displayed in the list.

5. Click the Zoom box arrow and then click Fit in View. If the Artistic filters are not displayed, click Artistic.

6. Click the Dry Brush thumbnail. Set the Brush Size to 7, the Brush Detail to 8, and the Texture to 2.

7. In the lower-right portion of the Filter Gallery, click the 'New effect layer' button to add another filter to the list.

8. Click the Cutout thumbnail. Set the Number of Levels to 5, the Edge Simplicity to 2, and the Edge Fidelity to 1.

9. Click the 'New effect layer' button to add another filter to the list.

10. Click the Rough Pastels thumbnail. Set the Stroke Length to 4, the Stroke Detail to 3, the Texture to Canvas, the Scaling to 120, the Relief to 24, and the Light to Bottom.

11. Click the OK button to close the Filter Gallery.

12. On the File menu, click Print to display the Print dialog box. Click the Scale to Fit Media check box so it is selected. In the upper-right corner, click the box arrow, and then click Color Management, if necessary. In the Print area, click the Proof option button. Click the Color Handling box arrow and then click Photoshop Manages Colors.

13. Ready the Printer. Click the Print button and then when your printer's Print dialog box is displayed, click its Print button. Turn in the printout to your instructor. Save the file again and then quit Photoshop.

Extend Your Knowledge

Extend the skills you learned in this chapter and experiment with new skills. You may need to use Help to complete the assignment.

Creating the Illusion of Flowing Water

Instructions: Start Photoshop and perform the customization steps found on pages PS 6 through PS 9. Open the Extend 6-1 Faucet file from the Chapter 06 folder of the Data Files for Students. See the inside back cover of this book for instructions on downloading the Data Files for Students, or contact your instructor for information about accessing the required files.

The Beta Faucet Company needs you to finish an ad for a new line of faucets. You are to add the appearance of water flowing from the end of the faucet, as shown in Figure 6–62.

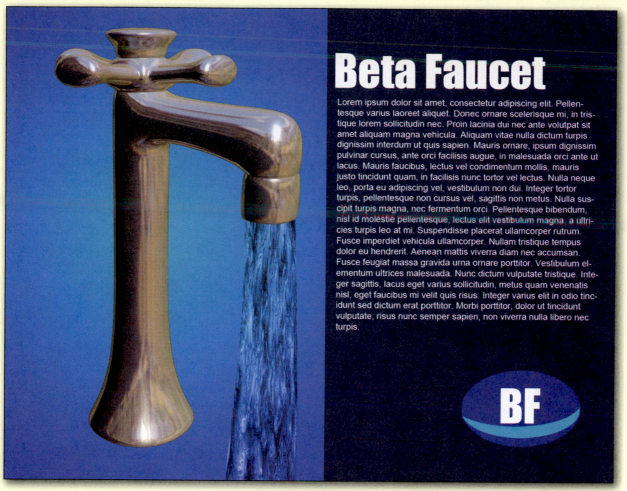

Figure 6–62

Perform the following tasks:

1. On the File menu, click Save As. Save the image on your USB flash drive as a PSD file, with the file name Extend 6-1 Faucet Edited. You will notice that several layers are not visible.

2. Click the visibility icons next to the light blue and dark blue layers.

3. On the Tools panel, click the 'Set foreground color' button to display the Color Picker dialog box. In the document window, click the light blue color to select it. Click the OK button to close the Color Picker dialog box.

4. Repeat Step 3 to assign the background color to the dark blue color in the document window.

5. Select the Background layer. On the Tools panel, select the Gradient Tool and create a radial gradient from left to right across the middle of the document window. Press SHIFT+CTRL+N to create a new layer above the background layer and name it, dark rectangle.

6. If a green ruler guide does not appear in the document window, click the View Extras button on the Application bar, and then click Show Guides. Use the Rectangular Marquee Tool to draw a rectangle enclosing the right side of the document window.

7. Change the foreground color to black and fill this new selection by using the Fill shortcut keys, ALT+BACKSPACE.

8. Deselect the marquee by clicking CTRL+D.

Continued >

9. On the Layers panel, change the opacity of the dark rectangle layer to 60%, creating a navy blue color.

10. Open the Extend 6-1 Single Faucet file from the Chapter 06 folder of the Data Files for Students.

11. Arrange the document windows side by side, and then move the faucet image into the Extend 6-1 Faucet Edited document window. Close the Extend 6-1 Single Faucet document window.

12. Press the D key to reset the default colors.

13. Create a new layer below the faucet layer with the name, water.

14. On the Filter menu, click Convert for Smart Filters to create a smart object. When Photoshop displays a dialog box, click the OK button.

15. On the Filter menu, point to Render, and then click Clouds.

16. On the Filter menu, point to Blur, and then click Gaussian Blur. Set the radius to 6, and then close the Gaussian Blur dialog box.

17. On the Filter menu, point to Blur, and then click Motion Blur. Enter the following settings, and then click the OK button:

    a. Angle 90

    b. Distance 80

18. On the Edit menu, point to Transform, and then click Scale. When Photoshop displays a dialog box, click the OK button.

19. On the options bar, set the width to 50% while leaving the height at 100%. Press the ENTER key to commit the transformation.

20. On the Filter menu, point to Artistic, and then click Plastic Wrap. Apply the filter with the following settings:

    a. Highlight Strength: 15

    b. Detail: 10

    c. Smoothness: 10

21. On the Filter menu, point to Sketch, then click Chrome. Apply the filter with the following settings:

    a. Detail: 0

    b. Smoothness: 8

    c. On the Edit menu, click Fade Chrome. Set the Opacity to 100% and the Mode to Hard Light.

22. On the Edit menu, point to Transform, then click Scale. On the options bar, set width to 30% while leaving the height at 100%. Press the ENTER key to commit the transformation.

23. On the Edit menu, point to Transform, and then click Warp. Drag the anchor points to simulate a stream of running water and move the layer to a location below the faucet in the document window. Press the ENTER key to commit the transformation.

24. On the Layers panel, change the blending mode to Hard Light.

25. Click the visibility icons for the rest of the layers to view the completed image.

26. Save the file as Extend 6-1 Faucet Complete and submit the assignment to your instructor in the specified format.

Make It Right

Analyze a document and correct all errors and/or improve the design.

Correcting Errors in a Poster

Instructions: Start Photoshop and perform the customization steps found on pages PS 6 through PS 9. Open the Make It Right 6-1 Fair Poster file from the Chapter 06 folder of the Data Files for Students. See the inside back cover of this book for instructions on downloading the Data Files for Students, or contact your instructor for information about accessing the required files.

The file contains a poster with black stripes that need to be straightened (Figure 6–63). The text also needs to stand out more.

Figure 6–63

Perform the following tasks:

Select the shirt layer. Use the Quick Selection Tool to select the second stripe from the left. Use the Refine Edge button on the options bar to increase the radius of the selection to include the slightly gray edges of the stripe. Click Edit on the menu bar, and then click Puppet Warp. Turn off the mesh, if necessary. Click to create four or five pins from one end of the stripe to the other. Drag inner pins to straighten the stripe. Repeat the process, using the appropriate selection tools for the third stripe from the left, the second stripe from the right, and the third stripe from the right. (*Hint:* you may need to use the Rectangular Marquee Tool to drag around the stripe, and then use the Magic Wand Tool and the 'Subtract from selection' button on the options bar to remove excess white in the selection.)

Continued >

STUDENT ASSIGNMENTS

Make It Right *continued*

The letters in each of the words need to be tracked, so one letter appears on each stripe. One at a time, select each text layer and the Horizontal Type Tool. Select all of the text in the word. Access the Character panel and track the letters. Finally, for each text layer, add a stroke layer style with a black 2 pt stroke.

Save the revised graphic with a new name and submit it in the format specified by your instructor.

In the Lab

Design and/or create a document using the guidelines, concepts, and skills presented in this chapter. Labs are listed in order of increasing difficulty.

Lab 1: Using the Liquify Filter

Problem: You are to enhance a music graphic on a poster by using the Liquify Filter. The completed poster is displayed in Figure 6–64.

Figure 6–64

Instructions: Perform the following tasks:

1. Start Photoshop. Perform the customization steps found on pages PS 6 through PS 9.

2. Open the file Lab 6-1 Recital Graphic from the Chapter 06 folder of the Data Files for Students. See the inside back cover of this book for instructions on downloading the Data Files for Students, or contact your instructor for information about accessing the required files.

3. Click the Save As command on the File menu. Type **Lab 6-1 Recital Graphic Solution** as the file name. Choose the Photoshop PSD format. Browse to your USB flash drive storage device. Click the Save button. If Photoshop displays a dialog box, click the OK button.

4. Using the Layers panel menu, create a duplicate layer of the music layer and name it, edits. Hide the Background layer and music layer.

5. On the Filter menu, click Liquify. When the Liquify dialog box is displayed, use the Zoom Tool and Hand Tool to position the music layer in the preview area, if necessary.

6. Set the Brush Size to 150.

7. Click the Bloat Tool, and then click at the beginning of the musical staff to inflate the area. Click in several other areas. Experiment with clicking several times in the same place.

8. Click the OK button to close the Filter Gallery.

9. Click the visibility icons beside the Background layer to make it visible.

10. Flatten the image, discarding hidden layers, and then save the file with the name, Lab 6-1 Recital Graphic Complete, in the TIFF format.

11. See your instructor for ways to print this poster-size image, if that service is available at your school. Otherwise, use the Image Size command on the Image menu to reduce the photo to fit on available printer paper. Print a hard proof using the instructions from the chapter.

In the Lab

Lab 2: Enhancing a Photo with Lighting and Text

Problem: You work for a small ad agency whose client is a cosmetics company named Your Way. Your supervisor has given you a photo to enhance with lighting effects and text. The completed advertising piece is displayed in Figure 6–65.

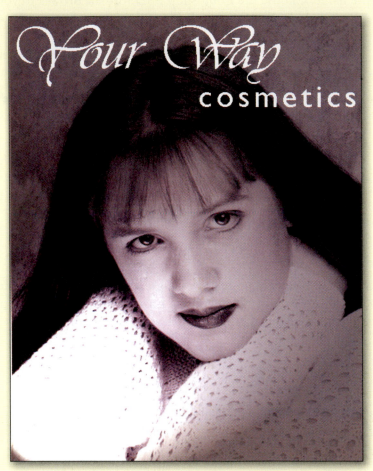

Figure 6–65

Instructions: Perform the following tasks:

1. Start Photoshop. Perform the customization steps found on pages PS 6 through PS 9.

2. Open the file Lab 6-2 Cosmetics from the Chapter 06 folder of the Data Files for Students. See the inside back cover of this book for instructions on downloading the Data Files for Students, or contact your instructor for information about accessing the required files.

3. Click the Save As command on the File menu. Type `Lab 6-2 Cosmetics Edited` as the file name. Browse to your USB flash drive storage device, and save the file in the PSD format.

4. On the Filter menu, point to Render, and then click Lighting Effects. When the Lighting Effects dialog box is displayed, change the Style setting to Default, if necessary. Click the Light type box arrow, and then click Spotlight in the list. In the preview, drag all handles toward the center so the entire ellipse is displayed. Then, in the following order, adjust the center point, the radial handle, and the ellipse handles to the positions shown in Figure 6–66. The position of each point on the ellipse, as well as the center point, is important.

5. Drag the Intensity slider to 34. Drag the Focus slider to 46. Drag the Gloss slider to –44. Drag the Material slider to 69 and the Ambience slider to 25. Reset the other sliders to zero, if necessary.

6. Click the OK button in the Lighting Effects dialog box.

7. When the document window again is displayed, press the T key to activate the Horizontal Type Tool.

8. On the options bar, click the 'Set the font family' box arrow and then click Vivaldi or a similar font. Type **4 8** pt in the 'Set the font size' box. Click the 'Set the anti-aliasing method' box arrow and then click Strong in the list. Click the 'Left align text' button.

9. On the options bar, click the 'Set the text color' button. When Photoshop displays the 'Select text color' dialog box, select a white color, and then click the OK button.

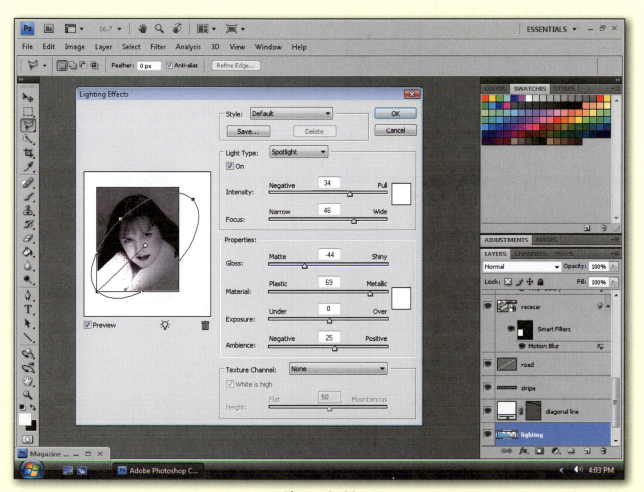

Figure 6–66

Continued >

In the Lab *continued*

10. In the document window, drag a type bounding box from the left margin to the right margin, approximately 1 inch tall near the top margin. In the box, type **Your Way** to complete the text. Click the 'Commit any current edits' button on the options bar to close the text box.

11. Drag a second type bounding box directly below the first type bounding box. On the options bar, click the 'Set the font family' box arrow, and then click Gill Sans MT, or a similar font. If necessary, click the 'Set the font style box' arrow, and then click Regular in the list. Type **24** in the 'Set the font size' box. Click the 'Right align text' button.

12. In the type bounding box, type **cosmetics** to complete the entry. Click the 'Commit any current edits' button on the options bar to close the text box.

13. Because there is too much space between the letters Y and o in the word, Your, and between the letters W and a in the word, Way, you will track those sets of letters with a negative value to improve the kerning by moving them closer together.

    a. Click the Your Way layer in the Layers panel. In the text box, drag to highlight the letter Y.

    b. On the options bar, click the Toggle the Character and Paragraph panels button.

    c. Click the Character tab, if necessary. Type **-180** in the Tracking box.

    d. Drag to highlight the letter W.

    e. Type **-240** in the Tracking box. On the options bar, click the 'Commit any current edits' button.

14. Because the word, cosmetics, would look better with more space between the letters, you will use a positive tracking value.

    a. In the type bounding box, drag to highlight the entire word, cosmetics.

    b. If necessary, click the Character tab. Type **120** in the Tracking box.

15. On the options bar, click the 'Commit any current edits' button.

16. Save the file again. Print hard proofs. Flatten the layers and then save the file in the TIFF file format, with the file name Lab 6-2 Cosmetics Complete. See your instructor for ways to submit this assignment.

In the Lab

Lab 3: Fizzy Root Beer Advertisement

Problem: The Fizzy Root Beer Company has a new label and needs you to finish the design for their latest advertisement. They want the background to look like bubbles, but they do not have any close ups of root beer bubbles for you to use. By combining several filters, you will create a bubbly background and add a spotlight effect as shown in Figure 6–67.

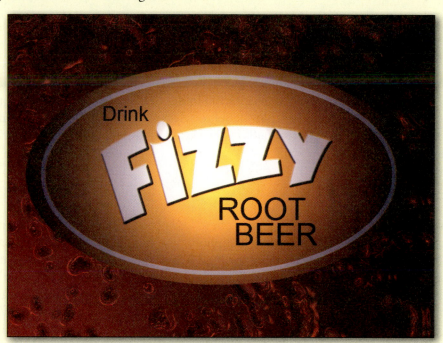

Figure 6–67

Instructions: Perform the following tasks:

Start Photoshop and perform the customization steps found on pages PS 6 through PS 9. Open the Lab 6-3 Fizzy file from the Data Files for Students. See the inside back cover of this book for instructions on downloading the Data Files for Students, or contact your instructor for information about accessing the required files. Save the image on your USB flash drive as a PSD file with the file name Lab 6-3 Fizzy Edited.

Hide the label layer. Select the background layer. Press the D key to reset the default colors. On the Filter menu, click Convert for Smart Filters, and then click the OK button. To simulate bubbles, apply the Render filter named Clouds. Apply the Stylize filter named Glowing Edges, setting the Edge width to 3, the Edge Brightness to 19, and the Smoothness to 15. Apply the Sketch filter named Plaster, setting the Image Balance to 16, and the Smoothness to 2.

To make the bubbles look like they are in liquid, add a lighting effect. On the Filter menu, point to Render, and then click Lighting Effects. Choose Blue Omni for the style. In the preview, drag the ellipse handles to create a circle that encompasses the entire preview. Drag the center point to the lower-left corner of the preview. Click the OK button to close the Lighting Effects dialog box.

Apply the Sketch filter named Chrome, setting the Detail to 8, and the Smoothness to 10.

To make the bubbles brown, click Hue/Saturation on the Adjustments panel. Select the Colorize check box so that it displays a check mark, set the Hue to 22, the Saturation to 70, and the Lightness to –25. Click the 'Clip to layer' button on the Adjustments panel status bar.

On the Layers panel, display and select the label layer. Add a spotlight filter to the label layer by pointing to Render on the Filter menu, and then clicking Lighting Effects. Select Flashlight as the Style and scale the light so that it covers the top and bottom of the label. Save the file again and submit it to your instructor in the specified format.

Cases and Places

Apply your creative thinking and problem solving skills to design and implement a solution.

Note: To complete these assignments, you may be required to use the Data Files for Students. See the inside back cover of this book for instructions on downloading the Data Files for Students, or contact your instructor for information about accessing the required files.

1: Create a Surface Blur

Academic

The photo of your campus, taken from the roof of its tallest building, was taken on a very cloudy day. The school would like to use the picture on its Web site, but would prefer a brighter sky. Open the file named Case 6-1 Cityscape from the Chapter 06 folder of the Data Files for Students. Select the sky and create a layer via cut. Use the Color panel to select a very light blue foreground color. Use the Render Filter named Clouds to create clouds in the sky. Flatten the file and save it for Web & Devices in the GIF format.

2: Create a Coloring Book

Personal

You decide to make a coloring book for your nephew. Use pets or go to the local zoo and take several digital pictures of various animals. Open the first photo. Use the Find Edges filter in the Stylize category. Save the file with a name such as Monkey Find Edges. Open the second photo and use the Trace Contour filter in the Stylize category. Adjust the level to 50 or a suitable value for your photo. Save the file with a name such as Tiger Trace Contour 50. Open the third photo and convert it to grayscale. Use the Photocopy filter in the Sketch category and adjust the settings to 8 and 11, or suitable values for your photo. Save the file with a name such as Zebra Photocopy 8 11. Open each of your other animal photos and experiment with different filters and settings to create areas that could be colored. Save each file with a name indicative of the filter and settings. Print a copy of each edited photo and staple them together in book form.

3: Develop a Filter Tutorial

Professional

As an intern with the state department of tourism, your job is to help create tourist pamphlets and posters. Your latest project is promoting a bridge run to support cancer research. Your supervisor has given you a photo of the bridge. She wants you to turn it into a poster, with filtering applied to the image edges and an added lens flare. Use the Brush Strokes filter named Accented Edges thumbnail. Type **2** in the Edge Width box, type **38** in the Edge Brightness box, and type **4** in the Smoothness box. Use the Render Filter named Lens Flare with a brightness of 100% and Lens type of 50–300mm Zoom. Make the text layer visible and apply any tracking or kerning as necessary.

7 Creating Color Channels and Actions

Objectives

You will have mastered the material in this chapter when you can:

- Create a master image
- View channel color separations
- Use the Channels panel to create alpha channels
- Use a brush in overlay mode to help define a selection
- Convert an image to black and white using different methods
- Create black-and-white, sepia, and duotone versions of an image
- Create an advertisement with warped text
- Create a new action set
- Record, save, edit, and play back an action
- Convert an RGB image to LAB color and then to CMYK
- List prepress activities
- Resize and resample images
- Print color separations

7 | Creating Color Channels and Actions

Introduction

Photographers and graphic artists routinely create different versions of the same image. Creating a master version, along with versions for the Web, for black-and-white advertising media, for color separations and tints, and for various color modes and sizes, enables maximum repurposing. Multiple versions of photos are used commonly in advertising, photo cataloging, and on photo Web sites. Portrait studios produce and sell a wide assortment of special effect portraits, which require a variety of image versions. Creating a reusable logo adds flexibility for business publications.

Another timesaving tool is the ability to record your steps as you work in Photoshop and play them back when needed. The saved recording, called a Photoshop action, is a powerful automation device. Tasks that you perform repeatedly, such as adding a logo to each publication, can be recorded and then played back with a single keystroke.

You will learn about channels, color changes, actions, resizing, and resampling as you work through this chapter.

Project — Toy Store Advertising

Chapter 7 uses Photoshop to edit a photograph for a store called Wild Thing Toys that sells animal themed toys and games. First, you will hide the background and create a masked piece of artwork that can be dropped into other backgrounds and page layout applications. Second, you will create warped text featuring the company name. A black-and-white version of the photo will be created for newspaper placement. Sepia and tinted versions will offer the store variety and styling, such as retro or filtered special effects. You will style the advertisement with a special effect, making it appear as though it was created with colored pencils, and resize it with an automated action. Finally, an image with exact size and resolution requirements will be created for an advertisement insert. The ad, complete with graphics and text, will be converted to the CMYK color model and printed with color separations. The images are shown in Figure 7–1.

Figure 7–1

Overview

As you read this chapter, you will learn how to create the images shown in Figure 7–1 by performing these general tasks:

- Add an alpha channel.
- Hide the background to create a floating image.
- Insert and warp text.
- Recolor images to produce black and white, sepia, and duotones.
- Use action sets.
- Record and play back an action.
- Resample and resize an image.
- Print color separations.

<table>
<tr><td>

General Project Guidelines

When editing a photo, the actions you perform and decisions you make will affect the appearance and characteristics of the finished product. As you edit photos, such as the one shown in Figure 7–1, you should follow these general guidelines:

1. **Plan your versions.** Always start with a high-quality photo and create a master image. Anticipate all the ways the image might be used or repurposed. Consider client needs as you create versions, such as color, masked images, black and white, tints, and color modes.

(continued)

</td><td>

Plan Ahead

</td></tr>
</table>

(continued)

2. **Choose the best tool for the job.** As you make decisions about how to edit your image, look at various ways to accomplish the same task. For example, compare using a simple delete command versus an alpha channel mask. Ask yourself if you will need to use the selection again. Is the background complicated? If you are considering a black-and-white version, decide whether a simple grayscale will be as effective as an adjustment layer where you can fine-tune the contrast.

3. **Record actions for repetitive tasks.** If you or your client have specialized, repetitive tasks that you perform several times a week, consider recording an action. This playback feature will not only save time, it will create consistency by applying revisions in the same way each time. Actions can give users flexibility by pausing for user decisions at critical points or by waiting for dialog box responses.

When necessary, more specific details concerning the above guidelines are presented at appropriate points in the chapter. The chapter also will identify the actions performed and decisions made regarding these guidelines during the creation of the edited photos shown in Figure 7–1 on the previous page.

To Start Photoshop

The following steps, which assume Windows 7 is running, start Photoshop based on a typical installation.

1 Click the Start button on the Windows 7 taskbar to display the Start menu.

2 Type **Photoshop CS5** as the search text in the 'Search programs and files' text box, and watch the search results appear on the Start menu.

3 Click Adobe Photoshop CS5 in the search results on the Start menu to start Photoshop.

4 After a few moments, when the Photoshop window is displayed, if the window is not maximized, click the Maximize button on the title bar to maximize the window.

To Reset the Workspace

The following steps reset the Essentials workspace.

1 Click the 'Show more workspaces and options' button on the Application bar.

2 If necessary, click Essentials to select the default workspace panels.

3 Click the 'Show more workspaces and options' button again to display the list, and then click Reset Essentials to restore the workspace to its default settings.

To Reset the Tools and the Options Bar

The following steps select the Rectangular Marquee Tool and reset all tool settings in the options bar.

1 If the tools in the Tools panel appear in two columns, click the double arrow at the top of the Tools panel.

2 If necessary, click the Rectangular Marquee Tool button on the Tools panel to select it.

3 Right-click the Rectangular Marquee Tool icon on the options bar to display the context menu, and then click Reset All Tools. When Photoshop displays a confirmation dialog box, click the OK button to restore the tools to their default settings.

To Reset the Default Colors

The following step resets the default colors.

1 Press the D key to reset the default foreground and background colors.

To Reset the Layers Panel

The following steps reset the Layers panel to make the thumbnails match the figures shown in this book.

1 Click the Layers panel menu button and then click Panel Options on the list to display the Layers Panel Options dialog box.

2 Click the option button for the smallest of the thumbnail sizes.

3 If necessary, click the Layer Bounds option button to select it.

4 If necessary, place a check mark next to each of the three check boxes at the bottom of the Layer Panel Options dialog box.

5 Click the OK button.

To Open a File and Save It in the PSD Format

When creating multiple versions of an image, you should create a master copy in PSD format. That way, new versions can be created from an original that remains unchanged. Recall that PSD is the only format that supports all Photoshop features. The following steps open an image and save it in a version that will serve as the master image for the project.

1 Open the Animals file from the Chapter 07 folder of the Data Files for Students, or a location specified by your instructor.

2 Change the magnification to 16.67%, if necessary, to view the entire image. If rulers do not appear, press CTRL+R to display them.

3 With your USB flash drive connected to one of the computer's USB ports, click File on the menu bar to display the File menu, and then click Save As to display the Save As dialog box.

4 Type **Animals Master** in the File name text box (Save As dialog box) to rename the file.

5 Click the Save in box arrow to display the list of available drives, and then click UDISK 2.0 (F:), or the location associated with your USB flash drive, in the list of available storage devices to select that drive as the new save location.

6 Click the Format button to display the list of available file formats, and then click Photoshop (*.PSD, *.PDD) in the list, if necessary.

7 Click the Save button (Save As dialog box) to save the file. If Photoshop displays a dialog box, click the OK button.

To Create an Edits Layer

The following steps create an edits layer on top of the Background layer.

1 Click the Layers panel tab to display the Layers panel, if necessary.

2 Right-click the Background layer and then click Duplicate Layer on the shortcut menu.

3 When the Duplicate Layer dialog box is displayed, type `edits` in the As box, and then click the OK button.

4 Click the visibility icon for the Background layer to hide it (Figure 7–2).

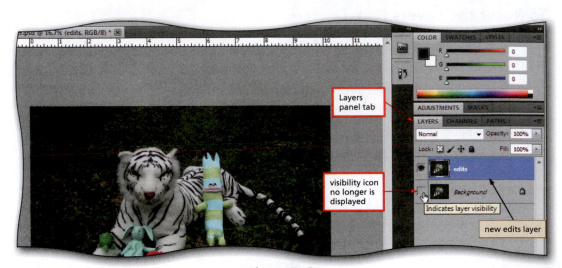

Figure 7–2

Using Channels

The first version of the photo will be a floating image without a background. **Floating images** have a transparent background so they can be placed in front of other pictures. There are many ways to remove a background, including methods you have used before, such as using the Eraser Tool, layer masks, or editing selections. Another way to isolate the background is to use Photoshop channels.

As you learned in previous chapters, digital images are made of many pixels, or tiny dots, each of which represents an abstract sample of color. Pixels use combinations of primary colors, or pigments. A **primary color** is one that cannot be created by mixing other colors in the gamut of a given color space. Traditionally, the colors red, yellow, and blue are considered primary colors. Those colors, however, are not the same hues as the red, yellow, and blue used on most computer monitors. Many modern computer applications and hardware devices use the primary additive colors of red, green, and blue, and the primary subtractive colors of magenta, yellow, and cyan. Recall that additive colors involve light emitted directly from a source. Subtractive colors absorb some wavelengths of light and reflect others. The two color modes RGB and CMYK are based respectively on the additive and subtractive primary colors.

Each of the primary colors creates a channel in Photoshop. In an image, a **channel** is all of the pixels of the same color, identified using the color modes. An image from a digital camera will have a red, green, and blue channel, while a printed image will have a cyan, magenta, yellow, and black channel. Channels are used in Photoshop to separate and store information about an image's colors so that users can manipulate them. Traditionally, **color separations** referred to the process of separating image colors into individual films or pattern plates of cyan, magenta, yellow, and black in preparation for printing. Photoshop takes that process one step further by automatically creating the color separation anytime you convert to the CMYK color mode.

Channels are created automatically when you open a new image. The color mode determines the number of color channels created. By default, bitmap, grayscale, duotone, and indexed-color images have one channel; RGB and LAB images have three, plus a composite; and CMYK images have four, plus a composite. You can add specialized channels to all image types except bitmap images.

In addition to the default color channels, extra channels, called alpha channels, are used for storing and editing selections as masks; spot color channels can be added to incorporate spot color plates for printing. A spot color plate is an extra part of the separation printing process that applies a single color to areas of the artwork.

Plan your versions.

Once you create a master image, plan for possible uses and versions. If you are creating a photo for a client or business, consider all the ways the image could be repurposed. **Repurposing** is the concept of using all or part of a photo for something other than its original purpose. Ask yourself these questions:

- Might the image need to be used with and without its background?
- Will the image be used in more than one medium, such as Web, newspaper, posters, flyers, etc.?
- Might you need both a color and black-and-white version?
- Would special tints, such as sepia or duotones, extend the possibilities for the image?
- Could you use all or part of the photo in another composite image?
- Can you save money by performing some prepress activities yourself?
- How will you organize your versions for maximum shelf life?

**Plan
Ahead**

The Channels Panel

The Channels panel (Figure 7–3) is used to create and manage channels. The panel lists all channels in the image — the composite channel first, then each individual color channel, followed by any spot color channels, and finally any alpha channels. As in the Layers panel, the Channels panel displays a visibility icon followed by a thumbnail of each channel's contents. The visibility icon is useful for viewing specific colors in the document window or to see how edits might affect a specific color.

BTW

Saving Channels
As long as you save a file in a format supporting color modes, the normal color channels are preserved. Alpha channels are saved only when using the PSD, PDF, PICT, Pixar, TIF, PNG, or camera raw formats.

BTW

Thumbnails
Viewing thumbnails is a convenient way of tracking channel contents; however, turning off the display of thumbnails can improve performance. To resize or hide channel thumbnails, choose Panel Options from the Channels panel menu. Click a thumbnail size to adjust the size of the display, or click None, to turn off the display of thumbnails.

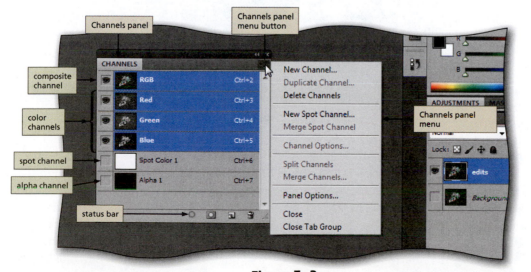

Figure 7–3

When you select one specific channel, it is displayed in grayscale in the document window by default. If more than one channel is selected, the document window displays the color combinations.

The Channels panel menu displays commands to create new channels, change the color overlay, or set other channel options.

To View Channels

The following steps open the Channels panel and allow you to view individual channels. As you view each channel, the channel color will appear almost white; other colors will appear in shades of gray.

- Click the Channels panel tab to access the Channels panel (Figure 7–4).

 **Experiment**

- One at a time, click each of the channels. Be sure to click the channel thumbnail or name – do not click the visibility icons. As you view each channel, look for strong contrast between the lightest and darkest colors in the image.

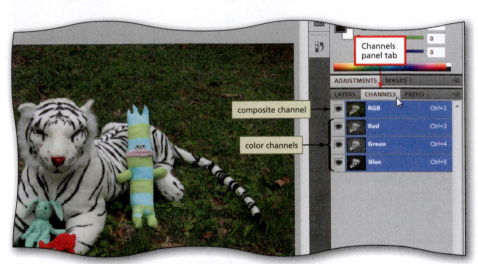

Figure 7–4

- Click the Red channel to display it (be sure to click the channel and not its visibility icon) (Figure 7–5).

 Q&A

Why does the Red channel appear in gray?

Photoshop creates a grayscale version of the image to provide the most contrast possible for editing purposes. Because you chose the Red channel, white (or light) areas indicate pixels with a high red content while black (or dark) areas indicate pixels with little red. Notice the red turtle appears almost white while the green turtle, which has virtually no red, appears almost black. Remember that in the RGB color mode, white is created by adding the maximum amounts of red, green, and blue. Therefore, the white tiger contains a high red content, which is why it appears nearly white in the channel.

Figure 7–5

● Click the Green channel to view the channel displaying the most contrast (because the turtle is red) with its background (Figure 7–6).

Figure 7–6

Other Ways

1. To display composite, press CTRL+2

2. To display first channel, press CTRL+3

3. To display second channel, press CTRL+4

4. To display third channel, press CTRL+5

To Zoom by Dragging

Sometimes you need to enlarge a specific area of the document as you work. Dragging with the Zoom Tool allows you to target a specific area of your document for zooming. The following step zooms in on the red turtle.

● With the Green channel still selected, click the Zoom Tool at the bottom of the Tools panel.

● Point to the top-left of the dark turtle, hold down the left mouse button and then drag down and to the right to draw a rectangular selection around the turtle with the Zoom Tool (Figure 7–7).

● Release the mouse button to apply the zoom.

Q&A What should I do if I zoomed out instead of in?

Figure 7–7

If you zoomed out, the Zoom tool setting on the Options bar is probably set to Zoom Out. Click the Zoom In button on the Options bar and then drag around the dark turtle again to zoom in.

To Select Using a Channel

The first goal in editing the Animals Master image is to isolate the red turtle and remove its background to create a floating image that can be repurposed. Recall that removing the background in an image involves isolating it in a selection area and then deleting or masking it. When you have a solid background, it is easy to select and delete. But often, the background is busy or shaded, requiring more creative steps to remove it. Variegated colors, such as shades of green in grassy areas or blue in sky areas, may be hard to delete as they appear behind, between, and around other objects. In a channel, those kinds of backgrounds appear as a single color; thus, they are isolated and selected easily.

The following step uses the Magnetic Lasso Tool to select as much of the red turtle as possible in the Green channel.

1

• Right-click the Lasso Tool on the Tools panel to display a shortcut menu, and then select Magnetic Lasso Tool.

• Click the edge of the dark turtle and then drag the mouse around it, staying close to the edges, to create a selection.

• Click the starting point as you finish to close the selection (Figure 7–8).

Q&A
Could I have used the Magic Wand Tool to select the turtle?

Yes, you could have, but it would have been tedious to get the tolerance setting correct.

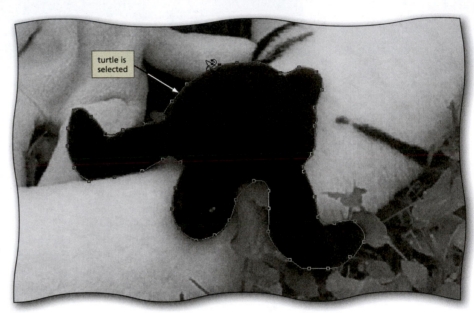

turtle is selected

Figure 7–8

Alpha Channels

When you create a new channel, by default it becomes an alpha channel. An **alpha channel**, or **alpha channel mask**, is a special channel that saves and loads selection marquees. It is similar to a new layer or layer mask in that it is used to edit or mask parts of an image. Alpha channel masking can be performed on the background layer, whereas masks created using the Layers panel cannot. Alpha channels represent selections and exist independently of any particular layer — for that reason, storing selections as alpha channels creates more permanent masks than saving as layer masks. You can reuse the stored selections or even load them into another image. The Channel Options command on the panel menu allows you to name the alpha channel and adjust settings related to editing.

Most commonly, alpha channels are used to isolate and protect areas of an image as you apply color changes, filters, or other effects to the rest of the image. Additionally, alpha channels are used for complex image editing, such as gradually applying color or filter effects to an image. For instance, viewing an alpha channel and the composite channel together allows you to see how changes made in the alpha channel relate to the entire image. When you display an alpha channel at the same time as a color channel, the alpha channel appears as a transparent color overlay in the document window.

To Create an Alpha Channel from a Selection

When making an alpha channel, you can create the channel first and then paint the selected area, or you can select the area first and then create the channel. The following step creates an alpha channel when a selection has already been made. You will use the 'Save selection as' channel button on the Channels status bar to create an alpha channel with colored overlay and adjustable opacity. You can edit the channel using any painting tool, or modify it with a filter.

1

- With the Green channel still selected in the Channels panel and the selection around the turtle still active, click the 'Save selection as channel' button to create an alpha channel.

- Click Select on the menu bar, and then click Deselect to deselect your selection.

- Click the visibility icon next to the Alpha 1 channel to display its color overlay (Figure 7–9).

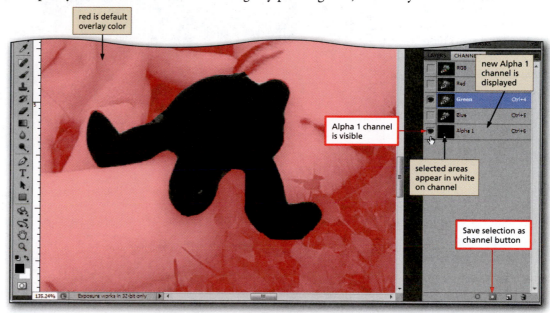

Figure 7–9

 **Experiment**

- Double-click the Alpha 1 channel thumbnail and view the name, color, and opacity settings. Click the OK button to close the dialog box.

Other Ways	
1. On Channels panel status bar, ALT+click 'Create new channel' button	2. On Channels panel menu, click New Channel, edit settings

To Edit an Alpha Channel

It is likely that after creating an initial selection and creating an alpha channel, you will need to edit the channel to modify what was selected. It is often easier to use the Brush Tool and paint with black or white. You can use any selection tool to make new selections on a channel and then fill them with black or white. The steps on the next page edit the turtle selection to create what will become a clean mask. Remember that as you paint with black the area you paint will turn red to match the red overlay.

1

- Click the Alpha 1 channel to select it. Be sure the visibility icons for both the Green and Alpha 1 channels are still displayed.

- Click the Brush Tool on the Tools panel to make it the active tool.

- Click the Brush Preset picker button on the Options bar to display the Brush Preset picker, double-click the value in the Size box, and then type **13** to set the brush size to 13 px.

- Double-click the value in the Hardness box and type **100** to set the hardness to 100% (Figure 7–10).

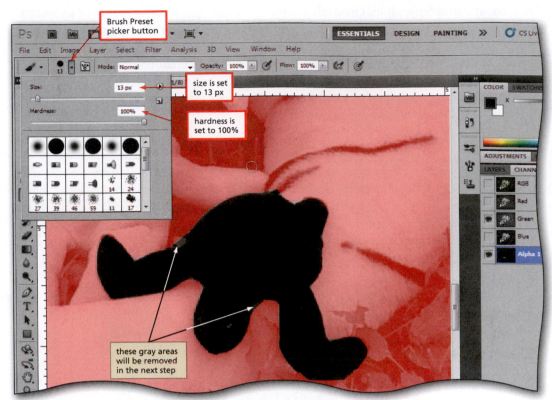

Figure 7–10

2

- Click the Brush Preset picker button again to close it.

- Drag the mouse pointer over any gray areas in the document window to paint over them, but do not paint over the turtle itself. Adjust the brush size as you paint to get in to the smaller spaces and corners around the turtle.

- If necessary, switch the foreground color to white and paint in any parts of the turtle that have been accidentally covered by the red overlay.

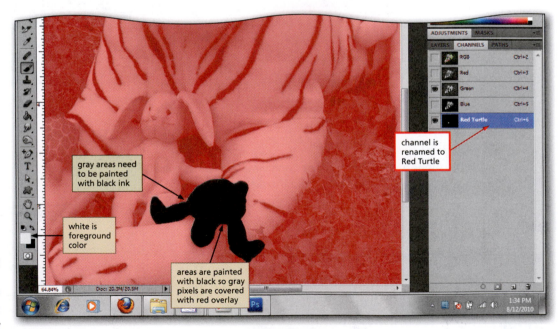

Figure 7–11

- Double-click the channel name Alpha 1, type **Red Turtle** to rename it, and then press the ENTER key to save the new name (Figure 7–11).

To Create a Second Alpha Channel

Photoshop allows you to create and save multiple alpha channels. This is helpful because it lets you store multiple selections for later use. The following steps create a second alpha channel to store a mask for the green turtle.

1 In the Animals Master document window, scroll up and to the left until you can see the other turtle.

2 Click the visibility icon beside the Red Turtle channel to hide it.

3 Click the Red channel to select it because it offers greater contrast between the second turtle and the background.

4 Click the visibility icon beside the Green channel to hide it.

5 Use the Magnetic Lasso Tool to create a rough selection around the green turtle.

6 Click the 'Save selection as channel' button.

7 Rename the new channel, Green Turtle.

8 Click CTRL+D to deselect.

9 If necessary, display the visibility icons for both the Green Turtle and Red channels (Figure 7–12).

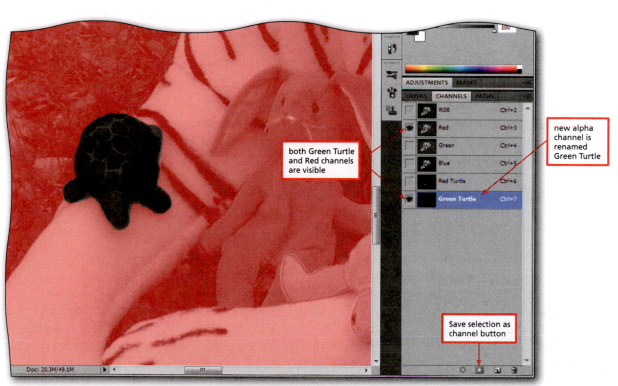

Figure 7–12

To Fine-Tune the Second Alpha Channel

The following step fine-tunes the rough selection around the green turtle to remove the portions of the gray background that still show through.

- With the Green Turtle channel selected, click the Brush Tool on the Tools panel.

- Press the D key to reset the default colors.

- Drag over any gray areas surrounding the turtle to mask them.

- If necessary, switch the foreground color to white and paint in any parts of the turtle that have been accidentally covered by the red overlay (Figure 7–13).

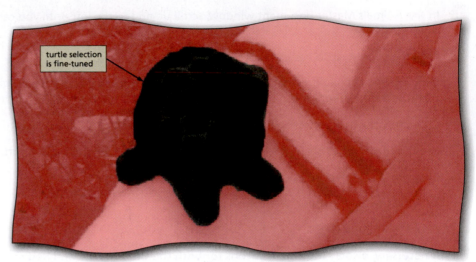

turtle selection is fine-tuned

Figure 7–13

Brush Overlay Mode

Using channels to create and fine-tune selections is an ideal way to make difficult selections, such as masking around hair, tree branches, or other small and thin objects that would be difficult to select with other tools. You have seen how to paint on an existing alpha channel with black and white to fine-tune a selection, but up until now you have used the brush in its default normal mode. Using a brush in overlay mode allows you to make finer selections.

When painting in overlay mode, painting with black makes dark areas darker without affecting light areas. Similarly, painting with white in overlay mode makes light areas lighter without affecting dark areas. This is ideal when working with the grayscale pixels in an alpha channel.

To Create an Alpha Channel from Scratch

Sometimes it is easier to create a selection completely with the Brush Tool rather than create a rough selection first. To do this, you should start with a new alpha channel to avoid painting directly on an existing color channel, which would permanently change the image's color information. The following step creates a new alpha channel that will contain information for the tiger's head.

- Double-click the Hand Tool on the Tools panel to zoom out so you can see the entire image.

- Click the visibility icons on the Green Turtle and Red channels to hide them.

- Click the Blue channel thumbnail to select the Blue channel, because it provides the most contrast between the tiger and its background.

- Right-click the Blue channel and choose Duplicate Channel from the context menu to display the Duplicate Channel dialog box.

Figure 7–14

- In the As text box, type `Tiger Head` as the channel name, and then click the OK button to close the Duplicate Channel dialog box.

- Display the Tiger Head channel and hide the visibility icon for the Blue channel (Figure 7–14).

To Make a Selection in Brush Overlay Mode

The following steps use the Brush Tool's overlay mode to isolate the tiger's head, mask out the background, and retain the fine wisps of hair. Using a soft edge retains the details of the hair.

- Click the Zoom Tool on the Tools panel, point to the tiger's head, and then drag from top-left to bottom-right to zoom in on it.

- Click the Brush Tool in the Tools panel.

- In the Options bar, click the Mode menu and select Overlay.

- Click the Brush Preset picker button to open the Brush Preset picker.

- Double-click the value in the Size box and type 70 to set the brush size to 70 px, then double-click the value in the Hardness box and type 0 , if necessary, to create a brush tip with a feathered edge (Figure 7–15).

- Click the Brush Preset picker button again to close the Brush Preset picker.

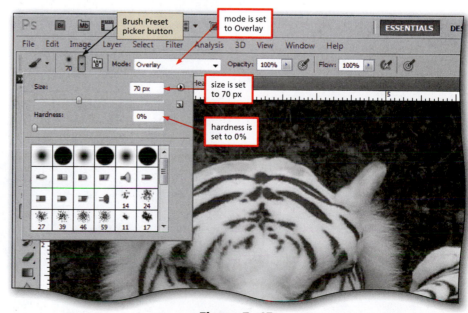

Figure 7–15

2

- If necessary, press the D key to reset the foreground/background colors so white is the foreground color.

- Point to the center of the left ear, then drag to begin to paint the ear white. As you paint, drag slightly outside the ear so the brush paints a little on the grass background. Continue until the ear is completely white (Figure 7–16).

Q&A

Why is the grass not turning white like the ear?

In overlay mode, light areas (like the ear) turn white when painted with white, but darker areas (like the grass) remain relatively unaffected.

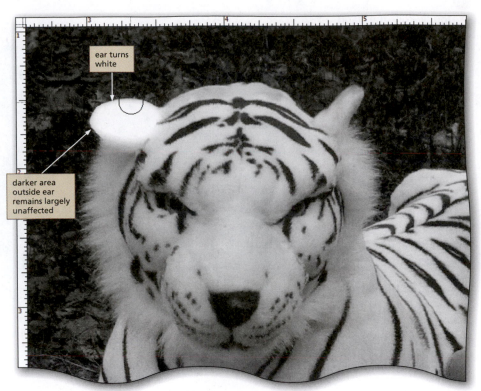

Figure 7–16

3

- Continue painting with white around the tiger's head. Be very careful to stay inside the edges of the mane (Figure 7–17).

Figure 7–17

4

- Press the x key to reverse the colors and set the foreground color to black.

- Drag the mouse pointer over the grassy background around the tiger to paint it black. Because you are in overlay mode, painting on the white parts will not affect them (Figure 7–18).

Figure 7–18

5

- Click any spots in the grass that did not turn black to include them (Figure 7–19).

Figure 7–19

- Continue dragging or clicking around the tiger's head, switching between the black and white brush colors as necessary, until you have isolated the edges of the head from the background. Do not worry about making the tiger's face white or the entire background black (Figure 7–20).

areas around mane are slightly gray and blurry

outline of tiger's head is clearly defined

Figure 7–20

To Fine-Tune the Selection

The goal is to create a channel that can be used as a mask, so the areas you want to hide must be completely black and the areas you want to keep visible must be completely white. Brush overlay mode does a great job at defining the edges of a difficult selection. For larger selections, such as the tiger's face and the rest of the grassy background, you can use simple selection tools to fill in the rest of the channel. The next steps fill in the rest of the channel, creating a black and white channel that can be used as a mask.

- Click the Lasso Tool on the Tools panel and draw a selection around the inside of the tiger's face. Be sure to stay within the solid white areas you defined in the previous steps (Figure 7–21).

selection around face

Figure 7–21

2

- Click Edit on the menu bar and then click Fill.

- Click the Use arrow to display the Use list, select White, and then click OK to fill the selection with white.

- Press CTRL+D to deselect the selection.

- Double-click the Hand Tool on the Tools panel to zoom out and view the entire image.

- Click the Brush Tool on the Tools panel to activate it.

- Click the Mode menu on the Options bar and set the mode back to Normal.

- Click the Brush Preset picker button on the Options bar to display the Brush Preset picker.

- Set the brush size to 400 px and the brush hardness to 100% (Figure 7–22).

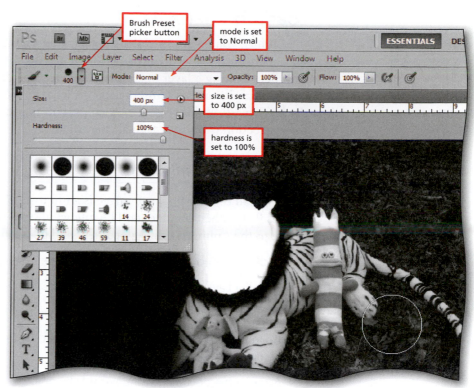

Figure 7–22

3

- Click the Brush Preset picker button to close the Brush Preset picker.

- If necessary, press the X key to change the foreground color to black.

- With black paint in normal mode, paint the rest of the background black, avoiding the white tiger head. You can increase the brush size to complete this step more quickly (Figure 7–23).

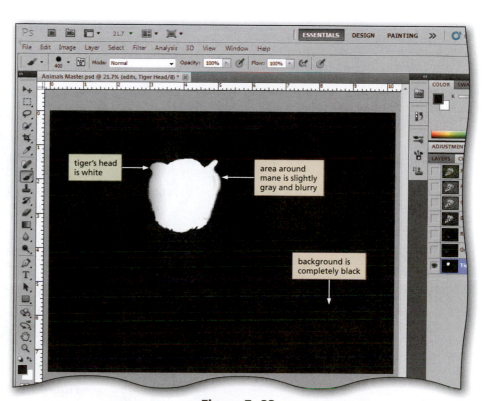

Figure 7–23

Loading Channels

Once you create an alpha channel, you can select it and use it to delete pixels, apply special effects, protect areas of a layer, or act as a mask. Loading a channel as a selection and then creating a layer mask from the selection allows you to edit and fine-tune the layer mask without affecting the original channel. This means you can experiment with the layer mask, and if you are not happy with the results, you can simply delete and load a fresh selection from the original channel.

To Create a Composite

Recall that a composite image is a Photoshop document that contains layers or images from other documents. The following steps copy a design frame from a second image to the Animals Master document and position it so the tiger's head shows through it.

1 Click the RGB channel in the Channels panel to hide and deselect the alpha channels.

2 Click the Layers tab to display the Layers panel.

3 Double-click the edits layer name and rename it, Tiger.

4 Open the Wild Things Frame file from the Chapter 07 folder of the Data Files for Students, or a location specified by your instructor.

5 Arrange the document windows side by side.

6 Drag the frame image from the Wild Things Frame window to the Animals Master document.

7 Close the Wild Things Frame document.

8 Use the Move Tool to position the frame over the tiger's head. The ears and chin should touch the inside of the circular frame (Figure 7–24).

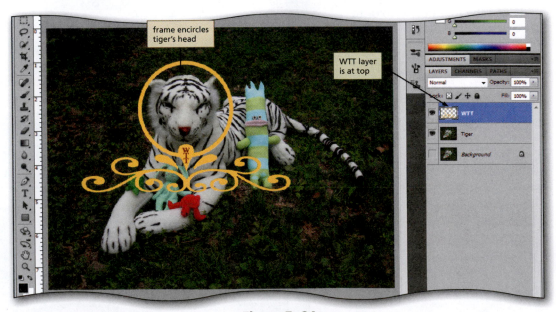

Figure 7–24

To Create a Layer Mask from an Alpha Channel

The following steps create a layer mask from a channel. The mask is used to hide the background so only the tiger's head shows through the frame.

- Click Select on the menu bar, and then click Load Selection to display the Load Selection dialog box.

- Click the Channel arrow to display the list, select Tiger Head to select the Tiger Head channel you created previously, and then click the OK button.

- Click the Tiger layer in the Layers panel to make it the active layer.

- Click the Add layer mask button to create a mask from the selection (Figure 7–25).

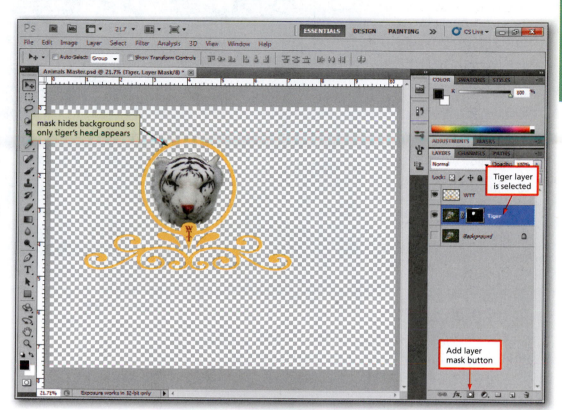

Figure 7–25

Q&A

What does the Load Selection dialog box do?

Loading a selection is the same process as making a selection, which you have previously done. Loading the channel as a selection selects the channel, displaying the dashed border visible around the tiger's head just as if you made a selection with a lasso tool.

2

- Right-click the Background layer and choose Duplicate Layer from the context menu to display the Duplicate Layer dialog box.

- In the As text box, type **Right Turtle** for the layer name, and then click the OK button to close the Duplicate Layer dialog box.

- Click the visibility icon on the Right Turtle layer to display it (Figure 7–26).

Q&A

Why do I see the background again?

The background was masked out on the Tiger layer, but the Right Turtle layer does not have anything masked and shows through the transparent areas of the Tiger layer.

Figure 7–26

3

- Click Select on the menu bar and select Load Selection.

- Click the Channel arrow to display its list, select the Red Turtle channel, and then click the OK button to load the channel as a selection.

- Click the 'Add layer mask' button to create a mask from the Red Turtle selection.

- Press the v key to activate the Move Tool, and then move the turtle to the right of the frame (Figure 7–27).

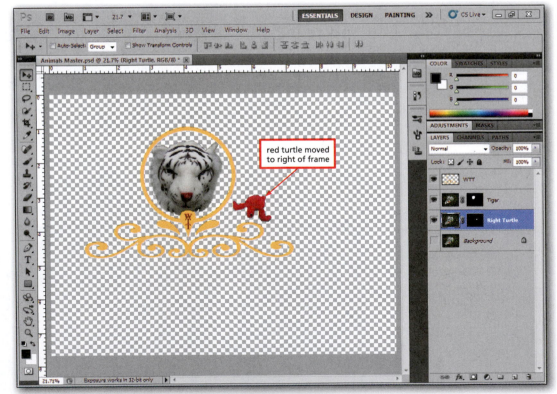

Figure 7–27

4

- Duplicate the Background layer again and name the new layer, Left Turtle.

- Click the visibility icon to turn the Left Turtle layer on.

- Click Select on the menu bar and then click Load Selection.

- Click the Channel arrow to display its list, select the Green Turtle channel, and click the OK button to load the channel as a selection.

Figure 7–28

- Click the Add a Layer Mask button to create a mask from the Green Turtle selection.

- Press the v key to activate the Move Tool if necessary, and then move the green turtle to the left of the frame (Figure 7–28).

To Add a Background and Crop

The transparent background created by the masks needs to be filled with a background for the advertisement. To reduce the background and emphasize the tiger image, you will crop the document to center the tiger. The following steps create a new layer and fill it with a texture.

1

- Click the Background layer to select it.

- Click the 'Create a new layer' button and name the new layer, Ad Background (Figure 7–29).

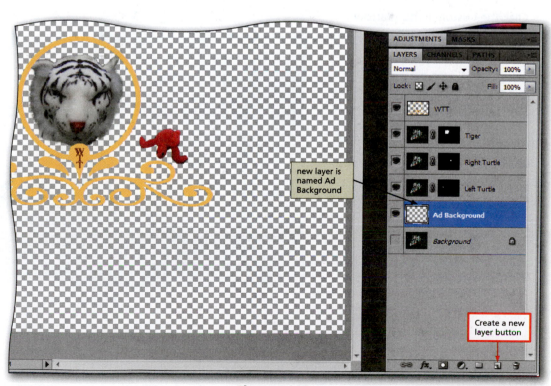

Figure 7–29

2

- Click Edit on the menu bar to display the Edit menu, and then click Fill to display the Fill dialog box.

- Click the Use arrow to display its list, and then click Pattern.

- Click the Custom Pattern arrow and then click the Custom Pattern options button to display the Custom Pattern menu (Figure 7–30).

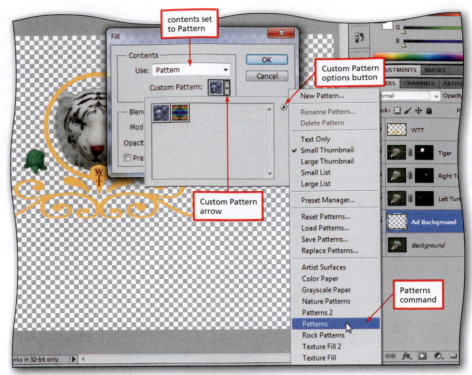

Figure 7–30

3

- Click Patterns and then click the OK button when prompted to replace the current patterns.

- Click the Custom Pattern arrow again to display the new thumbnails.

- Select the Woven pattern (the last one in the top row) and then click the OK button to close the Fill dialog box and apply the new background pattern (Figure 7–31).

Q&A

What am I replacing?

You are instructing Photoshop to no longer display the current patterns, and replace them with the patterns you have selected. This keeps the number of pattern thumbnails small. You will reset the patterns later in the chapter.

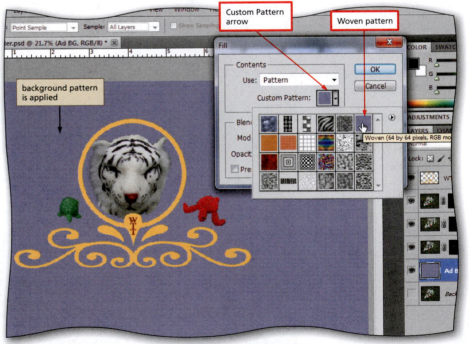

Figure 7–31

4

- Click the Crop Tool on the Tools panel.

- Drag from the top-left corner of the document and, using the rulers, create a crop area 8.25 inches wide by 5 inches tall (Figure 7–32).

Figure 7–32

5

- Press the ENTER key to apply the crop.

- Click Edit on the menu bar to display the Edit menu, click Fill, click the Use arrow to display its list, and then select Pattern.

- Click the Custom Pattern arrow and then click the Custom Pattern options menu button to display the Custom Pattern menu (Figure 7–33).

6

- Click Reset Patterns to reset the default pattern thumbnails.

- Click the OK button when prompted to reset the patterns.

- Click the Cancel button (Fill dialog box) without making any changes to the document.

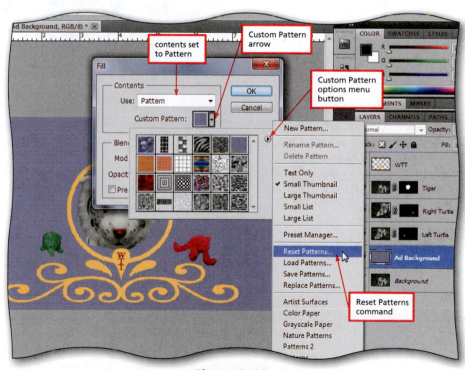

Figure 7–33

To Edit a Mask

When hiding areas of an image, it is better to use a mask than to erase pixels using one of the eraser tools because masks are non-destructive and allow you to restore pixels that may have been otherwise deleted. Recall that painting a mask with white allows pixels to show through. The following step makes a final adjustment to the tiger's head mask to remove the space beneath the tiger's head and redisplay some of the neck pixels.

1

- On the Layers panel, click the Tiger mask thumbnail, not the tiger thumbnail itself, to select it.

- On the Tools panel, activate the Brush Tool, and then press the x key to change the foreground color to white.

- Click the Brush Preset picker button on the options bar and change the size of your brush to 100.

- Click the Brush Preset picker button on the options bar again to close the Brush Preset picker.

- Carefully paint the area between the frame and the bottom of the tiger's head with white to allow those pixels to show through.

- If necessary, switch between black and white brushes to edit the mask further (Figure 7–34).

Q&A

I am not seeing the tiger's neck become visible. What should I do?

First verify you have selected the mask thumbnail and are painting on the mask. Second, check the options bar and confirm that the brush is in Normal mode and not Overlay mode.

bottom portion has been restored

Figure 7–34

Warped Text

Not only can text provide information for people to read, but it also can provide visual appeal and add interest to a design. Photoshop has tools that let you bend and warp text nondestructively. This means the text remains editable after it has been warped.

The advertisement for Wild Thing Toys needs the company name added in such a way as to provide information in addition to visual interest. The company name will be warped to follow the curvature of the frame and will be colored to match.

To Select a Text Color from the Image

The following steps sample a gold color from the frame to use as the text color.

- Select the Ad Background layer in the Layers panel.

- Press the T key to access the Horizontal Type Tool.

- In the options bar, click the 'Set the text color' button (Figure 7–35) to display the Set text color dialog box.

- If necessary, drag the dialog box out of the way so you can see some of the gold frame around the tiger.

- Click the gold color in the frame to set the text color to match the frame (Figure 7–35).

- Click the OK button ('Set text color' dialog box) to close the dialog box.

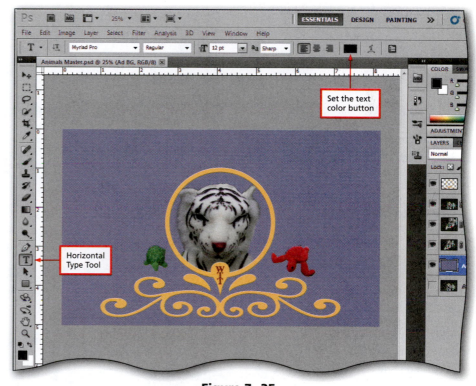

Figure 7–35

To Warp Text

One way to make your text eye-catching is to use the Warp Text dialog box. Photoshop has 15 different warp styles, each with adjustable settings, to create an endless number of possibilities for warped text. The steps on the next page create warped text for the advertisement.

1

- On the options bar, select the Algerian font or, if your computer does not have the Algerian font, choose an appropriate font for a wild animal themed toy store.

- Set the font size to 48 and click the 'Left align text' button, if necessary.

- Click in the top-left corner of the document to set the starting point for the text (Figure 7–36).

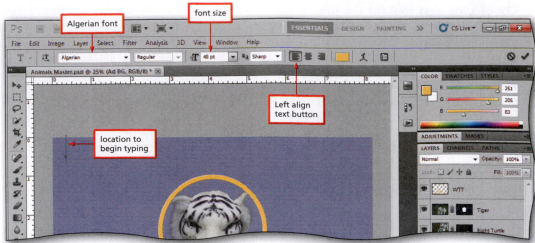

Figure 7–36

2

- Type **Wild Thing Toys**.

- On the options bar, click the 'Create warped text' button to display the Warp Text dialog box.

- Drag the dialog box title bar to move the dialog box to the side if necessary, so the text is fully visible.

- Click the Style box arrow (Warp Text dialog box) to display its list, and then click Arc to select a curved style.

- Drag the Bend slider to +100 to warp the text.

- In the document window, drag the text so it is centered above the circular frame.

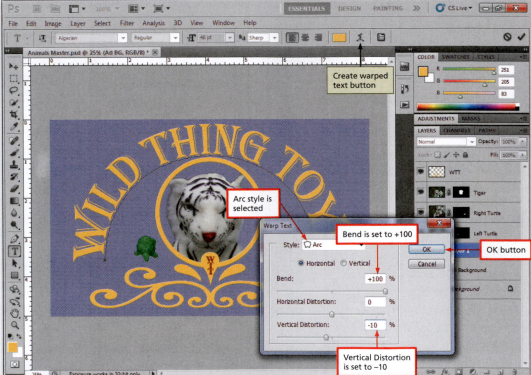

Figure 7–37

- Drag the Vertical Distortion slider (Warp Text dialog box) to –10 to increase the height of the letters (Figure 7–37).

 Q&A

Why is my text in all caps?

The Algerian font is an all caps font.

Experiment

- Drag the Horizontal Distortion and Vertical Distortion sliders to both the right and left, watching how they affect the text box. When finished, return Horizontal Distortion to 0 and Vertical Distortion to –10.

3

- Click the OK button (Warp Text dialog box).

- Click the 'Commit any current edits' button to commit the changes to the document (Figure 7–38).

Figure 7–38

- If necessary, use the Move Tool to reposition the text.

- Press CTRL+S to save the file.

To Merge and Save

The following steps merge the visible layers and then save the document with a new file name. Photoshop uses the name of the layer that was selected when the merge command was executed. Since the Wild Thing Toys type layer was selected when the merge command was executed, the new merged layer is named Wild Thing Toys.

1 Press SHIFT+CTRL+E to merge the visible layers into a single layer.

2 Click File on the menu bar and then click Save As to display the Save As dialog box.

3 Type **Animals Master merged** in the File name box and ensure the Format is set to Photoshop (*.PSD, *.PDD).

4 If necessary, browse to your storage location. Click the Save button to save the merged file.

5 If Photoshop displays a Photoshop Format Options dialog box, click OK.

> **Break Point:** If you wish to take a break, this is a good place to do so. You can quit Photoshop now. To resume at a later time, start Photoshop, open the file called Table Tent Card, and continue following the steps from this location forward.

Actions

An **action** is an automation task that stores a series of commands and keystrokes for repeated use later. For example, because of the large number of pixels generated by digital cameras, Photoshop typically imports those photos with very large document dimensions. If you use a digital camera often, you could save the resize process as an action. Then, each time you edit a photo from your camera, you could use a single command to play the action and perform the steps again. You can create your own actions, download sample actions from the Web, or use predefined actions that come with Photoshop.

An action is created in a manner similar to that of a tape or video recorder. The steps are recorded as they happen and then are saved in a location on your system. The next time you need it, the action can be loaded and played back. Action recording and playback steps are not recorded as states on the History panel. Actions are comparable to macros or functions in other software applications. Photoshop records nearly all commands and tools used in the Photoshop window; it will not record steps performed in other windows.

Actions might include **stops,** or places in the series of steps that pause during playback, waiting for the user to perform a task, such as choosing a brush size. Actions also might include **modal** controls that stop to let you enter values in a dialog box while playing an action. If there are no modal controls in an action, you can choose not to display the various dialog boxes. When you toggle modal controls off, the playback runs through the steps seamlessly, without any visible dialog boxes.

BTW

Droplets

The Droplet command automation feature converts an action into a standalone program with its own icon. Dragging a file icon onto the Droplet icon will start Photoshop and perform the action on the image. Droplets are cross-platform and transferable. Most graphic intensive publications — from yearbooks to church directories — use droplets to standardize size and resolution of photos.

BTW

Modal Icons

Each step in an action can have its own modality, which means that the action will stop at every dialog box. You might want the playback to stop at certain points to allow user decisions, while at other steps, you might want to mandate the settings. If an action set contains steps with mixed modalities, the modal icon beside the action set will be displayed in red. If all steps are modal, the modal icon will be displayed in black.

**Plan
Ahead**

Record actions for repetitive tasks.

If you or your client performs the same Photoshop tasks repeatedly, record the keystrokes for quick playback using an action. When creating and saving an action, the general work-flow is as follows:

1. Practice the action and write down the steps.

2. Create a new action set, or select one you have previously created.

3. Create a new action, giving it a name and keyboard shortcut.

4. Click the Record button.

5. Carefully proceed through the steps of your task.

6. Click the Stop button.

7. Turn on dialog boxes and then edit stop points as necessary.

8. Save the set as an atn file for use in other documents.

If you make a mistake while recording the action, the best solution may be to stop the recording and begin again. If you decide to edit an action, you can double-click an individual step in the Actions panel and then change its settings. To omit a recorded step during playback, click the Toggle item on/off box in the left column of the Actions panel.

BTW

Photoshop Actions
Many Photoshop actions use a beginning step of making a snapshot in the History panel. That way, you can see what the image looked like before the changes were made.

BTW

Actions with Prerequisites
If you see parentheses after the action name, the action only works at certain times. For example, if the word, Type, is in parentheses, you must have a text box selected. If the word, Selection, is in parentheses, the action will work only if you have a current selection marquee.

The Actions Panel

The Actions panel helps you manage actions you have created and those predefined actions that come with Photoshop (Figure 7–39). Each time you create a new action, it is added to the panel. An **action set** is an organizational folder that includes multiple actions, and can be opened or expanded by clicking the triangle to the left of the action set.

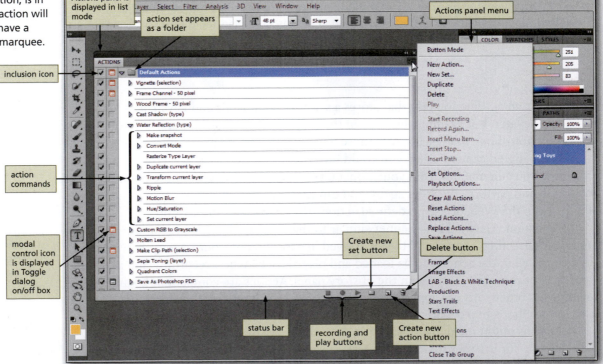

Figure 7–39

In Figure 7–39, the Default Actions set is expanded to display the predefined actions. The Water Reflection action is expanded to display the individual commands. On the left, a column of check marks indicates each command's inclusion in the action. Photoshop allows you to exclude specific commands during playback if you wish. The second column indicates whether the action is modal. Enabling the modal control creates an action generic enough to work with any image, pausing to allow the user to make adjustments. To enable modal controls, click the Toggle dialog on/off box on the Actions panel. On the panel's status bar are tape recorder-style buttons for stop, record, and play, as well as buttons to create sets and actions. The Actions panel menu displays commands to manage actions, set options, and load new sets of predefined actions. Action sets can be saved independently for use in other images. A saved action displays a file extension of atn. In the Save Action dialog box, Photoshop opens the folder where it stores other atn files by default.

The Actions panel can be displayed in two modes. The list mode, shown in Figure 7–39, allows you to make more choices about selecting, editing, playing, and managing your actions. The button mode, shown in Figure 7–40, is used for quick playbacks. To switch modes, choose the command from the Actions panel menu.

BTW

Organizing Actions
You can organize sets of actions for different types of work, such as online publishing or print publishing, and then transfer sets to other computers. Normally, user-defined action sets are stored with the file in which they are created. You can save your sets and actions to a separate actions file, however, so you can recover them if the file in which they were created is destroyed.

Figure 7–40

To Display the Actions Panel

The following step displays the Actions panel.

1
- Click Window on the menu bar and then click Actions to display the Actions panel (Figure 7–41).

Figure 7–41

To Append Action Sets

The Actions menu contains a default set that provides 12 different actions. In addition to the Default Actions set, seven other sets are available on the panel menu. In the following steps, you will append one of those sets to the list in the Actions panel.

1
- Click the Actions panel menu button to display the menu (Figure 7–42).

Q&A
What does the Load Actions command do?

It opens a dialog box so you can navigate to the location of an action set. Any actions or action sets not saved previously with the image must be loaded.

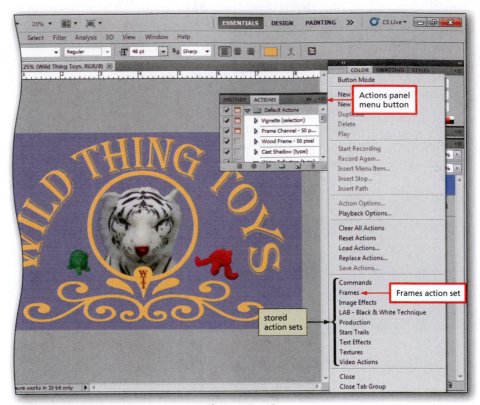

Figure 7–42

2
- Click Frames to select the action set.

- Scroll in the panel to display the Frames set, and then click the Brushed Aluminum Frame action to select it (Figure 7–43).

Figure 7–43

To Play an Action

To play an action, you click the Play selection button on the Actions panel status bar. In the step that follows, the Brushed Aluminum Frame action is played to create a picture frame around the advertisement. Later in this chapter, you will create a custom action.

- Point to the Play selection button on the Actions panel status bar (Figure 7–44).

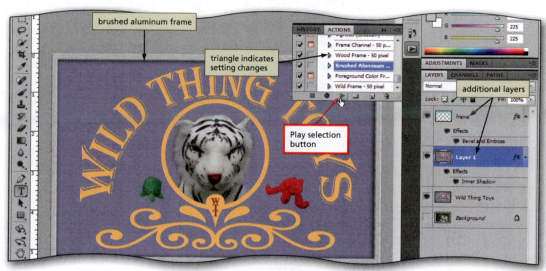

Figure 7–44

- Click the Play selection button to play the action (Figure 7–45).

- Click the Continue button (Message dialog box) to apply the action.

Q&A What are the right-pointing triangles on the Actions panel?

If you click a right-pointing triangle, Photoshop displays the steps taken in the action.

Figure 7–45

To Merge and Save the Document Again

The advertisement is complete. The next steps merge layers and save the file.

1 Press CTRL+SHIFT+E to merge the visible layers.

2 In the Layers panel, double-click the new merged layer's name, type `Wild Thing Toys` to rename the layer, and then press the ENTER key to apply the name change.

3 Press CTRL+S to save the file again. If Photoshop displays a dialog box, click the OK button.

BTW

Storing Actions
On most systems, the location of stored actions is C:\Program Files\Adobe\ Adobe Photoshop CS5\ Presets\Actions. If you are working in a lab setting, however, you should browse to your storage device in the Save Action dialog box and then save your action set.

To Create a New Action Set

The following step creates a new action set named Personal Actions in the Animals Master file. Saving your actions in a new action set keeps them separate from the built-in actions included in Photoshop.

1
- On the Actions panel status bar, click the 'Create new set' button to display the New Set dialog box.

- Type **Wild Thing Actions** in the Name text box to name the action set (Figure 7–46).

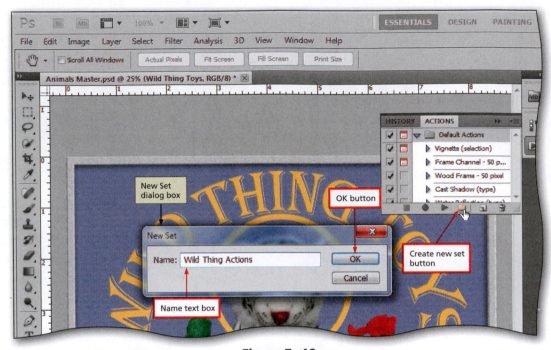

Figure 7–46

2
- Click the OK button (New Set dialog box) to create the action and add it to the Actions panel (Figure 7–47).

Figure 7–47

Other Ways
1. On Actions panel menu, click New Set

To Create a New Action

When you click the 'Create new action' button, the New Action dialog box is displayed. The New Action dialog box allows you to name the action, position it within a set, assign a function key, and choose a display color for the action in the panel. After editing the settings, the Record button begins the process. The following step creates a new action called Colored Pencil Thumbnail that applies a colored pencil special effect to the image.

- On the Actions panel status bar, click the 'Create new action' button to display the New Action dialog box.

- Type **Colored Pencil Thumbnail** in the Name text box to name the action.

- Click the Function Key box arrow and then click F11 in the list to assign a function key to the action.

- Click the Color box arrow and then click Red in the list to assign a color to the new action (Figure 7–48).

Figure 7–48

To Record an Action

The next steps record an action that applies the Colored Pencil artistic filter and reduces the size of the document to 300 px wide. This is an appropriate size to include on a Web page or to use for e-mailing a client a sample of the artwork.

- In the New Action dialog box, click the Begin recording button to close the dialog box and begin recording keystrokes (Figure 7–49).

Figure 7–49

- Press the D key to reset the default colors in preparation for the filter.

- Click Filter on the menu bar to display the Filter menu, point to the Artistic category, and then point to Colored Pencil (Figure 7–50).

- Click Colored Pencil to display the Colored Pencil dialog box and record the first step of the action.

Figure 7–50

3

- Click the OK button (Colored Pencil dialog box) to accept the default settings of the filter and apply the Colored Pencil filter.

- Click Image on the menu bar to display the Image menu.

- Click Image Size to display the Image Size dialog box.

- Ensure that the Scale Styles, Constrain Proportions, and Resample Image check boxes are all checked.

- Ensure the units are set to pixels.

- Type 300 in the Width box to set the new width to 300 pixels (Figure 7–51).

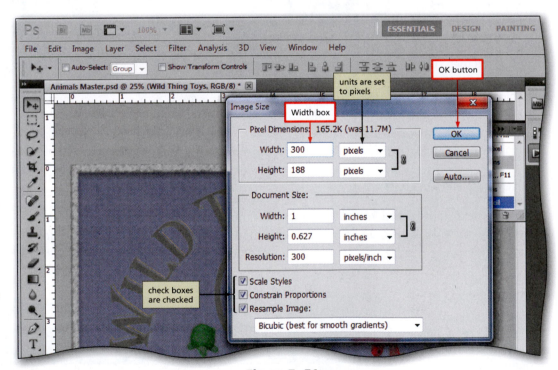

Figure 7–51

- Click the OK button to resize the image and close the Image Size dialog box.

Q&A | Why did the image get so small? It looks much smaller than 300 pixels.

The Image was resized to 300 pixels wide, but probably looks a lot smaller on your screen because you are not viewing it at 100%.

4

- Double-click the Zoom Tool at the bottom of the Tools panel to display the document at 100 percent.

What if I make a mistake while recording an action?

If you click inadvertently while creating an action, you can press CTRL+Z to cancel the recording and then start over.

- Click the 'Stop playing/recording' button to stop the recording (Figure 7–52).

Other Ways

1. On Actions panel menu, click Start/Stop Recording

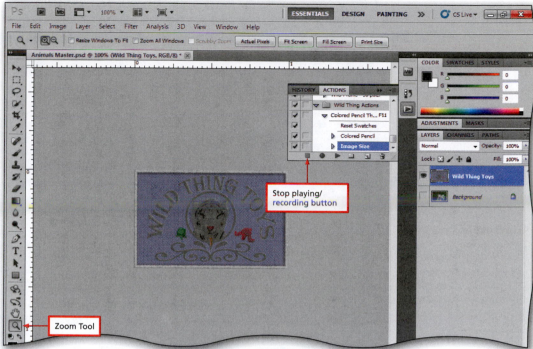

Stop playing/
recording button

Zoom Tool

Figure 7–52

To Save the File in the JPEG Format

The following steps save a copy of the altered file in a format appropriate for sharing with a client by e-mail. The file is then reverted back to its original state.

1 With your USB flash drive connected to one of the computer's USB ports, click File on the menu bar to display the File menu.

2 Click Save As to display the Save As dialog box.

3 When the Save As dialog box is displayed, click the Save in box arrow and then click UDISK 2.0 (F:), or the location associated with your USB flash drive, in the list.

4 Type `Wild Thing Sample` in the File name text box.

5 Click the Format menu and select JPEG (*.JPG, *.JPEG, *.JPE) from the list of options.

6 Click the Save button to save the document as a JPEG file (Figure 7–53) on the next page.

7 Click the OK button to accept the default settings in the JPEG Options dialog box.

8 Press the F12 key to revert the document to its last saved state and undo all the changes made by the action.

9 Double-click the Hand Tool at the bottom of the Tools panel to zoom out so you can see the entire document.

BTW

Creating Actions
You must be careful when you record actions that involve selecting a named layer. When you play back the action in a different file, Photoshop will look for that layer. If the named layer does not exist in the file, the action will not function correctly.

BTW

Editing Actions
Other edits that you can perform on the recorded steps include deselecting some check boxes, dragging a command to the Delete button on the status bar to remove it permanently, and setting playback options on the Actions panel menu.

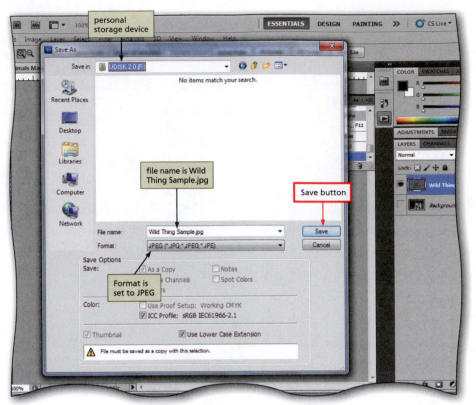

Figure 7–53

To Test the Action

To test the action, the following steps open a new file and then play back the action using the function key to confirm that it works.

- Open the file called Test Action from the Chapter 07 folder of the Data Files for Students, or a location specified by your instructor.

- Press the F11 key to play the action and apply the effect (Figure 7–54).

- Close the Test Action file.

- Click the No button to confirm closing the file without saving any changes.

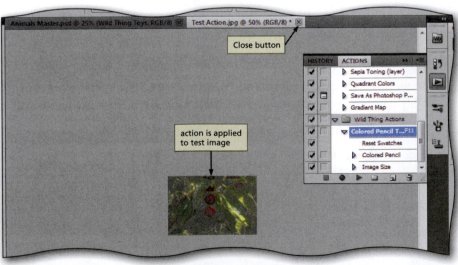

Figure 7–54

To Save an Action Set

The following steps save a new action set using the Actions panel menu.

- On the Actions panel, click the Wild Thing Actions set.

- Click the Actions panel menu button to display the menu (Figure 7–55).

Figure 7–55

- With your USB flash drive connected to one of the computer's USB ports, click Save Actions to display the Save dialog box.

- Click the Save in box arrow and then click UDISK 2.0 (F:), or the location associated with your USB flash drive, in the list (Figure 7–56).

Q&A

Could I save the action set in the Actions folder with the installed Photoshop actions?

Yes; however, saving on a personal storage device keeps lab installation actions unchanged for other students.

- Click the Save button to save the Action Set.

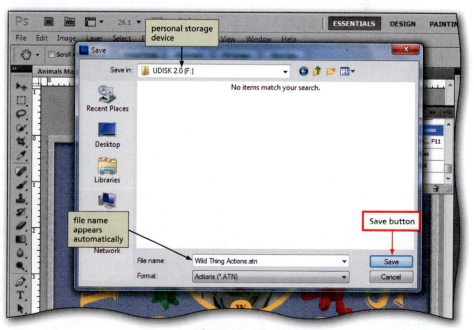

Figure 7–56

Color Toning and Conversions

Color toning is the process of changing or intensifying the color of a photograph after it has been processed by the camera. In traditional photography, toning was a darkroom technique that changed the black colors in a black-and-white photograph to a chosen color, such as sepia or blue. In digital photography, toning includes a variety of techniques, including converting to black and white, creating duotones or split tones, and adding tints.

Many of the color toning adjustments are located on the Adjustments panel, but some are available only through the menu system. Most of the tools work in the same way — they map or plot an existing range of pixel values to a new range of values. The main difference is the amount of control each tool provides. For example, the various color adjustment commands on the Image menu alter the pixels in the current layer. Another way to adjust color is to use an adjustment layer created using the Layer menu. This approach allows you to experiment with color and tonal adjustments first, before committing them to the image. Using an adjustment layer adds to the file size of the image, however; it also demands more random access memory (RAM) from your computer. Another way to access adjustments is to use the New Adjustment Layer submenu on the Layers menu. The difference is that when you access the settings using the menu system, Photoshop opens a dialog box allowing you to name and color the layer as you create it. You fine-tune the settings using the Adjustments panel either way.

Table 7–1 displays color adjustment commands that are not located on the Adjustments panel and therefore must be accessed through the menu system.

Table 7–1 Menu-Only Adjustment Commands

Command	Purpose	Menu Access
Desaturate	produces a grayscale image but leaves the image in the same color mode	Image | Adjustments
Equalize	redistributes the brightness values of all pixels so they represent the entire range of brightness levels more evenly	Image | Adjustments
Match Color	matches the color across selections, layers, or photos as well as adjusts luminance, color range, and color casts in an image	Image | Adjustments
Replace Color	replaces specified colors in an image with new color values	Image | Adjustments
Shadows/ Highlights	lightens or darkens based on surrounding pixels to correct photos with strong backlighting or other lighting errors	Image | Adjustments
Variations	adjusts the color balance, contrast, and saturation of an image using thumbnail samples	Image | Adjustments

BTW

Converting to Black and White
Another way to change to black and white is by converting the image to the LAB Color mode, creating a layer from the Lightness channel. Creating layers from channels offers you more control over contrast than some other conversion methods. It also offers you the flexibility of being able to change aspects of the conversion at any time in the future. Many design professionals prefer to use channels when converting to black and white because it permits precise control of shades, levels, and the conversion process.

Black and White

Recall that converting a color image to the Grayscale mode on the Image Mode submenu is one way to discard color information from the pixels in the image. If you change the color mode to LAB Color, a Lightness channel also creates a black-and-white image. Several settings on the Adjustments panel can be used to create a black-and-white or grayscale image. Additionally, some graphic artists create two adjustments layers, one for black and one for white, to emulate the film and filter process of traditional photography.

First, you will use the Desaturate command to view the image in grayscale; then, you will undo and use the Black & White settings on the Adjustments panel.

To Desaturate

The following steps use the Desaturate command on the Adjustments submenu to produce a grayscale image for use in black and white advertising or for use as on letterhead printed on a noncolor printer.

1

- Click the top layer, Wild Thing Toys, to select it in the Layers panel if necessary.

- On the menu bar, click Image and then point to Adjustments to display the submenu (Figure 7–57).

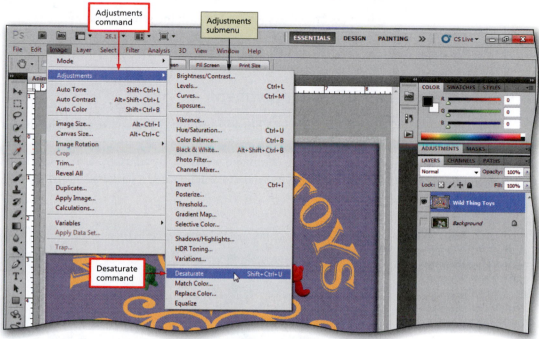

Figure 7–57

2

- Click Desaturate to produce a grayscale image (Figure 7–58).

Why can I no longer see the text?

The gold color of the text and the light blue background have similar luminosity levels. This means that without the color information they are almost identical. Desaturating the image removed all the color, resulting in poor contrast between the text and its background.

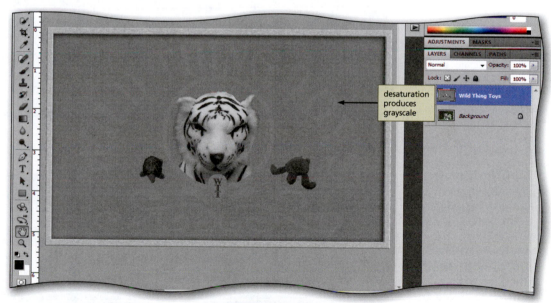

Figure 7–58

Other Ways
1. Press SHIFT+CTRL+U

To Undo the Desaturate Command and Save the File

While the Desaturate command is appropriate for technical illustrations or when you want to neutralize or de-emphasize a background, it leaves the image in the same color mode, usually rendering a flat, uninspiring version compared to other methods.

Additionally, it sometimes reduces the contrast between foreground and background objects making them difficult to see. Therefore, the following steps undo the Desaturate command and save the file.

1 Press CTRL+Z to undo the previous command.

2 Press CTRL+S to save the file with the same file name.

To Create a Black-and-White Adjustment

The Adjustments panel and its Black & White settings allow you to customize the shades of gray in the document window itself. By customizing the shades, you can create more diversity among the various shaded toys. For example, the text was almost invisible when the desaturate command was used. By adjusting a channel, the black-and-white version will appear with more variety. In the following steps, the text will be made a darker shade of gray.

1
• Click the Adjustments tab to display the Adjustments panel (Figure 7–59).

Figure 7–59

2
• Click the Black & White icon on the Adjustments panel to display the settings.

• In the Adjustments panel status bar, click the 'Clip to layer' button to create an adjustments layer.

• Click the 'Modify a slider' button to enable color changes in the document itself, and then move the mouse pointer into the document window and position it over an area of text, as shown in Figure 7–60.

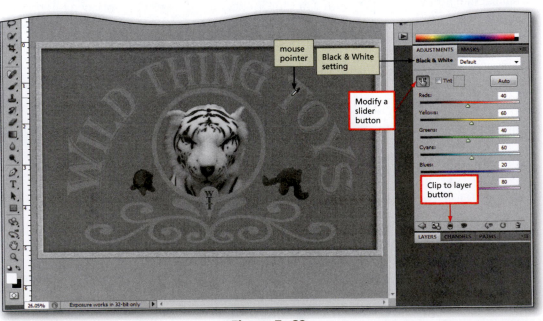

Figure 7–60

3

- In the document window, drag to the right to lighten the text and other areas of the frame (Figure 7–61).

Q&A Why did Photoshop change the yellow pixels?

Because you clicked the text (which was originally gold), Photoshop adjusts the darkness/lightness of all yellow pixels and darkens/lightens them as you drag.

Q&A Could I have used the sliders on the Adjustments panel to make the changes?

Yes, the sliders work the same way on the panel as they do in the document window.

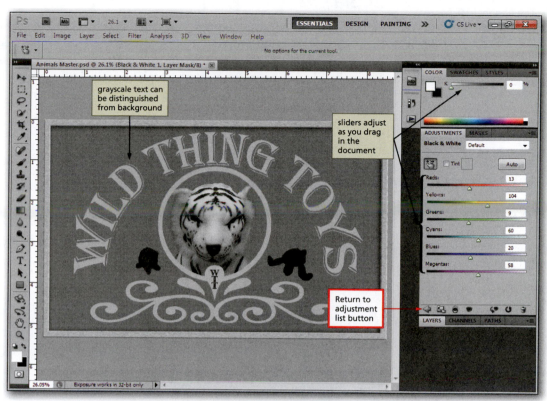

Figure 7–61

 Experiment

- Drag to the left to darken the text. Try dragging from either of the turtles to darken or lighten them. Continue dragging from the text and the turtles until you are satisfied with the changes.

4

- In the Adjustments panel status bar, click the 'Return to adjustment list' button to close the Black & White settings on the Adjustments panel.

Other Ways
1. On Image menu, point to Adjustments, click Black & White, change settings	2. On Layer menu, point to New Adjustment Layer, click Black & White, change settings	3. Press ALT+SHIFT+ CTRL+B, change settings

To Save the Black-and-White Image

The black-and-white image is complete. The next steps save the file.

1 Press SHIFT+CTRL+S to open the Save As dialog box.

2 Type `Wild Thing Black and White` to enter the file name.

3 Click the Save button to save the image. If Photoshop displays a dialog box, click the OK button.

The Channel Mixer
The Channel Mixer creates high-quality images by choosing the percentages from each color channel. It lends itself more toward artistic expression than for tasks related to simple restoration or technical graphics. Artists use the Channel Mixer to create a variety of tints, pastels, infrareds, and sepia tones.

Sepia

Sepia is a color toning technique resulting in a reddish-brown tint. Originally created through a pigmenting process for preservation of photos, it has become a popular kind of tinting to emulate older photos or for special effects. As with black-and-white conversions, Photoshop has many ways to create a sepia tone, including tints, channel mixing, selective coloring, filters, and processing raw data from a digital camera.

To Create a Sepia Image Using Selective Color

The following steps create a sepia version of the Animals Master ad using the Selective Color settings on the Adjustments panel.

1
• On the Adjustments panel, click the Selective Color icon to display its settings (Figure 7–62).

Figure 7–62

- Click the 'Clip to layer' button on the status bar to create an adjustment layer.

- Click the Colors box arrow to display its list (Figure 7–63).

Figure 7–63

- Click Neutrals to adjust the neutral colors in the image.

- Drag the Cyan slider to –53, drag the Magenta slider to –31, drag the Yellow slider to –18, and drag the Black slider to 49 until a warm brown color is attained (Figure 7–64).

Q&A

What do the Relative and Absolute option buttons do?

If you select the Relative option button, the percentage of change is multiplied by the current color. If you select the Absolute option button, the percentage of change is added to the current color.

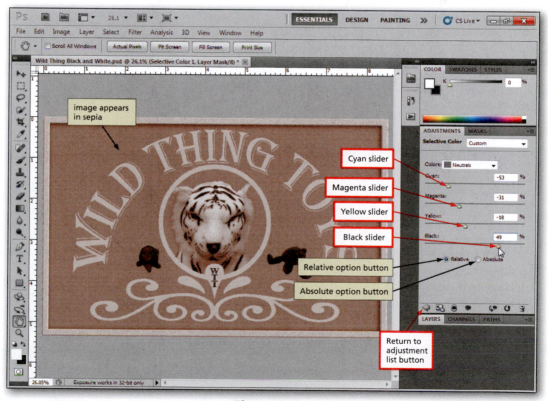

Figure 7–64

4

- In the Adjustments panel status bar, click the 'Return to adjustment list' button.

To Save the Sepia Image

The sepia image is complete. The next steps save the file.

1 Press SHIFT+CTRL+S to open the Save As dialog box.

2 Type `Wild Thing Sepia` as the file name.

3 Click the Save button to save the image. If Photoshop displays a dialog box, click the OK button.

Duotone

Duotone is a generic term for a variety of grayscale images printed with the addition of one, two, three, or four inks. In these images, colored inks, rather than different shades of gray, are used to reproduce tinted grays, increasing the tonal range of a grayscale image. Although a grayscale image displays up to 256 shades of gray, a printing press can reproduce only about 50 shades. For this reason, a grayscale image printed with only black ink can look significantly coarser than the same image on the screen. Printing with two, three, or four inks, each reproducing up to 50 levels of gray, produces an image with a slight tint and a wider dynamic range.

Because duotones affect only the gray levels, they contain only one channel; however, you can manipulate a wide range of tint using the Duotone Options dialog box.

To Convert an Image to Duotone

Because duotone requires a completely grayscale image, you will convert the current image to grayscale and then to duotone.

1

- On the Image menu, point to Mode and then click Grayscale.

- When Photoshop asks to discard adjustment layers, click the OK button.

- When Photoshop asks to discard color information, click the Discard button to accept the change (Figure 7–65).

image appears in grayscale

Figure 7–65

2

• On the Image menu, point to Mode and then click Duotone to display the Duotone Options dialog box. Click the Preview check box to preview the image, if necessary.

• Drag the title bar of the dialog box up and to the right to display more of the image (Figure 7–66).

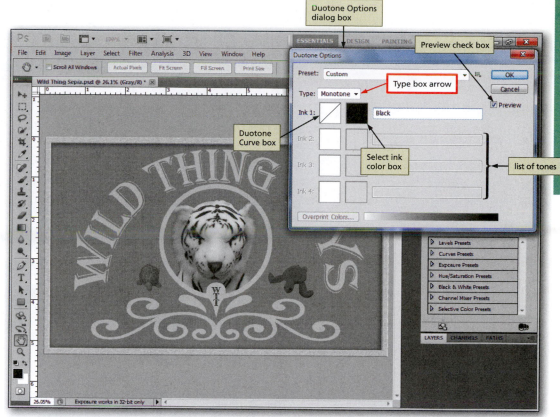

Figure 7–66

3

• Click the Type box arrow to display its list (Figure 7–67).

Q&A

What do the two boxes in front of the Black tone represent?

The first box is the curve that indicates how the color is spread across the image. The second box is the color itself. Clicking either box allows you to adjust the settings.

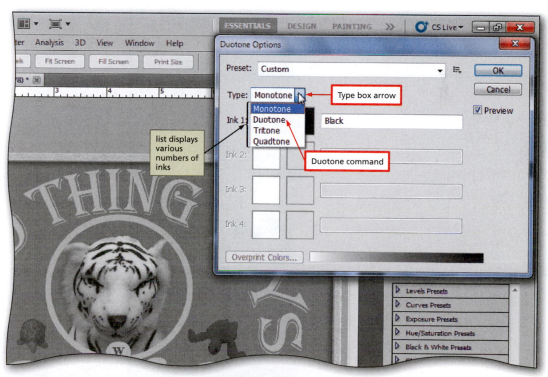

Figure 7–67

4

- Click Duotone to add one color to the original black (Figure 7–68).

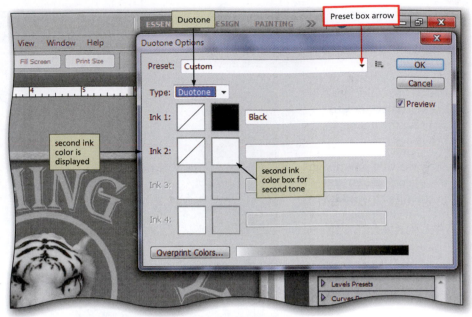

Figure 7–68

5

- To specify the second color, click the Preset box arrow to display its list (Figure 7–69).

Q&A

Could I just choose the color using the 'Select an ink' color box?

Yes, but the Preset box list includes standard colors that print shops and service bureaus can match easily.

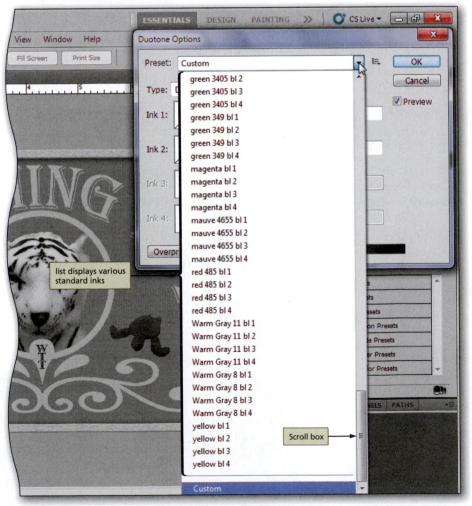

Figure 7–69

6

- Scroll as necessary and then click cyan bl 1 to select a blue duotone (Figure 7–70).

7

- Click the OK button (Duotone Options dialog box).

Figure 7–70

To Save the Duotone Image

The duotone image is complete. The next steps save the file.

1 Press SHIFT+CTRL+S to open the Save As dialog box.

2 Type **Wild Thing Duotone** to enter the file name.

3 Click the Save button to save the image. If Photoshop displays a dialog box, click the OK button.

To Close the Converted File and Reopen the Original File

You now have created color, black-and-white, sepia, and duotone versions of the Wild Thing Toys ad. Because you are finished with the color conversions, you will close the duotone file and open the original file in the following steps.

1 Click the Close button on the Wild Thing Duotone document window tab.

2 Open the Animals Master file from the Chapter 07 folder of the Data Files for Students, or a location specified by your instructor.

Break Point: If you wish to take a break, this is a good place to do so. You can quit Photoshop now. To resume at a later time, start Photoshop, open the file called Table Tent Card, and continue following the steps from this location forward.

Preparing for Four-Color Processing

Most digital cameras create an RGB file. While that is fine for online viewing and Web graphics, many traditional full-color printing presses can print only four colors: cyan, magenta, yellow, and black (CMYK). Other colors in the spectrum are simulated using various combinations of those colors. When you plan to print a photo professionally, you may have to convert it from one color model to the other. The tiger image was taken with a digital camera and uses the RGB color model. Wild Thing Toys wants a professional

BTW

Color Models vs. Color Modes
A color model is a numeric representation of the colors in digital images. A color mode determines which color model is used to display and print the image. A mode is based on a model.

color print of the advertisement. The service bureau that will print the ad uses the Trumatch 4-color matching system, which requires the CMYK color model.

Photoshop allows you to convert directly from RGB to CMYK; however, using the intermediary LAB color mode gives you more flexibility in color changes and contrast.

Using LAB Color

LAB Color is an internationally accepted color mode that defines colors mathematically using a lightness or luminance setting, and two color or chromatic channels — an A-axis color for colors from magenta to green, and a B-axis color for colors from yellow to blue. The LAB Color mode, which tries to emulate the colors viewable by the human eye, incorporates all the colors in the RGB and CMYK color spectrums, and often is used as an intermediary when converting from one format to another.

In Figure 7–71, the LAB color space is represented by the color spectrum. The black outline represents RGB's color space. The white outline represents CMYK's color space. RGB and CMYK are subsets, but they also are slanted in the color spectrum. For example, when converting from RGB to CMYK, you lose some of the blue's intensity but gain yellow. Reds and greens are better in RGB; cyans (blues) and magentas are better in CMYK, as you would suspect. Contrast, a result of how bright the white is and how dark the black is, is represented poorly in CMYK. The printer cannot make white any brighter than the paper on which it is printed. A solid black does not exist in CMYK on a display monitor. Therefore, when adjusting color and contrast during a conversion, it is appropriate to convert it to LAB Color, make your adjustments, and then convert it to CMYK.

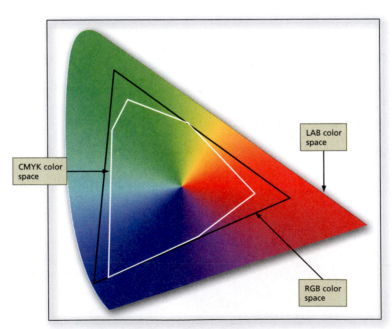

Figure 7–71

The LAB Color mode calculates each color description, rather than generating it from a combination, as is the case for RGB. Because RGB colors are combinations of colors, they may look different on different devices. For example, a row of televisions in a department store displaying the same program will look different because different television manufacturers combine red, green, and blue in slightly different ways. Working with LAB colors usually provides colors that are more consistent across platforms.

The LAB Color mode is independent of the type of device or media, and may be used for either display or printing. Many photo CD images use LAB colors where the luminance and color values are edited independently.

To Convert to LAB Color

The LAB Color mode will be used in the conversion process for the advertisement. Converting to LAB color rasterizes or changes vector-based text layers to pixel based images. The conversion process also merges the layers. The following step converts to LAB color.

1

- Click Image on the menu bar, point to Mode, and then click Lab Color to begin the conversion (Figure 7–72).

- When Photoshop displays a message about merging layers, click the Merge button.

Figure 7–72

To Convert to CMYK

Converting the file to CMYK allows you to make size, color, and tonal changes before printing. The following step converts to CMYK.

1 Click Image on the menu bar, point to Mode, and then click CMYK Color to convert the image to CMYK. If Photoshop displays a dialog box, click the OK button.

To Save the Advertisement

After the conversion to LAB and the conversion to CMYK, it is a good idea to save the file again.

1 Press CTRL+SHIFT+S to save the file.

2 Type **Wild Thing CMYK** to enter the file name.

3 Click the Save button to save the image. If Photoshop displays a dialog box, click the OK button.

BTW

Quick Reference
For a table that lists how to complete the tasks covered in this book using the mouse, shortcut menu, and keyboard, see the Quick Reference Summary at the back of this book or visit the Photoshop CS5 Quick Reference Web page (scsite.com/pscs5/qr).

Resizing, Resampling, and Interpolation

BTW

Resampling
In the General Preferences dialog box, you can specify which default interpolation method to use whenever you resample images using the Image Size or transformation commands. The Image Size command also lets you specify an interpolation method other than the default.

Recall that you used the Image Size dialog box to resize an image earlier in this chapter. Resizing an image can reduce the image quality. For example, when you resize an image to larger dimensions, the image may lose some detail and sharpness because Photoshop has to add or stretch pixels. When you make an image smaller, some pixels must be reduced or discarded and cannot be recovered once the image is saved. That is why you should always work with a copy of the original image, in case you do not like the changes.

Changing the document size, or physical size, of photos is one of the most common tasks in digital imagery, as is changing the file size, or number of required bytes to store the image.

Photoshop allows you to make the interpolation, resampling, and sizing changes yourself. Interpolation is the mathematical process of adding or subtracting pixels in an image, either to enlarge or reduce the size. Once the location of the interpolated pixels is determined, Photoshop uses a **resampling method** that assigns a new color value to pixels by taking a sample of the surrounding ones. Before you resample, however, it is important to check with your lab or service bureau, as some services automatically resample and resize at the time of printing. In those cases, retaining as much digital data as possible is the best choice. On the other hand, if a digital image must have a specific resolution and a specific size, then resampling may be warranted.

If you **downsample**, or decrease the number of pixels, information is deleted from the image. Downsampling reduces image data by representing a group of pixels with a single pixel. For instance, if an image needs to be reduced by 50 percent, Photoshop will have to destroy half of the pixels. If during the destruction, black-and-white pixels come next to each other, both pixels are changed using a complex calculation to produce a smoother tonal gradation of gray. The disadvantage of downsampling is the loss of data, or **lossiness**.

If you **upsample**, or increase the number of pixels, Photoshop assigns a new color to the added pixels based on an average interpolation. For example, if an image needs to be enlarged, the interpolation notes where a new pixel should be added. If that new pixel falls at the edge of a yellow insignia on a red sweater, the new pixel would be orange. Photoshop samples the two colors and averages the color values. At the pixel level, it would be hard to notice orange in the finished product; but it is something to keep in mind when upsampling. Remember that Photoshop cannot insert detailed information that was not captured from the original image. Photos will start to look softer, with less detail, as they are enlarged.

Table 7–2 lists the five interpolation methods offered by Photoshop; however, other interpolation methods can be downloaded from the Web.

Table 7–2 Photoshop Interpolation Methods	
Interpolation Method	**Description**
Bicubic (best for smooth gradients)	a slow, but precise, interpolation method based on an examination of the values of surrounding pixels — applies more complex calculations to produce smoother tonal gradations
Bicubic Sharper (best for reduction)	a bicubic interpolation method that works well for reducing images with enhanced sharpening while maintaining details
Bicubic Smoother (best for enlargement)	an interpolation method that works well for enlarging images with smoother results than bicubic alone
Bilinear	an interpolation method that produces medium-quality results by averaging the color values to produce new pixels
Nearest Neighbor (preserve hard edges)	a fast interpolation method that produces a smaller file size but may become jagged when scaling as it tries to preserve hard edges

No matter what resampling method you choose, it may introduce artifacts, or changed pixels, that do not look good and were not in the original image. Blurs or halos may be introduced. Jagged edges may appear when upsampling, and moiré patterns may appear when downsampling. A **moiré pattern** is an alternating of blurred and clear areas, forming thin stripes or dots on the screen. Table 7–3 describes some of the problems.

Table 7–3 Resampling Problems

Problem	Description	Possible Solution	Sample
Aliasing	jagged edges or moiré patterns	Set anti-aliasing options (during down-scaling)	
Blur	a loss of image sharpness, more visible at higher magnifications	Use the Unsharp Mask filter	
Halos	appears as a halo around edges — while a small amount may improve the perceived sharpness, a high amount does not look good	Use Defringe matting	

The Image Size Dialog Box

Recall that Photoshop uses the Image Size dialog box to make choices about the number of pixels, the document size, and the resampling method. Each setting in the Image Size dialog box makes a difference in the resulting type of file and document. Table 7–4 displays the settings and their effects. When resampling, pixels are added or subtracted during resizing. Without resampling, you are stretching or compressing the existing pixels by changing the resolution.

Table 7–4 Image Size Dialog Box Settings

Setting	Unit Of Measurement	Effect With Resampling	Effect Without Resampling
Pixel Dimensions	percent or pixels	The document size is adjusted in proportion to pixel dimensions, but the resolution does not change.	The pixel dimensions remain the same, but the resolution value changes to represent what the image can provide at that size.
Document Size	percent, inches, centimeters, millimeters, points, picas, or columns	The pixels are adjusted in proportion to document size, but the resolution does not change.	The pixel dimensions remain the same, but the resolution value changes to represent what the image can provide at that size.
Resolution	pixels per inch or pixels per centimeter	The pixel dimensions change and the document size remains the same.	The document size changes and the pixel dimensions remain the same.

If you make changes in the Image Size dialog box and wish to go back to the original dimensions or resolution, press and hold the ALT key before closing the dialog box. The Cancel button will change to a Reset button.

To Resize a File with Resampling

The current dimensions of the Wild Thing CMYK image are approximately 8.5 inches wide by 5.3 inches tall. The advertisement for the insert should be a half-page ad measuring approximately 5.5 inches wide. In addition, the printing service has specified a file resolution of 300 pixels per inch for best print results. The steps on the next page resize the file with resampling, which means the pixels will be downsampled using the Bicubic Sharper method because it works well for reducing images while maintaining details.

BTW

JPEG Artifacts
Sometimes, when converting from RGB to LAB color, a JPEG image will leave behind some small blotches of irregular color, called **artifacts,** because of the compression method involved. Sharpening the image will remove those kinds of artifacts.

BTW

Adjusting LAB Colors
Other adjustments that can be performed on the intermediary LAB color include filtering out noise.

- Click Image on the menu bar, and then click Image Size to display the Image Size dialog box.

- Click the Resample Image check box to select it, if necessary.

- Click the Constrain Proportions check box to select it, if necessary.

- Click the Resample Image box arrow to display the interpolation methods (Figure 7–73).

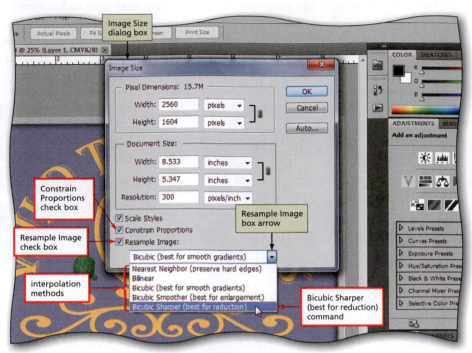

Figure 7–73

- Click Bicubic Sharper (best for reduction).

- If necessary, click the Width unit box arrow in the Document Size area and then click inches in the list.

- Type **5.5** in the Width box.

- Type **300** in the Resolution box, if necessary (Figure 7–74).

Q&A

Should I enter a height value?

No, Photoshop supplies the Height value automatically because Constrain Proportions is selected. Your document height might differ. The Pixel Dimensions settings also are adjusted.

- Click the OK button to close the dialog box and apply the settings.

- Change the magnification of the document window, if necessary.

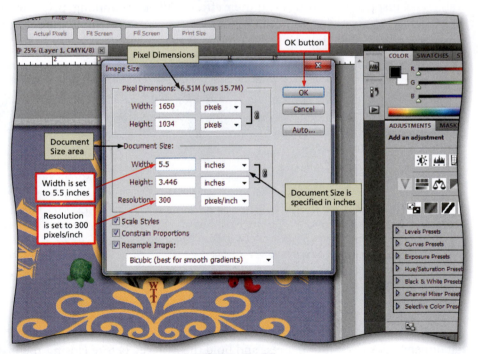

Figure 7–74

Printing Color Separations

Graphic professionals sometimes use print shops, labs, or service bureaus for their advanced printing needs. Service bureaus typically use image setters to create high quality prints. An **image setter** is a high-resolution output device that can transfer electronic files directly to photosensitive paper, plates, or film. While many service bureaus can resize and edit color at the time of printing, you save both time and money by performing these prepress tasks ahead of time in Photoshop. **Prepress tasks** are the various printing-related services performed before ink actually is put on the printed page.

When preparing your image for prepress, and working with CMYK images or images with spot color, you can print each color channel as a separate page. Photoshop also has a Split Channels command on the Channels panel menu that will split the channels into separate document windows for view and adjusting, if desired. Different service bureaus and labs require different kinds of submissions that are highly printer-dependent. Even when supplying a composite for reference by the service bureau, you might want to print color separations for proofing purposes. Separations help you see if your composite file will separate correctly and help you catch other problems that might not be apparent by looking at the composite.

BTW

Printing
The Photoshop Print dialog box displays many choices for printing locations, scaled versions, and page setup. If you want to print the color separations in landscape mode, click the Page Setup button, click the Layout tab, click the Orientation box arrow, and then click Landscape.

BTW

Scale Styles
If your image has layers with styles applied to them, select Scale Styles in the Image Size dialog box to scale the effects in the resized image. This option is available only if you select the Constrain Proportions check box.

To Print Color Separations

Printing the project in color separations allows you to determine whether your composite will separate properly and helps you spot problems before going to press. The following steps print the Wild Thing CMYK document as color separations.

1
- Ready the printer attached to your computer.
- Click File on the menu bar, and then click Print to display the Print dialog box.
- Click the Color Handling box arrow to display its list (Figure 7–75).

2
- Click Separations in the list.
- Click the Print button to display your printer-dependent Print dialog box.
- Click the Print button or the appropriate button for your printer to print the image as shown in Figure 7–1 on page PS 395.

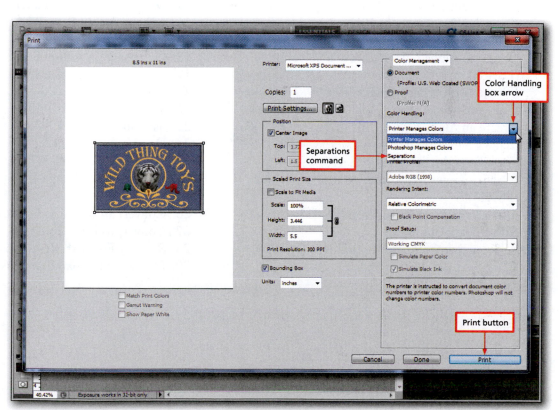

Figure 7–75

To Save and Close the Four-Color Version

The following steps save and close the CMYK four-color version of the Wild Thing Toys document.

1 Press CTRL+S to save the file with the same name.

2 Click the Close button on the document window title bar to close the image.

To Quit Photoshop

The chapter is complete. The final step is to quit Photoshop.

1 Click the Close button on the right side of the Photoshop title bar to quit Photoshop.

Chapter Summary

In this chapter, you used a master copy of an image as the basis for creating several new versions. First, you used channels to aid in the creation of complex selections, which were later used as masks. You added warped text and used an action to embellish the Image. You recorded an action to apply an artistic filter and resize a thumbnail version of the image. You learned various ways to create black-and-white, sepia, and duotone images. Finally, you converted the image to LAB Color mode, then converted it to CMYK color. Among the prepress activities, you resized and resampled the image, and then printed color separations.

The items listed below include all the new Photoshop skills you have learned in this chapter:

1. View Channels (PS 400)
2. Zoom by Dragging (PS 401)
3. Select Using a Channel (PS 402)
4. Create an Alpha Channel from a Selection (PS 403)
5. Edit an Alpha Channel (PS 403)
6. Fine-Tune the Second Alpha Channel (PS 406)
7. Create an Alpha Channel from Scratch (PS 406)
8. Make a Selection in Brush Overlay Mode (PS 407)
9. Fine-Tune the Selection (PS 410)
10. Create a Layer Mask from an Alpha Channel (PS 413)
11. Add a Background and Crop (PS 415)
12. Edit a Mask (PS 418)
13. Select a Text Color from the Image (PS 419)
14. Warp Text (PS 419)
15. Display the Actions Panel (PS 423)
16. Append Action Sets (PS 424)
17. Play an Action (PS 425)
18. Create a New Action Set (PS 426)
19. Create a New Action (PS 427)
20. Record an Action (PS 427)
21. Test the Action (PS 430)
22. Save an Action Set (PS 431)
23. Desaturate (PS 433)
24. Create a Black-and-White Adjustment (PS 434)
25. Create a Sepia Image Using Selective Color (PS 436)
26. Convert an Image to Duotone (PS 438)
27. Convert to LAB Color (PS 443)
28. Resize a File with Resampling (PS 445)
29. Print Color Separations (PS 447)

Learn It Online

Test your knowledge of chapter content and key terms.

Instructions: To complete the Learn It Online exercises, start your browser, click the Address bar, and then enter the Web address `scsite.com/pscs5/learn`. When the Photoshop CS5 Learn It Online page is displayed, click the link for the exercise you want to complete and then read the instructions.

Chapter Reinforcement TF, MC, and SA
A series of true/false, multiple choice, and short answer questions that test your knowledge of the chapter content.

Flash Cards
An interactive learning environment where you identify chapter key terms associated with displayed definitions.

Practice Test
A series of multiple choice questions that test your knowledge of chapter content and key terms.

Who Wants To Be a Computer Genius?
An interactive game that challenges your knowledge of chapter content in the style of a television quiz show.

Wheel of Terms
An interactive game that challenges your knowledge of chapter key terms in the style of the television show *Wheel of Fortune*.

Crossword Puzzle Challenge
A crossword puzzle that challenges your knowledge of key terms presented in the chapter.

Apply Your Knowledge

Reinforce the skills and apply the concepts you learned in this chapter.

Creating an Alpha Channel
Instructions: Start Photoshop and perform the customization steps found on pages PS 6 through PS 9. Open the Apply 7 - 1 Garden file from the Chapter 07 folder of the Data Files for Students. You can access the Data Files for Students on the CD that accompanies this book. See the inside back cover of this book for instructions on downloading the Data Files for Students, or contact your instructor for information about accessing the required files.

You will edit the file to create an alpha channel, hide the background, and insert a new background to create the photo shown in Figure 7–76.

Perform the following tasks:
1. On the File menu, click Save As. Save the image on your USB flash drive as a PSD file, with the file name Apply 7 - 1 Garden Edited.
2. On the Layers panel, right-click the Background layer and then click Duplicate Layer. Name the new layer, Foreground. Select only the Foreground layer, and hide the Background layer by clicking its visibility icon.

Figure 7–76

Continued >

3. Click the Channels panel and then, one at a time, view each channel independent of the others. Decide which channel has the most contrast to facilitate removing the mountains and sky background.

4. Right-click the Blue channel and then click Duplicate Channel. Name the new channel Old Background.

5. If necessary, click the Old Background channel to select it and ensure it is the only visible channel. All other channels should have their visibility icons toggled off.

6. To define the foreground:
   a. Use the Brush Tool set to Overlay mode and black as the foreground color. Drag across the top of the dark trees to paint them black. Be sure to drag across them only once or you may make the mountains too dark.
   b. Drag a second time across the trees below the initial swatch of black to paint more of the trees black.
   c. Change the brush to Normal mode and paint the rest of the bottom portion of the image black.

7. To define the background:
   a. Change the brush back to Overlay mode and change the foreground color to white.
   b. Drag just above the trees to paint the light mountains and sky white. You may need to click any trouble spots to turn them white.
   c. Continue painting the mountains and sky white where they are close to the trees.
   d. Change the brush to Normal mode and paint the remaining top portion of the image and the rest of the mountains and sky white.
   e. Continue to switch between black and white and Normal and Overlay modes until the top portion of the Image (mountains and sky) is completely white, and the foreground (garden and trees) is black.

8. Because the black areas will hide pixels when used as a mask while the white areas will allow the pixels to show through, you must reverse the colors within the channel. Black needs to become white, and white needs to become black. Press CTRL+I to invert the colors of the channel.

9. To view all channels and return to the Layers panel:
   a. Click the RGB channel.
   b. Click the Layers panel.
   c. Click the Foreground layer to select it, if necessary.

10. To load the channel as a selection and create a mask:
    a. Click Select on the menu bar.
    b. Click Load Selection.
    c. From the Channel menu, choose Old Background and click OK.
    d. Click the 'Add layer mask' button at the bottom of the Layers panel.

11. To insert the new background file:
    a. Open the Apply 7-1 Beach file from the Chapter 07 folder of the Data Files for Students.
    b. Position the two open documents side by side.
    c. Use the Move Tool to drag the beach image to the garden document.
    d. Close the Apply 7-1 Beach document.
    e. Rename the new layer, Layer 1, to New Sky.

12. To position the new background:

    a. Drag the layers in the Layers panel to restack them, if necessary, so the Foreground layer is on the top and the New Sky layer is beneath it.

    b. Use the Move Tool to position the New Sky layer as necessary.

13. Save the image.

14. To resize the image for printing on a desktop printer:

    a. On the Image menu, click Image Size.

    b. Click the Resample Image check box to deselect it.

    c. Type **9** in the Width box.

    d. Click the OK button.

15. Ready your printer. Print color separations in Landscape mode and turn them in to your instructor.

16. Quit Photoshop without saving the resized file.

Extend Your Knowledge

Extend the skills you learned in this chapter and experiment with new skills. You may need to use Help to complete the assignment.

Adding Spot Colors to a Print

Instructions: Start Photoshop and perform the customization steps found on pages PS 6 through PS 9. Open the Extend 7-1 Spot Color file from the Chapter 07 folder of the Data Files for Students. See the inside back cover of this book for instructions on downloading the Data Files for Students, or contact your instructor for information about accessing the required files. The purpose of this exercise is to add two spot colors to a four-color travel flyer. The two inks are PANTONE shades, not contained in the standard CMYK range. The file contains two extra channels with saved text selections that will be loaded and recolored. The final edited photo is displayed in Figure 7–77.

Perform the following tasks:

1. Press SHIFT+CTRL+S to save the image on your USB flash drive as a PSD file, with the file name Extend 7–1 Spot Color Complete.

2. To convert the image from RGB mode to CMYK mode:

    a. Point to Mode on the Image menu, then click CMYK Color.

    b. When Photoshop displays a dialog box, click the Don't Merge button, and then click the OK button to accept any default settings.

3. Click the Channels panel tab to activate the panel.

4. Click Select on the menu bar and then click Load Selection to open the Load Selection dialog box.

5. Click the Channel box arrow, click the Saint Basil's Cathedral channel, and then click the OK button to load the first text channel and display the selection marquee in the document window.

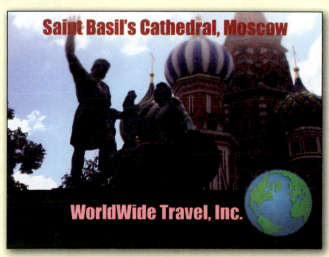

Figure 7–77

Continued >

Extend Your Knowledge *continued*

6. Click the Channels panel menu button and then click New Spot Channel to open the New Spot Channel dialog box.

7. Type **100** in the Solidity box and click the color box to access a color selection dialog box. If the Select Spot Color dialog box appears, click the Color Libraries button to display the Color Libraries dialog box.

8. Click the Book box arrow and then click PANTONE metallic coated in the list. Scroll in the color bar and select an appropriate color.

9. Click the OK button to close the Color Libraries dialog box. Click the OK button again to close the New Spot Channel dialog box.

10. Repeat Steps 4 through 9 for the WorldWide Travel, Inc. channel. Choose a color from the PANTONE pastel coated colors.

11. Save the image again.

12. Use the Save As command to save a copy of the file as Extend 7 - 1 Spot Color Complete in the Photoshop DCS 2.0 (*.EPS) in the format, which saves the file in a format that contains the extra spot channels.

13. Submit the assignment in the format specified by your instructor.

Make It Right

Analyze a project and correct all errors and/or improve the design.

Fixing a Grainy Photo Using Channels

Instructions: Start Photoshop and perform the customization steps found on pages PS 6 through PS 9. Open the Make It Right 7 - 1 Grainy file from the Data Files for Students and save it as Make It Right 7 - 1 Grainy Edited in the PSD file format.

You have a poor quality photo of an image (Figure 7 – 78) that you need for a brochure. Because the ISO settings on your camera were set too high, there is a lot of visual noise in the pixels, which makes the image appear grainy. You will use channels to fix the problem.

Perform the following tasks:

Access the Channels panel and click each color channel one at a time. Notice that the Red and Green channels appear fine but the Blue channel is full of noise and pixilation. With the Blue channel se-lected, click the visibility icon next to the RGB master channel. On the menu bar, click Filter, point to Blur, and then click Gaussian Blur to open the Gaussian Blur dialog box. Adjust the Radius, blurring the Blue channel to reduce some of the noise in the photo. On the menu bar, click Filter, point to Noise, and then click Re-duce Noise. Adjust the settings to reduce the noise and pixilation further. When you are happy with the outcome, save the file and turn it in to your instructor.

Figure 7–78

In the Lab

Design and/or create a publication using the guidelines, concepts, and skills presented in this chapter. Labs are listed in order of increasing difficulty.

Lab 1: Creating a Frost Effect Using Channels

Problem: You need a photo of a field with an early frost on the ground for a collage, but it is in the middle of the summer and everything is green. You will use your knowledge of channels to make the grass and trees look as though they have frost on them. The finished product is displayed in Figure 7–79.

Instructions: Perform the following tasks:

1. Start Photoshop. Perform the customization steps found on pages PS 6 through PS 9.

2. Open the file Lab 7-1 Green Grass from the Chapter 07 folder of the Data Files for Students. You can access the Data Files for Students on the CD that accompanies this book. See the inside back cover of this book for instructions on downloading the Data Files for Students, or contact your instructor for information about accessing the required files.

3. Save the file as Lab 7-1 White Frost. Browse to your USB flash drive storage device. Click the Save button. If Photoshop displays a dialog box, click the OK button.

Figure 7–79

4. If necessary, double-click the Layers panel tab to display the layers. Right-click the Background layer and then click Duplicate Layer on the context menu. Name the new layer, frost.

5. At the top of the Layers panel, click the Blending Mode box arrow and then click Lighten.

6. Click the Adjustments panel tab to access the Adjustments panel. Click the Channel Mixer icon to display its settings. (*Hint*: the Channel Mixer icon is the last one in the second row.)

   a. Click the Monochrome check box to select it.

   b. Type **200** in the Red box.

   c. Type **100** in the Green box.

   d. Type **−74** in the Blue box.

   e. Type **0** in the Contrast box, if necessary.

7. Click the Layers panel tab and then select the Background layer.

8. To select the sky:

   a. Click the Channels panel tab to access the Channels panel.

   b. Notice that an alpha channel has been created previously and was named, sky.

   c. Click the Layers panel tab.

   d. On the menu bar, click Select and then click Load Selection to display the Load Selection dialog box.

   e. Click the Channel box arrow and then click sky in the list, if necessary.

Continued >

In the Lab *continued*

    f. Click the OK button to close the Load Selection dialog box and to display the selection marquee in the document window.

    g. Press CTRL+J to create a new layer. Name the layer, sky.

    h. On the Layers panel, drag the new sky layer above the others.

  9. Save the file again.

10. To adjust the amount of frost:

    a. On the Layers panel, click the Channel Mixer layer.

    b. At the top of the Layers panel, change the opacity to 70%.

11. Flatten the image and then save the file in the JPEG format and submit it to your instructor as directed.

In the Lab

Lab 2: Using Predefined Actions

Problem: Your cousin wants you to use her senior picture to create an invitation to a graduation open house. You decide to investigate Photoshop's predefined actions to look for a specialized frame that you can apply to the photo. The finished product is displayed in Figure 7–80.

Instructions: Perform the following tasks:

1. Start Photoshop. Perform the customization steps found on pages PS 6 through PS 9.

2. Open the file Lab 7-2 Senior Picture from the Chapter 07 folder of the Data Files for Students. You can access the Data Files for Students on the CD that accompanies this book. See the inside back cover of this book for instructions on downloading the Data Files for Students, or contact your instructor for information about accessing the required files.

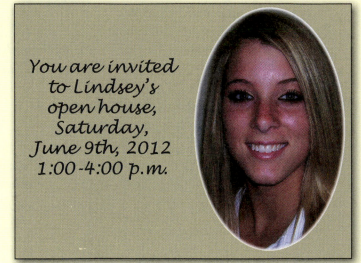

Figure 7–80

3. Click the Save As command on the File menu. Type `Lab 7-2 Invitation` as the file name and set the format to the Photoshop PSD format, if necessary. Browse to your USB flash drive storage device. Click the Save button. If Photoshop displays a dialog box, click the OK button.

4. Select the Elliptical Marquee Tool. On the options bar, click the New selection button, if necessary. Drag a large selection that encompasses the head and neck of the girl. Without clicking anywhere else, drag the selection to center it. Some of the selection may overlap the top and bottom edges.

5. Press ALT+F9 to display the Actions panel. If the Frames action set is not listed, click the panel menu button, and then click Frames. If necessary, click the right-pointing triangle of the Frames action set to display the actions stored in the set. Scroll down and click the Vignette (selection) action.

6. Click the Play selection button on the Actions panel status bar. When the action pauses to request a feather selection, type `5` in the Feather Radius box, if necessary. Click the OK button.

7. When the action is complete, close the Actions panel. On the Layers panel, select the layer of the vignette itself and then select the Move Tool. In the document window, drag the vignette to the right.

8. Select the Magic Wand Tool on the Tools panel. On the options bar, click the 'Add to selection' button, if necessary. In the document window, click to select the white areas around the vignette. Use the Color panel to choose a light or pale color of your choosing. Use the Paint Bucket Tool to fill the white areas with the color.

9. Click the Horizontal Type Tool button on the Tools panel.

10. To adjust the text settings:
    a. On the options bar, select the Lucida Handwriting font family or a similar font.
    b. Set the font style to Italic.
    c. Set the font size to 60.
    d. Set the anti-aliasing method to Smooth.
    e. Click the Center text button.
    f. Choose a black font color.

11. Drag a text box that fills the left side of the image. In the text box, type `You are invited to Lindsey's open house, Saturday, June 9th, 2012, 1:00 - 4:00 p.m.`, pressing the ENTER key as necessary to create the lines shown in Figure 7–80. When you are finished, click the 'Commit any current edits' button on the options bar. Use the Move Tool to adjust the placement of the text box if needed.

12. When you are finished, use the Flatten Image command to flatten all of the layers into the background. Discard hidden layers if Photoshop prompts you to do so. Save the flattened image.

13. E-mail your instructor with the Lab 7 - 2 Invitation file as an attachment, or see your instructor for another way to submit this assignment.

In the Lab

Lab 3: Changing Band Membership

Problem: A local band has contracted you to alter a concert photo to include their new bass player. They have provided you with a photo of their band in concert and a separate photo of the bass player. You are to edit the bass player photo and place him on the concert stage, creating a picture the band can use for promotional purposes. The edited photo is shown Figure 7–81.

Instructions: Perform the following tasks: Start Photoshop. Perform the customization steps found on pages PS 6 through PS 9. Open the Lab 7 - 3 Bassist photo from the Chapter 07 folder of the Data Files for Students. You can access the Data Files for Students on the CD that accompanies this book. See the inside back cover of this book for instructions on downloading the Data Files for Students, or contact your instructor for information about accessing the required files. Select the background and create an alpha channel. Hide or delete the background and edit as necessary to display only the bassist. Open the file named Lab 7 - 3 Concert. Arrange the documents side by side and then use the Move

Figure 7–81

Continued >

In the Lab *continued*

Tool to drag the bassist image into the Lab 7-3 Concert document window. Adjust and scale the layers as necessary. Use the Adjustments panel to adjust the levels and contrast so the bassist matches the concert scene. Delete portions of the bass player or create a mask so he appears behind the stage speakers and other band members. Create a Warped text box with the band name, as shown in Figure 7–81 on the previous page. Sample the blue in the guitar strap for the color of the text and apply a layer style to emphasize the text. Save the file as Lab 7-3 New Bass Player in the PSD format.

Cases and Places

Apply your creative thinking and problem-solving skills to design and implement a solution.

1: Converting to Black and White

Academic

Your school prints a monthly newsletter in black and white. Open the Case 7-1 School image that is located in the Chapter 07 folder of the Data Files for Students. Use the Adjustments panel and the Black & White adjustment to create a black-and-white version of the image that maintains good contrast and is not washed out. Write down the settings you used, and then revert the image to its original state. Using the Case 7-1 School image, record a new action named Convert to B&W and apply the settings you wrote down earlier as you record the action. Apply the saved action to the Case 7-1 Football and Case 7-1 Graduation images located in the Chapter 07 folder. Save the three black-and-white images with the description, B&W, appended to the end of the default file name.

2: Changing a Background

Personal

You are volunteering your expert graphic design skills to help a local ranch advertise horseback riding lessons. As part of the brochure, management wants to use an image of a horse on their own background. Open the Case 7-2 Horse image that is located in the Chapter 07 folder of the Data Files for Students. Determine the channel that offers the best contrast between the horse and its background and then duplicate the channel, naming it Horse. Paint in the Horse channel to make the background black and the horse white. (*Hint*: you might begin by making the horse black and the background white, then press CTRL+I to invert the colors.) Use any selection tool you believe is appropriate. (*Hint*: try using the Brush in overlay mode to help mask around the hair.) Load the channel as a selection and then apply the selection as a layer mask, hiding the background and leaving only the horse visible. Save the file as Case 7-2 Horse Masked.psd. Copy the masked horse to the Case 7-2 Trees file (also in the Chapter 07 folder) and resize and position as necessary. Add text in an appropriate font with the ranch's name, Fairview Ranch, and warp the text artistically. Save the file as Case 7-2 Trees Horse.psd and submit it to your instructor.

3: Converting to Duotone

Professional

A wedding planner wants to use a picture of a tulip on her business cards. The tulip is in full color, but her business cards are going to use brown spot color on ivory paper. Open the Case 7-3 Tulip image that is located in the Chapter 07 folder of the Data Files for Students. Save the image on your storage device with the name Case 7-3 Tulip Edited. Use an alpha channel to remove the background. Flatten the image. Convert the image to grayscale and then convert the image to duotone. When the Duotone dialog box is displayed, double-click the Color Picker and choose a sepia color. Type `sepia` in the Name text box. Click the OK button. Convert the image to CMYK color. Save the image again, and then print a copy.

8 | Working with Vector Graphics

Objectives

You will have mastered the material in this chapter when you can:

- Describe the characteristics of clip art and vector graphics
- Create and manage layer groups using the Layers panel
- Differentiate between vector and raster graphic images
- Create shape layers and paths with the Pen Tool
- Draw line segments and curved paths
- Add, delete, and convert anchor points

- Move and modify paths using the Path Selection and Direct Selection Tools
- Use the Freeform Pen Tool with the magnetic pen option
- Add detail to clip art images
- Use the Note Annotation Tool
- Enter text in a custom shape
- Apply effects to optimize clip art

8 | Working with Vector Graphics

Introduction

With the advent of page layout and word processing software, images have become common in all kinds of documents. Web sites without graphics are passé. Business stationery now includes artwork and logos in addition to the standard address and content data; lectures and oral presentations are considered uninteresting without graphics and multimedia effects; and textbooks are loaded with graphics to help improve students' focus and comprehension. Today, students routinely insert clip art into papers and presentations.

The term **clip art** refers to individual images or groups of graphics that can be transferred across computer applications and platforms. Clip art commonly is an illustrative, vibrant drawing featuring solid blocks of color, rather than a photo, but the term is applied loosely to any image that accompanies or decorates text, including black-and-white images. The term clip art also is applied to visual elements such as bullets, lines, shapes, and callouts. Photos, typically with full-color backgrounds, are referred to as **stock images** rather than clip art.

Project — Creating a Clip Art Image

A children's summer camp needs a kid-friendly graphic for a brochure and Web site. You will begin drawing waves freehand, then use a photograph of a sailboat to create an outline or tracing as the basis for a vector graphic of the same image. Additionally, you will insert text, convert the letters to shapes and then reshape the letters to create a custom lettering style. Using paths, opacity changes, and layer styles, portions of the image are recolored to create a cartoon look and feel. A custom shape with text also is added. The before and after images are displayed in Figure 8–1.

Figure 8–1

Overview

As you read this chapter, you will learn how to create the clip art image shown in Figure 8–1 by performing these general tasks:

- Create layer groups on a transparent background.
- Use paths to create vector graphics.
- Save paths using the Paths panel.
- Use the Path and Pen Tools to create shapes.
- Add detail to clip art.
- Annotate a clip art image using the Note Tool.
- Optimize clip art files for the Web.

Plan Ahead

> **General Project Guidelines**
>
> When editing a photo, the actions you perform and decisions you make will affect the appearance and characteristics of the finished product. As you edit photos, such as the one shown in Figure 8–1, you should follow these general guidelines:
>
> 1. **Plan and organize layers.** Organize your clip art from the back to the front in the document window, and from the bottom up on the Layers panel. Layer groups reduce clutter on the Layers panel and logically order the various parts of an image. Layer groups also can be used to apply attributes and masks to multiple layers simultaneously, which saves time and effort.
>
> 2. **Use vector graphics for clip art.** When creating clip art, use vector graphics. Vector graphics are high-quality graphics used in illustrations, typography, logos, and advertisements. They retain their crisp edges when resized, moved, or recolored. Vector graphics do not pixelate when transferred to other applications.
>
> 3. **Add detail to enhance clip art.** Good clip art uses strong lines and colors with enough detail to highlight the image's purpose. Keep the purpose, context, and audience in mind as you add detail to create movement, depth, light, and recognition to the clip art.
>
> 4. **Annotate graphics within the file.** Consider adding notes within the file itself, rather than using e-mail with an attached photo, to provide documentation and explanations. That way, the information stays with the graphic and can be accessed by others.
>
> When necessary, more specific details concerning the above guidelines are presented at appropriate points in the chapter. The chapter also will identify the actions performed and decisions made regarding these guidelines during the creation of the edited photos shown in Figure 8–1.

Clip Art

Clip art can be created from scratch, produced from a photo, copied and pasted from another source, or imported directly as a file into some applications. The use of clip art can save artists time and money; and in some cases, using clip art in a project allows artwork to be included when it would otherwise not be possible to do so. Clip art galleries that come with some page layout and word processing applications often contain hundreds of images.

Clip art comes in a variety of file formats. **Bitmap images** work best in the size and orientation at which they are created, and typically are stored in the GIF, JPG, BMP, TIF, or PNG formats. **Vector images** are resolution-independent and do not pixelate when resized. They commonly are stored as EPS, SVG, WMF, SWF, or PDF files. Choosing the appropriate file format often depends on the purpose of the graphic — print, Web, or file transfer — as well as the scalability and resolution.

For print publications, vector images can be resized, rotated, and stretched easily. The disadvantage is that many vector formats are specific to the software in which the image was created. For example, Windows Metafile is a format used with Microsoft products and associated clip art. It is saved with the extension WMF. A graphic created with Adobe Flash has the extension SWF. While you can copy and import those types of vector images, you might not be able to edit them without using the original software.

Clip art is not always free. Application software companies provide a license for registered users to import and distribute the clip art provided with the package without charge. Some Web clip art galleries might specify royalty-free images for one-time use, but not for commercial use intended to generate profit. For other uses, you must purchase clip art packages on CD or for download. It is important to read all licensing agreements carefully. Some artwork requires written permission. Copyright laws apply to all images equally — the right of legal use depends on the intended use and conditions of the copyright owner. All images are copyrighted, regardless of whether they are marked as copyrighted.

Table 8–1 displays some of the categories, descriptions, and usages of clip art sources.

BTW

Adding Metadata to Clip Art
Appendix C describes how to use Adobe Bridge to add metadata keywords to images to aid image searches.

Table 8–1 Categories of Clip Art

Clip Art Category	Warnings	Use
Free — An image that is given or provided free of charge	It is important to check the Web site owner's motive for giving away clip art. Some free graphics are unlabeled, copyrighted images. Images might contain spyware or viruses.	Appropriate for personal use and sometimes for educational purposes, but because the original source might be obscure, free clip art is not recommended for business use.
Published clip art — images in print or online	Ask for written permission to use the image. Do not use the image unless you can track it to its original source.	Published clip art is appropriate for personal use, educational purposes, and one-time use on a Web site. With permission, it may be used commercially.
Copyrighted — trademarked images that have legal owners	Do not use unless you have a written agreement with the copyright holder.	Copyrighted clip art has limited legal use. Only fully licensed resellers may use copyrighted clip art. It is not appropriate for any personal or educational use.
Royalty-free — images provided at little or no cost by the owner	Carefully read the rights and usages. Trading post Web sites require the permission of the artist or photographer. Even legitimate images might contain spyware or viruses.	With written permission from the owner, royalty-free clip art and stock images normally can be used by anyone — even for commercial use such as on Web sites and business stationery — but without redistribution rights.
Rights-protected — images created and sold for a specific use	You must buy the right to use the image exclusively. You may not use the image for any use other than its intended purpose.	Written businesses contract with artists to design rights-protected logos and artwork. The seller promises not to sell that image to anyone else for that purpose.
Editorial rights — photos used in public interest	Some editorial-use images also are copyrighted. Read the agreement carefully.	Editorial-rights images are used with written permission for news, sports, entertainment, and other public purposes with appropriate citation. These images are usually less restrictive and less expensive than rights-protected images.

In this chapter, you will create your own clip art — clip art that has no legal restrictions because you are designing it yourself. Artists, graphic design professionals, typographers, and casual users all use Photoshop to create specialized graphics such as clip art to avoid potential copyright problems.

Starting and Customizing Photoshop

The following steps start Photoshop and reset the default workspace, tools, colors, and Layers panel options.

To Start Photoshop

The following steps start Photoshop based on a typical installation. You may need to ask your instructor how to start Photoshop for your computer.

1 Click the Start button on the Windows 7 taskbar to display the Start menu.

2 Type `Photoshop CS5` as the search text in the 'Search programs and files' text box, and watch the search results appear on the Start menu.

3 Click Adobe Photoshop CS5 in the search results on the Start menu to start Photoshop.

4 After a few moments, when the Photoshop window is displayed, if the window is not maximized, click the Maximize button on the title bar to maximize the window.

To Reset the Workspace

The following steps use the Workspace switcher to select the Essentials workspace.

1 Click the 'Show more workspaces and options' button on the Application bar to display the names of saved workspaces and then, if necessary, click Essentials to select the default workspace panels.

2 Click the 'Show more workspaces and options' button again to display the list and then click Reset Essentials to restore the workspace to its default settings and reposition any panels that may have been moved.

To Reset the Tools and the Options Bar

The following steps select the Rectangular Marquee Tool and reset all tool settings on the options bar.

1 If the tools in the Tools panel appear in two columns, click the double arrow at the top of the Tools panel.

2 If necessary, click the Rectangular Marquee Tool button on the Tools panel to select it.

3 Right-click the Rectangular Marquee Tool icon on the options bar to display the context menu and then click Reset All Tools. When Photoshop displays a confirmation dialog box, click the OK button to restore the tools to their default settings.

To Reset the Default Colors

The following step resets the default colors.

1 Press the D key to reset the default foreground and background colors.

To Reset the Layers Panel

The following steps reset the Layers panel to make the thumbnails match the figures shown in this book.

1 Click the Layers panel menu button and then click Panel Options on the list to display the Layers Panel Options dialog box.

2 Click the option button for the smallest of the thumbnail sizes.

3 If necessary, click the Layer Bounds option button to select it.

4 If necessary, place a check mark next to each of the three check boxes at the bottom of the Layers Panel Options dialog box.

5 Click the OK button (Layers Panel Options dialog box) to close the dialog box, resetting the Layers panel.

Creating a New File with a Transparent Background

A desirable attribute of clip art is the transparent background. A clip art with **transparency** can be placed closer to text and other graphics when inserted into Web pages, slide presentations, and print publications. The graphic will appear without a white, cornered background obstructing the view. In Photoshop, when you create an image with transparent content, the image does not have a traditional Background layer. Each layer is neither drawn on, nor constrained by, the background; you can add layers anywhere in the document window.

To Create a File with a Transparent Background

The following steps use a shortcut key to display the New dialog box and then set the attributes for an image with a transparent background.

1 Press CTRL+N to display the New dialog box.

2 Type `Sailor Camp` in the Name box to name the graphic.

3 Click the Width unit box arrow and then click inches in the list, if necessary.

4 Set the width to 5 and the height to 3.

5 Set the resolution to 300 pixels/inch.

6 Set the Color Mode to RGB Color, 8 bit.

7 Set the Background Contents to Transparent (Figure 8–2).

8 Click the OK button (New dialog box) to create the document.

9 When the document window is displayed, if necessary, change the magnification to 33.33%. If the rulers do not appear in the document window, press CTRL+R.

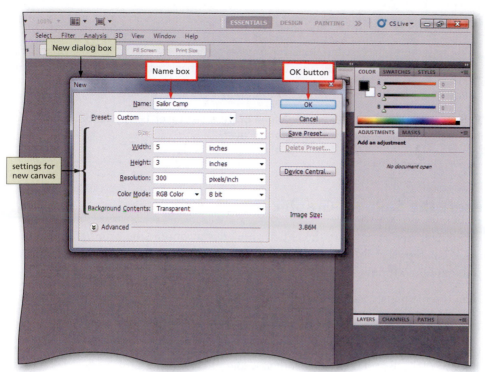

Figure 8–2

Plan and organize layers.	
As you build your clip art from the back to the front, keep the layers in order from bottom (back) to top (front) on the Layers panel. Always use a locked background and then organize other parts of the clip art in layer groups. Advantages of using layer groups include the ability to:	**Plan Ahead**

- Create a new document from a layer group.
- Move layer groups from one image to another.
- Nest layer groups within one another.
- Align and merge layer groups.
- Apply attributes and masks to multiple layers simultaneously.

Managing the Layers Panel

Converting a photo into clip art requires many steps with many layers. First, you must import the original photo onto your transparent background to use as a basis for drawing the clip art. Locking or partially locking the original photo is a good way to prevent accidental deletion of the image.

Each color you create in the clip art becomes a new path or shape, at least temporarily until the image is flattened and prepared for distribution. To manage the many layers, users find it easier to group multiple shapes and their special effects by style, category, or object.

The sections on the next page rename the transparent layer, import the photo, create layer groups, and save the file.

To Rename the Transparent Layer

The first step is to rename the layer that was created by choosing a transparent background. Later in this chapter, you will create a sky background on this transparent layer.

1 If necessary, click the Layers panel tab to display the Layers panel.

2 On the Layers panel, double-click the name of the layer, Layer 1. Type `sky background`, and then press the ENTER key to rename the layer.

To Insert the Sailboat Graphic

The next step in creating the clip art image is to import the original photo of a sailboat. The steps that follow open the Sailboat file and move the image into the Sailor Camp document window, creating a new layer.

1 Open the file named Sailboat from the Chapter 08 folder of the Data Files for Students.

2 Arrange the documents side by side.

3 Activate the Move Tool and then drag the sailboat image into the Sailor Camp document window. Close the Sailboat document window.

4 Position the image so it fills the canvas.

5 Rename the layer, original sailboat (Figure 8–3).

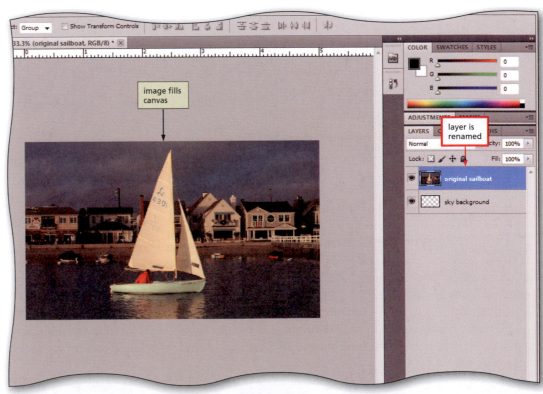

Figure 8–3

Locking Layers

Layers can be locked fully to prevent further editing or locked partially to allow movement of the layer without disturbing the effects and settings. Table 8–2 displays information about the four locking buttons.

Table 8–2 Layers Panel Locking Buttons		
Type of Lock	**Description**	**Button**
Lock transparent pixels	confines editing to the opaque portions of the layer	
Lock image pixels	prevents painting tool modifications of the layer	
Lock position	prevents the layer's pixels from being moved	
Lock all	locks transparent pixels, image pixels, and position	

To Lock Layers

The following steps use the Lock all button to lock the transparent sky background fully and use the Lock position button to partially lock the original sailboat layer. You later will unlock the sky background when you are ready to work with it. Partially locking the original sailboat will protect it from accidental movement.

1

- On the Layers panel, select the sky background layer.

- Click the Lock all button to lock the layer and to display the solid lock icon (Figure 8–4).

Q&A

When should I lock layers?

You might want to lock a layer fully when you finish working with it. You might want to lock a layer partially if it has the correct transparency and styles, but you still are deciding on the layer's position.

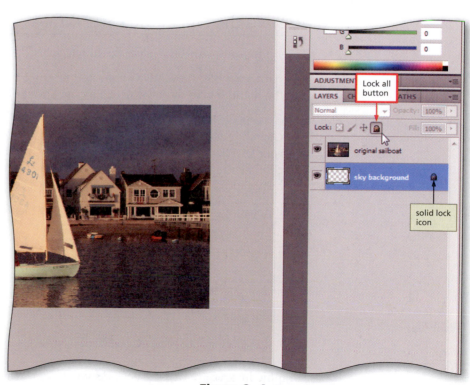

Figure 8–4

2

- Select the original sailboat layer.

- Click the Lock position button to lock the layer partially and to display a hollow lock icon (Figure 8–5).

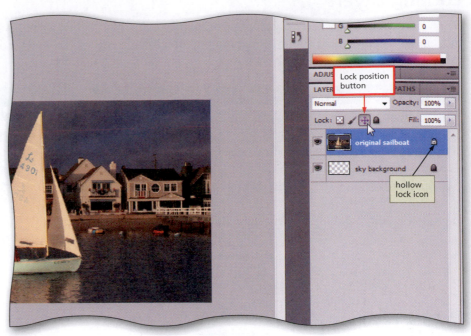

Figure 8–5

To Save the File in the PSD Format

The following steps save the file in the PSD format for maximum editing flexibility.

1 With your USB flash drive connected to one of the computer's USB ports, click File on the menu bar to display the File menu, and then click Save As to display the Save As dialog box.

2 Click the Save in box arrow and then click UDISK 2.0 (F:), or the location associated with your USB flash drive, in the list. If you want to create a folder for the photos in Chapter 8, click the Create New Folder button. Then when the new folder is displayed, type a chapter name, such as Chapter 08, and press the ENTER key.

3 If necessary, click the Format box arrow and then click Photoshop (*.PSD;*.PDD) in the list.

4 Click the Save button. If Photoshop displays a Photoshop Format Options dialog box, click the OK button.

Vector Graphics

Graphic images are of two types. As you have learned, vectors — also called vector graphics — are made up of shapes, lines, and curves that are defined by mathematical objects, or vectors. Vector graphics are high-quality graphics used in illustrations, typography, logos, and advertisements. Vector graphics retain their crisp edges when resized, moved, or recolored because they are made up of individual, scalable lines and objects rather than bitmapped pixels. Therefore, vector graphics are not directly editable at the pixel level. You can change a vector graphic, but not in the same way as you do a non-vector graphic. When you edit a vector graphic, you change its attributes such as color, fill, and outline. For example, if you create a circle as a shape layer, the vector graphic is generated using the current color scheme and style displayed on the options bar. The vector graphic neither can be edited with the brush or eraser tools, nor can it be filled with color using the Paint Bucket Tool. If you change your mind about the color, for instance, you must select the shape layer and then change the color using the options bar. Changing the attributes of a vector object does not affect the object itself; it merely applies the change as it shapes and transforms the layer along a path. In a previous chapter, you used the Shape layers button on the Shape options bar to create a vector graphic automatically. You might have seen or used vector graphics as clip art in page layout and word processing programs.

The other type of graphic image is a bitmap image, also called a raster image. **Raster images** are made up of pixels of color and are resolution dependent; thus, they are appropriate for photographs and artwork with continuous color, such as paintings. Images from scanners and digital cameras are raster images because they need to use continuous color to form the image.

Because vector graphics are drawn instead of compiled from pixels, they are more difficult to edit. For example, text must be converted from a vector graphic to a flat raster image, in a process called rasterizing, before editing. When you rasterize, you might need to set the pixel dimensions, color mode, anti-aliasing, dithering, and resolution. The disadvantage of rasterizing is that the image becomes resolution dependent, making it difficult to resize without sacrificing a degree of image quality. While raster images are scaled quite successfully in page layout programs, a permanent change in size is harder to interpolate.

Use vector graphics for clip art.
Begin with a good photo of the subject to use as a pattern. Study the shapes, angles, lines, and lighting. Because composition is such an important factor in clip art, consider using the photo as your outline to create the vector graphic or vector art. As you use paths to draw the vectors, experiment with different colors for each part of the vector graphic to differentiate it. Create each shape before adding detail.

By creating an original piece of vector art, you can express exactly what you or your client wants to convey through an image.

Plan Ahead

Path Lines and Anchor Points

While any of the shape tools can be used to create vector graphics, the most versatile are the Pen Tool and the Freeform Pen Tool, which create paths. A **path** is an outline that you can turn into a shape, turn into a selection, or fill and stroke with color. A path is different from a regular selection, not only in its vector graphic qualities, but also in the user's ability to use the pen tools for drawing and adjusting. When you use the pen tools to create path lines, each click in the document window becomes an anchor point, or node. An **anchor point** is a single handle created from a click along a path line or border. An anchor point is displayed as a small square. The current or latest anchor point is always a solid square, indicating that it is selected. Non-selected anchor points are displayed as hollow squares and are used to alter the shape and angle of line segments at adjacent segments along the path.

Not all paths have to be two-dimensional shapes; a path can be as simple as a line. To create a straight line path, you click the document window using the Pen Tool, creating an anchor point. When you click again, a second anchor point is displayed and a line connects the two in the document window.

When you want to create curved lines, you drag with the Pen Tool. Photoshop will display an anchor point and two direction lines with direction points (Figure 8–6). The direction lines move outward as you drag. The direction of the drag determines the eventual direction of the curve. For instance, if you drag to the right, the bump of the curve will be to the right. The length of the drag determines how much influence the anchor point will have over the curve — the longer the drag, the more exaggerated the curve. To create the other end of the curved line, simply click the desired end point and drag again. Dragging the end point in the opposite direction creates an arc; dragging in the same direction creates an S curve. Once the curve is completed, the direction lines no longer appear; the curve is the only thing that is displayed in the document window.

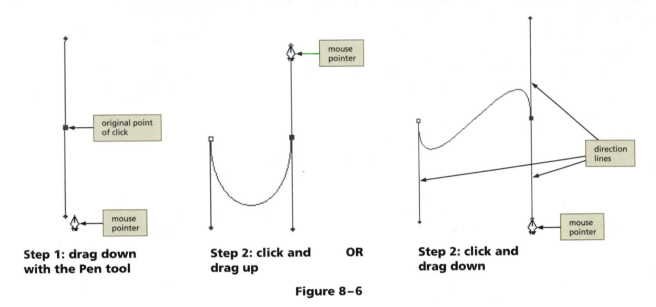

Figure 8–6

Whether straight or curved, when you are finished with a path, you have two choices: create an open path or a closed path. You can CTRL+click to create an open path. The ends of an **open path** do not connect, thus creating a line or curve, rather than a polygon or ellipse. Open paths can be used to create outlines or color strokes, or they can be used to place text such as words that display contoured along a curve. If you finish a path by joining the ends, it is called a **closed path** and creates a two-dimensional shape such as a rectangle, triangle, or oval. When your mouse pointer gets close to the first anchor point, a small circle is displayed next to the tip of the mouse pointer. Clicking then connects the anchor points.

Table 8–3 displays some of the possible tasks when creating path lines.

Table 8–3 Creating Path Lines		
Task	**Steps**	**Result**
Create a straight line path.	Click a beginning point. Click an ending point.	
Add an anchor point.	Click along a path.	
Delete an existing anchor point.	If the Auto Add/Delete option is selected on the options bar, you can click an existing point to delete it.	

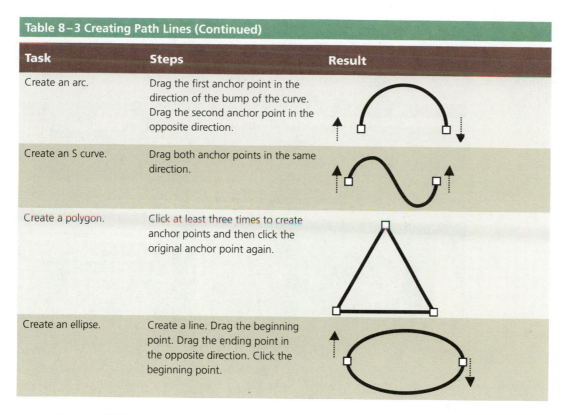

Task	Steps	Result
Create an arc.	Drag the first anchor point in the direction of the bump of the curve. Drag the second anchor point in the opposite direction.	
Create an S curve.	Drag both anchor points in the same direction.	
Create a polygon.	Click at least three times to create anchor points and then click the original anchor point again.	
Create an ellipse.	Create a line. Drag the beginning point. Drag the ending point in the opposite direction. Click the beginning point.	

Table 8–3 Creating Path Lines (Continued)

As you will learn in the next section, you have three basic choices or modes when creating paths. You can create a path that is a shape layer, a path on the Paths panel, or a non-vector, filled shape.

Shape Layers

As you create paths, if you select the Shape layers button on the options bar, Photoshop creates a shape on the Layers panel. Two clicks create a line path that is displayed in gray in the document window; a path with more than two points creates a fill with the current foreground color. A shape layer consists of a fill layer that defines the shape color and a linked vector mask that defines the path or shape outline. The outline of a shape appears as a path on the Paths panel as well, but the shape exists in its own layer on the Layers panel, making it easier to edit than other paths.

You can use the pen tools or other shape tools to create shape layer paths. Because they are easily moved, aligned, resized, and distributed, shape layers are ideal for making graphics for clip art and for Web pages. Additionally, you can create multiple shapes on a single layer.

To Create a Shape Layer Using the Pen Tool

An anchor point with direction lines that are straight sometimes is called a **smooth point**; when you drag the direction points, the resulting arc is curved smoothly. An anchor point without direction lines, or one with a direction line that creates an angle, sometimes is called a **corner point**; when you drag a corner point, the resulting line segments create a corner. When you add an anchor point, Photoshop automatically creates a smooth point. When you need to convert a smooth point to a corner point, you ALT+click the point or use the Convert Point Tool.

The steps on the next page create a closed path with the Pen Tool to simulate waves in a blue color as shown in Figure 8–1 on page PS 458. The path will become a shape layer on the Layers panel. Photoshop creates new shape layers above the selected layer on the Layers panel.

1
• Click the Swatches panel tab to display the Swatches panel and then click Pure Cyan to change the foreground color (Figure 8–7).

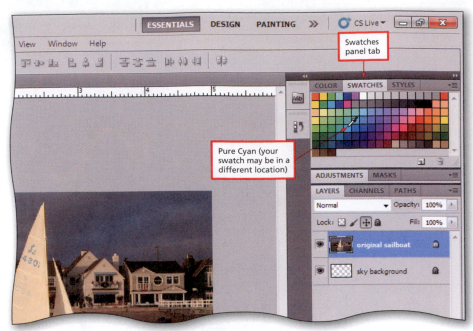

Figure 8–7

2
• On the Layers panel, select the original sailboat layer, if necessary.

• On the Tools panel, right-click the current Pen Tool button to display the context menu (Figure 8–8).

Q&A

If I locked that layer earlier, why am I selecting it?

Remember that layers — and paths — are created from the bottom up. The new path shape will appear above the layer in the Layers panel and in front of the original sailboat in the document window.

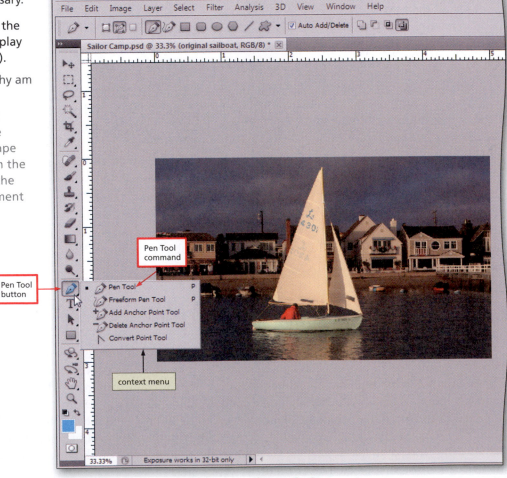

Figure 8–8

3
- Click the Pen Tool to select it.

- On the options bar, click the Shape layers button to set the Pen Tool to shape mode.

- In the document window, click the gray area to the left of the canvas about 2.5 inches down from the top of the canvas to display the first anchor point (Figure 8–9).

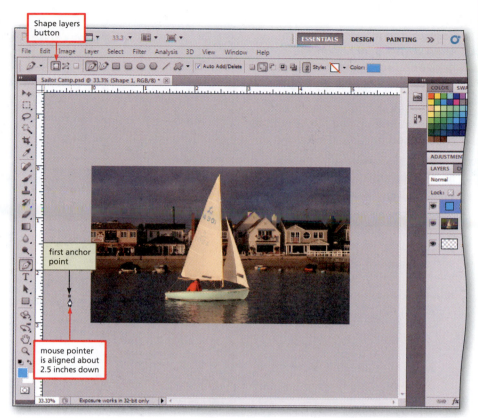

Figure 8–9

4
- Move the mouse pointer to the right to the 0.5 inch mark on the horizontal ruler.

- Click the location and drag the mouse pointer up and to the right to display the second anchor point and create the first curve (Figure 8–10).

Q&A

Why did a blue shape appear?

When you create more than two anchor points, Photoshop begins to fill the shape layer with the selected color.

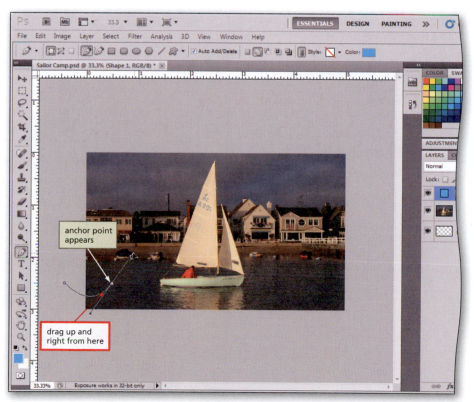

Figure 8–10

5

- Position the mouse pointer to align with 1.5 inches on the horizontal ruler and 2.5 inches on the vertical ruler.

- Click the location and drag the mouse pointer up and to the right to create another curve (Figure 8–11).

Q&A Why did the new line first curve up and then down?

The path is following the direction line created by the previous anchor point, which was dragged up and to the right. The wave should have a sharp point at the top, so the second anchor point must be converted to a corner point.

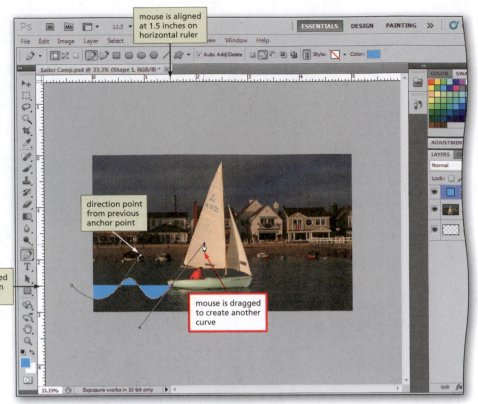

Figure 8–11

6

- Press the BACKSPACE key to delete the third anchor point.

- Click the second anchor point to reestablish the path (Figure 8–12).

Q&A Why did I have to click the second anchor point?

Clicking the last, or previous, anchor point selects the path so it can be continued.

Q&A How can I tell which anchor point is selected?

The selected anchor point displays a solid square. Other anchor points are hollow.

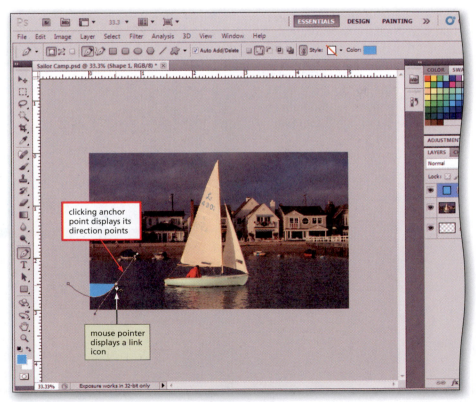

Figure 8–12

7

- ALT+click the second anchor point to remove the direction point and convert the point to a corner point.

- Position the mouse pointer to align with 1.5 inches on the horizontal ruler and 2.5 inches on the vertical ruler.

- Drag up and to the right to create another curve (Figure 8–13).

Q&A   Why does the wave now have a sharp point at the top instead of a curve?

By converting the second anchor point to a corner point, you removed the direction handles. Paths originating from a corner point do not begin with a curve, as there is no direction point to follow.

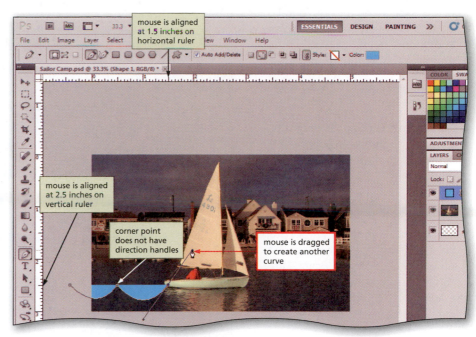

Figure 8–13

8

- ALT+click the last anchor point to remove the direction point and convert it to a corner point.

- Position the mouse pointer to align with 2.5 inches on the horizontal ruler and 2.5 inches on the vertical ruler.

- Drag up and to the right to create another wave.

- ALT+click the last anchor point to remove the direction point and convert it to a corner point (Figure 8–14).

- Position the mouse pointer to align with 3.5 inches on the horizontal ruler and 2.5 inches on the vertical ruler.

- Drag up and to the right to create another wave.

- ALT+click the last anchor point to remove the direction point and convert it to a corner point.

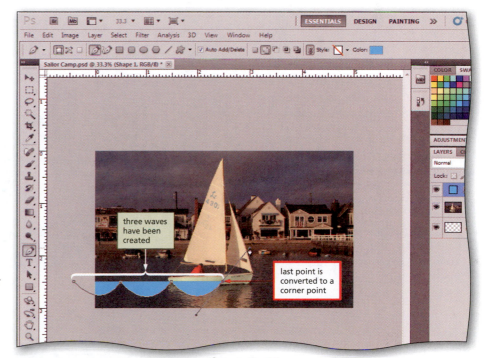

Figure 8–14

9

- Position the mouse pointer to align with 4.5 inches on the horizontal ruler and 2.5 inches on the vertical ruler.

- Drag up and to the right to create another wave.

- ALT+click the last anchor point to remove the direction point and convert it to a corner point.

- Position the mouse pointer to align with 5.5 inches on the horizontal ruler and 2.5 inches on the vertical ruler. Your mouse pointer will be in the gray area to the right of the canvas.

- Drag up and to the right to create another wave.

- ALT+click the last anchor point to remove the direction point and convert it to a corner point (Figure 8–15).

Q&A

What if I do not like the path or parts of it are wrong?

You can back up through your steps on the History panel or delete the path entirely and start again. Later in this chapter you will learn how to adjust path points by adding, deleting, converting, and moving them.

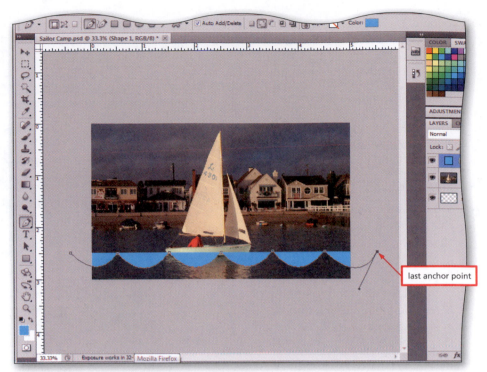

Figure 8–15

10

- Position the mouse pointer to align with 5.5 inches on the horizontal ruler and 3.5 inches on the vertical ruler, then click once to add an anchor point without dragging.

- Point to the starting anchor point so the mouse pointer shows a small circle next to the pen icon, then click to close the path (Figure 8–16).

Q&A

The waves do not look right. How can I fix them?

The path overlaps itself, creating an unwanted final result. You will add points in the next steps to fix this.

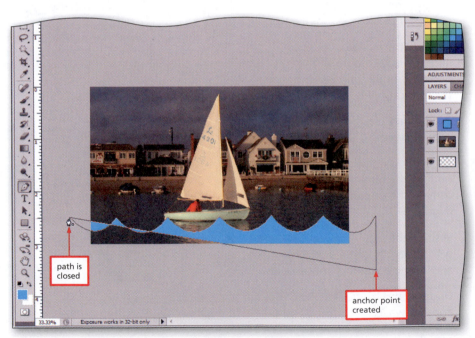

Figure 8–16

The Path Selection and Direct Selection Tools

Two tools are particularly useful to edit the shape and placement of paths by moving lines and anchor points. The Path Selection Tool moves the entire path. The Direct Selection Tool moves individual anchor points and direction points.

To Add Anchor Points to a Shape

For precise adjustments along path segments, you sometimes need to insert additional anchor points. Photoshop creates direction lines automatically with each added anchor point to give you more flexibility in editing. The following steps add anchor points using the Add Anchor Point Tool.

1
- On the Tools panel, right-click the Pen Tool button to display the context menu (Figure 8–17).

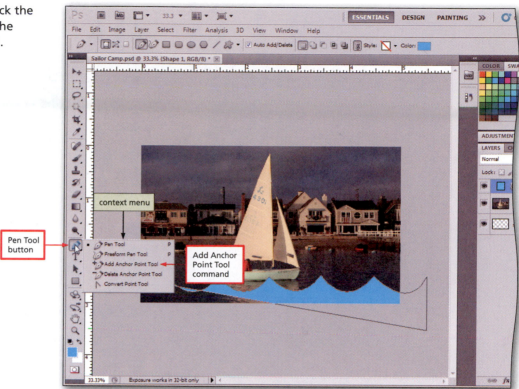

context menu

Pen Tool button

Add Anchor Point Tool command

Figure 8–17

2
- Click Add Anchor Point Tool in the list.

- In the document window, click the middle of the bottom edge of the path to add an anchor point (Figure 8–18).

Q&A Why did the mouse pointer display a plus sign?

The mouse pointer displays a plus sign (+) next to the tip of the pen when you add anchor points, and direction points appear.

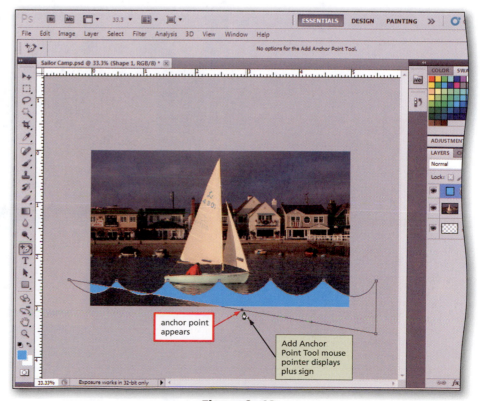

anchor point appears

Add Anchor Point Tool mouse pointer displays plus sign

Figure 8–18

3

- On the Tools panel, right-click the Path Selection Tool button to display the context menu.

- Click Direct Selection Tool in the list (Figure 8–19).

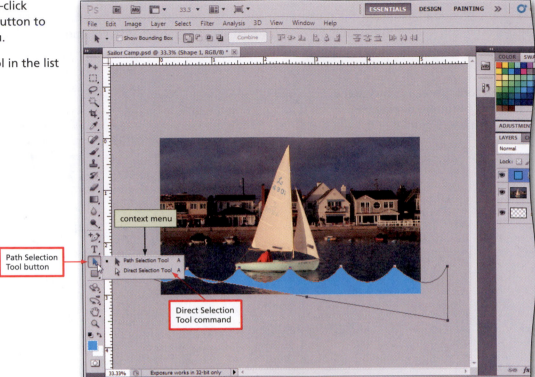

Figure 8–19

4

- Drag the new anchor point down and to the left to reposition the path so it no longer overlaps itself (Figure 8–20).

Other Ways

1. Right-click path, click Add Anchor Point

2. On Pen Tool options bar, click Auto Add/Delete, click path

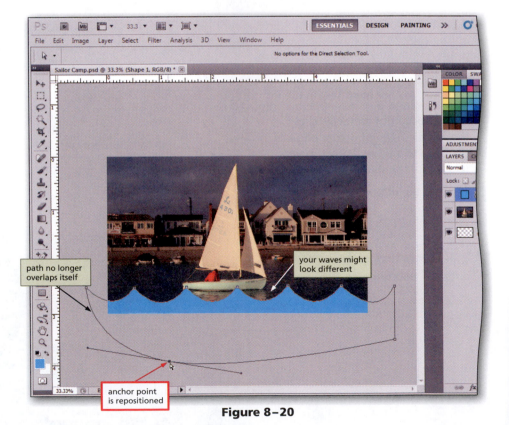

Figure 8–20

To Use Direction Points

Recall that anchor points contain a direction line that extends in opposite directions out from the anchor point. The direction line contains a direction point on either end, as well as the center anchor point itself. Dragging direction points alters the length and angle of the direction line, which in turn changes the shape of the path. Anchor points that have been converted to corner points contain a direction line that extends in a single direction on one side only of the anchor point. The following steps adjust the path using the direction points.

1
• With the Direct Selection Tool still active, click the starting anchor point at the top left of the path to select it.

• Drag the direction point up to make the wave a little shallower (Figure 8–21).

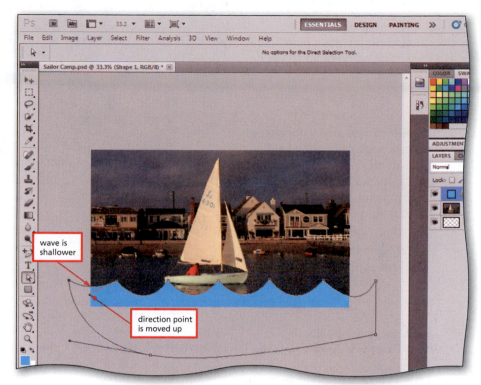

Figure 8–21

2
• Click the third top anchor point to display additional direction lines.

• Drag both direction points up slightly to the side to create shallower, different shaped waves (Figure 8–22).

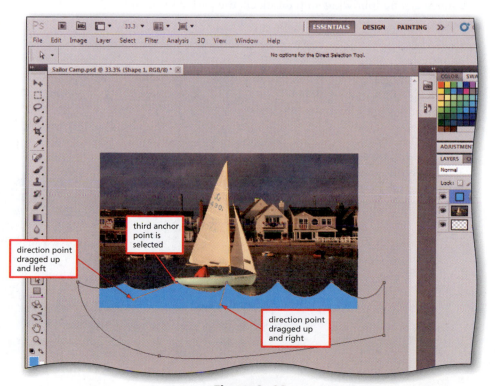

Figure 8–22

3
- Click the fifth top anchor point to display additional direction lines.
- Drag both direction points up and slightly to the side to create shallower, different shaped waves (Figure 8–23).

4
- Click the top-right anchor point and drag its direction point to your liking.

Q&A

Why would I ever want to delete an anchor point?

Sometimes deleting an anchor point will help you straighten path lines. To delete an anchor point, select the Delete Anchor Point Tool from the context menu on the Tools panel and then click the anchor point. A minus sign will appear next to the mouse pointer. The path then straightens between the two adjacent anchor points.

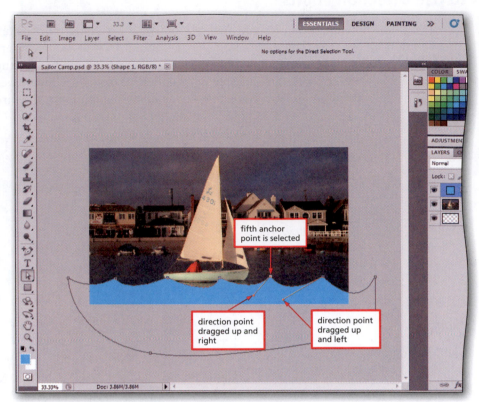

Figure 8–23

To Deselect Anchor Points and Rename the Layer

When you are finished adjusting anchor points and direction points, you should deselect the path so its outline is no longer visible. Deselecting makes it easier to work on other aspects of the document without the distraction of the outline. The following step deselects the path and renames the waves layer.

1
- Click the vector mask thumbnail on the Shape 1 layer to deselect the path (Figure 8–24).
- Double-click the Shape 1 layer name. Type **waves** and then press the ENTER key to rename the layer.

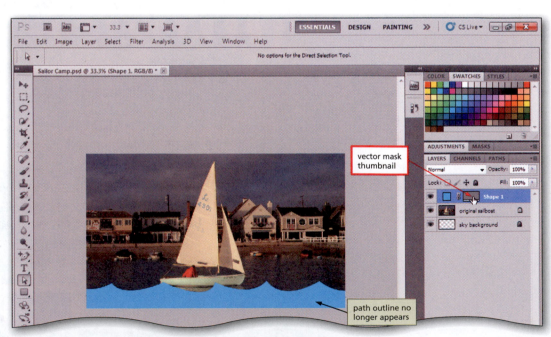

Figure 8–24

To Save the Document

The following step saves the document.

1 Press CTRL+S to save the document.

To Set the Foreground Color

The following steps set the foreground color for the sailboat body.

1 Click the visibility icon on the waves layer to hide the layer.

2 Click the original sailboat layer to select it.

3 Zoom to 66.67% and scroll as necessary to display the sailboat.

4 Click the 'Set foreground color' button to display the Color Picker (Foreground Color) dialog box.

5 Drag the title bar of the Color Picker dialog box, if necessary, to view the entire sailboat.

6 If necessary, remove the check mark in the Only Web Colors check box to access a greater variety of colors.

7 Click the shaded area on the sailboat hull or body to select the color (Figure 8–25).

8 Click the OK button (Color Picker dialog box) to close the Color Picker and set the foreground color.

BTW

Freeform Pen Settings
Clicking the Geometry options button on the options bar displays additional settings for the Freeform Pen Tool. Photoshop can detect edges within a specified distance from the mouse pointer. The Contrast setting determines what percentage of contrast is considered an edge; for example, 10% means very light differentiation. If you are working with a stylus tablet, you can select Pen Pressure in the Geometry options to adjust the width.

Figure 8–25

To Create a Shape Using the Magnetic Pen Tool

The following steps create a clip art version of the sailboat body. You will use the Magnetic option of the Freeform Pen Tool to draw around the front of the boat. The magnetism is similar to the Magnetic Lasso Tool in that the marquee is attracted to the edge of the object around which you drag. As you move the mouse pointer using the Magnetic option, work slowly. If the line goes astray, move the mouse backward. If several points become misaligned, press the ESC key and begin again.

1

• On the Tools panel, right-click the current Pen Tool button to display the context menu.

• Click Freeform Pen Tool to select it.

• On the options bar, click the Shape layers button.

• On the options bar, click the Magnetic check box so that it displays a check mark (Figure 8–26).

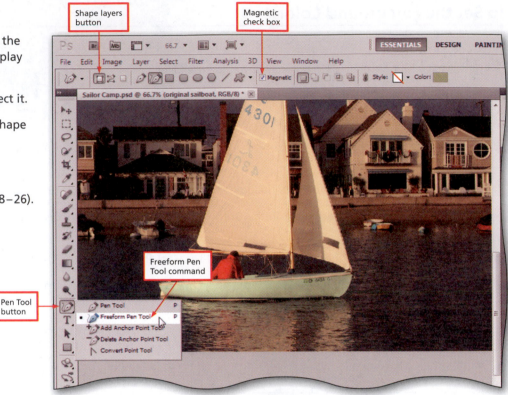

Figure 8–26

2

• Click the top-left corner of the sailboat body and slowly drag around it. Be sure to drag only around the side of the sailboat hull and not around the top portion that is visible inside the boat.

• Click the first anchor point to close the shape and fill it with the selected color (Figure 8–27).

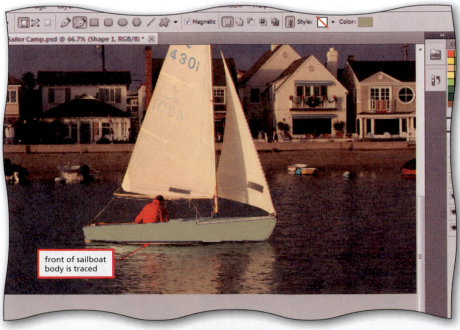

Figure 8–27

3

- Double-click the Shape 1 layer name to select it.

- Type **body front** and then press the ENTER key to rename the layer.

- Click the vector mask thumbnail on the body front layer to deselect the shape outline (Figure 8–28).

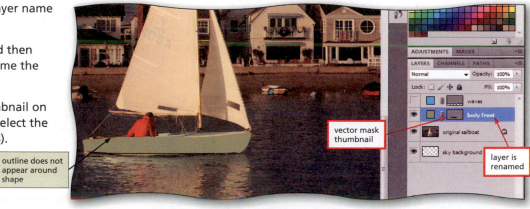

outline does not appear around shape

vector mask thumbnail

layer is renamed

Figure 8–28

To Set the Foreground Color

The following steps specify a darker color for the interior of the sailboat body by changing the foreground color.

1 Click the 'Set foreground color' button on the Tools panel to display the Color Picker (Foreground Color) dialog box.

2 Click the location shown in the figure to choose a darker shade (Figure 8–29).

3 Click the OK button (Color Picker dialog box) to set the new foreground color.

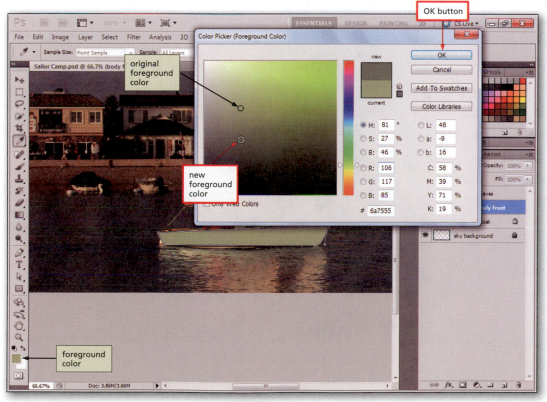

Figure 8–29

To Create the Top of the Sailboat Body Using the Freeform Pen Tool

Next you will draw a new shape that represents the top surface of the sailboat. The following steps create a new shape layer for the top of the sailboat body.

 1
- Zoom to 100% and scroll as necessary to display the top of the sailboat body.

- Right-click the current Freeform Pen Tool on the Tools Panel and click the Pen Tool to select it.

- Click the upper-left corner that defines the top of the sailboat body to create the first anchor point.

- Click the bottom-left corner of the top of the sailboat body to create the second anchor point and the first line.

- Click the upper-right corner of the sailboat body to continue the shape.

- Click the starting anchor point to close the shape (Figure 8–30).

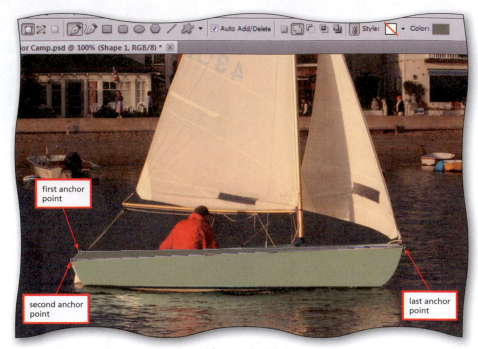

Figure 8–30

 2
- On the Tools Panel, click the Direct Selection Tool to select it.

- Drag the three anchor points so the edge of the shape lines up with the sailboat body shape. There should be no space between the two sailboat body shapes (Figure 8–31).

Q&A

I have some space showing between the top and body of the sailboat. How can I fix it?

Select the body front shape and adjust its anchor points with the Direct Selection Tool to minimize or eliminate the space between the parts.

 3
- In the Layers panel, double-click the Shape 1 layer name. Type **body top** and then press the ENTER key to rename the layer.

- Click the vector mask thumbnail on the body top layer to deselect the shape outline.

Figure 8–31

To Complete the Sailboat Body

The following steps adjust the anchor points of the sailboat body to give the appearance that the boat is in the waves.

1

- Double-click the Hand Tool on the Tools panel to fit the document window to the screen.

- Click the visibility icon on the waves layer to show it.

- Click the visibility icon on the original sailboat layer to hide it so it does not distract you as you work (Figure 8–32).

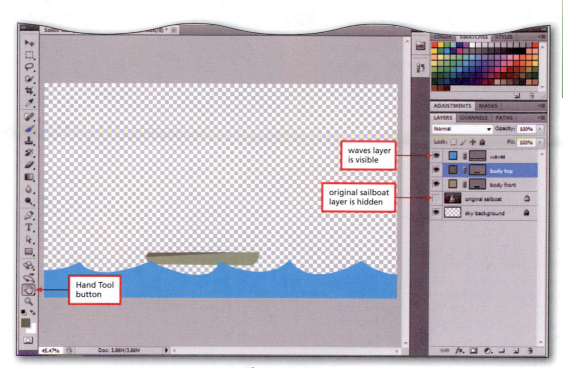

Figure 8–32

2

- Click the body front layer to select it.

- Click the Direct Selection Tool on the Tools panel to select it.

- Click the shape outline on the sailboat body to select it and display its anchor points (Figure 8–33).

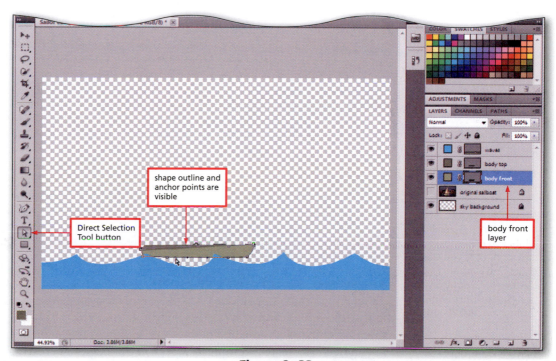

Figure 8–33

3

● Drag all the bottom anchor points down until there is no space between the sailboat body and the waves (Figure 8–34).

4

● Click the vector mask thumbnail on the body front layer to deselect the shape outline.

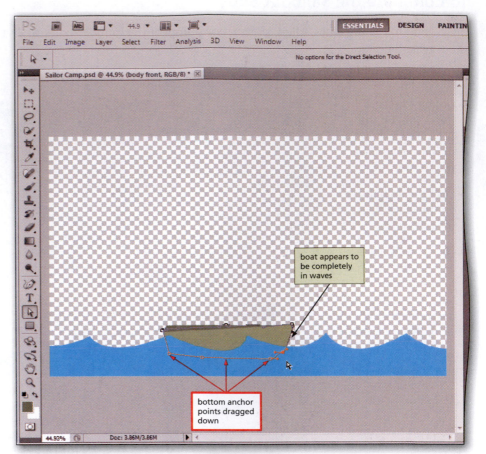

Figure 8–34

To Save the Document

The following step saves the document.

1 Press CTRL+S to save the document.

BTW

Viewing Anchor Points
If you want to see a line while you create new anchor points, you can click the Geometry options button on the options bar. One of the geometry options for the Pen tool is a Rubber Band check box. The Rubber Band feature helps guide the next anchor point by displaying a stretch line between anchor points, even before you click.

Paths

If you select the Paths button on the Shapes options bar, the path does not create a shape layer on the Layers panel; instead, it becomes a path or work path on the Paths panel. Once created, you can use a path to make a selection, create a vector mask, or fill and stroke with color to create raster graphics. A **work path** is a temporary path that opens in the Paths panel and defines the outline of the shape until you save or rename it. If you need to create a complex shape, you can begin by creating multiple paths and then combine them into a single shape.

The Paths panel (Figure 8–35) lists the name and a thumbnail image of each saved path, the current work path, and the current vector mask.

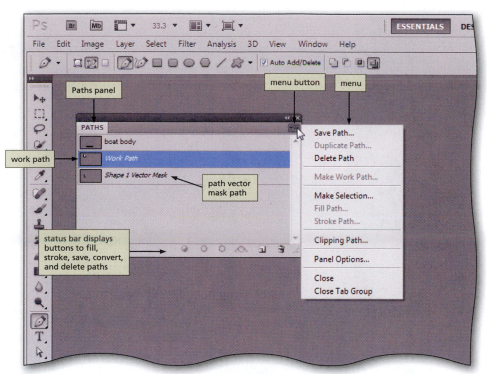

Figure 8–35

Auto Add/Delete Anchor Points
You can change the number of anchor points using the Auto Add/Delete box on the Pen tool's options bar. If the Auto Add/Delete check box is checked, clicking a path segment creates a new anchor automatically, and clicking an existing anchor point automatically deletes it.

To Create a Path Using the Pen Tool

In the Sailor Camp document window, you will use the Pen Tool to create two paths — one for the sails and one for the space between them. You will then combine the two paths into a single shape. The following steps create a path on the Paths panel with the Pen Tool.

1
- Click the visibility icon on the original sailboat layer to make it visible.

- On the Layers panel, click the original sailboat layer to select it.

- Select the Pen Tool.

- On the options bar, click the Paths button to choose the mode that creates a path on the Paths panel. If necessary, click the 'Add to path area' button to select it (Figure 8–36).

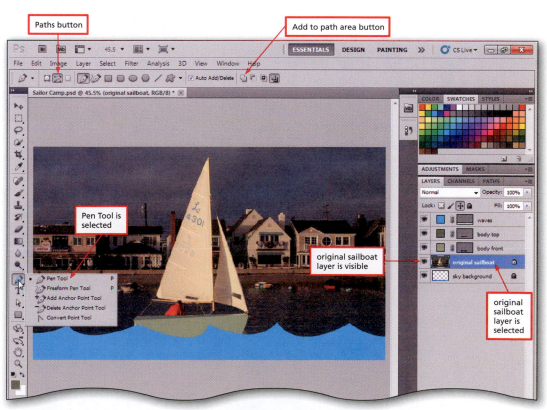

Figure 8–36

2

- Click the top of the large sail to create the first anchor point.

- Click the bottom-left corner of the large sail to create the third anchor point and drag slightly down and right to follow the curve of the sail.

- ALT+click the second anchor point to convert it to a corner point.

- Click the bottom-right corner of the large sail and drag slightly up and right to follow the curve (Figure 8–37).

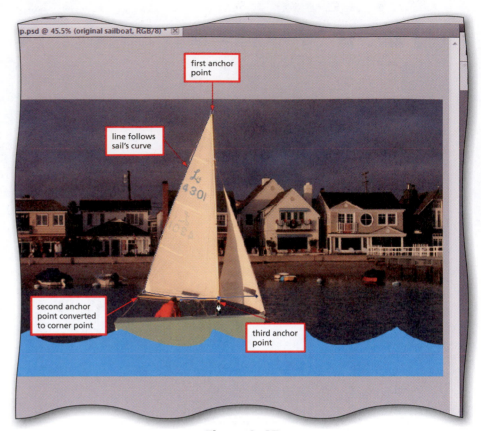

Figure 8–37

3

- ALT+click the third anchor point to convert it to a corner point.

- Click the lower-right corner of the small sail and drag slightly down and right to follow the curve of the sail.

- ALT+click the fourth anchor point to convert it to a corner point.

- Click the top corner of the small sail and drag slightly up and left to follow the curve.

- ALT+click the fifth anchor point to convert it to a corner point (Figure 8–38).

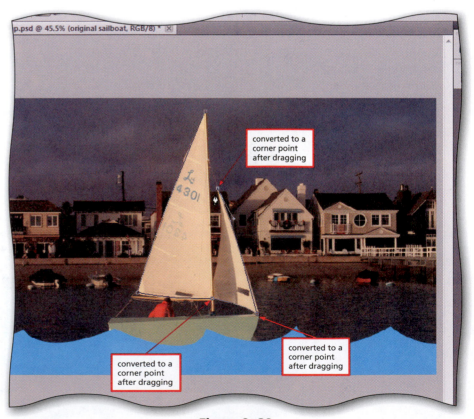

Figure 8–38

4

- Click toward the top of the right edge of the large sail.

- Click the starting point to close the path (Figure 8–39).

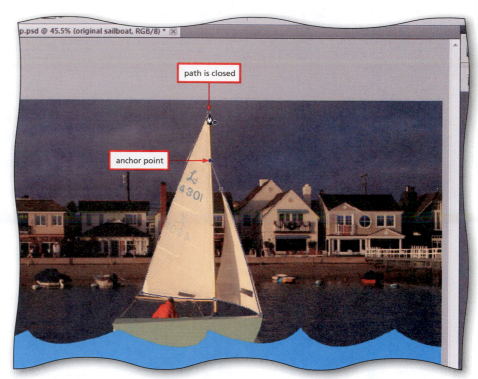

Figure 8–39

To Display the Paths Panel

The following step displays the Paths panel and the work path that was created in the previous steps.

1

- Click the Paths panel tab to display the Paths panel (Figure 8–40).

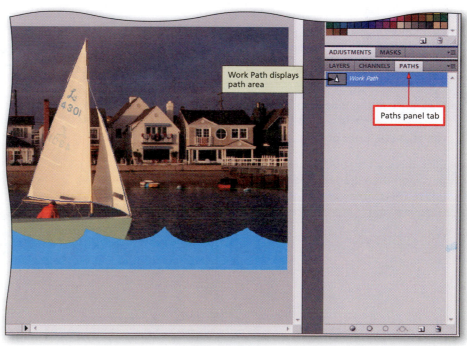

Figure 8–40

To Save a Work Path as a Named Path

Because work paths are temporary, the following step saves and names the path.

1

- On the Paths panel, double-click the Work Path name, type **sails**, and press ENTER to rename the path.

Q&A Why should I rename the path?

Renaming a Work Path saves the path. If you did not rename the Work Path, it would disappear as soon as the path was deselected.

- Click the gray area of the Paths panel below the sails path to deselect it (Figure 8–41).

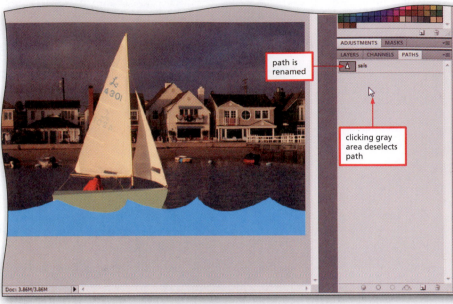

Other Ways

1. On Paths panel menu, click Save Path, enter name, deselect

Figure 8–41

To Create a Second Path

The following step creates a path around the space between the sails, which allows you to work with a single shape that includes both sails rather than two separate shapes for each sail.

1

- Click once on the right edge of the large sail just below the top of the space to create the first anchor point in the new path.

- Click once at the bottom of the space between the sails to create the second anchor point.

- Click the starting point to close the path and then drag up and to the left to follow the curve of the space (Figure 8–42).

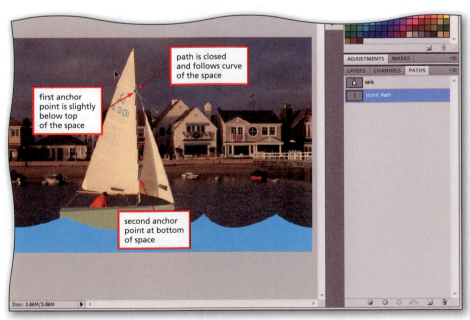

Figure 8–42

To Save the Second Path

The following step saves the path.

1 On the Paths panel, double-click the Work Path name, type **space**, and press ENTER to rename the path.

To Merge Paths

In the next steps, the paths are merged. Merging makes the sails and the space between them a single shape, so if you move the sails, the space between them moves too.

1

• On the Tools panel, right-click the Direct Selection Tool and click the Path Selection Tool to select it.

• Click the outline of the space path to select the path (Figure 8–43).

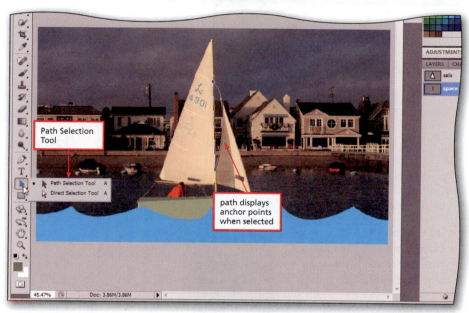

Figure 8–43

2

• Press CTRL+C to copy the path.

• On the Paths panel, click the sails path to select it.

• Press CTRL+V to paste the copied space path to the sails path.

• With the Path Selection Tool still selected, drag the pasted path down so it does not touch or overlap the outer sails path. It is fine if the outline no longer matches the space between the sails exactly (Figure 8–44).

Q&A

I cannot tell whether the pasted path is overlapping. The path outline is hard to see.

Drag the pasted path down and to the left until you can clearly see it is not overlapping. Then drag it back into position, making sure it does not overlap.

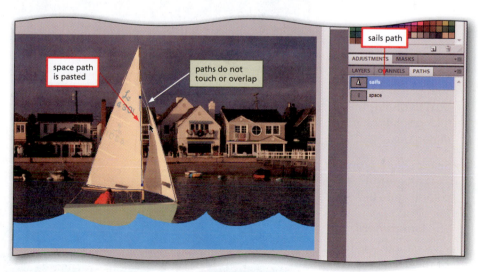

Figure 8–44

To Create a Shape Layer from a Path

The merged path now includes shapes that represent the two sails. The following steps create a new shape layer, consisting of the merged path that can be colored.

1

- With the sails path still selected, click Layer on the menu, and then point to New Fill Layer to display the fill choices (Figure 8–45).

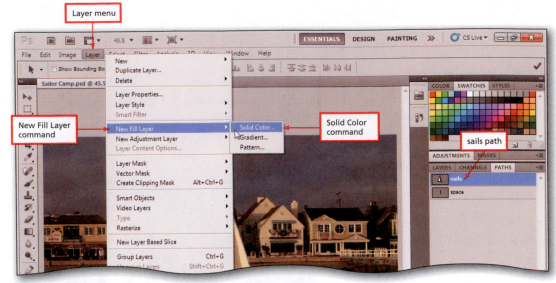

Figure 8–45

2

- Click Solid Color to display the New Layer dialog box.

- Type **sails complete** to name the new shape layer (Figure 8–46).

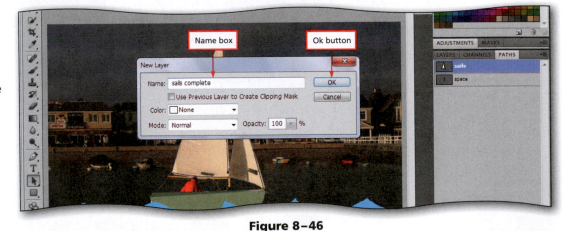

Figure 8–46

3

- Click the OK button (New Layer dialog box) to display the 'Pick a solid color' dialog box.

- Select a light brown or tan color for the sail color (Figure 8–47).

Experiment

- Click various locations of the document window to experiment with different colors for the sail's complete shape. Click the light brown or tan color.

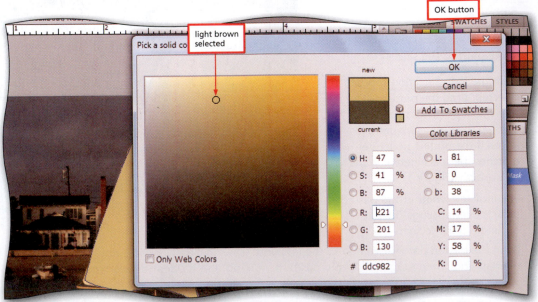

Figure 8–47

4
- Click the OK button (Pick a Solid Color dialog box) to close the color picker.

- Click the gray area below the paths in the Paths panel to deselect the path (Figure 8–48).

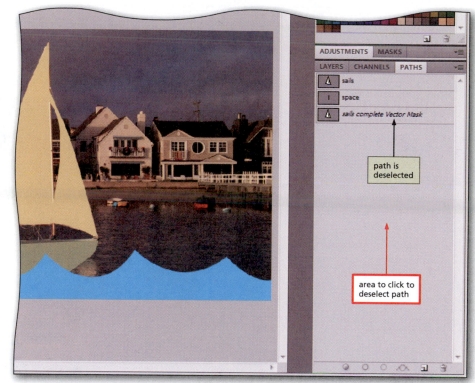

Figure 8–48

5
- Click the Layers tab to display the Layers panel and the new shape layer named sails complete (Figure 8–49).

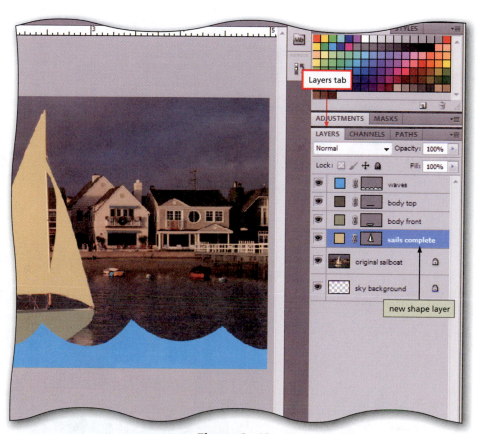

Figure 8–49

To Complete the Masts Using the Line Tool

Finally, to finish the sailboat, you will use the Line Tool to create the masts attaching the sails to the body.

1

- Right-click the current Shape tool on the Tools panel and click the Line Tool to select it (Figure 8–50).

Figure 8–50

2

- On the options bar, click the Shape layers button if necessary.

- Set the Weight to 10 px (Figure 8–51).

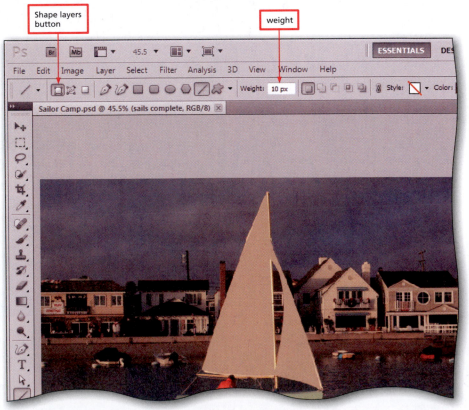

Figure 8–51

3

- If necessary, click the Swatches tab to display the Swatches panel.

- Click Darker Warm Brown to set it as the foreground color (Figure 8–52).

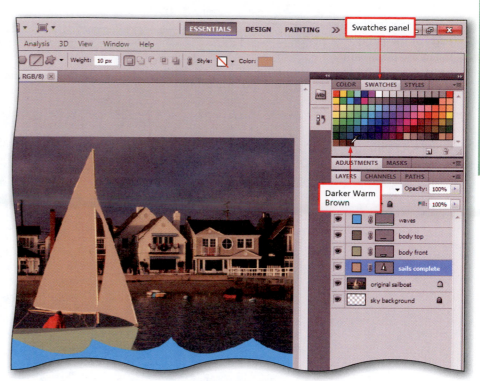

Figure 8–52

4

- Drag down the right edge of the large sail in the document window to create the vertical mast.

- Name the layer `vert mast` (Figure 8–53).

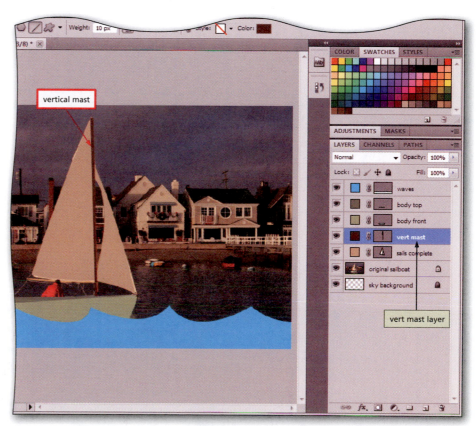

Figure 8–53

5

- Drag across the bottom edge of the large sail in the document window to create the horizontal mast.

- Name the layer `horiz mast` (Figure 8–54).

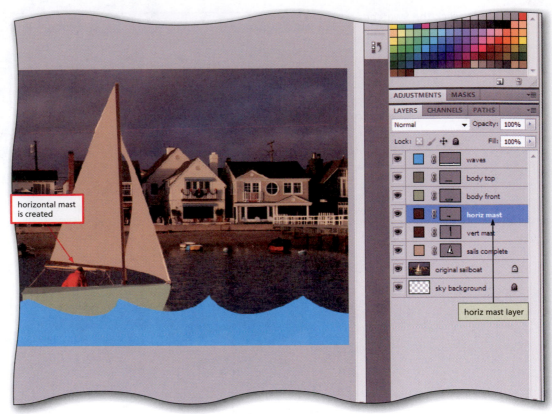

Figure 8–54

6

- Click the visibility icon on the original sailboat layer to hide it (Figure 8–55).

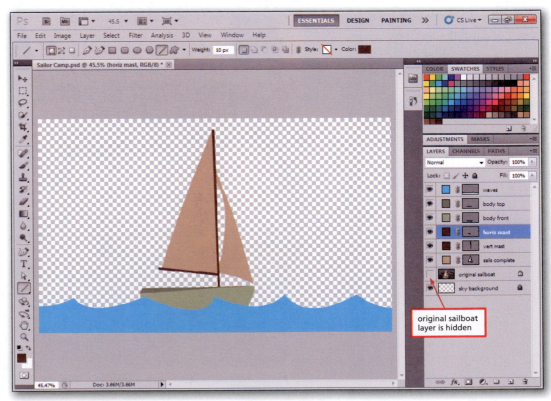

Figure 8–55

To Save the Document

The following step saves the document.

1 Press CTRL+s to save the document.

Layer Groups

A **layer group** is a named folder on the Layers panel that is used to contain a collection of layers. Layers can be created within the folder or moved into the folder. The number of additional layers, layer effects, and layer groups is limited only by the computer's memory capacity. The New Group command creates an empty group. The New Group from Layers command creates a group and places the selected layers in it.

When you create a new layer group, you can specify its name, its identifying color on the Layers panel, a blending mode, and an opacity setting. The settings apply to all layers created in, or moved to, the group. A layer group is displayed on the panel with a folder icon and with a triangle, called a Hide/Show layers icon, that points down to reveal the individual layers in the group, or points right to hide them (Figure 8–56). The icon does not affect the document window, however. The visibility icon determines whether the layer group is hidden or is displayed in the document window. Just like layers, a hidden layer group does not print.

Layer groups can be nested. This is helpful when you need to subdivide a large group into several smaller related groups. To nest layer groups, drag a layer group on top of another layer group in the Layers panel. To undo the nesting, drag the nested group out. Pay close attention to the Layers panel; as you drag, Photoshop displays borders to help identify the drop zones.

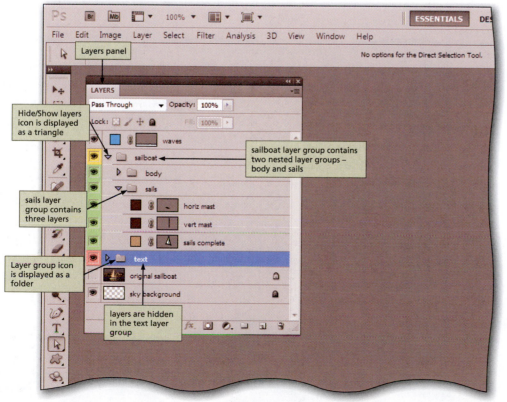

Figure 8–56

To Create a Layer Group from Layers

Four layer groups will be created for the Sailor Camp image: one to hold color and shapes related to the sailboat; two nested groups within the sailboat group separating the body from the sails; and one final group for the shapes related to the text.

- Click the body top layer in the Layers panel to select it.
- SHIFT+click the body front layer to select it in addition to the body top layer (Figure 8–57).

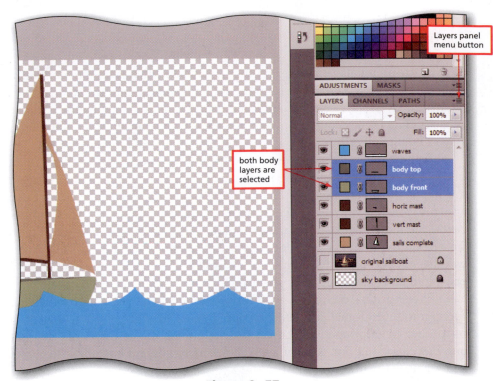

Figure 8–57

2

- Click the Layers panel menu button to display the menu (Figure 8–58).

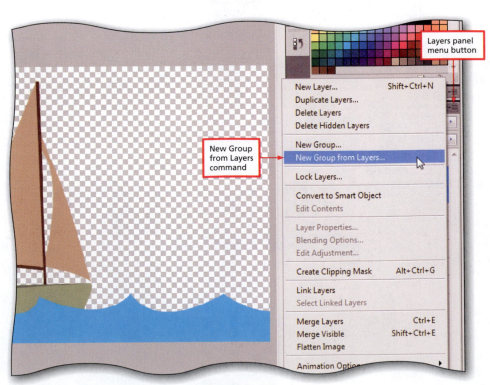

Figure 8–58

● Click New Group from Layers to display the New Group from Layers dialog box.

● Type **body** in the Name text box. Click the Color box arrow and then click Green in the list to change the settings for the new layer group (Figure 8–59).

Q&A What does Pass Through mean in the Mode box?

Pass Through is the default blending mode for layer groups and means the group will have no blending properties of its own.

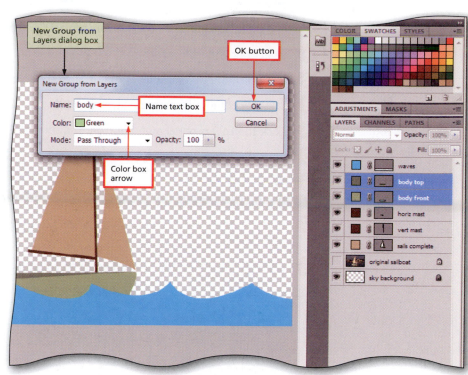

Figure 8–59

●④

● Click the OK button (New Group from Layers dialog box) to create the new layer group.

● Click the Hide/Show layers icon on the body layer group to expand it and see its contents (Figure 8-60).

Q&A How do I know that the body top and body front layers are inside the layer group?

On the Layers panel, layers within the layer group are indented.

● Click the Hide/Show layers icon again to collapse the layer group.

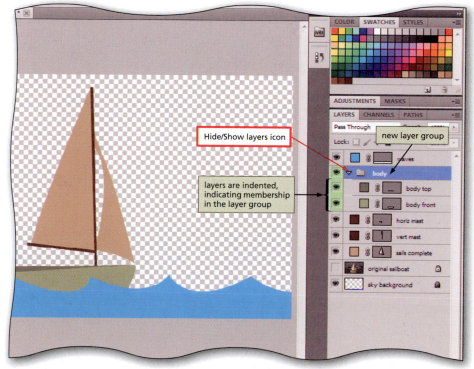

Figure 8–60

Other Ways

1. On Layer menu, point to New, click Group from Layers
2. Click 'Create a new group' button
3. Select layers, press CTRL+G

To Create More Groups from Layers

The following steps create four more layer groups.

1 Select horiz mast layer.

2 CTRL+click the vert mast layer to add it to the selection.

3 CTRL+click the sails complete layer to add it to the selection.

4 Click the Layers panel menu button to display the menu.

5 Click New Group from Layers to display the New Group from Layers dialog box.

6 Type `sails` in the Name box, select Green as the layer group color, and click the OK button (New Group from Layers dialog box) to create the layer group.

7 Click the Hide/Show layers icon to the left of the sails layer group to view its contents (Figure 8–61).

8 Click the Hide/Show layers icon again to collapse the layer group.

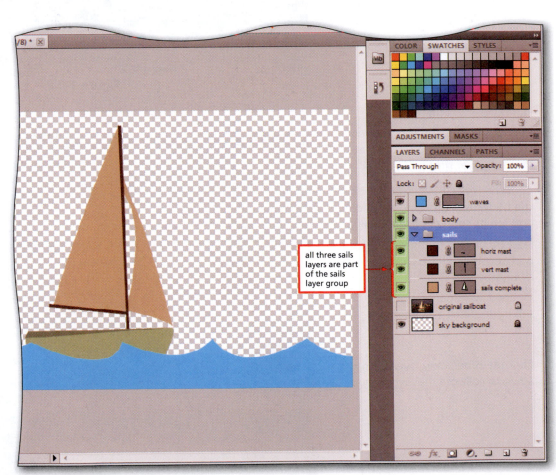

Figure 8–61

To Create a New Layer Group

The following step creates two new groups, rather than a single group from layers.

1

• Display the Layers panel menu and then click New Group (not New Group from Layers). Name the group, text, using the color Red.

• ALT+click the 'Create a new group' button at the bottom of the Layers panel to create a group named, sailboat, with the color Yellow (Figure 8–62).

Q&A

Why did I ALT+click the 'Create a new group' button rather than single click it?

When you ALT+click the 'Create a new group' button, the New Group dialog box appears, allowing you to name and set other options for the layer group.

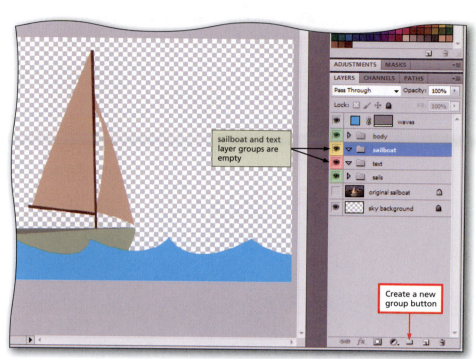

Figure 8–62

To Nest Layer Groups

Nest layer groups to help organize your content. The following step nests the sails and body groups inside the sailboat layer group.

1

• On the Layers panel, drag the body layer group on top of the sailboat layer group. Be sure the sailboat layer group displays a border around all four sides before you release the mouse button as this indicates that the dragged body layer group will be placed inside the sailboat layer group.

• Drag the sails layer group onto the sailboat layer to nest it (Figure 8–63).

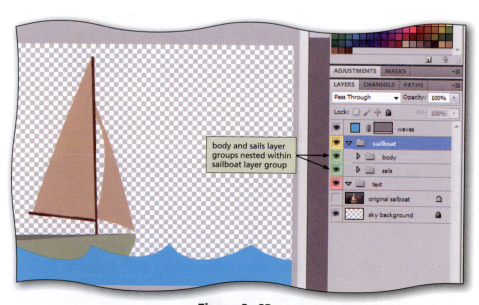

Figure 8–63

To Move Layer Groups

The following steps reposition the sailboat elements as a unit, then reposition just the sails.

1 On the Tools panel, click the Move Tool to select it.

2 On the Layers panel, click the sailboat layer group to select it, if necessary.

3 Drag the sailboat to center it in the document window. Notice that when you move the layer group, all elements contained within the group move (in this case, the sails, masts, boat top, and boat body).

4 Once the sailboat is positioned to your liking, click the nested sails layer group to select it.

5 Drag the sails to a different position in the document window. Notice that only the contents of the sails layer group (sails and masts) move.

6 Finally, position the sailboat in the horizontal center of the document window and move the sails to the front (right end) of the sailboat (Figure 8–64).

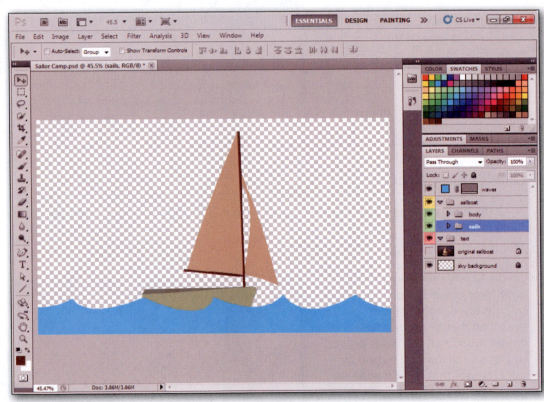

Figure 8–64

Using Text with Vector Shapes

The gold seal that is displayed in Figure 8–1 on page PS 458 is made up of a custom shape and a text element. You will append the Banners and Awards library of shapes using the Shape Preset picker. Then you will add the text. Text created in a vector shape will automatically adjust to fit the shape. Both components will become layers within the text layer group that you created earlier.

To Create the Award Seal Using a Custom Shape

On page PS 499, you created a layer group named, text. The following steps create the award shape in the text layer group using the Shape Preset picker.

1

- On the Layers panel, click the text layer group.

- On the Swatches panel, click the Pure Yellow color to change the foreground color.

- On the Tools panel, right-click the current Shape Tool button, and then click Custom Shape Tool.

- On the options bar, click the Shape layers button, if necessary, to select it.

- Click the Custom Shape picker button and then click the Custom Shape picker menu button to display the Shapes menu (Figure 8–65).

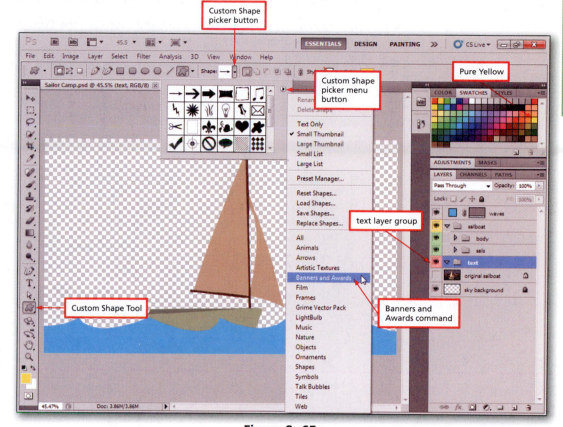

Figure 8–65

2

- Click Banners and Awards to load that set of shapes.

- Click the OK button when prompted to replace the current shapes.

- Click the Seal shape in the Custom Shape picker.

- In the document window, SHIFT+ drag a shape that almost fills the space to the left of the sailboat.

- If necessary, use the Move Tool to reposition the shape (Figure 8–66).

3

- Rename the new shape layer, seal.

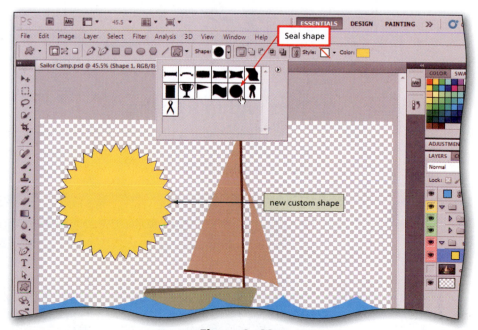

Figure 8–66

To Reset the Custom Shapes

The following steps reset the default shapes.

1 Click the Custom Shape Tool on the Tools panel to select it, if necessary.

2 Click the Custom Shape picker button and then click the Custom Shape picker menu button to display the Shapes menu.

3 Click Reset Shapes and then click the OK button to reset the custom shapes to the default settings (Figure 8–67).

4 Press the ESC key to close the Custom Shape picker.

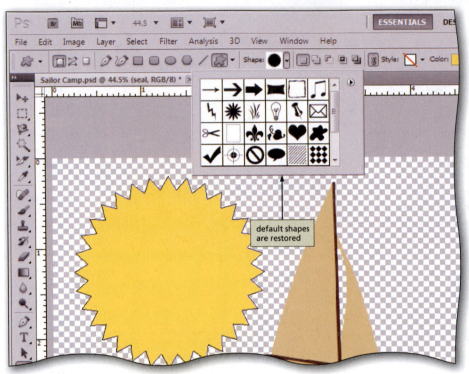

Figure 8–67

Text within a Shape

The next step is to create a type element within the seal. Text created in a vector shape will automatically adjust to fit the shape. The type settings for the seal shape are shown in Table 8–4.

Table 8–4 Type Tool Settings	
Type Option	**Setting**
Set the font family	Bookman Old Style or a similar font
Set the font style	Regular
Set the font size	14 pt
Set the anti-aliasing method	Smooth
Set the text alignment	Centered
Set the text color	Black

To Create Text within a Shape

The following steps create text in the seal.

 1

- With the vector mask thumbnail in the seal layer still selected, press the T key to access the current Type Tool.

- On the options bar, enter the settings from Table 8–4.

- In the document window, point to the seal (Figure 8–68).

Q&A

Why did the mouse pointer change?

The dotted oval shape around the mouse pointer indicates that the text will be created inside the shape, as opposed to in a new text box where the mouse pointer would display a rectangular shape around the insertion point.

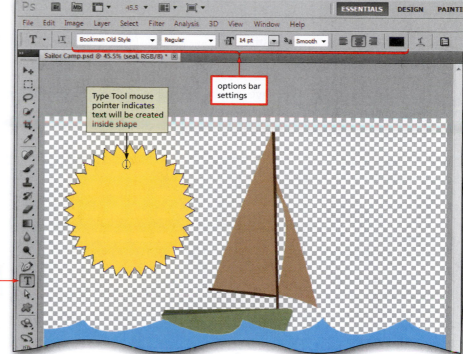

Figure 8–68

2

- Click the shape and then type **Voted #1 boating camp in Aquatic Parents Weekly** to enter the text (Figure 8–69).

- On the options bar, click the 'Commit any current edits' button to close the text box.

- On the Tools panel, click the Move Tool and reposition the text as necessary.

Q&A

What should I do if my text does not fit in the seal correctly?

Make the seal slightly larger by pressing CTRL+T to enter free transform mode. Drag the sizing handle of the bounding box to scale the shape and then press the ENTER key to apply the change. Alternatively, you can change the font size by a few points.

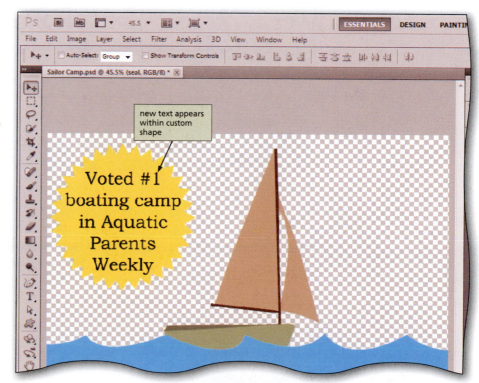

Figure 8–69

Converting Text to a Shape

If you cannot find the exact font you want, you can start with a font that is similar, and then convert the text to a shape. This converts the letters on the type layer to shapes, just as if you had drawn the letters with the Pen Tool. You then can use the Direct Selection Tool to alter the shape of each letter just as you would alter the anchor points and lines within a shape or path.

To Create a Type Layer

You will add a regular type layer to the right of the sailboat in the following steps. Later, you will convert the text to a shape and reshape the letters.

1

- On the Layers panel, select the seal layer if necessary.

- Press the T key to select the Horizontal Type Tool, if necessary.

- Click in the document window, to the right of the sailboat, to create a new type layer (Figure 8–70).

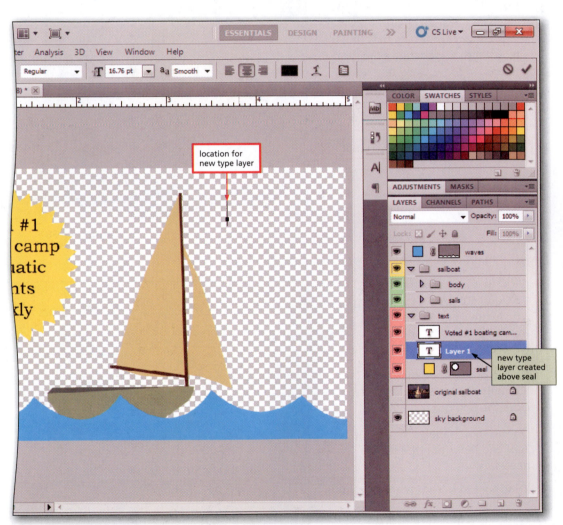

Figure 8–70

2

- On the options bar, set the font to Arial, the font style to Black, and the font size to 30.

- Click the 'Set the text color' box to display the Select text color dialog box.

- In the document window, click the dark green of the top of the sailboat body to select the color, and then click the OK button (Select text color dialog box) to set the color for the text.

- Type **Sailor** and then press the ENTER key. Type **Camp** to finish the text.

- On the options bar, click the 'Commit any current edits' button to close the text box.

- If necessary, use the Move Tool to reposition the text (Figure 8–71).

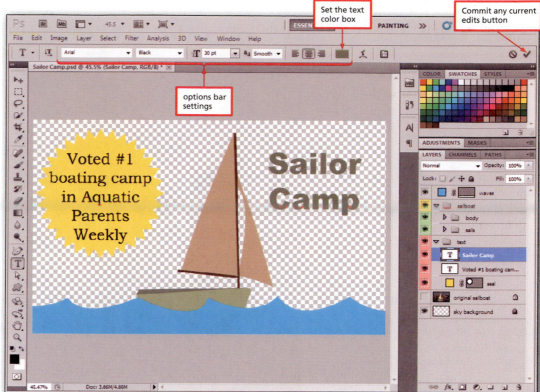

Figure 8–71

Q&A

My type is behind the sail. Is this a problem?

No, it is not a problem. You will adjust the text placement in a later step.

To Convert Text to a Shape

The following step converts the Sailor Camp text to a shape, which gives you the ability to manipulate the letters for visual interest.

1

- Click Layer on the menu and then point to Type.

- Click Convert to Shape to convert the text to a shape (Figure 8–72).

Figure 8–72

To Alter a Shape

The following steps alter the shape of the letters, giving the text an organic and childish feel.

1

- Zoom to 100% and scroll as necessary to display all of the Sailor Camp text.

- Press the A key to select the Direct Selection Tool.

- Click the outline of the capital S and move a few of the anchor points and direction points to change the shape of the letter (Figure 8–73).

Q&A

What if the Path Selection Tool was selected instead?

Because both the Path Selection Tool and the Direct Selection Tool use the same keyboard shortcut, A, you can press SHIFT+A to switch between the tools. If the Path Selection Tool is selected, press SHIFT+A to switch to the Direct Selection Tool.

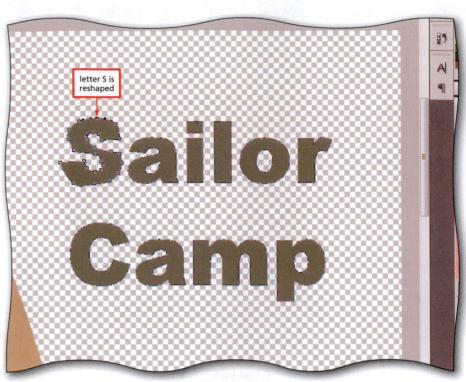

Figure 8–73

2

- Use the Direction Selection Tool to alter the shape of the remaining letters to create unique lettering (Figure 8–74).

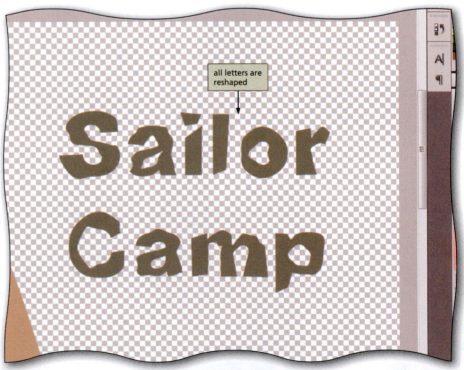

Figure 8–74

To Save the Document

The following step saves the document.

 Press CTRL+S to save the document.

Clip Art Detail

Good clip art uses strong lines and colors with enough detail to emphasize the purpose of the image. A clip art's purpose might be as simple as object identification requiring modest detail, or as complex as an idea within a context that might require intensive detail to get the point across. Movement, depth, and light play important roles in clip art; but without purpose, context, and visual detail, sometimes clip art is flat, static, and unsophisticated. In the following sections, you will add detail to the clip art, including overlays, layer styles, and shadows. Figure 8–75 displays examples of color overlays, shadows, and reflections.

Figure 8–75

Add detail to enhance clip art.
There are many ways to add detail to vector graphics and clip art, including overlays, layer styles, shadows, blending modes, and reflections. Make sure each of your edits is purposeful and not distracting. It is best to create a new layer for each enhancement.

Plan Ahead

To Fill a Shape with a Pattern

Clip art sometimes is created using layer styles to add detail. Recall that layer styles affect the appearance of the layer by adding depth, shadow, shading, texture, or overlay. In the steps on the next page, you will use a layer style to add texture to the sails.

1

- On the Tools panel, double-click the Hand Tool to fit the document to the screen.

- On the Layers panel, click the triangle to the left of the sailboat layer group to display its contents, if necessary.

- Click the triangle to the left of the sails layer group to display its contents, if necessary.

- Select the sails complete layer.

- Click the 'Add a layer style' button on the Layers panel status bar to display the list of layer styles.

- Click Pattern Overlay to display the Layer Style dialog box (Figure 8–76).

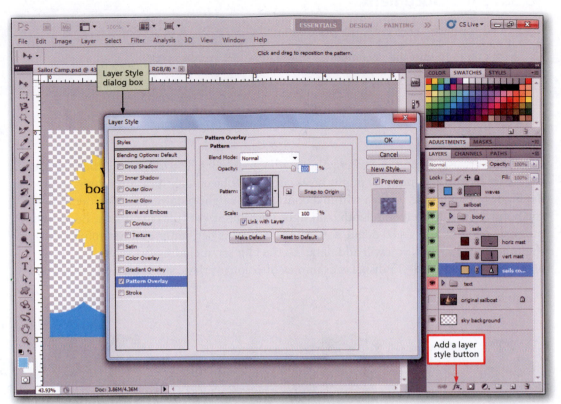

Figure 8–76

2

- In the Layer Style dialog box, click the Pattern picker to display thumbnails of the current patterns.

- Click the Pattern picker menu button to display the menu and then point to Artist Surfaces (Figure 8–77).

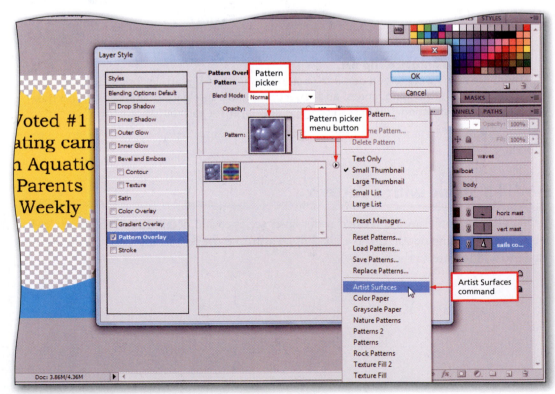

Figure 8–77

3
- Click Artist Surfaces and then click the OK button to append the current thumbnails with the new patterns.

- Click the third thumbnail, Burlap, to select it.

- Set the opacity to 50% (Figure 8–78).

4
- Click the OK button (Layer Style dialog box) to apply the pattern.

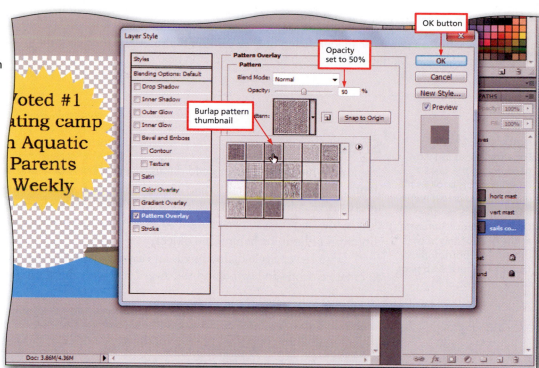

Figure 8–78

To Reset Patterns

The following steps reset the pattern thumbnails to their default settings. This is helpful for other students who might be using the same computer later. The Preset Manager is a dialog box where you can reset several different pop-up panels that display when you click picker buttons.

1
- On the menu bar, click Edit and then click Preset Manager to display the Preset Manager dialog box.

- Click the Preset Type box arrow and then click Patterns.

- Click the Preset Manager menu button to display the menu (Figure 8–79).

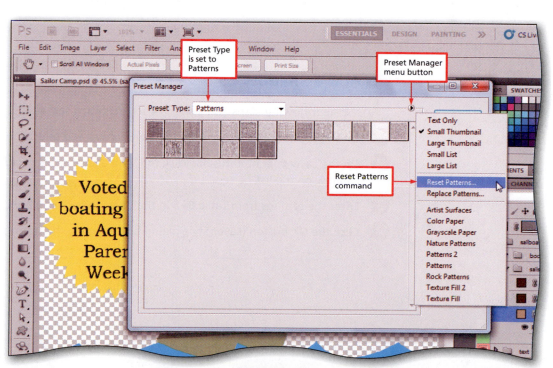

Figure 8–79

2

- Click Reset Patterns to reset the patterns.

- Click the OK button (Preset Manager dialog box) to confirm the reset and then click the Done button (Preset Manager dialog box) to close the dialog box.

BTW

Quick Reference
For a table that lists how to complete the tasks covered in this book using the mouse, shortcut menu, and keyboard, see the Quick Reference Summary at the back of this book or visit the Photoshop CS5 Quick Reference Web page (scsite.com/pscs5/qr).

Shadows

Another typical way to add detail to a clip art is by using shadows to represent depth. A **shadow** is a small extension on one or two sides of a graphic with a different, unobtrusive color, usually a shade of gray with no visible border. Shadows not only depict depth, but they also suggest a light source. A shadow is displayed opposite the perceived direction of light, or behind the object.

The Layer Style dialog box is an easy way to add a shadow. You will use a layer style to create a drop shadow behind the award seal with the settings shown in Table 8–5.

Table 8–5 Drop Shadow Settings	
Drop Shadow Effect	**Setting**
Blend Mode	Multiply
Opacity	80
Use Global Light	checked
Angle	150
Distance	7
Spread	10
Size	7
Noise	0
Contour	Linear
Layer Knocks Out Drop Shadow	checked

To Add a Shadow Using a Layer Style

The following steps add a shadow to the award seal shape.

1 On the Layers panel, expand the text layer group and select the seal layer.

2 On the Layers panel status bar, click the 'Add a layer style' button, and then click Drop Shadow on the list.

3 Enter the settings from Table 8–5 in the Layer Style dialog box.

4 Click the OK button (Layer Style dialog box) to apply the settings.

To Copy and Paste a Layer Style

The following steps copy and paste the shadow to the Sailor Camp shape layer.

1
- On the Layers panel, right-click the layer name, seal, to display the context menu. Do not click the layer thumbnail (Figure 8–80).

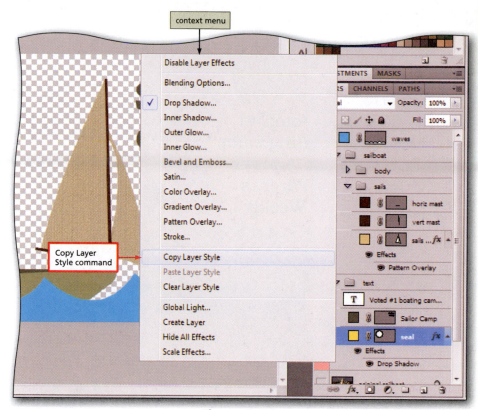

Figure 8–80

2
- Click Copy Layer Style to copy the style to the clipboard.

- Right-click the Sailor Camp shape layer to display the context menu (Figure 8–81).

- Click Paste Layer Style to apply the drop shadow.

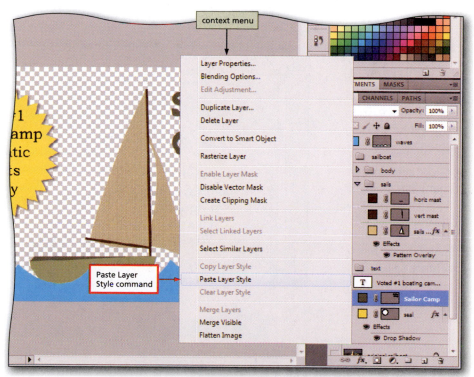

Figure 8–81

To Create a Background Gradient

The following steps complete the document by adding a gradient background.

1

- On the Layers panel, collapse any open layer groups so the Layers panel appears less cluttered.

- Click the bottom layer, sky background, to select it.

- Click the Lock all button to toggle the lock off (Figure 8–82).

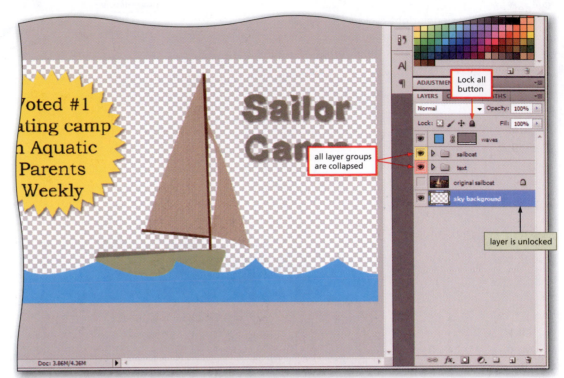

Figure 8–82

2

- Press the D key to reset the colors to their default settings of black and white.

- On the Swatches panel, click Pastel Cyan to set the foreground color.

- Click Layer on the menu bar, point to New Fill Layer, and click Gradient to display the New Layer dialog box (Figure 8–83).

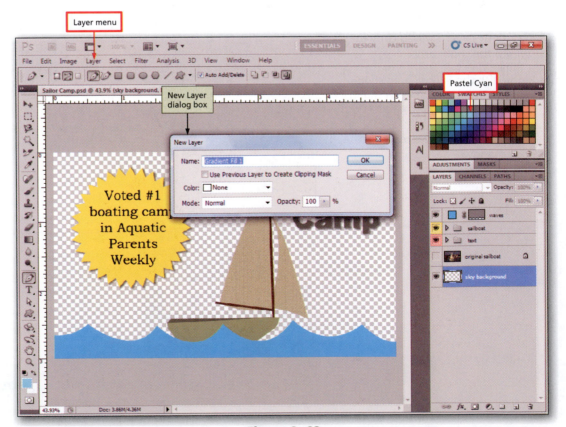

Figure 8–83

- Click the OK button (New Layer dialog box) to accept the default settings and display the Gradient Fill dialog box.

- Click the Gradient picker button (Gradient Fill dialog box) to display the Gradient picker (Figure 8–84).

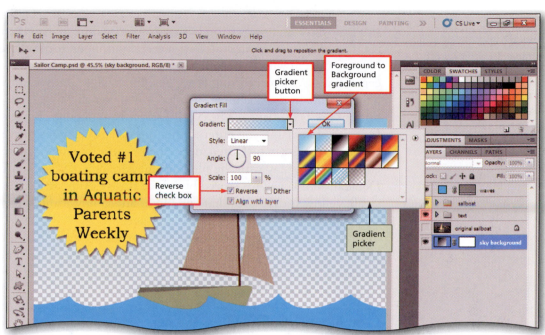

Figure 8–84

- Click the first gradient, Foreground to Background.

- Click the Gradient picker button again to close the Gradient picker.

- Click to display a check mark in the Reverse check box so the gradient goes from blue at the top to white at the bottom.

- Click the OK button (Gradient Fill dialog box) to apply the gradient (Figure 8–85).

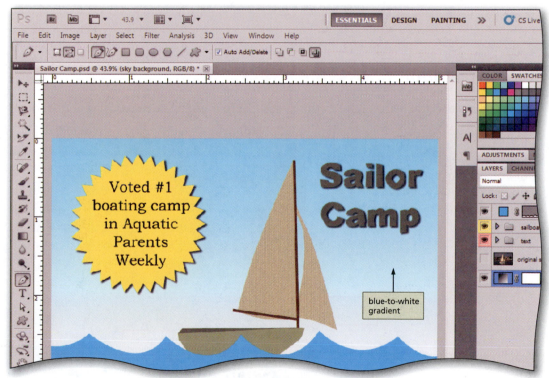

Figure 8–85

To Save the Document

The following step saves the document.

1 Press CTRL+S to save the document.

The Note Tool and Notes Panel

Photoshop Help
The best way to become familiar with Photoshop Help is to use it. Appendix D includes detailed information about Photoshop Help and exercises that will help you gain confidence in using it.

In Photoshop, an **annotation** is an explanatory note or comment included within the file itself. The Note Tool, included with the Eyedropper Tool on the Tools panel, opens the Notes panel, in which you can enter comments. Notes in the Notes panel have scrolling capabilities, standard editing functions, and a Close button in the corner. A yellow note icon appears in the document window when you click the Note Tool button and the Note options bar is displayed. The Note options bar contains choices for author, color, and font size. The name you enter in the Author box becomes the text on the Notes panel title bar. Notes can be edited, deleted, or repositioned anywhere on the image for greater emphasis; they stay with the file until they are deleted. These notes are different from the metadata and keywords stored by Adobe Bridge. Annotations are more like the popular, small, yellow sticky notes that you might attach physically, a comment inserted in many Office programs, or a short phone message.

Once created, to read a note, double-click it — you do not have to click the Note Tool to read notes. Notes do not print, and they are unique to Photoshop; a note in a Photoshop document is not visible in other graphic-editing software packages.

Plan Ahead

Annotate graphics within the file.
Photoshop gives you the opportunity to save notes with any image file. You might want to write a note to another person on your team about the use of the graphic, or you might want to keep some notes for yourself about which filter you used, or which settings you changed on a blend mode. Still other times, you might want to list some special instructions.

To Create a Note

The next steps create a note in the Sailor Camp image. The note will remind a coworker to add keywords to the clip art in Adobe Bridge.

• Right-click the Eyedropper Tool to display its context menu (Figure 8–86).

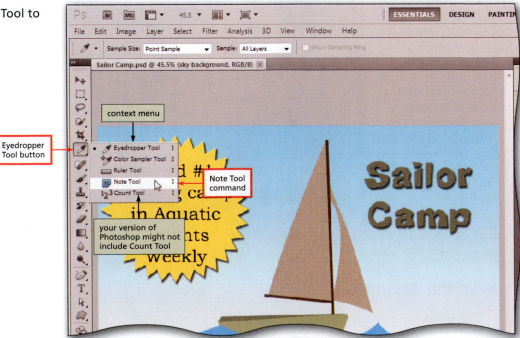

Figure 8–86

2

- Click Note Tool in the menu.

- Click the upper-left corner of the document window to open the Notes panel.

- In the Notes panel window, type **Anita, Don't forget to add keywords to this image using Adobe Bridge before you upload it to the server.** to complete the note (Figure 8–87).

3

- In the vertical panel group, click the Notes button to hide the panel.

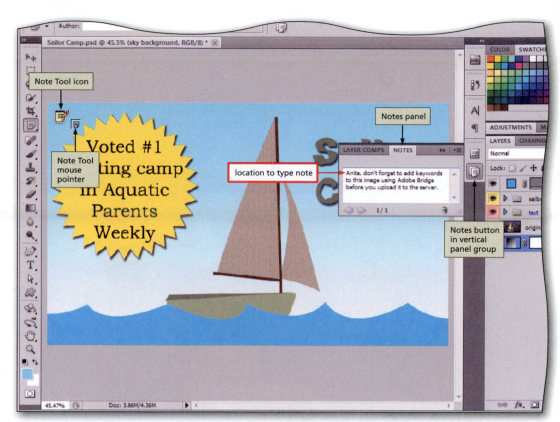

Figure 8–87

To Save the Document

The following step saves the fully layered, PSD version of the image.

1 Press CTRL+S.

Preparing the Image for Page Layout Applications

Currently, the Sailor Camp document features a gradient sky background. Oftentimes, clip art is created with a transparent background so the background of the page on which it is used shows through. In preparation for using the image in page layout applications, you will create a transparent background and convert the image to the PDF format. The PDF, or Portable Document Format, format produces a file consisting of all the Photoshop layers and also supports transparency. It is a format suitable for import to a page layout application and is also a format often requested by printing companies.

To Hide a Layer Creating a Transparent Background

In the following step, you will hide the gradient background to create a transparency.

1 Click the visibility icon on the sky background layer in the Layers panel to hide it (Figure 8–88).

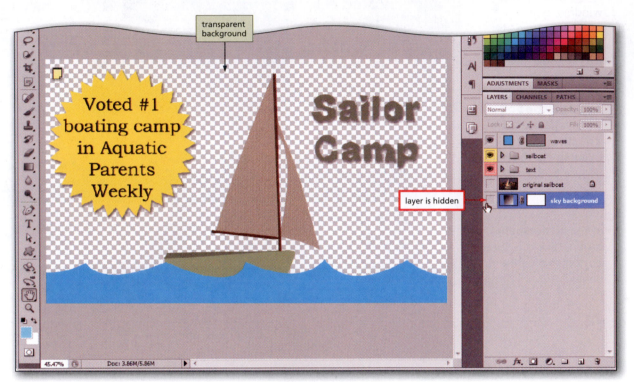

Figure 8–88

To Save in the PDF Format

The following steps save the file as a PDF suitable for import to a page layout program.

1 Press SHIFT+CTRL+S to display the Save As dialog box.

2 Type **Sailor Camp Transparency** in the File name box. Do not press the ENTER key.

3 Click the Format box arrow and then click Photoshop PDF (*.PDF, *.PDP) in the list.

4 In the Save Options section, ensure only the Layers and Notes boxes are checked.

5 Click the Save in box arrow and then click USB (F:), or the location associated with your USB flash drive, in the list.

6 Click the Save button (Save As dialog box) to display the Save Adobe PDF dialog box. Click the General category, if necessary.

7 Ensure only the first and third check boxes are checked (Figure 8–89).

8 Click the Save PDF button (Save Adobe PDF dialog box) to save the PDF.

9 If Photoshop displays a warning box about Photoshop editing capabilities, click the Yes button.

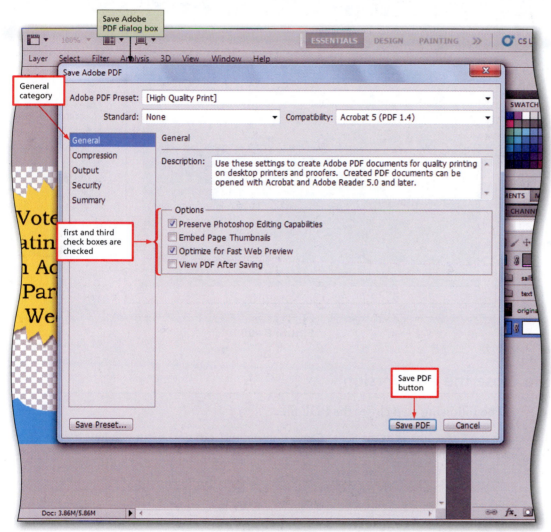

Figure 8–89

Displaying the Graphic in a Page Layout Program

The clip art now is ready to import to a page layout program. Figure 8–90 displays the PDF clip art file on a solid background in Adobe InDesign, a page layout program. As you can see, the graphic transparency is maintained, and it can be resized without any change in resolution.

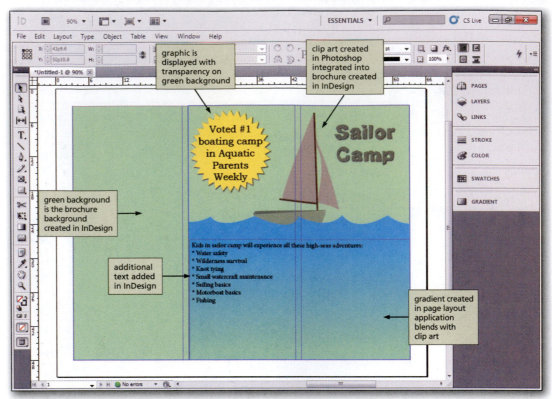

Figure 8–90

To Close the PDF Version

The following step closes the PDF file.

1 Click the Close button in the Sailor Camp Transparency.pdf document window. If Photoshop asks to save the file, click the No button.

Preparing the Image for the Web

Clip art for the Web, also called Web graphics, needs to load quickly and be stored in a format that makes coding a Web page easy. Recall that the standard format for Web graphics is GIF, or Graphics Interchange Format. The GIF format compresses the picture information, reducing file size. It also translates the digital image into a code that can be sent easily over the Internet. The GIF format is most effective on graphics that have contiguous areas of solid color. GIF files also support clip art transparency, so the graphics appear without a background of their own and can blend into the background of the canvas to which they are imported. An **interlaced** setting in a GIF format will display a low-resolution version of the image from the top down as the Web page loads. Interlacing makes download time seem shorter, but it also increases file size.

You will open the PSD version of the cartoon graphic and create an interlaced GIF version for the Web. You then will preview it in a browser.

To Create a Version for the Web

Recall that the Save for Web & Devices command allows you to create a version of an image that is optimized for the Web. The following steps create a Web-optimized version of the clip art.

1 Press CTRL+O and open the Sailor Camp.psd file.

2 On the File menu, click Save for Web & Devices to display the Save for Web & Devices dialog box.

3 Click the 4-Up tab, if necessary, to display the preview options.

4 In the Image size area, type 25 in the Percent box and press the ENTER key to reduce the size of the image so it is appropriate for use on the Web.

5 Click the Zoom Level box arrow and then click Fit in View to display the full graphic in each of the four preview panes.

6 Click the upper-right preview to select it.

7 In the upper-right portion of the dialog box, click the 'Optimized file format' button, and then click GIF in the list, if necessary.

8 Click the 'Specify the dither algorithm' box arrow and then click No Transparency Dither, if necessary.

9 Check both the Transparency and Interlaced check boxes for best display results on the Web.

10 In the lower-right portion of the dialog box, click the Quality box arrow and then click Nearest Neighbor, if necessary (Figure 8–91).

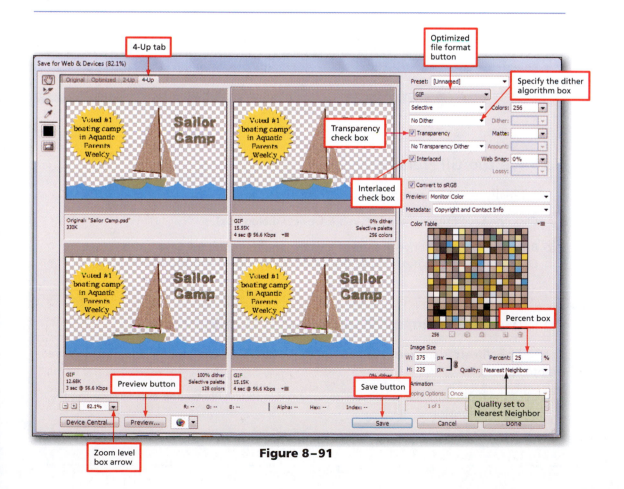

Figure 8–91

To Preview the Image

The steps that follow preview the GIF version of the clip art.

1 In the Save for Web & Devices dialog box, click the Preview button to view the image in a browser (Figure 8–92).

2 Close the browser window.

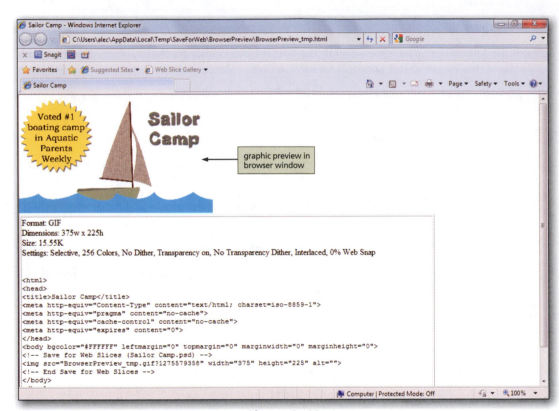

Figure 8–92

To Save the GIF Version

Finally, the steps that follow save the GIF version.

1 Click the Save button (Save for Web & Devices dialog box).

2 Browse to your USB drive or storage location and then click the Save button (Save Optimized As dialog box) to save the Web version with the name Sailor-Camp.gif.

To Close All Document Windows and Quit Photoshop

The clip art is complete, so you can close the document window and quit Photoshop.

1 Click the Close button in any open document window. If Photoshop asks to save the file, click the No button.

2 Click the Close button on the Photoshop title bar.

Chapter Summary

In this chapter, you converted a photo into clip art for a summer camp brochure and Web site using some colors that were chosen for their impact and other shades that were the colors of the original objects. You added details to give depth to the clip art. You learned about the general characteristics of clip art and transparency-based files destined for page layout applications and the difference between vector and raster graphics.

As you created layer groups and organized your objects, you created both paths and shape layers. You used the Pen and Freeform Pen Tools to draw line segments and anchor points. You added, subtracted, and converted anchor points to create straight lines and curves. The Path Selection and Direct Selection Tools helped position paths and shapes. You added detail to the clip art image, including background shape and color, shadows, blends, and impact lines. You used the Note Tool to annotate your file. Finally, you readied the clip art for use in a page layout application by converting it to the PDF format, and prepared the file for Web usage by saving it as a GIF file.

The items listed below include all the new Photoshop skills you have learned in this chapter:

1. Lock Layers (PS 465)
2. Create a Shape Layer Using the Pen Tool (PS 469)
3. Add Anchor Points to a Shape (PS 475)
4. Use Direction Points (PS 477)
5. Deselect Anchor Points and Rename the Layer (PS 478)
6. Create a Shape Using the Magnetic Pen Tool (PS 480)
7. Create the Top of the Sailboat Body Using the Freeform Pen Tool (PS 482)
8. Complete the Sailboat Body (PS 483)
9. Create a Path Using the Pen Tool (PS 485)
10. Display the Paths Panel (PS 487)
11. Save a Work Path as a Named Path (PS 488)
12. Create a Second Path (PS 488)
13. Merge Paths (PS 489)
14. Create a Shape Layer from a Path (PS 490)
15. Complete the Masts Using the Line Tool (PS 492)
16. Create a Layer Group from Layers (PS 496)
17. Create a New Layer Group (PS 499)
18. Nest Layer Groups (PS 499)
19. Create the Award Seal Using a Custom Shape (PS 501)
20. Create Text within a Shape (PS 503)
21. Create a Type Layer (PS 504)
22. Convert Text to a Shape (PS 505)
23. Alter a Shape (PS 506)
24. Fill a Shape with a Pattern (PS 507)
25. Reset Patterns (PS 509)
26. Copy and Paste a Layer Style (PS 511)
27. Create a Background Gradient (PS 512)
28. Create a Note (PS 514)

Learn It Online

Test your knowledge of chapter content and key terms.

Instructions: To complete the Learn It Online exercises, start your browser, click the Address bar, and then enter the Web address `scsite.com/pscs5/learn`. When the Photoshop CS5 Learn It Online page is displayed, click the link for the exercise you want to complete and then read the instructions.

Chapter Reinforcement TF, MC, and SA
A series of true/false, multiple choice, and short answer questions that test your knowledge of the chapter content.

Flash Cards
An interactive learning environment where you identify chapter key terms associated with displayed definitions.

Practice Test
A series of multiple choice questions that test your knowledge of chapter content and key terms.

Who Wants To Be a Computer Genius?
An interactive game that challenges your knowledge of chapter content in the style of a television quiz show.

Wheel of Terms
An interactive game that challenges your knowledge of chapter key terms in the style of the television show *Wheel of Fortune*.

Crossword Puzzle Challenge
A crossword puzzle that challenges your knowledge of key terms presented in the chapter.

Apply Your Knowledge

Reinforce the skills and apply the concepts you learned in this chapter.

Converting a Photo to Clip Art

Instructions: Start Photoshop and set the workspace and tools to default values. Open the Apply 8-1 Rocker file from the Chapter 08 folder of the Data Files for Students. See the inside back cover of this book for instructions on downloading the Data Files for Students, or contact your instructor for information about accessing the required files. The purpose of this exercise is to create a clip art image from a digital photograph. The photo you open is a picture of a rocking chair, shown on the left in Figure 8–93. You will convert the image to a clip art image as shown on the right.

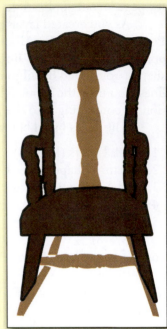

Figure 8–93

Perform the following tasks:

1. On the File menu, click Save As. Save the image on your USB flash drive as a PSD file, with the file name Apply 8-1 Rocker Clip-Art. If the Photoshop Format options dialog box is displayed, click the OK button.

2. On the Tools panel, click the Eyedropper Tool button. Sample a medium brown color in the rocker.

3. Select the Freeform Pen Tool on the Tools panel. On the options bar, click the Shape layers button. Click the Magnetic check box to select it, if necessary. If necessary, click the Style picker button and then click Default Style (None). Click the upper-left corner of the rocker and then move the mouse slowly around the headboard of the rocker. Do not drag. Click as you move over each rung, so the magnetism does not move down the rung. Do not include the rungs in the path. When you get all the way around the headboard, click the beginning point to close the path.

4. Click the 'Add to shape area' (+) button on the options bar. Repeat Step 3 to include the seat of the rocker. Repeat Step 3 to include the legs, arm rests, and back outer rungs. Rename the Shape 1 layer, **Brown**.

5. On the Layers panel, select the Background layer.

6. Select the Swatches panel and then click a tan color such as Pale Cool Brown.

7. Click the upper-left corner of the center rung on the back of the rocker. Move the mouse slowly around the rung. Do not drag. When you get all the way around the rung, click the beginning point to close the path and fill it with the tan shade.

8. Click the 'Add to shape area' (+) button on the options bar. Repeat Step 7 to include the rockers at the bottom of the image and the cross rung. Rename the Shape 1 layer, **Tan**.

9. Unlock the Background layer, if necessary, and delete it.

10. On the Layers panel, select the Brown layer. Click the 'Add a layer style' button. When the shortcut menu is displayed, click Stroke.

11. In the Layer Style dialog box, type **16** in the Size box. Click the Position box arrow and then click Outside in the list, if necessary. Click the Blend Mode box arrow and then click Normal in

the list, if necessary. Type **100%** in the Opacity box, if necessary. Click the Fill Type box arrow and then click Color in the list, if necessary. Click the Color box. When the 'Select stroke color' dialog box is displayed, select a black color, and then click the OK button.

12. Click the OK button (Layer Style dialog box) to apply the stroke.

13. To display the shape layer's bounding box, press CTRL+T. On the options bar, click the Switch between free transform and warp modes button.

14. When the side control handles are displayed, drag each of them slightly toward the center of the image to create a cartoon-like effect as shown in Figure 8–93.

15. Press the ENTER key to commit the changes.

16. Save the image again.

17. For extra credit, open a page layout program such as Microsoft Publisher, Microsoft Word, or Adobe InDesign. Insert the Rocker Clip Art file as a picture. Experiment with inline versus square graphic placement and scaling.

Extend Your Knowledge

Extend the skills you learned in this chapter and experiment with new skills. You may need to use Help to complete the assignment.

Create an Ant Anatomy Illustration

Instructions: Start Photoshop and perform the customization steps found on pages PS 6 through PS 9. Open the Extend 8-1 Anatomy file from the Chapter 08 folder of the Data Files for Students. See the inside back cover of this book for instructions on downloading the Data Files for Students, or contact your instructor for information about accessing the required files. You have been asked to create a scientific illustration of an ant, such as the one shown in Figure 8–94 on the following page. This illustration will teach students the basic body parts of an ant. The client has provided you with a photo of an ant but wants it to look more like an illustration than a photograph.

1. On the File menu, click Save As. Save the image on your USB flash drive as a PSD file, with the file name **Extend 8-1 Anatomy Edited**.

2. Look at the organization of the layers on the Layers panel. Click the visibility icon for the ant photo layer to display it.

3. Start with small items such as the eye. Use the Eyedropper Tool to sample the eye color, zooming as necessary.

4. Activate the Pen Tool. Click the Shape layers button on the options bar.

5. Click around the eye to create a path that covers the ant's eye. Double-click to close the path.

6. On the Layers panel, rename the layer, eye.

7. Create two more paths, one around each antenna. (*Hint:* As you click narrow images, such as the antenna, your path may fill temporarily at awkward-looking intersecting triangles. Just keep clicking close to the antennae.) Rename each layer.

8. Select the ant photo layer again. Use the Eyedropper Tool to select a lighter gray color from the head of the ant. Activate the Pen Tool again and click to create a closed path around the head.

9. Create additional paths for the legs, middle, and end of the ant. Experiment with bands of color as separate paths on the lower part of the ant's body. Rename each layer.

10. Hide and show the ant photo layer to view your work. Use the Direct Selection Tool to adjust any lines that are not smooth.

Continued >

Extend Your Knowledge *continued*

11. Create a different layer style for each part of the ant's body by selecting the layer and then clicking the 'Add a layer style' button on the Layers panel status bar. Use Photoshop Help as necessary to adjust the settings for the various layer styles.

12. Create layer groups to organize the layers. Group the leg layers into one group; the head, antenna, and eye layers into another group; and finally the middle and end body parts into another group.

13. To create a label for the diagram, activate the Custom Shape Tool. Click the

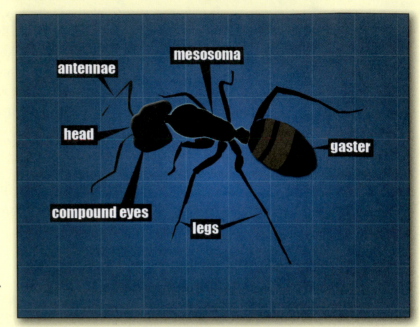

Figure 8–94

Shape picker button on the options bar to display its panel and then click the panel menu button. Select Talk Bubbles and choose to append them to the panel. Select one of the Talk Bubble shapes. Choose a gray color. Drag in the document window to create a shape above the ant's head.

14. Activate the Horizontal Type Tool. Choose a sans serif font, such as Impact, with a font size of 36 points and a color of white. Click the shape and type `head` to create text within the shape.

15. Create additional labels for mesosoma, gaster, compound eyes, antennae, and legs, as shown in Figure 8–94.

16. Hide the ant photo layer, if necessary.

17. Save the file again and turn it in to your instructor.

Make It Right

Analyze a project and correct all errors and/or improve the design.

Centerville Baseball Team Logo

Problem: The Centerville baseball team needs help completing a new logo. A previous graphic designer started the project but did not finish it. A photo of a batter needs to be converted to a silhouette.

Instructions: Perform the following tasks:

1. Start Photoshop and perform the customization steps found on pages PS 6 through PS 9. Open the file Make It Right 8-1 Team Logo file from the Data Files for Students and save it as Make It Right 8-1 Team Logo Edited in the PSD file format.

2. Look through the layers on the Layers panel (Figure 8–95). Hide all layers except the batter layer and then select the batter layer, if necessary. Use the Pen Tool with the Paths button to trace slowly around the entire outline of the batter and the bat. If necessary, use the Direct Selection Tool to make adjustments. To create the space between the batter's legs, click the 'Subtract from path area' button and then trace the inside of the legs.

3. Show all layers. Create a new layer and name it, silhouette. Click the Paths panel tab and notice that the batter outline is named Work Path in the panel. On the status bar, click the 'Load path as

a selection' button. Use the Eyedropper Tool to sample the gold color from the text surrounding the logo. Press ALT+BACKSPACE to fill the selection with gold. Click the Layers panel tab to switch to the Layers panel. Press CTRL+D to deselect the selection. Click the batter layer visibility icon to hide the layer and then select the silhouette layer. Move the silhouette layer so the batter is centered in the logo. In the Layers panel, drag the silhouette layer down below the gold ring layer.

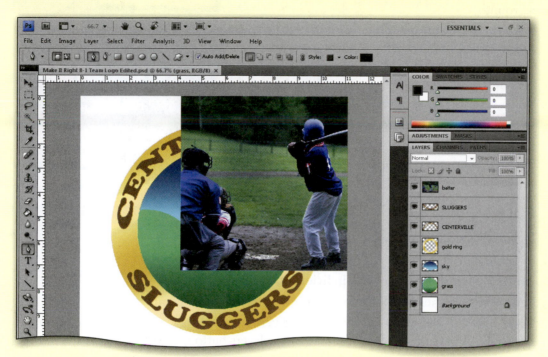

Figure 8–95

4. Add at least three layer effects of your choice to the logo. Try adding a soft glow around the silhouette. Add a stroke and bevel to the gold ring layer. Experiment with drop shadows on the text, CENTERVILLE and SLUGGERS. Save this file as Make it Right 8-1 Team Logo Complete, and turn it in to your instructor when you are happy with the results.

In the Lab

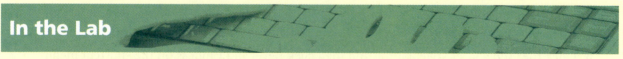

Design and/or create a publication using the guidelines, concepts, and skills presented in this chapter. Labs are listed in order of increasing difficulty.

Lab 1: Creating a Sign

Problem: Your summer job is working at the public library. Your supervisor has asked you to make a sign for the Bookworm Corner — a section of the children's library with carpeting and bean bag chairs. He would like the same image in a scalable format for use in the desktop publishing products of the library. You have taken a picture of some books and have decided to add a clip art of a worm, as shown in Figure 8–96 on the following page. You will save it in both the PSD and PNG formats to preserve the transparency.

Perform the following tasks:
1. Start Photoshop. Perform the customization steps found on pages PS 6 through PS 9.
2. Open the file Lab 8-1 Books from the Chapter 08 folder of the Data Files for Students. See the inside back cover of this book for instructions on downloading the Data Files for Students, or contact your instructor for information about accessing the required files.

Continued >

In the Lab *continued*

3. Save the file on your storage device with the name, **Lab 8-1 Books Clip Art**.

4. To create a transparent background:

   a. Press the w key to access the Magic Wand Tool. On the options bar, click the 'Add to selection' button.

   b. Select all of the white areas.

   c. On the Select menu, click Inverse.

   d. On the Layer menu, point to New, and then click Layer via Cut. Name the new layer, books.

   e. Delete the background layer.

   f. Save the file.

Figure 8–96

5. To create a color shape layer of an individual book:

   a. Select the Swatches panel. Choose a bright color in the red family.

   b. On the Tools panel, right-click the current Pen Tool to display the context menu, and then click Pen Tool. On the options bar, click the Shape layers button, if necessary.

   c. Choose a book in the document window and then click each corner to create a red shape layer.

   d. Add and subtract anchor points as necessary to match the edges. Convert any anchor points that need moving. Use the Path Selection Tool to adjust anchor points along the path. Press the ENTER key when you are satisfied with the path.

   e. Click the books layer.

   f. Save the file.

6. Repeat Step 5, choosing a different color from the Swatches panel for each book.

7. Hide the books layer.

8. To add a special effect:

   a. Select the Shape 1 layer.

   b. Click the 'Add a layer style' button and then click Bevel and Emboss on the shortcut menu. When the Layer Style dialog box is displayed, apply the settings displayed in Table 8–6.

Table 8–6 Layer Style Settings for the Lab 8-1 Books Clip Art	
Name	**Setting**
Style	Inner Bevel
Technique	Smooth
Depth	100
Direction	Down
Size	24
Soften	3
Angle	−138
Use Global Light	checked

Table 8–6 Layer Style Settings for the Lab 8-1 Books Clip Art (Continued)

Name	Setting
Altitude	21
Gloss Contour	Linear
Highlight Mode	Screen
Highlight Mode Opacity	75
Shadow Mode	Multiply
Color	Black
Shadow Mode Opacity	75

9. To copy the layer style to the other shape layers:

   a. Right-click the Shape 1 layer. When the context menu is displayed, click Copy Layer Style.

   b. SHIFT+CLICK each of the other shape layers to select them all.

   c. Right-click the selected layers and then click Paste Layer Style on the context menu.

   d. Save the file.

10. To add the worm graphic:

    a. Click the books layer.

    b. Press CTRL+O and then open the file named Lab 8-1 Worm from the Chapter 08 folder of the Data Files for Students. When the Lab 8-1 Worm document window is displayed, arrange the windows so both can be seen.

    c. Using the Rectangular Marquee Tool, drag a rectangle around the right half of the worm. Use the Move Tool to drag the selection and drop it in the Lab 8-1 Books Clip Art window. Name the layer, right worm. Place it on the right side of the books, as shown in Figure 8–96. Press CTRL+T and resize the layer as necessary. On the Layers panel, move the right worm layer to a location below the center books, but above the books on the right, as necessary.

    d. Repeat Step 10c for the left half of the worm.

    e. Close the Lab 8-1 Worm document window.

    f. Save the file.

11. To create the text:

    a. On the Layers panel, select the top layer.

    b. On the Tools panel, select the Horizontal Type Tool. On the options bar, select Myriad Pro or a similar font, a font style of bold, a font size of 14, strong anti-aliasing, left text alignment, and a text color of black.

    c. Click the bottom-left area of the image and then type **Wiggle on over to Bookworm Corner**, to enter the text along the path.

    d. On the options bar, click the 'Commit any current edits' button to accept the changes.

    e. On the options bar, click the 'Create warped text' button. Select the Flag style with a bend of 100%.

    f. Add an outer glow layer style. Set the Blend Mode to Normal, the Spread to 15%, and the Size to 55 px.

    g. Use the Move Tool to position the text at the bottom of the canvas.

    h. Save the file.

12. Create a new layer above the books layer. Name the new layer, background, and fill it with white. Save the file.

In the Lab

Lab 2: Using Saved Paths

Problem: The Bow-Wow dog treat company needs help in finishing the packaging for its newest variety of dog treats. Most of the artwork has been created in Adobe Illustrator and saved as paths in the main document. The art director has provided instructions for you to complete the layout. The final version is shown in Figure 8–97.

Perform the following tasks:

1. Start Photoshop. Perform the customization steps found on pages PS 6 through PS 9. Open the file Lab 8-2 Bow-Wow from the Chapter 08 folder of the Data Files for Students. See the inside back cover of this book for instructions on downloading the Data Files for Students, or contact your instructor for information about accessing the required files. Save the file as Lab 8-2 Bow-Wow Edited on your USB drive.

2. The file contains a layer named color swatches. The swatch colors were provided for your use as you create the various packaging elements. Select the color swatches layer. Press SHIFT+CTRL+N to create a new layer above the color swatches layer and name it, package.

3. Click the Paths tab to display the Paths panel.

4. To create the package background:

   a. Click the package path to select it, if necessary.

   b. To convert the path into a selection, right-click the package path to display the context menu. Click Make Selection to display the Make Selection dialog box and then click the OK button.

   c. Press the D key to reset the foreground and background colors to their default settings. Verify that the foreground color is black. Use the Eyedropper Tool to sample the tan color in the document window. Depending on your monitor, the swatch might look more yellow than tan. You want to use the second-to-last sample color.

   d. Activate the Gradient Tool. On the options bar, click the Radial Gradient button. If necessary, click the Gradient picker and then double-click the Foreground to Background preset.

   e. Create a radial gradient from the bottom of the selection to the top. Deselect the selection.

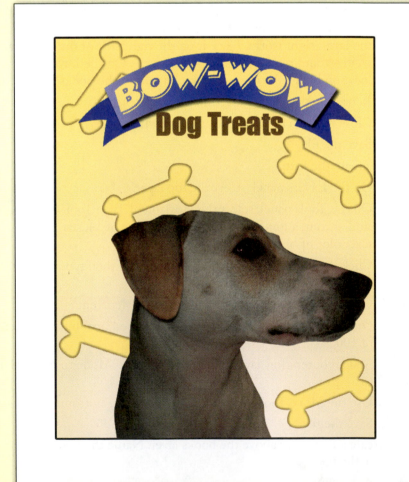

Figure 8–97

On the Layers panel, click the 'Add a layer style' button, and then click Stroke. Use a black 3-px wide stroke around the package layer. Keep all other default settings.

5. To create a bone-shaped background:

a. On the Paths panel, select the bone path, and then click the Load path as a selection button to create a selection marquee of the bone.

b. On the Layers panel create a new layer named, bone.

c. Press ALT+BACKSPACE to fill the selection. Deselect the bone selection. Add a stroke layer style to the bone layer using a size of 3 and the color black.

d. Activate the Move Tool. ALT+drag to create a few copies of the bone and then rotate the copies in various angles by pressing CTRL+T and dragging outside of the transform handles. Press the ENTER key to confirm each transformation.

6. To create a title banner:

a. Create a new layer above the bone copy layers named, banner caps.

b. On the Paths panel, select the banner caps path and then click the Load path as a selection button.

c. Use the Eyedropper Tool to sample the dark blue color in the document window. Press ALT+BACKSPACE to fill the selection. Deselect the banner caps path.

d. On the Layers panel, create a new layer above the banner caps layer named, banner.

e. On the Paths panel, select the banner path and create a selection.

f. Press the X key to reverse the foreground and background colors so the light blue is the background color.

g. Sample from the light blue color in the document window to make it the foreground color, using the Eyedropper Tool.

h. Activate the Gradient Tool and drag from the middle of the banner selection outward. Deselect the banner.

i. Add a Drop Shadow layer style to the banner layer using the default values for the Drop Shadow.

j. Create a new layer above the banner layer and name the new layer, Bow-Wow.

k. On the Paths panel, load the Bow-Wow path as a selection.

l. Sample the yellow/tan color, press ALT+BACKSPACE to fill the path, and then deselect.

7. To create the dog layer:

a. On the Layers panel, click the visibility icon to show the dog layer. Drag the layer to the top of the Layers panel.

b. Activate the Freeform Pen Tool. On the options bar, click the Paths button and turn on the Magnetic option.

c. Carefully trace around the dog's head and neck.

d. To remove the background around the dog, click Layer on the menu bar, point to Vector Mask, and then click Current Path.

e. Use the Move Tool to position the dog at the bottom of the package outline.

f. Create a new layer named, package bottom.

8. Activate the Horizontal Type Tool. Drag a type box under the Bow-Wow banner, approximately 3 inches wide and .5 inches tall. Type **Dog Treats**, using Impact or a similar font, a size of 48, and a color sampled from the document window.

9. Hide the color swatches layer. Save the file again. Flatten the image and save it as Lab 8-2 Bow-Wow Complete in the TIF format. If Photoshop displays a warning about discarding hidden layers, click the OK button.

In the Lab

Lab 3: Creating a Promotional Flyer

Problem: A local bakery is hosting their annual "cupcake day" when they will sell their gourmet cupcakes (normally $3 each) for only 50¢. They have asked you to create a promotion flyer for the event in the style of a postage stamp (Figure 8–98).

Instructions: Start Photoshop. Perform the customization steps found on pages PS 6 through PS 9. Create a new document with a white background, 3 inches wide and 4 inches tall, and save the file (in the Photoshop PSD format) as Lab 8-3 Cupcake Flyer on your USB drive.

Use the Custom Shape Tool to create a gray stamp shape. (*Hint:* Load the Objects category of shapes from the Custom Shape Picker to find a stamp shape.) Overlap a white rectangle and apply a Gradient Overlay layer style with the colors of your choice to add texture to the background. Add text similar to that shown in Figure 8–98. Create a layer group named, stamp, and drag the shape layers into it. Create a layer group named, type, and drag the type layers into it.

Open the file Lab 8-3 Cupcake from the Chapter 08 folder of the Data Files for Students. See the inside back cover of this book for instructions on downloading the Data Files for Students, or contact your instructor for information about accessing the required files. Drag the cupcake photo into the Lab 8-3 Cupcake Flyer document. Hide the stamp and type layer groups so you can focus on the cupcake. Use the Pen Tool and Freeform Pen Tool to trace the different parts of the cupcake. It may be helpful to zoom in so the cupcake is enlarged. Color the shapes appropriately and add layer styles, such as a Pattern Overlay, to add texture. Create a new layer group named, cupcake, to store all the cupcake layers. Delete the original cupcake photo layer and resize the cupcake layer group to enlarge your clip art cupcake. Rearrange the stacking order of the layer groups to your liking.

Figure 8–98

Rotate, resize, and reposition any layers to your liking. Apply any additional layer styles you think benefit the design. Save the file.

Cases and Places

Apply your creative thinking and problem-solving skills to design and implement a solution.

Note: To complete these assignments, you may be required to use the Data Files for Students. See the inside back cover of this book for instructions on downloading the Data Files for Students, or contact your instructor for information about accessing the required files.

1: Mapping Demographics

Academic

Your political science professor has given you the assignment of creating an electoral map for your state from the last presidential election. Find a free graphic of your state map that shows county outlines. Research county election data using your state government's Web site. With the Freeform Pen Tool and the Shape layers button, draw around each county, filling it with either red for Republican or blue for Democrat. Save and print the file.

2: Creating a Vector Self-Portrait

Personal

You have decided to run for student council and need a photo to use in posters around campus. Create a new document in Photoshop with a solid, bright background. Have a friend take a digital picture of you. Copy the photo into your new document and then convert everything from the neck down into vector graphics, maintaining size and proportion. Use subtle colors that complement the background. Create other shadows, reflections, and blends that enhance the poster. Use the Horizontal Type Tool to insert your name, slogan, or office above your picture. Save the file in the format specified by your instructor.

3: Creating a Game Graphic

Professional

You recently took a job with a company that produces graphical adventure games for computers. Your assignment is to convert an image of a historical ruin into a clip art type of graphic to display on the CD liner. The photo, Archway, is located in the Chapter 08 folder of the Data Files for Students. Open the photo and create a layer group named Columns. Use the Pen Tool to create shape layers with the group for each column. Fill the area with a dark tan color. Use the Shape layers button along with the Pen Tool, Freeform Pen Tool, and anchor point tools to draw around other parts of the archway with darker and lighter shades. Do not recolor the blue sky. Save the file as a PDF format and submit a copy to your instructor.

9 | Creating Web Pages and Animations

Objectives

You will have mastered the material in this chapter when you can:

- Explain why planning is the most important step in Web design

- Organize photos for inclusion in a Web gallery

- Generate a Web gallery

- Differentiate between a Web page and a Web site

- Slice an image

- Apply slice settings

- Create animation frames

- Describe the process of creating an animation and optimization

- Tween an animation

- Loop an animation

- Optimize an animation

- Preview an animation

9 | Creating Web Pages and Animations

Introduction

Photoshop has several tools to help you design Web pages. While Photoshop is not Web page creation software, it can be used to mock up or create a simple Web page, as a sample or prototype in advance of creating a fully featured site. In a typical Web page design workflow, you create individual files and then combine them into a single unified design using Photoshop. Using Adobe Bridge, you can create a **Web gallery**, which is a Web page (or set of Web pages within a Web site) that features a thumbnail page with small preview versions of your photos. Photoshop optimizes Web pages using slices with hyperlinks or hot spots. Designers use the Animation panel to animate graphics and then optimize them for display on the Web. In this chapter, you will create an interactive Web site for a fictitious horse stable, complete with animation and a working photo gallery.

Project — Web Site for Horseshoe Stables

This chapter examines some of the Web tools used by Photoshop and Bridge as you create a home page for a fictitious horse stable. A **home page** is a Web page designated as the first page and point of entry into a **Web site,** which is a collection of related Web pages. Also called the **main page** or **index page**, a home page typically welcomes the viewer by introducing the purpose of the site, indicating the business name or personal name of the Web site owner, and providing links to the lower-level pages of the site.

In the Horseshoe Stables home page, a light brown background area connotes the dusty feel of a horse stable. A **masthead** is the top portion of a design and is usually the first thing people notice when looking at a Web page. Therefore, the masthead is the ideal place to locate the company name, exciting imagery, contact information, and anything else you want to be sure your users see. A set of links to other Web pages appears below the masthead. One of the links will take visitors to a Web gallery generated with a Bridge automation command. Finally, when the home page first appears, a horseshoe will rotate and move into the Web page in an animated special effect. The Web page is illustrated in Figure 9–1a. The area below the links is intentionally left blank at this stage of the design as it is reserved for content provided by the client. The Web gallery, opened from a link on the Web page, is illustrated in Figure 9–1b.

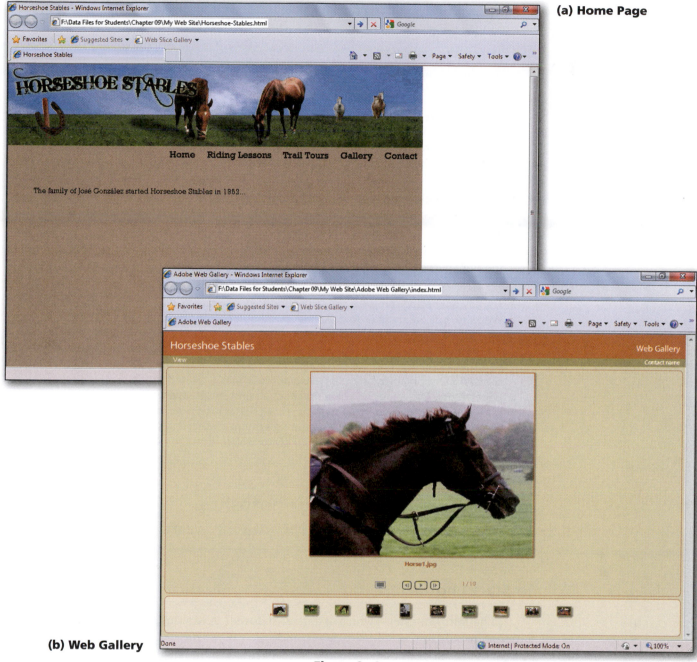

(a) Home Page

(b) Web Gallery

Figure 9–1

Overview

As you read this chapter, you will learn how to create the Web site shown in Figure 9–1 by performing these general tasks:

- Create a folder and copy files in the Bridge Output workspace.
- Set options and save a Web gallery.
- Create slices from text for navigation.
- Set slice options for hyperlinks.
- Create multiple layers and position them for animation.
- Create frames in the Animation panel.

- Create new frames using tweening.
- Use the Animation panel to set animation options.
- Preview the animation.
- Save the Web page, optimized for animation.

**Plan
Ahead**

General Project Guidelines

When creating a Web site design, the actions you perform and decisions you make will affect the appearance and characteristics of the finished product. As you create Web sites, such as the one shown in Figure 9–1 on the previous page, you should follow these general guidelines:

1. **Organize photos for a Web site and gallery pages.** Collect the photos you will need and store them in a Windows folder. Make sure each photo and the folder are named appropriately.

2. **Use standard Web design and planning principles.** As you develop the site, keep in mind the site's purpose, the audience, the elements you plan to include, the visual impact, and the placement of the pages within the Web site structure.

3. **Employ animation carefully.** Use animation to draw attention to or create interest in a Web site, but do not overdo it. Animations that loop continuously make it difficult for users to focus on content; scrolling marquees are difficult to read and distract from the purpose of the Web page. You should use animation to draw the viewer's attention to a specific element on the page, alert readers to updated information, or create hot spots. Animation always should have a purpose that is related to the content in the page. Weigh the value the animation adds against its disadvantages: animation reduces performance, uses more system resources, increases load time, and seldom runs optimally on both low-end and high-end computing systems. Research also suggests that animation is distracting and reduces the user's ability to seek information on the Web page.

Starting and Customizing Photoshop

The steps on the next page start Photoshop and reset the default workspace, tools, colors, and Layers panel options.

To Start Photoshop

The following steps, which assume Windows 7 is running, start Photoshop based on a typical installation.

1 Click the Start button on the Windows 7 taskbar to display the Start menu.

2 Type `Photoshop CS5` as the search text in the 'Search programs and files' text box, and watch the search results appear on the Start menu.

3 Click Adobe Photoshop CS5 in the search results on the Start menu to start Photoshop.

4 After a few moments, when the Photoshop window is displayed, if the window is not maximized, click the Maximize button on the title bar to maximize the window.

To Reset the Workspace

The following steps reset the Essentials workspace.

1 Click the 'Show more workspaces and options' button on the Application bar.

2 If necessary, click Essentials to select the default workspace panels.

3 Click the 'Show more workspaces and options' button again to display the list, and then click Reset Essentials to restore the workspace to its default settings.

To Reset the Tools and the Options Bar

The following steps select the Rectangular Marquee Tool and reset all tool settings in the options bar.

1 If the tools in the Tools panel appear in two columns, click the double arrow at the top of the Tools panel.

2 If necessary, click the Rectangular Marquee Tool button on the Tools panel to select it.

3 Right-click the Rectangular Marquee Tool icon on the options bar to display the context menu, and then click Reset All Tools. When Photoshop displays a confirmation dialog box, click the OK button to restore the tools to their default settings.

To Reset the Default Colors

The following step resets the default colors.

1 Press the D key to reset the default foreground and background colors.

To Reset the Layers Panel

The following steps reset the Layers panel to make the thumbnails match the figures shown in this book.

1 Click the Layers panel menu button, and then click Panel Options on the list to display the Layers Panel Options dialog box.

2 Click the option button for the smallest of the thumbnail sizes.

3 If necessary, click the Layer Bounds option button to select it.

4 If necessary, place a check mark next to each of the three check boxes at the bottom of the Layer Panel Options dialog box.

5 Click the OK button.

BTW

Photoshop Help
The best way to become familiar with Photoshop Help is to use it. Appendix D includes detailed information about Photoshop Help and exercises that will help you gain confidence in using it.

Web Galleries

Anyone who creates graphics or digital photos appreciates the opportunity to show them off. In today's technology-oriented world, distribution of your personal artwork and photographs commonly is done on the Web. In addition, clients often want collections of photographs on their Web site that feature their products, location, work samples, employees, or more. Adobe Bridge provides a set of tools to create a display of images on the Web. In a Web gallery, each thumbnail is linked to a gallery page that displays a full-size image. The home page and each gallery page contain links that allow visitors to navigate your gallery site.

Plan Ahead

> **Organize photos for a Web site and gallery pages.**
> You should organize the photos that you plan to use for the Web site, Web gallery, or animation into a Windows folder for more efficient manipulation. Put the photos in the order in which they will appear in the gallery or automation before you create the Web gallery. Use descriptive names for both the photos and the folder.

To Launch Bridge

BTW

Picture Package
The Picture Package feature and several other automation commands are now included in Bridge CS5. The Picture Package, typically used for school or other photo packages, places multiple copies of a source image on a single page and allows you to choose from a variety of size and placement options.

The first step is to launch Adobe Bridge because the command to create a Web gallery is in Bridge.

1 With your USB flash drive connected to one of the computer's USB ports, click the Launch Bridge button on the Photoshop Application bar to open Adobe Bridge in a new window. Click No if Photoshop asks you to start Bridge at login. Click the Maximize button to maximize the Bridge window, if necessary.

2 Click Essentials on the Bridge Application bar to set the workspace to Essentials.

3 Click Computer in the Favorites panel to display the locations.

4 In the lower-right corner of the Adobe Bridge window, click the 'View content as thumbnails' button, if necessary (Figure 9–2).

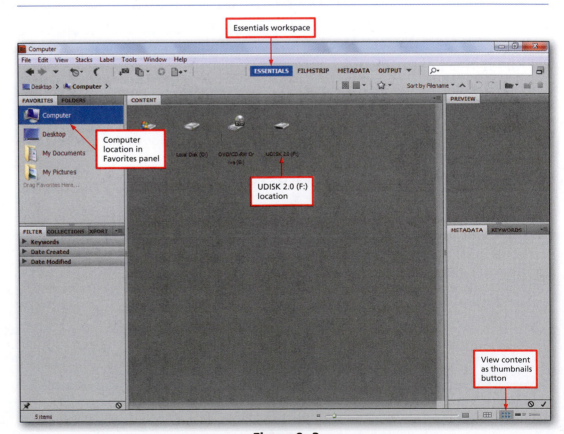

Figure 9–2

Organizing Photos

You should store the photos that you use for the Web gallery or for any of Photoshop's automation options in a dedicated folder for more efficient organization. The 10 files included in the steps on the next page come from a folder and its subfolders within the Chapter 09 folder of the Data Files for Students.

To Create a Folder in Bridge

The following steps create a folder for storing the gallery images and copy the 10 files into the new folder.

1

- In the Content panel, navigate to the location of the Data Files for Students, and then double-click the Chapter 09 folder to display its contents in Bridge.

- Right-click a blank area of the Content panel to display its context menu (Figure 9–3).

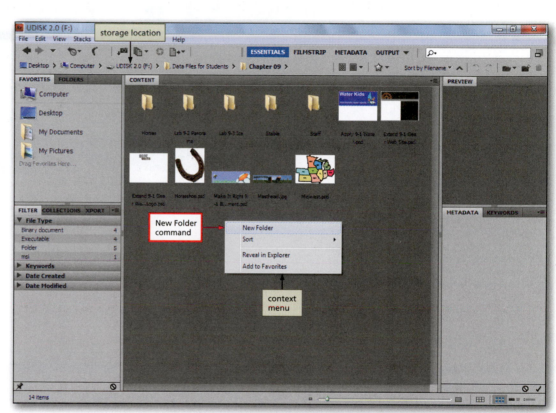

Figure 9–3

Q&A | Why do my Bridge window and context menu look different?

You may store your files in a different location, so the Bridge window will look different. Context menus are user dependent. You might have different files selected, or your system Clipboard might contain content, so the Paste command might be displayed.

2

- Click New Folder to create a new folder on your storage device.

- When the new folder is displayed, type **My Web Site**, and then press the ENTER key to rename the folder.

- Click away from the new folder icon for better viewing (Figure 9–4).

Q&A How much storage space will I need for my Web site?

Because a Web gallery contains many pictures, and later in the chapter, you will create an animation, you will need approximately 145 Mb of storage to save all the files. If you want to include different pictures in your Web gallery, your storage needs will change.

Figure 9–4

Other Ways

1. On Bridge File menu, click New Folder
2. In Windows 7 Explorer window, right-click content pane, point to New, click Folder

To Copy and Paste Files in Bridge

The following steps use context menus to copy and paste files into the My Web Site folder. The location of your files might differ.

1

- Double-click the Horses folder to display its contents (five images) in Bridge.

- Press CTRL+A to select all five images.

- Press CTRL+C to copy the files to the system clipboard (Figure 9–5).

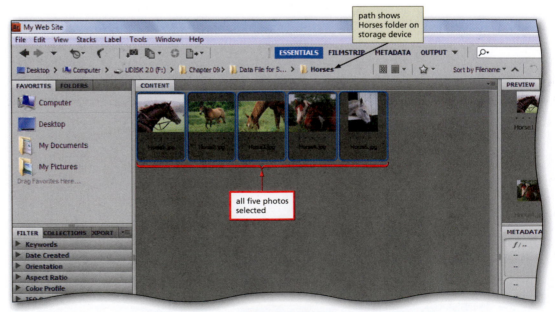

Figure 9–5

2

- At the top of the Bridge window, click Chapter 09 to return to the Chapter 09 folder.

- Double-click the My Web Site folder to open it in Bridge.

- Press CTRL+V to paste the files into the folder (Figure 9–6).

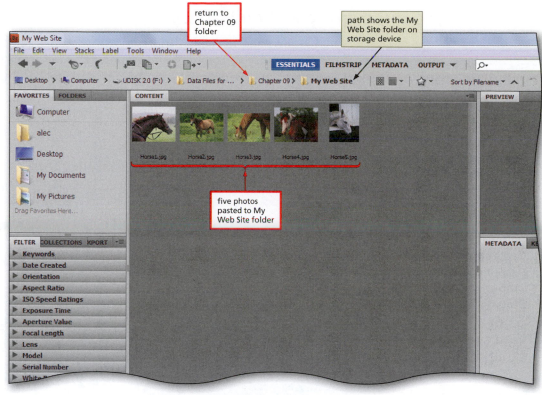

Figure 9–6

3

- At the top of the Bridge window, click Chapter 09 to return to the Chapter 09 folder.

- Repeat Steps 1 and 2 for the files in the Stable and Staff folders, both of which are in the Chapter 09 folder.

- Double-click the My Web Site folder to display its contents, 10 images.

- Press CTRL+A to select all the photos (Figure 9–7).

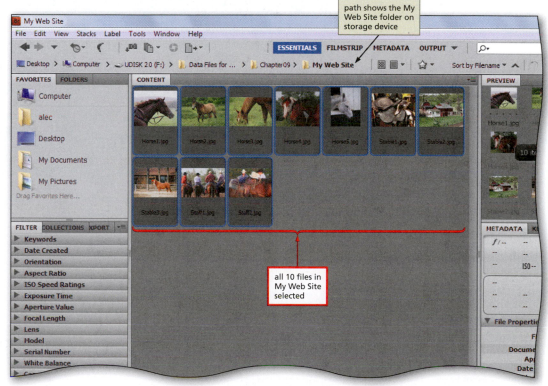

Figure 9–7

Other Ways
1. To copy, right-click file, click Copy
2. To copy, on Edit menu, click Copy
3. To paste, right-click Content pane, click Paste
4. To paste, on Edit menu, click Paste

Creating a Web Gallery

The Output panel in Adobe Bridge contains settings and buttons to generate the Web pages that display your photos and graphic creations in a gallery format. Once you select the photos, you can choose a template and style to determine the layout and design of the Web gallery pages, specify the gallery title, edit colors, and change the appearance of the gallery before saving or uploading the site.

To Display the Bridge Output Panel

The following step displays the selected photos in the Bridge Output workspace and the Output panel.

1

• On the Bridge Application bar, click Output to display the Output workspace (Figure 9–8).

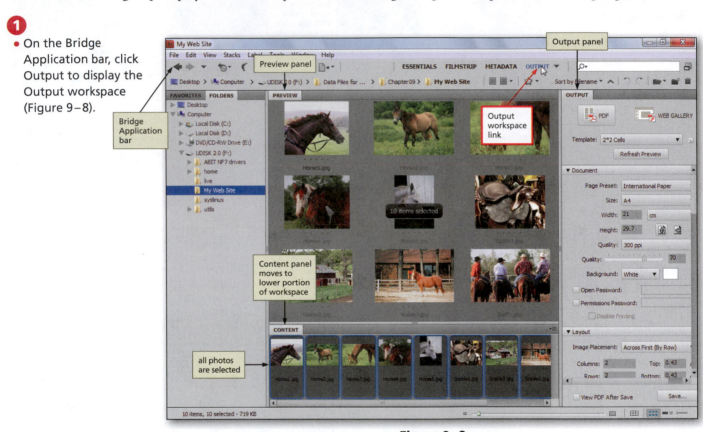

Figure 9–8

Q&A

Where is the Output workspace link?

It is possible that another user has changed the default links. Press CTRL+F4 to display the Output workspace.

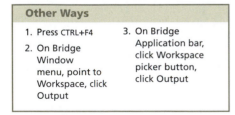

Other Ways

1. Press CTRL+F4
2. On Bridge Window menu, point to Workspace, click Output
3. On Bridge Application bar, click Workspace picker button, click Output

To Choose a Template and Style

You will choose the Lightroom Flash Gallery template and the Warm Day style in the steps that follow. Bridge includes the template and style, in addition to others, to offer you quick formatting of a professional looking Web gallery.

1

- On the Output panel, click the Web Gallery button, if necessary.

- Click the Template button to display the list of templates (Figure 9–9).

Q&A

What does the PDF button do?

The PDF button displays options for placing a photo in a PDF layout, along with paper sizes, templates, a watermark, and the option to apply a password. A Save button then saves the layout in the PDF format.

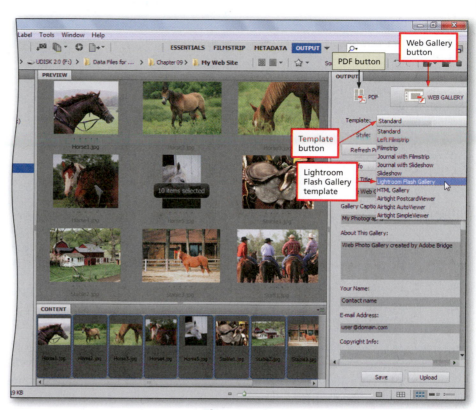

Figure 9–9

2

- Click Lightroom Flash Gallery to select it as the applied template for the gallery.

- Click the Style button to display the list of styles (Figure 9–10).

Figure 9–10

3
- Click Warm Day to apply the style.
- Click the Refresh Preview button to create the gallery (Figure 9–11).

🔍 **Experiment**
- Apply other templates and styles, and then click the Refresh Preview button to display the different Web galleries. When you are finished, return the template to Lightroom Flash Gallery and return the style to Warm Day. Refresh the preview if necessary.

Figure 9–11

To Edit Site Information

The site information fields allow Bridge to create headings, descriptions, and contact information that will appear in the Web gallery. The Site Title will appear across the top of the gallery. The Collection Title will appear as a subheading in the upper-right corner of the gallery. The Contact information will appear just below the subheading. The following steps edit the site information fields.

1
- In the Site Info area, select the text in the Site Title box, and then type **Horseshoe Stables** to replace the text.
- Type **Web Gallery** in the Collection Title box.
- Type your name in the Contact Info box and type your e-mail address in the E-mail or Web Address box (Figure 9–12).

Q&A
What should I type in the Collection Description box?

You may leave the default text in the box, or type further information about your work in Photoshop and your design skills. The Collection Description appears when accessing the About this Gallery command on the gallery's View menu.

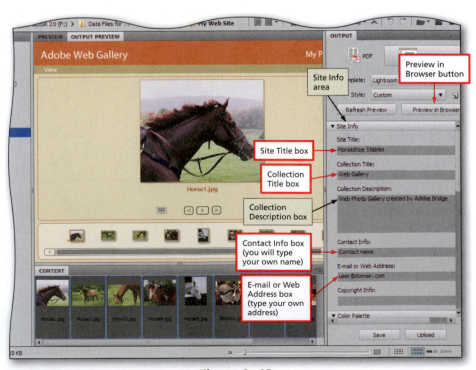

Figure 9–12

To Preview the Web Gallery

It is a good idea to view the Web gallery in a browser to ensure that it appears as you expected. The following steps preview the Web gallery in a browser window.

- On the Output panel, click the Preview in Browser button to open a browser window.

- When the browser window opens, double-click the title bar to maximize the window, if necessary (Figure 9–13).

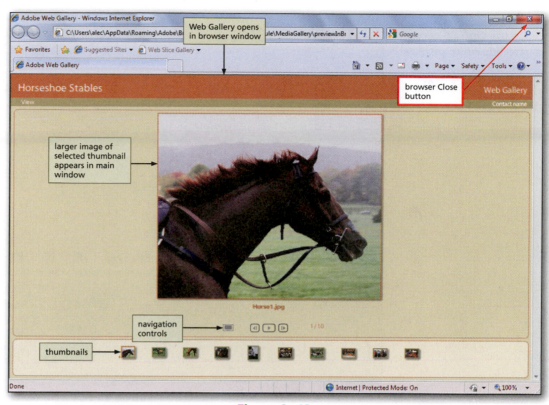

Figure 9–13

Experiment

- Click any of the links or navigation buttons to experiment with navigating the site.

- When you are finished, click the Close button in the browser window title bar to return to Bridge.

To Save the Web Gallery

In the steps that follow, you will save the gallery files to your USB storage device or a location specified by your instructor. Optionally, Bridge allows you to upload the files directly to a server if you have server space and uploading privileges.

1
- On the Output panel, scroll down to display the Create Gallery area (Figure 9–14).

Figure 9–14

2
- Click the Browse button to display the Choose a Folder dialog box.

- Click Computer in the list, and then click UDISK 2.0 (F:) or the location of your storage device to display its files and folders.

- Navigate to the My Web Site folder to select it as the storage location (Figure 9–15).

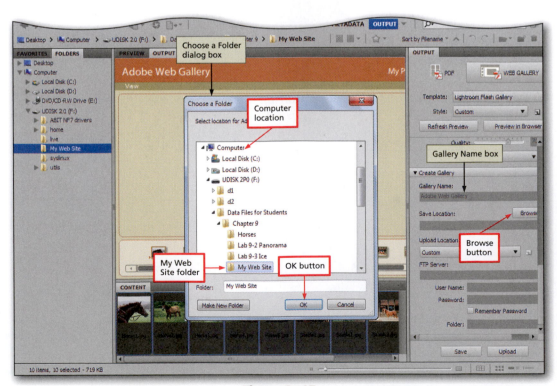

Figure 9–15

3

- Click the OK button to accept the location.

- In the Output panel, click the Save button to start the Save process (Figure 9–16).

How do I adjust the width of the output panel to see more of the buttons and settings?

Drag the border between panels to adjust the width.

4

- Click the OK button in the Create Gallery dialog box to create the gallery.

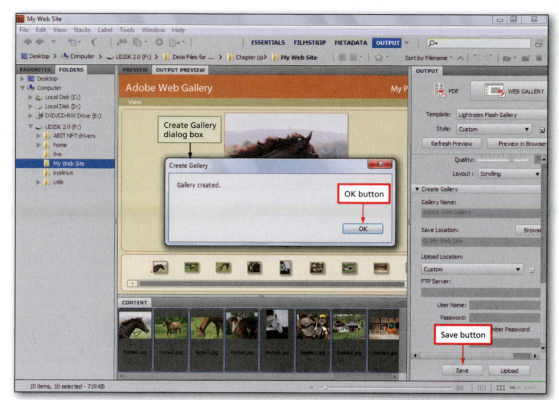

Figure 9–16

Web Gallery Files

When a user views your Web gallery, he or she will see them in the order in which they are displayed in the gallery folder in Bridge. If you prefer a different order, change the order of the files using Adobe Bridge by dragging them in the Content pane. By default, Bridge creates a start page for the gallery with the name, index.html, in a folder named Adobe Web Gallery. It also creates a set of accompanying files and folders in the Adobe Web Gallery folder. Because you will use the My Web Site folder and its index. html page later in the chapter, it is a good idea to write down the exact drive and location of your folder for future reference. In the previous steps, the location was F:\Data Files for Students\Chapter 09\My Web Site.

Posting Web Pages
If you want to **post**, or upload, your Web pages or Web site to the Web, you will need access to a Web server. Most Web servers have an easy-to-use software interface that allows you to drag and drop your files to the server space. For the Web site to work properly, you must post all of the HTML files and any supporting file folders.

To Close Bridge

Because you are done with Adobe Bridge, the following step closes the application.

1 Click the Close button on the Bridge title bar.

Designing a Web Page

Planning is the most important step when designing Web pages and Web sites. A **Web page** is a browser-accessible single page of graphics and information. A **Web site** is a collection of Web pages that are linked logically, and located together on a hosting computer. Web pages within Web sites typically share a common design and are navigated, or browsed, using some kind of navigation system. To be an effective Web designer, you need to understand and apply principles of Web design and programming protocols, and become proficient with many planning and design tools, including Web programming languages and scripting tools. As a graphic designer, however, you may use Photoshop to prepare graphics for the Web page, or to plan the site with galleries, graphics, color, links, and animation. Without the visual impact of color, shapes, and contrast, Web pages are neither interesting nor motivating.

The purpose of the Web page designed in this chapter is to serve as a home page or starting place from which to access several other pages, including informational pages about horseback riding, trail tours, group rentals, and the Web gallery created in the previous steps. Therefore, a heading and links are important elements of the home page. For visual impact, an animation will attract attention when the page is loaded.

Plan Ahead

Use standard Web design and planning principles.
When planning Web pages, several important issues must be considered:

- **Purpose** — Decide on the site's intended use; for example, advertising, direct sales, business-to-business tasks, prospect generation, employee communications, customer support, information, or education.

- **Audience** — Take into account the target population, characteristics, preferences, Web experience, and computer systems of the audience, and adapt the site design accordingly.

- **Viewer expectations** — Examine the Web page to see if links and other elements are located in common places, test the ease of navigation and form fields, check for usability issues, and so on. Navigation elements, such as buttons and tabs, typically are placed on the top or left side of a Web page.

- **Nature of planned elements or content** —Make sure that text, images, color, and animation are used judiciously and with purpose.

- **Viewer's visual impact** — Research shows that Web users form first impressions of Web pages in as little as 50 milliseconds, making nearly instantaneous judgments of a Web site's visual appeal, including the loading speed, perceived credibility, usability, and attraction.

- **Page's placement within the Web site structure** — Careful planning of the home page, secondary page(s), links, and accompanying folders involves standard naming conventions, file hierarchy, and structure.

To Select a Background Color Using the Swatches Panel

The first step in creating the Web page for this chapter will be to select a color scheme. Because this is a Web site for a horse stable, you will choose a light brown background to give a down-to-earth feel similar to the stable atmosphere. The following step selects a light brown color for the background of the Web page. Later, you will create a new blank document that uses this background color as the canvas color.

1

- Click the Adobe Photoshop button on your system's taskbar, if necessary, to display the Photoshop workspace.

- Click the Swatches panel tab to display the color swatches.

- CTRL+click the Pale Cool Brown swatch to assign it to the background color (Figure 9–17).

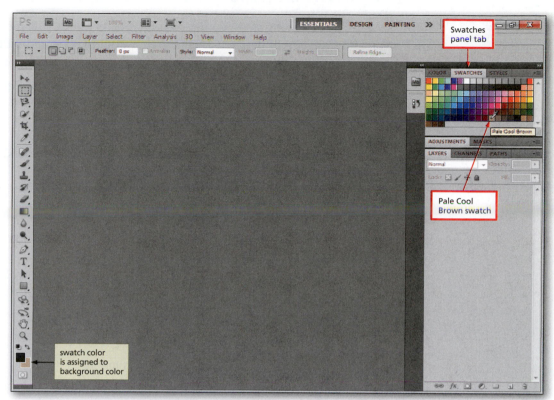

Figure 9–17

Setting Web Page Dimensions

While Web pages come in a variety of sizes, most pages usually fall within certain height and width limits. It is important to choose a size for your Web page that will accommodate the majority of user monitors and screen size settings. Oversized Web pages, designed on larger screens with resolutions of 1024 × 768 or higher, become unreadable when viewing the page using narrower browser widths. The graphics may be too wide to fit the browser window, and unwrapped text may create long, unreadable lines. Most Web users do not want to scroll from side to side; they also prefer limited vertical scrolling. Therefore, when designing Web pages, you should choose a page size used by a majority of users. Web designers constantly analyze and compare existing Web sites for usage guidelines related to screen colors, screen size, scrolling, graphics, and readability of text.

Another consideration is the possibility that the site visitor will want to print the Web page. Setting the dimensions of the Web page to 800 × 600 pixels will accommodate most users visually, but for Web pages destined for print on 8.5 × 11-inch paper, you should try to keep text and graphics within 760 pixels wide and 410 pixels high to account for margins when printed.

BTW

Using Pixels on the Rulers
Using pixels as the unit of measurement on the rulers allows you to keep in mind the page layout, both for browsers and for printing of graphics and text. By using 800 × 600 pixels, most visitors to the Web page will not have to scroll to see your information. Later, as part of a complete Web site solution, HTML code could be added to create more flexibility and to adjust screen size further.

To Set Attributes for a New Document

The following steps use the New command on the File menu to set the attributes for a new document destined for the Web. Recall that a common resolution for Web products is 72 pixels per inch (PPI).

1 Click File on the menu bar and then click New. When the New dialog box is displayed, type **Horseshoe Stables** in the Name text box.

2 Click the Preset box arrow and then click Custom, if necessary.

3 Double-click the Width box and then type **800** as the entry. Click the Width unit box arrow and then click pixels in the list, if necessary.

4 Double-click the Height box and then type **600** as the entry. If necessary, click the Height unit box arrow, and then click pixels in the list.

5 Double-click the Resolution box and then type **72** as the entry. Click the Resolution unit box arrow and then click pixels/inch in the list, if necessary.

6 Click the Color Mode box arrow. If necessary, click RGB Color in the list. If necessary, click the Color Mode unit box arrow and then click 8 bit in the list.

7 If necessary, click the Background Contents box arrow and then click Background Color in the list to finish setting the attributes for the new file (Figure 9–18).

8 Click the OK button to create the new document.

9 If the rulers are not displayed in the document window, press CTRL+R.

10 Right-click either of the rulers and then click Pixels in the list.

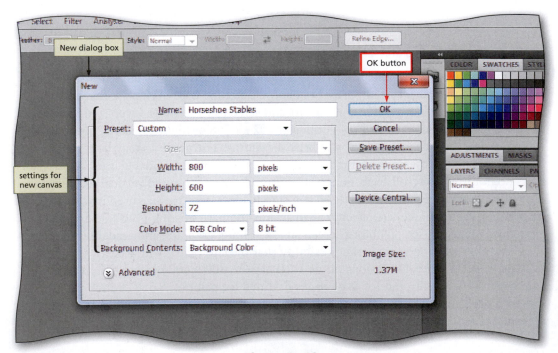

Figure 9–18

To Save the New Document

With the settings complete, it is a good practice to save the new blank document on a storage device as described in the following steps. You will save it in the PSD format for now; later in the chapter, you will save it in the HTML Web format.

1 With your USB flash drive connected to one of the computer's USB ports, click File on the menu bar, and then click Save As.

2 Click the Save in box arrow and then click UDISK 2.0 (F:), or the location associated with your USB flash drive, in the list. Navigate to the My Web Site folder.

3 Click the Format button to display the list of available file formats and then click Photoshop (*.PSD; *.PDD) in the list.

4 Click the Save button.

To Add a Masthead Background Graphic

The following steps insert a graphic to use as a masthead for the Horseshoe Stables Web site.

1 Open the file named Masthead from the Chapter 09 folder of the Data Files for Students.

2 Arrange the documents side by side.

3 Activate the Move Tool, and then drag the Masthead image into the Horseshoe Stables document window. Close the Masthead document window.

4 Position the image at the top of the Horseshoe Stables document window. It should span the full width of the canvas.

5 Double-click Layer 1 in the Layers panel, type **Masthead**, and press the ENTER key to rename the layer (Figure 9–19).

Figure 9–19

To Add an Image to the Masthead

The next steps insert a graphic to use as a masthead background.

1 Open the file named Horseshoe from the Chapter 09 folder of the Data Files for Students.

2 Arrange the documents side by side.

3 Activate the Move Tool and then drag the Horseshoe image into the Horseshoe Stables document window. Close the Horseshoe document window.

4 Position the image at the upper-right corner of the Horseshoe Stables document window (Figure 9–20). You will animate the horseshoe later in this chapter.

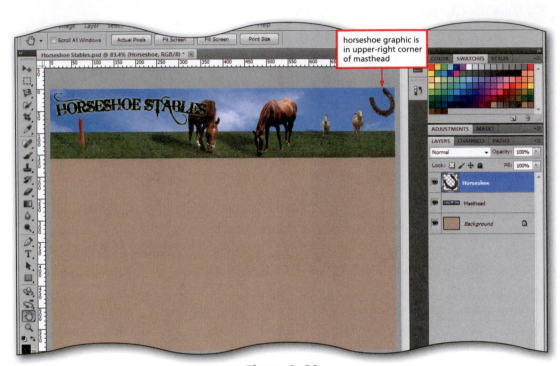

horseshoe graphic is in upper-right corner of masthead

Figure 9–20

BTW

Special Characters
A list of available special characters is called the **Character Map**. To view the Character Map, click the Start button, click All Programs, click Accessories, click System Tools, and then click Character Map. The special character code is listed at the bottom as you click each symbol. Special characters also can be copied to the Clipboard and then pasted into any application.

Inserting Text

After looking at the masthead to identify the Web site, most users will look for a text heading or **navigation bar** to identify page content. A navigation bar is an area on a Web page that contains the links to other pages in the site. It is important to use placement, font size, and font style appropriately and consistently to emphasize the text so users can find, and differentiate between, the heading, navigation bar links, and regular page content. Color is a secondary consideration for text because not all users will be able to distinguish colors. Choosing colors with high contrast is the best choice for accessibility and readability. In this chapter, you will use the Photoshop Horizontal Type Tool to create the navigation element, and then later add functionality using slices.

Web pages sometimes require **special characters**, such as letters with diacritical marks. These characters do not appear on the standard keyboard. Photoshop's type tools use the ALT key combined with a character code to create letters such as é, ñ, or ü, among others. You must type the character codes using the numeric keypad rather than the numbers on the standard keyboard.

To Insert Text with Special Characters

When designing a Web site, your focus is typically on imagery and layout. The Web site programmer normally adds the actual text on a Web page with HTML code after receiving it from the client. Therefore, Web designers commonly insert placeholder text with the understanding that it will be replaced at a later time when the Web page is coded with HTML. Including the placeholder text in Photoshop allows the client to preview the design and offer feedback before the actual Web page is coded. Additionally, the coders find the placeholder text useful as a guide in formatting the text with the Web page code. The following steps insert placeholder text that includes special characters.

- Press the D key to reset the colors.

- Double-click the Zoom Tool at the bottom of the Tools panel to zoom the document view to 100%.

- If necessary, scroll the document window until you see the upper-left portion of the canvas.

- Press the T key. If the Horizontal Type Tool is not active, right-click the current type tool button, and then click Horizontal Type Tool in the list.

- Using the box arrows on the options bar, select Arial, Regular, 14 pt, None, Left align, and black text as the text characteristics.

- In the document window, position the mouse pointer at 50 pixels on the horizontal ruler and 250 pixels on the vertical ruler, then drag a box that spans the width of the canvas and is about 50 pixels tall to create a text box and place the insertion point.

Figure 9–21

- In the document window, click in the text box, and then type **The family of Jos** to begin entering the placeholder text (Figure 9–21).

②

- Using the numeric keypad, press ALT+0233 to create the special character, é, at the end of the name.

Q&A

My laptop does not have a numeric keypad. How can I type the accented e?

You can use the Windows 7 Character map. Click the Start button, click All Programs, click Accessories, click System Tools, and then click Character Map. Click the character, click the Select button, and then click the Copy button. Close the Character Map dialog box, and then click CTRL+V to paste the character into the Photoshop text box.

③

- Press the SPACEBAR and then type `Gonz` to begin the last name.

- Using the numeric keypad, press ALT+0225 to create the special character, á, or use the Windows 7 Character Map to do so, if necessary.

- Type `lez` to complete the last name.

- Press the SPACEBAR and then type `started Horseshoe Stables in 1952...` to finish the placeholder text (Figure 9–22).

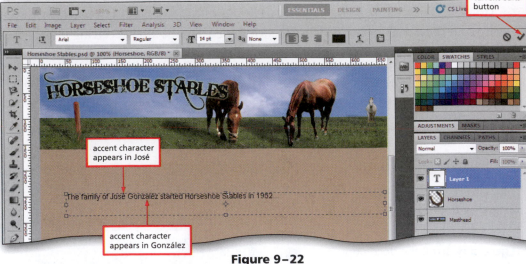

Figure 9–22

Why am I leaving so much empty space at the bottom of the canvas?

You are typing placeholder text, which, in a professional setting, would give the Web page HTML programmer an idea of where to position the text. If necessary, the site owner or client would instruct the programmer to place any additional text here. The HTML coder will add the real (and complete) text when the Web site is coded with HTML.

④

- On the options bar, click the 'Commit any current edits' button.

To Create the Navigation Bar

The following steps create the text that will later become the navigation bar. The navigation bar will include the elements that allow a user to navigate around the site.

①

- Double-click the Hand Tool on the Tools panel to fit the canvas to the screen.

- Press the T key to activate the Horizontal Type Tool. If necessary, right-click the current type tool button, and then click Horizontal Type Tool in the list.

- Click in the document window at about 350 pixels on the vertical ruler and about 50 on the horizontal ruler. You will move the navigation bar into position after you type.

- Using the box arrows on the options bar, select Rockwell, Regular, 18 pt, Sharp, and Left align text. Choose a different appropriate font if your computer does not have Rockwell (Figure 9–23).

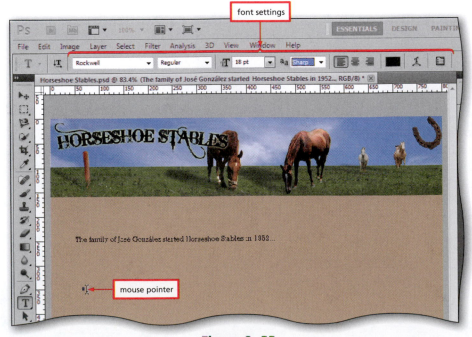

Figure 9–23

2

- Type **Home** and then press the SPACEBAR five times.

- Type **Riding Lessons** and then press the SPACEBAR five times.

- Type **Trail Tours** and then press the SPACEBAR five times.

- Type **Gallery** and then press the SPACEBAR five times.

- Type **Contact** to complete the navigation bar text.

- On the options bar, click the 'Commit any current edits' button to complete the creation of the navigation bar.

3

- Click the Move Tool on the Tools panel.

- Drag the navigation bar to the right side of the canvas below the masthead. Be sure to leave some space around the top and right side of the navigation bar so it is not cramped (Figure 9–24).

Q&A

Why does my text look jagged and distorted?

You are not viewing the document at 100% so the text is not clear. If you zoom to 100%, the text will be sharp and clear.

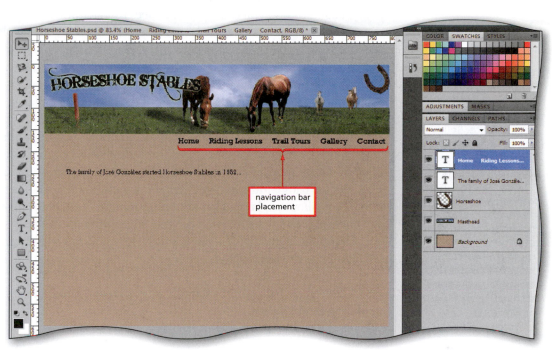

Figure 9–24

To Save the File Again

Because you have completed entering the text for the site, the following step saves the file.

1 Press CTRL+S. If Photoshop displays a dialog box, click the OK button.

Break Point: If you wish to take a break, this is a good place to do so. You can quit Photoshop now. To resume at a later time, start Photoshop, open the file called Horseshoe Stables, and continue following the steps from this location forward.

Creating Slices

You will assign the Web site navigation functionality to the navigation bar you just created using slices. A **slice** is a defined rectangular area in a picture that performs a specific function when the page is viewed in a Web browser. You might want to designate an area of an image to act as a hyperlink that, when clicked, opens a different Web page or document in a user's browser. Designers can use slices to create image maps. An **image map** is a graphic containing one or more invisible regions, called **hot spots**, which are hyperlinked. For example, you could slice a map of the United States into an image map by assigning hot spots to each state. Clicking an individual state then would cause the browser to perform a designated task such as displaying a different Web page or moving to another location on the current page. Slices give you better control over the function and file size of your image because you can optimize slices to load individually. An image may have many slices — all of which are reassembled when the Web page is displayed. When you save a sliced image for the Web, each slice is saved as an independent file with its own settings and color table; the slice preserves hyperlinks and special effects.

You create a slice by using the Slice Tool or by creating layer-based slices, which are slices that are created automatically from the contents of a layer. The Slice Tool is located with the Crop Tool on the Tools panel. Once you create a slice, you can select, move, resize, or align it. You can assign each slice an individual hyperlink.

When you create a slice, Photoshop displays a number and a badge. A **slice badge** is an icon that appears next to the slice number, indicating certain information about the slice. A slice badge indicates whether the slice is image based, layer based, or has no content. Photoshop displays a blue slice number and blue slice badge on user-defined slices; automatically created slices display gray slice numbers and gray slice badges.

Numbering of slices is from left to right and top to bottom, beginning in the upper-left corner of the image. If you change the arrangement or total number of slices, Photoshop updates the slice numbers to reflect the new order.

The Slice Tool options bar allows you to designate an exact size for the slice or use guides to create a slice.

To Create Slices

The following steps create slices in the Horseshoe Stables file that will serve as links to various parts of the Web site.

- On the Tools panel, right-click the Crop Tool button to display the context menu (Figure 9–25).

Figure 9–25

2

- Click Slice Tool to select it.

- In the document window, drag a rectangle around the word, Home (Figure 9–26). The size of your slices may differ from the figure. Just be sure to include the entire word in your slice.

Q&A What are all those symbols and lines?

Photoshop slices the page into five numbered pieces: one slice around the word, Home, and slices on each of the four sides. In the slice badge, a mountain icon indicates that the slice has image content. The mouse pointer displays a slice icon.

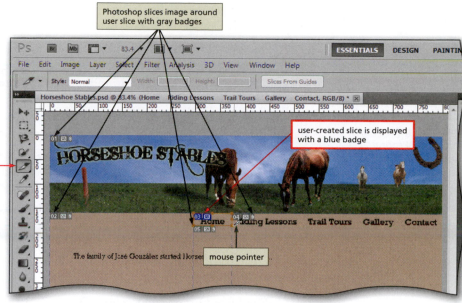

Figure 9–26

3

- In the document window, drag a rectangle around the phrase, Riding Lessons, to create a slice. As you drag, allow Photoshop to snap the slice into position so it is the same height as the Home slice (Figure 9–27).

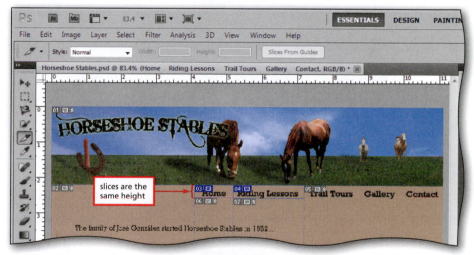

Figure 9–27

4

- Create slices for the Trail Tours, Gallery, and Contact phrases (Figure 9–28).

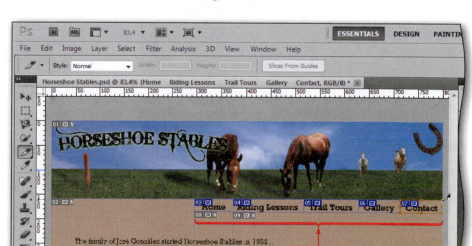

Figure 9–28

Other Ways

1. On Layer menu, click New Layer Based Slice

The Slice Select Tool

Once you create a slice, you can select, move, resize, align, distribute, and assign attributes using the Slice Select Tool. With the Slice Select Tool activated, to select a slice, click it. To move a slice, click within the slice and drag. To resize a slice, drag its border or drag a handle. The Slice Select Tool options bar displays many buttons to reorder, align, and distribute (Figure 9–29). Other Slice Select Tool options — including the ability to delete, divide, and reorder — are available by right-clicking the slice.

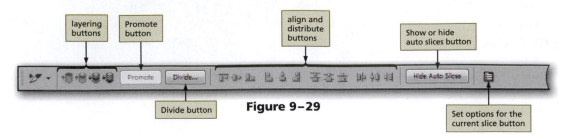

layering buttons

Promote button

align and distribute buttons

Show or hide auto slices button

Divide button

Figure 9–29

Set options for the current slice button

The Slice Options dialog box (Figure 9–30) appears when you double-click a slice; you can use it to set values associated with a slice.

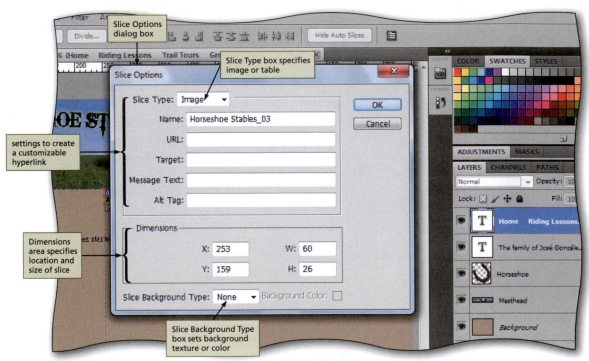

Slice Options dialog box

Slice Type box specifies image or table

settings to create a customizable hyperlink

Dimensions area specifies location and size of slice

Slice Background Type box sets background texture or color

Figure 9–30

Each slice becomes a small image when converted to HTML. The Name box of the Slice Options dialog box automatically generates the name of that image, although you can change it. The URL box holds the Web page address or a relative location of the hyperlink. The Target box allows you to specify how the link will open — in a new browser window (or browser tab) or as a replacement of the current page. For example, a target setting of _blank will cause the hyperlink to open the Web page in a new browser window or tab. The Message Text box allows you to specify text that will be displayed in the browser's status bar when a user points to the hyperlink. You can use the Alt Tag box to create alternative text used by screen readers. The alternative text also becomes a tool tip in most browsers; it appears as placeholder text if a user chooses not to download graphics. At the bottom of the Slice Options dialog box are dimension settings and the background type setting.

To Select the Slice Select Tool

The following step selects the Slice Select Tool.

- Right-click the Slice Tool button to display the context menu (Figure 9–31).

- Click Slice Select Tool to choose the tool.

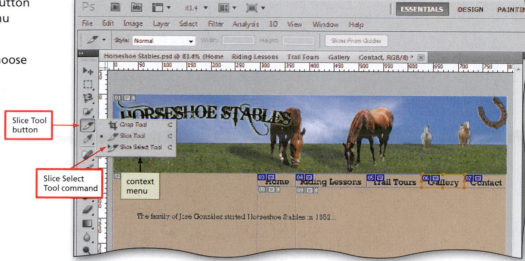

Figure 9–31

To Enter Slice Settings

In the Horseshoe Stables image, you will enter hyperlink settings for the Gallery slice. The link will take Web page visitors to the index.html page of the Web gallery. The Message Text setting defines text that appears at the bottom of a Web browser window when a user points to a slice on the Web page. The Alt Tag setting provides alternative text that is displayed on the Web page if the Web browser cannot display the image. The Alt Tag text is also read aloud by some computers. This allows a visually impaired user to know where a hyperlinked slice will take them without physically seeing the Web page.

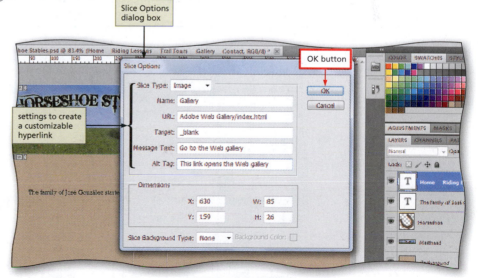

- Double-click the Gallery slice to display the Slice Options dialog box.

- Drag to select any existing text in the Name box, then type **Gallery**.

- Click the URL box and then type **Adobe Web Gallery/index.html** as the entry. Recall this is the name and location of the Web gallery start page, Bridge, created earlier.

- Click the Target box and then type **_blank** as the entry.

- Click the Message Text box and then type **Go to the Web gallery** as the entry.

- Click the Alt Tag box and then type **This link opens the Web gallery** as the entry (Figure 9–32).

Figure 9–32

What are the parts of the URL entry?

Adobe Web Gallery is the folder that Bridge created automatically. The file, index.html, is the name of the first page in the Web gallery. The / (slash) in the URL separates the name of the folder and the file name. Because this is a relative reference, the My Web Site folder location is not necessary.

2

• Click the OK button to apply the settings and close the dialog box.

<table>
<tr><td colspan="2">**Other Ways**</td></tr>
<tr><td>1. Right-click slice, click Edit Slice Options, enter settings, click OK</td><td>2. On options bar, click 'Set options for current slice' button, enter settings, click OK</td></tr>
</table>

To Enter More Slice Settings

The following steps set the options for the remaining slices.

1 Double-click the Home slice to display the Slice Options dialog box, select any existing type in the Name text box, and then type `Home`.

2 Click the URL box, select any existing text, and then type `index.html` as the entry (Figure 9–33).

3 Click the OK button to apply the settings and close the dialog box.

4 Double-click the Riding Lessons slice to display the Slice Options dialog box.

5 Type `Riding Lessons` in the Name box, type `lessons.html` in the URL box, and then click the OK button to apply the settings and close the dialog box.

6 Double-click the Trail Tours slice to display the Slice Options dialog box and then type `Trail Tours` in the Name box and `tours.html` in the URL box.

7 Click the OK button to apply the settings and close the dialog box.

8 Double-click the Contact slice to display the Slice Options dialog box, type `Contact` in the Name text box, type `contact.html` in the URL box, and then click the OK button to apply the settings and close the dialog box.

Figure 9–33

Previewing the Web Page

Photoshop uses the Save for Web & Devices dialog box to preview the image or Web page within a browser. While that is fine for viewing the page and its settings, it will not navigate the hyperlinks unless you are connected to the Web. Because the preview is created in a temporary location, also known as a temp file on your system, the preview will not connect to relative links at all. Relative links point to files in a location that is different from the location of the original file.

To Preview the Hyperlink

The following steps preview the hyperlink settings.

1
- Click File on the menu bar, and then click Save for Web & Devices to display the Save for Web & Devices dialog box (Figure 9–34).

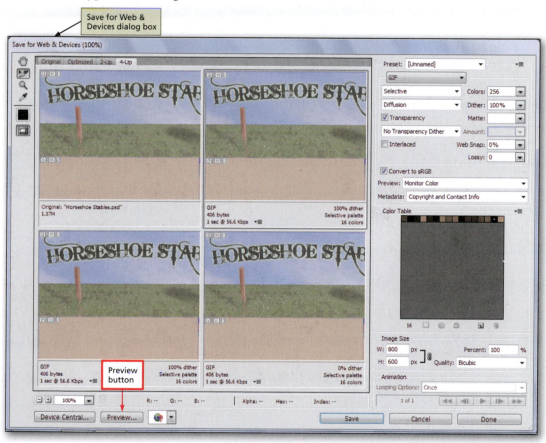

Figure 9–34

2

- Click the Preview button (Save for Web & Devices dialog box).

- When the browser window opens, if a yellow security bar appears across the top of the window, click it, and then click Allow Blocked Content on the shortcut menu.

- If Windows displays a security warning dialog box, click the Yes button.

- If necessary, maximize the browser window.

- Move the mouse pointer over the Gallery link to display the hand icon, tool tip, and Status bar message (Figure 9–35).

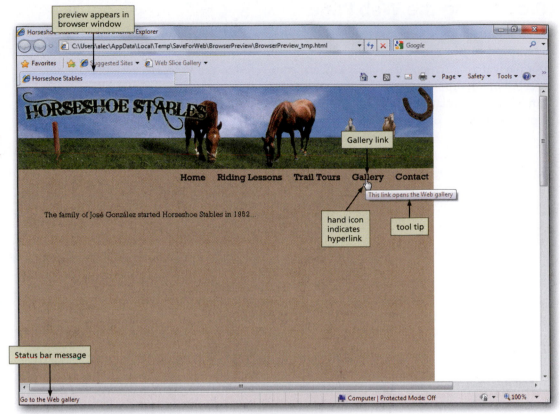

Figure 9–35

Q&A Can I click the Gallery link to display the Web gallery?

The preview is stored in a temporary location that cannot access the index.html page of the gallery. Later in the chapter, you will save the Web page and test the link.

 3

- Close the browser window.

- Return to Photoshop, if necessary, and click the Cancel button in the Save for Web & Devices dialog box.

To Save the File

The following step saves the file again.

1 Press CTRL+S.

Animation

An **animation** is a sequence of frames or images, displayed over time to convey movement. A **frame** is a single view of the image within the sequence, which can be edited and optimized. Each frame in an animation varies slightly from the preceding frame by changing effects, filters, or repositioning objects. This variation creates the illusion of movement when the frames are viewed or played in quick succession. Professional animators create hundreds or thousands of frames, each with a tiny change from frame to frame, to emulate smooth movement. In small animations that are used on the Web, such as **animated GIFs**, the number of frames varies, but commonly includes from five to 50 frames and can run several seconds or longer, depending on how the timing for the animation is set.

Designers create animations using a wide variety of application software. While Photoshop is a high-end graphic editing tool, it is not intended for the creation of advanced animations with film or movie quality. You can create basic animations in Photoshop, however.

To learn all of the animation and optimization features in Photoshop takes time and practice. In this chapter, you will create a simple animation with approximately 30 frames. Building this animation presents you with an introduction to the basic techniques and tools used in animation and optimization. Further study will be required to master these tools and techniques.

Plan Ahead

Employ animation carefully.

The judicious use of animation in a Web site can add impact and increase comprehension, but a little goes a long way. Animations that illustrate a dynamic process, that enliven a logo, or pace the delivery of information are best. Keep in mind the following rules when creating animations:

- Animations should enhance content. All Web sites present information, so animated effects should support the content by delivering information, identifying key elements or purpose, or clarifying a complex process.

- Simple animations are more effective than complex ones. Animated effects should enhance, not distract, from content. Choose subtle effects such as dissolves and fades.

- Keep your animations consistent; do not try to do too many different kinds of animations on a Web site.

Creating the Animation Graphic for the Horseshoe Stables Web Page

The animation in the Horseshoe Stables Web page creates a rotating horseshoe that starts in the upper-right corner and finishes around a stake in the lower-left corner of the masthead, similar to a horseshoe toss game. First, you will temporarily hide the slices and layers that are not involved in the animation. Then, you will create a layer group, and open and copy it to multiple layers, placing them in different locations on the page. Relocation of the layer groups gives the illusion of motion when viewed in quick succession. You will align and distribute the layers evenly. Finally, you will place each layer as a frame in the animation and have Photoshop create additional frames for smooth transitions.

BTW

Creating Animations
Adobe Flash CS5 is an authoring environment for creating animations and interactivity. Flash animations are platform-independent and can be displayed on a variety of devices.

To Hide Layers and Slices

The following step temporarily hides layers that are not involved in the animation. You also will hide the slices.

- Display the Layers panel.

- Hide the Background and the two type layers so they are not visible in the document window.

- Press CTRL+H to hide extras (such as guides, grids, bounding boxes, and selections) and hide the slices (Figure 9–36).

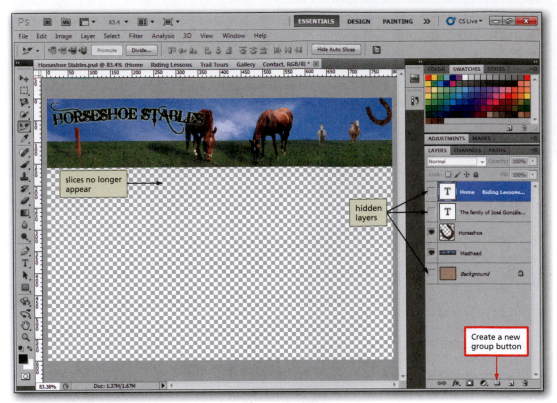

Figure 9–36

To Create a Layer Group

The steps that follow create a layer group named Toss.

1 On the Layers panel, click the 'Create a new group' button.

2 Name the layer group, Toss.

3 On the Layers panel, drag to move the new layer group to the location immediately above the Masthead layer.

To Move the Horseshoe Layer

The following steps move the Horseshoe layer into the Toss group.

1 On the Layers panel, drag the Horseshoe layer onto the Toss group to move it into the group. The Horseshoe layer should now appear indented below the Toss group.

2 If necessary, click the Hide/Show layers icon to the left of the Toss group to expand its contents (Figure 9–37).

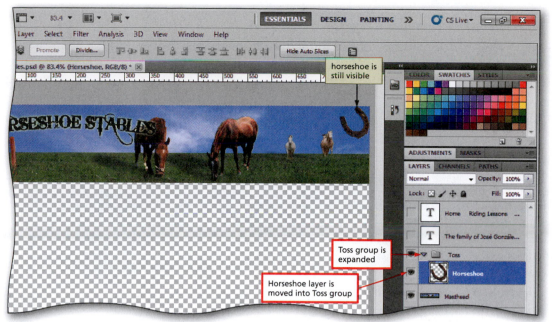

Figure 9–37

To Create Copies of the Horseshoe Layer

The steps that follow create copies of the horseshoe layer, numbering them from 2 to 7; the layers will be used to create animation frames.

1 On the Layers panel, right-click the Horseshoe layer, and then click Duplicate Layer on the context menu to display the Duplicate Layer dialog box.

2 Type `Horseshoe 2` in the As text box and then click the OK button to create the new layer.

3 Repeat Steps 1 and 2 to create a total of seven layers named Horseshoe, and Horseshoe 2 through Horseshoe 7.

4 Drag the Horseshoe layers within the Toss group to rearrange them, if necessary, as shown in Figure 9–38.

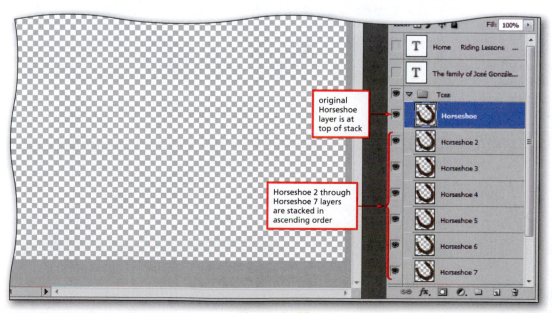

Figure 9–38

To Move the Layers

The following steps move the layers to locations diagonally across the document window.

- With Horseshoe 7 selected on the Layers panel, press the v key to activate the Move Tool.

- In the document window, drag the horseshoe to a location on top of the stake on the left side of the masthead. This represents the final resting state of the animation. Be sure the horseshoe does not extend beyond the masthead and appears to be landing around the stake, as shown in Figure 9–39.

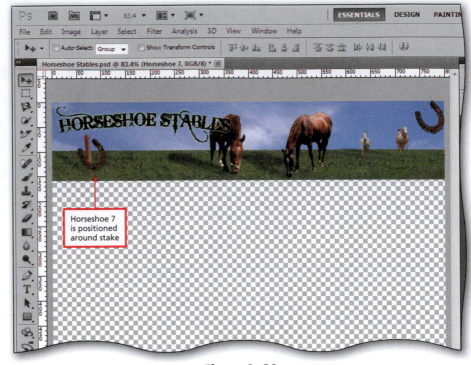

Figure 9–39

- On the Layers panel, select the Horseshoe 6 layer. In the document window, drag it to a location to the right and slightly above the Horseshoe 7 layer.

- Repeat the previous step, moving layers 5, 4, 3, and 2 to locations to the right and slightly above the previous layer (Figure 9–40). Do not be concerned with spacing the horseshoes evenly. You will use a Photoshop command to distribute the horseshoes equally later in this chapter.

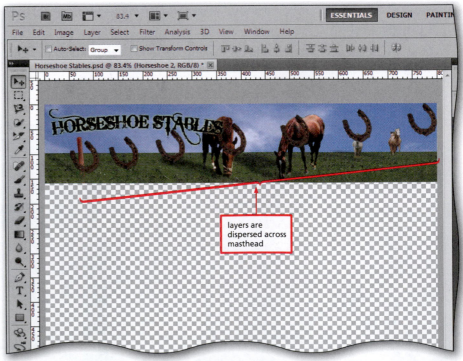

Figure 9–40

To Rotate the Layers

The following steps rotate each layer 45° clockwise so the animated horseshoe will appear to be rotating.

- On the Layers panel, select the Horseshoe 6 layer, if necessary. Press CTRL+T to display the bounding box.

- Position the mouse pointer just outside the upper-right corner of the bounding box to display the rotation handle (Figure 9–41).

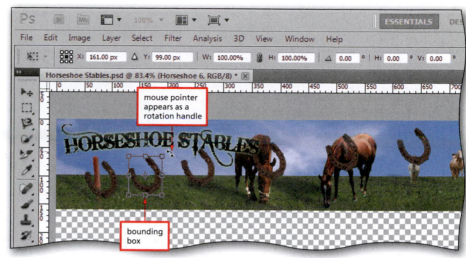

Figure 9–41

- Drag the layer approximately 45° clockwise. Press the ENTER key to confirm the transformation (Figure 9–42).

Q&A

How can I tell when I am close to 45°?

Look in the Options bar and locate the Set rotation box. The value in this box changes in real time as you rotate the layer, giving you the exact degree measurement. You can also hold the SHIFT key as you rotate the layer to rotate in 15° increments.

Figure 9–42

- Repeat Steps 1 and 2 for the layers named Horseshoe 5, 4, 3, and 2, adding an additional 45° to each successive rotation (Figure 9–43).

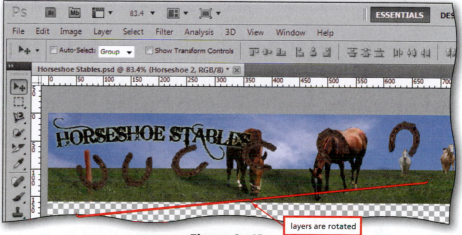

Figure 9–43

To Distribute the Layers

The following steps distribute the layers evenly across the image using buttons on the options bar. Distributing the layers improves the smoothness of the animation.

- CTRL+click each of the Horseshoe layers to select them all.

- On the options bar, click the 'Distribute vertical centers' button to evenly space the layers (Figure 9–44).

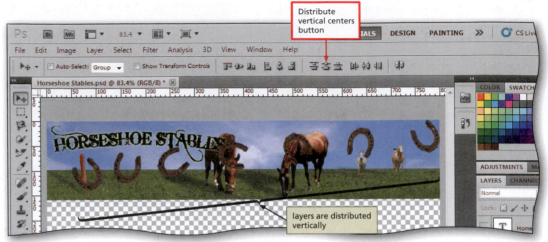

Figure 9–44

- On the options bar, click the 'Distribute horizontal centers' button (Figure 9–45).

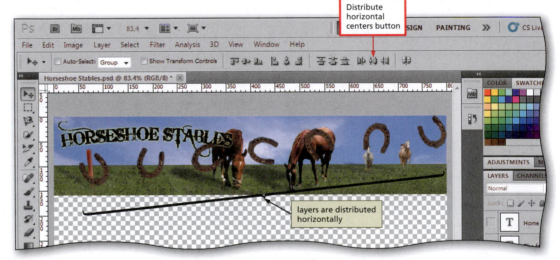

Figure 9–45

The Animation Panel

You will use the Animation panel in conjunction with the Layers panel to create animation frames (Figure 9–46). The panel usually opens at the bottom of the Photoshop window, with one frame visible to start. To create an animation, you insert a new frame from the panel menu, and then edit the layers. As you create them, frames are added sequentially from left to right in the panel.

The panel menu displays commands to create, manipulate, and optimize the frames. Below each frame is a button used to set the timing or delay between the current frame and the next frame.

The Animation panel displays buttons along the bottom that are used to manipulate the frames. The buttons allow you to do the following: edit how the animation loops; play, rewind, and fast-forward the animation; and tween, duplicate, and delete frames.

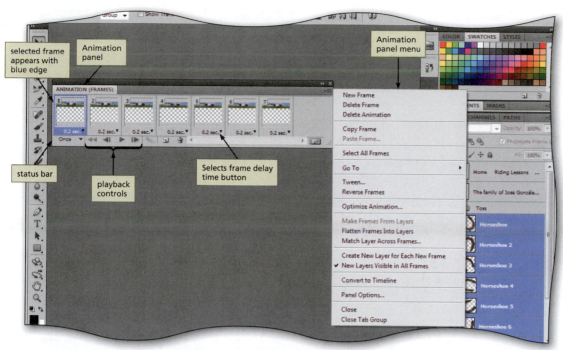

Figure 9–46

To Display the Animation Panel

The following step uses the menu system to open the Animation panel.

1

- Click Window on the menu bar to display the menu.

- Click Animation to display the Animation panel. If the Animation (Timeline) panel of Photoshop is displayed, click the Animation panel menu button, and then click Convert to Frame animation (Figure 9–47).

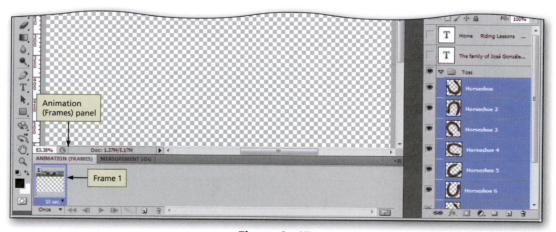

Figure 9–47

To Display Appropriate Layers

When the animation begins, you will want only the Masthead and Horseshoe layers to appear in the document window to display the starting state of the animation. The following step shows the proper layers.

1 Click the visibility icon for the Horseshoe 2 through Horseshoe 7 layers to hide them (Figure 9–48 on the next page).

Figure 9–48

To Set the Timing

The amount of time that Photoshop takes to move from one frame to another during playback is called the **delay time**. By default, Photoshop sets the delay time to 10 seconds, but you can change it depending on your purpose. In the following steps, you will set the time to .2 seconds so very little time elapses between frames. The delay time that you specify in Frame 1 automatically applies to subsequent frames as they are created.

1
• Click the 'Selects frame delay time' button to display the list of timings (Figure 9–49).

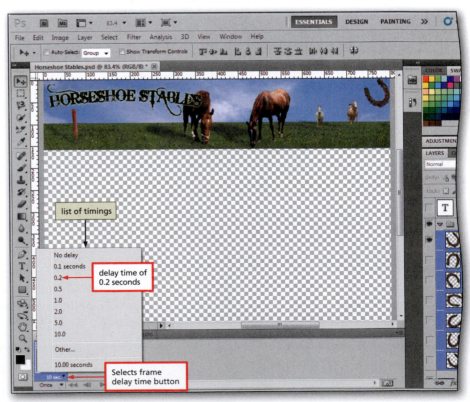

Figure 9–49

2

● Click 0.2 in the list to delay the next frame by two-tenths of a second (Figure 9–50).

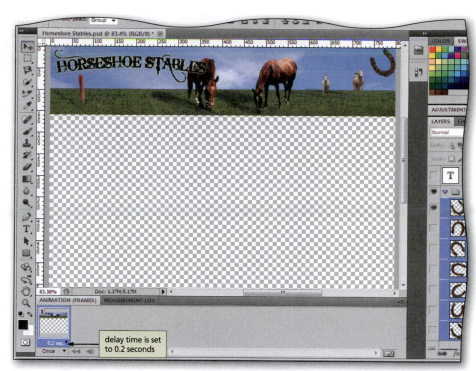

delay time is set to 0.2 seconds

Figure 9–50

To Create New Frames

The following steps build the animation using the Animation panel. As you duplicate each frame, you will hide the previous horseshoe and display the next one.

1

● On the Animation panel status bar, click the 'Duplicates selected frames' button to display the second frame (Figure 9–51).

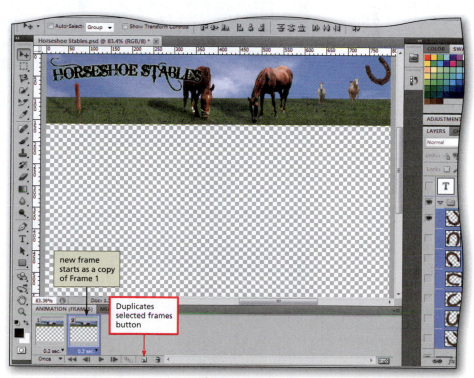

new frame starts as a copy of Frame 1

Duplicates selected frames button

Figure 9–51

2

● Hide the visibility of the Horseshoe layer and turn on the visibility of the Horseshoe 2 layer (Figure 9–52).

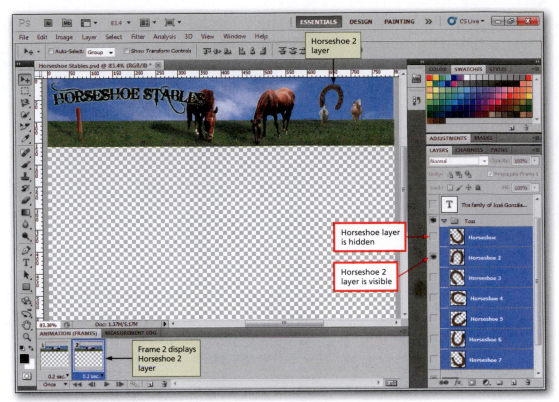

Figure 9–52

3

● Repeat Steps 1 and 2, hiding and showing each subsequent horseshoe layer until Horseshoe 7 is displayed in the seventh frame (Figure 9–53).

Q&A

How many frames should I have?

A total of seven frames should appear in the Animation panel. Each frame will have a horseshoe displayed at a different spot.

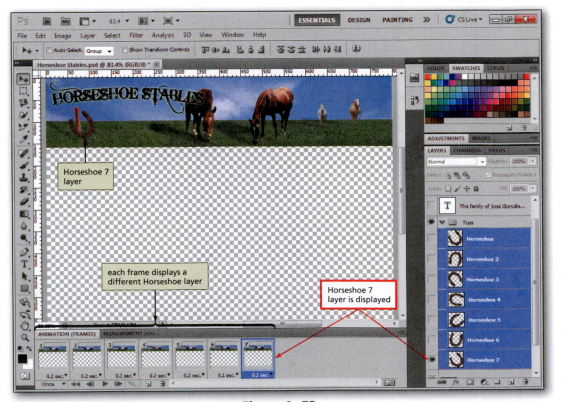

Figure 9–53

Other Ways

1. On Animation panel menu, click Copy Frame, click Paste Frame

To Preview the Animation

The following steps preview the animation by clicking the Plays animation button at the bottom of the Animation panel.

1

• On the Animation panel, click Frame 1 to select it (Figure 9–54).

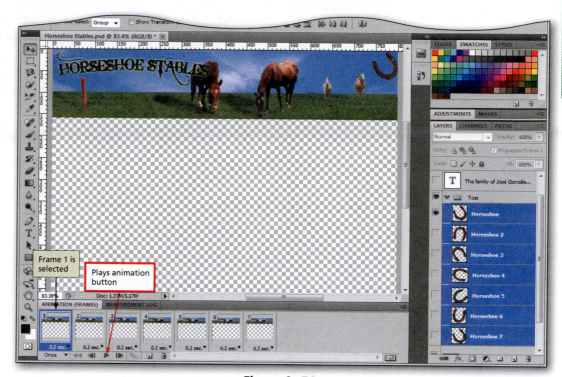

Figure 9–54

2

• On the Animation panel status bar, click the Plays animation button to preview the animation (Figure 9–55). The Plays animation button becomes a Stop button after you click it and then becomes the Plays animation button at frame 7.

• After viewing the animation a few times, click the Stop button to stop playing the animation.

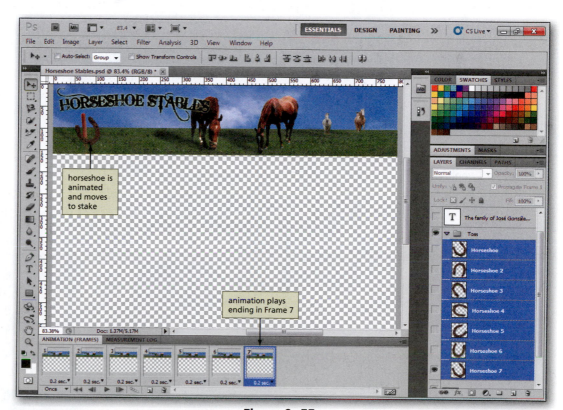

Figure 9–55

Tweening

Tweening, a corruption of the phrase in-between, is a way to allow Photoshop to create new frames automatically between two existing frames. When you tween between two frames, Photoshop parses the data equally in the frames, creating graduated changes. Photoshop reduces the opacity of the layer evenly across the new frames and increments the layer position equally, and any special effects are interpolated across the new frames. For example, if two frames contain an opacity change from 50% to 100%, Photoshop creates a tween frame with 75% opacity. Similarly, if two frames display an object that has been moved, the tween frame will display the object placed halfway between the two. Tweening significantly reduces the time required to create animation effects, but is more effective with images that are simpler in composition; a highly complex animation does not generate a great result with tweening. Tweened frames are fully editable.

To Tween

The following steps create three new frames between each of the current frames, tweening the animation.

1

- In the Animation panel, click Frame 7 to select it, if necessary.

- On the Animation status bar, click the Tweens animation frames button to display the Tween dialog box (Figure 9–56).

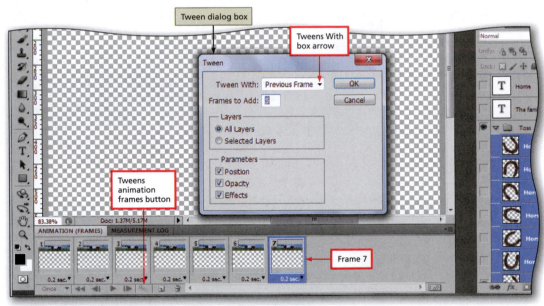

Figure 9–56

2

- Click the Tween With box arrow to display the list (Figure 9–57).

Q&A

How does Photoshop create the tween?

Photoshop adds a new frame, interpolating the layer properties evenly between the two surrounding frames.

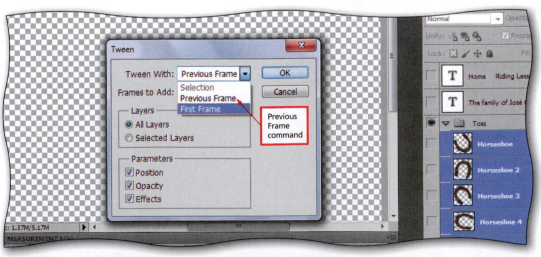

Figure 9–57

3

- Click Previous Frame to create tween frames between Frames 6 and 7.

- Type 3 in the Frames to Add box to create three frames between Frames 6 and 7.

- If necessary, click the All Layers option button to select it. Click to display a check mark in each of the check boxes in the Parameters area, as shown in Figure 9–58.

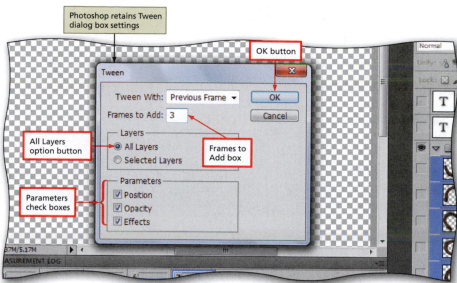

Photoshop retains Tween dialog box settings

OK button

All Layers option button

Frames to Add box

Parameters check boxes

Figure 9–58

Q&A

What does the All Layers option button do?

If the frame contains more than one layer with movement or opacity changes, the All Layers option will tween each layer. If you do not select the option, only the layer selected on the Layers panel will be tweened.

4

- Click the OK button to create the tween frames (Figure 9–59).

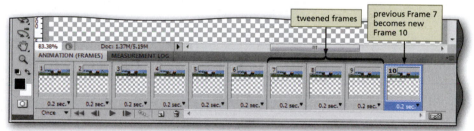

tweened frames

previous Frame 7 becomes new Frame 10

Figure 9–59

5

- Click Frame 6 and then click the 'Tweens animation frames' button. Repeat Steps 2 through 4 to create three frames that tween between Frames 5 and 6.

- Click Frame 5 and then click the 'Tweens animation frames' button. Repeat Steps 2 through 4 to create three frames that tween between Frames 4 and 5.

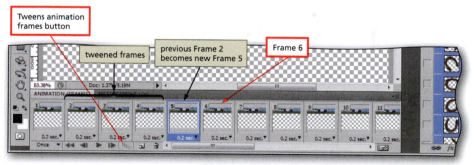

Tweens animation frames button

tweened frames

previous Frame 2 becomes new Frame 5

Frame 6

Figure 9–60

- Click Frame 4 and then click the 'Tweens animation frames' button. Repeat Steps 2 through 4 to create three frames that tween between Frames 3 and 4.

- Click Frame 3 and then click the 'Tweens animation frames' button. Repeat Steps 2 through 4 to create three frames that tween between Frames 2 and 3.

- Click Frame 2 and then click the 'Tweens animation frames' button. Repeat Steps 2 through 4 to create three frames that tween between Frames 1 and 2 (Figure 9–60).

Q&A

How many total frames is that?

You should have 25 frames: the original 7 plus 3 between each one.

Other Ways

1. Select frames, on panel menu, click Tween

To View Tween Frames

To look at the interpolation Photoshop creates in order to tween, the following step views a tween frame.

1

- Click Frame 2 to view how Photoshop tweens (Figure 9–61).

🔍 **Experiment**

- Continue clicking each frame, one at a time, and watch the opacity and movement changes.

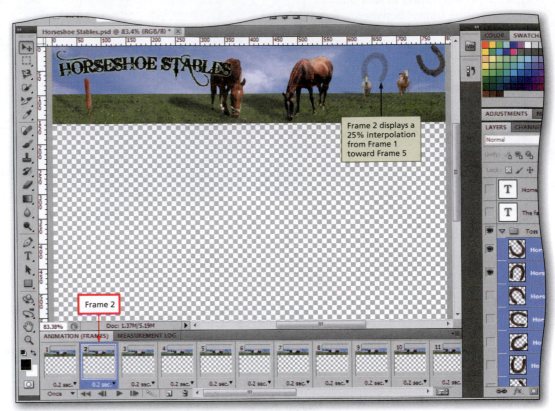

Frame 2 displays a 25% interpolation from Frame 1 toward Frame 5

Frame 2

Figure 9–61

To Preview the Animation Again

The following steps preview the animation again by clicking the Plays animation button at the bottom of the Animation panel.

1 On the Animation panel, scroll the frames to the left, and then click Frame 1 to select it (Figure 9–62).

2 If necessary, click the 'Selects looping options' arrow and set the looping to Once.

3 On the Animation panel status bar, click the Plays animation button to preview the animation.

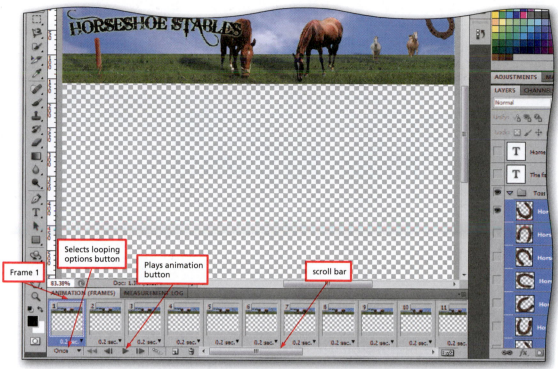

Figure 9–62

To Offset for Animation

If you want to create an animation that moves an object without any rotation, you can use a special filter in Photoshop to specify the exact movement in pixels. For example, if you wanted to create a ball that bounces across the screen, you would perform the following steps.

1. Duplicate the layer that contains the ball.
2. With the new layer selected, click Filter on the menu bar, point to Other, and then click Offset.
3. In the Offset dialog box, specify exactly how many pixels to move the object both horizontally and vertically.
4. On the Animation panel, in the first frame, make only the original layer visible.
5. Duplicate Frame 1 and make only the filtered frame visible.
6. Repeat Steps 1 through 5 for each new position of the bouncing ball.

Animation Settings

You can choose to have an animation display just once, a specified number of times, or repeat continuously, which is called **looping**. The animation you created displayed once. The animation display choices are available through the 'Selects looping options' button, shown in Figure 9–62, at the bottom of the Animation panel.

Additionally, you can optimize the animation for both performance and storage with two settings on the Animation panel menu. When optimizing, the Bounding Box setting crops each frame to only the area that has changed from the preceding frame, which can reduce the file size and lessen the time needed to download the animation when viewed on a Web page. The Redundant Pixel Removal setting makes transparent the pixels in a frame that are unchanged from the preceding frame. Later, when you save the file as a GIF or HTML file, you must select the Transparency option on the Optimize panel for the setting to work properly.

BTW

Disposing Frames
The **Dispose** command, available on each frame's context menu, discards the current frame before displaying the next frame. When displayed on the Web, the disposal prevents flickering and provides a more consistent flow of animation. For the best animation effect, you should choose a disposal method for frames that include background transparency to specify whether the current frame will be visible through the transparent areas of the next frame.

To Optimize the Animation

The following steps set the optimization for the animation.

 1
- Click the Animation panel menu button to display the menu (Figure 9–63).

Q&A What does the Match Layer Across Frames command do?

If you added an animation to an existing image, the Match command would make sure the background appeared throughout every frame of the animation.

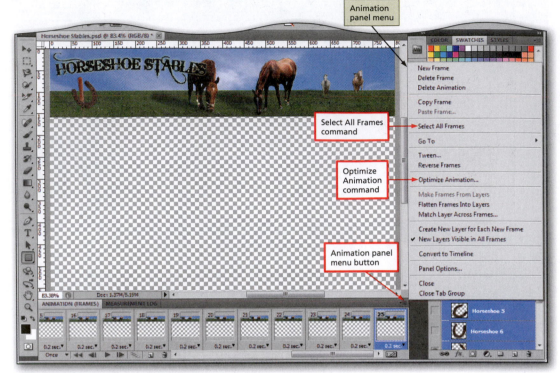

Figure 9–63

2
- Click Select All Frames to include all of the frames in the animation.

- Click the Animation panel menu button, and then click Optimize Animation to display the Optimize Animation dialog box.

- If necessary, click both the Bounding Box and Redundant Pixel Removal check boxes to select them (Figure 9–64).

3
- Click the OK button to close the dialog box.

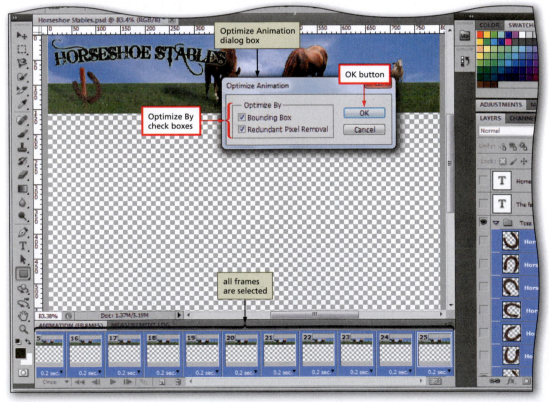

Figure 9–64

To Save the File with the Animation

Saving the file preserves the animation. Because you have used appropriate sizes and slices, you do not need to specify further optimization. Photoshop files that contain animation are larger than other files. Make sure you have enough room on your storage device to hold the file, which is approximately 2.6 Mb. If you do not have enough space, you will have to save your file to another location.

1 Click the Hide/Show layers icon to the left of the Toss group on the Layers panel to collapse it.

2 Click the visibility icons to show the three hidden layers so that all the layers are visible.

3 Click the Animation panel menu button and then click Close Tab Group to close the Animation panel.

4 Press CTRL+S to save the file again.

To Save the File as a Web Page

In the next steps, you will save the file in the HTML format that can be uploaded to a Web server.

1

- On the File menu, click Save for Web & Devices to display the Save for Web & Devices dialog box.

- Click the preview with the smallest file size, and then click the Save button to display the Save Optimized As dialog box.

- If necessary, click the Save in box arrow and navigate to the My Web Site folder or the location of your storage device.

- Click the Format box arrow to display the format options.

- Click HTML and Images in the list (Figure 9–65). Do not click the Save button.

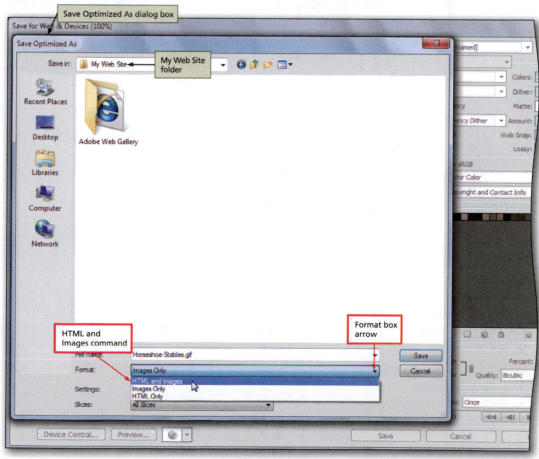

Figure 9–65

2

- Click the Slices box arrow to display the options (Figure 9–66).

3

- Click All Slices in the list.

- Click the Save button to save the file and a folder of images on the storage device.

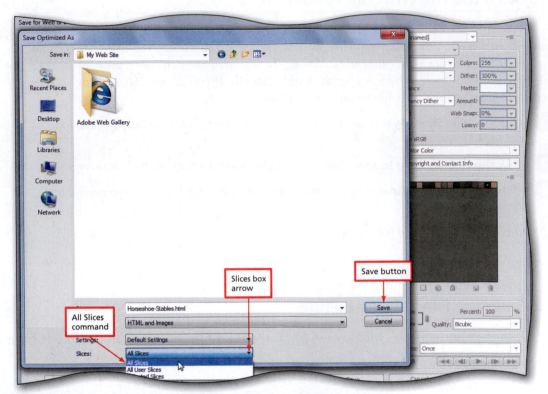

Figure 9–66

To Close the File and Quit Photoshop

The Web page is complete. The final step is to close the file and quit Photoshop.

1 Click the Close button on the Photoshop title bar. If Photoshop displays a message about saving the file, click the No button.

To View the Web Page Interactively

To make a final check of the interactivity of the Web page, the following steps open the Horseshoe Stables HTML file with a browser for viewing the animation. After you click the Gallery link, the Web gallery will open.

1

- Click the Start button on the Windows 7 taskbar and then click Computer on the Start menu.

- When the Computer window opens, navigate to your USB storage drive and open the folder named My Web Site.

- If necessary, click More options on the toolbar and then click List to display a list of all the files (Figure 9–67).

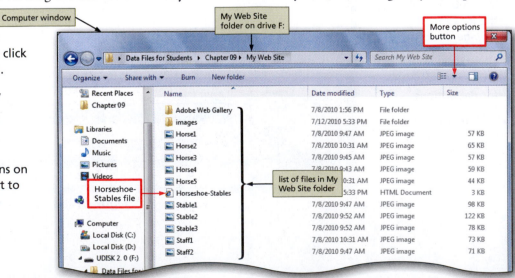

Figure 9–67

2

- Double-click the HTML file, Horseshoe-Stables, to launch your default Web browser, load the page, and view the animation (Figure 9–68).

- If a yellow bar is displayed below the browser toolbars, click the yellow bar, click Allow Blocked Content, and then click Yes in the Security Warning dialog box.

Q&A My animation did not appear. Did I do something wrong?

If your animation does not play, your browser might not permit ActiveX controls. See your instructor for ways to play the animation in your browser.

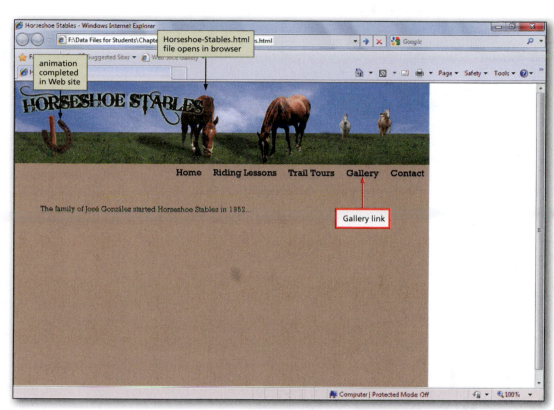

Figure 9–68

3

- When the animation is finished, click the Gallery link to open the Web gallery in a new window.

- Click any of the thumbnails or use the navigation buttons to display a larger view of each image (Figure 9–69).

4

- Close all of the open windows.

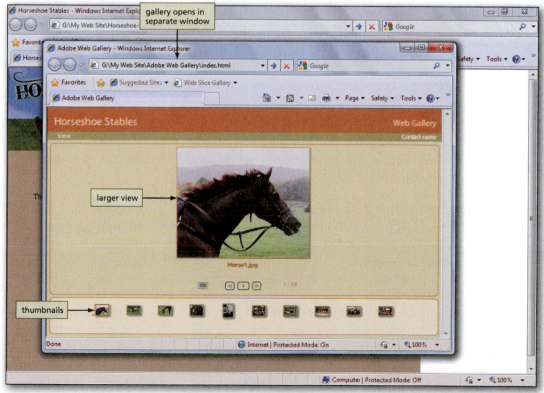

Figure 9–69

Chapter Summary

In this chapter, you created a Web site for Horseshoe Stables. First, you organized images in a folder and created a Web gallery using an automation feature in Bridge. After inserting a masthead, you added placeholder text and a navigation bar. You entered text to serve as hyperlinks when the Web page is viewed in a browser. You sliced the image into multiple sections, one for each hyperlink. You used the Slice Options dialog box panel to enter specific settings for the hyperlink, such as the destination URL and Status bar message.

Finally, you created a series of frames that animated a graphic of a horseshoe moving onto a stake, similar to a horseshoe toss game. You created each part of the animation as a separate layer and then displayed each layer in its own animation frame. You learned about the Animation panel and animation techniques such as looping, tweening, and optimizing. The completed animation was added to the home page of the Web site. With the Web site complete, you tested the animation and the hyperlink in a Web browser.

The items listed below include all the new Photoshop skills you have learned in this chapter:

1. Create a Folder in Bridge (PS 539)
2. Copy and Paste Files in Bridge (PS 540)
3. Display the Bridge Output Panel (PS 542)
4. Choose a Template and Style (PS 543)
5. Edit Site Information (PS 544)
6. Preview the Web Gallery (PS 545)
7. Save the Web Gallery (PS 546)
8. Select a Background Color Using the Swatches Panel (PS 548)
9. Insert Text with Special Characters (PS 553)
10. Create the Navigation Bar (PS 554)
11. Create Slices (PS 556)
12. Select the Slice Select Tool (PS 559)
13. Enter Slice Settings (PS 559)
14. Preview the Hyperlink (PS 561)
15. Hide Layers and Slices (PS 564)
16. Move the Layers (PS 566)
17. Rotate the Layers (PS 567)
18. Distribute the Layers (PS 568)
19. Display the Animation Panel (PS 569)
20. Set the Timing (PS 570)
21. Create New Frames (PS 571)
22. Preview the Animation (PS 573)
23. Tween (PS 574)
24. View Tween Frames (PS 576)
25. Offset for Animation (PS 577)
26. Optimize the Animation (PS 578)
27. Save the File as a Web Page (PS 579)
28. View the Web Page Interactively (PS 580)

Learn It Online

Test your knowledge of chapter content and key terms.

Instructions: To complete the Learn It Online exercises, start your browser, click the Address bar, and then enter the Web address `scsite.com/pscs5/learn`. When the Photoshop CS5 Learn It Online page is displayed, click the link for the exercise you want to complete, and then read the instructions.

Chapter Reinforcement TF, MC, and SA

A series of true/false, multiple choice, and short answer questions that tests your knowledge of the chapter content.

Flash Cards

An interactive learning environment where you identify chapter key terms associated with displayed definitions.

Practice Test

A series of multiple choice questions that test your knowledge of chapter content and key terms.

Who Wants To Be a Computer Genius?

An interactive game that challenges your knowledge of chapter content in the style of a television quiz show.

Wheel of Terms

An interactive game that challenges your knowledge of chapter key terms in the style of the television show *Wheel of Fortune*.

Crossword Puzzle Challenge

A crossword puzzle that challenges your knowledge of key terms presented in the chapter.

Apply Your Knowledge

Reinforce the skills and apply the concepts you learned in this chapter.

Creating a Web Banner

Instructions: Start Photoshop and perform the customization steps found on pages PS 6 through PS 9. Open the Apply 9-1 Water file from the Chapter 09 folder of the Data Files for Students. See the inside back cover of this book for instructions on downloading the Data Files for Students, or contact your instructor for information about accessing the required files.

The purpose of this exercise is to create a Web banner for a company that specializes in kid-friendly water sports. The file you open is a banner with the name of the company, a logo, and a slogan. You are to create a folder to hold all of the associated files, animate the company's logo, and add text slices in preparation for hyperlink entries. The final product is shown in Figure 9–70.

Perform the following tasks:

1. On the File menu, click Save As. When the Save As dialog box is displayed, navigate to your storage device. If you created a Chapter 09 folder, double-click to open it, and then click the Create New Folder button on the toolbar. When the new folder is displayed, type `Water Kids Web Site` as the name, and then press the ENTER key to rename the folder. If necessary, double-click the Water Kids Web Site folder to open it. In the File name text box, type `Water Edited` to name the file. If necessary, click the Format box arrow, and then click Photoshop (*.PSD;*.PDD) in the list. Click the Save button. If Photoshop displays an options dialog box, click the OK button.

Figure 9–70

Continued >

Apply Your Knowledge *continued*

2. To create the text hyperlinks:

a. On the Tools panel, click the Horizontal Type Tool button. On the options bar, set the font to Georgia, set the font style to Bold, set the size to 10, and set the color to match the blue in the shape.

b. Drag a box on the left side of the document window, just below the blue shape. Type `Our Activities` in the type bounding box and then click the 'Commit any current edits' button on the options bar.

c. Press the v key to access the Move Tool. ALT+drag four copies of the type bounding box and position them along the left edge, below each other. One at a time, select each new layer and type the words shown in Figure 9–70 on the previous page.

d. Select the five type layers you added on the Layers panel. On the Tools panel, select the Move Tool. On the options bar, click the 'Distribute vertical centers' button and the 'Align left edges' button.

3. To slice the text:

a. On the Layers panel, select the Our Activities text layer.

b. On the Tools panel, click the Slice Tool button.

c. Draw a slice around the Our Activities text element.

d. Repeat the process for the remaining four new layers.

4. To create new layers for the animation:

a. On the Layers panel, right-click the Boat layer, and then click Duplicate Layer. Repeat the process until you have the Boat layer and four copies. Rename the five Boat layers `Boat 22`, `Boat 44`, `Boat 66`, `Boat 88`, and `Boat 100` respectively.

b. Click the Boat 22 layer and press CTRL+T to display the Transform options bar. In the Options bar, click the 'Maintain aspect ratio' button, if necessary, to select it. In the Set horizontal scale box, type `22` to resize the layer to 22 percent of its original size. Press the ENTER key to accept your entry, then press ENTER again to commit the change.

c. Repeat Step 4b for the Boat 44, Boat 66, and Boat 88 layers, resizing them to the 44, 66, and 88 percent, respectively.

d. On the Layers panel, turn off the visibility of all the boat layers except Boat 22.

5. To create animation frames:

a. On the Window menu, click Animation. If necessary, click the Animation panel menu button, and then click Convert to Frame Animation. When the Animation (Frames) panel is displayed, click the 'Duplicates selected frames' button.

b. On the Layers panel, turn off the visibility of the Boat 22 layer and turn on the visibility of the Boat 44 layer.

c. Create a third frame. On the Layers panel, turn off the visibility of the Boat 44 layer and turn on the visibility of the Boat 66 layer.

d. Create a fourth frame. On the Layers panel, turn off the visibility of the Boat 66 layer and turn on the visibility of the Boat 88 layer.

e. Create a fifth frame. On the Layers panel, turn off the visibility of the Boat 88 layer and turn on the visibility of the Boat 100 layer.

6. To create tweens:

   a. On the Animation panel, click Frame 5 to select it, if necessary.

   b. Click the 'Tweens animation frames' button.

   c. Ensure the Tween With box is set to Previous Frame and set the Frames to Add box to 3.

   d. Ensure the All Layers option is selected and all three Parameters check boxes are checked, then click OK.

   e. Click Frame 4 and repeat steps 6b through 6d to create tweened frames between frames 3 and 4.

   f. Click Frame 3 and repeat steps 6b through 6d to create tweened frames between frames 2 and 3.

   g. Click Frame 2 and repeat steps 6b through 6d to create tweened frames between frames 1 and 2.

   h. If desired, change the time delay by selecting all of the frames and then clicking the 'Selects frame time delay' button. When you are done, click Frame 1 to select it.

   i. If necessary, set the Selects looping options menu to Once.

7. To save the file, press CTRL+S.

8. Click File on the menu bar and then click Save for Web & Devices. When the Save for Web & Devices dialog box appears, select the best preview, and then click the Preview button. Wait for the browser window to open; if necessary, click the yellow bar, click Allow Blocked Content, and then click Yes in the Security Warning dialog box. Watch the animation. Close the browser window.

9. Click the Save button. If necessary, navigate to the Water Kids Web Site folder. If necessary, type **Water-Edited** in the File name box. If necessary, click the Format box, and then select HTML and Images in the list. Click the Save button.

10. Close the Water Edited document window. If Photoshop asks if you want to save the file again, click the No button. Quit Photoshop.

11. Submit the Water Kids Web Site folder in the format specified by your instructor.

Extend Your Knowledge

Extend the skills you learned in this chapter and experiment with new skills. You may need to use Help to complete the assignment.

Animating and Slicing a Web Page Header

Instructions: Start Photoshop and perform the customization steps found on pages PS 6 through PS 9. Open the Extend 9-1 Gear Web Site file from the Chapter 09 folder of the Data Files for Students. See inside the back cover of this book for instructions on downloading Data Files for Students, or contact your instructor for information about accessing the required files. You have just finished a mock-up of a new Web site for the company, Gear Werks. After looking at the design of the header, you have decided to animate the main gear illustration. You also need to slice the design for production.

1. Press SHIFT+CTRL+S to save the image on your USB flash drive as a PSD file, with the file name Extend 9-1 Gear Web Site Edited.

2. Click Window on the menu bar, and then click Animation to view the Animation panel. If necessary, click the 'Convert to frame' animation button on the Animation panel status bar.

Continued >

Extend Your Knowledge *continued*

3. To create the animation:

    a. On the Layers panel, click the Big Gear layer to make it active. Drag the layer down to the status bar and drop it on the 'Create a new layer' button to create a duplicate of the layer.

    b. Rename the duplicate layer, Big Gear 2.

    c. Press CTRL+T to transform the Big Gear 2 layer. On the options bar, enter **18** in the Set Rotation box. Click the Commit transform (Return) button to commit the transformation.

    d. On the Layers panel, drag the Big Gear 2 layer down to the 'Create a new layer' button to create another duplicate. Name the layer Big Gear 3. Repeat Step 3c to rotate this layer another 18 degrees.

    e. Repeat to create two more rotated duplications. Name the layers Big Gear 4 and Big Gear 5.

    f. Turn off the visibility for the Big Gear 2 through Big Gear 5 layers.

    g. On the Animation panel, click the 'Selects frame delay time' button in Frame 1 and set the timing to 1.0 seconds.

    h. Duplicate the frame and turn off the visibility for the Big Gear layer. Turn on the visibility for the Big Gear 2 layer. Repeat the process for each of the Big Gear layers, creating a total of five frames.

    i. Click the Play button to preview the animation.

4. Click File on the menu bar and then click Place. Navigate to the Chapter 09 folder of the Data Files for Students and then double-click the file named, Extend 9-1 Gear Werks Logo. Press the ENTER key to confirm the placement.

5. On the Animation panel, click the Animation panel menu button. Click Select all frames. On the Layers panel, turn on the visibility of the Navigation and Content layer groups to add them to the animation.

6. To create the slices:

    a. Select the Slice Tool on the Tools panel. Drag to create a slice over the top portion of the image, including the gear and the logo. Do not cover the navigation buttons. Right-click the slice and then click Edit Slice options on the context menu to open the Slice Options dialog box. Type **Header** in the Name box and then click the OK button to close the dialog box.

    b. Create a slice over the about us button. Right-click the slice and then click Edit Slice Options. Enter the name, **btn about us**.

    c. Create a slice over each of the remaining buttons and name them accordingly.

    d. Create one last slice that covers the rest of the Web site mock-up. Right-click the slice and then click Edit slice options. Name this slice, content.

7. On the File menu, click Save for Web & Devices. When the Save for Web & Devices dialog box opens, click the Optimized tab.

8. Click the Header slice and choose GIF 128 No Dither using the Preset box arrow. At the bottom of the dialog box, change the Animation Looping Options from Once to Forever. One at a time, click each remaining slice and change its preset to GIF 128 No Dither. Navigate in the preview as necessary.

9. Click the Save button. When the Saved Optimized As dialog box is displayed, navigate to your storage location and click the Create New Folder button and name the new folder, Gear Web Site. Double-click the Gear Web Site folder to open it. Name the file, Gear_Web_Site. Click the Format box arrow, and then click HTML and Images, if necessary. Click the Settings box arrow and then click All Slices.

10. Click the Save button to create the images and HTML code.

11. When the image is displayed again, click Save As on the File menu and then save the file with the name, Extend 9-1 Gear Web Site Complete.

12. Navigate to the Gear Web Site folder and double-click the file named Gear_Web_Site.html to view it in your Web browser (Figure 9–71).

Figure 9–71

Make It Right

Analyze a publication and correct all errors and/or improve the design.

Improving a Florist Web Banner Advertisement

Problem: The Busy-Bee Florist has a Web banner that needs to grab the attention of visitors to their Web site. They have started work on an animated GIF banner using Photoshop's frame animation but it has several problems: the background disappears after one second, the animation is too fast, the phone number flashes, and the path of the bee is incorrect.

Instructions: Perform the following tasks:
Start Photoshop and perform the customization steps found on pages PS 6 through PS 9. Open the Make It Right 9-1 Bee Advertisement file from the Chapter 09 folder of the Data Files for Students. See inside the back cover of this book for instructions on downloading the Data Files for Students, or contact your instructor for information about accessing the required files. Press SHIFT+CTRL+S to save the image on your USB flash drive as a PSD file, with the file name Make It Right 9-1 Bee Ad Edited in the PSD format.

Continued >

Make It Right *continued*

1. Open the Animation panel. If the Animation (Timeline) is displayed, click the 'Convert to frame animation' button. Play the animation and notice how the blue sky disappears after the first frame. The phone number flashes on and off. Notice also that the bee disappears, then reappears out of nowhere and flies back and forth rather than straight for the flower. Finally, the animation is too fast (Figure 9–72).

2. Click Frame 1 on the Animation panel. Select the Background layer on the Layers panel. Click the Animation panel menu button and then click Match Layer Across Frames. When the dialog box appears, click the OK button.

3. Click the visibility icon to show all three layers of text (Busy Bee, Florist, and 1–800). Click the 1–800 layer and then SHIFT+click the Busy Bee layer to select all three layers. Click the Animation panel menu button and then click Match Layer Across Frames. When the Match Layer dialog box appears, click the OK button.

4. On the Layers panel, select the Bee layer. Use the Move Tool to drag the Bee layer to the far left side of the workspace, just off of the document window. Click Frame 2 and then use the Move Tool to position the bee to the right of its location in the previous frame. Continue clicking the frames and moving the Bee layer so the bee's path moves from left to right. Frame 7 should display the bee in the center of the flower.

5. With Frame 7 selected, add four tween frames between Frames 7 and 6. Select Frame 6 and add two tween frames between Frames 6 and 5. Select all the frames and change their timings from 0.1 sec. to 0.2 sec.

6. Play the animation again and check for accuracy. Fix any other problems and adjust the timing as necessary. Use the Save for Web & Devices command to save the file in the GIF format with the name, Make-It-Right-9-1-Bee-Ad-Animated. Be sure to set the Format box to Images Only so only the GIF, and not the HTML files, is created. Save the PSD file again with the name Make It Right 9-1 Bee Ad Final. See your instructor for ways to submit this assignment.

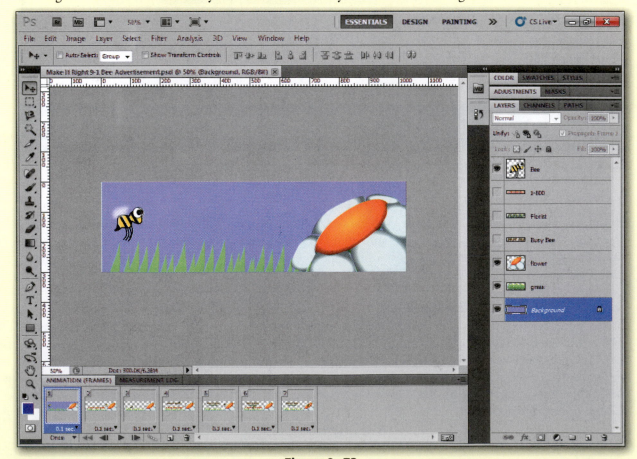

Figure 9–72

In the Lab

Design and/or create a publication using the guidelines, concepts, and skills presented in this chapter. Labs are listed in order of increasing difficulty.

Lab 1: Creating an Image Map

Problem: As an assignment for your geography class, you decide to make an image map of the Midwest portion of the United States with links to each state's Web site. When users view the image map, clicking any state in the graphic will link them to the state's Web site. Table 9–1 shows the URL of each state's Web site.

Table 9–1 Midwest States Web Sites

State	URL
Illinois	http://www.illinois.gov
Indiana	http://www.indiana.gov
Iowa	http://www.iowa.gov
Kansas	http://www.kansas.gov
Michigan	http://www.michigan.gov
Minnesota	http://www.minnesota.gov
Missouri	http://www.missouri.gov
Nebraska	http://www.nebraska.gov
Ohio	http://www.ohio.gov
Wisconsin	http://www.wisconsin.gov

Perform the following tasks:

1. Use Windows Explorer to open the Computer window, navigate to your storage device, and create a new folder named Image Map.

2. Start Photoshop. Perform the customization steps found on pages PS 6 through PS 9.

3. Open the file Midwest from the Chapter 09 folder of the Data Files for Students. See the inside back cover of this book for instructions on downloading the Data Files for Students, or contact your instructor for information about accessing the required files.

4. Click the Save As command on the File menu. Type **Lab 9-1   Midwest Image Map** as the file name. Select the PSD format. Browse to the Image Map folder on your USB flash drive storage device click the Save button. If Photoshop displays an options dialog box, click the OK button.

5. To create a slice for each state:
   a. On the Tools panel, select the Slice Tool.
   b. Drag a rectangle around the outline of the state of Nebraska. Stay as close to the border as possible.
   c. Press SHIFT+C to activate the Select Slice Tool. On the options bar, click the 'Set options for the current slice' button to display the Slice Options dialog box. Type **Nebraska** in the Name box. Enter the URL from Table 9–1. Leave the Target box blank. In the Message Text box, type **State of Nebraska** as the entry. In the Alt Tag box, type **Click here to go to the official Web site of Nebraska**. Click the OK button.
   d. Repeat Steps 5b and 5c for each state. In state outlines that are not rectangular, draw as large a slice as possible that does not overlap any other state. You can create two slices that point to the same Web site for the two parts of Michigan, if desired.

Continued >

In the Lab *continued*

6. When all the states are complete, click the Save for Web & Devices command on the Photoshop File menu. Choose the best optimization and save the file with the name, Lab-9-1-Midwest-Image-Map, using the HTML and Images format, in the Image Map folder.

7. Save the PSD file again and then quit Photoshop. Preview the Web site using a browser. The image map is displayed in a browser in Figure 9–73.

8. See your instructor for ways to submit this assignment.

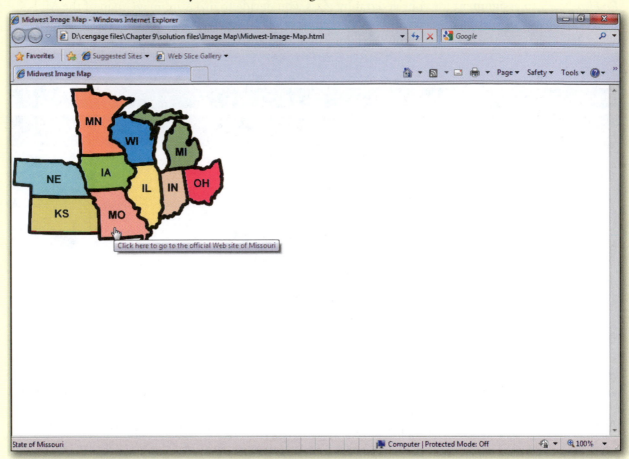

Figure 9–73

In the Lab

Lab 2: Creating a Panoramic Photo

Problem: You have been asked to create a wide-screen, panoramic photo of Lake Patoka for a new travel brochure. Unfortunately, you do not have a camera that takes panoramic photographs, but you do have several photos that were taken from the same location at different angles at the lake. Using Photoshop's Photomerge function, you can create a panoramic photo without the use of expensive cameras or lenses (Figure 9–74).

Figure 9–74

Perform the following tasks:

1. Start Photoshop. Perform the customization steps found on pages PS 6 through PS 9.

2. On the File menu, point to Automate, and then click Photomerge.

3. When the Photomerge dialog box is displayed, click the Use box arrow, and then click Folder.

4. Click the Browse button and then navigate to the Chapter 09 folder of the Data Files for Students. See inside the back cover of this book for instructions on downloading Data Files for Students, or contact your instructor for information about accessing the required files. Open the Lab 9-2 Panorama folder. Click the OK button to display the names of the five source files.

5. On the left side of the Photomerge window, click the Auto option button, if necessary. Click the OK button to start the automation process. The Photomerge process will take several minutes.

6. Select the Crop Tool on the Tools panel.

7. Drag a crop rectangle across the entire canvas. Press the CTRL key as you drag the top edge of the crop border down to eliminate the transparent pixels at the top. Repeat on the other three sides to exclude all transparent pixels. Press the ENTER key to crop the image.

8. Flatten the image and save the file with the file name, Lab 9-2 Panorama Complete, using the TIFF file format.

In the Lab

Lab 3: Creating a Web Site Animation

Problem: As an intern for a Web design company, you have been assigned to create an animated GIF for an air conditioning service shop (Figure 9–75). The client has provided several photos of an ice cube melting, which are included with the Data Files for Students. See inside the back cover of this book for instructions on downloading Data Files for Students, or contact your instructor for information about accessing the required files. In the Chapter 09 folder, the photos are stored in a folder named Lab 9-3 Ice.

Instructions: Perform the following tasks:

Open the Lab 9-3 Ice Banner file in the Lab 9-3 Ice folder. Notice the dimensions of this file are 120 pixels wide × 240 pixels tall – standard dimensions for a vertical Web banner ad. Open each of the Ice photos in the Lab 9-3 Ice folder and use the Move Tool to copy each photo into the Lab 9-3 Ice Banner document. Move the Blend layer to the top of the layer stack and arrange the ice photos in order from solid to melted. Create a new text layer at the top of the document with the phrase, Air Conditioner Problems Burning You Up? Select an appropriate font and color so the phrase is readable on top of the black background. Create another new text layer at the bottom of the document with the company name and phone number, AirPros 1-800-555-1212. Select an appropriate font and color so the name and phone number are readable on top of the white background. Create a 10-frame animation that animates the ice melting. The text should be visible throughout all frames. Set the animation speed to 1 second for the first frame and 0.2 seconds for all remaining frames. Set the looping to repeat once. Save the file to the Lab 9-3 Ice folder with the name, Lab 9-3 Ice Banner Animated. Save the file for Web & Devices, in the HTML and Images format, to the Lab 9-3 Ice folder with the name, Ice-Animated. View it in a browser to watch the ice cube melt.

Figure 9–75

Cases and Places

Apply your creative thinking and problem solving skills to design and implement a solution.

Note: To complete these assignments, you may be required to use the Data Files for Students. See the inside back cover of this book for instructions on downloading the Data Files for Students, or contact your instructor for information about accessing the required files.

1: Create a Photoshop Resources Web Page

Academic

Your Web design instructor has given you an assignment to create a Web page that includes links to some useful Web sites. Create a folder in your storage location named Photoshop Resources. Use a light muted color and draw a large shape for the background. Use the Vertical Type Tool to create a text element down the left edge of the page. Use a contrasting color for the text. Type your name in the type bounding box. Using the same text color, create a horizontal text element heading that says, Photoshop Resources. Below the heading and to the right of your name, create five more horizontal text elements in a complementary font, but use a smaller font size. Using your favorite search tool, find several Web sites that offer Photoshop tutorials or other Photoshop resources (such as custom brush or shape downloads). Type the name (not the URL) of one such Web site into the first of the five text elements. Type the names of four additional Web sites into the remaining text elements. Slice each text element. Use the Slice Options dialog box to insert a URL, a _blank target specification, an Alt tag, and a Status bar message for each slice. Save the file to your Photoshop Resources folder in the PSD format with the name, My Photoshop Resources. Preview the Web page and make any necessary changes. Save the page as HTML and Images to the Photoshop Resources folder with the name, My_Photoshop_Resources. Exchange your Photoshop Resources folder with another student and explore their Photoshop resources Web pages.

2: Design a Personalized Web Banner

Personal

You have decided to put your name up in lights! Create a Web banner with a bold background color. Create a type bounding box using a large font in a contrasting color. Type your name. Add a layer effect to enhance the text. On the Layers panel, make sure the opacity is set to 100%. Duplicate the layer and set the opacity of the copy to 10%. Turn the visibility off on both text layers. Open the Animation panel. In the first frame, turn on the visibility of the 10% layer. Create a second frame in which you turn off the 10% layer and turn on the 100% layer. Set the time delay on each frame to .5 seconds. Set the animation to play only once. Tween the two frames with 10 frames in between, applying only opacity changes. Create a folder in your storage location named Personalized Banner. Save the file in the PSD format to the Personalized Banner folder with the name My Banner. Save the file optimized for the Web in HTML format in the Personalized Banner folder with the name My-Banner. View your name up in lights using a browser window.

3: Customize Navigation Buttons

Professional

You need to make buttons for an upcoming slide show presentation and want something more than the traditional clip art buttons that come with your presentation software. Create a new file in Photoshop with a transparent background. Press the U key to access the Rectangle Tool. Draw four rectangles approximately 200 pixels square. The layers will be displayed on the Layers panel. Open the Styles panel and choose a different style for each rectangle. Press the T key to access the Type Tool. One at a time, click each button. On the options bar, choose a contrasting color for the text that complements the button. On the buttons, type Home, Back, Forward, and End, respectively. On the Layers panel, add a shadow effect on each text layer. For each button, point the shadow in a different direction. Order the layers so each text layer is displayed just above its button. One set at a time, click the button layer, and then SHIFT+click the button's text layer. On the panel menu, click Link Layers to link the button and its text together. Save the file to your storage location with the name Buttons. Have your instructor choose the best of the four buttons and then copy and paste it into a presentation.

Appendix A
Project Planning Guidelines

Using Project Planning Guidelines

The process of communicating specific information to others is a learned, rational skill. Computers and software, especially Adobe Photoshop CS5, can help you develop ideas and present detailed information to a particular audience.

Using Adobe Photoshop CS5, you can edit photos and create original graphics. Computer hardware and productivity software, such as Adobe Photoshop CS5, reduces much of the laborious work of drafting and revising projects. Some design professionals use sketch pads or storyboards, others compose directly on the computer, and others have developed unique strategies that work for their own particular thinking and artistic styles.

No matter what method you use to plan a project, follow specific guidelines to arrive at a final product that presents an image or images clearly and effectively (Figure A–1). Use some aspects of these guidelines every time you undertake a project, and others as needed in specific instances. For example, in determining content for a project, you may decide an original graphic would communicate the idea more effectively than an existing photo. If so, you would create this graphical element from scratch.

Determine the Project's Purpose

Begin by clearly defining why you are undertaking this assignment. For example, you may want to correct camera errors and adjust image flaws. Or you may want to create a graphic for a specific publishing or marketing purpose. Once you clearly understand the purpose of your task, begin to draft ideas of how best to communicate this information.

Analyze Your Audience

Learn about the people who will use, analyze, or view your work. Where are they employed? What are their educational backgrounds? What are their expectations? What questions do they have? Design experts suggest drawing a mental picture of these people or finding photographs of people who fit this profile so that you can develop a project with the audience in mind.

PROJECT PLANNING GUIDELINES

1. DETERMINE THE PROJECT'S PURPOSE
Why are you undertaking the project?

2. ANALYZE YOUR AUDIENCE
Who are the people who will use your work?

3. GATHER POSSIBLE CONTENT
What graphics exist, and in what forms?

4. DETERMINE WHAT CONTENT TO PRESENT TO YOUR AUDIENCE
What image will communicate the project's purpose to your audience in the most effective manner?

Figure A–1

By knowing your audience members, you can tailor a project to meet their interests and needs. You will not present them with information they already possess, and you will not omit the information they need to know.

Example: Your assignment is to raise the profile of your college's nursing program in the community. Your project should address questions such as the following: How much does the audience know about your college and the nursing curriculum? What are the admission requirements? How many of the applicants admitted complete the program? What percent of participants pass the state nursing boards?

Gather Possible Content

Rarely are you in a position to develop all the material for a project. Typically, you would begin by gathering existing images and photos, or designing new graphics based on information that may reside in spreadsheets or databases. Design work for clients often must align with and adhere to existing marketing campaigns or publicity materials. Web sites, pamphlets, magazine and newspaper articles, and books could provide insights of how others have approached your topic. Personal interviews often provide perspectives not available by any other means. Consider video and audio clips as potential sources for material that might complement or support the factual data you uncover. Make sure you have all legal rights to any photographs you plan to use.

Determine What Content to Present to Your Audience

Experienced designers recommend writing three or four major ideas you want an audience member to remember after viewing your project. It also is helpful to envision your project's endpoint, the key fact or universal theme that you wish to emphasize. All project elements should lead to this ending point.

As you make content decisions, you also need to think about other factors. Presentation of the project content is an important consideration. For example, will your brochure be printed on thick, colored paper or transparencies? Will your photo be viewed in a classroom with excellent lighting and a bright projector, or will it be viewed on a notebook computer monitor? Determine relevant time factors, such as the length of time to develop the project, how long editors will spend reviewing your project, or the amount of time allocated for presenting your designs to the customer. Your project will need to accommodate all of these constraints.

Decide whether a graphic, photograph, or artistic element can express or emphasize a particular concept. The right hemisphere of the brain processes images by attaching an emotion to them, so in the long run, audience members are more apt to recall themes from graphics rather than those from the text.

Finally, review your project to make sure the theme still easily is identifiable and has been emphasized successfully. Is the focal point clear and presented without distraction? Does the project satisfy the requirements?

Summary

When creating a project, it is beneficial to follow some basic guidelines from the outset. By taking some time at the beginning of the process to determine the project's purpose, analyze the audience, gather possible content, and determine what content to present to the audience, you can produce a project that is informative, relevant, and effective.

Appendix B

Graphic Design Overview

Understanding Design Principles

Understanding a few basic design principles can catapult you to the next level of digital artistry. Beyond knowing how to use software, a graphic designer must know how to create effective and readable layouts no matter what the product type. In this Appendix, you will learn the design principles, color theory, typography, and other technical knowledge required to create usable and successful graphic designs.

A major goal in graphic design work, whether for print or Web page layout, is to guide the viewer's eyes toward some key point. Another major goal of design work is to convey a certain emotion — a project can have the effect of making the viewer feel relaxed, energetic, hungry, hopeful, or even anxious. By implementing a few basic principles of design, you can control your viewers' physical focus so they look where you want them to look as you steer them toward a desired emotion. Design principles typically include the following:

- Balance
- Contrast
- Dominance
- Proximity
- Repetition
- Closure
- Continuance
- Negative space
- Unity

Balance

Visual elements can be **balanced** within a design, just as items may be balanced on either side of a scale. Unbalanced designs can cause viewers to feel anxious or uncomfortable, or even like they are falling sideways out of their seats. Balance may be achieved symmetrically or asymmetrically. Symmetrical balance mirrors a visual element to achieve equilibrium (Figure B–1). Asymmetrical balance can be achieved by balancing a small, dark element with a large, light element (Figure B–2) or balancing one large element with several smaller elements (Figure B–3).

with symmetrical balance, the left and right halves are mirror reflections, and the two trees, which are identical in size and shape, balance the composition

Figure B–1

left-heavy design with sparse right sidebar that is too white to add much weight

balanced design with a darker right sidebar adding weight to the right side

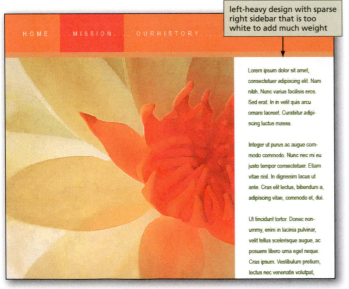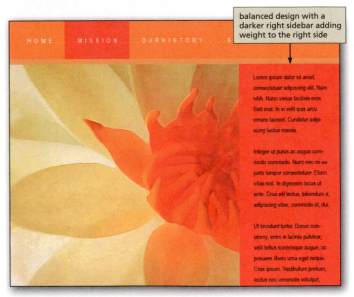

Figure B–2

large photo at right is asymmetrically balanced by the multiple small thumbnails on left

Figure B–3

Contrast

Contrast describes the visual differences between elements; it adds variety to a design and helps to draw the viewer's focus. Differences in color, scale, quantity, or other characteristics of visual elements help to achieve contrast. The element that is different from the others draws the viewer's attention. In Figure B–4, the words in white contrast against the other words on the page, and the viewer's eye is drawn to the contrasting sentence.

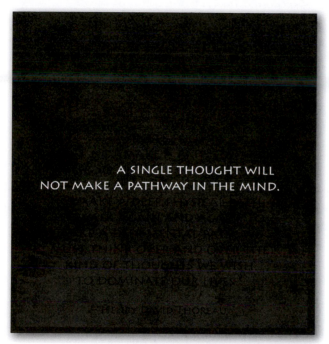

Figure B–4

Dominance

Dominance is a critical principle in controlling viewer focus. The dominant element in a design is the one to which a viewer's eyes and attention usually move first. An element's position within a design or its contrast to other elements can establish dominance. If you want your viewer to focus on a certain area of your design or on a specific design element, make it dominant, like the yellow V.I.P. banner in the discount card shown in Figure B–5.

grabbing your attention with its contrasting color, the V.I.P. banner is the dominant element in the design even though it is not the largest

Figure B–5

Proximity

Proximity describes the relative space between elements. Related elements should be close to each other. Headings should be close to their related paragraph text, and product names should be close to their photos and prices. As shown in Figure B–6, when related items are not within close proximity of each other (Figure B–6a), the viewer may not know the items are related. When elements are too close, the design looks cluttered and text can become difficult to read. Strive for balance in your proximity, as in Figure B–6b.

(a) Items Without Proximity Are Not Clearly Related

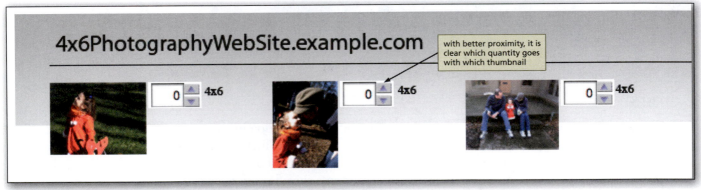

(b) Items With Close Proximity Are Clearly Related

Figure B–6

BTW

Natural Repetition
Repetition occurs naturally in the petals around a flower, patterns on snakeskin, and polygons on turtle shells.

Repetition

Repeating a visual element helps to tie a design together. **Repetition** of color, shape, texture, and other characteristics can help to unify your design (Figure B–7), create patterns, or impart a sense of movement. Most Web sites repeat a design theme across all the pages so users know they are on the same site as they navigate from page to page. Repeated colors and layouts help to unify the overall Web site design.

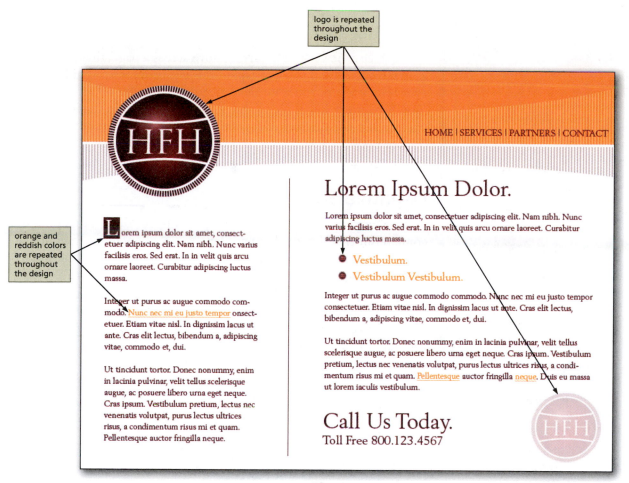

logo is repeated throughout the design

orange and reddish colors are repeated throughout the design

HOME | SERVICES | PARTNERS | CONTACT

Lorem Ipsum Dolor.

Lorem ipsum dolor sit amet, consectetuer adipiscing elit. Nam nibh. Nunc varius facilisis eros. Sed erat. In in velit quis arcu ornare laoreet. Curabitur adipiscing luctus massa.

- Vestibulum.
- Vestibulum Vestibulum.

Integer ut purus ac augue commodo commodo. Nunc nec mi eu justo tempor consectetuer. Etiam vitae nisl. In dignissim lacus ut ante. Cras elit lectus, bibendum a, adipiscing vitae, commodo et, dui.

Ut tincidunt tortor. Donec nonummy, enim in lacinia pulvinar, velit tellus scelerisque augue, ac posuere libero urna eget neque. Cras ipsum. Vestibulum pretium, lectus nec venenatis volutpat, purus lectus ultrices risus, a condimentum risus mi et quam. Pellentesque auctor fringilla neque. Duis eu massa ut lorem iaculis vestibulum.

Call Us Today.
Toll Free 800.123.4567

Lorem ipsum dolor sit amet, consectetuer adipiscing elit. Nam nibh. Nunc varius facilisis eros. Sed erat. In in velit quis arcu ornare laoreet. Curabitur adipiscing luctus massa.

Integer ut purus ac augue commodo commodo. Nunc nec mi eu justo tempor onsectetuer. Etiam vitae nisl. In dignissim lacus ut ante. Cras elit lectus, bibendum a, adipiscing vitae, commodo et, dui.

Ut tincidunt tortor. Donec nonummy, enim in lacinia pulvinar, velit tellus scelerisque augue, ac posuere libero urna eget neque. Cras ipsum. Vestibulum pretium, lectus nec venenatis volutpat, purus lectus ultrices risus, a condimentum risus mi et quam. Pellentesque auctor fringilla neque.

Figure B–7

Closure

Not everything in a design must be composed of solid lines. Composing objects from small parts and spaces allows a design to breathe and creates visual interest. Under the concept of **closure**, the human brain will fill in the blanks to close or complete the object (Figure B–8).

your brain fills in the remainder of the triangular shape

Figure B–8

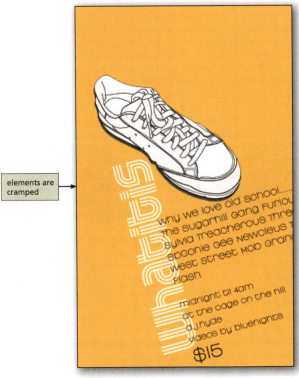

large dominant dancer captures your attention and her arms direct your eyes straight to the message

Figure B–9

Continuance

Once a viewer's eyes start to move across a page, they tend to keep moving — and you can exploit this **continuance** to guide their eyes exactly where you want them to go. A dominant object can capture the viewer's initial focus, and diagonal lines within that dominant object can guide the viewer's eyes toward the focal point of your design (Figure B–9).

Negative Space

Negative space refers to the space in your design that does not contain information, or the space between elements. For example, the space between the vertical heading and descriptive text or the space between a logo and the vertical heading, as shown in Figure B–10, is negative space. Without negative space, your design will feel cluttered, and viewers will have difficulty identifying on the focal point. Note that negative space, also called **white space**, does not literally translate to "white space," as negative space does not have to be white (Figure B–10).

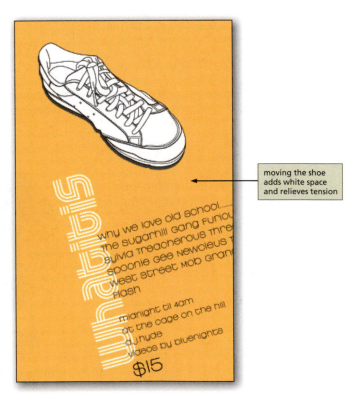

elements are cramped

moving the shoe adds white space and relieves tension

Figure B–10

BTW

Unity
Unity is not limited to elements in a specific piece of work; it can apply to multiple pieces. For example, a business card, Web site, letterhead, and product packaging that feature a similar color and style can help unify a business's identity.

Unity

Unity refers to the concept that all elements within a design work well together to form a whole. The individual images, textures, text, and negative space join together to create a single unified message or meaning. Unity can be created by applying a combination of basic design principles. Balanced elements alone do not produce a visually appealing design. The same is true for elements with appropriate proximity and negative space, good contrast, or clear dominance. No single design principle is responsible for a pleasing design. Instead, the combination of these principles creates a single unified design. Without unity, a design degrades into chaos and loses meaning. Of course, that is not a bad thing if chaos is the intentional message.

Layout Grids

A graphic designer needs to know where to place elements within a document or Web page. The use of grids makes it easy to align objects to each other and can help with balance and proximity. There are many standard grids that can be applied to Web page layouts or print layouts for standard paper sizes. One very popular grid system uses thirds, which is derived from the golden ratio.

BTW

Dominant Object Placement
Placing an object at a certain location within a grid, such as the intersection of thirds or slightly above and to the right of center, helps to establish dominance.

Rule of Thirds and Golden Ratio   The rule of thirds specifies that splitting a segment into thirds produces an aesthetically pleasing ratio. The rule of thirds is derived from a more complex mathematical concept called the golden ratio, which specifies segment ratios of long segment divided by short segment equal to about 1.618 — which is close enough to the rule of thirds that designers typically apply the rule of thirds rather than break out their slide rulers (Figure B–11).

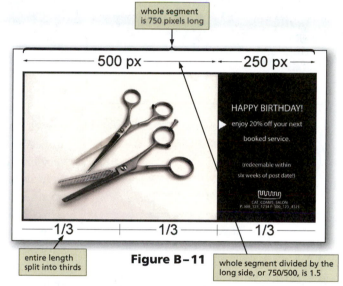

Figure B–11

Color Theory

Color can have a profound effect on the overall message a design conveys. Certain colors evoke specific emotions, and the way colors are combined can make the difference between readable copy and copy that is unable to be read.

Color Properties

Before you begin to work with color, it is important to understand the properties of color, which include hue, saturation, shade, tint, and value.

Hue refers to the tone, or actual color, such as red, yellow, or blue. Many color theorists interpret hue to mean pure color. A pure color, or hue, can be modified to create color variations. A basic color wheel, shown in Figure B–12, displays hue.

Saturation refers to the intensity of a color. As hues become less saturated, they create muted tones and pastels as they approach gray. As hues become more saturated, they appear very bright (Figure B–13).

Figure B–12

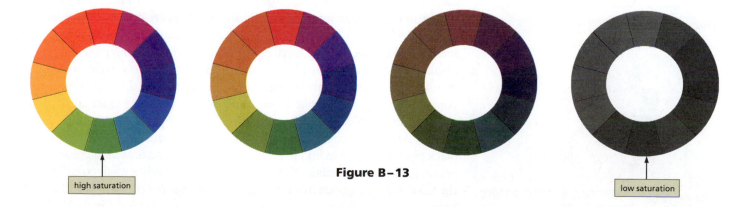

Figure B–13

desaturated hues can have calming effect

Figure B–14

oversaturated hues can be hard on the eyes

Figure B–15

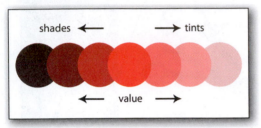

shades ← → tints

← value →

Figure B–16

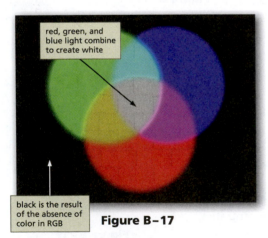

red, green, and blue light combine to create white

black is the result of the absence of color in RGB

Figure B–17

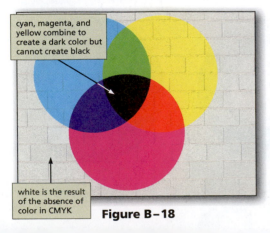

cyan, magenta, and yellow combine to create a dark color but cannot create black

white is the result of the absence of color in CMYK

Figure B–18

Desaturated colors can produce mellow tones and evoke calm feelings (Figure B–14). Oversaturated colors can produce almost neon colors and cause excitement (Figure B–15). Sometimes it is appropriate to use very bright colors, such as in a picture book for children or a high-energy advertisement for a sports drink. Other times, bright, saturated colors produce the wrong feeling for your work.

A **shade** is a mixture of a hue and black, producing a darker color. A **tint** is a mixture of a hue and white, producing a lighter color. A color's **value** describes its overall lightness or darkness. A tint has a higher value, while a shade has a lower value (Figure B–16). Mixing a hue with its shades, tints, and variations of saturation can lead to very harmonious color combinations.

Color Modes

A color mode describes the way in which colors combine to create other colors. The most commonly used color modes are RGB, CMYK, and LAB. Each mode has its strengths and weaknesses, and each is appropriate for a specific type of work.

The **RGB** color mode mixes red, green, and blue light to create other colors. Computer monitors and TV screens use the RGB color mode. All images used on a Web site must use the RGB color mode because few Web browsers can display CMYK images. RGB is an additive color mode, meaning colored light combines (light waves are added) to create other colors. The absence of all color in the RGB mode results in black. As colored light is added, white is created, as shown in Figure B–17. RGB is also device dependent, because the colors you see depend on the viewing device. Different computer screens will display colors in the same photograph differently due to variances in the manufacturing process and component wear over time. Do not waste your time trying to get your Web site to display the same exact colors consistently from computer to computer. It is not possible.

The **CMYK** color mode mixes physical cyan, magenta, yellow, and black pigments (such as ink) to create other colors, and is used in color printing. CMYK is a subtractive color mode. The absence of all color in the CMYK mode results in white light, and, as colored pigment is added, light wavelengths are absorbed or subtracted, creating color (Figure B–18).

Cyan, magenta, and yellow alone cannot create black; thus, the need for pure black in the CMYK mode.

Unlike RGB and CMYK, which combine individual well-defined colors, the **LAB** color mode combines levels of lightness with two color channels, a and b. One color channel ranges from green to magenta, while the other includes blue through yellow. By combining color ranges with lightness values, LAB is able to closely approximate the true human perception of color and thus is able to produce more colors than either RGB or CMYK. This makes it an ideal color mode for photographers wanting to have access to every possible color in a photograph. LAB typically is used during photographic retouching and color correction. The image then is converted to RGB or CMYK for use with electronic media or print.

BTW

LAB
LAB is sometimes written as L*a*b for lightness, color channel a, and color channel b.

Psychological Considerations of Color

Colors can evoke both positive and negative emotions in people, and the influence of a color can differ among individuals and cultures. While the effect of color on people is not an exact science, there are some generalities.

White often is associated with cleanliness, purity, and hope. Doctors and brides in most Western cultures wear white. However, white is associated with death and mourning attire in some Eastern cultures. White is the most popular background color and offers great contrast for highly readable dark text.

Black often is used to represent evil, death, or mourning, but also mystery, intelligence, elegance, and power. Black text on a white background is the easiest to read.

Red is used in Western cultures to signify love, passion, and comfort — but also is used to represent sin, hell, and danger. Use dark reds to imply indulgence or fine living and brownish reds for designs dealing with Thanksgiving, harvest, or the fall season in general.

Green symbolizes many positives such as growth, tranquility, luck, money, ecology, environmentalism, and health, but it also symbolizes jealousy. Green can have a calming effect.

Blue often is cited as the favorite color by men. Like green, it evokes feelings of calmness and serenity. Blue implies authority, stability, loyalty, and confidence. However, it is one of the least appetizing colors, as there are few naturally blue foods. It also is associated with sadness and bad luck, as evidenced in blues music or phrases like "I've got the blues."

Yellow generally makes people happy. It is a highly visible and active color. However, too much yellow can lead to frustration and eye fatigue. Babies cry more in yellow rooms. Avoid using yellow as a page background and use it instead in smaller areas to draw attention.

Print Considerations for Color

The printing process cannot reproduce every color. Gamut refers to the range of printable colors and colors that cannot be printed are said to be *out of gamut*. If an out of gamut color exists in your document, the printer you are using will simply get as close to it as it can — but it will not be exact. Depending on the printer you have installed, the actual color produced can vary. Photoshop identifies out of gamut colors in the Color Picker with a small icon. If your document contains out of gamut colors, you have two options: change or replace the out of gamut color with one that is in gamut; or accept that the final print may not be exactly what you expected.

Web Considerations for Color

When working with color for the Web, the most important thing to remember is that colors will appear differently on different computers. Web sites look similar, but not exactly the same, from computer to computer. Years ago, Web designers used only the **Web-safe colors**, which was a set of 216 colors that supposedly appear the same on all monitors. This was due to the limitations of video subsystems at the time, as computer monitors could display only 256 specific colors. Microsoft Windows supported 256 specific colors, and Apple Macintosh supported a different 256 colors. Of the two sets, 216 were the same across both platforms; these 216 became the Web-safe palette. However, designers soon realized that only 22 of those 216 were truly the same between Windows and Macintosh; this subset was called the **really Web-safe colors**.

Photoshop displays a warning in the Color Picker for non-Web-safe colors. Modern computers (as well as cell phone browsers) can display millions of distinct colors, so limiting yourself to 216 Web-safe colors is no longer a necessity. In fact, it is extremely limiting, because the 216 Web-safe colors are generally very bright or very dark with few choices for pastels or saturation and value variances. Most designers do not use Web-safe colors for their designs.

Relativity

A color's relative lightness/darkness value can appear different depending on what other color neighbors it. The gray block in Figure B–19 looks lighter when against the brown background and darker when against the light yellow background. Keep this in mind as you choose background/foreground relationships. A certain hue (or tint or shade) might look great when it is by itself, but you may not be so fond of it when used in close proximity to another certain color.

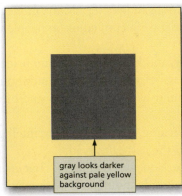

gray looks lighter against maroon background

gray looks darker against pale yellow background

Figure B–19

Color Schemes and Matching

Choosing colors that work well together and enforce the design's message can be challenging but worth the effort. Successful color matching requires an understanding of **color schemes**, which simply describes an organized method of matching colors based on their positions on a color wheel. The color scheme can make or break a design.

Figure B–12 on page APP 9 displayed a color wheel. While there are various color wheel models, the most popular uses the primary colors red, blue, and yellow (Figure B–20a). Primary colors combine to create the secondary colors green, orange, and purple (Figure B–20b). A primary and a secondary color combine to create a tertiary (third level) color (Figure B–20c). More complex color wheels can include gradients to show varying saturation, tints, and shades (Figure B–21).

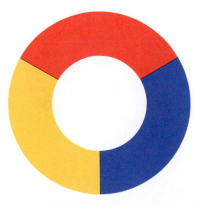
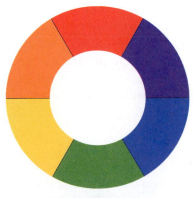
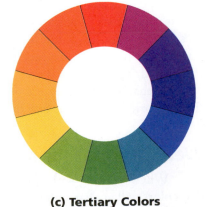

(a) Primary Colors

(b) Secondary Colors

(c) Tertiary Colors

Figure B–20

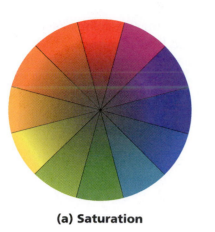

(a) Saturation

(b) Tints

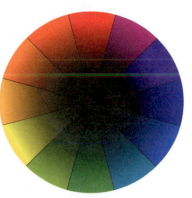

(c) Shades

Figure B–21

Color Schemes   A **monochromatic color scheme** is one that uses a single hue with a variety of shades and tints (Figure B–22). This is an easy color scheme to create. While a monochromatic color scheme can appear soothing, the lack of hue variance can leave it looking a bit boring.

BTW

Color Scheme Web Sites
Stand-alone color scheme software programs are available for purchase, but Adobe offers a free online service at kuler.adobe.com that lets you browse color schemes created by other users, modify them, and create and save your own.

Figure B–22

A **complementary color scheme** uses colors directly across from each other on the color wheel. Their high contrast can look vibrant but also can be hard on the eyes. Avoid using complementary pairs in a foreground/background relationship, as shown in Figure B–23. Adjusting the saturation or substituting tints and shades makes this color scheme more workable.

bright complementary colors do not work well in a foreground/background relationship

adjusting the arrangement of the colors or using a variety of values or saturation can help

Figure B–23

An **analogous color scheme** uses colors next to each other on the color wheel. This color scheme is generally very appealing and evokes positive feelings (Figure B–24). Be careful not to choose colors that are too far apart. A very wide range of analogous colors can appear mismatched.

Figure B–24

The **split-complementary scheme** uses a base color and, instead of its direct complement, the two colors on either side of its complement (Figure B–25). This scheme offers a lot of hue variance, and therefore excitement. However, if all the hues are overly saturated, split-complementary colors can be very harsh. Try keeping one hue saturated and use tints, shades, or desaturated colors for the rest of the scheme.

Figure B–25

Other color schemes such as triadic, tetradic, neutral, and an infinite number of custom schemes also exist. Using a color matching resource such as software or a Web site is a good way to help you get started choosing colors and allows you to experiment to see what you and your client like.

Typography

Typography is the art of working with text. Perhaps the two most important factors for graphic designers to address when working with text are visual appeal and readability. A dull text heading will not entice viewers to read the rest of the advertisement, but a text heading that looks beautiful can be useless if it is not readable (Figure B–26).

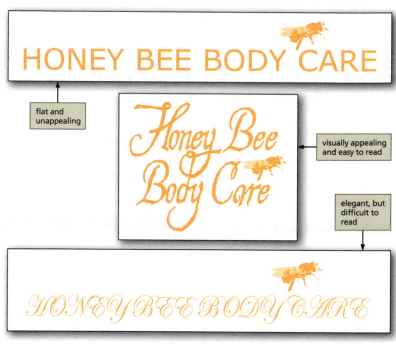

Figure B–26

Readability

Readability is the measurement of how comfortable or easy it is for readers to read the text. Many factors contribute to overall readability. Commonly accepted readability factors include the following:

- Large text passages written in lowercase are easier to read than long text passages in uppercase.

- Regular text is easier to read than italicized text.

- Black text on a white background is easier to read than white text on a black background.

- Legibility affects readability.

- Line length, letterforms, and appearance all influence readability.

Before learning the details of readability, you must understand some type basics. A **font** is a set of characters of a specific family, size, and style. For example, the description Times New Roman, 11 points, italic is a font. What most people consider a font is actually a **typeface** (Times New Roman, in this example). A font represents only a single specific size and style within a family, while a typeface is a set or family of one or more fonts.

Legibility refers to the ease with which a reader can determine what a letter actually is. If readers cannot figure out the letter, they cannot read the text, resulting in low readability and failed message delivery. The difference between legibility and readability is subtle. Figure B–27 shows an exit sign — something that needs to be legible.

Line length refers to the physical length of a line of text. When lines are too long, the reader's eyes can get lost trying to go all the way back to the left side of the page to find the next line. There is no conclusive magic number for how long a line of text should be. Optimal line lengths differ for adults and children, and for people with dyslexia and without. The best choices for line length differ based on the media of the message; printed newspapers, books, text on a Web site, and the subject lines in an e-mail message all require different line lengths. Some studies recommend line lengths based on physical lengths in inches, while other studies recommend a maximum number of characters per line. However, many designers follow the guideline that line lengths should not exceed 70 characters (about two-and-a-half alphabets' worth of characters).

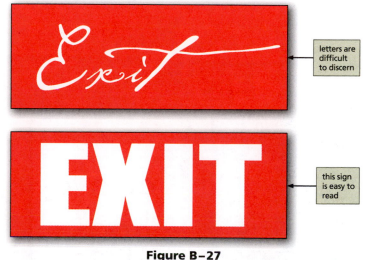

Figure B–27

BTW

DON'T YELL
Not only is typing in all uppercase difficult to read, but it connotes yelling at your reader.

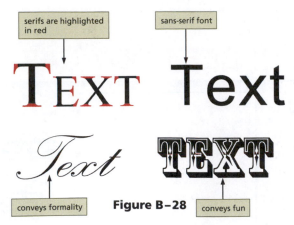

serifs are highlighted in red

sans-serif font

conveys formality

Figure B–28

conveys fun

Typeface Categories

Typefaces are organized into several categories, including serif, sans-serif, script, and display. Serif fonts include additional appendages, while sans-serif fonts do not (Figure B–28). It is generally accepted that large passages of serif text in print are easy to read, while sans-serif text is easier to read on a Web page. Because headlines are typically small, either serif or sans-serif is appropriate. Varying the headline typeface style from the body copy typeface style is an effective method of adding some visual excitement to an otherwise dull page of text. Script fonts look like handwriting, and display fonts are decorative.

In addition to differences in readability, the choice of a serif, sans-serif, or other font can help to create an emotion much like the selection of a color scheme. Wedding invitations often use a script font to signify elegance, while headlines using display fonts can grab a reader's attention. The same phrase written in different typefaces can have different implications (Figure B–29). Similarly, differences in the size, weight (boldness), or spacing of a font also can influence emotion or meaning (Figure B–30).

typeface implies a fancy party or elegant gathering

typeface implies the event will be fun, zany, or whimsical

Figure B–29

you are asked to remove your shoes, but you are still made to feel welcome

you are being ordered to remove your shoes, and emphasis on remove and before may cause resentment

Figure B–30

Designing for Web vs. Print

Graphic designers must be aware of subtle differences in how print and Web projects are created and perceived when designing for these media. While many design principles are common to both, it takes a different mindset to successfully create a design for either medium. Print designs are static, as the layout never varies from print to print (though differences in color may appear due to inconsistencies with the printer or printing press). The appearance of Web designs can vary, depending on the device used to view them. Some print designers struggle with the device dependency and fluidity of Web page designs. Some Web designers unnecessarily concern themselves about accommodating fluid or shifting content when designing a print advertisement.

Device Dependency and Fluidity

The main differences between print and Web design are related to device dependency and fluidity. Web pages are **device dependent**, meaning that the appearance of the page varies depending on the device (computer, cell phone, or PDA) on which they are viewed (Figure B–31). Discrepancies in monitor color calibration, screen resolution, and browser window size can affect how a Web page appears to the viewer. Colors can change, objects can shift, and text can wrap to a new line on different words from one device to another. In comparison, a newspaper or magazine looks the same no matter where it is purchased or where it is read.

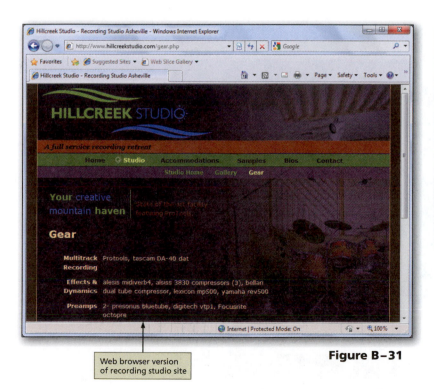

cell phone browser of the same page with relocated page elements

Web browser version of recording studio site

Figure B–31

Pixels, Dimensions, and Resolution

A pixel is the smallest element of a digital image. Magnifying an image reveals the individual pixels (Figure B–32). A pixel, unlike an inch or centimeter, is not an absolute measurement. The physical size of a pixel can change depending on device resolution.

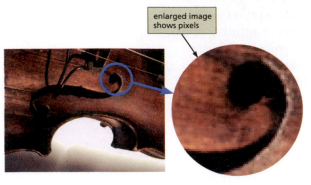

enlarged image shows pixels

Figure B–32

As you learned in Chapter 1, resolution refers to the number of pixels displayed on a computer screen. More pixels gives greater detail. When referring to an image file, the phrase, document dimensions, is used to describe the number of pixels in the file. For example, an image may have the dimensions of 450×337, meaning it contains 450 pixels across and 337 pixels vertically, for a total of 151,650 pixels. File size is directly related to pixel dimension. The more pixels there are in a document, the larger the file size.

When used to describe an image file, the word, resolution, also is used to describe the printed output. The print resolution is given in pixels per inch (PPI); for example, 72 PPI or 300 PPI. PPI is a linear measurement: 72 PPI means that, when printed, the output will contain 72 pixels across every linear inch. If the document dimensions were 450×337, those 450 horizontal pixels would print in groups of 72 PPI, resulting in a printout just over six inches wide (Figure B–33). If the resolution, but not the dimensions, was

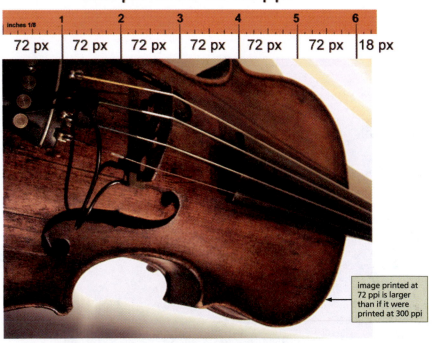

450 px wide at 72 ppi

inches 1/8	1	2	3	4	5	6
72 px	72 px	72 px	72 px	72 px	72 px	18 px

image printed at 72 ppi is larger than if it were printed at 300 ppi

450 px wide at 300 ppi

Note: The rulers are not to scale

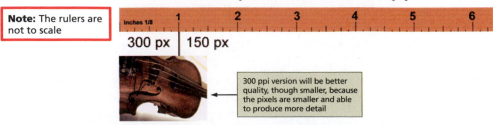

inches 1/8	1	2	3	4	5	6
300 px	150 px					

300 ppi version will be better quality, though smaller, because the pixels are smaller and able to produce more detail

Figure B–33

increased to 300 PPI, then those same 450 pixels would print in groups of 300 per inch, producing a final output about 1.5 inches wide.

Key points to remember when working with resolution are:

- A pixel is not a static measurement. Pixels change in size. They get smaller or larger to fill an inch as defined in the PPI setting.
- Changing the resolution of an image file has no effect on the file size. It affects the physical size of the printed output.
- Changing the document dimensions does affect the file size.

When printing documents, printers create each individual pixel with a group of microscopic dots of ink (or toner or other pigment). The number of dots a printer can generate is measured in dots per inch (DPI). People sometimes incorrectly use the term DPI when they really mean PPI. A printer with a resolution of 2400 DPI means it can squeeze 2400 dots of ink (not pixels) into a single inch. The more dots used to create a pixel, the truer color each pixel can have — resulting in a higher quality print.

A common misconception related to creating image files is that all graphics for use on the Web should be created at a resolution of 72 PPI. However, because PPI affects the output of printing only, the PPI setting has no effect on the screen display of an image.

It is common practice to save Web images at 72 PPI, not because it optimizes images for the Web, but because the 72 DPI Myth so widely is believed, saving Web images at 72 PPI simply is very common.

BTW

Resolution and Print Quality
The higher the resolution, the smaller the pixels and the printout, and the better the quality.

BTW

PPI and Printing
An image with the dimensions of 800 x 600 at 72 PPI will look exactly the same on screen as the same image at 300 PPI. In fact, the file sizes will be identical. There will only be a difference when printed. For Web images, you can save them at 0 PPI, and they would work just as well, and have the same file size, as if you saved them at 1200 PPI. However, when printed, they will differ.

Working as a Graphic Designer

The business world offers many opportunities for people with creativity and an eye for design. From automotive design to fashion to advertising, the need for talented graphic artists is vast. Many industry experts believe there are generally three levels of professionals working in the graphics field: graphic artists, graphic designers, and people who own graphics editing/design software.

Graphic artists typically receive extensive schooling as art majors and know a lot about design principles and art history. However, schooling does not necessarily mean formal education in a school environment. A graphic artist can be self-educated. The key to the "artist" designation revolves around a personal need to creatively express oneself beyond that of producing commercial work for hire. While graphic artists work with software, they typically also produce art with more traditional media such as paints, pencils, fiber, metals, or other physical materials. Graphic artists may hold the same job as a graphic designer, but very often graphic artists will create and sell their own original artwork. This personal drive to create and the resulting independent production of original artwork is what distinguishes graphic artists from graphic designers.

The line separating graphic artists from graphic designers is a fine one. A **graphic designer** often is knowledgeable about design principles and may possess a wealth of information about art history, but not all graphic designers are graphic artists. They usually create design products for others, such as brochures, advertisements, or Web sites, using software, but do not create their own original works.

The third category of graphic designers includes people who own and use graphics design software for various purposes. This category, **software owners**, is not a true graphic design designation. Simply owning a copy of Photoshop or knowing how to use a certain software program does not make you a graphic artist/designer. Whereas artists and designers understand principles of design, effective use of color, and possess a certain degree of artistic ability or raw talent, design amateurs rely on the power of the software to help them create projects. Of course, it is possible for an amateur to become a professional designer or artist — but doing so requires education and training, not just purchasing a software suite.

Jobs in Graphic Design

An understanding of design principles and software skills opens the door to many opportunities in the professional graphics industry. Jobs for graphic designers range from freelance work and self-employment to full-time careers with advertising agencies, Web design firms, print houses, software companies, or the marketing team within an organization such as a school or commercial or nonprofit business. Perhaps the most important questions to ask yourself when considering a job in this field are:

- Do I want to work for myself or for someone else?
- Am I truly an artist? Am I creative? Or do I simply follow direction well, understand basic design principles, and know how to use graphics software?
- What is my preferred medium — physical (print) or electronic (Web, software interface)?

Once you have secured a position in the graphics field, you will be assigned projects that will call on your design skills and other abilities.

Design Projects

A successful project always begins with solid planning. Proper planning helps you to stay focused and reduces the potential for wasted time and money — both yours and your client's. A project plan must specify the following aspects of the project:

- Scope of design work
- Roles and responsibilities of designer and client
- Expectations and specifications for final product, including time frame

When you and your client agree on the scope of the work and are clear on what the final product should look like, you as the designer know exactly what it is you need to produce. It is better to take the time to plan a project before sitting down with Photoshop, so you have a good idea of what to do once you start the software.

Client and Designer Roles

Both the client and the designer have specific jobs. Defining and agreeing on these roles is crucial for the success of the collaboration.

Simply put, the client must clearly communicate his or her expectations. Clients often need help articulating their wants and needs, and the designer must be able to help draw this information from the client. Additionally, the client must be available to provide feedback when the designer offers a draft for feedback or proofing. A client's responsibilities include the following:

- Clearly communicate the needs of the project
- Provide timely and constructive feedback
- Trust the designer's expertise
- Pay the bills on time

Aside from the obvious (creating the product), the designer also is responsible for making sure the client knows their own responsibilities and avoids poor design choices. Sometimes, a client will request something that is just bad — like certain colors that do not work well together or make text unreadable. The designer is responsible for respectfully steering the client away from the bad options and toward a better alternative.

In a highly competitive job market, you must determine what sets you apart from your competition. A potential client might choose one designer over another not because one is a better or more creative artist, but simply because they like the other designer more.

Customer service is part of your job, as well. Treat your client and your client's time and money with respect, be personable, and appreciate your client, and you will have more to offer than your competitors will. In addition to meeting the responsibilities previously defined, you should do the following:

- Be on time to meetings
- Meet or beat your deadlines so you don't submit work late
- Treat your clients and their time and money with respect
- Be able to explain your design choices
- Ensure adherence to copyright law

Defining the Project

As a designer, you must understand you are acting in the role of a hired hand — not an artist with complete creative control. You are being hired to create what your client wants, not what you necessarily prefer. While you need to educate your client as to best practices in design, ultimately the client is paying the bill, so he or she has the final word when it comes to making decisions.

Specifying Project Details

Project details should be discussed with the client and agreed upon before any design work begins. One detail to consider is what the client needs for files. For example, does the client require a 300 PPI TIF file or a layered Photoshop file? How will the files be delivered? Will they be sent by e-mail, burned to a CD and mailed, or downloaded from a Web site or FTP server? Additionally, a timeline of deliverables should be stated. A first draft of the design should be sent to the client for approval by a certain date, and pending timely client feedback, the final version should be delivered by the project deadline. The client may have a desired time frame, and the designer must be able to deliver the work within that time frame. Sometimes a compromise must be reached.

Collecting Materials

Existing materials help to speed up the design process. If you are hired to create a Web site or brochure, ask your client for copies of their existing promotional materials, such as a business card, letterhead, or logo. Ask your client what they like and dislike about these materials and if the product you are creating should be stylistically similar. This approach can prevent you from going down the wrong path, inadvertently creating something the client does not like or need. Additionally, you will need to collect any photographs your client has earmarked for the project.

Next, you must gather other assets for the project; specifically, high-quality artwork and photographs.

Original Artwork   If you have the raw artistic ability or own quality camera equipment, you can create your own original artwork or take your own photographs if you are a professional-level photographer. You can outsource some of this work to professional artists or photographers — just be sure to get your client's approval for the cost. Your other option is to use stock art.

Stock Art   **Stock art** includes existing artwork and photographs that can be licensed for use. The cost of a single picture can range from zero to several thousand dollars, depending on the source and license restrictions. Realistically, you should expect to pay between $5 and $40 for each print-quality digital file if you cannot find free sources.

BTW

Photos on CD or DVD
If possible, get photos and images on a CD or DVD. Many times a collection of photographs and other materials are too large to send by e-mail, and even if they are successfully sent, e-mails accidentally get deleted. Having all the materials on CD or DVD also guarantees you always have a backup of the original files as you modify copies with Photoshop or other software.

BTW

Public Domain vs. Commercial Stock Art
Public domain stock art sites can be difficult to use because they do not have the funding for the more intuitive style of interface found on the commercial sites. You can often find exactly what you want in the public domain. However, sometimes it is worth the $5 to more easily find exactly what you want on a commercial Web site.

Stock art is commercially available from many companies, most with a Web presence — meaning you can download images or purchase whole collections of stock art on CD or DVD from a Web site. Thousands of companies sell commercial stock art online. Some of the most popular resources are fotosearch.com, corbis.com, and gettyimages.com.

When searching for stock art, be sure to seek out **royalty-free images**. Images that are royalty free can be reused without paying additional fees. For example, you could spend $100 to purchase an image that is not royalty free and use it on a Web site. If you want to use the same image in a brochure or another client's Web site, you might have to pay another fee to reuse the image. Royalty free means that once the initial payment is made, there are no re-usage fees.

If you do not want to pay anything for your images, look into finding **public domain** artwork or photographs. Images in the public domain are completely free to use. The only trick is finding quality artwork in the public domain. Whereas commercial stock art Web sites typically have millions of high-quality images from which to choose, public domain stock art Web sites often have far fewer choices. Public domain stock art sites include Flickr, Morgue File, and Uncle Sam's Photos.

Other Licenses   There are usage licenses allowing free unrestricted use of images, audio, video, text, and other content similar to that of the public domain. These licenses include Copyleft, Creative Commons, education use, fair use, GNU general public license, and open source. The definitions of these alternative licenses read like a law book, but it is helpful to recognize the names. Laws related to these licenses allow for limited use of copyright-protected material without requiring the permission of the copyright owner. If you find images or other content offered as one of these alternatives, there is a good chance it will be completely free to use.

Whatever the source for your images, be sure to read the license and usage rights and restrictions carefully. No matter your source for artwork, you need to document its origin. The documentation serves two important purposes. First, it provides a record of the image's origin in case you need to get additional similar artwork. Second, it provides peace of mind should you or your client ever face legal action for copyright infringement. The documentation does not have to be fancy; it can simply be a list of where an image is used in a project and where that image was acquired.

Summary

Successful design uses the principles of balance, contrast, dominance, proximity, repetition, closure, continuance, negative space, and unity. The properties of color include hue, saturation, shade, tint, and value. Color modes include RGB for Web images, CMYK for images you intend to print, and LAB for access to the largest color space possible when working with digital photographs. Adherence to Web-safe colors is unnecessary. Colors can have emotional implications and should be used in harmony with neighboring colors. Color schemes include monochrome, complementary, analogous, and split-complementary.

Typeface selections can affect text readability, as can line lengths. Typefaces are organized into several categories, including serif, sans-serif, script, and display. The same Web site can look different from one monitor or computer to another.

Pixels per inch (PPI) determines the number of pixels printed per inch and affects the printed size of an image only, not how it appears onscreen or its file size. Higher PPI settings produce better quality printouts but have no effect on how an image appears onscreen. Dots per inch (DPI) refers to printer capabilities and defines how many dots of ink a printer can print in a linear inch. Pixel dimensions, not image resolution, affect how large an image appears on-screen and the size of a file.

Working in graphic design can incorporate a range of creative roles; working with clients in a design role requires specifying project expectations and the responsibilities of both designer and client.

Appendix C

Changing Screen Resolution and Editing Preferences

This appendix explains how to change the screen resolution in Windows 7 to the resolution used in this book. It also describes how to customize the Photoshop window by setting preferences and resetting user changes.

Screen Resolution

Screen resolution indicates the number of pixels (dots) that the computer uses to display the graphics, text, and background you see on the screen. The screen resolution usually is stated as the product of two numbers, such as 1024×768. That resolution results in a display of 1,024 distinct pixels on each of 768 lines, or about 786,432 pixels. The figures in this book were created using a screen resolution of 1024×768.

To Change Screen Resolution

The following steps change your screen's resolution to 1024×768 pixels. Your computer already may be set to 1024×768 or some other resolution.

- If necessary, minimize all programs so that the Windows 7 desktop is displayed.

- Right-click the Windows 7 desktop to display the desktop shortcut menu (Figure C–1).

Figure C–1

2

• Click Screen resolution on the shortcut menu to open the Screen Resolution window. Maximize the window if necessary (Figure C–2).

Screen Resolution window

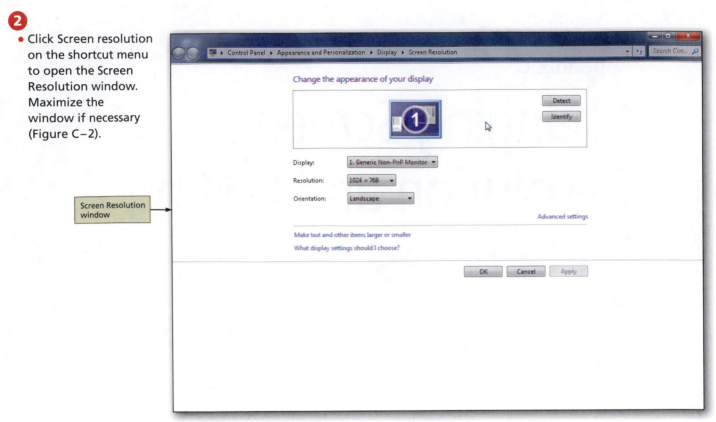

Figure C–2

3

• Click the Resolution button to display the list of available resolutions (Figure C–3).

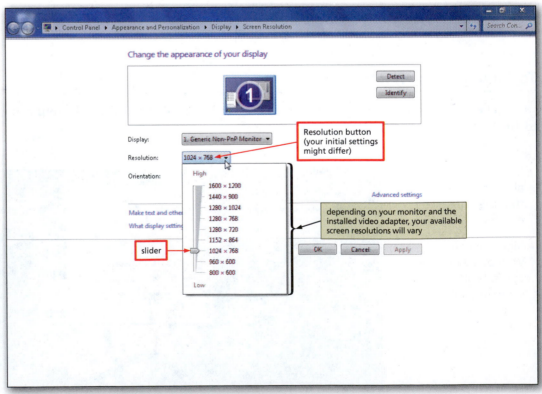

Figure C–3

4
- Drag the slider in the Resolution list so that the screen resolution changes to 1024 × 768, if necessary (Figure C–4).

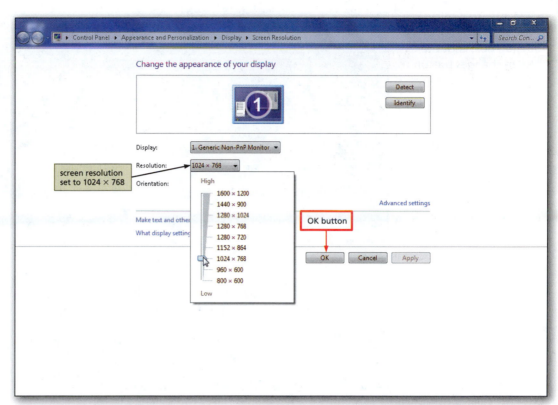

Figure C–4

5
- Click outside of the list to close the list. Click the OK button to change the screen resolution (Figure C–5).

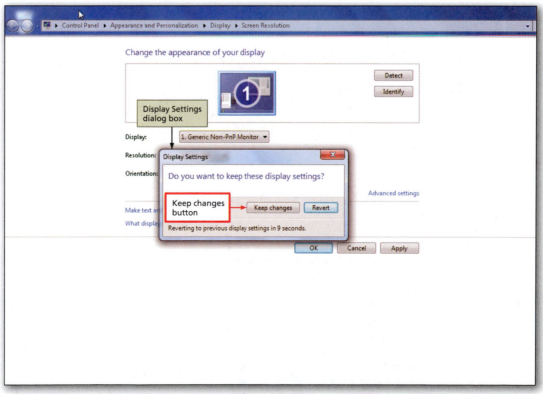

Figure C–5

6

• If Windows displays the Display Settings dialog box, click the Keep changes button to accept the changes (Figure C–6).

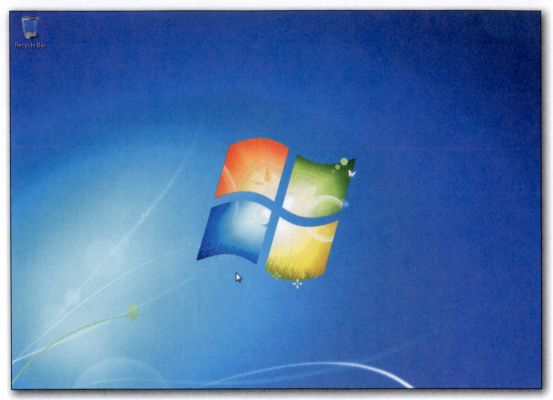

Figure C–6

Screen Resolutions
When you increase the screen resolution, Windows displays more information on the screen, but the information decreases in size. The reverse also is true; as you decrease the screen resolution, Windows displays less information on the screen, but the information increases in size.

Editing Photoshop Preferences

In Chapter 1, you learned how to start Photoshop and reset the default workspace, select the default tool, and reset all tools to their default settings. There are other preferences and settings you can edit to customize the Photoshop workspace and maximize your efficiency.

Editing General Preferences

General preferences include how Photoshop displays and stores your work. For example, you can change how many states are saved in the History panel, change the number of files shown on the Open Recent menu, or reset the display and cursors.

To Edit General Preferences

In the following steps, you will traverse through several Preferences dialog boxes to reset values and change preferences. You can access this set of dialog boxes by pressing CTRL+K or by clicking Preferences on the Edit menu.

1

- Start Photoshop CS5 for your system.

- Press CTRL+K to display the Preferences dialog box.

- Make sure the check boxes in the Options area are selected as shown in Figure C–7.

- Click the Reset All Warning Dialogs button, so your dialog boxes will match the ones in this book.

- When Photoshop displays a Preferences dialog box, click the OK button.

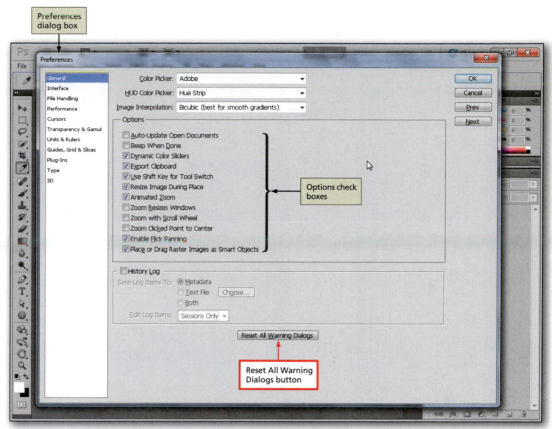

Figure C–7

2

- Click File Handling in the list of Preferences.

- Click the File Extension box arrow and then click Use Lower Case, if necessary, so Photoshop will use lowercase letters when saving.

- Make sure your check boxes are selected as shown in Figure C–8.

- Click the Maximize PSD and PSB File Compatibility box arrow and then click Ask, if necessary, so that Photoshop asks about saving files in PSD format.

- Type 10 in the Recent File List Contains box, if necessary, to specify that Photoshop will display the last 10 files.

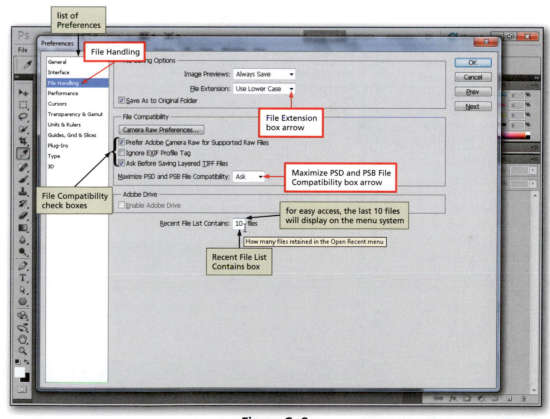

Figure C–8

3

• Click Performance in the list of Preferences.

• If necessary, type 20 in the History States box, so Photoshop will allow you to back up through the last 20 steps of any editing session (Figure C–9).

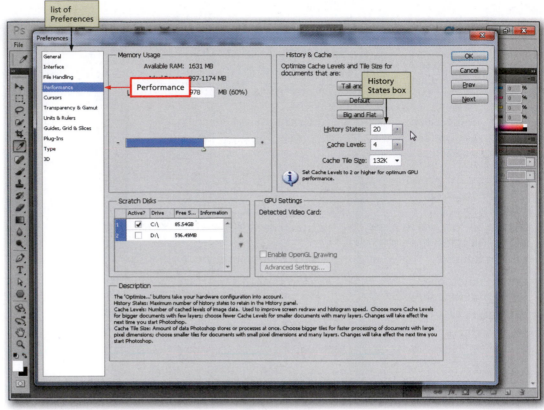

Figure C–9

4

• Click Cursors in the list of Preferences.

• If necessary, select Normal Brush Tip in the Painting Cursors area and Standard in the Other Cursors area, to reset those options back to their default values (Figure C–10).

5

• When you are finished, click the OK button (Preferences Dialog Box).

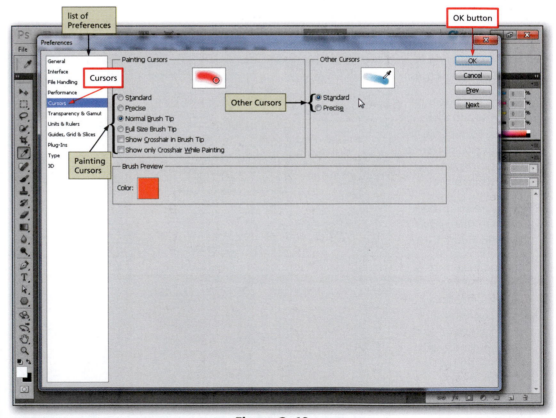

Figure C–10

Other Ways

1. On Edit menu, point to Preferences, click General, select individual preferences

The Preferences dialog boxes contain a variety of settings that can be changed to suit individual needs and styles. The Reset All Warning Dialogs button in Figure C–7 on page APP 27 especially is useful to display the dialog boxes if someone has turned them off by clicking the Don't show again check box.

In Figure C–10, Normal Brush Tip causes the mouse pointer outline to correspond to approximately 50 percent of the area that the tool will affect. This option shows the pixels that would be most visibly affected. It is easier to work with Normal Brush Tip than Full Size Brush Tip, especially when using larger brushes. A Standard painting cursor displays mouse pointers as tool icons; a Precise painting cursor displays the mouse pointer as a crosshair.

Menu Command Preferences

Photoshop allows users to customize both the application menus and the panel menus in several ways. You can hide commands that you seldom use. You can set colors on the menu structure to highlight or organize your favorite commands. Or, you can let Photoshop organize your menus with color based on functionality. If changes have been made to the menu structure, you can reset the menus back to their default states.

Hiding and Showing Menu Commands

If there are menu commands that you seldom use, you can hide them to access other commands more quickly. A hidden command is a menu command that does not appear currently on a menu. If menu commands have been hidden, a Show All Menu Items command will be displayed at the bottom of the menu list. When you click the Show All Menu Items command or press and hold the CTRL key as you click the menu name, Photoshop displays all menu commands, including hidden ones.

To Hide and Show Menu Commands

The following steps hide a menu command and then redisplay it.

1

• Click Edit on the menu bar, and then click Menus to display the Keyboard Shortcuts and Menus dialog box (Figure C–11).

BTW

Changing Preferences
If there is one particular setting you wish to change, you can open that specific Preferences dialog box from the menu. For example, if you want to change the color of a ruler guide, you can point to Preferences on the Edit menu and then click Guides, Grid & Slices on the Preferences submenu to go directly to those settings and make your edits.

BTW

Resetting Preferences
To restore all preferences to their default settings, you can press and hold ALT+CTRL+SHIFT as you start Photoshop, which causes the system to prompt that you are about to delete the current settings.

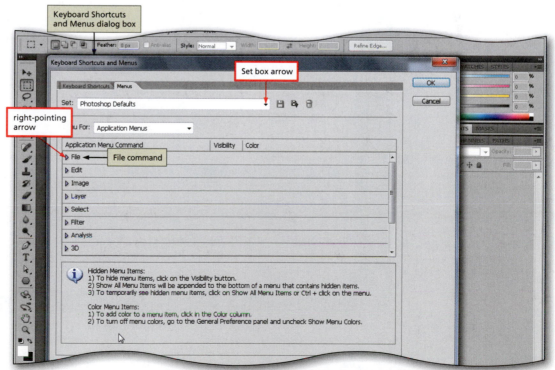

Figure C–11

2

• If necessary, click the Set box arrow and then click Photoshop Defaults.

• Click the right-pointing arrow next to the word File to display the File commands (Figure C–12).

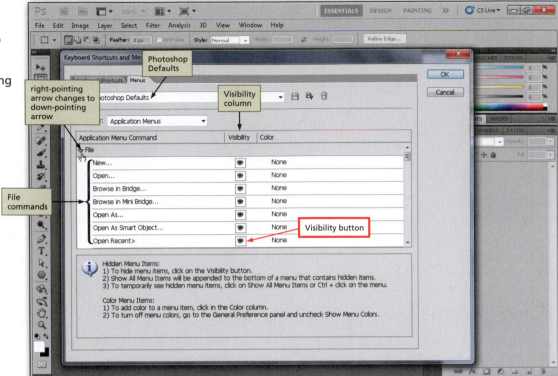

Figure C–12

3

• In the Visibility column, click the Visibility button next to the Open Recent command so it no longer is displayed (Figure C–13).

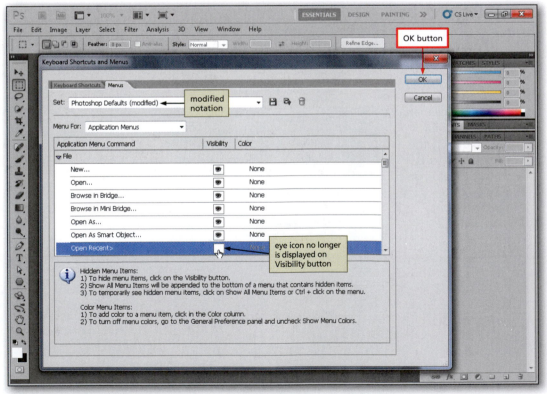

Figure C–13

4

- Click the OK button (Keyboard Shortcuts and Menus dialog box) to apply the settings.

- Click File on the menu bar to display the File menu (Figure C–14).

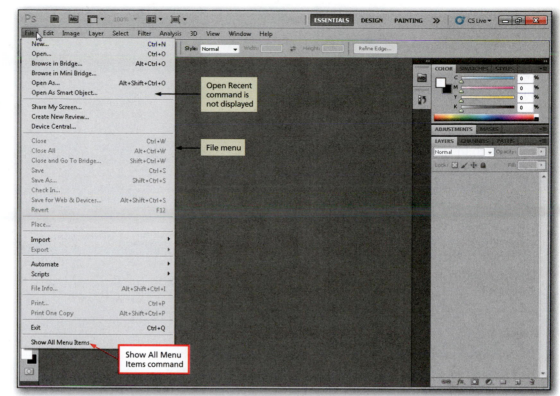

Figure C–14

5

- On the File menu, click Show All Menu Items to redisplay the command that you hid in Step 3 (Figure C–15).

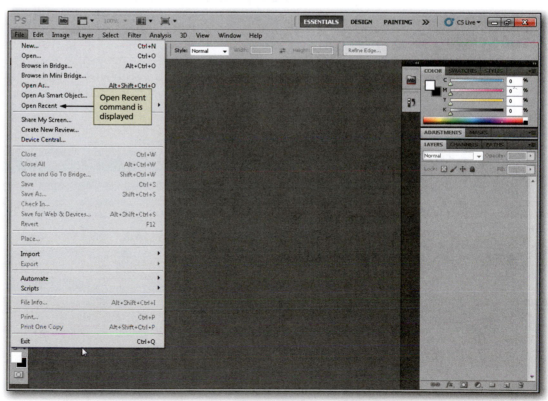

Figure C–15

• Click Edit on the menu bar and then click Menus to display the Keyboard Shortcuts and Menus dialog box again.

• If the arrow beside the word, File, is pointing to the right, click it to display the File list.

• Click the Visibility button next to the Open Recent command so it again is displayed (Figure C–16).

Other Ways

1. On Window menu, point to Workspace, click Keyboard Shortcuts & Menus

2. Press ALT+SHIFT+CTRL+M

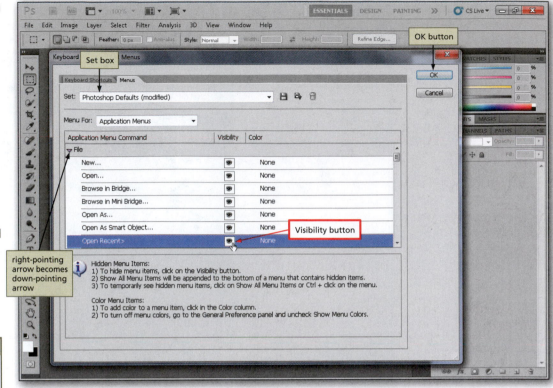

Figure C–16

To Add Color to Menu Commands

You can add color to menu commands to help you find them easily or to organize them into groups based on personal preferences. The following steps change the color of the Open and Open As commands.

• With the Keyboard Shortcuts and Menus dialog box still displayed, click the word, None, in the row associated with the Open command to display a list of colors (Figure C–17).

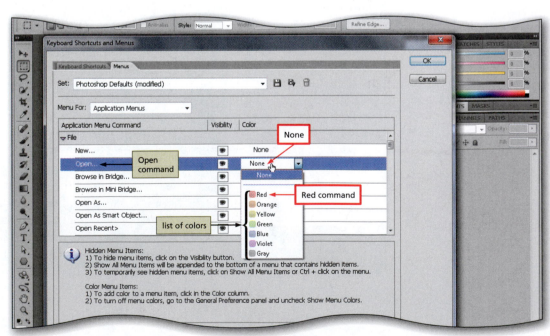

Figure C–17

2

- Click Red in the list to select a red color for the Open command.

- Click the word, None, in the row associated with the Open As command, and then click Red in the list to select a red color for the Open As command (Figure C–18).

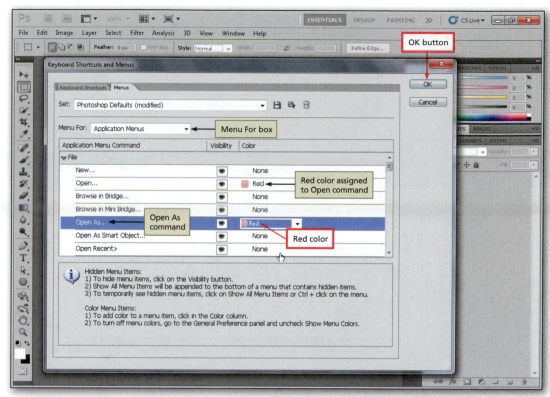

Figure C–18

3

- Click the OK button (Keyboard Shortcuts and Menus dialog box) to close the dialog box.

- Click File on the menu bar to display the new color settings (Figure C–19).

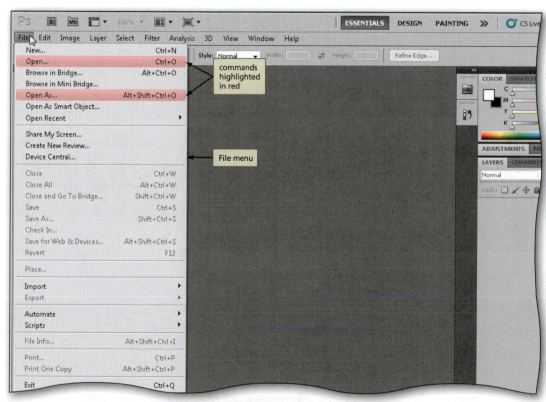

Figure C–19

Menu Box
The Menu For box (Figure C–18 on the previous page) allows you to set options for Application Menus or Panel Menus.

The Set box (Figure C–20) lists three sets of stored menu commands: Photoshop Defaults, New in CS5, and Photoshop Defaults (modified), which you created in the previous steps. Choosing a set causes Photoshop to display related commands with color. For example, if you choose New in CS5, the commands on all menus that are new will appear in blue.

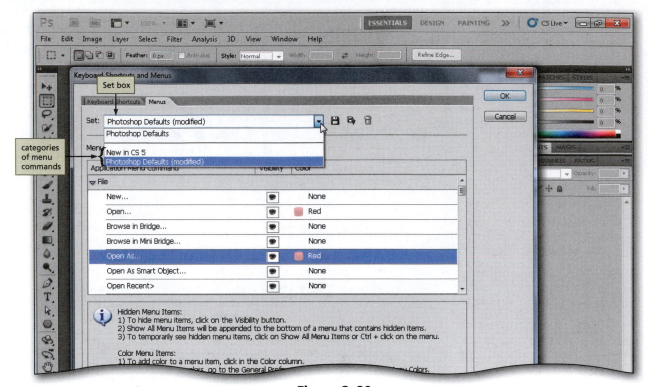

Figure C–20

To Reset the Menus

The following steps reset the menus, removing the red color from the Open commands.

1 Click Edit on the menu bar and then click Menus to display the Keyboard Shortcuts and Menus dialog box.

2 Click the Set box arrow and then click Photoshop Defaults in the list.

3 When Photoshop asks if you want to save your changes before switching sets, click the No button.

4 Click the OK button (Keyboard Shortcuts and Menus dialog box).

Resetting the Panels, Keyboard Shortcuts, and Menus

A **tool preset** is a way to store settings from the options bar. Besides the default settings for each tool, Photoshop contains tool presets for many of the tools that automatically change the options bar. For example, the Crop tool contains a preset to crop for a 5 × 7 photo. You can load other tool presets, edit current presets, or create new presets.

In a lab situation, if you notice that some tools are not working they way they are supposed to, or some presets are missing, someone may have changed the settings. The following steps reload all of the default tool presets.

To Reset Tool Presets

 1

- On the options bar, click the current tool's Preset picker and then click the menu button to display the Tool Preset menu (Figure C–21).

 2

- Click Reset Tool Presets.

- If Photoshop displays a dialog box, click the OK button to reload all of the default tool presets.

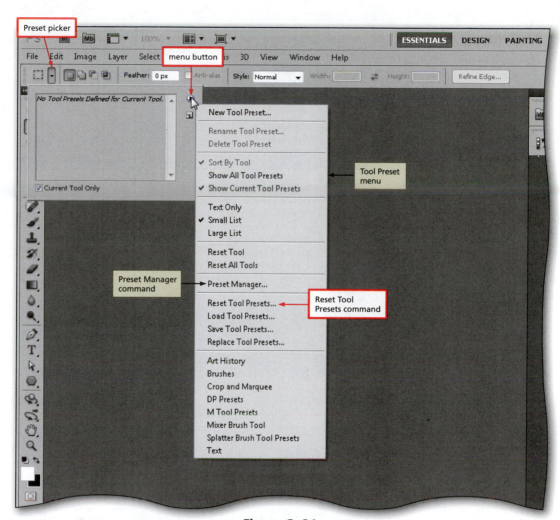

Figure C–21

Other Ways

1. From any panel menu, click Reset Tool Presets, click OK

Resetting Panel Components

Many panels, including the Brushes, Swatches, and Styles panels, display preset samples with preset shapes, colors, and sizes. A few options bars, including the Gradient and Shape options bars, as well as the Contours box in the Layer Style dialog box, also display similar components — all of which may need to be reset at some time.

You can reset these presets using the Preset Manager (Figure C–21), or each panel menu.

To Reset Panel Presets

The steps on the next page reset all panels that use presets.

- On the options bar, click the current tool's Preset picker and then click the menu button to display the Tool Preset menu.

- Click Preset Manager to display the Preset Manager dialog box.

- Click the Preset Type box arrow to display the list of panels that contain presets (Figure C–22).

- Click Brushes to select the Brush presets.

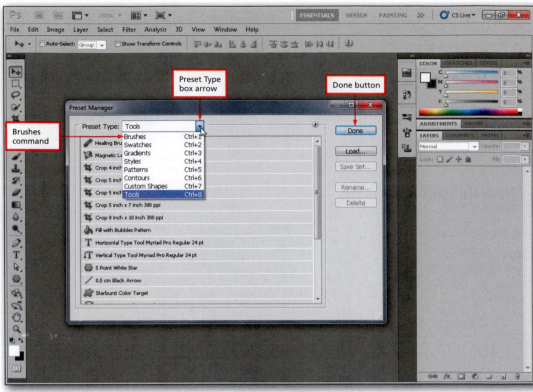

Figure C–22

- Click the Preset Manager menu button (Preset Manager dialog box) to display the list of commands and preset libraries (Figure C–23).

- Click Reset Brushes to reset the Brush presets. When Photoshop displays a confirmation dialog box, click the OK button.

- Repeat Steps 2 and 3 for each of the other panels that appear on the Preset Type box arrow list.

- When you are finished resetting all panels, click the Done button (Preset Manager dialog box) to close the dialog box.

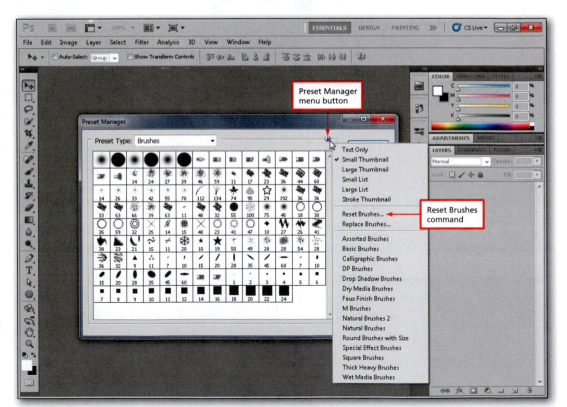

Figure C–23

Other Ways

1. On each panel menu, click Reset command, click OK button

Changing Preferences

Changing the Color and Style of Guides, Grid, and Slices

Instructions: You would like to use some different colors and styles for grids and guides because the current colors are very similar to the colors in your image, making them hard to see. You decide to change the color and style preferences on your system as described in the following steps.

1. Start Photoshop CS5.

2. On the Edit menu, point to Preferences, and then click Guides, Grid, & Slices.

3. When the Preferences dialog box is displayed, change the Color and Style settings as shown in Figure C–24.

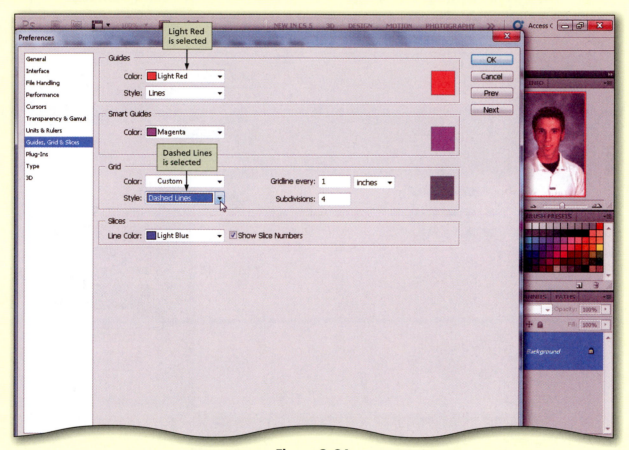

Figure C–24

4. Click the OK button.

5. Open any image file you have saved on your system and drag a guide from the horizontal ruler. Note the Light Red colored line.

6. On the View menu, point to Show, and then click Grid. Note the grid with dashed gray lines.

7. To clear the guides, on the View menu, click Clear Guides.

8. To hide the grid, on the View menu, point to Show and then click Grid.

9. To reset the colors and styles, either change the guide color back to Cyan and the grid style back to Lines, or quit Photoshop and then restart Photoshop while pressing ALT+CTRL+SHIFT. If Photoshop asks if you wish to delete the previous settings, click the Yes button.

Resetting Styles

Instructions: Someone has loaded many styles into the style box, making it difficult to find the common styles you are used to. You decide to reset the styles using the following steps.

1. Start Photoshop CS5.
2. On the Edit menu, click Preset Manager to display the Preset Manager dialog box.
3. Click the Preset Type box arrow to display the Preset list, and then click Styles in the list (Figure C–25).
4. Click the Preset Manager menu button to display a list of commands about the Styles Presets. Click Reset Styles in the list.
5. When Photoshop asks if you want to replace the styles with the default set, click the OK button.
6. Click the Done button to close the Preset Manager dialog box.
7. Quit Photoshop.

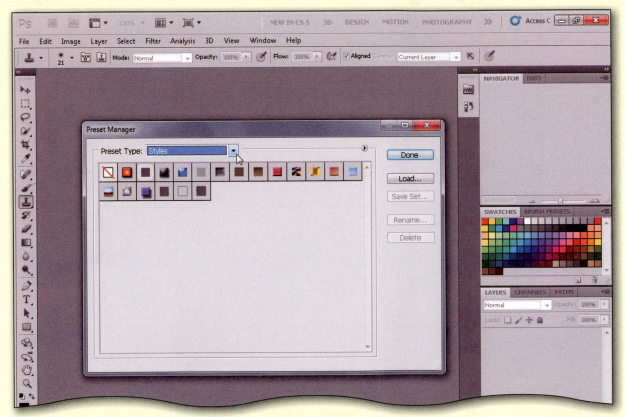

Figure C–25

Searching the Web

Instructions: You want to learn more about optimizing Photoshop settings and your computer system's memory by setting preferences for file size, history states, and cached views. Perform a Web search by using the Google search engine at google.com (or any major search engine) to display and print three Web pages that pertain to optimizing Photoshop CS5. On each printout, highlight something new that you learned by reading the Web page.

Appendix D
Using Photoshop Help

This appendix shows you how to use Photoshop Help. At anytime, whether you are accessing Photoshop currently or not, there are ways to interact with Photoshop Help and display information on any Photoshop topic. The help system is a complete reference manual at your fingertips.

Photoshop Help

Photoshop Help documentation for Photoshop CS5 is available in several formats, as shown in Figure D–1 on the next page. The first format is a Web-based help system that was introduced in Chapter 1. If you press the F1 key or choose Photoshop Help on the Help menu, Adobe Community Help appears in your default browser. You then can use the Web page to search for help topics. The Adobe Community Help page also contains many other kinds of assistance, including tutorials and videos. Your computer must be connected to the Web to use this form of Photoshop Help.

A second form of Photoshop Help is available as a PDF file. Again, pressing the F1 key or choosing Photoshop Help on the Help menu opens the Adobe Community Help page on the Web. Then, you can click the View Help PDF link to open a searchable help documentation, called Using Adobe Photoshop CS5, in book format. You can save this help file on your storage device, or continue to use it on the Web. Additionally, you can open a browser window and go directly to the Using Adobe Photoshop CS5 file by typing http://help.adobe.com/en_US/photoshop/cs/using/photoshop_cs5_help.pdf

Using Adobe Photoshop CS5 is packaged with Photoshop if you purchase the software on a DVD. To view the documentation, open the Documents folder on the installation or content DVD for your software, and then double-click Photoshop Help. If you prefer to view documentation in print form, you can print the Photoshop Help PDF file.

Photoshop Help displays two main panes. The left pane displays a search system. The right pane displays help information on the selected topic. Using Adobe Photoshop CS5 displays a chapter navigation system on the left, and pages from Photoshop Help documentation on the right.

Searching for Help Using Words and Phrases

The quickest way to navigate the Photoshop help system is through the **Search box** in the upper-left corner of the Adobe Community Help Web page. Here you can type words, such as *layer mask*, *hue*, or *file formats*; or you can type phrases, such as *preview a Web graphic*, or *drawing with the Pen tool*. Adobe Community Help responds by displaying search results with a list of topics you can click.

Here are some tips regarding the words or phrases you enter to initiate a search:

1. Check the spelling of the word or phrase.
2. Keep your search specific, with fewer than seven words, to return the most accurate results.
3. If you search using a specific phrase, such as *shape tool*, put quotation marks around the phrase — the search returns only those topics containing all words in the phrase.
4. If a search term does not yield the desired results, try using a synonym, such as Web instead of Internet.

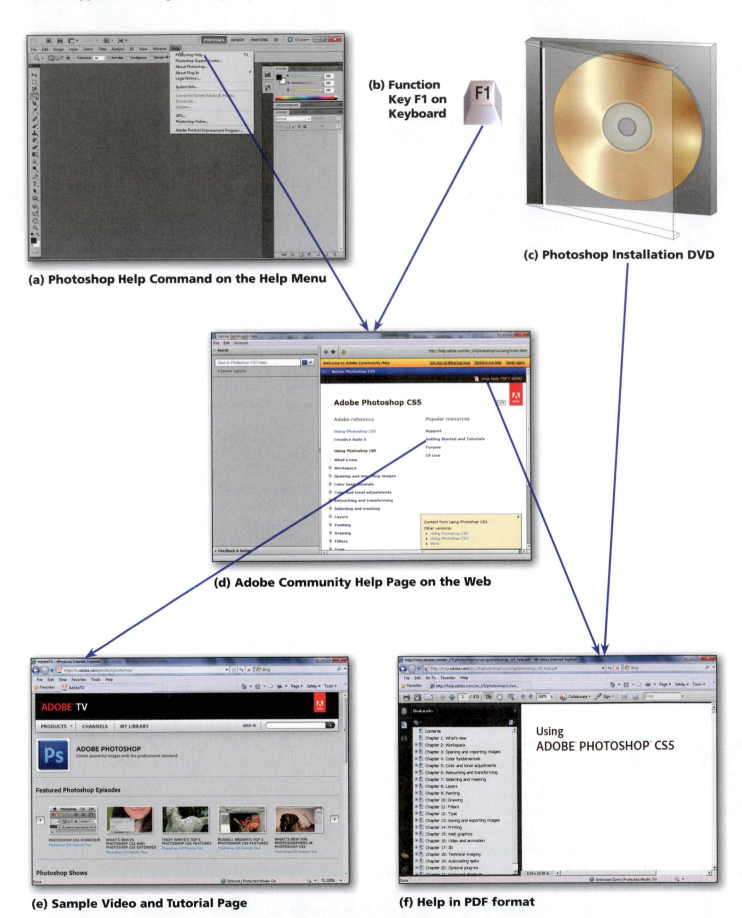

(a) Photoshop Help Command on the Help Menu

(b) Function Key F1 on Keyboard

(c) Photoshop Installation DVD

(d) Adobe Community Help Page on the Web

(e) Sample Video and Tutorial Page

(f) Help in PDF format

Figure D–1

To Obtain Help Using the Adobe Community Help Search Box

The following steps show how to open Adobe Community Help and use the Search box to obtain useful information by entering the keywords, ruler origin.

1
- With Photoshop running on your system, press the F1 key to display the Adobe Community Help window.

- When the Adobe Community Help window is displayed, double-click the title bar to maximize the window, if necessary.

- If the yellow informational slide-in tab is expanded, click the collapse button (Figure D–2).

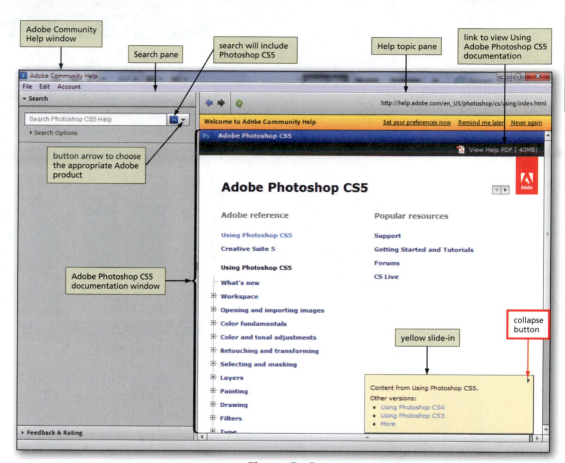

Figure D–2

Q&A I do not see a Search pane. Did I do something wrong?

No, someone might have closed the Search pane. To redisplay it, press CTRL+K, and then click the Off button in the Accessibility Mode area. Click the Done button to close the Preferences dialog box.

Q&A My help screen is asking me to download an update. Should I do that?

If you are in a lab situation, you should check with your instructor. If you are working on your own computer, the choice is yours. Downloading updates provide you with the latest help topics, videos, and tutorials, but the download takes time and disk space. You must be online to download the updates, and Photoshop may require you to restart your system.

2

- Click the Search box in the Search pane.

- Type **ruler origin** and then press the ENTER key to display the search results (Figure D–3).

- Click the Back button to return to the Adobe Photoshop CS5 page.

Q&A

What is the Adobe Community Help bar?

The Adobe Community Help bar contains links to assist you in setting Help preferences. If your system does not display a yellow bar, you can still set Help preferences by pressing CTRL+K.

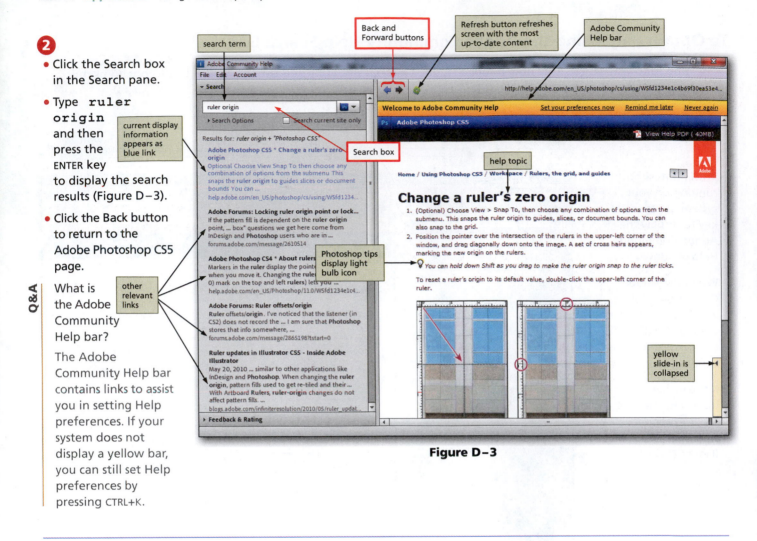

Figure D–3

On the right, Photoshop Help displays information about the topic, instructions, and a graphic. A light bulb icon indicates a Photoshop tip.

If none of the topics presents the information you want, you can refine the search by entering another word or phrase in the Search box. Or, you can click the Search Options button to filter or search other locations.

Adobe Community Help remembers the topics you visited and allows you to redisplay the pages visited during a session by clicking the Back and Forward buttons (shown in Figure D–3).

Using the Topics List

The Topics List is similar to a table of contents in a book. To use the Topics List, click any plus sign on the left side of Photoshop Help to display subtopics, as shown in the following steps.

To Use the Topics List

The following steps use the topics list to look up information about layers.

1

• In the Adobe Photoshop CS5 documentation window, scroll down and then click the plus sign next to the word, Layers, and then click the plus sign next to the words, Layer basics, to expand the list of topics (Figure D–4).

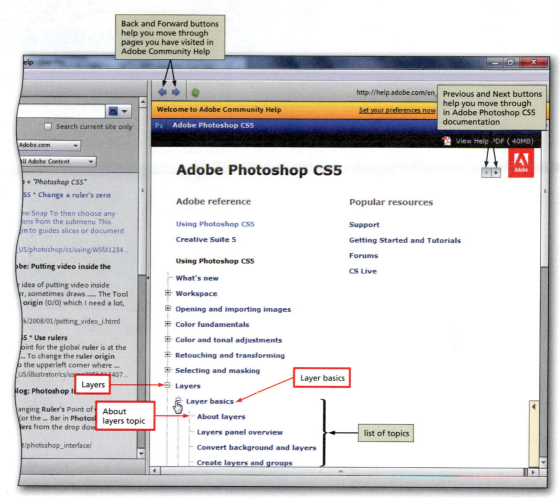

Figure D–4

2

- Click About layers to display information about Photoshop layers (Figure D–5).

Q&A

How do I get back to the table of contents?

Adobe Photoshop CS5's help documentation uses a breadcrumb trail navigation aid to help you see where you are within the documentation. A **breadcrumb trail** is a horizontal navigation that moves through the hierarchy of folders and files in a user interface. Click the Home link in the breadcrumb trail to return to the table of contents.

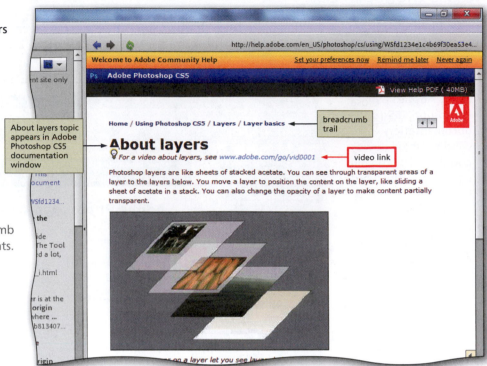

Figure D–5

To View a Video

Using Photoshop Help while connected to the Web, you can view online videos and tutorials, as done in the following steps.

1

- Click the video link www.adobe.com/go/vid0001 to start a video about creating layers (Figure D–6).

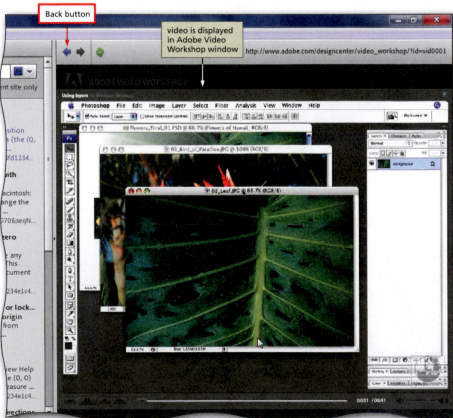

Figure D–6

2
- When the video is finished playing, click the Back button to return to the previous help topic (Figure D–7).

Q&A

Could I use the Close button on the Using Layers title bar?

The Close button closes the video and displays the Adobe Video Workshop home page.

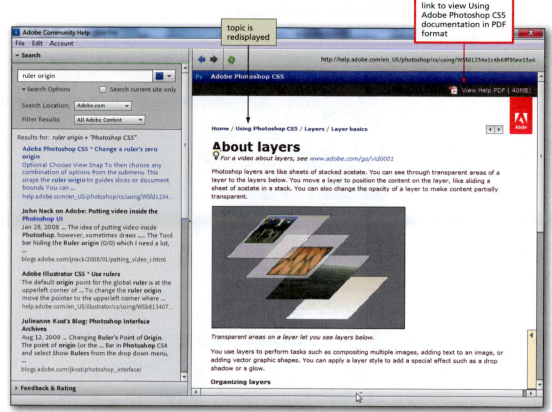

Figure D–7

Using Adobe Photoshop CS5 Documentation

Using Adobe Photoshop CS5 is a complete set of documentation for using Photoshop CS5. The PDF file is organized into 22 chapters with a table of contents like a regular book. You can access Using Adobe Photoshop CS5 by clicking the link on the Adobe Community Help page or by opening the file from the installation DVD.

To Open Using Adobe Photoshop CS5

The following steps open Using Adobe Photoshop CS5 from the Adobe Community Help page. You will use Adobe Acrobat to view the documentation.

- Click the link, View Help PDF in the upper-right corner of the Adobe Community Help window, to open the Using Adobe Photoshop CS5 documentation. (Figure D–8).

Q&A

The file would not open because I don't have Adobe Acrobat on my system.

See your instructor for ways to access the file.

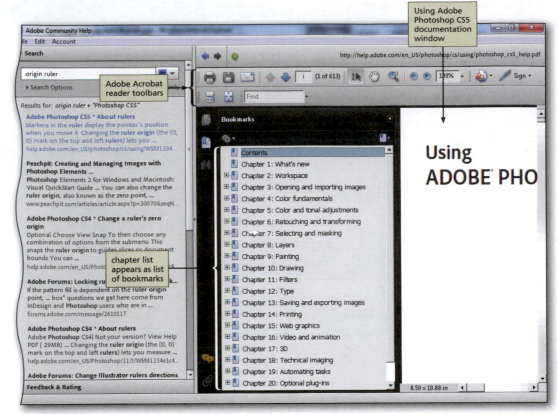

Figure D–8

To Navigate the Documentation by Chapter

The following steps use the left pane of the documentation window to find information related to color.

- With the Using Adobe Photoshop CS5 documentation file still displayed, click the plus sign next to the words, Chapter 4: Color fundamentals, and then click the plus sign next to the words, About color, to display the topics (Figure D–9).

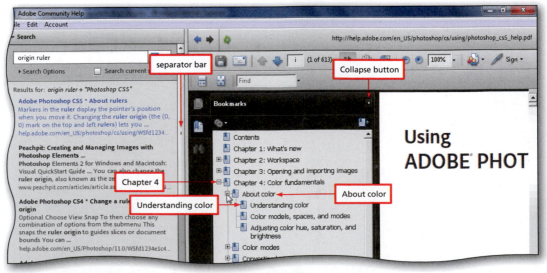

Figure D–9

2

- Click the words, Understanding color, to display the information on the right side of the window.

- Click the separator bar to hide the Search pane (Figure D–10).

Q&A

How can I redisplay the Search page?

Click the separator bar again to expand the pane.

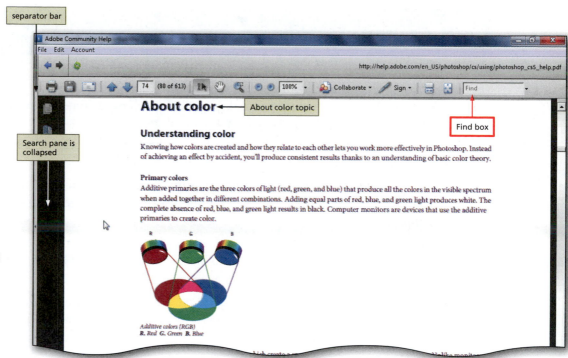

Figure D–10

To Use the Find Box

The following steps search the documentation information about the topic, knockout, using the Adobe Acrobat Find box.

1

- With the Using Adobe Photoshop CS5 documentation window still displayed, click the Find box in the Adobe Acrobat toolbar and then type **knockout**.

- Press the ENTER key to search for the term (Figure D–11).

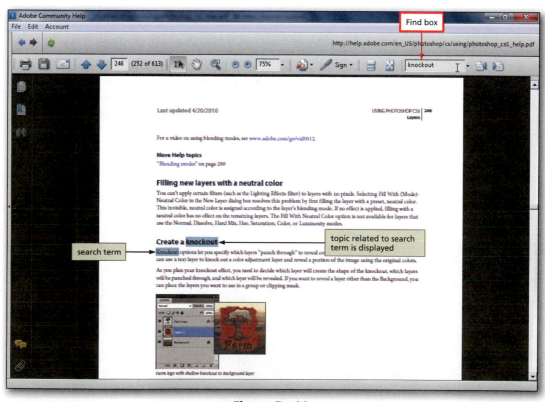

Figure D–11

Use Help

1: Using Adobe Help on the Web

Instructions: Perform the following tasks using Adobe Community Help.

1. If necessary, click the separator bar to display the Search pane. Type `pencil tool` in the Search box to obtain help on using the Pencil tool.

2. When the topics are displayed, click the topic, Adobe Photoshop CS5 * Paint with the Brush tool or Pencil tool.

3. One at a time, click two additional links and print the information. Hand in the printouts to your instructor. Use the Back to previous page and Forward to next page buttons to return to the original page.

4. Use the Search box to search for information on alignment. Click the Automatically align image layers topic in the search results. Read and print the information. One at a time, click the links on the page and print the information for any new page that is displayed.

5. Use the Search box to search for information on tutorials. Navigate to a tutorial of your choice and follow the directions. Write three paragraphs describing your experience, including how easy or difficult it was to follow the tutorial and what you learned. Turn in the paragraphs to your instructor.

6. Close Adobe Community Help.

Use Help

2: Using Adobe Photoshop CS5 Documentation

Instructions: Use the Using Adobe Photoshop CS5 documentation to understand the topics better and answer the questions listed below. Answer the questions on your own paper, or hand in the printed Help information to your instructor.

1. Use the Using Adobe Photoshop CS5 documentation to find help on snapping. Use the Find box, and enter `use snapping` as the term. Click the search result entitled, Use snapping, and then print the page. Hand in the printouts to your instructor.

2. Use the Using Adobe Photoshop CS5 documentation and expand the bookmarks, if necessary. Navigate to Chapter 10: Drawing, and then click the plus sign to expand the topic. Click the plus sign next to Drawing Shapes. One at a time, click each link and print the page. Hand in the printouts to your instructor.

Appendix E

Using Adobe Bridge CS5

This appendix shows you how to use Adobe Bridge CS5. Adobe Bridge is a file exploration tool similar to Windows Explorer, but with added functionality related to images. Adobe Bridge replaces previous file browsing techniques, and now is the control center for the Adobe Creative Suite. Bridge is used to organize, browse, and locate the assets you need to create content for print, the Web, and mobile devices with drag-and-drop functionality.

Adobe Bridge

You can access Adobe Bridge from Photoshop or from the Windows 7 Start menu. Adobe Bridge can run independently from Photoshop as a stand-alone program.

To Start Bridge Using Windows

The following steps start Adobe Bridge from the Windows 7 Start menu.

1

- Click the Start button on the Windows 7 taskbar to display the Start menu.

- Type **Bridge CS5** as the search text in the 'Search programs and files' text box, and watch the search results appear on the Start menu (Figure E–1).

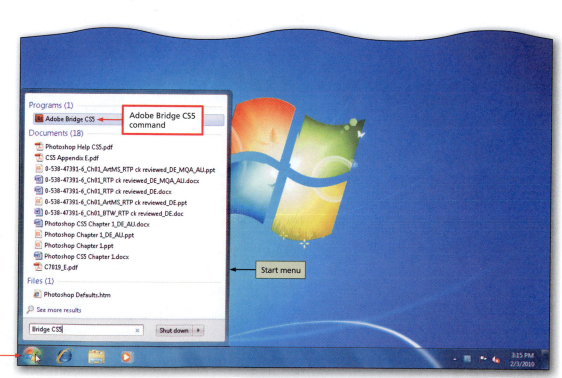

Figure E–1

2

- Click Adobe Bridge CS5 in the search results on the Start menu to start Bridge.

- When the Adobe Bridge window is displayed, double-click its title bar to maximize the window, if necessary (Figure E–2).

Other Ways

1. In Photoshop, click File on menu bar, click Browse in Bridge
2. In Photoshop, click Launch Bridge button on Applications Bar
3. Press ATL+CTRL+O

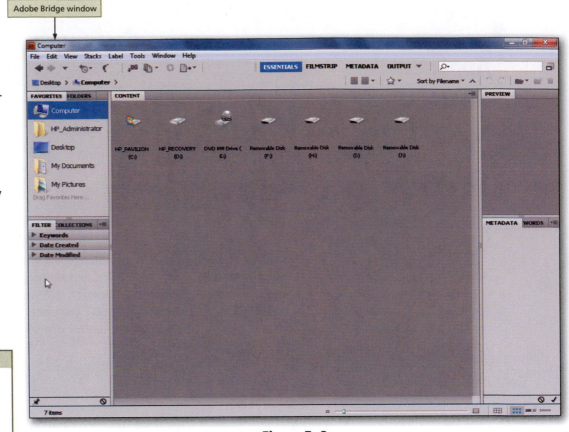

Adobe Bridge window

Figure E–2

To Reset the Workspace

To make your installation of Adobe Bridge match the figures in this book, you will reset the workspace to its default settings in the following steps.

1

- Click Window on the menu bar, and then point to Workspace to display the Workspace submenu (Figure E–3).

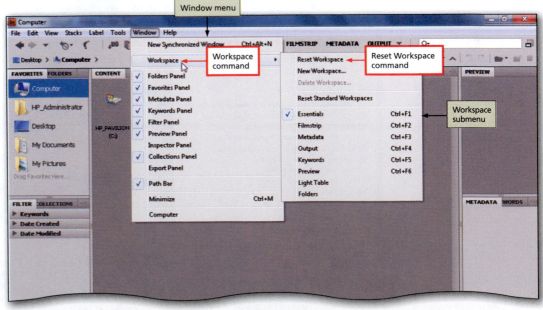

Window menu

Workspace command

Reset Workspace command

Workspace submenu

Figure E–3

2

- Click Reset Workspace on the Workspace submenu.

- In the Favorites panel, click Computer to display the files and folders, if necessary (Figure E–4).

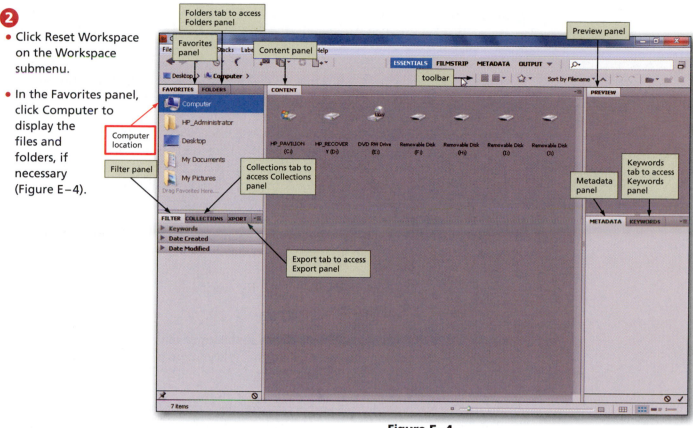

Figure E–4

Other Ways

1. Press CTRL+F1

The Adobe Bridge Window

The parts of the Adobe Bridge window are displayed in Figure E–4. The window is divided into panels and includes a toolbar and status bar.

The Panels

Several panels are displayed in the Bridge workspace in default view. To select a panel, click its tab. You can change the location of the panels by dragging their tabs. You can enlarge or reduce the size of the panels by dragging their borders. Some panels include buttons and menus to help you organize displayed information.

Favorites Panel   The Favorites panel allows quick access to common locations and folders, as well as access to other Adobe applications. Click a location to display its contents in the Content panel.

Folders Panel   The Folders panel shows the folder hierarchy in a display similar to that of Windows Explorer. Users click the plus sign to expand folders and the minus sign to collapse them.

Content Panel   The Content panel is displayed in a large pane in the center of the Adobe Bridge window. The content panel includes a view of each file and folder, its name, the creation date, and other information about each item. The Content panel is used to select files and open folders. To select a file, click it. To open a folder, double-click it. You can change how the Content panel is displayed on the Bridge status bar.

Preview Panel The Preview panel displays a preview of the selected file that is usually larger than the thumbnail displayed in the Content panel. If the panel is resized, the preview also is resized.

Filter Panel The Filter panel is displayed in the lower-left region of the Adobe Bridge window. The Filter panel includes many categories of criteria used to filter or control which files display in the Content panel. By default, three categories are displayed when you first start Bridge: Keywords, Date Created, and Date Modified. As you click files, the criteria categories change to include metadata that is generated dynamically depending on the file type. For example if you click an image in the Content panel, the Filter panel includes criteria such as camera data. If you click an audio file, the criteria include artist, album genre, and so on.

Collections Panel The Collections panel is displayed in the lower-left region of the Adobe Bridge window. **Collections** are a way to group photos in one place for easy viewing, even if the images are located in different folders or on different hard drives. The Collections panel allows you to create and display previously created collections, by identifying files or by saving previous searches.

Export Panel The Export panel is displayed in the lower-left region of the Adobe Bridge window. The panel helps with saving and uploading to photo-sharing Web sites, including Facebook, Flickr, and Photoshop.com.

Metadata Panel The Metadata panel contains metadata information for the selected file. Recall that metadata is information about the file including properties, camera data, creation and modification data, and other pieces of information. If multiple files are selected, shared data is listed such as keywords, date created, and exposure settings.

Keywords Panel The Keywords panel allows you to assign keywords using categories designed by Bridge, or you can create new ones. The keywords help you organize and search your images.

Toolbars and Buttons

Bridge displays several toolbars and sets of buttons to help you work more efficiently (Figure E–5).

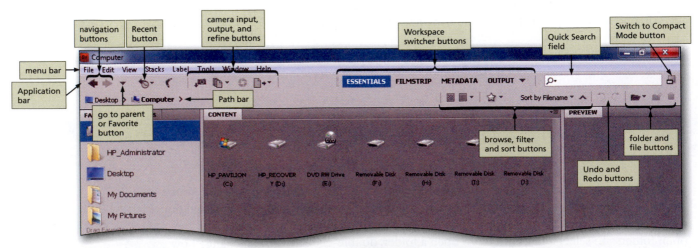

Figure E–5

Menu Bar   The menu bar is displayed at the top of the Bridge window and contains commands specific to Bridge.

Application Bar   Below the menu bar is the Application bar, which includes the navigation buttons, file retrieval and output buttons, buttons for switching workspaces, and other buttons to search for files.

Path Bar   The path bar displays the path for the current file. On the right side of the Path bar are shortcut buttons to help you work with your files. Browse, Filter, and Sort buttons change the display in the Content panel. The Create a new folder button inserts a new folder in the current location. The rotate buttons are active when an image file is selected in the Content panel. The Delete item button deletes the selected item.

Status Bar   At the bottom of the Bridge window, the status bar displays information and contains buttons (Figure E–6). On the left side of the status bar is information regarding the number of items in the current location and how many files are selected, if any. On the right side of the status bar, the Thumbnail slider sets the size of the thumbnails. To the right of the slider are four buttons used to change the display of the Content panel, including the 'Click to lock thumbnail grid' button, the 'View content as thumbnail' button, the 'View content as details' button, and the 'View content as list' button.

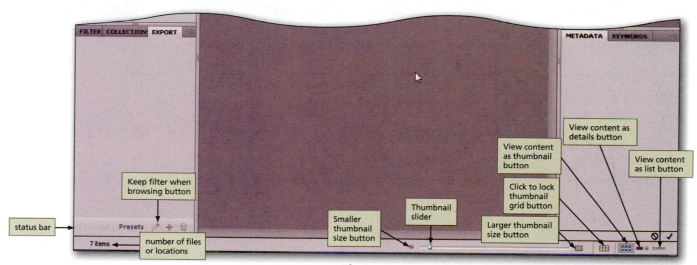

Figure E–6

Bridge Navigation and File Viewing

The advantages of using Bridge to navigate through the files and folders on your computer system include an interface that looks the same in all folders, the ability to see the images quickly, and the ease with which you can open the files in Photoshop or other image editing software. Besides the four kinds of displays represented by the Workspace switcher buttons on the right side of the status bar, Bridge offers several other configurations or layouts of the workspace accessible on the Workspace submenu on the Window menu (Figure E–3 on page APP 50).

To Navigate and View Files Using Bridge

The following step navigates to a CD to view files. Your instructor might specify a different location for these files. You then will use the Workspace switcher buttons to view the Content panel in different styles.

1
- Insert the CD that accompanies this book into your CD drive.

- After a few seconds, if Windows displays a dialog box, click its Close button.

- In the Content panel, double-click the CD icon associated with your CD drive.

- When the folders and files of the CD are displayed, double-click the Chapter 01 folder to display the files (Figure E–7).

Experiment
- One at a time, click each of the workspace buttons on the options bar and note how the Content panel changes.

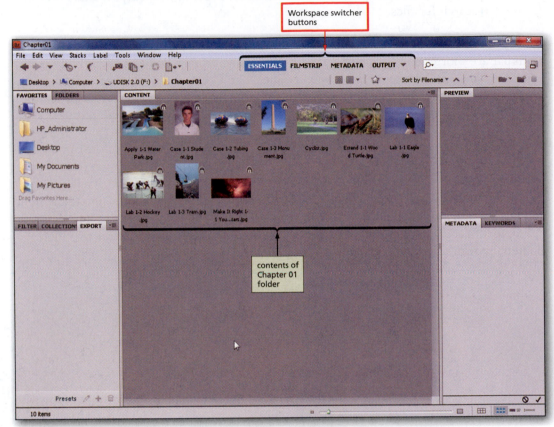

Figure E–7

Other Ways

1. To view Filmstrip workspace, press CTRL+F2	4. To view Keywords workspace, press CTRL+F5
2. To view Metadata workspace, press CTRL+F3	5. To view Preview workspace, press CTRL+F6
3. To view Output workspace, press CTRL+F4	

Duplicating Files
Bridge also offers a Duplicate command on the Edit menu (Figure E–8) that makes a copy in the same folder. Bridge renames the second file with the word, Copy, appended to the file name.

Managing Files

If you want to move a file to a folder that currently is displayed in the Content panel, you can drag and drop the file. The right-drag option is not available. If you want to copy a file, you can choose Copy on the Edit menu, navigate to the new folder and then choose Paste on the Edit menu. At anytime you can press the DELETE key to delete a file or folder, or right-click and then click Delete on the context menu. To rename a photo in Bridge, right-click the file and then click Rename. Type the new name.

To Copy a File

The following steps copy a file from a CD to a USB flash drive using Bridge.

- With the Chapter 01 folder contents still displaying in the Content panel, click the Case 1-2 Tubing thumbnail to select it.

- Click Edit on the menu bar to display the Edit menu (Figure E–8).

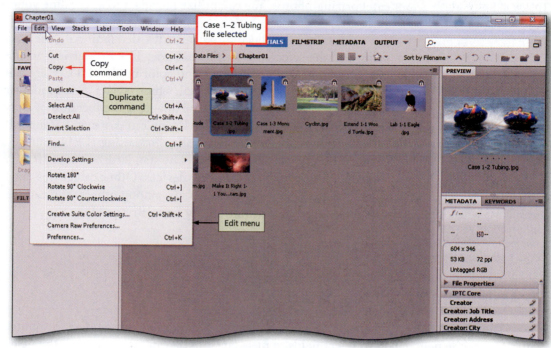

Figure E–8

- Click Copy on the Edit menu.

- In the Favorites panel, click Computer.

- When the Computer locations are displayed in the Content panel, double-click drive G or the drive associated with your USB flash drive.

- Click Edit on the menu bar, and then click Paste to display the copy in its new location (Figure E–9).

Other Ways

1. To copy, press CTRL+C
2. To paste, press CTRL+V

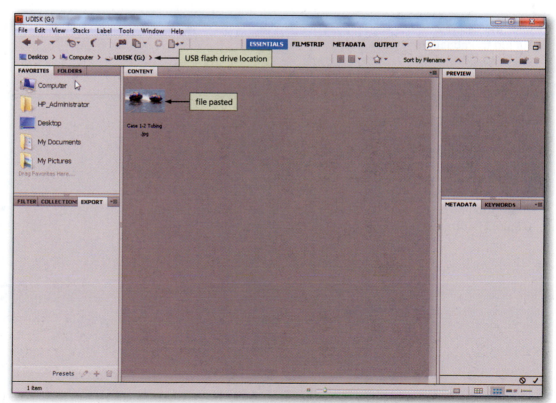

Figure E–9

Metadata

This extended set of metadata is particularly useful for large businesses, such as the newspaper industry, which contracts with many photographers and must maintain photo history.

Metadata Panel Menu

The Metadata panel menu button displays options to change the font size of the fields in the panel, options to set preferences, and ways to find and add new fields. For example, if your digital camera records global positioning system (GPS) information, you can use the menu to append that data to the digital photos.

Metadata

A popular use for Bridge allows you to assign metadata to files. Metadata, such as information about the file, author, resolution, color space, and copyright, is used for searching and categorizing photos. You can utilize metadata to streamline your workflow and organize your files.

Metadata is divided into categories, depending on the type of software you are using and the selected files. The category File Properties includes things like file type, creation date, dimensions, and color mode. IPTC Core stands for International Press Telecommunications Council, which is data used to identify transmitted text and images, such as data describing the image or the location of a photo. Camera Data (Exif) refers to the Exchangeable Image File Format, a standard for storing interchange information in image files, especially those using JPEG compression. Most digital cameras now use the Exif format. The standardization of IPTC and Exif encourages interoperability between imaging devices. Other categories may include Audio, Video, Fonts, Camera Raw and Version Cue, among others. You can see a list of all the metadata categories and their definitions by using Bridge Help.

To Assign and View Metadata

The Metadata Focus workspace makes it easier to assign or enter metadata for photos. In the Metadata panel, you can click the pencil icon to select fields of metadata, or you can move through the fields by pressing the TAB key. The following steps enter description and location information for the selected file.

1
- Click the Case 1-2 Tubing thumbnail to select it.

- In the Metadata panel, scroll down and if necessary, click the right-pointing arrow next to IPTC Core to display its fields.

- Scroll down to the Description field (Figure E–10).

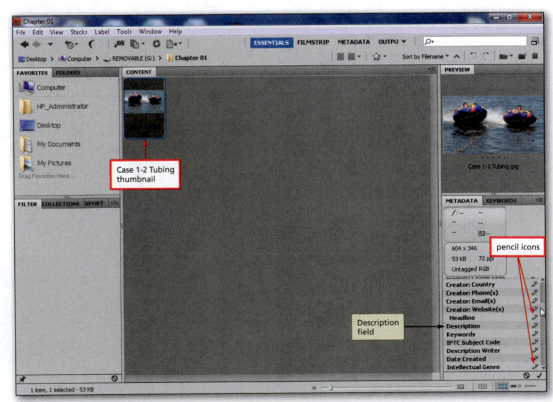

Figure E–10

2

• Click the pencil icon to the right of the Description field. Type **Tubing Adventure** as the description.

• Scroll as needed and then click the pencil icon to the right of the Sublocation field. Type **Raccoon Lake** as the location.

• Press the TAB key, Type **Rockville** as the city.

• Press the TAB key. Type **Indiana** as the state (Figure E–11).

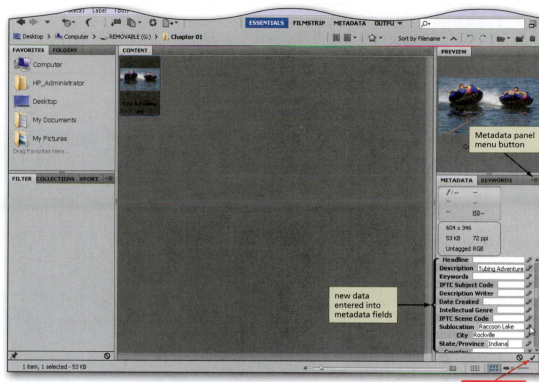

Figure E–11

3

• Click the Apply button at the bottom of the Metadata panel to assign the metadata to the photo.

• Click File on the menu bar and then click File Info to display the Case 1-2 Tubing.jpg dialog box (Figure E–12).

• Click the OK button to close the dialog box.

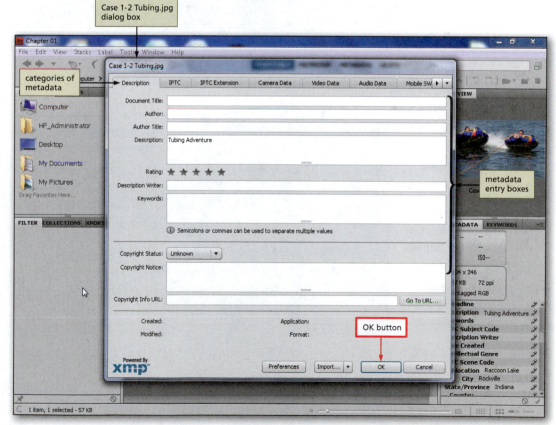

Figure E–12

Other Ways

1. Press CTRL+F4, enter data

To Enter a New Keyword

The Keywords panel lets you create and apply Bridge **keywords** to files. Keywords can be organized into categories called **sets.** Using keywords and sets, you identify and search for files based on their content. To assign keywords, you click the box to the left of the keyword in the Keywords panel, as shown in the following steps.

1
- With the Case 1-2 Tubing image still selected, click the Keywords tab to display the Keywords panel.

- Right-click the word, Places, to display the context menu (Figure E–13).

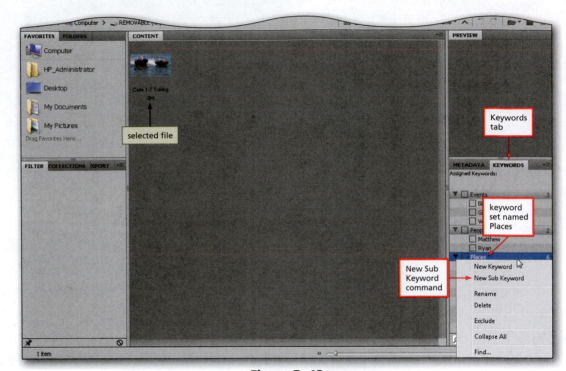

Figure E–13

2
- Click New Sub Keyword on the context menu.

- When the new field is displayed in the Keywords panel, type **Indiana** and then press the ENTER key to create the new item in Places.

- Click the check box to the left of Indiana to assign an Indiana keyword to the picture (Figure E–14).

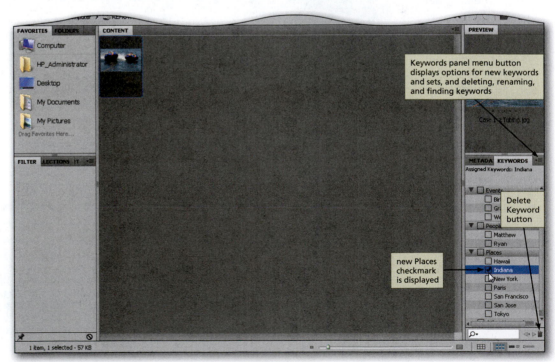

Figure E–14

To Rate a Photo

A rating system from zero stars to five stars is available in Bridge to rate your images and photos. A rating system helps you organize and flag your favorite, or best, files. Many photographers transfer their digital photos from a camera into Bridge and then look back through them, rating and grouping the photos. You can rate a photo using the Label menu or using shortcut keys. Once the photo is rated, stars are displayed below or above the file name depending on the workspace view. To change a rating, click Label on the menu bar and then either increase or decrease the rating. To remove all stars, click Label on the menu bar and then click No Rating. In some views, you can change a rating by clicking stars or dots that display below the thumbnail. You can remove the rating by clicking left of the stars.

The following step adds a rating to a photo file in Bridge.

- With the Case 1-2 Tubing image still selected in the Content panel, press CTRL+3 to assign a three star rating (Figure E–15).

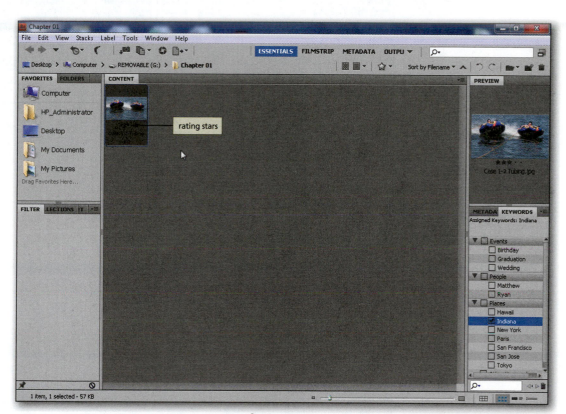

Figure E–15

Other Ways
1. On Label menu, select desired rating

To Label a Photo with Color-Coding

Another way to group photos in Bridge is to use a color-coding system. Bridge provides five colors with which users can label or group their photos. Each color has a category keyword that can be used to group photos. Keywords such as Approved, Second, or Review are used in photojournalism to indicate the status of the photo for future usage. Some companies use the colors for sorting and selecting only. The steps on the next page add a green color indicating approval to the Case 1-2 Tubing image using the menu system. Shortcut keys also are available for labeling photos with color-coding.

1

- With the Case 1-2 Tubing image still selected in the Content panel, click Label on the menu bar to display the Label menu (Figure E–16).

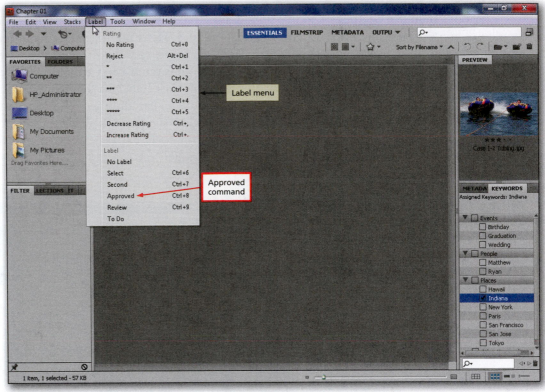

Figure E–16

2

- Click Approved.

- If Bridge displays a dialog box, click its OK button to apply the color (Figure E–17).

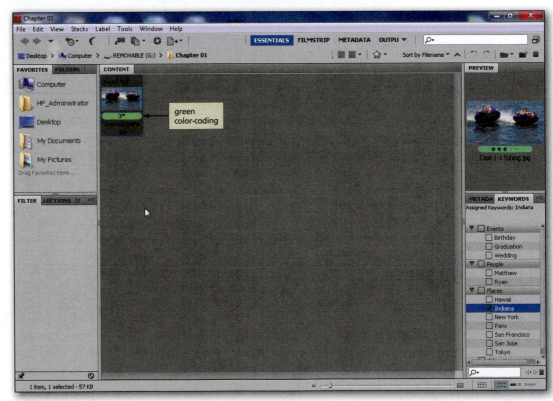

Figure E–17

Other Ways

1. Press CTRL+8

Searching Bridge

Searching is a powerful tool in Adobe Bridge, especially as the number of stored image files increases on your computer system. It is a good idea to enter keywords, or metadata, for every image file you store, to make searching more efficient. Without Adobe Bridge and the search tool, you would have to view all files as filmstrips in Windows, and then look at them a screen at a time until you found what you wanted.

Using the Find Command

In Bridge, you can enter the kind of data or field that you want to search, parameters for that field, and the text you are looking for using the Find command. For example, you could search for all files with a rating of three stars or better, for files less than 1 megabyte in size, or files that begin with the letter, m.

To Use the Find Command

The Find dialog box displays many boxes and buttons to help you search effectively. In the following steps, you will look for all files with metadata that includes the word, lake.

1

- Click Edit on the menu bar, and then click Find to display the Find dialog box (Figure E–18).

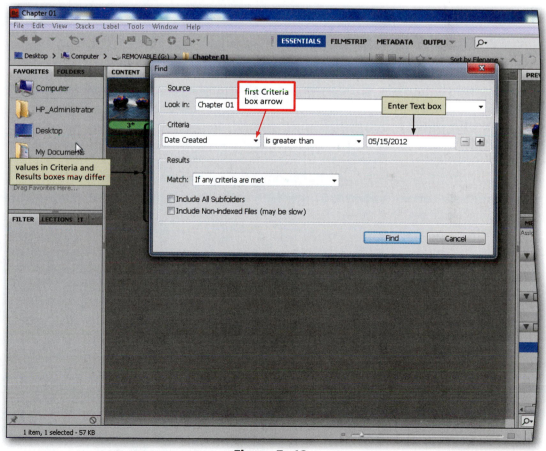

Figure E–18

● If necessary, click
the first Criteria box
arrow, scroll down as
necessary, and then
click All Metadata
to search all of the
metadata fields.

● Press the TAB key
twice, and then
type **lake** in the
Enter Text box to
enter the criteria
(Figure E–19).

Figure E–19

● Click the Find button
to display all files
that have the word,
lake, in any part
of their metadata
(Figure E–20).

● Click the Cancel button
in the Search title bar.

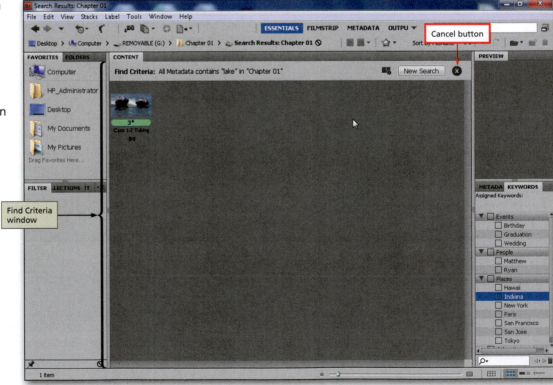

Figure E–20

Other Ways

1. Press CTRL+F, enter search
   criteria, click Find button

The plus sign to the right of the search boxes in the Find dialog box allows you to search multiple fields. When you click the plus sign, a second line of search boxes is displayed. For example, if you needed to find photos that were created last winter from your vacation in the Rockies, you could search for the date in the first line of boxes, click the plus button, and then enter the keyword to narrow your search even further in the second line of boxes (Figure E–21). When clicked, the Match box arrow allows you to match any or all criteria.

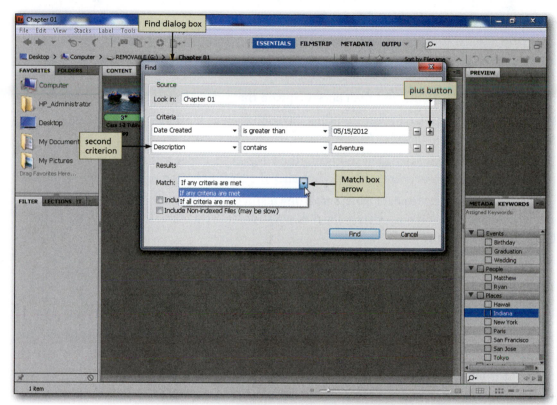

Figure E–21

Bridge offers you a way to save common searches as a **collection** for use later. For example, if you were working for a grocery wholesaler who stores many files for artwork in advertising, searching for pictures related to dairy products would be a common search. Looking through folders of images for pictures of milk or cheese would be very time consuming. Bridge then offers to name the search and store it. To display stored collections, click Collections in the Favorites panel. Then to perform the search again, double-click the collection. With metadata and collection searches, Bridge saves a lot of time.

To Quit Bridge

The final step quits Adobe Bridge.

1 Click the Close button on the Adobe Bridge title bar.

Using Bridge

1: Assigning Metadata

Instructions: You would like to assign metadata to some of the photos you worked on in previous chapters in this book. The photos can be found on the CD containing the Data Files for Students that accompanies this book, or your instructor may direct you to a different location. You will copy the photos from the CD to a local storage device and then assign metadata using Adobe Bridge.

1. Insert the CD that accompanies this book or see your instructor for the location of the data files.

2. Start Adobe Bridge on your system. When the Adobe Bridge window is displayed, on the Favorites tab, click Computer. In the Content panel, double-click the CD that accompanies this book, or navigate to the location specified by your instructor.

3. Right-click the Chapter 01 folder, and then click Copy on the context menu.

4. Using the Favorites tab, click Computer, and then navigate to your USB flash drive or other storage location.

5. On the Edit menu, click Paste. After a few moments, the Chapter 01 folder will appear in the right pane. Double-click the folder to open it. If necessary, click the Default button on the Bridge status bar.

6. Click the first photo. In the Metadata pane, scroll down and click the pencil icon next to the word, Description. In the description box, enter a short description of the picture. Click the Description Writer box. Enter your name.

7. With the first photo still selected, click the Keywords tab. When the Adobe Bridge dialog box appears, click Apply to apply the changes you just made in the Metadata pane. On the Keywords tab, click to place a check mark next to any keywords that apply to the photo.

8. Scroll to the bottom of the keywords list. Right-click the Other Keywords category and then click New Keyword on the context menu. When the new keyword box appears at the top of the panel, type a new keyword relating to the selected photo.

9. Repeat Steps 6 through 8 for each photo in the right pane of the Adobe Bridge window.

Using Bridge

2: Rating and Categorizing Photos

Instructions: You would like to rate and categorize some of the photos you worked on in previous chapters in this book. The photos can be found on the CD that accompanies this book, or your instructor may direct you to a different location.

1. If you did not perform exercise 1, Assigning Metadata, perform steps 1 through 5 from Exercise 1 to copy images to your storage location.

2. With the photos from the Chapter 01 folder displayed in the Content pane of the Adobe Bridge window, click the first photo. Assign a rating to the photo on a scale from 1 to 5 with 1 being the worst photo in the group and 5 being the best photo in the group. On the Label menu, click the number of stars that corresponds to your rating. Repeat the process for each of the photos in the folder.

3. Click the first photo again to select it. Click Label on the menu bar. Choose a label setting, such as Approved. Repeat the process for each of the photos in the folder, choosing different label settings.

4. Choose your favorite photo in the folder and right-click the image. Click Add to Favorites on the context menu.

5. Consult with at least three other members of your class to compare your ratings.

Quick Reference Summary

Adobe Photoshop CS5 Quick Reference Summary

Task	Page Number	Mouse	Menu	Context Menu	Keyboard Shortcut
Action Sets, Append	PS 424		Actions panel menu | select action set, select action		
Action, Play	PS 425	Select action, click Play selection button on Actions panel status bar	Actions panel menu | Play		
Action, Record	PS 427	'Create new action' button on Actions panel, Record button (New Action dialog box), perform action to record, click 'Stop playing/recording' button	Actions panel menu | Start/Stop Recording		
Action, Save	PS 431		Actions panel menu | Save Actions		
Action, Test	PS 430				Assigned function key
Actions Panel, Display	PS 423		Window | Actions		ALT+F9
Adjustment Layer	PS 187	'Create new fill or adjustment layer' button on Adjustments panel	Layer | New Adjustment Layer		
Alpha Channel, Create from Scratch	PS 406			Right-click source channel in Channels panel | Duplicate Channel command	
Alpha Channel, Create from Selection	PS 403	'Save selection as channel' button	Channels panel menu | New Channel, edit settings		
Anchor Points, Add to a Shape	PS 475	Auto Add/Delete button on Pen Tool options bar, click path		Right-click Pen Tool button | Add Anchor Point Tool, click in document window to add anchor points	
Anchor Points, Deselect	PS 478	Vector mask thumbnail on Layers panel			
Animation Panel, Display	PS 569		Window | Animation		

Adobe Photoshop CS5 Quick Reference Summary (continued)

Task	Page Number	Mouse	Menu	Context Menu	Keyboard Shortcut
Animation Timing, Set	PS 570	'Selects frame delay time' button on Animation panel			
Animation, Optimize	PS 578		Animation panel menu | Optimize Animation		
Animation, Preview	PS 573	Plays animation button on Animation panel			
Background Eraser Tool	PS 168	Background Eraser Tool button on Tools panel			SHIFT+E
Black-and-White Adjustment, Create	PS 434	Black & White button on Adjustments panel	Image | Adjustments | Black & White or Layer | New Adjustment Layer | Black & White		ALT+SHIFT+CTRL+B
Blending Mode	PS 288	Mode box arrow on Layers panel or Mode box arrow on Brush options bar			
Blur Tool	PS 320	Blur Tool button on Tools panel			
Border, Create	PS 35		Select All | Edit | Stroke	Stroke	
Border, Modify	PS 38		Select | Modify | Border		
Bridge Output Panel, Display	PS 542	Output on Bridge Application bar or Workspace picker button on Bridge Application bar, click Output	Bridge Window menu | point to Workspace, click Output		CTRL+F4
Brightness/Contrast, Adjust	PS 185	Brightness/Contrast icon on Adjustments panel or 'Create new fill or adjustment layer' button on Layers panel, Brightness/Contrast	Layer | New Adjustment Layer | Brightness/Contrast		
Brush Options, Set	PS 236	Brush Tip Shape button on Brush panel			
Brush Overlay Mode	PS 407	Painting Mode box arrow on Brush options bar | Overlay			
Brush Panel, Display	PS 235	Toggle the Brush panel on Brush options bar	Window | Brush		F5
Brush Presets, Append	PS 231		Brush Preset picker menu | click desired preset or Brush Presets panel menu | click desired preset		
Brush Tool	PS 229	Brush Tool button on Tools panel			B
Brush, Change Size and Hardness	PS 232	Size or Hardness slider on Brush Preset panel			
Brush, Select	PS 232	Brush Preset picker panel, select brush			
Burn Tool	PS 312	Burn Tool button on Tools panel			SHIFT+O
Canvas, Rotate	PS 257		Image | Image Rotation		
Channels, View	PS 400	Channel on Channels tab			CTRL+2 for composite, CTRL+3 for first channel, CTRL+4 for second channel, CTRL+5 for third channel
Character Panel	PS 371	Toggle the Character and Paragraph panels on Brush options bar	Window | Character		

Adobe Photoshop CS5 Quick Reference Summary *(continued)*

Task	Page Number	Mouse	Menu	Context Menu	Keyboard Shortcut
Clone Stamp Tool	PS 192	Clone Stamp Tool button on Tools panel			S
Close	PS 42	Close button on document window tab	File | Close		CTRL+W
Color Separations, Print	PS 447		File | Print | Color Handling box arrow | Separations | Print button		
Color, Choose on Swatches Panel	PS 227	Swatches panel tab, select color			
Color, Select using Color Panel	PS 336	Color ramp on Color panel or enter values in C,M,Y, and K boxes on Color panel			
Colors, Reset Default	PS 14	Default Foreground and Background Colors button on Tools panel			D
Colors, Switch Between Background and Foreground	PS 40	Switch Foreground and Background Colors button on Tools panel			X
Commit Change	PS 118	Commit transform (Return) button on options bar			ENTER
Content-Aware	PS 294		Edit | Fill | Use box arrow | Content Aware		DELETE
Custom Shape	PS 501	Shape Tool button, Custom Shape Tool button on Shape Tool options bar			
Desaturate	PS 433		Image | Adjustments | Desaturate		SHIFT+CTRL+U
Direction Points, Use	PS 477			Right-click Path Selection Tool button | Direct Selection Tool, click anchor point	
Document Windows, Arrange	PS 152	Arrange Documents button on Application bar	Window | Arrange		
Dodge Tool	PS 311	Dodge Tool button on Tools panel			O
Download Speed, Choose	PS 49	'Select download speed' button (Save for Web & Devices dialog box)	File | Save for Web & Devices | 'Select download speed' button		
Drop Shadow	PS 242	'Add a layer style' button, Drop Shadow			
Elliptical Marquee Tool	PS 80	Elliptical Marquee Tool button on Tools panel			SHIFT+M
Eraser Tool	PS 164	Eraser Tool button on Tools panel			E
Essentials Workspace, Select	PS 7	Essentials button on Application bar or 'Show more workspaces and options' button, click Essentials	Window | Workspace | Essentials		
Extend Edges	PS 317	Edge box arrow (Lens Correction dialog box), Edge Extension			
Eyedropper Tool	PS 248	Eyedropper Tool button on Tools panel			I
Files, Copy and Paste in Bridge	PS 540		Edit | Copy, Edit | Paste	Right-click file, click Copy | right-click Content pane, click Paste	CTRL+C, CTRL+V

Adobe Photoshop CS5 Quick Reference Summary *(continued)*

Task	Page Number	Mouse	Menu	Context Menu	Keyboard Shortcut
Filter Gallery	PS 354		Filter | Filter Gallery | select filter and settings		
Folder, Create in Bridge	PS 539		File | New Folder	Right-click Content panel | New Folder	
Font Options, Set	PS 253	Font buttons on Horizontal Text Tool options bar or font buttons on Character panel			
Freeform Pen Tool, Use Magnetic	PS 480			Right-click Pen Tool button | Freeform Pen Tool, click Shape layers button on options bar, click Magnetic check box	
Gradient Tool	PS 219	Gradient Tool button on Tools panel			G
Grid, Hide or Show	PS 101	View Extras button on Application bar	View | Show | Grid		CTRL+APOSTROPHE (')
Guides, Create	PS 103	Drag from ruler	View | New Guide		
Guides, Hide or Show	PS 101	View Extras button on the Application bar	View | Show | Guides		CTRL+SEMICOLON (;)
Hand Tool	PS 27	Hand Tool button on Tools panel			H
Hard Proof, Print	PS 377	Proof option button (Print dialog box), OK button	File | Print		CTRL+P
Healing Brush Tool	PS 301	Healing Brush Tool button on Tools panel			SHIFT+J
Help	PS 58, APP 39		Help | Photoshop Help		F1
History, Step Backward in	PS 93	Click state on History panel	History panel menu | Step Backward		CTRL+ALT+Z
History, Step Forward in	PS 93	Click state on History panel	History panel menu | Step Forward		CTRL+SHIFT+Z
Horizontal Type Tool	PS 252	Horizontal Type Tool button on Tools panel			T
Hue/Saturation, Adjust	PS 185	Hue/Saturation icon on Adjustment panel or 'Create new fill or adjustment layer' button on Layers panel, Hue/Saturation	Layer | New Adjustment Layer | Hue/Saturation		CTRL+U
Hyperlink, Preview	PS 561		File | Save for Web & Devices | Preview button		
Image, Convert to Duotone	PS 438		Image | Mode | Duotone		
Image, Convert to LAB Color	PS 443		Image | Mode | Lab Color		
Image, Crop	PS 33	Crop Tool button on Tools panel	Image | Crop		C
Image, Flatten	PS 195		Layer | Flatten Image or Layers panel menu | Flatten Image	Flatten Image	
Image, Resize	PS 44		Image | Image Size		ALT+CTRL+I
Keyboard Shortcuts, Create	PS 122		Edit | Keyboard Shortcuts		ALT+SHIFT+CTRL+K
Keyboard Shortcuts, Reset Default	PS 126		Edit | Keyboard Shortcuts | Photoshop Defaults		

Adobe Photoshop CS5 Quick Reference Summary *(continued)*

Task	Page Number	Mouse	Menu	Context Menu	Keyboard Shortcut
Lasso Tool	PS 108	Lasso Tool button on Tools panel			L
Layer Effects, Hide	PS 190	'Reveals layer effects in the panel' button on Layers panel			
Layer from Background	PS 283		Layer | New | Layer from Background	Background layer | Layer from Background	
Layer Group, Create from Layers	PS 496		Layers panel menu | New Group from Layers		
Layer Group, Create New	PS 499	ALT+click Create a New Group button	Layers panel menu | New Group		
Layer Groups, Nest	PS 499	Drag subordinate group(s) onto primary group on Layers panel			
Layer Mask, Create	PS 174	'Add layer mask' button on Layers panel			
Layer Mask, Create from Alpha Channel	PS 413		Select | Load Selection | select channel, click Layer in Layers panel, 'Add layer mask' button		
Layer Properties, Assign	PS 148, PS 154		Layer | Layer Properties or Layers panel menu | Layer Properties	Layer Properties	
Layer Style, Add	PS 189	'Add a layer style' button on Layers panel	Layer | Layer Style		
Layer Style, Copy	PS 187		Layer | Layer Style | Copy Layer Style	Copy Layer Style	
Layer Style, Copy and Paste	PS 511			Right-click layer name, click Copy Layer style, right-click layer name, click Paste Layer style	
Layer Style, Paste	PS 187		Layer | Layer Style | Paste Layer Style	Paste Layer Style	
Layer via Cut, Create	PS 147		Layer | New | Layer via Cut	Layer via Cut	SHIFT+CTRL+J
Layer, Color	PS 148		Layers panel menu | Layer Properties | select color	Right-click 'Indicates layer visibility' button | click color	
Layer, Create	PS 163	Drag new image into document window	Layer | New | Layer or Layers panel menu | New Layer		SHIFT+CTRL+N
Layer, Hide	PS 149		Layer | Hide Layers	Right-click 'Indicates layer visibility' button | click Hide this layer	
Layer, Lock	PS 465	Lock all button on Layers panel			/

Adobe Photoshop CS5 Quick Reference Summary *(continued)*

Task	Page Number	Mouse	Menu	Context Menu	Keyboard Shortcut
Layer, Name	PS 148	Double-click layer name, enter new name on Layers panel	Layers panel menu | Layer Properties | enter new name	Layer Properties | enter new name	
Layer, Show	PS 149	'Indicates layer visibility' button on Layers panel	Layer | Show Layers		
Layer, Show Only Current	PS 163	ALT+click 'Indicates layer visibility' button on Layers panel			
Layers Panel Options, Set	PS 145		Layers panel menu | Panel Options		
Layers, Arrange	PS 171	Drag layer on Layers panel			CTRL+LEFT BRACKET ([) or CTRL+RIGHT BRACKET (])
Layers, Distribute	PS 568	'Distribute vertical centers' button or 'Distribute horizontal centers' button			
Layers, Rotate	PS 567		Edit | Transform | Rotate		CTRL+T, drag
Lens Correction	PS 315		Filter | Lens Correction		SHIFT+CTRL+R
Levels, Adjust	PS 183	Levels icon on Adjustments panel or 'Create new fill or adjustment layer' button on Layers panel, Levels	Image | Adjustments | Levels		CTRL+L
Lighting Effects	PS 339		Filter | Render | Lighting Effects		
Lock Transparent Pixels	PS 291	On Layers panel, click 'Lock transparent pixels' button			
Magic Eraser Tool	PS 161	Magic Eraser Tool button on Tools panel			SHIFT+E
Magic Wand Tool	PS 110	Magic Wand Tool button on Tools panel			SHIFT+W
Magnetic Lasso Tool	PS 114	Magnetic Lasso Tool button on Tools panel			SHIFT+L
Magnification, Change	PS 27	Enter number in Magnification box on Status bar or enter number in Zoom Level box on Application bar or Zoom Level box arrow, desired percentage			
Menus, Edit	APP 29		Edit | Menus		ALT+SHIFT+CTRL+M
Mini Bridge, View Files	PS 54	Launch Mini Bridge button on the Application bar	File | Browse in Mini Bridge		
Move Tool	PS 84	Move Tool button on Tools panel			V
New Action Set, Create	PS 426	'Create new set' button on Actions panel status bar	Actions panel menu | New Set		
New Action, Create	PS 427	'Create new action' button on Actions panel status bar	Actions panel menu | New Action		
New Adjustment Layer	PS 284	'Create new fill or adjustment layer' button on Layers panel status bar, select adjustment	Layer | New Adjustment Layer | select adjustment		
New Frames, Duplicate	PS 571	'Duplicates selected frames' button on Animation panel status bar	Actions panel menu | Copy Frame, Actions panel menu | Paste Frame		
New Photoshop File	PS 215		File | New		CTRL+N
Noise Gradient Preset	PS 221	Gradient Editor box, Presets menu button (Gradient Editor dialog box)			
Note, Create	PS 514	Note Tool button on Tools panel			I
Offset for Animation	PS 577		Filter | Other | Offset		

Adobe Photoshop CS5 Quick Reference Summary (continued)

Task	Page Number	Mouse	Menu	Context Menu	Keyboard Shortcut
Opacity, Change	PS 180	Drag Opacity scrubby slider on Layers panel			
Open	PS 10		File | Open	Right-click document tab | click Open Document	CTRL+O
Open Recent	PS 43		File | Open Recent		
Paint Bucket Tool	PS 369	Paint Bucket Tool button on Tools panel			SHIFT+G
Painting Workspace, Select	PS 214	Painting button on Application bar or 'Show more workspaces and options' button on Application bar, click Painting	Window | Workspace | Painting		
Panel, Collapse	PS 57	Collapse to Icons button on panel		Right-click panel tab | click Collapse to Icons	
Panel, Open	PS 55	Panel button on vertical docking of panels	Window | panel name		
Paste	PS 98		Edit | Paste	Paste	CTRL+V
Patch Tool	PS 303	Patch Tool button on Tools panel			SHIFT+J
Path, Create using Pen Tool	PS 485	Paths button on Pen Tool options bar, click Add to Path button			
Paths Panel, Display	PS 487		Window | Paths		
Pattern Stamp Tool	PS 191	Pattern Stamp Tool button on Tools panel			SHIFT+S
Pattern, Define	PS 367		Edit | Define		
Pattern, Delete	PS 370	'Set source for fill area' button on Gradient options bar, click Pattern, Pattern Picker box arrow on Gradient options bar, right-click pattern, click Delete Pattern			
Pattern, Use	PS 368	'Set source for fill area' button on Gradient options bar, click Pattern, Pattern Picker box arrow on Gradient options bar, select pattern			
Patterns, Reset	PS 509		Edit | Preset Manager | Preset Type box arrow | Patterns | Preset Manager menu | Reset Patterns		
Polygonal Lasso Tool	PS 105	Polygonal Lasso Tool button on Tools panel			SHIFT+L
Preferences, Edit	APP 26		Edit | Preferences | General		CTRL+K
Preview, Web	PS 48, PS 51	Preview button (Save for Web & Devices dialog box)	File | Save for Web & Devices | Preview button		ALT+CTRL+SHIFT+S
Print	PS 47		File | Print		CTRL+P
Print One Copy	PS 47		File | Print One Copy		ALT+SHIFT+CTRL+P
Puppet Warp	PS 345		Edit | Puppet Warp		
Purge Cached Settings	PS 366		Edit | Purge | All		
Quick Selection Tool	PS 90	Quick Selection Tool button on Tools panel			W
Quit Photoshop	PS 60	Close button	File | Exit		CTRL+Q
Rectangular Marquee Tool	PS 83	Rectangular Marquee Tool button on Tools panel			M

Adobe Photoshop CS5 Quick Reference Summary *(continued)*

Task	Page Number	Mouse	Menu	Context Menu	Keyboard Shortcut
Red Eye Tool	PS 307	Red Eye Tool button on Tools panel			SHIFT+J
Refine Edge	PS 96	Refine Edge button on options bar	Select | Refine Edge	Refine Edge	ALT+CTRL+R
Reset All Tools	PS 8			Reset All Tools	
Resize with Resampling	PS 445		Image | Image Size | Resample Image		
Rule of Thirds Overlay, Position	PS 33	Drag overlay			
Rulers, Show or Hide	PS 30	View Extras button on Application bar	View | Rulers		CTRL+R
Save	PS 19		File | Save		CTRL+S
Save for Web	PS 52		File | Save for Web & Devices		ALT+SHIFT+CTRL+S
Save in PDF Format	PS 120		File | Save As | click Format box arrow | click Photoshop PDF (*.PDF; *.PDP)		
Save with New Name	PS 19		File | Save As | enter new name		SHIFT+CTRL+S
Screen Mode, Change	PS 28	Screen Mode button on Applications bar	View | Screen Mode | select mode		F
Select All	PS 36		Select | All		CTRL+A
Selection, Add To	PS 115	'Add to selection' button on options bar			SHIFT+drag
Selection, Deselect	PS 41	Click document window	Select | Deselect		CTRL+D
Selection, Distort	PS 86	Enter rotation percentage on options bar	Edit | Transform | Distort	Free Transform mode | Distort	
Selection, Duplicate	PS 98		Edit | Copy | Edit Paste		CTRL+ALT+drag
Selection, Flip Horizontal	PS 111		Edit | Transform | Flip Horizontal	Free Transform mode | Flip Horizontal	
Selection, Flip Vertical	PS 111		Edit | Transform | Flip Vertical	Free Transform mode | Flip Vertical	
Selection, Free Transform	PS 86		Edit | Free Transform	Free Transform	CTRL+T
Selection, Grow	PS 107		Select | Grow		
Selection, Intersect with	PS 104	'Intersect with selection' button on options bar			
Selection, Rotate	PS 8	Enter degree rotation on options bar	Edit | Transform | Rotate	Free Transform mode | Rotate	
Selection, Rotate 180°	PS 86	Enter degree rotation on options bar	Edit | Transform | Rotate 180°	Free Transform mode | Rotate 180°	
Selection, Rotate 90° CCW	PS 86	Enter degree rotation on options bar	Edit | Transform | Rotate 90° CCW	Free Transform mode | Rotate 90° CCW	
Selection, Rotate 90° CW	PS 86	Enter degree rotation on options bar	Edit | Transform | Rotate 90° CW	Free Transform mode | Rotate 90° CW	
Selection, Scale	PS 99	SHIFT+drag corner sizing handle	Edit | Transform | Scale	Free Transform mode | Scale	
Selection, Skew	PS 8		Edit | Transform | Skew	Free Transform mode | Skew	
Selection, Snap	PS 106	Drag selection near object or guide			

Adobe Photoshop CS5 Quick Reference Summary *(continued)*

Task	Page Number	Mouse	Menu	Context Menu	Keyboard Shortcut
Selection, Subtract From	PS 110	'Subtract from selection' button on options bar			ALT+drag
Selection, Transform Perspective	PS 86		Edit | Transform | Perspective	Free Transform mode | Perspective	
Selection, Warp	PS 86	Warp button on Transform options bar	Edit | Transform | Warp	Free Transform mode | Warp	
Sepia Image, Create	PS 436	Selective Color button on Adjustments panel, click Colors box arrow, click Neutrals			
Set Tracking	PS 373	'Set the tracking for the selected characters' text box on Character panel			
Shape Layer, Create from Path	PS 490		Layer | New Fill Layer | Solid Color		
Shape Layer, Create using Pen Tool	PS 469			Right-click Pen Tool button | click Shape layers button on options bar, click document window	
Shape Tool	PS 241	Shape Tool button on Tools panel			U
Shape, Alter	PS 506	Direct Selection Tool, drag anchor points			
Shape, Fill with Pattern	PS 507	'Add a layer style' button on Layers panel, Pattern Overlay			
Sharpen Tool	PS 320	Sharpen Tool button on Tools panel			
Single Column Marquee Tool	PS 80, PS 82	Single Column Marquee Tool button on Tools panel			
Single Row Marquee Tool	PS 80, PS 82	Single Row Marquee Tool button on Tools panel			
Site Information, Edit	PS 544	On Bridge Application bar, click Output workspace link, on Output panel, enter site title in Site Title box, enter description in Collection Title box, enter name in Contact Info box, enter e-mail address in E-mail or Web Address box			
Slice Settings, Enter	PS 559	Double-click slice		Right-click slice | click Edit Slice Options	
Slices, Create	PS 556	Slice Tool button on Tools panel	Layer | New Layer Based Slice		C
Smart Object, Create	PS 362		Filter | Convert for Smart Filters	Convert to Smart Object	
Smart Object, Layer	PS 179		Layer | Smart Objects | Convert to Smart Object or Layers panel menu | Convert to Smart Object	Convert to Smart Object	
Smooth, Modify	PS 38, PS 39		Select | Modify | Smooth		
Smudge Tool	PS 321	Smudge Tool button on Tools panel			
Snapping, Turn On	PS 107		View | Snap		SHIFT+CTRL+;
Spot Healing Brush Tool	PS 298	Spot Healing Brush Tool button on Tools panel			J

Adobe Photoshop CS5 Quick Reference Summary *(continued)*

Task	Page Number	Mouse	Menu	Context Menu	Keyboard Shortcut
Straighten Tool	PS 316	Straighten Tool button (Lens Correction dialog box)			
Stroke	PS 256	'Add a layer style' button on Layers panel, Stroke			
Text Color, Select from Image	PS 419	'Set the text color' button on Horizontal Type Tool options bar			
Text within Shape, Create	PS 503	Select vector mask thumbnail, Horizontal Type Tool button on Tools panel			
Text, Convert to Shape	PS 505		Layer | Type | Convert to Shape		
Text, Warp	PS 419	'Create warped text' button on Horizontal Type Tool options bar			
Transform Controls, Display	PS 84	Show Transform Controls check box on options bar	Edit | Free Transform		CTRL+T
Tween	PS 574	'Tweens animation frames' button on Animation panel status bar	Actions panel menu | Tween		
Undo	PS 33	Click previous state on History panel	Edit | Undo		CTRL+Z
Unsharp Mask Filter, Apply	PS 290		Filter | Sharpen | Unsharp Mask		
Web Gallery Template and Style, Apply	PS 543	On Bridge Application bar, click Output workspace link, on Output panel, click Web Gallery button, click Template button, select template, click Style button, select style, click Refresh Preview button			
Web Gallery, Preview	PS 545	On Bridge Application bar, click Output workspace link, on Output panel, click Preview in Browser button			
Web Gallery, Save	PS 546	On Bridge Application bar, click Output workspace link, on Output panel, display Create Gallery area, click Browse button, navigate to storage location, click OK button, click Save button, click OK button (Create Gallery dialog box)			
Web Page, View Interactively	PS 580	Double-click HTML file			
Windows, Consolidate	PS 173	Arrange Documents button on Application bar, Consolidate All button	Window | Arrange | Consolidate All to Tabs	Right-click document tab | click Consolidate All to Here	
Work Path, Save as Named Path	PS 488	Double-click work path name on Paths panel			
Zoom by Dragging	PS 401	Zoom Tool button, drag selection			
Zoom In	PS 23	Zoom In button on Navigator panel	View | Zoom In	Zoom In	CTRL+PLUS SIGN (+)
Zoom Out	PS 23	Zoom Out button on Navigator panel	View | Zoom Out	Zoom Out	CTRL+MINUS SIGN (−)
Zoom Tool	PS 23	Zoom Tool button on Tools panel			Z
Zoomify	PS 47		File | Export | Zoomify		

Index

Note: Page numbers in boldface type indicate key terms and the location in the text where they are defined.